AVIATION IN NORTHERN CALIFORNIA
1910-1939
Volume II: Yuba, Sutter, and Butte Counties

Previously titled *Golden Wings over the Feather River*

Allen Herr

Curtiss B-2 and Keystone LB-6 bombers near Mather Field during the April 1930 U.S. Army Air Corps air maneuvers.

STANSBURY
PUBLISHING
Chico, Ca.

AVIATION IN NORTHERN CALIFORNIA 1910–1939
Volume II, Yuba, Sutter, and Butte Counties

Copyright © 2015, 2019 by H. Allen Herr

ISBN 978-1-935807-46-9

Library of Congress Control Number 2015935230

This is the third printing of *Golden Wings over the Feather River* ISBN 978-1-935807-14-8, 2015 but with a new title and ISBN, additional facts, thirty-four more photos, and a new cover illustration.

Stansbury Publishing is an imprint of Heidelberg Graphics

All rights reserved. No part of this book maybe be reproduced or transmitted in any form or by any means, electronic or mechanical, including photocopying, recording, or by any information storage and retrieval system without permission in writing from the copyright holders or publisher, except for reviews.

Front cover: Friesley Falcon on a flight through the Sutter Buttes in August 1921. The highest peak in the buttes, South Butte, towers over the rest and is in the background with West Butte off center in the foreground.

Back cover: A Standard Model Curtiss (Pusher) in the foreground with a JN-4 Jenny behind over the Feather River.

Both cover paintings are by Allen Herr

TABLE OF CONTENTS

CHAPTER 1 -- p. 1
First flights in the Sacramento Valley – Frank Johnson at Marysville – Thaddeus Kerns and "Bud Mars" attempt to fly – Charlie Hamilton flies the valley's first professional exhibition – Knight Park racetrack becomes an airport – Kingsford-Smith stranded in Yuba City – Friesley Falcon flies the baseball team – Barnstormers at Marysville

CHAPTER 2 -- p. 39
The Angel Flying Circus comes to Marysville – Jimmie Angel meets Dr. Johnson – Angel's career before Yuba City – Dr. Johnson, founder of Yuba City's first airport – Angel Airport – Angel brothers' hurried departure – Johnson struggles to keep the airport open

CHAPTER 3 -- p. 75
James E. Read leads search for new airport site – Heiman Cheim donates airport site in Marysville – Dr. Johnson is still in the game – Cheim Field is created – Jim Read is named airport manager – Sierra Aircraft Company – Cheim Field dedication – Western Auto transfers Jim Read south

CHAPTER 4 -- p. 97
James Read leaves Marysville – Jimmie Angel moves south – Dr. Johnson's final years – Marysville supports Cheim Field – Yuba City searches for another airport site – Yuba-Sutter Flying Club is founded – First crop dusting in the Sacramento Valley

CHAPTER 5 -- p. 127
Continental Air Express – Airwar over the Twin Cities – Consolidated Air Lines (CAL) begins service – CAL inauguration air show – Dewey Ashford – Yuba-Sutter Flying Club activities – Harold F. Brown's civilian flying career

CHAPTER 6 -- p. 163
Sutter Air Terminal is founded – Yuba-Sutter aviation in the first years of the Depression – Consolidated Air Lines' rebirth and Twin Cities aviation in the

remaining Depression years – Cheim Field aviators prepare for war

CHAPTER 7 -- p. 195
Butte County airships and aeronauts – Colonel Frank Johnson at Chico – Thaddeus Kerns – Orvar "Swede" Meyerhoffer – Butte County aviators at the 1911 San Francisco International Air Meet – Harry Roderick and Harry Newhart – The Mar/McAuliffe fiasco

CHAPTER 8 -- p. 227
Orvar Meyeroffer and his new aviation business – California Aviation Company customers – Thad Kerns' flying career – Hamilton, Scott, and Martin fly at Chico – Kerns' last months

CHAPTER 9 -- p. 253
Orvar Meyerhoffer after leaving the Bay Area – Lyman and Jeanette Doty learn to fly

CHAPTER 10 -- p. 275
Army Air Service begins forest fire patrols – Fire patrols of 1919 – Oroville opens an airport –Army fire patrols at Oroville – Fire patrol moves to Redding – The Air Service, dissatisfied, moves from Redding to Red Bluff – Fire patrols of 1920 at Red Bluff – Fire patrols of 1921 at Corning – Fire patrols from 1925 and beyond

CHAPTER 11 -- p. 303
Postwar civilian flying at Oroville – E. H. Pendleton – Ogle W. Merwin – Friesley Aircraft Corporation – Bond Spencer, designer, builder, pilot – Friesley development

CHAPTER 12 -- p. 323
The Friesley Falcon flies – Friesley hires Roy Francis – Bond Spencer after the Falcon – The Friesley Falcon finale – Oroville flying activities after the forest patrol moves on

CHAPTER 13 -- p. 351
Postwar aviation at Chico – Merwin and Pendleton – Flying at the Chico Auto Show – More barnstormers – Jimmie Angel at Chico – Royle Air Lines – Sierra Aircraft Corp. at Chico – Garrison Patrick

CHAPTER 14 -- p. 381
Early fliers and barnstormers at Gridley – Friesley's influence – The California Association for the Promotion of Aeronautics – Harvey Bolton

ABBREVIATIONS -- p. 399
ENDNOTES -- p. 401
BIBLIOGRAPHY -- p. 413
PHOTOGRAPH CREDITS -- p. 413
INDEX -- p. 417
ABOUT THE AUTHOR -- p. 427

LIST OF PHOTOGRAPHS AND ILLUSTRATIONS

p. Title page USAAC bombers near Mather 1930
p. vi Paulhan in his Farman at Dominguez Hills
p. xii Weldon Cooke, Lan Maupin's aviator
p. xiv Ryan B-3 Brougham at Redding
p. 3 Johnson, Curtiss, Paulhan, and Hamilton
p. 4 Johnson at Knight Park, Marysville
p. 6 Hamilton at Knight Park
p. 7 Hamilton at Knight Park
p. 13 Knight Park, Marysville
p. 17 George Bihlmann
p. 21 Jackson Bottoms, Yuba City
p. 31 Map of Knight Park & Cheim Field
p. 36 Yolo Fliers Club Field in 1993
p. 37 Aircraft side-view
p. 38 Curtiss JN-4 (top)
p. 38 Mather Field fly-by (bottom)
p. 42 Dr. Julian P. Johnson
p. 52 Eddie Angel
p. 55 Dominic DiFiore
p. 57 Angel Airport location 1937
p. 72 Dudley Cunningham 1927
p. 73 Jim Read & Dudley Cunningham
p. 74 Cheim Field location 2004
p. 88 Avis Sutfin Bielefeld 1934
p. 89 Jewel Danley 1930s
p. 96 Cheim Field w/ planes lined up
p. 107 Jimmie Angel
p. 116 Lan B. Maupin & Diamond 1930
p. 125 Ashford's Travel Air
p.126 J. Angel&Huang - Bristol F2B - TM Scout
p. 133 Army Air Maneuvers 1930
p. 136 Curtiss Kingbird
p. 152 Johns Multiplane
p. 153 Johns Multiplane
p. 154 Ashford and his Stearman
p. 155 Ashford's logbook
p. 156 Ashford's Fairchild 24
p. 162 H&B Stinson – Ashford, Moore & Davis

p. 164 Sutter Air Terminal 1937
p. 182 Fokker Super Universal
p. 186 Fokker Trimotor at Cheim
p. 188 Earhart Lockheed Vega
p. 190 Cheim Field circa 1939
p. 193 Sutter County Airport 1947
p. 194 Brander crash – Fagerskog – Travel Air
p. 207 Thad Kerns aircraft
p. 209 Orvar Meyerhoffer circa 1919
p. 217 Meyerhoffer V-plane
p. 218 Roderick & Newhart aircraft
p. 225 Sacramento Muni Airport 1938
p. 226 Langley Field, VA 1918
p. 252 Willows Airport – Boeing 40B
p. 261 Meyerhoffer at Ft. Bidwell
p. 263 Lyman & Jeanette Doty
p. 273 Del Paso Airport 1928
p. 274 De Havilland DH-4
p. 278 Riley Field, Oroville
p. 302 Corning Airport 1990
p. 322 Friesley's First Hangar SF
p. 334 Friesley Falcon at Gridley
p. 335 Friesley Falcon at Woodland
p. 350 Oroville Airport 1994
p. 362 Edgar Slough airports Chico
p. 369 Bill Royle and Oakland pilots
p. 376 Franklin Rose circa 1926
p. 380 Chico Airport 1994 – Ford Tri-motor
p. 387 Cloddy Field, Honcut 2014
p. 388 Harry Middleton
p. 389 James Giffin & Gold
p. 390 First Crop Dusting
p. 397 Curtiss R-4 – Airmail DH-4
p. 398 Alicia Airport – Alicia Main Hangar Burns
p. 400 Yuba County Airport (current)
p. 428 Planes on river barge – McClellan Field
p. 429 Bach Tri-motor on Crissy Field
p. 430 N11MF over Sutter Co. Airport 1978

Louis Paulhan in his Farman biplane dominated America's first aviation meet in the Dominguez Hills near Los Angeles during January 1910.

INTRODUCTION

This volume is about the first aviators in Yuba, Sutter, and Butte counties and the many aviation pioneers who followed them. It is a record of the flying activities of those early aviators, their aircraft, and their airports.

Aeroplane flying began on the East Coast of America in December 1903, but it didn't begin on the West Coast until 1910. Someone once said that progress always moves west, but in this case surprisingly slow. Aviation had already progressed from discovery to what has been termed its Exhibition Years (1909–1914) by the time the first manned, powered, controlled, and sustained flight was made in California at the Dominguez Hills in January 1910.

The narrative structure of this book is simple; it is chronological and anecdotal. There are an abundance of aviators, airports, flying activities, and aviation events introduced in this work that will interest even the most jaded airplane nut. The reader will know exactly where he is in the progression of aviation history as the multitude of aviators and events are presented. Their stories are expanded whenever possible to clarify their importance and their relationship to each other in the march of the new technology.

The available literature concerning aviation during the Exhibition Years in America deals mainly with the activities and accomplishments of Orville and Wilbur Wright and their disciples, who trained in the East, or of Glenn Curtiss and his early students. The first fliers in the West began training later and have been ignored.

Glenn Curtiss made the first successful powered, controlled, and sustained aeroplane flight on the West Coast on January 9, 1910, at the Los

Angeles International Air Meet in the Dominguez Hills of Southern California; the day before the meet opened. At least this is the first such flight in the state that can be corroborated. Glenn Martin and few others claimed to have flown in 1909, but corroboration of their flights is woefully inadequate in meeting the definition of a successful aeroplane flight agreed upon by most aviation historians. That definition being the flight must be manned, powered, controlled, and sustained.

Within the month, successful aeroplane flight was carried out in the San Francisco Bay Area and a week-and-a-half after that in the Sacramento Valley.

For one who wishes to write about the aeronautical activities occurring in the various cities, towns, and communities in the north state during the years 1910 through 1939, the time span of this book, one must determine who the aviators were plus when, where, and what they flew. The following explains how I went about this task.

The aeroplane was such an amazing new machine involving the mind-bending field of aerodynamics and allowing people to use the vertical dimension in a way never before possible. Because of this, the press recorded most public flights whenever and wherever they occurred—from the Wright brothers' developmental flights on the Huffman Prairie through America's entry into the Great War. These flights were recorded in newspaper reports often with numerous photographs.

In California the building and flying of aeroplanes was front-page news in small town newspapers through the Exhibition Years and well into the 1920s. In big city newspapers, such articles fell off the front pages in 1914 with the start of the Great War, but they could still be found on page two or three. Once the war ended and the brief ban on civilian flying in America was lifted, front-page articles on aviation in the larger newspapers were usually about record flights, air shows, air races, and famous aviators. The daily activities at the city airport were still of great interest and could be found deeper in the pages of those same newspapers.

Newspaper articles describing aerial events were good sources of information about local flying history, but the dates of these events must be known in advance for historians to search the mountains of newspaper microfilm in a timely manner.

During the Exhibition Years, flying schedules and exhibition results of the nation's professional exhibition fliers were published regularly in aviation weeklies and magazines like *Aeronautics*, *Aero* (later *Aero and Hydro*),

Aerial Age Weekly, Aviation, and *The Ace.* The activities and accomplishments of professional aviators, many of the amateur aviators, and aeroplane builders in the East, Midwest, and even in the West were described in these now rare and obscure publications.

For the postwar years through the 1930s, the best information on the activities of the country's aviators, airplane manufacturers, aeronautical expositions, air races, air meets and air shows is found in less rare magazines like *Western Flying, Popular Aviation, Sportsman Pilot,* and *Aero Digest.* Of course to expand on the dates found of aerial activities, further research was required in pertinent newspapers, books, journals, logbooks, and interviews.

Organized flying schools in the state began with H. V. Schiller's flying school founded in the Dominguez Hills—site of America's first air meet—soon after the meet ended in January 1910. Schiller's school was followed quickly by Jay Gage's flying school at Griffith Park in Los Angeles. Later, Glenn Curtiss started his outstanding flying school on North Island in San Diego. The near perfect climate for flying in the south state was a strong factor in the founding of these first schools.

Climate aside, interest in flying may have been more prevalent in the north state than in the south during the Exhibition Years due to the larger population base in the north initiated by the Gold Rush in 1849 and not exceeded in Southern California until 1920. Another important stimulus to early flying in the Bay Area was the 1915 Panama–Pacific International Exposition. There was much promotional flying for the exposition beginning in 1913 and later during its ten months of operation ending in December 1915.

Jay Gage's flying school influenced flying in the San Francisco Bay Area more than any other Southern California flying school after the Bay Area's first professional pilots trained there. Frank Bryant learned to fly at Gage's school before he moved in 1911 to the Bay Area where he became the first truly proficient flying instructor. Gage also taught Roy Francis to fly and built him an excellent twin-propeller tractor aeroplane. Francis brought the plane back to San Francisco and became a popular local exhibition pilot. It wasn't long before he and Bryant together made a barnstorming tour of California's Great Central Valley. They were the first team of Northern California exhibition pilots to do so.

Frank Bryant may not have been the first flying instructor in the Bay Area, but the local aviation community considered him the best. He taught Silas Christofferson to fly, and Silas opened a flying school that would become the only successful aviation school in the Bay Area during the prewar years. After Silas opened Christofferson Aviation School, he immediately hired Frank Bryant as chief instructor.

As you read this book, the relationship between Bay Area aviation and the north state becomes apparent. The support from Bay Area aviation manufacturing and supply houses to fledgling north state aeroplane builders was considerable; one of which had been supplying aeronauts and glider enthusiasts since 1909. These supply houses, which were often also bicycle supply houses, carried everything for aviators and aeronauts from motors, wheels, and premade wing ribs to fabric and propellers. In some cases, they even helped build customers' flying machines in their shops.

After the Great War, the determined individuals in the Bay Area and the Sacramento Valley who had the vision and courage to start the first flying businesses and, in some cases, open their own airports, are in this book. The story is told of their struggle to expand business opportunities with obsolescent airplanes left over from the war—airplanes that glutted the aircraft market until the middle to late 1920s. Lack of government regulation, customer fear of flying, and the added economic steamroller of the Great Depression were for some aviation businesses too overwhelming. Some businesses were able to survive, and some were even successful. Failure, success, or bread and beans survival—their efforts are recorded here. This book is about failure as much as it is about success.

Insight into the creation of airports in the Bay Area is gained by examining the first generation of airports—the local horse racing tracks. Second-generation airports were those laid out on land developed and dedicated specifically for the housing, servicing, and flying of aircraft. Third generation airports, those built to replace the previous generation due to residential encroachment or the need for longer runways, are mentioned very seldom in this book because most of those were built after 1939.

Also in this work are those fliers who paid the ultimate price for living their dreams. So many aviators were killed during the Exhibition Years that a concentrated effort was made by the Bay Area aviation community to have the Column of Progress, which survived the Panama-Pacific International Exposition, standing next to Marina Green in San Francisco, dedicated to the aviators who gave their lives in the development of aeronautics.

It is my hope the rich aviation history of the three Sacramento Valley counties through which the Feather River passes, described in this work, will fill the void in current aviation literature on this subject.

Introduction

Certain nomenclature used throughout this work needs explanation. It did not feel right to use the word airplane when writing about the flying machines used prior to the Great War. It took fifteen years following the Wrights' first flight for the word aeroplane to morph into airplane. So, in this work aeroplane is used until World War I starts and thereafter airplane takes its place. The British still use the word aeroplane.

When America entered the Great War, US Army aviators were under command of the Army Signal Corps' Aviation Section. In late May 1918, the Army Air Service was born. The term Air Service is used throughout this book when referring to army aviation during the war regardless of the date.

The Bay Area is used when referring to the San Francisco Bay Area even though that name didn't completely evolve until the 1950s. The many books, newspapers, and magazine references of the day refer to the location as San Francisco bay district or San Francisco bay region or, heaven forbid—"Frisco"—a name offensive to San Franciscans. Often there was no distinction made of other cities on the bay, they were all lumped together as San Francisco.

I believe Northern California is a cultural entity thus the capital N. The same goes for Southern California. If a city is cited in this work without a state location it is in California. Out of state cities are usually identified with their states unless they are mentioned multiple times.

World War I is referred to as the Great War, the World War, or just the war. The terms refer to the largest conflict to take place during the scope of this work. Hostilities began in August 1914 in Europe with the United States entering the conflict on April 6, 1917. It ended on November 11, 1918.

Military aviation is mentioned often in this work, but only as it effected the civilian population or the civilian flying community. The histories of the military airfields mentioned in this work have been well covered in aviation literature. My favorite is Stephen A. Haller's excellent book, *The Last Word in Airfields—San Francisco's Crissy Field*.

Dirigibles, a transitional technology, and other lighter-than-air aircraft are mentioned for the attitude they created towards the coming heavier-than-air technology that would replace them in the public's eye. Their history is not a theme here.

Throughout the time span covered in this work, model numbers of the various aircraft manufacturers were rarely mentioned in periodicals. An example would be the identification of a Curtiss OX-5 powered Travel Air biplane as an "OX-5 Travel Air"; not the more correct designation, Travel Air 2000. An Alexander Eaglerock would be described as an "OX-5 Eaglerock," or if powered by a Wright J-5 Whirlwind motor it was identified as a "Whirlwind Eaglerock." I make my apologies now to the aircraft identification experts for using the less precise method of model identification.

One troubling reference must be questioned, what to call the ubiquitous Curtiss Pusher biplane? During the Exhibition Years it was responsible, more than any other design, for bringing aviation to the people of Northern California and, I believe, the rest of the country. It is generally referred to today as the Curtiss Pusher, but in the aviation reports of the day it was rarely referred to in that manner. The experts now refer to the aircraft as the Curtiss Model D. Technically that may be correct, but I found in the periodicals of the day it was referred to as the Standard Model Curtiss with a capital S and capital M and the word Curtiss always at the end of the designation. This designation for the Curtiss is used throughout this work, but I'm sure you will discover, as above, that I sometimes refer to it as a Curtiss Pusher.

Weldon Cooke won over $7,000 flying Lan Maupin and B. Lanteri's Curtiss Pusher copy at the 1912 Dominguez Air Meet.

ACKNOWLEDGEMENTS AND DEDICATION

Valuable assistance was given to me by the diligent employees of the Richmond Annex of the University of California at Berkeley's Doe Library. Through them I obtained the rare aeronautical trade papers and magazines of aviation's Exhibition Years and the early 1920s.

The folks at the circulation desk in the California Room of the California State Library at Sacramento were wonderful in helping with the aviation trade magazines of the mid-1920s and early '30s. They also allowed me to view the correspondence and papers of the California Aviation Company in their rare book room and were ever so patient with my all day binges, twice weekly, for three years in their newspaper microfilm lab.

When this project began, I had vital assistance in the search for photographs from Gordon Werne, Hiller Aviation Museum archivist, in San Carlos and Pat Johnson of the Sacramento Archives & Museum Collection Center. Now, fifteen years later as the project winds down, Ms. Debbie Seracini, an archivist at the San Diego Air & Space Museum Library & Archives has given me wise advice and generous help in the often times painful search for the right photographs. The Sutter County Library, San Mateo County Museum, Sacramento City Library, Miriam Library at Chico, Butte County Museum, Gridley Museum, Yolo County Archives, Marysville's Mary Aaron Memorial Museum, and the Yuba County Library all provided helpful assistance during my years of research.

Special thanks must be given to Ms. Julie Stark, curator of the Community Memorial Museum of Sutter County for allowing me to be co-curator of the exhibition, *Taking Off*, a collection of photographs and information about early aviation in Sutter and Yuba Counties.

I must also thank James Lenhoff for his vast knowledge of the history of Butte County, for his expansive photo collection, and for his friendship.

My respect and thanks to Larry Jackson, publisher.

The late Richard Sanders Allen, my good friend, was an inspiration in the writing of this book. He was the author of *Revolution in the Sky* about the early Lockheed aircraft, and *The Northrop Story*. I have never known anyone so kind, helpful, and generous as Richard.

This book is dedicated to H. T. Herr and Kathe Herr. My father, H. T. "Ted" Herr, was responsible for my love of airplanes and flying. He loved flying and began taking lessons in 1947. After obtaining his pilot license, he bought a Piper J-3 Cub. In 1965 after a fifteen year hiatus from flying, he bought a partnership in an Aeronca Champ, as did I, and in 1975 he, my wife, and I purchased a Bellanca Decathlon. He flew it often until shortly before he passed on in 2002.

The love of my life, Kathe, has provided unwavering support for this project. She dragged me kicking and screaming into the computer age and has supplied technical support for the infernal device, which is my never-ending requirement. She constantly reminds me of the necessity of correct grammar and style as only a retired educator could. She has been extremely tolerant of the thousands of aviation books and magazines, which line the walls of our house. She and I have made hundreds of wonderful flights together over the past forty years. I am so lucky that she is my wife, my friend, and my copilot and I hers.

—Allen Herr, Yuba City, Calif., April 2019

Rose Air Service's Ryan B-3 Brougham believed to be parked at Benton Field, Redding, circa 1930s

CHAPTER 1

First flights in the Sacramento Valley – Frank Johnson at Marysville – Thaddeus Kerns and "Bud Mars" attempt to fly – Charlie Hamilton flies the valley's first professional exhibition – Knight Park racetrack becomes an airport – Kingsford-Smith stranded in Yuba City – Friesley Falcon flies the baseball team – Barnstormers at Marysville

Louis Paulhan, a French aviator, made the first successful aeroplane flight in Northern California at Tanforan Park near San Francisco on January 24, 1910. At Los Angeles a week earlier, he flew so well at America's first international air meet, he won the most prize money.

The first flight in the Sacramento Valley took place February 12, 1910, at Marysville, the county seat of Yuba County. Aviation history of Sutter County goes hand in hand with that of Yuba County because Yuba City, the county seat of Sutter County, is less than a mile from Marysville. They are separated by the Feather River and today are connected by two automobile bridges and two railroad bridges. The Twin Cities, as they are sometimes called, are indeed one community.

One of the earliest flying events in the Yuba-Sutter area happened in 1893 when Thomas J. Godfrey made his first parachute jump from a balloon at a community picnic in the Sutter County town of Meridian on the Sacramento River. At the time, Godfrey was working as a shepherd in the Sutter Buttes where he made his own balloon and parachute from crude materials. He was then offered twenty dollars to jump at the picnic. After landing successfully from the balloon, he decided to give the people of Meridian an even bigger thrill and attempt an illuminated night jump. The balloon caught fire and Godfrey was almost killed. He returned to sheepherding.

It wasn't long before he made another balloon and developed a reputation as a parachutist. He made jumps at many Yuba and Sutter county festivities. In his later years, he was a photographer living in Jackson. Godfrey died in a car accident in El Dorado County June 1929.

It was reported in May 1897 that, "The airship being built on the Schillig place in Sutter County will be ready to fly in about three weeks. Davenport, the inventor, says it will weigh three thousand pounds. and cost three thousand dollars." Whether this airship was ever built is a mystery. It is not clear what sort of airship it was. Was it a balloon, as implied by the use of the word airship, or was it an aeroplane? It may have been one of Godfrey's balloons.[1]

There was much balloon activity in California prior to the turn of the century. Dirigible flight began in the state just after the twentieth century began. Thomas Baldwin, Ivy Baldwin, Capt. Park Van Tassall, Frank Hamilton, and Roy Knabenshue were the most well-known aeronauts of the period to fly in Northern California. However, lighter-than-air machines are beyond the scope of this work except on those occasions when they mingled with aeroplanes or made exceptional flights that influenced community attitudes towards flying.

The first Sacramento Valley successful manned, powered, controlled, and sustained aeroplane flight took place at Knight Park in Marysville. Frank H. Johnson made the flight in his factory-built Standard Model Curtiss (Pusher) biplane.[2]

Many years prior to Johnson's flight, another event occurred in the Yuba-Sutter community that would effect aviation in Northern California. John J. Montgomery, the man considered by some as the father of basic flying, was born just across the Feather River from Marysville in Yuba City on February 15, 1858. Montgomery, who may have been the first man to successfully make a flight in a glider, left Yuba City with his parents when he was five years old.

Montgomery would later claim he made the world's first successful glider flight in 1884 at Otay Mesa near the California–Mexico border. Unfortunately, adequate corroboration is lacking that this "first" glider flight ever took place.

Montgomery was a successful engineer whose career in aeronautics, electricity, and teaching took place mostly in Santa Clara County. He never experimented with powered flight—only gliders. His heirs were convinced Montgomery had some rights to controlled flight and sued the Wright brothers over their patent. The heirs lost in a court fight that was minor

Chapter 1

1. Frank Johnson, 2. Glenn Curtiss, 3. Louis Pulhan, and 4. Charlie Hamilton.

compared to the Wright's legal battle over the same patent with Glenn Curtiss.

IN FEBRUARY 1910 it was reported, "The aviator [Frank] Johnson will attempt to encircle the Sutter Buttes," during his flying exhibition at Marysville on February 12 and 13. This first flying exhibition in the valley brought the largest group of spectators to date ever to assemble in Marysville.[3]

Frank H. Johnson, a self-proclaimed millionaire from a merchant family in San Rafael, claimed to be a colonel. Supposedly, Governor J. N. Gillett had given him the rank for his work on the governor's staff with the state militia. It is more likely he adopted the rank in the manner of the many balloon aeronauts, who exhibited during earlier decades, and adopted stage names that were always preceded by either the rank of captain or professor. Since Johnson was wealthy, he reportedly gave all the money he was paid for flying to the men who traveled with him for taking care of his aeroplane. The Marysville Chamber of Commerce paid Johnson three hundred dollars for flying at Marysville.[6]

Knight Park, location for this exhibition, would become the local flying field for organized flying events in the Yuba-Sutter area for the next sixteen years. This park had a horse racing track and a large surrounding recreation area. Even today there remains a large recreation area on the site, which is now the location of Marysville High School. The original park grounds extended from the railroad tracks on the city's northern border, south to the city's then-undeveloped eastern portion of Ellis Lake.

Frank Johnson's advance man, Mr. Price, reportedly claimed Johnson would be making a flight around the Sutter Buttes. It was predicted tens of thousands of people would come by the trainloads to witness such a flight. In fact, ten to fifteen thousand spectators did come to see Johnson fly!

On February 12, 1910, Frank Johnson made the first aeroplane flight in the Sacramento Valley at Marysville's Knight Park. Johnson made several flights at the park that day and this remarkable photo depicts one of those flights.

Chapter 1

Johnson's first flight, on Saturday the twelfth, was a race against Marysville auto racing driver J. Rupert Foster. The aviator won the one-mile race flying around and above the track, beating Foster to the finish line. There were complaints from the audience that Johnson didn't fly high enough. He never exceeded eighty feet.

Johnson's second flight, a cross-country flight of approximately six miles, ended when Johnson returned to the track and landed at the exact spot from which he had taken off. Some crowd members were perturbed that Johnson didn't fly around the Sutter Buttes as promised.[4]

Johnson made several more flights that day, but Sunday's flights were more problematic. Marysville's levees surrounding Knight Park on two sides were jammed with spectators, as was the grandstand in the park.[5] Many of the spectators felt he should have been more daring.

Johnson made seven successful flights on the first day, and the six-mile flight was the longest. On his last flight of the day, as he was cruising along twenty-five feet above the track, his engine quit. The stall speed of Johnson's 40hp. Curtiss Pusher was only a little less than its cruising speed. In any event, the aircraft dropped onto the inside boundary fence of the racetrack. Johnson was thrown violently to the ground, yet walked away with minor injuries. The machine suffered some damage, but the Curtiss was repaired overnight and ready to fly the next day.[7]

On Sunday, Johnson landed on a fence once again. This time he had just taken off from a point some distance from the finish line in front of the grandstand. He was in the air flying down the homestretch at his favorite cruising altitude of thirty feet when the biplane began to veer towards the grandstand. Johnson couldn't stop the turn so he shut the engine down. The Curtiss dropped like a rock. It fell on the picket fence that marked the last one hundred feet of the track's homestretch before the finish line.

The plane's box-kite-appearing elevator mounted on the forward booms was destroyed, as were a couple of struts between the wings. Johnson considered the damage insignificant. What was significant were the several men and two women who were either knocked down or fell down trying to escape the sweep of the biplane's wings as it hurtled towards them. Luckily, they escaped injury by falling toward the fence, which held the wing up and off of them. It turned out the cause of the accident was a wire used in the repairs made after Saturday's accident. The wire came loose and caught in the propeller pulling tension on one wing and causing the aircraft to turn uncontrollably. Johnson was slightly injured on his side and one wrist from his encounters with the fences.

Each day, Johnson made a flight to the north from Knight Park. He flew over the fence surrounding the park, then turned eastward past the powder house and on around the slaughterhouse of Valley Meat Company—eventually turning back to the racetrack. Johnson made this entire flight at a height of thirty feet. Many of the spectators who paid their fifty cents to get into the park and many, who sat on the levees outside the park, were critical of Johnson's low flying. Again, they were disappointed that he did not fly around the Sutter Buttes as wrongly predicted. Johnson was never out of the sight of spectators during his flights.

Unfortunately for the Marysville Chamber of Commerce, as packed as the grandstand was, more people sat on the levees and the railroad berms around the park than those who paid and went into the park. It was a problem that became universal and plagued air show promoters and barnstormers forever.[8]

THE NEXT FLYING EXHIBITION in the area came about as the result of a hoax perpetrated on the citizens of the Yuba-Sutter community and, presumably, on Thaddeus Kerns, a young aviator from Chico.

Someone telephoned a Marysville city official on Friday, November 17, 1911, and introduced himself as Bud Mar. The official was led to believe he was speaking with famous Curtiss exhibition flyer James C. "Bud" Mars. He said his name was McAuliff and implied Bud Mar was his stage name.

Mar said he planned to make two exhibition flights in Marysville, his old hometown, on the coming Sunday. His airplane was undergoing repairs, he claimed, and he was going to use a plane belonging to the flying prodigy from Chico, Thaddeus Kerns. He said he and Kerns would alternate their

During Hamilton's March exhibition at Marysville, he raced against E. E. Foss who was driving a Regal 20 racing automobile.

Chapter 1

Hamilton landing on the racetrack at Knight Park with spectators who seem to be unaware of how dangerously close they are to the landing aircraft.

exhibition flights. Mar said it would take a week to repair his plane, but on Thanksgiving Day, three days after the exhibition flights, he planned to fly over Marysville on his way east following Western Pacific's railroad tracks up the Feather River Canyon and across the Sierra Nevada. The two aviators planned their exhibition flights to be at Knight Park on Sunday, November 19.

That Sunday morning the local paper reported Bud Mar was one of the best exhibition flyers "… in the business and all those who go out to Knight Park will see a birdman go up in the air who understands his machine, and who is perfectly able to give a good exhibition." It also reported Mar would fly around the Sutter Buttes. Mar was to arrive that morning from Sacramento and proceed directly to Knight Park where he would examine Kern's aeroplane and test-fly it. Later in the afternoon, Kerns was to make a flight. Kerns was an amateur, but "… he has the pluck and perseverance to make good."

Bud Mar never showed, but the exhibition was reported a success. Thad Kerns, "… the eighteen-year-old wonder from Chico," flew an excellent exhibition after working the bugs out of his engine. He flew for a large crowd assembled at Knight Park and on the nearby levees. It took Kerns quite awhile before he was ready to fly, and when he was ready it was late. People were beginning to leave the site. Kerns took off and made a large circling flight around the slaughterhouse and back to the racetrack, a distance of three miles. He was at least one hundred feet in the air at the highest point of his flight, and the crowd went home satisfied they had seen a flight.⁹

The Bud Mar/McAuliff character set up another aviation meet for Sacramento on December 16, 1911. This meet would also involve Thaddeus Kerns. In Sacramento, the hoax of McAuliff/Mar not showing up as promised, which slipped by those in Marysville, was finally revealed. McAuliff was vilified and Kerns was embarrassed.

CHARLES K. HAMILTON FLEW to the racetrack at Marysville's Knight Park on March 15, 1912. At last the citizens of Yuba, Sutter, and the surrounding counties would enjoy a flying exhibition by one of the most skilled fliers in the United States. He was arguably the most famous "fancy flier" in the nation at the time.

Charlie made one long continuous flight to Marysville from Sacramento in thirty-three minutes. He did this during a time in aviation history when exhibition pilots usually moved their planes around the country on trains because most early aircraft didn't have the fuel capacity or engine dependability for extended cross-country flights.¹⁰

Hamilton flew in a large air meet at Sacramento's Agricultural Park two weeks before the Marysville engagement. He and five other aviators were part of a flying exhibition assembled by aeronautical impresario Dick Ferris, the man who managed America's first air meet in the Dominguez Hills near Los Angeles in January 1910. After the Sacramento meet, the other flyers went to Chico for the Spring Festival air meet. Hamilton had been negotiating to fly an exhibition at Reno, Nevada, but after the Sacramento meet something soured him on Reno, and he took the Marysville engagement instead. The high altitude of 4,400 feet at Reno made flying these early low-powered aircraft a deadly endeavor.¹¹

The Marysville newspaper ballyhooed Hamilton's flight from Sacramento to Marysville as an unofficial world record. Hamilton made the forty-two-mile flight at an average speed of 78.9 miles per hour. Aviator Harry Atwood previously held the long distance speed record for a flight he made between Chicago and South Bend, Indiana, in thirty minutes for a speed of 71.75 miles per hour.

Charlie Hamilton left Sacramento at 4:27 PM and landed at Knight Park at 5:04. After overflying Marysville at 5:00 PM, he flew a wide circle over Yuba City, on the opposite side of the Feather River, before landing. Thousands of people in Marysville were waiting to see him. They crowded the levees surrounding the town, the D Street Bridge, and the tops of various structures to catch a glimpse of the approaching aircraft.[12]

The next day Hamilton put on an exciting aerial demonstration at Knight Park. Photos of the event show the aviator doing a corkscrew maneuver over the grandstand. He is shown landing on the racetrack with a throng of spectators crowding the track, oblivious to the danger of being so close to a landing aircraft.

Hamilton flew exhibitions on the seventeenth and the eighteenth. He carried out stunts such as racing local auto speedster, E. E. Foss, around the track. Foss was driving his Regal 20 automobile, and Hamilton was flying his all black, slightly larger version of a Standard Model Curtiss pusher biplane, named the *Hamiltonian*. Charlie tossed baseballs from his biplane to a couple of professional ballplayers from the Sacramento Coast League. The stunt failed because Hamilton was unable to land the balls close enough. The same thing happened two weeks earlier when he tried it in Sacramento.

It was estimated on one day there were six thousand spectators inside and outside Knight Park. This was important to Hamilton. He had agreed to fly at Marysville for 50 percent of the gate. He was paid nothing for those outside the gate.[13]

THE NEXT AERIAL EXHIBITION in the Yuba-Sutter area was to be flown, once again, by Thaddeus Kerns on Sunday, March 30, 1913. It was over a year since Charlie Hamilton had flown there.

Thad Kerns had recently turned professional and was starting a small barnstorming tour from Chico, his hometown, to Sacramento. He first put on an impressive exhibition in Chico. Moving on south, he was forced to land in the Biggs area, north of Gridley, due to bad weather. He decided to put on an exhibition at Gridley on March 25. He flew the short distance to Gridley from Biggs. After circling Gridley he landed in the Onstott pasture northeast of town. A number of the townsfolk came out to the pasture to watch Kerns fly his exhibition and were pleased with the results. The Onstott pasture became the city's de facto landing field for many years.

The next day Kerns took off for Marysville in mid-morning. As he was climbing away from the pasture and before he had reached his cruising speed, he hit a downdraft or stalled, possibly both, and dropped two hundred feet to the ground. His plane hit with such force the wheels were driven into the ground and the machine was badly damaged. Kerns was lucky to escape with only minor abrasions. His barnstorming tour was over. The March 30 exhibition at Marysville would have to wait until April after he rebuilt his machine. His barnstorming tour had gotten him only twenty-eight miles from home.[14]

KNIGHT PARK BECAME Marysville's official aviation field after America's entry into the Great War. The creation of a huge military flying field, twelve miles east of Sacramento at Mills Station, would make aircraft a slightly more common sight over towns in the Sacramento Valley. The airfield at Mills Station was eventually renamed Mather Field for Lt. Carl Mather, killed in a Texas flying accident. Mather Field was to provide primary flying training for United States Army Air Service flying cadets. As part of the training, cadets were to make cross-country flights away from their home field. That meant auxiliary landing fields had to be established at various distances from Mather Field. There were no airports in the Sacramento Valley; the army would have to create them or have them created.

America entered the Great War on April 6, 1917, with a military desperate for airplanes and aviators. A massive six hundred million dollar program was funded by congress to establish pilot training bases and build aircraft enabling America to help its allies England, France, and Italy defeat Germany and the Central Powers.

When America entered the conflict, US Army aviation was under the control of the Army's Signal Corps. On May 20, 1918, control of aviation was removed from the Signal Corps by President Woodrow Wilson and given to the newly formed Division of Military Aeronautics. By August it was renamed the Army Air Service.

The French trained a small number of American volunteers as pilots and assigned them to the Lafayette Escadrille prior to America's entry into the war. The British had American volunteers flying in the Royal Flying Corps as early as 1915.

The French continued training American soldiers to become aviators after America entered the conflict. The top scoring American ace, Eddie Rickenbacker, was trained as an aviator by the French after the American Army sent him to France as a chauffeur. Meanwhile, in the United States, men who signed up to become US Army aviators either sat around waiting for their training bases to be built or were ordered to help build them.

Word got out that an enlistee who had trained as a pilot before he enlisted would have a leg up on those who hadn't. Some men who had the money sought training from civilian flying schools in America prior to enlisting. After the US entered the war, the first man from the Yuba-Sutter area to get his training from such a school was Victor G. Strain, son of one of Yuba County's pioneer ranchers, G. Strain. Victor spent months at Frank Bryant's Redwood Aviation School in Redwood City learning to fly. In March 1918, he was awarded Aero Club of America/Federation Aeronautique Internationale (ACA/FAI) license No. 1406. He then enlisted in the army and served as a lieutenant instructing cadets in the United States. After the war, Strain became a successful rancher and automobile dealer in Butte County.[15]

Because there were no airports in Sacramento Valley when America entered the war, the army set about creating them. It wasn't hard. Every community wanted to do its part to help the war effort. It was only a matter of the army coordinating with a chosen town to get a landing field developed.

Major Reuben H. Fleet was sent to Sacramento in 1918 to direct the establishment of Mather Field as a major base of operations for flight training. His job was to get the field up and running. Part of his duties entailed flying around the Great Central Valley to towns like Marysville, Woodland, Colusa, and others to establish auxiliary airfields for cross-country training flights. In this manner, the US Army got the first airports developed in the Sacramento and San Joaquin valleys.

C. H. Chace, secretary of the Marysville Chamber of Commerce, wrote a letter to Fleet in the early spring of 1918 asking what the government required of a city to establish an auxiliary landing field. Fleet made Marysville a stop on his July aerial tour when he was evaluating prospective landing spots around the Sacramento Valley and telling prospects what needed to be done to secure an airport.

At 10:20 AM on July 17, Major Fleet and First Lt. A. F. Hogland, flying a Curtiss JN-4D with No. 3654 painted on the side of the fuselage, landed at Marysville's Knight Park. It was the first time a government airplane had landed there.

Mr. Chace and councilman Clarence E. Swift met the Jenny as it landed. The four men discussed the possibility of making Knight Park an auxiliary field for Mather's flying cadets. They toured the grounds in Swift's automobile with Fleet explaining carefully what changes would have to be made to the park for it to be an adequate landing field. He told them there was little work needed to make it into an airport. He said it was already one of the best sites in the north state. The ground needed to be leveled and made smooth enough an automobile traveling from the center of the field could move at a speed of twenty miles per hour with ease. It would be necessary to build a large wind tee sixty-feet long in the center of the field and another wind tee thirty-feet long where the planes would touch down when landing. At the latter wind tee, a six-foot pole should be placed with an eighteen-inch-wide by five-foot long streamer attached so pilots could determine the wind direction. Pilots always landed into the wind whenever possible. Fleet said a mailbox would have to be placed with a lock on it near the latter wind tee. On cross-country flights, aviators were required to drop a postcard with their signature in a mailbox, indicating their time of arrival at the field. Contents of the box were to be mailed to headquarters at Mather Field once a week.

Fleet reiterated the necessity of making the field very smooth. The Curtiss JN-4D Jenny training plane landed at forty miles per hour. If it hit a rough spot it was possible there would be damage to the plane. Fleet told the men planes were expensive; he said the plane he flew in that day was a Curtiss Jenny built in Sacramento at a cost of twelve thousand dollars each. This particular aircraft was one of the first on Mather Field.

Finishing his talk about the necessary field requirements, Fleet said a small gas station had to be built, then five gallons each of water, oil, and gasoline must be on hand at all times for the army aircraft. He made it clear the city must send him an authoritative letter stating it would comply with the requirements and would begin to prepare the field immediately.

Fleet outlined the government's intention to have landing fields at Marysville, Woodland, Colusa, and Arbuckle. Once the cadets started training, they would fly a circuit of those cities each day. He anticipated such flights would begin in about three weeks. As an afterthought, Fleet explained once the landing field was established, no one was allowed to enter the field when a plane was landing or departing, and at no time was anyone to come within twenty feet of an aircraft.

With their conference completed, Fleet and Hogland climbed back into their Jenny and left Knight Park. They ascended to five hundred feet and decided to put on a little exhibition for the folks who had gathered in the park to see the airplane. They first dove at the crowd and came so close everyone dropped to the ground believing they might be struck by the plane. The pilot pulled out of the dive, climbed to twenty-five hundred feet, then put the plane into a spiral nosedive. People watching at Seventh and B streets in Marysville said the plane came so close to the ground it clipped the tops of some orange trees in a yard nearby.

Secretary Chace mailed the required letter to Major Fleet at Mather

CHAPTER I   13

A mosaic reconnaissance photo of Marysville believed to have been taken by the US Army Air Service circa 1920. This part of the photo shows the racetrack in Knight Park.

Field. In the letter, he described Knight Park as being in the northeast corner of the city on land consisting of an unused municipal racetrack property, eighty acres in size. There was an adjoining property of forty additional acres available if necessary, and the entire 120 acres could be leased by the city for a nominal sum should the site be chosen as a landing site for Mather's aviation cadets.[16]

Fleet returned to Marysville a week later on a flight to Red Bluff in the company of another airplane. He met, once again, with Secretary Chace, and they discussed Knight Park. Chace said the city council would take up the matter of turning the park over to the Air Service sometime that week. He also said the work of making the park ready for airplanes would cost less than a hundred dollars. Fleet, before departing to Red Bluff to look at another prospective landing site, said he hoped the airfield would be ready the next time he came to Marysville. The army plane accompanying Fleet landed across the river in Sutter County—Fleet gave no details as to where or why it landed there.

The next night at the Marysville City Council meeting, there was confusion among the members. Some believed the city would forfeit title to Knight Park to the heirs of the late D. E. Knight, who donated the property, if it were used for anything other than horse racing. After a council member investigated, it was discovered there was no such provision in the deed. W. M. Meek, the city engineer, was then told to begin preparations of Knight Park immediately for use as an airfield by Mather aviators. He said he would begin tomorrow, and the work would take two days.[17]

Marysville's landing field was declared ready by Meek at the council meeting in August. Major Fleet was to be notified immediately. It was predicted as soon as the other cities had their landing fields prepared around the valley, the student flyers from Mather would begin their cross-country flights.[18]

Long flights from Mather Field had been limited to qualified Army Reserve pilots or by qualified flying officers at Mather. The students would not be flying any fixed route or distance. The landing fields they would fly to would depend on the current weather conditions and the particular student's abilities. Wind velocity and direction would also be determining factors in the fields used on any given day. The students had several choices to fly to from Marysville. They could fly to Woodland in the west and Fresno in the south in addition to a few other available airfields. The auxiliary fields were mostly forty to fifty acres in size with Marysville being one of the largest. The students were not allowed to make night flights away from Mather Field. They were trained in night flying only over Mather. Rated flying officers were allowed to fly away from the field at night. Night flights were carefully planned in advance. The students would be trained in nighttime cross-country flying after graduating from Mather and moving on to an advanced training base elsewhere.[19]

Major Fleet flew up to Knight Park in the company of another officer, Dellos C. Emmons, on August 8. City officials Chace and Swift met their plane in the park and from Swift's car they inspected the newly developed landing field. Fleet was pleased with the leveling job, but he felt more should be done to keep spectators off the field. He explained to the two civilians Willows residents wanted a landing field for their town, but spectators refused to stay off the field, so the army refused to use Willows as an auxiliary field.[20]

A few days later, three Curtiss Jennies landed at Knight Park. Lt. Leo F. Post, who had recently been appointed officer in charge of advanced cross-country flying, Lt. L. Long, and senior civilian flight instructor Charles McHenry Pond were piloting the planes. They came to deliver plans and specifications for the fuel station and other small structures needed to complete the site as an army auxiliary landing field. Lt. Post was impressed with the condition of the field. Due to its size, he felt it could accommodate thirty aircraft at one time. Lt. Post repeated Fleet's earlier warning about keeping people out of the racetrack oval. Secretary Chace and Mayor Arnoldy assured Post if the signs didn't work, a police officer would be sent to the field to enforce the rules. Chase and Arnoldy told Lt. Post, who had been a resident of nearby Gridley when he was young, the field would be leased to the government at the next city council meeting, and the rules would be strictly enforced. Post told the two men the landing field would, hereafter, be known as Mather Field, Auxiliary No. 1 Marysville.[21]

Lieutenant Post flew to Knight Park, once again, on August 19 to make final arrangements for the field's use, which he predicted would start in less than a week; however, later he let slip that flights wouldn't start until all of the auxiliary fields were ready. Once flights began, he said there would be fifteen to twenty planes a day going into Knight Park.[22]

The lieutenant took a letter from the Marysville baseball committee back with him to Mather Field. It was addressed to the post baseball team welcoming them to Marysville the following Sunday for a game against the Marysville Giants. It was said to be the first airmail letter ever sent from Marysville.[23]

Three sisters, Bernice, Manila, and Dorothy Reissinger, responded to a recent newspaper article requesting a flag for the Knight Park airfield. The three sisters gave a six-by-nine-foot American flag to Secretary Chace to be flown at the landing site. He announced it would (unwisely) be flown from a staff in the center of the airfield where every landing cadet could dip his wing to it.[24]

The Mather Field baseball team visited Marysville to play the Marysville

Giants on August 25. An unauthorized article was published in the newspaper stating the team would arrive by airplane. Hundreds of local citizens turned out to watch the planes. When the team arrived by other means, there was great disappointment. Major Fleet, who was in temporary command of Mather Field, heard about the disappointed citizens and made them a promise he would send a plane to the area on Admission Day to put on an exhibition of stunt flying for the day's celebration.[25]

For Admission Day, a patriotic celebration was held at Bert's Feather River Resort on the river between Marysville and Yuba City. One of the afternoon events was a stunt-flying exhibition by Lieutenant Jacobson. He did every maneuver in his repertoire thrilling the good citizens of the Twin Cities. Fleet, who would be leaving Mather Field in a week for duty in the East, had kept his promise.

Reuben Fleet would, after the war, become a giant in the aviation industry. He founded Consolidated Aircraft at San Diego, the company that designed and built the B-24 bomber used in World War II. His company was later renamed Convair and built thousands of aircraft for the Army Air Corps and later the US Air Force.[26]

Lieutenant Post notified Chace student pilots from Mather Field would begin visiting the auxiliary fields in groups of twenty to thirty airplanes beginning September 12. The first group was supposed to visit Knight Park that day. Post would be in charge of the group, and they would get their supplies and meals in Marysville. The group was to remain all day and in the future come to Marysville about five times per month. He invited the public to witness the flying, but stay off the field. The group flights may or may not have occurred. This author has not been able to discover any record of aerial activities taking place at Knight Park on the twelfth nor any group of training flights coming to Knight Park. They probably did, but written records of cadets landing at Knight Park have not surfaced. The World War ended two months later on November 11, 1918, and training at Mather Field was drastically curtailed.[27]

Two aviators from Mather caused quite a stir in the duck hunting gun clubs of Sutter County in mid-November. The two flew up to Sutter County in their Curtiss JNs, and after bagging their limits of ducks and geese, they cranked up their Jennies and put on an exhibition for the gun club members. They chased the ducks and geese all about the sky. Diving through the large formations of geese, they broke the formations up into clouds of confused birds scrambling to get out of the way of this new threat to their sky. The maneuvers amazed the hunters on the ground.[28]

Miss Laura Thornbrough, formerly of Meridian in Sutter County, became one of the first Red Cross nurses to fly in an airplane ambulance in the state. Thornbrough, a US Army nurse in charge of the hospital at Mather Field, went up with Lt. John D. Swain in a new aerial ambulance created from a Curtiss JN-4 in Mather's machine shops. The flying ambulance held a single person on a belted stretcher lying horizontally in the fuselage with his head towards the front of the plane.[29]

Five aircraft, probably Curtiss JN-4s, departed Mather Field on December 10 at 9:35 AM and landed at Knight Park forty minutes later. They were on a "pathfinder flight." Leaving Knight Park, they would fly to Gridley and land—then on to Chico. From there they were to proceed to Red Bluff for the night. The following day they would return to Mather. These pathfinder missions were being carried out from most military airfields around the United States during December 1918 and January 1919. The purpose was to gather information for the Army Air Service's Navigation Branch with special attention paid to air navigation routes, landing fields, description of

Lieutenant George Bihlmann (first on the right) during his training as a bomber (later termed bombardier) in Texas during the Great War.

terrain overflown, and weather conditions on the flight, etc. In addition to navigational research, the flights were intended to inform the public of the services that army aviation could provide for the public and what the Air Service's postwar potential could be.[30]

Mather Field had graduated 201 Reserve Military Aviators by December 5, 1918. To accomplish this, the Curtiss JN-4Ds at Mather flew 29,939 hours.[31]

Major Walter Wynns of Mather Field sent a message on January 22, 1919, to the city of Marysville stating the Army Air Service would no longer need Knight Park as a landing field. The park was returned to city control. City officials believed Marysville might be used as an airmail stop in the near future, and they let it be known the park would continue to be used as a flying field.[32]

After the World War ended, local soldiers who had served in the Army Air Service were returning home. From the Yuba-Sutter community, Al Makepeace, Rennie J. Mahon, Erling S. Norby, and George H. Bihlman served as aviators. Allen Cunningham spent twenty-one months in England with the Air Service as an electrician, and Lon C. Fugitt served as an aviation mechanic at a mechanic's training school in Saint Paul, Minnesota.[33]

Only one aviator from the Yuba-Sutter community made it to France, Rennie J. Mahon, and he arrived there too late to see any action.

Nelson Dewey Ashford was assigned to a photography squadron at Langley, Virginia, where he logged 120 flying hours before being mustered out of the army. He would become a dedicated pilot and aviation enthusiast in the Yuba-Sutter community for the next sixty years.[34]

George Bihlman had the unusual job of bomber (later designated as bombardier) in the Air Service. He became an instructor of bombing at Ellington Field, Houston, Texas. He had left Stanford University in his senior year and enlisted in the Army Air Service. Towards the end of his service, he learned to fly. The job of bombardier was rare in the US Army Air Service in 1918; there were few aircraft in service large enough to carry a special crewmember to act as bombardier.[35] After the war, Bihlman participated in the 1920 Olympic Games as a shot putter on the American team.[36]

In April 1919, the Army Air Service began a barnstorming campaign across the nation utilizing three separate flying circuses made up of Air Service planes and personnel flying to eighty-eight cities in forty-five states. The flying circus for the Eastern states was from Hazelhurst Field, New York. The one working the Midwest was out of Ellington Field, Texas. The group performing for the Western states was from Rockwell Field, San Diego. Major Carl Spatz, (who later changed his name to Spaatz) commanded this latter group. The reason for the army barnstorming tours was to promote the Victory Loan campaign and stimulate the citizenry to buy Liberty Bonds to pay for America's participation in the World War. The Air Service also used the barnstorming tours to encourage enlistment in the Air Service and continue its pathfinder research. Air Service command naively believed the Air Service would be maintained at the congressionally mandated number of fifteen thousand men. Unfortunately, the funds to support such a number were not approved. [37]

Sgt. William Wingfield, army recruiting officer for the Yuba-Sutter area, was notified by Col. Henry Watson, officer in charge of flying at Mather Field, that a squadron of aircraft would arrive at Knight Park for the dual purposes of promoting the sale of Victory Loan Bonds and obtaining recruits for the Air Service. Watson announced that the two people in each county who purchased the most bonds and who sold the most bonds, would be taken for a ride in an army aircraft. Army regulations prohibited civilians from riding in army aircraft, however, it was agreed the service would waive the regulations for the war bond tours.[38]

At Mather Field, army fliers formed a small Northern California flying circus for Major Spatz. They were: squadron commander Col. H. L. Watson, Capt. Hopkins, lieutenants Krull, Gardner, and Schwartz, and sergeant pilots Buckley and McKee.

Lt. James S. Krull flew into Knight Park on March 8 at 12:50 PM in a de Havilland DH-4 bomber, No. 18, carrying five bundles of the *San Francisco Call*. He had picked up the newspapers at San Francisco's Marina Field only two hours before. He flew over Vallejo, Vacaville, Woodland, and Knight's Landing to Marysville. He had a thirty-mile per hour wind blowing and excellent visibility when he crossed the bay, but upon reaching the Great Central Valley it became very hazy, and he had difficulty locating the towns. Finally making it to Marysville, he delivered the newspapers and joined the other Air Service pilots at Knight Park.

The army pilots put on a spectacular air show of stunt flying. The four people who won airplane rides were Catherine Gill and George Boyd, who had sold the most Liberty Bonds. Ed Johnson and Ruth Harter got rides because they had purchased the most bonds. When these four went up, they were subjected to every aerobatic maneuver the pilots could muster.

The business district of Marysville was deserted, and the schools in

Marysville and across the river in Yuba City were closed so students could get to the park and watch the stunt flying.[39]

Henry Neimeyer, secretary of the Yuba County Chamber of Commerce, made arrangements with Marysville's Mayor Arnoldy and members of the city council to officially announce re-establishment of a landing field at Knight Park. E. H. Pendleton, manager of the Sacramento Aviation Field, was considering an office at Knight Park for the sale of airplanes and accessories to private aircraft owners.[40]

Sacramento Aviation Company sent L. J. Reese to Marysville on August 1, 1919, to book passengers for rides in the company's Curtiss Jennies the following weekend at Knight Park. Reese was remembered in the city as one of the speakers for the Victory Loan train, which had passed through town some time back. At the time, he told of his experiences in some of the biggest air battles on the Western Front during the war. Now, he was promoting the Sacramento Aviation Company as having the best fliers around and said they had been hired to carry out night flying stunts for the upcoming California State Fair.

Reese told everyone the price for an airplane ride was one dollar a minute for a gentle conservative fifteen-minute ride. Reese advised people to take their ride on Saturday, if possible, because on the previous Sunday the pilots had to refuse flights to twenty people because there wasn't enough daylight left to take them up. Reese said his company's home airfield was in the Cutter Tract of Sacramento's Curtiss Park, east of today's McClatchy High School.[41]

The Sacramento Aviation Company plane arrived at Knight Park on the morning of the second. Ex-Lieutenant Mess flew Schillig Thayer of Grimes as his passenger. Anxiously waiting for the plane at the park was the first paying passenger, Walter Lewis, manager of Garret Company. Soon Lewis was taking his first plane ride at thirty-five hundred feet over Marysville and loving it.[42]

The results of Sacramento Aviation Company's barnstorming tour to Marysville were reported a week later. The folks who lived out of town were charged less for their airplane rides than those who lived in town. It was reported, "Recently an aviation outfit gave our people (in town) a ride at one dollar a minute, trips averaging in cost fifteen dollars. This past week a Stockton concern has been giving farmers of the Grimes and Meridian sections rides at fifty cents per minute, or a ten minute voyage in the blue sky for five dollars. This same outfit will give the residents of Sutter City a

Chapter 1   21

From the earlier mentioned USAAS mosaic reconnaissance photo of 1918-1920, Jackson Bottoms, adjacent to Yuba City, is depicted in the upper left quadrant of the photo from the diagonal road (Garden Highway) to the Feather River. This was the makeshift airfield used by Charles Kingsford-Smith in April 1920 and in later years by many others.

chance at aerial joyriding this coming week. The aviators are said to be Canadian flyers."

H. L. "Bud" Coffee, a Bay Area aviator, landed at Knight Park in early April 1920. He was flying Roy Mires, the Lexington Six auto dealer, to Red Bluff and back from San Francisco.[43]

The municipal golf club asked the city council to use Knight Park as the site for a city golf course. They wanted to put a fence around the course. Since there was a possibility the park would be utilized in the future by the US Air Mail Service, they felt justified in asking the city for twenty-five hundred dollars to help with fencing costs. In November, contractors began tearing down all of the old buildings on the park grounds. The golf course was laid out with the help of Professor Selkirk of Edinburgh, Scotland, who was in charge of the Del Paso Park Golf Course near Sacramento. Marysville's course was to be finished in January 1921.[44]

CHARLES KINGSFORD-SMITH (CKS), who would become Australia's and United Kingdom's most famous aviator, flew into Jackson Bottoms at Yuba City in early April 1920. Jackson Bottoms was the name local folks called the river bottom area of southeastern Yuba City.

Jackson Bottoms was a level and reasonably unobstructed acreage that was unused and undeveloped in the 1920s. It belonged to a Dr. Jackson who lived in a large house built at the northern tip of the property, where B Street turns south and becomes Garden Highway today. Dr. Jackson divided his time living in this house and his other residence in Sacramento. The bottoms were a long narrow property bounded on the north and east by the Sutter County levee that ran along the Feather River and by a much older and smaller bow levee paralleling Garden Highway on the western and southern boundaries. This small levee shielded the activities that took place in the bottoms from the highway and the rest of the city. Those activities included a yearly Easter egg hunt and occasional dog races at a makeshift track. The southwestern section of the bottoms became home for a seasonal auto camp for itinerant fruit pickers.

When Kingsford-Smith landed in Jackson Bottoms, he was unknown, broke, and flying a borrowed Jenny. The plane belonged to his employer, Edmund J. Moffett, owner of Moffett Aero Service, a company whose various addresses in the early 1920s were in Sacramento, Colusa, Willows, and Woodland. Kingsford-Smith or "Smithy," (pronounced Smitty) as he was known, was worried at the time about that most serious threat to a barnstormer's health—starvation. Ed Von Geldern, the city engineer who lived a block from Jackson Bottoms, helped out and took Smithy in during his monthlong stay in Yuba City.

The Hispano-Suiza (Hisso) powered Jenny that CKS brought to Yuba City was in dilapidated condition and was kept flying only by using spare parts from two of Moffett's other Jennies that had been wrecked, undoubtedly, during the 1919 duck herding season.

Ed's son, Rick, later told of his family's memories of Charles Kingsford-Smith's stay with them. Kingsford-Smith, with Ed Von Geldern riding along, was flying the Jenny one spring day over Hammonton, a small town (that no longer exists) in the Sierra foothill gold dredging fields east of Marysville and Yuba City. Smithy got a little warm in the plane and climbed out to stand on the lower wing to cool off after telling Von Geldern to hold the stick steady. Smithy's coat was flapping in the slipstream and his military discharge papers along with his aviator's credentials blew out of his pocket and scattered in the wind over the endless mounds of cobblestones in the dredger fields. A ground search was carried out later, but the documents were never found.

When CKS took Red Dowell, a Yuba City auto dealer, up for his first airplane ride, he had to make several runs across the airfield to burn off enough gasoline to lighten the Jenny enough to get off the ground. At the end of the flight, he landed hard with Dowell and broke the tailskid on the JN. The next morning while making his first flight of the day, the entire tailskid assembly fell off of the Jenny. When Smithy landed, the absence of the skid put so much ground drag on the Jenny it was pulled into two pieces. A telephone order was placed for parts from Moffett's two wrecked Jennies to get Smithy's plane airworthy once again.[45]

Kingsford-Smith wasn't paid a steady wage as a pilot with Moffett Aero Service. He was loaned the airplane and only made money by giving plane rides—taking up photographers and other businessmen who could benefit from the aerial views. He had to kick back some of his money to the Jenny's owner. This was the situation CKS was in until mid-August when Moffett's contracts with various rice farmers went into effect. CKS made a salary based on the number of acres he flew for the rice growers. His job for the growers was chasing ducks and geese from their fields. It was a disgustingly dangerous job. There are photos extant of the airplane after one of the missions flown just a couple of feet above the rice crop that show the wings, fuselage, and aviator covered with duck feathers, blood, and guts. One wonders how such a light and flimsy airplane could stay airborne after multiple goose strikes on the airframe.[46]

In an effort to make a little more money, Smithy was able to get the local newspaper to print a brief notice that a Moffett Aero Service plane, flown by Lt. C. K. Smith, would be giving rides for ten dollars each at River Road (now Garden Highway), Yuba City, opposite Tom Giblin's ranch. The Giblin property was located on the west side of Garden Highway, five hundred to one thousand feet south of present day Franklin Road, directly across the road from the bow levee and Jackson Bottoms.[47]

The advertisement stated E. J. Moffett, the organizer and (possible) originator of duck herding in Colusa and Glenn counties, with British ace (actually Australian), Lt. C. K. Smith would be giving airplane rides and an aerial exhibition from Giblin's ranch at Yuba City on April 19–20. There has been no evidence found that Moffett, himself, did any flying at Yuba City or was even capable of flying.[48]

The same ad was published the following day with an additional notice to, "See our movie of the rice patrol showing at the Lyric tonight and the Liberty Sunday. A Thriller don't miss it. Moffett Aero Service. The Tested Ships with Tested Crews. Moffett Aero Service of Sacramento."[49]

More evidence of CKS' flying work at Yuba City is reflected in the following news notice: "Farm advisor Sullivan to take pictures from a plane over Yuba City and Marysville."[50]

On April 23, 1920, a news reporter photographed Catherine Gill sitting on the fuselage of Smithy's Jenny with him standing next to her. They were both in flying togs and leather helmets. They had just come down from a half-hour flight over Marysville promoting the opening of the chamber of commerce campaign to recruit members and raise money for a fifteen thousand dollar service fund.

When asked if she wasn't a little afraid during the flight, Gill replied, "That depends on who is piloting the plane. With a British ace having eleven Boches to his credit it would be foolish to be fearful even in the slightest degree."[51] Actually, Kingsford-Smith was officially credited with four aerial victories and forcing down nine German observation balloons during the war.[52]

A week later, Smithy flew Ed Von Geldern from Yuba City to the Nicolaus area to attend a surveying job. They made the twenty-mile trip in seventeen minutes in Smithy's Jenny.[53]

In early May, Kingsford-Smith left Yuba City. There were no reports of him again until late June when he turned up at an air show in Sacramento flying for Ed Moffett. This time Moffett had acquired two Avro 504K biplanes from Robert Fowler in San Francisco. Fowler was a West Coast dealer for Allied Aircraft Ltd., an Eastern concern that sold British military surplus aircraft in Canada and the United States after the war. The Avro 504K was the standard primary training aircraft for the British Royal Flying Corps during the World War. The Avro was considered a better airplane than either the Jenny or the Standard J-1 trainers.

Some 504Ks sold in America had three seats making them very desirable for passenger hopping. The Avro was powered by a Le Rhone rotary engine, which was a drawback for sales. The engine, spinning with the propeller, produced considerable torque requiring more opposite rudder application on takeoff, a disconcerting response for American ex-military pilots who never flew rotary engine aircraft. The Le Rhone wasn't throttle controlled; it ran at full speed, half speed, or was shut-off completely by pressing a "blip" switch on the control stick. This switch regulated the amount of spark to the spark plugs on the spinning engine. CKS, having flown many hours in 504Ks during his wartime training, probably did his best to persuade Moffett to acquire the Avros.[54]

CKS made his dream of flying the Pacific Ocean known to all after *Aerial Age Weekly*, an important aviation trade magazine, published in June 1920 a brief paragraph about the aviator that read, "Lt. Charles Edward K. Smith of Oakland, California, is making preparations to attempt to be the first man to fly across the Pacific Ocean … although nothing definite has been decided he will use a seaplane similar to the NC-4 [untrue], which made the transatlantic flight. He has hopes of joining Sir Arthur Brown [would never happen], navigator on the first (nonstop) Atlantic crossing with Captain Alcock in a Vickers."[55]

Reportedly Kingsford-Smith and Ed Moffett would take part in what was described as, "A monster air circus at South Curtis Oaks Field," in Curtis Park of the Cutter Tract of Sacramento. A. E. Wagner, a north state air show promoter, assembled the participants for the event under the auspices of the American War Mothers of Sacramento. The event was to take place on Sunday, June 27, 1920. On Wednesday, the twenty-third, Kingsford-Smith and E. E. Mouton landed at South Curtis Oaks Field in Moffett's two Avro 504K biplanes. If Moffett was there he was not flying.[56]

The air show for the American War Mothers did not go as advertised due to high winds on the twenty-seventh and smoke from small fires caused by spectators tossing their cigarette butts into the grass stubble on the airfield. However, the biggest problem was greed on the part of a few aviators. Only five planes showed up for the "monster air show." The pilots only wanted to give rides (at ten dollars each) instead of performing stunts for the three thousand people who came to see an air show. Two thousand of them paid fifty cents each to see stunt flying, and all they saw was an occasional loop performed by an aviator trying to thrill his paying passenger. The results of this disappointing show caused the War Mothers to withhold payment to the promoter for a short time. CKS mentions in his autobiography that he was never paid for his air circus flying because someone ran off with the money. He may have been referring to this Sacramento air show.[57]

It was around this time that CKS went to Hollywood seeking the "big money" he believed could be made in movie flying. In a recent biography of Kingsford-Smith there is an image of him hanging from the undercarriage of an Avro 504K while flying over the California desert during a film shoot. During that shoot, he hung upside down from the landing gear axle pinned by the wind speed, barely having the strength to recover. His movie-flying career ended after witnessing the death of Ormer Locklear, Hollywood's most famous early stunt flyer, on August 2, 1920. Locklear was filming a night shoot not far from DeMille Field, Los Angeles, and while doing a night aerobatic scene he was blinded by spotlights used to illuminate his aircraft for the cameras. In the ensuing crash, Locklear and fellow pilot, Milton "Skeets" Elliott, were killed.

Kingsford-Smith hadn't been in Hollywood long enough to "pay his dues." He couldn't get enough film work to keep him in bread and beans. He was there long enough to learn that various cliques and guilds got most of the work, and they would never allow an outsider, who just showed up on their doorstep to get much work, regardless of his war record. Another factor in his leaving Los Angeles was CKS' commitment to E. J. Moffett's duck herding contracts in Colusa and Glenn counties scheduled to begin August 15, 1920.[58]

Smithy really didn't owe Ed Moffett any loyalty for the amount he was paid to scare ducks off rice fields, but Moffett had Smithy on a hook. He had made promises to CKS he might bankroll a future Pacific flight for the young Australian.[59] Both men dreamed of a Pacific flight—Smithy to make such a flight and Moffett to promote one. They didn't fulfill their dreams as a team. Smithy's dream would come true in 1928. Moffett's dream came apart after he promoted the less-than-successful Smith-Carter Hawaiian flight in June 1927.

CKS must have come to the realization near the end of duck herding season that Moffett would never have the kind of money necessary to finance a Pacific flight to Australia, and Smithy had run out of ideas to obtain the funds. He decided to go back to Australia soon by way of ship.

Charles Kingsford-Smith came to Yuba City once again in his lifetime. He came in the tri-motor Fokker he would fly to fame. The Fokker's name *Southern Cross* was changed temporarily to the *Spirit of California* for an unrefueled endurance record CKS was attempting to set in December 1927. He believed the fame of setting a new endurance record would make it easier to get financial backing for his planned flight to Australia from California.

Smithy hired George Pond to be his copilot for the endurance flight because of Pond's experience flying multi-engine transports. They departed Mills Field, San Francisco, and flew great circles above the Bay Area. Smithy extended one of his circles all the way up to Marysville on the day he started his final record attempt, January 17, 1928. He circled Marysville and Yuba City at 12:55 PM. Of course he didn't land, but in his own way, he paid his respects to the citizens of the Twin Cities area where he was once stranded and broke.

CHAPTER I   27

CKS had to exceed fifty-one hours in nonstop flight to break the record. His longest attempt was his first on December 20, but he ran out of fuel after forty-nine hours and had to land at Mills Field. He made four more attempts over the next month but all failed, although he did gain valuable multi-engine experience flying the Fokker with Pond.[60]

Following Kingsford-Smith's monthlong stay in Yuba City, another aviator who would one day become famous, "dropped in," literally, on the Yuba-Sutter community. Major Carl Spatz and his pilot suffered engine problems with the de Havilland DH-4 they were flying on a cross-country trip in June 1920. They were forced to land in a grain field belonging to Rob Anderson, three miles south of Marysville.

Spatz and his pilot were cruising at two thousand feet when the engine developed problems, and they began their glide to land. After they descended to one hundred feet, a wind gust pushed the plane's tail up forcing the nose down. The pilot responded quickly, but the DH still struck the ground nose down and was damaged. Both men were uninjured. They located a telephone and called for assistance from Mather Field. A salvage crew brought a truck, dismantled the de Havilland, and took it back to Mather.

Major Spatz was flying from Red Bluff to Mather when the incident occurred.[61] The spot where Spatz's DH-4 came down was very close to the current location of Marysville's Yuba County Airport.

Major Spatz, (later Spaatz) would eventually command the Eighth Air Force in England during World War II. After that he became the commanding general of the newly created and independent, US Air Force in September 1947.

ANOTHER LOCAL AVIATION MILESTONE, which surprised many citizens of the Yuba-Sutter community, was the first flight of the Friesley Falcon airliner on April 6, 1921. Two Yuba-Sutter men in a car were driving along the state highway (now Highway 99) from Gridley to Live Oak when, two miles south of Gridley from Friesly Field, the company airport, a large twin-engine biplane suddenly sped by them on the dirt runway and took to the air. The startled driver nearly lost control of the car from the surprise.

For the past year the Falcon was being built in a large hangar constructed on the west side of the railroad track which parallels Highway 99 on the east side. The two men stopped their car across from the hangar and asked if the airplane was indeed the "big fellow," which many folks in the community had heard and read about in the local papers for months. Some had even purchased stock in the Friesley Company. One of the men called the Marysville newspaper as soon as they got to a phone and reported what had happened. The Falcon had just made an unexpected half-hour flight. The twelve-passenger plane would be making its official "first" flight in front of ten to fifteen thousand spectators in just ten days from Friesley Field.[62]

The son of Mrs. Lottie Cunningham, Dudley, built a model of the Friesley Falcon in woodshop at Marysville High School. It was considered one of the most attractive exhibits at the high school and later took an award at the State Fair. Dudley Cunningham was an important figure in Yuba-Sutter aviation from 1927 through the 1950s. He became the caretaker and manager, sometimes paid and sometimes unpaid, of Cheim Field, the only permanent civilian airport in the Yuba-Sutter area, which operated successfully from 1929 until a few years after the end of World War II.[63]

The Marysville City Council, in July 1921, discussed the necessity of establishing an airport in the city. Numerous town councils were realizing the need to take advantage of the progress being made in aerial transportation. Airports, approved by the federal government, were placed on the makeshift maps and pilot's notes of every aviator in the nation. Marysville once had an ideal landing field at Knight Park, but it was converted into a golf course. The city council agreed to find a new site for an airfield. They believed Yuba County would become an attractive destination for aviation business if two of its towns, Hammonton and Marysville, each had airports,. It was suggested land to the east of Knight Park be considered for a new airfield. In September, the city council received an offer for seventy acres east of the park for an airport. The property was offered on a lease basis at sixty dollars an acre. Councilmen Arnoldy, Cook, and Booth were chosen as the city council's airport committee and assigned to investigate the proposal.[64]

The Friesley Falcon was flying around the Yuba-Sutter area regularly since its maiden flight in April. It was making three to four flights a week from Gridley and Marysville areas carrying over four hundred passengers during seventy flights made by August 15, 1921. Bonifield "Bond" M. Spencer, the plane's designer and builder, and later Roy Francis, a Bay Area pioneer aviator, carried out all of the Falcon's flights.[65]

On August 7, the Friesley Falcon made its best-known contribution to aviation and baseball history. The Marysville Merchants baseball team was flown from Friesley Field near Gridley to Yolo Fliers' Club Field, a new airfield near the ballpark at Woodland. At the time, it was said this was the first baseball team to ever travel by airplane to a game. It was a publicity stunt designed to bring attention to the plane and its manufacturer. The stunt was effective; newspapers all around the country picked up the story. Using the nation's pastime as the hook the stunt was a great public relations event for the Friesley. Locally, the photo of the baseball team standing in front of the Friesley was hung in many a saloon and barbershop in the Twin Cities. It still hangs in a few.

The famous photo (see p. 334) shows the team standing in front of the Falcon in a group of fifteen. It was good advertising for the Friesley Company; it implied the plane could carry more than it did. The Falcon was advertised as a twelve-passenger aircraft. Actually, it could only seat ten in the passenger cabin and two crewmen in the cockpit.

The team flew to Woodland and played the Woodland American Legion team. It was a sad showing for Marysville. The Merchants were handicapped by the absence of their starting catcher Charles Hust and outfielder Gerald Trayner. Both were unable to make the flight due to illness—or was it because there wasn't room in the plane?

Highlights of the game began when pitcher Cliff Gotwals was "driven from the mound in the third ... and Bryden Kelly took his place. Kelly twirled a nice brand of ball but by that time the Woodland team had put the game on ice." "[Tyrell] Brooks was the hitting star of the day ..." for Marysville after "... he drove one into a haystack in deep left center for a homer. He also secured a three-bagger and a single," but Woodland won the game 15–3.

Other players who flew with the team were: Harvey Eich the manager, Charles Brown, Lewis Wilcoxen, Willis Laughlin, Lou Anthony, Clyde Manwell, Allen Eich, Warren Eich, and batboy Wilton Eich. The Falcon's crew consisted of Bond Spencer, pilot; Grafton Reed, mechanic; and Roy Francis as copilot.[66]

The flight to Woodland took the Friesley thirty minutes cruising at an altitude of three thousand feet. Once the city of Woodland was observed, Spencer took the airliner down to one thousand feet to spot the airfield easier. It was discovered quickly four miles west of town. The landing tee, inside a circle outlined in white, could be seen for several miles. The Liberty engines were brought back to idle and the Friesley descended to land. After the game, the flight back home to Marysville was by way of Sacramento.[67]

This was the first time in history a baseball team flew to a game *on the same plane*, but it was *not* the first time a baseball team had flown to a game. (see chapter 12).

IN SPRING 1923, there was a flurry of aviation activity in the Yuba-Sutter community. Full-page advertisements in a Sacramento newspaper promoted land for sale in Yuba County's Tolosano tract in early March. The tract was located ten miles north of Marysville near the Butte County line southwest of Honcut.[68]

Aviator Joe McKinney flew north in a Curtiss JN-4 Jenny from Sacramento with assistant publisher of the *Sacramento Union*, Victor H. Werlhof on March 19. They landed at Wonderland Farms, seven miles north of Marysville in the southern Tolosano tract. Earlier they had flown up from San Diego where McKinney optioned to buy three hundred JN-4s from the US government for resale.

A young Yuba County farmer, who was in the Air Service during the war, T. M. Blake, bought a Jenny from McKinney. Blake lived near the Tolosano tract.

McKinney was manager of Sierra Aircraft Company's flying school in Sacramento. He flew between Sacramento and San Diego in a French Salmson, a modified warplane, in four hours and fifty minutes, which he claimed was a new record. McKinney was negotiating with organizers of the Yuba-Sutter Peach Day celebration to bring three of Sierra Aircraft Company's Jennies to Yuba City for stunt flying and passenger hopping operations during the festivities.[69]

Two days after McKinney and Werlhof met with Sutter County Chamber of Commerce member A. A. Mullen, it was agreed that McKinney would bring the trio of airplanes to Yuba City for Peach Day June 1–2. The planes would fly an exhibition each afternoon and another after dark with fireworks shooting from the aircraft. McKinney said he would paint advertising signs on his aircraft for Peach Day.[70]

On March 23, McKinney took the editor of the *Marysville Democrat* for a ride in a Jenny. They took off from the landing strip at Jackson Bottoms, Yuba City, which the locals were beginning to call Jackson Field.[71]

McKinney reported his plans to buy a hundred acres of flat ground south of Yuba City to build a one hundred by three hundred-foot factory to manufacture airplanes, employing four hundred workers. McKinney dealt with chamber member A. A. Mullen. When asked about using hydroplanes on the Feather River, McKinney said it would be too dangerous. He

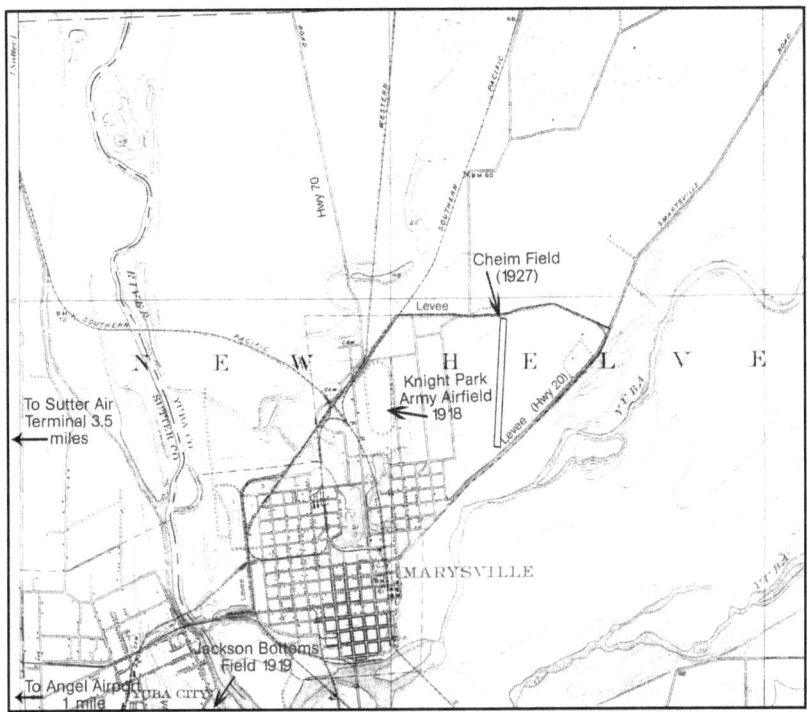

Map of Yuba-Sutter airport sites 1918–1928.

reiterated he had more than thirty aircraft on his field in Sacramento. The Yuba City land and aircraft factory deal never materialized.

McKinney wanted to establish a flying community on Tolosano's land. He offered any former AEF (American Expeditionary Forces) aviator from the Great War a free Curtiss Jenny if he would buy land in the Tolosano tract and become a Yuba County rancher (farmer). McKinney claimed he had three hundred Curtiss JNs worth $300 to $750 each. Mr. Tolosano was even more specific; he stated that anyone who would buy a forty-acre plot of land would receive a free airplane.[72]

Joe McKinney's first name was actually Ive. This fact was revealed in a newspaper article that placed Ive McKinney and Robert Clohecy, both pilots, with Jack Shalk, an Orpheum acrobat, and seventy-three other aviators, as participating in the 1923 Mother's Day flying meet in Sacramento. This meant Ive "Joe" McKinney was, undoubtedly, the same Ive McKinney who in 1926 joined the Gates Flying Circus, one of the largest flying circuses in the United States, and one of the most successful. Ivan R. Gates, an early Bay Area aviation promoter, Lowell Yerex, and Clyde "Upside-Down" Pangborn, as chief pilot, led the Gates Flying Circus. This barnstorming group of aviators flew together from 1919 until its last performance at Palo Alto in 1931. Gates' pilots, wing walkers, and parachutists changed from time to time, as they came and went or were killed, but the group was in continuous service throughout those years. For most of those years, the group was known as the Gates Flying Circus and was at the pinnacle of its success in 1927 when it was eleven aircraft strong. At that time, its pilots were flying Jennies, Standards, a Curtiss R, and a Bellanca.

The Department of Commerce (DOC) Aeronautics Branch, under William P. MacCracken, began applying pressure in 1927 to end barnstorming. Within the next four years federal regulations stopped the use of war surplus aircraft (Jennies and Standards) and banned wing walking and stunt flying without the participants wearing parachutes. The DOC singled out Gates Flying Circus, the biggest and most successful barnstormers, and Gates left the business by 1928.[73] Clyde Pangborn renamed it the Flying Fleet.

There was a local connection in the upcoming Peach Day aerial activities. W. J. Obele of Marysville had been a participant in the 1923 Mother's Day air show in Sacramento. The event took place at Sierra Aircraft Company's east Sacramento airfield managed by Joe McKinney. Obele and his wife, in earlier times ran the A&W Root Beer stand in the Western Hotel in downtown Marysville. Obele also happened to be a parachute jumper. Peach Day officials were in talks to get him to jump on June 2 during the celebration.[74]

On May 18, 1923, Robert J. Clohercy and J. L. Flanders, in a Sierra Aircraft Company plane were caught in a sudden thunderstorm a few miles south of Yuba City. The heavy rain blinded them and forced a landing a couple of miles from town. Their destination was Chico for an exhibition. Flanders was also scheduled to fly with Joe McKinney for Yuba City's Peach Day celebration in a couple weeks.[75]

Joe McKinney, with passenger Victor Werlhof, flew up the valley advertising the Peach Day celebration at Yuba City. McKinney had California Peach Day painted on the top and bottom of his wings. He planned to do loops over neighboring towns to advertise the event.[76]

The Peach Day schedule included an illuminated airplane flight at 10:00 PM on June 1 and stunt flying at 3:30 PM the next day, which would include a parachute jump. Flying would take place over the Jackson Bottoms airfield at Yuba City. At 4:30 PM there would be hound races on the Jackson Bottoms course adjoining the flying field, and events would finish with another illuminated airplane flight at 10:00 PM.[77]

Flanders and Clohercy air dropped fifteen thousand air show programs on towns around the valley. They flew from Sierra Field in Sacramento to various valley towns and then on to Yuba City, landing at Jackson Bottoms.[78]

The Peach Day flying activities were a great success. Passenger flights were given continuously throughout the celebrations, and the stunt flying went off with only one small hitch. Bill Obele did his wing walking but was unable to parachute jump. A chute for him could not be found. Joe McKinney did the stunt flying after dark.[79]

Bill Obele was requested by the Dobbins Farm Center, two months later, to skywrite the word Dobbins over Marysville and Yuba City using one of Sierra Aircraft Company's Jennies. It was to promote their upcoming Buck Stew celebration. Skywriting required specially equipped airplanes and the Jenny was too underpowered to accomplish the task successfully; it is doubtful this request was carried out.[80]

Jackson Bottoms was used for more dog racing in June 1923. By late July, it was returned to use as a growers' auto camp for migrant fruit workers. The committee in charge of the camp reported that unless the local orchardists kicked in adequate financial support, the two hundred occupants would be evicted, and the growers' labor source would be cut off. On August 1, the camp was closed.[81]

Sierra Aircraft Company's Jack Shalk came to Marysville on August 1 to finalize a deal to fly exhibitions on the following weekend. He picked suitable ground next to the state highway (now Highway 65) near the intersection of Hammonton Road as a landing field for the exhibitions.[82]

Joe McKinney and Bill Obele flew to Mexico and back to Marysville in early August. At a later date, these same pilots crashed into San Francisco Bay between Alcatraz and Angel Island. Their destination was San Francisco's Marina Field, but they found it fogged in and turned back. They either ran out of gas or spun in because of the fog. They survived crashing in the bay with minor injuries. They planned to be flying again for Buck Stew Day and to fly an aerial golf match at Marysville.[83]

The Army Air Service's Round-The-World Flight of Douglas Cruisers returned to the United States in early September 1924. Local Yuba City druggist L. C. White of the Kirk-White Drug Company was overjoyed by the news. His cousin was Lowell H. Smith, commander of the flight.[84]

Capt. Lowell H. Smith was going to Sacramento for a reserve officers military ball February 20, 1925, put on by the 361st Infantry. Twenty-three aviators were to fly in for the event. Captain Smith was scheduled to come from San Diego in his thirty thousand dollar Waldo Waterman copy of an army LePere biplane given to him by Glendale millionaire L. C. Brand for the great work Smith did leading the Round-The-World Flight. The original commander, Major Fredrick Martin, crashed when leading the flight early on.[85]

Erling Norby, a Yuba County attorney who was commander of the Yuba-Sutter American Legion Post, heard about Captain Smith coming to Sacramento. He called mutual friends of Smith's in Sacramento and invited the captain to visit Marysville for the dedication and grand ball for the new Memorial Auditorium. Norby and Smith were old friends from the Air Service during the World War. Smith was also remembered as vice president of the Friesley Aircraft Company of Gridley.[86]

Norby's efforts to invite the now famous aviator to Marysville for the auditorium dedication sparked the interest of James E. Read, manager of Western Auto Supply in Marysville. Read had been in Marysville since December 1924. Upon reading of Norby, Read decided to look him up wondering if Norby was his old flying buddy from Rockwell Field, San Diego, during the war. He was the same man, and they had a grand reunion. Lowell Smith was unable to come to Marysville for the new auditorium dedication, but Norby and Read were reunited and would both play important roles in the future of aviation in Yuba and Sutter counties.[87]

Lt. Oakley G. Kelly and Lt. H. C. Miller were forced to land at Marysville on the night of December 23, 1924. Nightfall and worsening weather were believed to be reasons they landed. They were flying from Vancouver, Washington, to Crissy Field. Premature reports had gone out stating they were lost. Kelly was famous for flying the first nonstop transcontinental flight across America with John Macready a year-and-a-half before.

THE CLOSURE OF THE AIRFIELD in Knight Park was foreshadowed when the city council deeded sixty-six acres of the old racetrack in the park to the Marysville High School District in February 1925.

That same month, Norman J. Laughlin, who taught agriculture at Yuba City Union High School, spoke to the students about his activities as a pilot in the Royal Flying Corps during the war.[88] A complete list of local men killed in the World War was released that February. The only local man in the aviation service to die in the war was Joseph M. Burns. He died aboard a ship on his way to Europe.[89]

CHAPTER 1

MAGNOLIA PARK, A TRACT OF LAND south of Marysville, had occasionally been used as an aircraft landing field. It was eventually developed into a housing subdivision. The Yuba County site was located at the intersection of Hammonton Road and the state highway (now Highway 65). The Magnolia Park site was unnamed and was the only Yuba-Sutter landing field listed in the January 1926 *Western Flying* airport guide. It was listed as south of Marysville between two paved highways and was the principal landing field for the area. It was described as an open one hundred-acre field with no services, gas, or oil available.[90]

To assist aviators flying over the Marysville, a locator name was painted on the roof of the Standard Oil Co. warehouse in February 1926. It spelled out MARYSVILLE in letters fifteen feet high and had an arrow forty feet long pointing north.[91]

Walter T. Varney, the San Francisco aviation entrepreneur and head of Checker Air Service—a new flying service in the Great Central Valley—made a trial flight for the service from San Francisco to Fresno on March 25, 1925. Checker Air Service would operate nine aircraft throughout the valley to and from the Bay Area. It was not a scheduled airline. It flew charter trips that were met at various airfields in the valley by taxis of the Checker Cab Company, the financial backer behind the air service.[92]

In January 1926, the California State Corporation Department in Sacramento refused permits for stock sales of air transportation companies because the possibilities of investors making any return on life savings invested in such companies was nonexistent.[93]

Fred Hoyt, another aviator friend of Erling Norby, flew into Marysville in early March to visit. Hoyt instructed flying students at Rockwell Field during the war and was currently with Travel Air Aircraft Company. While visiting, he told a local reporter Marysville needed an adequate airport. Hoyt was the California distributor for Travel Air.[94]

An earlier incident brought the lack of a permanent Yuba-Sutter airport to the attention of the community on June 7, 1925. That evening, once again, Lt. Oakley G. Kelly, the transcontinental flier, had to land near Marysville on Scheu's farm in District Ten because daylight was dwindling and his plane needed repairs. District Ten is north of Marysville's protective levee, extending to Honcut Creek. Kelly and his passengers were driven into Marysville for the night. The following morning they departed District Ten to the north. Their only complaint was the lack of a landing field at Marysville or Yuba City.[95]

Knight Park was being used for recreational purposes during the first seven or eight months of 1926, even though the land had been given to the school district for construction of a new high school. Special events were still held at the racetrack since construction on the new school had not yet started. Auto races were held there on New Year's Day 1926 and, sadly, a driver was killed during the races.[96]

Final disposition of Knight Park was announced July 1, 1926. The old golf course, which took up most of the park, had been abandoned. Yuba-Sutter Golf and Country Club would build a thirty-five thousand dollar club house and swimming pool on a new course constructed at Plumas Lake, several miles south of Marysville. A new high school was to be built on the old golf course and racetrack.[97]

Yolo Fliers Club Field, currently known as Woodland-Watts Airport, is shown in this 1993 photo. The Fliers Club and golf course is just left of the runway.

The three principal aircraft types flown in the Sacramento Valley in 1918–1926.

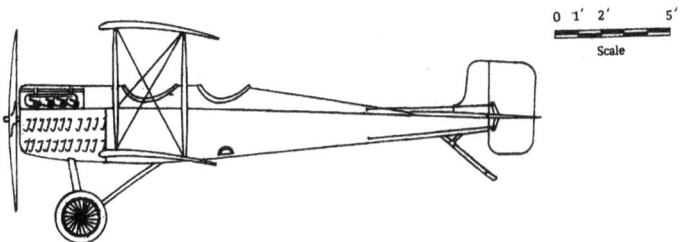

Martin TT: This design was not prolific in the Sacramento Valley but it was present in 1918-1919.

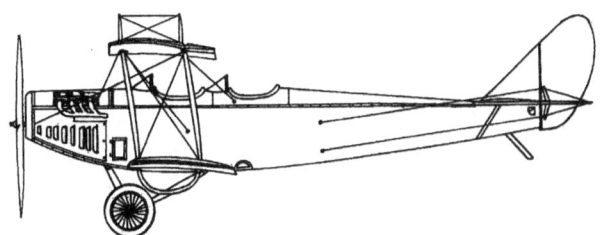

Curtiss JN-4D Jenny: After the Great War ended, war surplus Jennies, some reconditioned by the Curtiss Company, dominated the US aircraft market. The domination of these obsolescent aircraft on the market stifled the design and construction of modern civilian aircraft for many years after the war, jeopardizing flying safety, and delaying the progress of commercial aviation.

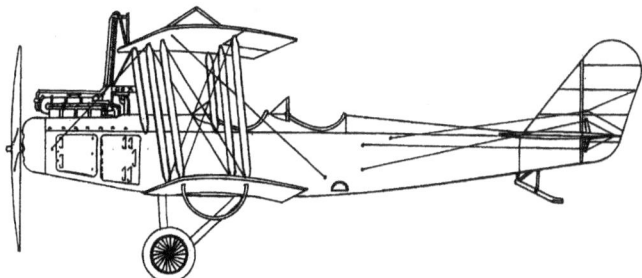

Standard J-1: The Standard J-1 was produced in large numbers during the war, although not near as many as the Jenny. It was not popular with pilots during the war due to the proclivity of its Hall-Scott motor to catch fire. Following the war, many ex-military pilots purchased Standards and replaced the Hall-Scott motors with more powerful and reliable Hisso (Hispano-Suiza) motors. This made the Standard a more desirable aircraft than even a Hisso powered Jenny. The Standard could easily carry two passengers in the front seat and later models could carry four.

A Curtiss JN-4, Jenny, used by the Army Air Service on a Victory Loan Campaign following the end of the Great War.

Mather Field during a pass and review fly-by of the bombers participating in the April 1930 Air Corps Air Maneuvers.

CHAPTER 2

The Angel Flying Circus comes to Marysville – Jimmie Angel meets Dr. Johnson – Angel's career before Yuba City – Dr. Johnson, founder of Yuba City's first airport – Angel Airport – Angel brothers' hurried departure – Johnson struggles to keep the airport open

Marysville city officials planned a grand air show at Knight Park one last time before the high school construction began. They contacted A. J. Edwards, director of the 13 Black Cats, a flying circus formed in 1925 at Burdett Airport in Los Angeles. Their first priority was to perform stunt flying, wing walking, parachute jumps, and plane crashes for the movies. Their price list was sent out to all of the movie producers and directors in Hollywood. The list contained over twenty various stunts and maneuvers they would perform for cameras. The cheapest was a spin with the plane on fire without crashing for fifty dollars. A parachute jump was eighty dollars. A spin with the plane on fire and crashing was twelve hundred dollars. A plane blowing up in the air with the pilot parachuting to safety was the most expensive at fifteen hundred dollars.[1]

Flying for the cameras was all well and good, but like any business there were dry spells of little film work. When that happened, the Black Cats would go barnstorming up through the state with two or three planes, leaving an equal number of machines and pilots in Los Angeles to cover any movie work that might come up.

Edwards promised Marysville officials on a Monday in April 1926 the Black Cats would land on the golf course in Knight Park Thursday. They were supposed to bring six aircraft, three of which would do stunt flying with Miss Gladys Ingle walking the wings.[2]

Two days before this event, Howard Batt, one of Edward's best pilots and a veteran movie flyer, force landed in a vineyard near Modesto. Batt and his two passengers were scratched up a little, suffering no serious injuries, but his plane was seriously damaged.[3]

The Black Cats contacted Marysville air show officials and explained the situation. They had to push back their arrival to May 1 while Batt recovered. He was their star aerobatic pilot. Before May 1 for unknown reasons, they postponed the air show again.[4]

That was the final straw for the air show officials. The Black Cats were cancelled and another air circus would be hired. The next day a short announcement about the on-again, off-again, air show was published in the local newspaper. The air show was rescheduled for the Fourth of July celebration of 1926.[5]

Leo J. Smith, an official for the Fourth of July celebration, called Jimmie Angel at his headquarters in San Jose and hired the Angel Brothers' Flying Circus to perform at Marysville on July 3–5.

The first Angel Brothers' Flying Circus plane landed on the golf course at Knight Park on the evening of July 1. Jimmie Angel, while looking over the site, told Leo Smith he would bring three planes for the three-day celebration. One of the pilots expected was Charley Ming, a Chinese pilot whose brother lived in Marysville, according to Angel. An unusual aspect of this air show was Angel agreeing to allow two local aviators, Erling Norby and Jimmie Read, to fly his aircraft in an exhibition of their aerobatic skills for the home crowd. Angel promised Smith three exhibitions a day with passenger hops given throughout each day of the celebration.[6]

The two strangers planning to fly Angel's planes had both been experienced instructor pilots during the war, but eight years had passed since the war ended. Norby had flown a recruiting drive the length of the West Coast from border to border for the Army Air Service in 1919. He had flown an aerobatic routine over every town he came to during the flight. Jimmie Read was fairly new in town and unknown to locals. Unbeknownst to everyone except Norby, who had flown with him at Rockwell Field, Read was an excellent pilot, but neither man had an airplane.[7]

Whether Norby and Read flew during the Fourth of July celebration of 1926 is unknown. There was no mention of them in newspaper reports about the air show. Instead of three planes, which Jimmie Angel promised, the plane that came into Knight Park on the evening of the first was the only one to arrive for the air show. Angel claimed to have eleven airplanes at an airfield in San Jose, but like so much of what Jimmie Angel said there was only a thin strand of truth to it. Angel exaggerated continuously; truth was something that totally escaped Jimmie at times. His flying stories cannot be trusted in any form. Angel was a fearless pilot and would fly anything, anywhere, anytime for a price. Unless someone saw him do it, there was no way his description of an event would bear any resemblance to what really happened. Jimmie was very good at selling himself. He could talk people into giving him airplane parts, gasoline, their airplanes, and even their last dollar if he needed it, and he usually did.

The only record of what happened at the air show during the three-day July Fourth celebration was the following sketchy report.

George N. Mitchell, a veteran parachute jumper from the Bay Area, jumped from Jimmie's plane at three thousand feet during the air show. The plan was for him to jump from five thousand feet, but a strong south wind was blowing and it was feared he would come down somewhere north of Marysville in District Ten if he jumped from that altitude. Mitchell opened his chute just after exiting the plane and landed in a field that joined Knight Park. There were thousands of people at the park to watch and with the high wind they were expecting the worst.

After the show, Angel reported he would be returning to Marysville soon to perform again since his pilots only brought one plane for the Fourth of July air show. The other plane scheduled for the show had an engine failure as Jimmie was flying back to San Jose the previous week. He said he hadn't time to replace the engine. Angel then returned to San Jose in Charley Ming's plane.[8]

The three-day celebration was not only for the Fourth of July but also for Marysville's Diamond Jubilee. It was the most successful celebration ever held in the city—an estimated fifteen thousand people attended. Considering Marysville's population then was about five thousand and Yuba City's was three thousand the event did well. Reportedly, no houses were broken into nor any fires started, which apparently was a pleasant surprise.[9]

Jim Read gave a speech at a local service club luncheon in late July. It was a stirring account of his time in Africa. From Cape Colony, South Africa, to Lake Victoria Falls, he hunted wild game, worked for gold mining operations at Johannesburg, and suffered primitive transportation of the region while cutting his way through jungles.[10]

AT SOME POINT DURING the Fourth of July celebration, Jimmie Angel met Dr. Julian P. Johnson. It was a match made in … well, you pick. Jimmie

Dr. Julian P. Johnson with his daughter, Joyce Adele, circa 1931. The 60-year-old Johnson not only opened Yuba City's first airport in 1926, he opened the town's first hospital in 1924.

was always looking for a moneyed flying enthusiast—a sugar daddy, if you will. Of course, Jimmie wasn't alone in this quest. Many aviators at this point in the evolution of aviation were looking for someone with enough money and ability to see the benefits of this new technology. Time-saving speed, aerial exploration, and ease of transportation into difficult areas were the best reasons to fly in 1926. However, flying safety, dependable equipment, and a lack of airports were still problems for commercial operations.

Dr. Johnson was a person who wanted to learn and experience new ideas. As a man of science, he embraced technology. He not only wanted to learn to fly, he wanted to get in on the ground floor of the fledgling aviation industry.

Dr. Johnson and Jimmie Angel became partners in a flying business. Together they opened the first true airport at Yuba City. Their airport included a flying service, which specialized in flight instruction and air taxi service. The new airfield was named Angel Airport, of course, after Jimmie and his brothers. Dr. Johnson was named airport manager and Jimmie chief pilot. Their advertising slogan was, "Fly with the Angels."

Who were these two men who were determined to open the first purposely built civilian airport and flying business in the postwar Yuba-Sutter community? Mid-1926 wasn't the best time to start a flying business. The industry was in doldrums. The surge in aviation interest following the Great War had subsided. Barnstormers were lucky to get two and a half dollars a head for a passenger hop. Government regulation creating public confidence in the safety of airplanes and pilots was still a year away, as was the biggest boost to aviation interest—Lindbergh's flight to Paris.

Jimmie Angel has his niche carved out in aviation history as the man who discovered the world's tallest waterfall. While flying the high plateaus of Venezuela looking for possible gold mining sites in 1933, Jimmie discovered Angel Falls, which were named for him.

JAMES CRAWFORD ANGEL WAS BORN near Cedar Valley, Missouri, August 1, 1899. He was the oldest of six children. When growing up, he was called Crawford because his grandfather was named James. As a young adult, he preferred being called Jimmie and would correct anyone who spelled his name with a Y. His appearance belied American Indian blood, which he told people he was. His mother, Margret Belle Marshall Angel, was part Cherokee.[11]

When Jimmie learned to fly is a mystery. Once again, it must be stated nothing Angel said about his past can be trusted. We must examine what Jimmie claimed against what others said and witnessed. Jimmie claimed he flew during the Great War with Eddie Rickenbacker in the 94th Aero Squadron in France.

Karen Angel, Jimmie's niece, is president of the Jimmie Angel Historical Project (JAHP). In 1997 she interviewed Harry Middleton, who for the first half of his life worked as an aircraft mechanic. Harry met Jimmie for the first time at an airfield in Texarkana, Texas, in 1920 or '21. He said Jimmie was a mechanic, just out of the army, and was learning to fly at Twin City Flying Service. Later, he was told Jimmie had soloed and was flying passengers.

By 1930, Harry Middleton was working for Aerovias Centrales, a Mexican subsidiary of Pan American Airways. One of the line's pilots was K. K. Hoffman. Hoffman told Harry that during the Great War he was a lieutenant assigned to the 94th Aero Squadron. Harry must have mentioned Jimmie to Hoffman because Hoffman told Harry, Jimmie Angel had been a crew chief (mechanic) with the 94th during the war and not a pilot. In the 1920 Census, Jimmie was registered working as a mechanic and living with his parents in West Plains, Missouri.[12]

If Harry Middleton was correct, Angel learned to fly after the war. For sure, Jimmie was flying for pay in 1921.[13]

As to Jimmie Angel's claims to have flown in the war with the 94th Aero Squadron, there is a photo in the JAHP archive of the Angel family after a funeral in May 1921. Jimmie is there in his army uniform and the caption states he had just come from Kelly Field, Texas, to his sister Goldie Angel's funeral service in Hominy, Oklahoma. His rank is not visible in the photo, and he is wearing leggings with his uniform. Karen Angel also has a letter from the US Department of Veterans Affairs to Marie Angel, Jimmie's second wife, stating Jimmie enlisted in the US Army under the name Crawford Jas [sic] Angel on August 5, 1917, and on August 9, he was honorably discharged because he was underweight.

In the JAHP archive, there is a postcard from Jimmie to his mother sent on September 10, 1917, from Little Rock, Arkansas. The postcard illustration is of Uncle Sam rolling up his sleeves for a fight and on the card Jimmie wrote, "I am having a good time.... We will get our new clothes today, there is no chance to get homesick here. I am feeling good now." The card implied that, regardless of his discharge, he was back at a military training camp the following month. The question is what kind of training?

Another reference that Jimmie was flying by 1921 came from Clyde Angel, his brother, who remembered Jimmie visited the Angel family at Independence, Kansas, in the fall of 1921 and took his mother and Clyde up for their first airplane rides.[14]

It is possible that Jimmie rejoined the army, as the above evidence suggests, and made it to France as an airplane mechanic during the war. Also, service as an aviation mechanic during the war may have gotten him a slot in pilot training at Kelly Field after the armistice.

Eyir "Slonnie" Slonniger, who would one day be American Airlines' most senior airline pilot, had one of the earliest encounters with Jimmie Angel documented in aviation literature. Slonniger went to Mexico in July 1921 to fly payroll for crews working on drilling rigs in the huge oil field at Tampico. Slonnie contracted malaria. After nine months of flying, his malaria attacks were coming every week, so he decided it was time to leave. He later confided that he left pilots Tittle and Jimmie Angel to fly the payroll. There is a photo in Slonniger's biography, which shows Slonniger and a very thin Jimmie Angel standing beside a Lincoln-Standard. This was the make of plane they flew for Eastern Mexican Aviation Company, which was owned by the same people who owned Nebraska Aircraft Company, the company that manufactured the Lincoln-Standard airplane. In the photo, Slonniger and Angel are wearing the same knee-length boots, jodhpurs, mid-length leather jackets, and newsboy caps. The photo suggests it was taken at Tampico during their employment in Mexico.

Slonniger was quoted describing a meeting with Angel at the airport in Lincoln, Nebraska, not long after their employment in Mexico. Jimmie had just landed in a Canuck (a Canadian built Jenny) with a bad carburetor.

Slonnie had an extra carburetor and Jimmie begged it off of him with the promise he would send him a new one as soon as he got to Oklahoma City. It was obvious to Slonniger, Jimmie was, once again, broke. Several years afterward, Angel stopped off at Fort Worth's airport where Slonniger was chief pilot. Jimmie was headed for Mexico with a wealthy Osage Indian woman. Jimmie told Slonniger he found a cave there where an ancient Indian civilization had hidden their jewels. At that point in the conversation, Slonniger asked Jimmie, " Where the hell was the new carburetor ..." he was supposed to have returned. Jimmie claimed he had sent it, but it was obvious he hadn't because he then promised Slonnie he would send him a handful of emeralds from Mexico. He said there were bushels of jewels in his cave. Slonniger never got anything from Angel.[15]

Jimmie Angel met Virginia Martin during his travels. They were married in August 1922 in Coffeyville, Kansas. She became a member of the Angel Brothers Flying Circus and performed as a wing walker and parachutist.[16]

So, reputable evidence puts Jimmie Angel in Missouri, Oklahoma, Kansas, and possibly in France as an aircraft mechanic during the World War; at Kelly Field in early 1921; in Mexico during latter 1921; and in Kansas in mid-1922. This author believes Jimmie Angel remained in the Southern states of the Midwest until late 1923.

Jimmie's next reported appearance, found by this author, was in November 1924. He and his passenger walked away from a crash after spinning in from eighteen hundred feet near Chico. Angel was reported as living on N Street in Sacramento. A month later, it was reported Angel was going to start a passenger service connecting Chico, Sacramento, and the Bay Area.[17]

Reports of Angel's crash during the last two months of 1924 may have prompted his arrest in Sacramento on January 6, 1925, from an outstanding telegraphic warrant from Sheriff George Jackson of Mt. Ida, Arkansas. Angel was arrested when he went to the Sacramento Sheriff's Office to discuss the outstanding warrant. Angel said later, "My arrest is due either to the fact that I owe money at Mt. Ida or because of a wrecked airplane. ... I did no wrong while I was at Mt. Ida. I was there for eight months and participated in an aerial circus during which a plane was wrecked." The report went on to say Angel served during the recent war with the Aviation Corps and was under Rickenbacker. It stated Angel served as a test pilot in France. Jimmie must have given this information to the reporter.[18]

The sheriff of Mt. Ida never replied to a telegram from the Sacramento County sheriff stating Angel had been picked up on the warrant and asked for clarification of the two felony charges against Angel. He wanted to know what Angel had done and how to proceed with the prisoner. When no answer came from Mt. Ida, the Sacramento County sheriff had no choice but release Angel from custody after he spent two nights in jail.[19]

Angel Flying Company opened for business and was bent on starting a daily air service between Chico, Sacramento, and San Francisco. Jimmie's plan was to use four planes making two round trips daily from Chico to the Bay Area. He would use Lincoln-Standard biplanes with 220 horsepower Hisso engines that could carry five passengers with two hundred pounds of luggage at one hundred miles per hour. Angel reported his headquarters would be at Chico with repair and supply facilities in Sacramento.

Angel planned to use the airfield on Upper Stockton Road (Stockton Boulevard today) near the Sacramento city limits. He claimed all pilots flying for his company would be ex-army aviators who flew overseas during the war. He also reported the company was backed financially by capitalists from Sacramento, Chico, and Stockton, but he would not reveal their names. Typical of Jimmie Angel, he would not reveal the amount of the company's capitalization.

He threw in another gimmick that was unusual for a startup flying service. He promised a blanket insurance policy for each passenger. As a passenger bought a ticket to fly, he or she would sign up for a policy covering the passenger and his company in case of an accident. In 1924, before federal air regulations had been instituted, it would have been very difficult to obtain such insurance at a reasonable price.

At the time of Angel's press release about the creation of his air service, he admitted he didn't have a starting date yet, due, he said, to the company having problems acquiring proper landing fields in Chico and San Francisco. Negotiations with Chico were pending, but if a field couldn't be found in San Francisco (of San Francisco's early municipal airports, Marina Field closed in late 1924 and Mills Field wouldn't open until 1927), it would make Durant Field in Oakland his best possibility.[20]

It is clear Jimmie believed he was still in good standing with Nebraska Aircraft Company, the outfit that employed him to fly payrolls to Tampico, Mexico. Through Walter Varney, they would supply the Lincoln-Standard biplanes that Jimmie planned to use for his Chico to San Francisco air service.

Jimmie and his brother, Eddie, who was sometimes referred to as an aeronautical engineer (actually, a mechanic and pilot), had planned to create a large airplane manufacturing plant in Sacramento. They claimed they were already constructing several planes on a temporary site at the ranch of Roy White on the H Street road, east of Sacramento. One aircraft had been finished by January 1, 1925. Ultimately, they planned to build two five-passenger planes per month. In addition to building planes for their Chico to San Francisco air service, they planned to build planes on special order for anyone interested in owning their own airplane. Jimmie reported the planes used for their passenger service would never be used for stunt flying. Stunt flying, he said, weakened the airframes more than any other type of flying.[21]

It is doubtful Jimmie and Eddie had means to construct an aircraft from scratch; it would have been too expensive and time consuming. More likely they were simply assembling Lincoln-Standards shipped in crates from Nebraska destined for Walter Varney, who would have shipped them on to the Angels in Sacramento to be assembled. Or the brothers may have planned to assemble JN-4s from crates acquired as war surplus from Rockwell Field, San Diego. To believe they were building any airplanes on White's farm at all, one will have to accept Jimmie's reports to the newspaper as being true.

Jimmie was flying with A. J. Wilson on January 18 when an air line [sic] failed on their aircraft causing them to make a forced landing at Thirty-first and M Streets in Sacramento. It was reported Wilson was acting as pilot.

The two men were test flying the aircraft to make sure it would be ready for the inaugural flight of their planned passenger service from Chico to San Francisco. They were flying in a wide circle over Sacramento at one thousand feet when the problem arose. Wilson spotted a large vacant field where he could put the airplane down, then set up his glide to the field. He brought the plane in a little too low striking a large tree on the west side of Thirty-first Street smashing the wings. The aircraft went under the trolley wires that ran along Thirty-first Street and hit a fence enclosing a vacant field. Both wings were severely damaged, but the plane remained upright throughout the crash, which the two pilots attributed to their lack of injuries. They both walked away from the crash. Jimmie Angel told a reporter, "The plane will be ready for flight within a week, and soon after that time, I believe the airplane service between San Francisco, Sacramento, and Chico will be established." Only Jimmie Angel would use an airplane crash to promote his new flying service.[22]

Angel's air service to the Bay Area from Chico never got off the ground, but Jimmie and Eddie Angel remained in the area still trying to find a home field for their flying ventures. It appears Jimmie's activities in Sacramento were his most notable venture, since leaving Oklahoma two steps ahead of the sheriff.

The Sacramento Aviation Club put on the largest civilian air meet ever held at Mather Field on May 9–10, 1925. Ninety-two aircraft flew in for the meet at Mather, twelve miles east of Sacramento. The majority of the aircraft were military planes from Crissy Field, Rockwell Field, and Riverside's March Field. For the civilian stunt flying portion of the meet, H. G. "Andy" Andrews and Jimmie Angel were hired to fly. Jimmie performed daredevil feats from two thousand feet and Andrews did loops, spins, and other maneuvers.[23]

After the crash at Thirty-first Street in Sacramento, Jimmie may have lost his credibility with financiers for his passenger service, if there actually were any. Nothing more was said about the service or whether Jimmie had replaced the wrecked plane.

Jimmie may have given up on establishing a passenger service from Chico to the Bay Area, but during his search for Bay Area landing fields, he met Peter Allinio of El Cerrito.

Bordering Richmond, El Cerrito was a small northeastern Bay Area town. Marshall Boggs had landed a Bristol Tourer biplane at the new Richmond city airport in June 1923. El Cerrito didn't have a developed landing field that could safely accommodate the modified ex-World War fighter-bomber. The two-place warplane had been converted into a passenger plane with an open cockpit for the pilot and an enclosed cabin for as many as four passengers.

Boggs landed at Richmond with a passenger, Peter Allinio, the new owner of the Bristol. Allinio learned to fly on Sunset Field at Alameda in 1912 and was a Bay Area aviation pioneer. Allinio was said to have built and flown planes from ground along Stockton Street and Fairmont Avenue in El Cerrito in 1908. It is doubtful he made powered, sustained, and controlled flights at that early date, and no corroboration for such flights has turned up. It is possible he may have flown gliders there around that time.[24]

On the day they landed at Richmond, the press reported Boggs and Allinio had just flown from Oklahoma in the new plane. Allinio was said to have converted the ex-fighter bomber himself and was searching for a suitable East Bay site to carry out the conversion of more Bristol airplanes.[25]

The story is interesting, but the facts are the Bristol company in England made the exact same passenger conversions of their ex-wartime F.2B fighter-bombers and shipped them for sale to Canada and the United States by the Arbon-Bristol Aeroplane Company of Toronto and New York. Walter T. Varney, based at Redwood City Airport and San Francisco's Marina Field, was the exclusive Northern California distributor for Arbon-Bristol. He had been selling airplanes identical to Allinio's since 1920.[26]

Allinio met Jimmie Angel in early 1925 when Jimmie was looking for a Bay Area terminus for his proposed Chico to San Francisco air service. Allinio may have diverted Jimmie's plans with his own plan. With Jimmie as his chief pilot, Allinio could start a charter service to anywhere in the United States from Richmond. He could begin regular service to Los Angeles nonstop—a three-and-a-half-hour flight in the Bristol. He and Jimmie were confident that businessmen and others would jump at the chance to save valuable time with such flights. Jimmie entered into negotiations with the Richmond Chamber of Commerce to use the new Richmond Airport at Clam Flat, located at the end of Fourteenth Street and south of Cutting Boulevard on Tank Farm Hill. The chamber maintained the airport and negotiated all leases for commercial and private pilots wanting to operate from the field.[27]

Jimmie was to fly Allinio's Bristol in a handicap race on May 9, 1925, from Richmond Airport to Mather Field. The race was intended to show mutual support and cooperation amongst the few municipal airports in existence in Northern California at this early date. The race was also intended to bolster aerial participation in flying events and closed course racing at the big air show on Mather Field. Two Jennies flown by E. W. Farrow and Richard Duke and a French Morane belonging to Dr. Sterling Bunnell of San Francisco were the only aircraft from Richmond to participate in the race. E. W. Farrow, a commercial operator at Richmond, owned the two Jennies in the race. The Sonoma County Aero Club was supposed to have two planes at Richmond to start the race, but they didn't show. Allinio's Bristol was on the field, but Jimmie Angel was not. One wonders if Jimmie had bothered to tell Allinio he had gotten a better offer. Jimmie was already at Mather Field; he had been hired to do stunt flying for the air show.

Richard Duke, winner of the race, received a seventy-five dollar loving cup. The race, from smaller outlying airports to a central port, was the first of its kind in the state, and, mistakenly, it was believed it would promote similar events linking more California airports.[28]

An aero technique for "curing" deafness was popular in the 1920s. A pilot would haul his deaf passenger to ten thousand feet, which, in a Jenny, would take over twenty minutes—making the cure expensive. Upon reaching the desired altitude, the pilot would push the nose down into a painful, screaming, ear-popping dive, pulling out at a thousand feet. It was more scam than cure.

Jimmie Angel was an aerial shaman for the miraculous cure and demonstrated it to E. L. Barger of Berkeley on June 9. The cure took place over Jimmie's new base of operations on Richmond Airport. Jimmie gave Barger a "limited" treatment meaning he only took the patient to sixty-five hundred feet and from there dove to one thousand feet. After landing, Mr. Barger was stunned; he could hear an ordinary conversation without any problems. Also, the ringing in his ears that had plagued him for the previous two months was gone. People who for the last ten years had had to speak very loudly for him to understand no longer had to.

Angel was planning to fly a deaf friend of Barger's that same afternoon for the cure, but the results were never reported.[29]

An air meet was planned for the dedication of the new Richmond Airport two weeks later, and Jimmie was scheduled to provide stunt flying for the two-day event. Were his "flights for the cure" a way to get his name in the local papers for the coming events?

The flights to cure deafness were such a scam and became so prevalent in the 1920s that the medical community debunked and proved the flights a useless cure. Jimmie's cure flights were reported in the Richmond newspaper on the same page right next to publicity about the upcoming air show at Richmond Airport on June 27 and 28.[30]

The air meet and air show at Richmond garnered much interest amongst Bay Area aviators. It was to be one of the largest held in the Bay Area in years. The Army Air Service, the Naval Air Service, the Marine Corps Air Service, and the Air Mail Service were all involved in planning the event, and they would all send aircraft to the meet.[31]

On the first day, Saturday, June 27, sixty aircraft flew into Richmond Airport. On Sunday, slightly less flew into the airfield. It was the largest gathering of aircraft to occur at a civilian airport in the Bay Area to date. For the Sunday event, more than five thousand automobiles were parked next to the airport, and at least fifteen thousand spectators were inside the airport fence.

At midday on Saturday, the dedication ceremony for Richmond Municipal Airport began. Speeches were made and Ernestine Clark, winner of the Miss East Bay beauty contest, christened the field and raised the American flag, while the 30th Infantry Army Band from the Presidio played the "Star

Spangled Banner." The airport was officially accepted by representatives of the military services and Superintendent O. C. Richerson of the US Air Mail Service at San Francisco.

Jimmie Angel flew the fastest time of one race in the A. P. Allinio Aircraft Corporation's Bristol Tourer. Other race winners were: Red Williams in his Canuck, E. W. Farrow of Richmond, in a Hisso Jenny, and Chris Meyling of Fresno in his OX-5 Jenny. Frank Sheitz from the San Joaquin Valley Aeronautical Association won the handicap race to Richmond from Fresno in an OX-5 Jenny. Frank Schultz won the dead-stick landing contest with Art Starbuck placing second.

Naval aviators demonstrated formation flying and did some stunt flying; the army fought a sham battle with aircraft against artillery and machine guns firing blanks. This spectacular battle was carried out against troops from Battery B, 143rd Artillery and A and D companies of the 159th Infantry of the California National Guard.

Lieutenant Dowling, flying an army observation plane with Sergeant Faxon as observer, crashed while taking off. There were no injuries. The plane lost power while departing and dropped off on a wing from fifty feet. The plane was from the 316th Army Reserve Squadron.

Lt. Ben H. Wyatt led an exhibition of flying by a group of navy pilots. Wyatt was commander of the San Diego Naval Air Station at the time. Two years later at Oakland, he would test the navigators for the ill-fated Dole Race to Hawaii.

Popular musical theater singer Wentella La Pierre was hired to sing during the Sunday afternoon portion of the air show. Jimmie Angel flew the Allinio Bristol Tourer to Santa Rosa to fetch her, but Jimmie was late, so she hired a local pilot and plane to fly her to Richmond.

Army Major Powell and naval Lt. Ben Wyatt presented Mother Tusch with a gift as a token of affection from all the flyers she befriended during the war. Her home on Union Street in Berkeley was known as "The Hangar." It had been a gathering place for aviators since the Great War. The Hangar was considered a shrine by the military and civilian flying community.

Saturday's aerial events included several handicap races from various cities one of which was Santa Rosa. Art Starbuck, a pioneer airmail pilot, won the race from Santa Rosa against pilots Jack Barham, George Buck, and John Gugileimetti. While these racers were landing at Richmond Airport, Jimmie and Eddie Angel were doing their stunt flying and wing walking routine. They also took parachutist H. W. Booth aloft to jump for the crowd.

Booth was representing Lincoln-Standard Aircraft Co. of Lincoln, Nebraska. Jimmie carried Booth to fifteen hundred feet; Booth jumped and landed perfectly. On Saturday, Eddie Angel impressed the audience when he climbed onto the top wing of Jimmie's Jenny and did a headstand, then moved between the wings before Jimmie did a loop over the airport.

A large flight of Army Reserve pilots from Crissy Field demonstrated formation flying followed by smaller flight exhibitions of marine and navy aircraft. Jimmie Angel in the Allinio Bristol and R. W. Gilbert's Hudson

Eddie Angel, Jimmie's brother and his right hand in running the Angel Brothers' Flying Circus. Harry Middleton, who knew both brothers, thought Eddie was the better pilot.

automobile had a tug-of-war on the ground in front of the crowd Saturday but not on Sunday. A military band performed between aerial events during the two-day air show and played for the spectators as they departed the airfield once the show ended.[32]

For a year after the airport dedication at Richmond, Jimmie Angel had found a home with the Allinio Aircraft Company and for his flying circus at Richmond Airport. For reasons unknown, it didn't last. The best supposition is city airports, even today, sign exclusive contracts with one or two companies to run the flying businesses on their airports excluding other competition. Jimmie may have tried to expand the Allinio Aircraft Company's service from air-taxi work to include flying instruction and air show work, stepping on the toes of E. W. Farrow whose flying business was established on Richmond Airport before Jimmie Angel came on the scene.

Jimmie moved at least a part of his flying operations in May 1926 to San Jose joining Harold Hall, a pioneer aviator and engine designer. Hall had developed a six-cylinder aircraft engine, and Jimmie supplied his Lincoln-Standard as a test bed for it. If the operational tests were successful, the engine would be sent on to the army and navy for further tests.

Hall had formed a company and during the last days of May, Jimmie took several members of the company for rides over San Jose to demonstrate the new engine. Louis Silverstein, secretary of the corporation, and stockholder John Annear were among those given rides in the Lincoln-Standard.

Hall said he had designed the motor during the World War and was given assistance from the war department to build one engine. After it was assembled, he took the motor to the East Coast to demonstrate it for the military services. Military and civilian engineers, who agreed it was capable of unusual performance, tested the motor. Hall still owned the design and had never tried to manufacture the engine until Jimmie met him.

According to Hall, the motor was unusually economical in oil and gasoline consumption. Though it was a high compression engine, it was designed to not require constant overhaul. In one test the motor was run five hundred hours on a stand before needing the valves ground and the bearings replaced.[33]

The motor, rated at three hundred horsepower, was put on a rebuilt Fokker D. VII. The Fokker served as the new test bed for the Hall motor.

Robert Straight, who joined Jimmie's air circus in 1926, remembered working on the Fokker continuously at San Jose. He said the engine cooling method simply would not work; it was always overheating.

While trying to work out the problems with the Hall experimental motor at San Jose, Jimmie and his flying circus became "squatters" on another aviator's airfield at San Jose.

On June 4, 1926, R. B. Patterson, manager of Patterson's Airport at Alum Rock Road and Capitol Avenue, took Jimmie Angel and E. R. Sturtevant, who may have been Jimmie's latest moneyman, to court. Angel and Sturtevant moved onto the airport on May 8 and began flying operations. Patterson wanted an injunction forcing them to cease and desist. He also wanted five thousand dollars in damages, which he claimed his business lost since they started operations. He told the judge he had a one-year lease for his exclusive use of the property as an airport and to advertise the American City subdivision nearby for the developers.

Jimmie, upon setting up shop on the property, named his business Angel's Airport and continued to do so after Patterson asked him to stop.

In court the judge told Jimmie he could continue operating at the airport on Alum Rock Road, but he could not continue to call it Angel's Airport. He made Jimmie post a five hundred dollar bond pending trial.[34]

How the trial turned out is unknown, but a clue was revealed in another court action on June 14. Landowners Carl Crosby and Harriett Howell filed suit to recover possession of the airport land on Alum Rock Road from R. B. Patterson. They had leased the land to Patterson March 13, not January 1, on a monthly basis to be used as a landing field for one airplane. On May 12, they served notice on Patterson his tenancy would terminate on June 12; he was to vacate the property by that date. Patterson refused to vacate, and the landowners wanted the court to restore their property to them plus award them lost rental fees.[35]

Jimmie was in court, once again, on June 19. This time, John Mendoza, a rancher whose horse pasture adjoined the same airport on Alum Rock Road, brought suit against Angel. He claimed Jimmie flew his aircraft so low over his horses they became hysterical. He wanted the court to find against Angel for cruelty to animals.

Mendoza didn't show for the trial. The judge said horses grazing in a field will frolic, and, as the airplanes were not mingling with them in the field, it was not cruelty to animals. Jimmie walked again. Obviously he was still on the Alum Rock airport.[36]

The same day as his last court appearance, Jimmie announced Angel Brothers' Air Service of San Jose was hiring San Jose aviator Dominic DiFiore. (Jimmie had changed his business name from Angel's Airport to Angel Brother's Air Service.) DiFiore had an outstanding flying record and had just returned home to San Jose after a long stint flying for Johnson's Flying Service in Missoula, Montana where he did extensive, dangerous mountain flying. Upon hiring DiFiore, Jimmie told the press, "I am proud of the flying record of our organization. In six years of commercial aviation none of our pilots have ever crashed with a passenger. ..." This quote suggests Jimmie had been flying for hire since 1920, and it supports the belief that he learned to fly after the war, but again they're Jimmie's words.

During his announcement of hiring DiFiore, Angel stated all of his planes would be at the airport next to the American City subdivision at Alum Rock Road and Capitol Avenue for an exhibition of stunt flying the following day. Jimmie never missed a chance for free publicity. Jimmie was still at the airport on Alum Rock Road and used it as his Bay Area base of operations for a while.[37]

Dominic DiFiore and the Oakland Airport mascot, Contact, in 1928. DiFiore went to work flying for Jimmie Angel at San Jose and Yuba City in 1926. DiFiore had just returned from an extensive stint flying for Bob Johnson in Missoula, Montana. Johnson thought DiFiore was an outstanding aviator and was sorry to see him go.

When Jimmie came to Yuba City to fly the 1926 Fourth of July exhibition, it was doubtful he could start another airport. He had the planes and crew, mostly his brothers, but he didn't have the cash until he met the local doctor, Julian P. Johnson. Dr. Johnson was the moneyman and the other half of the partnership that would develop the first postwar commercial airport for the Yuba-Sutter community.

DR. JOHNSON CAME TO YUBA CITY in 1924. He previously had a medical practice in Ashland, Oregon. By August 1925, he had the first hospital in Yuba City. It was a modified home surrounded by bungalows located at what was then, the north end of Plumas Street on the Tahoe-Ukiah Highway (now Highway 20). As of this writing the building is still there. It has been an antique store for many years. The bungalows behind the store were torn down in 2010.[38]

Dr. Johnson was a multifaceted individual. He once told the Kiwanis Club of Yuba City in a speech, "Yuba City needs a broader vision; a vision of beautiful homes, more business houses and greater civic progress." He spoke of three kinds of visions—individual, community, and national. For national vision, he said, "The United States often seemed lacking in national vision." He cited an example of one kind of national vision, "That of Japan, which is an ambition for supremacy, not a desirable vision, but nevertheless an example of national vision."

As for his personal vision, he declared, "... systems of mind healing depended largely on the right vision. This is the secret of the Coue system of healing. By keeping a vision of a perfect body and physical perfection before the mind ... the result would result [sic] in physical perfection."[39]

Dr. Johnson embraced new technology. His hospital had one of the first X-ray machines in the area. After meeting Angel, Johnson became enamored with aviation. His talks with Jimmie during the Fourth of July festivities inspired him. He went into the aviation business utilizing all of his oratory skills and most importantly a lot of his own money.

A deal between Dr. Johnson and Jimmie Angel had been struck. It is unknown which one convinced the other; both were skilled at getting what they wanted. They agreed to go into the flying business together at a new site, Glenn Onstott's ranch, a mile west of the Yuba City limits on the southwest corner of Walton Avenue and Tahoe-Ukiah Highway.

Dr. Johnson with Jimmie Angel flying the plane travelled from Yuba City to San Jose on August 3. Angel claimed having eight aircraft at his home field in San Jose and said he would bring six of those planes to the new airport at Yuba City. Angel planned to leave two aircraft at San Jose for his students there to complete their training. Once they were trained, the aircraft would join the others at Yuba City. Jimmie planned a flying business like the one he had in San Jose.[40]

Jimmie and Dr. Johnson left San Jose for Yuba City the next day. Once in the air, they discovered a leak in the plane's radiator. It was 2:15 PM, and they

CHAPTER 2

had just left the airport. Rather than risk an accident, Jimmie put the plane down at Oakland's Durant Field for repairs. The airplane was a three-passenger plane Angel was moving to Yuba City. He had planned to land on the

Angel Airport was one mile west of the 1926 city limits of Yuba City on the southwest corner of what is now Highway 20 and Walton Avenue. Here an aerial photo taken of the site in 1937 shows all evidence of the airport gone.

newly graded runway at his new airport. Earlier in the week, Jimmie came to Yuba City in a smaller plane, a Jenny, landing near the Shell Oil plant. At that time the new airfield wasn't ready for planes.[41]

Dr. Johnson and another minor partner in the airport venture, Hugh Pryce Jones, leased the airport land from Glenn Onstott for three years. Johnson reported hangars and a plant containing thirty thousand dollars worth of equipment to build and repair airplanes would be provided to Jimmy Angel to operate as a flying service and flight school. Angel said in addition to his airplanes, he would bring his staff of aeronautical experts from San Jose, which included Harold Hall, Robert McCullough, and Eddie Angel. Dominic DiFiore, Parker Angel, and Robert Straight would soon follow.[42]

The plane Jimmie and Dr. Johnson flew to Yuba City from San Jose was Jimmie's Lincoln-Standard, equipped to haul three passengers. They brought Jimmie's chief mechanic, Robert McCullough, with them, which was a good thing because of the forced landing and repairs needed at Durant Field.

The trip from San Jose must have shaken Dr. Johnson's vision of the new technology. After their forced landing at Durant Field and making necessary repairs, they took off for Yuba City only to make several more forced landings and temporary repairs to the radiator before reaching their home field. Jimmie returned to bring another airplane up from San Jose. Soon, the railroad shipment of Angel's equipment arrived from San Jose, and they set up their repair shop. Jimmie was supposed to bring up a five-place cabin plane and a pursuit ship, a Tommy Morse Scout, during the next couple of weeks.[43]

On August 13, Jimmie was going to fly another plane up from San Jose, but his brother, Parker Angel, phoned Dr. Johnson to say Jimmie was sick, and it would be a few days before he brought another plane to Yuba City. In the meantime, the foundation of the 250-foot hangar was laid out. The hangar was planned to house six aircraft.[44]

Jimmie and Dr. Johnson flew to Sacramento on August 17 to get construction plans for the new hangar's trusses. They were also going to examine the Meteor aircraft being manufactured in Sacramento by its designer, Jack Irwin.

TWO PLANES WERE NOW on the Angel Airport at Yuba City, and six more were to be dismantled and shipped by rail to Yuba City where they would be assembled and put into service. It is doubtful this ever happened. The six were basket cases and by rail was the only way they could travel. It is doubtful there were enough usable parts for more than two flyable planes. There were never more than four planes of Angel's parked on the airport at Yuba City.

A few days later, Angel flew into the Yuba City in a Jenny. He had with him Leslie Goebel from his staff in San Jose. Goebel was the brother of Art Goebel, who in August 1927 would win the Dole Race to Hawaii. During that race his was one of only two planes to reach the islands.[45]

Jimmie acquired the first big flying contract for his new flying service at Yuba City. It was aerial photography work for the *San Francisco Examiner*, so he rented a special camera from Eastman Company in Rochester, New York. Jimmie claimed it was a one-of-a-kind camera that could take absolutely clear pictures from a distance of five miles. He planned to operate the camera himself while Dominic DiFiore flew Angel's Lincoln-Standard.

The job was to fly directly to Mount Lassen from Yuba City, and "If the volcano was not erupting," (Jimmie's words) their plan was to drop down inside the crater and take the first pictures of the molten lava inside. Dr. Johnson planned to go along as a passenger.

Angel carried out the photo mission on August 25. DiFiore, from an altitude of one thousand feet above the crater, descended and flew the Lincoln-Standard around the crater below its rim while Jimmie took forty photographs said to be the first taken of the inside of Lassen crater. Jimmie reported the *San Francisco Examiner* commissioned the photos to be taken and that some would be sold to Associated Press. Dr. Johnson was a passenger on the trip as planned.[46]

Dominic DiFiore, Jimmie's pilot for this dangerous photo mission, claimed he was an ace in the Italian Air Service during the Great War, but no facts have been found to support this. He was highly thought of as a mountain pilot by Bob Johnson when DiFiore flew for Johnson in Montana prior to returning to the Bay Area and going to work for Jimmie Angel.[47]

On the Sunday prior to the flight over the Mount Lassen volcano, Jimmie's planes were giving rides over Angel Airport all day long. Two transient airplanes dropped into the port, possibly, the first out-of-town aviators to fly into Angel Airport since it opened. The pilots were Claude Wilson and J. C. Bassford, who flew up from Salinas. DiFiore flew down to San Jose on business that day accompanied by Mrs. Ester Marshall of Yuba City. Angel Airport now had four of Jimmie's airplanes on the field, and the hangar was going up rapidly.⁴⁸

J. S. Ferrera, a pilot associated with Angel Airport, gave a talk to the local Kiwanis Club on the safety of flying. He was an experienced war veteran who had served as a military aviator in the United States and France. He told the Kiwanis it was more dangerous to ride a mule than it was to fly in an airplane. He was asked many questions about the cost of flying and the possibility of spraying or dusting peach orchards with airplanes.⁴⁹

Jimmie negotiated with a Bay Area supply house to deliver retail goods to Angel Airport using his planes. No further mention was made of such deliveries.

Dr. Johnson and Jimmie Angel arranged to buy a five-passenger Bristol Tourer. They flew to San Francisco to acquire the aircraft, which, Jimmie claimed erroneously, had a speed of two hundred miles per hour. It is possible the plane they acquired was the Allinio Bristol that Jimmie flew when he was at Richmond in 1925.⁵⁰

With DiFiore along, they purchased the Bristol, which was to be delivered to Angel Airport in Yuba City within two weeks.⁵¹

Angel and Dr. Johnson made several flights together in September. They flew to Aetna Springs on the seventeenth. On the return flight, they flew over Clear Lake. A week later, they flew to Fresno to discuss a contract for flying two thousand pounds of freight from Fresno to Bakersfield with Angel's planes from Yuba City. The biggest problem hauling the freight was the distance the planes would have to fly from Yuba City just to pick up the freight. Another job for the Angel Air Service was to fly Miss Mildred Sowles of Yuba City on a promotional flight for a dance to raise funds for an armored automobile for local traffic officers.⁵²

Angel Air Service added the five-passenger Bristol to its stable. The dismantled aircraft arrived by rail at Yuba City on the twenty-ninth and was quickly assembled at Angel Airport.⁵³

Dr. Johnson, in September 1926, placed an ad in the local paper which started with the catch phrase, "FLY With the Angels at the Angel Airport, Yuba City, Calif. Established by the California Airways Company." It went on to say the company offered a school of aviation with full courses in flight instruction, engine repair, and airplane construction. On completion of the courses, the student would be given a pilot's license issued by the American Aeronautical Association (A nonexistent organization named as a cover for a worthless certificate, or, possibly, it was a mistake by Dr. Johnson who may have meant the ad to read the National Aeronautic Association, which may, at that late date, still have been issuing FAI pilot's licenses). The ad ended with the reassuring phrase, "Careful, skilled pilots and dependable ships." The last two words were stretching the truth. The students were taught in Jennies, which by 1926 were wearing out beyond reasonable repair. In October Dr. Johnson bought a new Alexander Eaglerock biplane giving the business a new more dependable aircraft making training safer. The ad ended with Dr. Johnson named as manager and Jimmie Angel, chief pilot. Revealed in the ad, for the first time, was the name of Dr. Johnson's new aviation business, California Airways Company.[54]

Dr. Johnson's broader vision came into play when he outlined Yuba City's part in the development of aviation in Sacramento Valley. It is not difficult to see the influence of Jimmie Angel in the doctor's plans.

Johnson reported on September 10 he planned to follow the establishment of Angel Airport with a startup corporation he claimed would make the town the most important and leading aeronautical center on the West Coast. The next step was establishing air passenger service from Yuba City to San Francisco via Sacramento. He predicted the service would be up and running within a month.

California Airways was to be capitalized with sales of stock. The doctor reiterated the passenger service, freight hauling, aircraft construction, and other aspects of his flying service would make Yuba City the aviation hub for the entire north state. He intended, in the future, to extend passenger and freight service as far south as Bakersfield and, eventually, Los Angeles. His service to the north would extend to the Oregon border.

All of his company's pilots would be registered and bonded. The company's airplanes were to be insured and every passenger would also be insured and fully protected in every possible way. All stunting and trick flying with passengers was strictly forbidden. The doctor said all of the company's flying would conform to the laws regulating aviation (there were none in September 1926) and any pilot who infringed the law would be immediately dismissed. Johnson, as manager of the company, pledged his word "… to enforce these rules from this date on to the best of my ability."

Dr. Johnson concluded a letter to the editor of the *Marysville Appeal* by emphasizing, "Legitimate flying in modern airplanes is safer than travel in automobiles on our highways. No one in the country or towns is endangered by our planes passing over them. Practically all accidents in flying are due to the same causes which bring about automobile accidents, namely, booze, selfish vanity, and thoughtless violation of the rules governing such traffic.

The unfortunate smashup of a visiting plane on our field a few days ago was entirely due to the above-mentioned causes. Aviation is coming by astonishing leaps and bounds and the near future will see the world of men and merchandise traveling through the air as the chief mode of transportation."[55]

The same day Dr. Johnson made his speech, Jimmie Angel was returning from Tacoma, Washington, to Yuba City and was forced to land due to a blinding rainstorm. Jimmie had flown a passenger to Tacoma and after passing Medford, Oregon, on his way back he encountered the storm. He made headway into it but lost all forward visibility and decided it was time to get on the ground. He landed near the foot of Mt. Shasta. The next day he got word to Dr. Johnson the storm was still raging. He eventually made it back to Angel Airport.[56]

Dr. Johnson invited William H. Phillips, a friend and an aviation enthusiast, to give a speech to the local Kiwanis Club encouraging its members to support Jimmie Angel and the new airport. Phillips, an orchardist from Porterville, also spoke of the advancements made in aviation and its commercial value to the community. Phillips was an investor in Johnson's new corporation, California Airways. Another speaker for the evening was the man who flew Phillips to Yuba City from Porterville, W. L. Lamkin. He was the Northern California distributor for Alexander Eaglerock airplanes. Lamkin was headquartered in Porterville. He had recently sold Dr. Johnson his new Eaglerock, which Jimmie Angel was already using for flying instruction at Angel Airport.[57]

A week later, Dr. Johnson revealed his grand plans for California Airways Company on the front page of the *Marysville Appeal*. The sale of stock in the new company would begin with the First National Bank of Yuba City acting as trustee of the stock fund. The stock subscription committee was made up of the main promoters of the company other than Dr. Johnson. They were: W. M. Phillips, Hugh Pryce Jones, and R. W. Skinner. Johnson reported that if the corporation went through to completion, Yuba City would become an aerial hub with Seattle as its northern terminus and San Diego as the southern terminus. Affiliation with other companies would permit air service from those cities into Mexico and Canada.

The same day his grand plans were revealed, Dr. Johnson flew to Oroville and delivered his pitch to its service clubs. Dominic DiFiore would deliver a similar speech to the Marysville Achaean Club.[58]

Dr. Johnson gave a banquet on October 19 at Hotel Marysville. It was free to anyone willing to hear W. M. Phillips speak about investing in the new California Airways Company.[59]

The banquet was well attended. Warren Woodson, the "Daddy" of Corning, came down with his wife to attend the banquet. At one point during the evening, he told the assemblage, "Get the ear of the people and this thing is sold. The man who is wise will anticipate air transport and what it will mean in the very near future. At Corning we are strong for this thing. If you folks don't go, I will." Woodson founded Corning's city airport soon after he spoke in Yuba City.

Hugh Pryce Jones acted as toastmaster for the banquet. Among those who spoke were: R. W. Skinner, Carl Schnabel, G. Fred Otis, Dr. Johnson, Walter M. Phillips, James Long, Erling S. Norby, and Julius Duservoir, the experimental engineer for the Durant Motor Company of Oakland. (An early aviator wanna-be, Mr. Duservoir in 1910 couldn't get his self-built monoplane to fly at Luna Park, San Jose, and later he failed to fly Frank Johnson's Curtiss Pusher at Alameda that same year.) It was announced at the banquet, California Airway's first plan was to establish air service from the Yuba-Sutter community to Sacramento and San Francisco with aircraft departing on an hourly schedule from 7:00 AM to 6:00 PM every day.[60]

It is difficult to believe anyone in 1926 could assume there were enough air-minded residents in the Marysville-Yuba City area to fill the seats in those airplanes daily, much less hourly, even with only two or three passengers in each plane. The scheduled air service never happened.

In Marysville, construction workers began preparing the land at the old Knight Park for a new high school, east of the old golf course, in the park. Across the highway from the park, the county agriculture department put in four acres of experimental fields. All of this work put an end to Marysville's first airport. All new progress in aviation during 1926 would take place across the Feather River at Yuba City.[61]

Angel Airport suffered its first major flying accident on October 7. Basil Russell, flying for the Blue Stage Line Company, was blown off course in a Fokker transport while en route to San Francisco from Oregon and landed at Angel Airport. After getting his bearings, Russell and his passenger prepared to depart. When it became obvious he intended to take off to the south with a thirty mile per hour north wind blowing, Dominic DiFiore walked out to the Fokker and advised Russell not to take off downwind with such a strong tailwind. Russell told DiFiore he could make the take off easily and hit the throttle. He began his takeoff roll on the dirt runway that paralleled Walton Avenue. As the Fokker broke ground, the slightly cross tailwind blew him over Walton Avenue into F. S. Walton's peach trees. There were no injuries, but the wings, landing gear, and propeller were destroyed in the crash. The fuselage and engine were not damaged. This was the crash Dr. Johnson had mentioned in a letter to the editor of the *Marysville Appeal*.[62]

The next day an unusual occurrence happened. Eddie Angel took off from Angel Airport in his Lincoln-Standard. He circled the field after takeoff and turned on a heading for Sacramento. He was carrying two passengers on a charter flight to the Bay Area. As he was turning onto his heading, people on the ground saw one of the wheels fall off of his airplane. Of course Eddie, unable to see the wheels without sticking his head over the edge of the cockpit, had no idea what had happened. He leveled off at his cruising altitude heading south.

Dominic DiFiore was on duty at the airport that day. He saw what happened, ran to Dr. Johnson's Eaglerock, and took off to catch Eddie. He intercepted Eddie near Sacramento. DiFiore circled Eddie's plane making hand gestures to let Eddie know what had happened. Eddie finally figured out what DiFiore was trying to convey to him and immediately turned back for Yuba City.

Eddie and Dominic circled Angel Airport for quite some time while Eddie burned off fuel and tried to decide how to land with the least damage to the plane and passengers. At first he thought he might land in the river, but wisely he ruled that idea out. He finally made his decision and shut his engine down for his approach to land. As he neared the ground, Eddie raised the wheelless side of the plane and touched down gently on the remaining wheel. He managed to hold the wheelless side up until the aircraft had almost stopped its forward motion. He stopped the prop before touching down and miraculously there was no damage whatsoever to the airplane nor harm to his passengers.

W. L. Lamkin, the Eaglerock dealer, was on the field that day and claimed in his ten years of flying he had seen only two other one-wheel landings, but he had never seen one where the aircraft escaped all damage. From that time forward, he said he would call Eddie, "One Wheel Angel."[63]

On Sundays, the Angel brothers and their air circus crew usually put on a mini-air show at the airport. This brought people out from Yuba City and Marysville to watch Jimmie do aerobatics in his rotary engine Thomas Morse Scout. Many travelers on Tahoe-Ukiah Highway stopped to watch Eddie Angel, Parker Angel, or Robert Straight walk the wings on one of the company's Jennies as it flew over the airport. After they stopped and got out of their cars, Parker Angel or one of the Angels' wives would try to sell them a ticket for an airplane ride.

Dr. Johnson's interest in actually flying himself waned after he had a serious accident on October 18. Johnson was taught to fly by Jimmie Angel and other pilots on Angel's staff. When he soloed is unknown, but surely he did. If he hadn't, it is doubtful Jimmie or any of his staff would have allowed Johnson to take his nephew, Herbert Winn, for a ride in a Jenny.

Johnson lifted off from Angel Airport in the JN-4 rising to seventy feet then hit a downdraft. Sensing the airplane losing altitude rapidly, Johnson pulled the stick back too far. Already at full power, the JN stalled and snapped over into a spin crashing to the ground. It was reported Johnson and Winn were alternately controlling the plane, which on take off, near the ground, is extremely dangerous. They told a reporter that each misunderstood the other's signals as to whom was flying the plane. The Jenny spun the short distance to ground nose first. It was totally destroyed, but Johnson and Winn climbed out of the wreckage unharmed. One of the few advantages of flying a Jenny was it flew so slowly that when it crashed its occupants often survived.

Dr. Johnson said the JN-4 was built during the war for the government and was obsolete. He claimed few were still flying (not true), and it was expected the government would soon condemn the type. Angel Airport officials had already made plans to dispose of the aircraft before it crashed. Johnson said the crash "... was a good way of getting rid of the Jenny."[64]

A month later, plans for local Kiwanis Club members to fly to San Jose for the district convention of Kiwanis Clubs in November. James Read was to fly the California Airways five-passenger Bristol Tourer to the convention with Kiwanis president Hugh Pryce Jones, Mr. and Mrs. George Fred Otis, Arthur Coats, and Dr. Johnson as his passengers.[65]

The partnership between Jimmie Angel and Dr. Johnson came to an abrupt end at the end of November 1926. Newspaper headlines exclaimed, a TRIPLE ELECTRIC STORM hit Marysville and Yuba City with torrential rain November 26. The worst damage to the two communities occurred at Angel Airport. The sole hangar blew down after being hit by a heavy gust of wind a little after 10 AM.

The hangar was a frame building with a corrugated iron sheeting roof over a bare ground floor. The rain softened the ground and caused the structure to settle—opening part of the building to the wind. Strong gusts got under the roof causing center timbers to buckle and fall. The hangar, with the exception of the east section, collapsed. A center beam fell on Dr. Johnson's Eaglerock smashing the wings and airframe but missing the engine. The Bristol Tourer was also damaged.

Dr. Johnson reported the hangar would be rebuilt immediately and stronger than before. He said the storm caused about eighteen hundred dollars damage to the hangar, the Eaglerock suffered one thousand dollars of damage, and the Bristol had about five hundred dollars damage.[66]

ROBERT STRAIGHT, WHO WORKED and lived with the Angel families in a rooming house at 618 G Street in Marysville, described Jimmie Angel's response to the hangar collapse on the airplanes. "We picked up and moved back to San Jose the next day." Straight said Jimmie lost a couple of his planes in the collapsed hangar. He believed they were the Tommie Morse Scout and one of the Jennies, but there doesn't seem to be any written record of the loss. It's possible the planes were such flying junk they had little value. Jimmie didn't care, he wanted out. He had lost three planes in a month-and-a-half. The hangar collapse was the final straw. Jimmie's dissatisfaction had been building for a while. The lack of a population base large enough to support his dream of running a successful flying business in the community had already signaled an end of the partnership. Angel and his crew deserted Dr. Johnson leaving Angel Airport and California Airways with a collapsed hangar, an Eaglerock airplane with smashed wings, no pilots, and no operable aircraft. One man stayed behind with Dr. Johnson, crack mechanic Bob McCullough.[67]

Less than a week after the hangar had blown down at Angel Airport, two attempts were made to steal a rotary engine from an airplane inside the collapsed hangar. The fact there was still an airplane inside the collapsed hangar supports Bob Straight's belief Angel's Thomas Morse Scout was destroyed in the hangar. The Scout was the only aircraft Angel had at Yuba City equipped with a rotary engine.

The first attempt to steal the engine occurred a day or two after the hangar collapsed. Ray Dorme, the night watchman, was sleeping in the part of the hangar that did not come down. At 2:00 AM, a noise awakened him. Someone was trying to remove the rotary engine. He yelled and they ran away. The previous day an airport employee witnessed three men closely inspecting the rotary engine. He thought the men were just visiting the airport and nothing more.

CHAPTER 2   67

The second attempt to steal the engine was more organized. It was thwarted by accident. Ray Dorme went to spend the night of December 1 at the airport. After he got there, he stepped into the partially collapsed hangar to refill his lantern. It was pitch dark, but he knew where the lantern was and began groping for it. In the darkness, someone knocked him to the ground with a blow to his head. Dorme believed he was struck with a pistol butt. He was a bit stunned, but recovered in time to see two men sprinting from the hangar. He ran after the intruders and fired his revolver at the shorter of the two. He believed he hit one of the thieves. A man fell to the ground with a loud groan, got up, turned, fired two shots from his pistol at Dorme, and escaped into the darkness.

Dorme had just been dropped off by Mrs. J. Marshall, a nurse at Dr. Johnson's emergency hospital, before he entered the darkened hangar. After the shots were fired, he ran back to the car and told Mrs. Marshall to hurry back to the hospital and telephone for help.

She sped back to Yuba City and returned with Frank Winn, Dr. Johnson's nephew, who had armed himself with the doctor's pistol. Winn entered the airport hangar and found a third intruder hiding behind the Bristol Tourer. As Winn approached him, the suspect made a dash for freedom. Winn raised his pistol, aimed at the fleeing man, and pulled the trigger. The gun was not loaded and didn't fire.

The three intruders escaped in different directions. It was believed they made their separate ways back to an automobile parked near the Sacramento Northern rail tracks across the state highway from the airport. The thieves, most likely, planned to haul the engine away in the car. The three men had already removed and taken the heavy engine about twenty-five feet before they were discovered. Dr. Johnson told a reporter armed men would protect the airport in the future.[68]

There are many unanswered questions following Angel's departure. Was it necessary to have armed security at the hangar in such a small rural community? Were threats made between Angel and Johnson when Angel left the partnership? Did California Airways own the Scout and the Bristol as corporation assets, or did Jimmie have a right to them?

The first Pacific Air Transport plane visited the Yuba-Sutter area on December 1, 1926, but not by choice. Ralph Virden, the airmail pilot who flew the regular run from the old Air Mail Service's airfield (Diablo Field) at Concord to Seattle, Washington, made a forced landing south of the confluence of the Yuba and Feather rivers near Marysville.

Virden's usual route up the valley was flown west of the Sacramento River, but on this particular day Virden departed the airfield at Concord at 7:00 AM and immediately had to climb above a cloud layer. Upon reaching the Siskiyou Mountains, north of Redding, he couldn't go any further due to a severe storm. Still above the cloud layer, he turned around and flew back south looking for a hole in the clouds to get down through and land. He was running low on gas. Finally finding a hole, he made it down in a field south of Marysville at 11:15 AM.

E. P. Cogswell, who had been a flying student at Angel Field across the river, was passing nearby in his automobile and saw Virden land in a farmer's alfalfa field. He stopped and gave Virden, with his mailbag, a ride to the Marysville post office. The mail was placed aboard a northbound Southern Pacific train at 11:50 AM. Later, Virden got gasoline and took off for Concord.[69]

Dr. Johnson, with Jimmie Angel and his crew gone, would need help if California Airways were to survive. Johnson was new to flying and still very much wanted to be in the aviation business. Although the Lindbergh "surge" was still months away and the Yuba-Sutter area was in an out-of-the-way locale, Dr. Johnson was devoted to his newly found religion—flying.

Jimmie Angel, barnstorming around the state with his brothers and crew, was always looking for an airport he could adopt and start a successful flying business. But barnstorming was a dead end; there was no future in hopping passengers for ten-minute rides, and it was still too soon to successfully fly scheduled passenger routes. The Angel brothers moved back to San Jose from Yuba City, then on to Fresno in their quest for work and keeping the family together.

Eventually, Jimmie had had enough. He realized he couldn't set his crew up on an airport and expect business to come to him. He had to move where the work was, so he and Eddie went their separate ways. Occasionally, they would work together, but Jimmie was restless, and for a while he could be found on practically any airport in Southern California depending on what day it was.

Meanwhile, Dr. Johnson had convinced his friend, Walter M. Phillips, to come back to Yuba City and take over organizing and financing California Airways.

After extolling Phillips' business acumen, Johnson reported, "The time is not only ripe for commercial aviation, but every day the most splendid opportunities for a big paying business are opening up all over the country. The wide-awake people are taking advantage of them. Airways companies are being organized daily. Yuba City and Marysville are not going to lag behind now. I take this opportunity to say that I have eliminated every objectionable element from the personnel and management of the airport. And from now on the entire business will be under the management of Mr. Phillips. I have endeavored to take the necessary steps to get commercial aviation established in our own community. I am confident that it will succeed."[70]

Unfortunately for Dr. Johnson, Mr. Phillips had second thoughts about neglecting his orange groves at Porterville to come to Yuba City and take over a struggling aviation company with no flyable airplanes and its only hangar partially destroyed. Phillips was never again mentioned in news releases concerning Angel Airport or California Airways.

James E. Read and Erling S. Norby made an attempt to save Angel Airport by forming the Feather River Flying Club. Read and Norby were the most active ex-wartime fliers in the Yuba-Sutter area, and they wanted to get other ex-military aviators interested in a flying club on the airport. Norby and Read were also stumping to have the state of California create a National Guard air unit based at Angel Airport. In another scheme, they contacted the US War Department about the possibility of an Army Reserve Air Corps squadron at Yuba City.[71] These efforts failed, and soon Dr. Johnson gave up his lease for the airport location.

He desperately needed help with the aviation business, but he had other pressing matters. The father of a boy whom Dr. Johnson had tended for a broken leg sued the doctor for malpractice.[72]

Eva Bronson and Dr. Johnson announced their engagement in early February 1927. They were married on the twenty-sixth. Even though Johnson was in his late fifties, it may have been his first marriage.[73]

In March, Dr. Johnson made a statement about the need for the establishment of an airport at Yuba City. He related how he had carried on the crusade to establish an airport practically alone, and he felt the time had come for the rest of the local citizenry to support the idea. He said even the state legislature had acknowledged the need of landing fields for the state's towns and cities. Johnson didn't feel Sutter County should depend on neighboring counties for such facilities. He said the only ground used for airplane landings at the time was across the river in Yuba County, south of Marysville.[74] Johnson was correct. He was referring to a landing strip in the

Cline Bull Tract used by transient aircraft on occasion.

Dr. Johnson's bride, Eva Bronson Johnson, filed suit seeking an annulment of her marriage. An angry Dr. Johnson publicly responded to the charge (that he was physically unfit to enter the state of marriage) with a denial in the newspaper. In court he testified he had never been at the time of his marriage or any other time, "... physically incapable of entering into the marriage state. Wherefore—the defendant prays to be hence dismissed with his costs and that the plaintiff take nothing by reason of her said complaint."[75]

On the heels of his divorce problems, the doctor's new Peerless sedan was stolen from the front of his hospital on Plumas Street. It was found a few days later near Santa Rosa wrecked and abandoned in a ditch.[76]

William J. Obele flew to Marysville from Sacramento on May 3 looking for a field near town where several aircraft could land. It was his second trip to Marysville; he had visited in February with the same goal in mind. He wanted a date and place to bring a flying circus he was forming for an air show in the Yuba-Sutter area.

Obele, three years prior, ran a soft drink stand in the Marysville Western Hotel, and was now an accomplished aviator and wing walker. He had just finished touring the Midwest performing at air shows. While assembling his flying circus, he was based at Sacramento's Del Paso Airport. He said his pilots included Ive McKinney, who in earlier days had flown under the Fifth Street Bridge at Yuba City. He claimed McKinney had quit the famous Gates Flying Circus and was to join Obele soon as were Ingvald Fagerskog and H. G. "Andy" Andrews, both popular Sacramento aviators.[77]

It is doubtful Obele was able to arrange his air show in the Yuba-Sutter area. His scheduling for it was in 1927 when the Yuba-Sutter community had no adequate landing field. Obele claimed having contracts for his aviators to fly for the '49er Celebration at the fairgrounds in Sacramento late in May, and to fly for the opening of the Carquinez Straits Bridge in the Bay Area.

This is a good time to mention pilot Allan Barrie who was born in the Cordua area of Yuba County near Marysville in 1903. He joined the Army Air Corps in 1926 or '27 after graduation from the University of California at Berkeley. He was sent to Brooks Field in Texas where he learned to fly and served out his enlistment as an army flight instructor. After military service, he worked for a few commercial operators, and then got a flying job for Western Air Express. He logged thirteen thousand hours of flying time

CHAPTER 2   71

over his career. Barrie served as vice president of several airlines including Western Airlines. He was decorated during World War II for outstanding work as assistant chief of staff of the Ferrying Division, Army Air Transport Command, and during his flying career he served with the 40th Division Aviation of the California National Guard.[78]

Reportedly, Dr. Julian Johnson was planning to reenter commercial aviation in the Yuba-Sutter area and looking for a new airport site since the land on which his collapsed hangar sat was no longer available to him. Robert McCullough, Johnson's mechanic from San Jose, was rebuilding the doctor's Eaglerock so it could be used for commercial flying. Jim Read had purchased his own Curtiss JN-4 and, like Dr. Johnson, was in need of an airfield where he could park his plane.

Read and Johnson were looking at a site adjacent to the old Knight Park, but it was small and the government had new regulations against placing an airport too near a school. Another site they were considering was on the Browns Valley Road (Highway 20 now), and there were other sites they hadn't yet examined.[79]

With Lindbergh's flight to Paris exciting the public, there was a sudden demand for airfields at many cities and towns in the nation. Also, the enactment of civil aviation law by the federal government created a perceived validation of flying as a safe viable mode of transportation. By mid-1927, there were several airline startup rumors flying about in the Sacramento Valley and San Francisco Bay Area.

One rumor that would affect the Yuba-Sutter area, if true, was spread by J. Spaulding Edwards of Valley Air Service Inc., who made grandiose claims of eighteen tri-motor airliners serving all of the major cities in the state. A key sentence in his spiel stated the, "… development in interior valley points depends on creation of airfields. …"[80]

City officials at Marysville, Chico, and Oroville took Spaulding Edwards' statements to heart and began planning for airports in their communities.[81]

JIM READ, WHO BECAME the Yuba-Sutter area's sole active civilian pilot once Angel and his crew departed, revealed another talent to the community during the conclusion of the infamous Dole Race to Hawaii on August 16, 1927. He would monitor the radio of pilot William Erwin, who was searching for the two planes that disappeared during the Dole Race.

Before William Erwin took off on August 19 to look for the missing race planes, he had a radio installed in his Swallow aircraft, the *Dallas Spirit*.

Erwin planned to maintain radio contact with the mainland as long as possible during his flight. He had been an entrant in the Dole Race, but after take off on August 16, he returned to Oakland within minutes with a strip of his plane's fabric trailing behind him. On August 19, he wanted to search for those of his friends who were lost during the race, and continue on from Hawaii to Hong Kong to win the Easterbrook Prize of twenty-five thousand dollars.

Jim Read's hobby was wireless telegraphy. He was a ham radio operator and maintained a licensed ham radio station since the end of the war. He was very interested in Erwin's flight to Hawaii, so he tuned in and was able to pick up Erwin's short wave messages during the flight.

Read heard Erwin's navigator, Aichwoldt, on the radio communicate, "All is well." That Morse code message was followed a short time later by an SOS call with a description of the spin they were in and their approximate position. Then another SOS call of two or three letters, which Read could not distinguish came a few minutes later. The messages were carried on the forty-meter wavelength and could not be heard on ordinary radios that didn't operate under two hundred-meters wavelength. Telegraphy was

Dudley Cunningham (left) on his first day at work for Dr. Johnson, September 26, 1927. He is assisting Robert McCullough in repairing the doctor's Alexander Eaglerock at Johnson's new hangar in east Marysville. In less than a year the site would become Marysville's Cheim Field, the Yuba-Sutter community's first successful airport.

CHAPTER 2   73

still used in early aviation radio as voice communication was still a year or so in the future.

Read reported he heard the SOS call and knew something bad happened. He didn't hold much hope for the survival of Erwin and his navigator. He was right. Erwin and his navigator were lost at sea like the two planes he was searching for never to be seen again.[82]

Meanwhile, Dr. Johnson was continuing his return to the flying business. Bob McCullough with his new apprentice, Dudley Cunningham, a young Marysville resident, spent the summer of 1927 at Dr. Johnson's new hangar, east of the old Knight Park in Marysville, rebuilding and reconditioning Johnson's Eaglerock. Jimmie Read claimed the plane was finished in better condition than it came out of the factory.

Dr. Johnson obtained permission from Glenn Onstott to use the old Angel Airport landing strip at Yuba City for a few days to make his grand return to the flying game. On October 23, Jim Read flew passengers in the Eaglerock around the Sutter Buttes for $7.50 each, some opted for a shorter $3.00 ride. The Alexander Eaglerock had seating capacity for a pilot and two passengers.[83]

At the doctor's new hangar in Marysville, Robert McCullough, James E. Read, and Dudley Cunningham with his dog, stand by Dr. Johnson's Eaglerock. This was the day Read made the first flights in the newly refurbished biplane since its wings were destroyed in the hangar collapse at Angel Airport over a year before.

A current photo of Hall Street in east Marysville, the exact position and length of the runway for Cheim Field, the Yuba-Sutter community's most successful pre-World War II airport.

CHAPTER 3

James E. Read leads search for new airport site – Heiman Cheim donates airport site in Marysville – Dr. Johnson is still in the game – Cheim Field is created – Jim Read is named airport manager – Sierra Aircraft Company – Cheim Field dedication – Western Auto transfers Jim Read south

One of the first offers of land for a community airport came from a realtor/developer, M. Norins, who was developing a twenty-five-thousand-acre project northeast of Marysville. He was creating a new town in the foothills southeast of Honcut named Iowa City. He wanted Iowa City to have an airport serving Yuba County. He claimed his chosen site was only eight miles east of Marysville on Tahoe-Ukiah Highway (Highway 20). Iowa City is actually twelve miles northeast of Marysville and four and a-half miles north of Tahoe-Ukiah Highway.[1]

No action was taken on Norins' proposal, which was probably fortunate. The project turned out to be a scam due to a complete lack of water for the land. A large canal was dug for the town, but it had no water source, and it went nowhere.[2]

Aviation was the main topic of the August 1927 Kiwanis Club meeting. Gus Kirk talked about the Dole Race to Hawaii, then Dr. Johnson spoke about the community's need for an airport more so now than ever with the huge push given aviation by Lindbergh's flight and the flights to Hawaii. Assemblyman Fred B. Noyes spoke about the menace of hydraulic mining in the Sierra Nevada.[3]

Jim Read planned to fly Julius Wheeler and Wes Owen to the Cal–Stanford football game at Berkeley Stadium in Dr. Johnson's Eaglerock. Read had a landing field picked out near the stadium.[4]

Read later took part in an air show on a December Sunday at an undisclosed location. He joined Al Gilhausen and Ted Penney. Gilhausen flew Penney who entertained spectators with wing walking and a parachute jump. Al, in his Hisso Standard J-1, and Read, in Johnson's Eaglerock, spent the rest of the day giving rides for a penny a pound.[5]

Dr. Johnson joined the Sacramento Region Citizens Council's Aeronautical Committee in his ongoing campaign to establish an airport in the Yuba-Sutter area. In December, Jim Read and Army Reserve pilot Erling Norby were added to the committee.

Dr. Johnson and Read, the only urban owners of airplanes, and Russell Hill of San Jose, who was moving to the area with his own plane, needed a permanent airfield.

Dr. Johnson pointed out an airport was not just for airplane owners; it was a necessity for the community. There had to be a place planes could land to drop off passengers traveling to the area, and a place to land vital cargo necessary for the community. He emphasized an airport was important for a community to thrive. California was leading the states, he said, in designated landing fields with fifty-eight developed, marked, and equipped. Landing sites were indicated on maps used by aviators. He said of the fifty-eight, only four were designated as emergency landing fields. Marysville and Yuba City had no designated airfields, not even for an emergency.

Johnson and Read were keeping their planes at a site north of Marysville in district ten. It was a farmer's field, and he would be plowing soon; they would have to move their planes. He said they would probably move them to Jackson Bottoms, Yuba City.

Johnson praised Jackson Bottoms where Charles Kingsford-Smith operated from in 1920. Johnson said the state had passed legislation, which permitted funds to be used jointly with counties to purchase land such as Jackson Bottoms, for airport development.[6]

The Yuba County Chamber of Commerce met in December and discussed the quest for a local airport. Newly elected District Attorney Erling Norby broached the matter. Chairman Mat Arnoldy appointed Jim Read head of a committee to find a location for a permanent airport along with Ed Johnson and J. S. O'Brien.[7]

Read's committee came back quickly with a site in Marysville. It was property owned by Heiman Cheim and the former site of Valley Meat Company slaughterhouse. Marysville is encircled by a levee higher than all those around it. It protects the city from flooding by the Yuba River on the city's southeastern border and from the Feather River on the western border. The proposed airport site was inside the encircling levee in the city's northeastern quadrant adjoining Tahoe-Ukiah Highway (Highway 20).[8]

Ed Johnson, local head of Pacific Gas & Electric Company and a member of Read's airport committee, discovered that Jim Stack, a Los Angeles millionaire sportsman, had an airplane and flew through the area quite often to bird hunt near Live Oak. Johnson contacted Stack and asked if he would use an airport at Marysville if the city had one. Stack replied he would be happy to use an airport at Marysville.

Stack owned a Ryan Brougham aircraft, very similar to Lindbergh's *Spirit of St. Louis*. It was a high-wing monoplane that seated four people. Stack told Johnson he had flown over Marysville often on the way to Jim Stack Lodge. His nearest fuel stop was the Sacramento airport in Del Paso Park, and his duck-hunting lodge was west of Live Oak. He recently purchased another hundred acres adjoining the lodge to develop a landing strip for his plane. He said he made three trips up the valley to his lodge during the year so far. It was a four-hour flight from his home in Los Angeles to his hunting lodge, and Marysville would be a much more convenient fuel stop than Sacramento.[9]

AFTER READ'S AIRPORT COMMITTEE studied the site thoroughly, they met with Heiman Cheim and told him of their plan. Cheim agreed it would be an excellent use of the property, and he generously offered its use for free. The land was not in the city's development plan and was unlikely to be sold for a very long time. Cheim told the committee any buildings built on the land belonged to the owners and were removable by the owners at anytime. The committee said a hangar would have to be built, and a runway needed to be developed. An aircraft parking area and a gasoline station would have to be constructed. They chose a 350 x 2,000-foot strip of Cheim's land as the final site.

Everyone at the meeting agreed the committee should present the plan to the full city council in February. They would also present it to the county board of supervisors the same month.

The airport committee and chamber of commerce directors were of the opinion the community had to have an airport so it wouldn't be left out of the nation's economic and technological progress.[10]

Jim Read spoke to the Gridley Rotary Club in January 1928. Again, he spoke of the twelve years he spent in Africa working in the gold and diamond mining business. He talked about aviation's progress and urged people of Gridley to build an airport. The time when every community would need an airport to accommodate the expanding growth of air travel, he said, was near.[11]

Dr. Johnson made headlines in the local paper once again. With his new wife, Laura, he was the first person in the community to elope in an airplane.

To say this marriage was unusual and spur of the moment was an understatement.

Dr. Johnson was in his late fifties at the time, and his new wife was in her mid-thirties. They had known each other only two weeks. This episode of love at first sight began around the first of the year. Laura Riddle was brought into Johnson's Emergency Hospital with the small bones in both of her ankles broken. She had fallen off a ladder while painting her home in Sutter. Johnson treated her injuries, and she remained in the hospital for over a week. She was discharged a few days before their elopement still disabled and on crutches.

SATURDAY AT 11:15 AM, January 14, the couple climbed aboard Dr. Johnson's Eaglerock, parked temporarily in a District Ten farm field, for an elopement by plane. The plane, flown by Johnson's newly hired pilot Russell Hill, took off for Reno, Nevada.

Three days later, Mr. and Mrs. Julian P. Johnson returned to Yuba City—not from Reno, but from Medford, Oregon.

Instead of flying to Reno as originally planned, they went to Ashland, Oregon, to spend Sunday with the doctor's friends. Dr. Johnson practiced medicine in Ashland before coming to Yuba City. On Monday, they flew to Medford and were married in the rear seat of a taxi, while their witnesses sat in the front seat. They had to be married sitting in the taxi due to the bride's healing broken ankles.

The newlyweds left Medford around noon on Monday. As they crossed a mountain range, the engine in the Eaglerock quit. They were cruising at six thousand feet and Hill could see no safe place to land. He set the plane up for its maximum gliding distance with a dead engine and hoped for the best. They glided about six miles when Hill spotted an open field and landed safely. He checked the engine and discovered a spring in a magneto was broken.

Dr. Johnson telephoned Yuba City and arranged a magneto spring be driven to their forced landing site by his car. The spring was installed and the three took off at 10:30 AM Tuesday, landing at Yuba City two hours

CHAPTER 3

later. Dr. and Mrs. Johnson later reported a beautiful flight over the snow clad mountain peaks of the Cascade Range on their Oregon trip.

Twenty-five minutes after they landed, Charles Kingsford-Smith and George Pond swept over Marysville and Yuba City in a large arc without landing Smithy's tri-motor Fokker during his attempt to set a new endurance record. It was the Fokker crew's first trip this far north on their final attempt for a new record, which eluded them.

Dr. Johnson had lived in Yuba City four years, and Laura Riddle lived in the town of Sutter for several years before they married. The doctor had recently built a home and office in the seven hundred block of B Street in Yuba City. The newlyweds started their lives together in the new home.[12]

Mrs. Johnson joined the doctor, as a staff member, at his hospital. As soon as she could walk, she took charge of the hospital kitchen. Dr. Johnson reported he was very happy and felt, "... sure that only happiness awaits him and his bride in the marriage venture."[13]

Two days later after the Johnsons returned from Oregon, Jim Read took Henry Sackrider, Marysville's professional photographer, up in his Jenny for aerial photos of Marysville, Yuba City, and surrounding countryside for the upcoming edition of the *Marysville Appeal-Democrat's* yearbook. It was the second photo flight in three weeks. Sackrider was using his new Graflex camera.[14]

Yuba City's "Flying Doctor" was at it again; Johnson had Russell Hill fly him and his wife to Red Bluff to attend to his niece, Mrs. Ruby Salz. He found his niece in need of hospital care. He immediately phoned his aircraft mechanic apprentice, Dudley Cunningham, to drive Johnson's car to Red Bluff. The doctor drove Mrs. Salz and the small son of E. W. Drennan to Yuba City for treatment at his hospital. Dudley Cunningham returned in the Eaglerock with Russell Hill.

While waiting for his car, the doctor and his wife attended a Sciots ceremony. He had planned to place the word Sciot in electric lights on the Eaglerock for a night flight over town, but the lights couldn't be installed in time. His pilot, Hill, hopped passengers from Red Bluff's new municipal airport on the Sunday they were there.[15]

Sutter is a small town eight air miles west of Yuba City at the southeastern foot of the Sutter Buttes, known then as Marysville Buttes. The small mountain range rising up in the Sacramento Valley midway between the Coast Range and the Sierra Nevada is locally known as "the Buttes." The Yuba-Sutter community suffered its first airplane crash with serious injuries on January 25, 1928. Russell Hill crashed Dr. Johnson's Eaglerock while giving rides to high school students from a farmer's field across South Butte Road from Sutter High School.

Russell Hill was flying Dr. Johnson's Eaglerock, the plane in which he had flown the Johnsons on their elopement to Oregon the week before. Students Otto Thomasson, seventeen, and Francis Yates, twenty, sat in the wide front cockpit. Hill piloted from the rear cockpit.

At two hundred feet the plane went out of control. Hill was unable to recover and nosedived onto the Rind property in northeastern Sutter.

Otto Thomasson's head hit the instrument panel. He suffered a fractured skull, a broken arm, and possible internal injuries. Otto was taken to Marysville by his brother, Albert, and treated by Dr. E. E. Gray. The boy was said to be near death.

Francis Yates and Russell Hill were not seriously injured but still taken to Johnson's Emergency Hospital for treatment. Yates had two long gashes on his forehead from striking the instrument panel. Hill had cuts on his nose and a badly bruised eye. Dr. Johnson treated the pair. Hill said he believed a broken control wire caused the accident.[16]

The next day, Dr. Johnson gave a speech at a Sign of Progress Club luncheon about aviation being the greatest sign of progress in the world today. He said he had not been able to develop aviation in the community as he hoped in the last two years, but he expected to be around another fifty years to see its grand future. His support given to the aviation industry locally had cost him seven thousand dollars. He also talked about the accident involving his plane the previous day. He mentioned the injuries to the pilot and passengers and said his plane was a total loss.[17]

By January 26, Otto Thomasson was showing some improvement. After a long convelescence he would recover. A fourth person had also been injured at the crash scene. Carrie Rockholt suffered lacerations from a barbed wire fence while running to the accident.[18]

Jim Read claimed the crash was not caused by a broken control wire as written in the first accident report. Read, the most experienced aviator in the community, personally investigated the accident. He reported, "Airplanes are built today to a standard set by the Department of Commerce and have a safety (factor) eight times in excess of actual necessity." Unbelievably, he wrote, "Mechanical faults and structural weaknesses are therefore impossible in a government approved type [sic]."

Read and Dr. Johnson called in a DOC aviation inspector to investigate the cause and verify Read's opinions. "Had (the) pilot ... confined his activities to straight flying as he was instructed by Dr. Johnson and had not attempted stunts with which he was unfamiliar he would not have lost control of the ship," declared Read. [19]

THE YUBA COUNTY Chamber of Commerce, in February, announced an airport site had been acquired and work on it had begun. Also, the chamber revealed that inquiries from two companies wanting to start passenger and freight service to the new airport had been made. The first was from Dick Spracklin of Dick's Express in Oakland, and the second was from W. J. Smith of Valley Air Express in Berkeley. Golden State Aircraft Company sent a request to the chamber for communication with Marysville High School to offer instruction in aeronautical courses.[20]

Dr. Johnson and Dudley Cunningham trucked the doctor's wrecked Eaglerock to the high school in Galt and spent the day looking over the facilities.[21] Galt High School planned to rebuild the doctor's Eaglerock as a training project for the aviation students. It would cost the doctor much less for the rebuild, but take more time to accomplish.

Johnson returned from Galt singing praise for the school, which had a one-of-a-kind aviation program embraced by nearly the entire male student body. Principal William Rutherford set up a complete program of aeronautical instruction. Students spent several hours daily learning how to build an airplane. Weekends they were taught how to fly. Johnson was quite excited about the program and recommended Yuba and Sutter county high schools add such courses to their curriculum. He claimed the Galt program was so exceptional Los Angeles high schools and others around the country were examining Galt's methods for use at their facilities.

WORK CEASED AT the new airport site on the Cheim property due to the winter rainy season, and restarted by May 1, 1928. General contractor L. J. Fallon resumed grading and smoothing the two thousand-foot runway after he finished grading and leveling the new high school grounds not far away at old Knight Park. Jim Read said private funds were paying for the work, but it was expected the city and county would sponsor the new airfield soon and assist financially in its development. He also reported two fliers had flown to the community recently and, at first, could find no place to land. After flying over the Twin Cities for twenty minutes, they landed at Jackson Bottoms in Yuba City. Earlier in the week, Dudley Steele of

Richfield Oil landed south of Marysville, probably at the Cline Bull Tract, to meet with Dr. Johnson and Jim Read. The community definitely needed the new airfield to be finished.[22]

In March, the Yuba County Chamber of Commerce named the new airport in east Marysville Cheim Field in recognition of the man who donated use of his property to the community. A culvert was installed at the entrance of the airfield making it accessible from the Tahoe-Ukiah Highway, and grading was scheduled to make the ground smooth for landing aircraft and proper drainage.[23]

An illuminated airplane, flown by Donald Templeman of Los Angeles, flew over the Yuba-Sutter area the night of April 17. It carried lights that flashed advertising for its sponsor, Richfield Oil. It came from Sacramento but would not land; Cheim Field was not finished and had no night lighting.[24]

THE YUBA COUNTY Chamber of Commerce chose Jim Read, who led efforts to get the airport site chosen and developed, as its first superintendent. Read told the chamber aviators were already questioning him about applications to use the new airport and available hangar space. He said Dr. Johnson would probably be the first to build a hangar on the field. Johnson had already asked Read where on the field would be the best location for a hangar. Roy Bostic of Warren Construction Co. volunteered two big steamrollers to further pack the runway under development.[25]

Residents of the Yuba-Sutter community realized the importance of their new airport on May 15, 1928, when Capital Airlines, a Sacramento air service, began scheduled passenger service between Sacramento and Oakland. The company announced the service would, in the future, be extended to Marysville, Chico, Redding, and southward to various San Joaquin Valley cities.[26]

Marysville's Cheim Field had its first aerial visitor on May 24, 1928. Hudson S. Meade, a prominent pilot at San Jose's airport, used Cheim Field for several landings and takeoffs. Meade landed, the day before at the temporary field in District Ten after buzzing J. J. Jacobs Motor Company in Marysville. Meade's brother-in-law, J. W. Squires, was a Studebaker salesman for the company and the buzz job was Meade letting him know he would need transportation from District Ten to Squires' home to visit his sister. The following morning he met his relatives at Cheim Field and gave them all rides in his Eaglerock. Meade was pleased with the airfield's

CHAPTER 3

location and its condition.[27]

Jim Read announced in June that Dr. Johnson was building a new hangar on Cheim Field, and it would soon be ready for use. Johnson expected to have a new plane in the hangar. It is not clear whether he was getting his rebuilt Eaglerock back from Galt or a new one from the Alexander factory.

It is believed Dr. Johnson had a hangar on or near the Marysville airport site in 1927, where Dudley Cunningham and Bob McCollough rebuilt his Eaglerock after the hangar collapsed on it in Yuba City. Heiman Cheim may have allowed him to use the site as a landing field a year before the city became interested in the site.

Read said, in June 1928, a new office building for Cheim Field was to be constructed immediately.

Two aircraft arrived and were tied down overnight at Cheim Field for the first time in June. They were both from out of the area. One brought Albert E. Hastings and Don Cornell, the Eaglerock dealer for Northern California who were meeting prospective customers at the Hotel Marysville. They landed in Sutter County first because they were unable to find Cheim Field. The grounds had not yet been marked as an airport. When told of its location, they took off and landed at Cheim.

The other airplane with former Eaglerock dealer James Mayberry at the controls overflew Marysville and landed in a field north of Live Oak. The field was rough and the plane's wheels struck a depression in the ground causing the tips of the propeller to be chewed off. Mayberry examined the tips and decided the propeller had been shortened equally on each end, so he flew back to Cheim Field. He tied the aircraft down and waited overnight for a new prop to arrive. It was the first time a transient aircraft remained overnight at Cheim Field.

Jim Read, the new airport superintendent, reported Cheim Field had not been marked as an airport yet because the field had no water supply, and other improvements were needed. Water was important because many aircraft of the period used Curtiss OX-5 or Hisso engines, which were water-cooled.[28]

Mr. Mayberry's problems were not over. He became Cheim Field's first aircraft accident victim. After he installed a new prop on his Eaglerock and made repairs to his damaged landing gear, he was ready to fly back to his home field at Oakland. He had to hand prop his engine to get it started, but there were no wheel chocks available on the new airport. So, while Mayberry propped the Eaglerock, he had someone else hold the airplane and adjust the throttle while standing outside the airplane next to the cockpit. Airplanes of this era had no parking brake, no wheel brakes, and no self-starters. The planes had to be hand propped by someone standing in front of the propeller. The wheels should have been chocked while someone else sat in the cockpit possibly with the throttle advanced slightly. The person in the cockpit had to reduce the throttle setting once the engine started. Depending on the experience of the people involved, it could be a dangerous procedure but unavoidable at this earlier stage of the technology. Sometimes the person minding the throttle was a passenger with no flying experience or, worse yet, the passenger would hand prop the airplane with little or no prior experience.

The problems with this procedure were numerous, but again unavoidable. When a pilot was ready to depart, there might not be anyone available to sit in or stand by the cockpit to mind the throttle. There might not be any wheel chocks available and not all pilots carried their own. There might not be anyone to pull the chocks from the wheels once the pilot got the engine started and got in the plane. One can see the problems pilot's had in these early days just getting their engines started.

In Mayberry's situation, the person working the throttle should have pulled the throttle back to the point where he could hold the airplane from rolling forward, but instead he advanced the throttle full on, and the airplane began rolling. Mayberry was able to grab the tailskid as the plane rolled by him. He tried to hang on hoping to reach the cockpit and kill the engine. With the throttle full forward, the plane accelerated more and more. Mayberry was forced to let go. The plane took off with no one in it. It bounced into the air, then came down hard, careening into a fence that paralleled the new runway. After going through the fence, the Eaglerock flipped upside down and crashed, damaging the upper wing and destroying the new propeller. No one was injured, but Mayberry would long remember his first flight to Cheim Field. His plane was shipped to Oakland for repairs within hours after the crash.[29]

ALBERT E. HASTINGS and Don M. Cornell came to Marysville about this time not only to sell Eaglerocks but also to set up a commercial aviation business at Marysville's new airport. Their company was Sierra Aircraft Corporation and, according to company president Hastings, it had been incorporated only a short time ago. Don Cornell was vice president and sales manager.

CHAPTER 3   85

In addition to selling Eaglerocks, the company would provide a flying school, general aviation business, and air taxi service. Aircraft were to be available for licensed pilots to rent. After airport buildings at Cheim Field were completed, the company's repair shop and supply house would occupy them. Sierra Aircraft Company would open offices on airports at Chico and Oakland soon after the opening in Marysville.

Jim Read assisted the company and did most of its flying work. He reported forty people had signed up for flying instruction.

Hastings already had one Eaglerock on the field and another would be at Cheim in a few days. The Alexander factory in Denver, Colorado, was to deliver a third in one month.[30]

There may have been a connection with a business of the same name opened at Sierra Airport in Sierra Madre, November 1919. Sierra Madre was a small community two miles east of Pasadena in the south state. Leon T. Eliel, president of Sierra Aircraft Company, an aerial survey business, managed the airport. Eliel went on to preside over Fairchild Aerial Surveys. The reason it is believed there was some connection between the two companies, other than the fact their names are identical, was the Sierra Airport in Sierra Madre, which only existed until 1922, was also called Hastings Airport, possibly for Albert Hastings who became president of the Marysville company.

Dr. Johnson traveled to Galt in search of a new plane to buy. His demolished Eaglerock may have been too far gone to rebuild.[31]

Herbert Keeler, shop teacher at Marysville High School, enrolled in Jim Read's new aviation ground school at Sierra Aviation Company, Cheim Field. Keeler was sure aeronautical education would soon be added to the high school curriculum, and he wanted to be the one to teach it.[32]

Keeler went to San Diego during the summer of 1928 and learned much at the Ryan School of Aeronautics. He learned all about aircraft by actually building airplanes at the Ryan factory. His efforts paid off. He was chosen to teach a complete course in aeronautics at Yuba Junior College and Marysville High School when school began in September 1928.[33]

Marysville city officials realized they needed a lease agreement with Heiman Cheim for use of the airport land. They wanted to financially support the airport but couldn't legally do so until there was a lease agreement for the land use.

Cheim Field needed to be graded once again in the fall to improve drainage making it usable during the winter months.

Jim Read asked the city council to enact regulations to govern flying. He gave the council a copy of the regulations enacted the year before by the US Department of Commerce's Aeronautics Branch as a guide in preparing a city ordinance. He told them that all principal cities were setting up such laws. The highest priority regulations would prevent unlicensed pilots and planes from transporting passengers out of the local airport, would designate the altitude at which pilots could fly over town, and would prohibit stunting over town.

Read cited an official report stating there had been no deaths from flying by government licensed pilots or planes. If the report were true, odds are it wouldn't be long before a licensed pilot was killed in an accident somewhere in the nation.[34]

After Congress passed the Air Commerce Act of 1926, there was confusion about who would enforce the new regulations and how. In the interim, states and cities duplicated the regulations allowing them to use their own law enforcement officers and courts to catch and punish offenders, which was why Read was pushing for a city ordinance.[35]

Eventually, federal regulations and enforcement superseded all other air laws—cities and states gave up their regulation and enforcement efforts.

At Cheim Field, Julius Wheeler and Wes Owen took off in a Sierra Aircraft Company Eaglerock with Jim Read at the controls. It was a night flight and required automobiles to park near the runway with their lights on so Read could see the runway when landing. A Sierra Aircraft Company representative reported the company planned to make night flights a specialty.[36]

Around this time, July 2, Dr. Johnson's sixteen-year-old stepdaughter, Mildred Riddle, died in his hospital after an appendicitis operation.[37]

Cheim Field was falling into poor condition by July 1928. It lacked necessary equipment and no funds had been provided to improve the situation. Dust was the field's biggest problem. Whenever an airplane started its motor, huge dust clouds billowed, got into the engines, and caused damage. Roiling clouds of dust covered everything with layers grit. Mrs. Marie Schmipf who lived in the vicinity, offered to pay for all the gravel needed to cover the runway. Unfortunately, gravel damages propellers and aircraft fabric. Her offer wasn't accepted.

Martin Jensen, who took second place in the Dole Race to Hawaii less than a year before, flew over Marysville on his way to a reception for him at the Redding airport. He was flying his yellow Breese monoplane *Aloha*, the plane he flew to Hawaii. He wanted to land because Jensen was a friend of Sierra Aircraft Company president Albert Hastings of Marysville, but city officials hadn't provided an incentive for him to stop. The two men had worked together for Golden State Aircraft at Oakland before Jensen flew to fame in the Dole Race.[38]

Yuba County Sheriff C. J. McCoy assigned Jim Read as flying deputy sheriff to enforce air laws and regulations. Jim was also appointed to help pursue fugitives. For Read's personal safety, the sheriff made it quite clear to the public that Read was *not* hired to search the river bottoms around Marysville or the canyons in the mountainous part of the county for moonshine stills.[39]

Sierra Aircraft kept an office in Marysville's Ellis Building on Second Street since early June. After city officials and Heiman Cheim signed a lease agreement, the company moved temporarily into one of the hangars on the field while a new office building was being built. Warren Construction planned to dig a ditch for electrical lines running into the airfield from the highway. Hemstreet & Bell Construction Company of Marysville donated ten truckloads of dirt to fill the ditch paralleling Tahoe-Ukiah Highway. To help control the dust, Pacific Gas and Electric hauled in coal cinders to spread on the runway, roads, and parking areas.

Julius Wheeler and Jim Read planned to fly from Cheim Field to San Jose in mid-July. Albert Hastings flew to San Francisco to watch the arrival of the 1928 national air tour. Later, Hastings, Read, and Felix Dreyfus, Cheim Field's first aviation mechanic, flew to Sacramento for Hastings and Dreyfus to take flight physicals while Read attended a meeting of the California Development Board.[40] Also that month, lights were installed on the new hangar and office at Cheim Field, but no runway lights were installed.[41]

The Marysville Merchants Association and the Yuba County Chamber of Commerce approved plans for an air show at Cheim Field to dedicate the new airport and let the state's flying community know Marysville had developed a first class landing field. Jimmy Read and the head of the California Association for the Promotion of Aviation, Don Castle, laid out an air show proposal for the two organizations to consider.[42]

In his letter to a friend, Jimmy Read wrote about the magnificent cooperation he received from local businesses and service clubs during construction of the new airport. He listed those that hadn't yet been publicly mentioned. They were: Valley Concrete Pipe, donating the culvert pipe needed to construct a driveway; the Exchange Club, whose members paid for a new water well and pump; the Lions Club donation of the underground conduit for the power lines; Hemstreet & Bell Construction's loan of an engine and pump to develop and clean up the new well; S. E. Price of Price's Super Service Station who donated and installed a gasoline pump and underground gasoline storage tank; E. M. Smith who donated one hundred dollars toward lighting the field; the *Appeal Democrat*'s free publicity for the project; and Carrol Fike and Fire Chief Goss who gave their time, at all hours of the day or night, whenever they were asked.[43]

The new airport was included in *Western Flying*'s "Airports in the West" article in its August issue. The article stated, "Marysville—Located about five minutes ride from the city hall, the Marysville airport is now complete and is able to handle any type of aircraft, according to E. Johnson, division manager of the Pacific Gas and Electric Company. At the present time, however, lights have not been installed, so the field is not safe for night landing. The field has a runway of approximately three thousand feet, which has been leveled. It is located about one mile northeast of the Marysville gas (plant), and at an early date an arrow will be placed on the tank to indicate the direction of the field."

Avis Sutfin Bielefeld, born and raised in Yuba County, learned to fly in Sacramento in 1934. She is shown here with her flying instructor, Ivor Whitney.

With the exception of the glaring error of the field's length, the article was a reasonable description of Cheim Airport. At the time, the runway length was only two thousand feet, not three thousand feet.[44]

Jimmy Read began instructing flying students for Sierra Aircraft Company at Cheim Field in late July. Among his first group of students was Miss Estal Burch, who would become the Yuba-Sutter area's first woman pilot. She gained that distinction when she got her student pilot license on August 9 from the DOC. Miss Burch, secretary to the Sutter County farm advisor, was Read's only female student and first of his student group to get a student license. The license permitted her to make flights with her instructor, Read, and solo flights within gliding distance of Cheim Field. So far she had three flying hours of instruction under Read and would soon be starting his advanced instruction, which included solo flight.[45]

Another Yuba County aviatrix of the 1930s was Jewel Danley shown here hand propping Garick's biplane at Cheim Field.

THE AIRPORT DEDICATION and air show for Cheim Field was scheduled August 25–27, 1928. The Marysville *Appeal-Democrat* ran large photographs on its front page of Estal Burch and Jimmy Read, who were chosen as Queen Estal and King Jimmy for the upcoming dedication festivities.[46]

Standard Oil Company would send their big tri-motor Ford named *Standard of California* to Cheim Field for the celebration. Pilots, F. V. Tompkins and his assistant, R. S. Allen, would take up invited guests for a number of flights on Sunday, the twenty-seventh. The Ford was fitted out to haul six passengers in luxury rather than the usual fourteen in wicker seats.[47]

Bob Barbour was hired to make parachute jumps during the air show. Barbour, age thirty-five, was a well-known parachutist on the air show circuit. He had jumped at many of the big national air shows according to Don Castle, who was hiring the talent for the air show at Cheim. Castle said

Barbour had been hired to make fourteen jumps for the 1928 National Air Races at Los Angeles in September. Barbour claimed to hold three world records for parachuting. The first was his claim to have made more jumps than anyone in the business. His second claim was to have jumped from a higher altitude than anyone else. His third was one that no one would be able to surpass and few believed, and that was his claim of having made the most jumps during the Great War. (The when, where, and why he was making parachute jumps during the Great War remains a mystery. The only Americans to use parachutes during the Great War were observers in tethered observation balloons.) It was said that he added more thrills to his jumps by not opening his chute until he was close to the ground. Barbour said he began his parachuting career in 1913. Unfortunately, no one was recording or officiating parachute jumping during 1913–1928.[48]

When Barbour got to Marysville on the twenty-third, it wasn't long before he demonstrated a technique of generating free publicity from local newspapers that was used by many air show parachutists.

After dinner and meeting some friends, Barbour got back to his hotel room around 3:00 AM and found the parachute he would be using for the Cheim event was out of its case. The shrouds were all tangled and slits cut in strategic places that would cause the chute to rip open when he jumped sending him to his death.

Barbour called Darrell LaFortune, the Marysville chief of police, to the hotel, and the chute was examined then taken to the police station.

Barbour surmised to the press that he returned to his room sooner than expected and interrupted the person who was trying to kill him. He assumed the perpetrator escaped from the room before he entered and was unable to put the chute back in its case and return it to where it was stored.

Barbour asked the chief for protection for the rest of the night but was told it was unnecessary. Even so, Barbour was able to get a good night's sleep following the incident.

He claimed that two previous attempts to sabotage his parachutes had occurred. One, supposedly, resulted in the death of Sandy Sanders, a popular Oakland aviator who died just a week before. Sanders' parachute had belonged to Barbour and had been sabotaged before Sanders borrowed it.

Barbour could offer little as to why anyone would want to kill him other than his belief that it might be a wartime grudge against him. He thought a German might be trying to kill him. He made sure the last line in the story read "he would not change his plans." He would jump during the upcoming air show at Cheim Field in two days.[49]

Leo Moore flew into Cheim at 8:00 AM on the twenty-fourth to pick up Queen Estal Burch for a publicity flight. He flew her to his home field on Auburn Boulevard in Del Paso Park. Moore had signed to do stunt flying for the air show at Cheim Field.[50]

On the morning of Saturday, August 25, aircraft began arriving at Cheim Field. It seemed to many that planes were raining from the skies, but obviously it would seem like rain to observers at an airport so new that the most planes ever seen parking together were two.

Saturday morning and early afternoon were for aircraft arrivals, which were so unusual to the townspeople of Marysville and Yuba City that carloads of people began arriving on the adjacent Tahoe-Ukiah Highway.

Two aces from the Great War arrived at 1:00 PM. They were H. E. "Tex" Frolich, who said he was the first American pilot to be decorated by the English for valor in bringing down German planes, and Capt. Bernard Foster from the Oakland Airport. They each claimed downing seven German planes during the war. Frolich had been shot up pretty badly and was partially disabled. This author has been unable or corroborate the pairs' victory claims.

The aces flew up from Oakland in a Lockheed Vega called *Copper Princess* belonging to the short-lived Nevada Airlines. It was a yellow aircraft powered by a Wright Whirlwind with an aluminum propeller. The pilot said he had to climb to five thousand feet near Fairfield to get over the fog on his way to Marysville.

Jack Ness, George A. Heddinger, and T. S. Marlor flew into Cheim Saturday morning in a Travel Air with plans to participate in the flying events. They came up from San Francisco.

Leo Moore, as noted, arrived in his Travel Air *Miss Sacramento*.

Also arriving Saturday morning by car was H. A. Sanders, the father, and Mrs. Sanders, the widow of Sandy Sanders, the Oakland aviator recently killed in a crash near Oakland Airport.

The pilot of the plane in which Sanders was killed, Louise McPhetridge (later Thaden), was supposed to come to the Cheim dedication and participate. She did not—she was recuperating from injuries suffered in the crash.[51]

Sanders's fatal crash occurred during a short low-level flight from an Alameda airport to the Oakland Airport, a distance of about three miles. The plane never reached an altitude where a parachute could safely be used. So,

Bob Barbour's concocted story about one of his sabotaged parachutes causing Sanders' death was a fabrication.

Over a thousand spectators came out to Cheim Field to watch Saturday's arrivals and a short air show that afternoon. Bob Barbour made a parachute jump and Leo Moore flew aerobatics. Because of heavy fog at Fairfield, arrival of some participants was delayed, and the scheduled fifteen-mile free-for-all race was cancelled. A much larger crowd was expected the next day for the scheduled military flying, stunt flying, air races, and airplane rides.

An aviators' ball was held Saturday night at the Moon Dance Pavilion across the river near Sutter with a large crowd attending.

Sunday saw an enormous throng of automobiles creep slowly out of Marysville north along Tahoe-Ukiah Highway. The highway paralleled the levee that keeps the Yuba River out of Marysville during the rainy winter months. The highway, also known as Brown's Valley Road, was constructed on raised ground along the western toe of the levee. As cars reached the entrance to Cheim Field they decended onto the field and had to quickly turn south into an area set aside for parking.

Twelve thousand spectators arrived on Sunday. The combined force of the Yuba and Sutter county traffic officers, plus a group of national guardsmen, were nearly overwhelmed by the numbers.

Again, the delay of planes due to fog in the Bay Area caused cancellation of much of the dedication ceremony, but the crowd was pleased with what they saw.

Queen Estal Burch and King Jimmy Read arrived an hour late at 3:00 PM in a plane flown by Jerry Andrews. Theirs was the first "official" landing on Cheim Field. Following the royal couple, planes landed carrying ceremonial princesses Anita Doyle, Irene Anderson, Siri Johnson, Carol Counter, and Eleanor Burroughs.

The crowd watched every plane with great interest. While the various flying events were taking place, five veteran pilots from the Bay Area and Sacramento were giving passenger rides, for a fee, from 9:00 AM until 7:00 PM. These five airplanes were in the air throughout day.

Standard Oil's tri-motor Ford roared in for a landing at 9:00 AM attracting thousands of spectators to its static display. Just before noon, the Ford took off with a load of invited guests for a short ride around the Twin Cities. After returning, it was decided the runway was a little too short for further passenger flights in the Ford. It sat on display for the remainder of the day. For its late afternoon departure, the Ford's pilots decided to give the audience a thrill. They put the big airliner through a series of maneuvers thought impossible for an aircraft of such size.

After lunch the military aircraft finally arrived. The two observation planes from the Presidio's Crissy Field had been held up by fog. Marine ground support planes came up from Mather Field; the three planes were part of a squadron temporarily stationed there for the summer of 1928.

Marine pilots, led by Lieutenant Cushman, put on a spectacular demonstration of tactical maneuvers, and then the army did some stunt flying for the crowd, and when finished departed for Crissy Field at 4:00 PM. The race planned between the army and navy aircraft had to be cancelled due to heavy fog forming along their route back to the Bay Area. They had to leave at once, and all of the other races were cancelled.

Leo Moore took to the sky doing loops, rolls, and spins in his Travel Air *Miss Sacramento*. He demonstrated great expertise as an aerobatic pilot and filled the time slot left by the departing military aircraft and race cancellations.

Bob Barbour made another parachute jump Sunday afternoon, only this time things didn't go quite as he expected. He jumped from twenty-six hundred feet, but his chute didn't fully deploy. He came down much faster than expected, receiving a severe jar upon landing. He was rushed to the hospital where his injuries were determined not serious.

Air show officials timed Barbour's jumps Saturday and Sunday. He jumped from the same altitude both days. His descent on Saturday took fifty-four seconds. His descent on Sunday took only twenty-two seconds. His survival of the second jump with only a sprained neck and minor spinal displacement baffled everyone.

The last event at Cheim on Sunday was a performance by the municipal band directed by Wilson McRae.[52]

Of the twenty airplanes that came to Cheim Field for the dedication, two were army Douglas O-2 observation aircraft from Crissy Field. Lt. Harold F. Brown, a former Marysville lad, flew one of the Douglas planes. Brown was said to be one of the youngest pilots in the Army Air Corps. He would soon become a fixture in Yuba-Sutter aviation following his military career.[53]

A WEEK BEFORE the airport dedication and air show, Jim Read, after all his work pushing through the development of Marysville's first civilian airport, announced he would be leaving at the beginning of September to work in Los Angeles. He was being transferred by his employer, Western Auto Supply Co., to head the new aeronautical department of Western Auto. His new position was said to put Read in command of the largest aeronautical accessory enterprise in the country.

Read was particularly well suited for the job; he had been a flying instructor during the Great War and had a respected reputation as an aviator. He was also an accomplished engineer and designer of aircraft and an excellent radio engineer having designed a special broadcasting set at his home in Yuba City.[54]

Whatever feelings Read's colleagues and flying students had upon learning about his coming departure were put on hold for the next six days while everyone prepared for the upcoming airport dedication. However, on Sunday night after the air show was over and the last spectators had gone home, a big send-off was planned for Jimmy Read at the Idylwild Inn.

It was not only a party for Jimmy Read, it was also an after party for the aviators and organizers of the airport dedication. The toastmaster was District Attorney Erling Norby.

At the party, Norby gave the dedication speech for the new airport, which he couldn't make during the air show because the program changed after the military cancellations. In his speech he gave credit to Heiman Cheim for providing the land and to Roy Bostic, Ed Johnson, and those who actually did the development work on the airport. But it was Jimmy Read whom he credited for getting the airport built. He said the crowd saw some fine flying on Sunday, and he felt the air show put Marysville on the air maps that day. He also said further development of the airfield would have to happen soon.

After Norby finished speaking, Read got up and refused any honor for his part in the endeavor. He said it was the unselfish cooperation of those already mentioned, and the businessmen in the community who created the airport.

Read said he regretted having to leave the community, but he felt the field was in good hands. He agreed with Norby, the runway needed to be lengthened and further improved. He ended his brief speech by saying he would always look on Marysville as his home port.

Others speaking were: Jerry Andrews, Tex Frolich, Leo Moore, Bernard Foster, attorney Marias, and few other event participants. They all made short speeches. W. R. Schanhals, a local insurance man who had served in the Army Air Service and expected to soon have an airplane on the field, also gave a short talk.

Bob Barbour, with his neck dislocated, was at the party but spent most of his time lying on a couch. The dedication committee voted him one of the silver loving cups, which he greatly appreciated. Another cup was given to Jack Ness, a San Francisco aviator. Leo Moore received a third cup for his aerobatic flying. Tex Frolich thanked the committee for the excellent air show, the aviator's reception, and for the night's entertainment.

A vote of appreciation was given to Don Castle, an ex-Royal Flying Corps pilot, and Bryan Lake, both from the California Association for the Promotion of Aviation, for organizing all of the events and the aviators who participated in the air show.

Later in the evening, National Theater manager W. H. Cornwell arrived from his theater with several vaudeville entertainers who were on the evening's bill. They got the party going, which continued into the wee hours.[55]

In early September, Marysville Mayor Walter Kynoch and Roy Bostic met with Heiman Cheim. The three men worked out a plan enabling the city to own and operate Cheim Field. It would allow the city to lease the ground for five years at one dollar a year with an option to buy at the end of the lease.[56]

September 20 saw the start of a trial in which Otto Thomasson sued Dr. Julian Johnson for five thousand dollars in damages for injuries he received in the crash of Dr. Johnson's Alexander Eaglerock at Sutter.

Dr. Johnson represented himself, and attorney Arthur Coats represented Thomasson. Judge Eugene McDaniel presided over a twelve-member jury. Dr. Johnson represented himself because in an earlier malpractice case against him, he also represented himself and won. He thought highly of his own legal prowess.

During the trial, the plaintiff claimed Dr. Johnson owned the airplane flown by Russell Hill at the time of the crash. Dr. Johnson replied that he had sold the airplane prior to the crash, and he produced the bill of sale for the court.

The plaintiff produced seven witnesses for the trial and Dr. Johnson only two, his wife Laura Johnson and himself.

Once again, Dr. Johnson won his case. It took the jury only forty minutes to bring in a verdict. Dr. Johnson stressed two points as the basis for his defense: the first was negligence on the part of the pilot had not been proven, and the second point was the plane was not the property of the doctor when it crashed. The bill of sale was produced, at the last minute, in court as proof.[57]

The jury's verdict was amazing when one considers Jim Read's comments to the newspaper on February 3, just after the crash. Read had criticized the pilot for not following Dr. Johnson's instructions to fly straight and level. Read also condemned the pilot for his inexperience and lack of judgment. And if the plane was sold, why did Dr. Johnson truck the remains to Galt High School to be rebuilt for himself?

Yuba City High School began the 1928 school year with a new aeronautics program. The school had recently received a four hundred horsepower Liberty engine to use in Jack C. Roberts' class on aviation mechanics. The engine came free from the government; it was one of twelve thousand Liberty engines leftover from the war. Norman J. Laughlin taught the theory of flight. Roberts, Laughlin, and also J. E. Tolman, all teachers at the school, were fliers during the World War. Roberts had worked with Jim Read in Modesto before Read was transferred by Western Auto to Marysville.[58]

Lester Benson, a restaurant employee at Hotel Marysville, purchased Jim Read's Curtiss Jenny before he left for Los Angeles. Read had been working on the Jenny, but it was not in flying condition. Benson took the wings off and moved it to his backyard in Marysville. While attempting to restore it he liked to run the engine, resulting in dust and noise, which irritated his neighbors.[59]

Marysville's Cheim Field circa 1938.

CHAPTER 4

James Read leaves Marysville – Jimmie Angel moves south – Dr. Johnson's final years – Marysville supports Cheim Field – Yuba City searches for another airport site – Yuba-Sutter Flying Club is founded – First crop dusting in the Sacramento Valley

Jim Read left Twin Cities in September 1928. His energy and enthusiasm for flying, which contributed so much for the community, would be sorely missed. Dr. Johnson was still hanging on, but his interest and finances were being usurped by his medical practice and a difficult marriage.

Read moved to Los Angeles to take over the aforementioned Western Auto aviation products job, but lost the job after the Depression hit and, eventually, was hired by the Department of Commerce (DOC) Aeronautics Branch as an aviation inspector. By the mid-1930s, he worked mainly out of Union Air Terminal in Burbank. He was involved with inspection of several aircraft prototypes built in Southern California during the 1930s and '40s, including the ill-conceived Lockheed Orion/Explorer hybrid in which Wily Post and Will Rogers were killed. In 1939, he was a member of the Civil Aeronautics Authority (CAA) team that conducted Approved Type Certificate (ATC) certification of the Douglas DC-4 airliner. James E. Read was an active member of the Los Angeles Hangar of Quiet Birdmen. Read's name is often misspelled in various books and resources as Reed instead of Read.[1]

JIMMIE ANGEL'S CAREER after leaving the Yuba-Sutter community was more diverse than Read's. Two months after he abandoned Dr. Johnson and Angel Airport at Yuba City, Angel pursued his usual backup plan when flying jobs were scarce or when his situation in the states got too hot for him. He returned to flying payroll, mail, gold, and freight for mines in Mexico. Angel went to work for Copalitos Mining Company. The company wanted an OX-5 Standard J-1 flown from Clover Field, Santa Monica, to Guamuchil, Mexico. Jimmie flew the plane to the border with Leslie Dutro along as mechanic. Mexicali authorities refused to allow the plane to cross the border due possibly to a lack of paperwork, an insufficient bribe, or Jimmie's past activities in Mexico, so Jimmie lost his job with Copalitos.[2]

Jimmie then joined an old friend, Charles Ming, on a flying job at Long Beach in July 1927. Ming, who was Asian, called himself, "One Wing Low" in the flying business, possibly to get ahead of more serious racial bias of the times. After their work was completed, Ming and Angel flew back to the Bay Area from Long Beach via Visalia.[3]

The Long Beach work was training Chinese pilots for military and airmail jobs in China. It was the beginning of occasional contract work that Jimmie, and later with his brother Eddie, took at various Southern California airports from 1927 through 1932.

The Angel Brothers Air Circus went back to Alum Rock Airport in San Jose after the hangar blew down at Yuba City, but according to wing walker Bob Straight, they didn't stay long. Robert Eccles and Robert Leroy were running the Alum Rock and Capitol Avenue airport by November 1927 when the Angel Brothers Air Circus broke up with Straight and the Angels each going their own way. That same month Eccles and Leroy were served with an injunction from the local district attorney declaring the use of the airfield a public nuisance and closed it down. Motorists and nearby residents had complained of the choking dust generated by aircraft.[4]

Jimmie Angel's parents and his youngest brother, Clyde, had moved from Wichita, Kansas, to Long Beach, California, in September 1927 and stayed with Jimmie and his first wife, Virginia. Soon the parents found a place to live in Compton. The brothers worked sporadically in the Great Central Valley and Southern California as pilots through the 1930s. Jimmie was close to his mother and from time to time would visit while flying out of Compton Airport.[5]

Jimmie and Eddie moved to Fresno in March 1928. Jimmie had been hired as field superintendent for Beacon Airways. Beacon had offices in the Bay Area and Los Angeles, but its main headquarters and flying field was Fresno Airport, six miles northwest of the city. Harold Hall, Angel Air Circus' chief mechanic at Yuba City, was listed as Beacon's "aeronautical engineer."

CHAPTER 4
99

F. W. Hemingway, Beacon president, and Presho Stephenson, vice president, required Jimmie and Eddie Angel to obtain government flying licenses. They took the test for transport licenses right away. Jimmie listed his address as Beacon Airways, Fresno, California, and Eddie listed Beacon's downtown Fresno address as his own. They received DOC Transport Pilot Licenses, No. 1987 for Jimmie and No. 2121 for Eddie.[6]

The Richmond Airport, which Angel Brothers Air Circus helped dedicate in 1925, had died many deaths since then and was reborn a number of times. It was leased in February 1928 to Frank Pebbles to be born once again and listed as being an active airport in 1928, but by 1935 the Richmond Airport disappeared forever.[7]

The Angels moved to Fresno in late 1927 or January 1928. Jimmie had a new moneyman on the hook. It was Presho Stephenson or Frank W. Hemingway or maybe both.

This became evident after Beacon officials announced to the press that after having taken on the Prudden all-metal aircraft distributorship, they were also going to develop the three hundred horsepower, six-cylinder engine built by Harold Hall. They hoped to put the inline, water-cooled motor into production. They would use a Fokker D. VII aircraft as the engine's test bed. The company planned to use the engine on a 1,750-mile nonstop flight from Fresno to Mexico City later in the month.[8] This was the same engine and plane that Jimmie and his crew were working on with Harold Hall at San Jose.

The Mexico City flight did not happen. Jimmie said he had planned to use the Hall-powered Fokker on a photography tour of South America, but the D.VII, with the Hall engine, had an unusually high landing speed of *eighty* (!) miles per hour. Jimmie explained that was "too fast for backyard landings." Angel said he had purchased, "... the Bach cabin job owned by Stanley Short to use on the tour." The D.VII, he said, was to compete in the upcoming National Air Races. As usual with most of Jimmie's grandiose plans, getting the D.VII to the races didn't happen.[9]

Besides the Fokker D.VII and Hall's overheating engine, Jimmie sold Hemingway and Stephenson on his plan to film an aerial tour of South America. What better way for Jimmie to get to the land of his dreams where caches of gold and emeralds were just waiting to be found?

The film tour was given the go-ahead. The expedition acquired a CS-1 from Los Angeles aircraft designer and builder Morton Bach. Bach created the CS-1 by attaching the wings from a World War SE-5 British fighter to the modified fuselage of an Italian Ansaldo warplane and hung a 180 horsepower Hisso on it. He built an enclosed cabin for three people, but Jimmie reported he would carry four people plus their baggage and camera equipment in the Bach for the tour.[10]

The tour route was from Fresno to Cape Horn at the southern tip of South America. The crew for the tour were: Jimmie as pilot; William Benton, copilot and mechanic; and Presho Stephenson who went along to keep an eye on Jimmie and pay the bills. At Guaymas, Mexico, William Beri would join them as cameraman to record the trip into South America. Movie film would be shot from Guaymas to Cape Horn.[11]

The tour started well from Fresno Airport, but, once again, Jimmie had problems with customs at Mexicali. Was it Angel's reputation with Mexican officials from prior work in Mexico that caused him so much trouble?

Jimmie was no saint, for sure, but he suffered a reputation that was not always deserved. D. W. Tomlinson reveals a disturbing meeting with a pilot named Jim in his autobiography. There is no date for this meeting, but given the chronology of Tomlinson's book it would have taken place in the early 1920s prior to January 1923.

Tomlinson and Earl Daugherty flew into a small airfield at the end of Broadway in San Diego where Jim was converting a Sopwith two-place aircraft into one that would carry more passengers. He was putting an OXX-6 engine on the plane for more power. Tomlinson and Daugherty had heard about the conversion and wanted to see this adaptation.

While inspecting the plane, Tomlinson noticed the passengers' cockpit was moved back from under the wing on the fuselage, and inside the passenger's cockpit he had walled it with thin plywood. There wasn't anything a passenger could hang on to nor were there any seat belts in that cockpit. When Tomlinson had a chance to get Jim alone, he asked him about the walled cockpit and the answer he got "shook [his] faith in humanity." Jim told him he rebuilt the cockpit without handholds or seat belts for smuggling Chinese into the country from Mexico. If government planes began chasing him, he said he would swing fifteen or twenty miles out over the Pacific Ocean, and turn the plane upside down dumping the passengers!

A journalist claimed in a newspaper article about Angel, the Jim in Tomlinson's book was Jimmie Angel. In fairness to Angel, Tomlinson's book never mentions Jim's last name.

There is a photograph extant of Jimmie standing by his plane in December 1931 with a score of artifacts he brought out of Mexico. When he

Chapter 4

acquired these artifacts is a mystery. Whether he smuggled them out during his many payroll flights to the mines and oil fields or brought them out legally, a photo of such artifacts published in a Washington, D. C., newspaper could easily lead to a misunderstanding with the Mexican government; allowing the photo to be published was not a wise decision on Jimmie's part.

During Jimmie's epic flight to Cape Horn, another problem arose when Jimmie and his crew reached Mexicali in addition to the problems with customs officials. They began to experience problems with the Bach's Hisso engine. A leaky oil line further delayed their departure from Mexicali. While Benton, the copilot and mechanic, repaired the oil line, Angel spoke with Capt. Louis Farrel, who was coming out of Mexico and had just flown the route from the Mexican mainland to Mexicali.

After Angel told Farrel the route he was going to fly—directly from Mexicali over the Gulf of California and down to Guaymas along the coast of mainland Mexico—Captain Farrel immediately advised against such a course. He told Angel that to fly over the gulf for such a long flight would put him and his passengers in jeopardy. There was only uninhabited desert on both sides of the gulf. It would be fatal if one had engine problems. Farrel suggested Angel take a more easterly route to the town of Santa Ana. From there, it was a straight shot due south to Guaymas. This route would put Angel within reach of several towns and villages should he have to make a forced landing.[12]

Without a doubt, Angel's conversation with Captain Farrel saved his and his passenger's lives. Jimmie followed Farrel's advice and struck out for Santa Ana from Mexicali. The Hisso engine just wasn't up to a long flight. The oil pressure dropped, and Jimmie had to put the Bach down somewhere on the Sonoran prairie. Once again, the oil line was broken but fixable.

Soon the Bach was back in the air headed for Santa Ana, and the engine quit once more. Jimmie made a safe landing on a sandbar in the Rio Altar. He found the cause to be lack of fuel. A leaky fuel pump had lost all of the plane's gasoline. While Benton fixed the pump, Jimmie found someone with a horse, which he borrowed and rode many miles to a mountain gold mine. There he acquired enough gasoline to get the plane to Hermosillo. He brought the gas back to the plane by oxcart.[13]

Jimmie landed on the outskirts of Hermosillo, Mexico, April 24, 1928. He and his crew were exhausted. They had spent the previous day scrounging the gasoline and then fueling the Bach. Jimmie had a cold when they left Fresno, and it became much worse. After landing at Hermosillo, he said he felt bad and was admitted to the local hospital for the Southern Pacific of Mexico Railroad. It seems this illness may have also prolonged the holdup at Mexicali.

After three nights of rest in Hermosillo, Angel and his crew flew on to Empalme Airport at Guaymas and met their cameraman, William Beri. From Guaymas on the Gulf of California, they had planned to fly across the Mexican mainland to Tampico on the Gulf of Mexico. From Tampico, they would follow the eastern coast of Mexico, Central America, and South America to Cape Horn. That was the route Jimmie had ballyhooed to the press over and over.[14]

Presho Stephenson, the financial officer for the tour and Beacon vice president, decided Jimmie's plan was not in the cards. He realized after the scary night on the sandbar of the Rio Altar, the Bach's Hisso engine was not up for a prolonged flight. That realization wasn't difficult after two forced landings within three hundred miles of the United States border and thousands of miles to go. Stephenson surely knew the only dependable American engines for long distance flying in April 1928 were the new air-cooled Wright Whirlwind and the Pratt & Whitney Wasp.

On May 6, Angel tried to save the trip from total failure. He flew north from the airport at Empalme, serving Guaymas, to the Mexican army headquarters for the state of Sonora at Ortiz.

Notification of this flight was sent to the Associated Press from the military radio station at Guaymas. An amateur radio operator in Los Angeles had picked up the message and forwarded it to a news agancy. The message had to have been sent by Jimmie letting Beacon officials know he was still on the job.

The message said Jimmie was meeting with Gen. Francisco R. Mazo to explore the possibilities of an airmail service connecting the states of Sonora and Sinaloa with Baja California. It also said that a landing field had been surveyed at Guaymas and a hundred troops had been sent to clean the field and prepare it for military and commercial service. According to the message, Jimmie Angel was planning to spend some time in Mexico. This was the time of the Cristados uprising, and it is possible Jimmie was trying to negotiate work as a mercenary.[15]

A press report from Fresno on May 16, 1928, stated Angel had abandoned the Cape Horn tour for a year, implying he was home again in Fresno, and would be returning to Guaymas the following week to fly aerial survey and photography flights for the government of Mexico. Also, it said he

CHAPTER 4

would be instructing at a flight school he was planning to open at Guaymas. Jimmie said he would be flying a seaplane from Los Angeles to Guaymas, which he would then use to transport the mail from Lepase across the Gulf of California to Guaymas.[16]

It is doubtful that Jimmie ever followed through with his Baja airmail plan. It was just a face-saving publicity statement to cover the fact that Beacon Airways was through with Jimmie Angel.

Angel is known to have test flown an all-metal, 120 horsepower Gnome rotary powered aircraft designed and built by Harvey Crawford at Dycer Airport, Los Angeles, in August 1928. Crawford claimed his new all-aluminum sportplane had a safety factor of 30 to 1, and that most wooden airplanes were rated at 6 to 1. Jimmie must have taken Crawford's safety statistics to heart because he was forever after associated with all-metal aircraft when most pilots were still flying ragwing (fabric covered) planes.[17]

In December 1927, Major Tien Lai Huang, said to be commander of the Chinese Nationalist Air Force, visited Dallas, Texas, where he filled out an application for the Easterwood Prize for the first aviator to successfully fly the Pacific Ocean from Dallas to Hong Kong or vice versa. Initially, Huang reported he would be using a Chinese built plane for the flight, and would make the flight in the spring of 1928.[18]

Spring came and went and the flight had yet to happen. By September, Huang had dropped the rank of major and was referred to in the press as Dr. Tien Lai Huang. He no longer claimed to be commander of the Chinese Air Force; he was now a goodwill flier and student of international problems. He wasn't flying from Hong Kong to Dallas; he was going to go the opposite direction. He would not be flying a Chinese plane; he was planning to use an all-metal tri-motor Junkers purchased in Germany. Huang reported the flight would no longer be made from Dallas; it would start from San Francisco with stops at Honolulu and Midway Island.

Huang named Jimmie Angel as his copilot or chief pilot, depending on which report one reads, and Jack Leach of Butte, Montana, as his navigator. This last publicity about Huang's proposed flight in September was also the swansong for Huang's plans. He dropped out of sight and the flight never took place, but there is an excellent publicity photo extant of Huang and Angel standing together in front of a metal plane.[19]

In 1928 and 1929 Jimmie took on several test-flying jobs, while his brother, Eddie, remained in Fresno. Jimmie had burned his bridge there after the failure of the Cape Horn tour. Eddie, said to be a better pilot than

Jimmie, remained with Beacon a while longer. Jimmie moved back to the Los Angeles area and picked up various flight-test jobs that were dangerous but lucrative.

In September 1928, Jimmie was test-flying a Hisso powered Waterhouse biplane and crashed while landing at Long Beach. He had the owner, Langar Gornall, riding along as his passenger. The DOC accident report listed Jimmie as the pilot and gave his address as 927 West 166th Street, Gardena. The cause of the accident was listed as landing with a heavy load causing the landing gear to collapse. The airplane was termed a washout with damage to the gear, propeller, and left wings.

The Waterhouse biplane had been flown a total of twenty-five hours before the crash. Martin, Gornall, and Abergast of Long Beach had reconditioned the plane prior to the crash. The aircraft was to be used in the nonstop, New York to Los Angeles Race [sic]. The X (experimental) registration number had been wired to T. S. Lundgren of Los Angeles for the race.[20]

Jimmie did test-flying in Otto and Wally Timm's new design called the Collegiate in 1928. The Collegiate was a parasol wing dual cockpit monoplane powered by a 120 horsepower Anzani radial engine. Jimmie, Frank Clarke, and Charles LaJotte all tested the Timm design and found it to be a superior airplane especially for aerobatics. Jimmie, who claimed to be chief pilot for the Airflite Flying School at the time, put the plane through a rigorous flight test in December 1928, and reported that Airflite was considering an order for four planes for their training school.[21]

Jimmie made the first flight of the Tunison Scout on December 21, 1928. The low-wing monoplane was designed by M. C. Tunison and built by Scout Airplane Company of Los Angeles. It was a radical sleek design powered by a Wright-Hispano H3 three hundred horsepower engine with a top speed reported to be two hundred miles per hour. The airplane, with the exception of its wheel pants on fixed landing gear and awkward appearing rudder, looked a dozen years ahead of its time. Jimmie spent weeks flight-testing the Scout at Eddie Martin's airport in Santa Ana.[22]

Jimmie next got involved in development of the Zenith Albatross in 1929. This aircraft was said to be the largest aircraft ever built to date in Southern California when it was rolled out of the Zenith factory in January 1928. It had a wingspan of ninety feet and was powered by three German-made 140 horsepower Seimens-Halske engines. Jimmie was first hired to flight-test a Zenith single-engine design, the Z-6-A (or B). The flight-testing Jimmie did for Zenith was also done from Eddie Martin's airport, the

CHAPTER 4

Zenith Company's home field.[23]

Jimmie may have bought the Albatross cheap because Zenith wanted to be rid of it due to its poor performance. It was seriously underpowered for its size. The company managed to sell out to a group of Guatamalan investors, who claimed to represent "Guatamala Air Service," a mysterious Central American airline. The group immediately renamed themselves Albatross Airplane Company.

The new company took over the Albatross project and Jimmie remained as test pilot. After flying the Albatross, he complained about its lack of power. He recommended the Seimans-Halske motors be replaced with more powerful engines. They were taken off and replaced with three 150 horsepower Axelson engines. The result was a loss of ten miles per hour in cruising speed![24]

When Zenith had the Albatross, they tried a few times to set a new endurance record. The aircraft was built with a thirteen hundred-gallon fuel capacity just for the purpose of setting records. The manufacturers felt that setting records was necessary to keep investors interested. When Jimmie later took control of the project, he had a similar idea to interest investors.

Jimmie decided to fly the Albatross for a new endurance record on December 14, 1930. He had a crew of five help him since the Albatross was to be refueled in the air. Sam Hopkins was to fly the refueling plane. This record attempt may have been the reason for an extant photo showing five of the crew standing in front of the Albatross wearing dark airline uniforms with white service hats. Jimmie is standing in the middle with a large bandage on his right cheek. It covered a burn he suffered when the instrument panel in a plane he was testing caught fire. What plane this occurred in is unknown.[25]

Jimmie and the crew departed from Grand Central Air Terminal at Glendale. After the Albatross left the runway, both pilots had to push full forward on the control columns to keep the plane from stalling. Jimmie yelled for someone to check the tail section. Behind the rear bulkhead lying on the longerons, they discovered a stowaway—a terrified young woman. The crew was afraid to move her; she might step between the longerons and fall through the fabric to her death. Jimmie and the copilot made a wide shallow turn and landed back at Glendale. The tailskid snapped off from the full fuel tank on landing. The endurance attempt lasted twenty-eight minutes.[26]

While waiting for a new tailskid to arrive, Jimmie sold the copilot's job on the next endurance try to a friend for a healthy investment check. The friend was furious when he discovered that several other "copilots" had also made the same purchase for a flight that, unfortunately, would never happen. More than once after that, Jimmie tried to secretly fly the Albatross to Guatamala, but mechanical problems foiled each of his attempts.[27]

Jimmie was probably the "Guatamala Air Service." He was reported being manager of operations and announced to the press in June 1929 the new company would be establishing an airline between Tiajuana, Mexico, and Guatamala City, Guatamala. Jimmie was to make the airline's inaugural flight in the Albatross—a one-way trip between the two cities that would take two days by air compared to nine days by rail. Once again, like so many of Angel's plans, the flight never took place.

Jimmie had made quite a nest egg working as a test pilot and other flying jobs, legal and otherwise. He liked the Albatross and felt it had potential. Jimmie invested his savings in the Albatross.[28]

The Albatross failed as a viable transport plane. It was never mated with the proper engines. Wright Whirlwinds, which it desperately needed, were too expensive. It would eventually sit on the ground as an automobile gas station in Southern California and never fly again. Jimmie lost all of his money and, as always, he returned south of the border to recoup his losses.[29]

Mexico and points south were a difficult and dangerous job market for American aviators during the twenties and thirties. By the mid-1930s, there were many landing fields in Mexico, but many of the countries of Central and South America were not as developed. Flying was, in many cases, the only way to get to some mines and villages in these undeveloped countries; roads were often only ox-cart trails or nonexistent. Airstrips were rough and usually fuel was unavailable. It took tough, skilled bush pilots to fly and survive in this environment and Jimmie Angel fit the bill.[30]

After completing another contract training Chinese pilots in Los Angeles in May 1931, Jimmie was in Mexico by January 1932.

He was forced to crash land in the surf along the shore at Aguamelula, supposedly because of the onset of darkness. The tri-motor Ford he was flying was damaged in the landing. Jimmie was carrying seven passengers including his wife and a Mrs. Don Glass with her baby. There were no injuries during the crash landing. Don Glass flew to the aid of the passengers in a Travel Air with the Mexican registration XBAFE.

From Macuapana in the state of Tabasco, Glass made attempts to hire a barge from Acapulco to retrieve the Ford from the water and take it to a

Chapter 4

Jimmie Angel (first on the right) with Chinese Flying Students in Los Angeles circa 1931. Jimmie opened Yuba City's first airport, Angel Airport, in partnership with Yuba City physician, Dr. Julian P. Johnson in August 1926. Their flying business, California Airways Co. was the first commercial aviation business in the Yuba-Sutter area.

repair station. G. E. Flaherty was listed as its owner. DOC records indicate the plane was a Ford 4-AT-A; c/n 4-AT-12; US registration No. 1781. It was registered in Mexico as X-BAFF with the letters on its fuselage. Its Mexican license was reported cancelled by 1933.[31]

Jimmie Angel, from this point in time, moved his flying operations to Mexico, then Central America, and finally South America. His name is immortalized in the identification of the world's tallest (longest falling with a drop of 3,212 feet) waterfall: Angel Falls in Venezuela. Jimmie discovered the falls in November 1933 while flying alone over the area searching for places he could land to look for gold.[32]

During his career flying in South America, Jimmie took part in several scientific expeditions in which he acted as pilot including at least one for *National Geographic* magazine.

Jimmie had his dark side and a big part of that was a story, which he would reel-off usually after a few drinks, about an old miner he met in Venezuela. The miner, whose name he said was MacCracken, hired Jimmie to fly him to a mountain that had a long plateau on top. (Was the same surname as that of the assistant secretary of commerce for aeronautics, MacCracken, chosen by Jimmie so he would always keep his story straight, as he spread it among gullible investors?) Before taking-off, the miner, MacCracken, covered Jimmie's compass and told Jimmie to follow his directions. After they departed, the miner gave Jimmie plenty of turning directions to confuse him before eventually pointing out a stream on a mountain plateau. After landing on rough terrain next to the stream, they got out of the plane and were able to pick up gold nuggets by the handful from the stream. After gathering all they could carry in the plane, they took off and made the same turning, confusing trip back to the airfield so Jimmie wouldn't be able to find it on his own. Afterwards, MacCracken had to make a quick trip back to the states. He was supposed to return and he and Jimmie would fly back to the site to pick up more gold. MacCracken never came back. According to Jimmie, he died in the states.

After telling this story, Jimmie would hit up his listener to buy a partnership in his newest search expedition to locate the mysterious mountain plateau with the stream full of gold nuggets. Some of his listeners believed him, but those who knew Jimmie knew better. Some believed Jimmie had told the story so often he believed it himself. What happened next tends to support that theory.

On October 9, 1937, Jimmie purposely landed his plane, an all-metal Halpin Flamingo C-W-2, NC 9487, named *El Rio Caroni*, on the plateau of Auyantepui, a table mountain in southeastern Venezuela. The plan was to land and search for gold on the plateau. The landing went well at first, but as the Flamingo slowed on what appeared to be flat grassy turf, its wheels sank into marsh-like wet ground hidden by the plant life growing from it. The Flamingo went down on its nose damaging the left wing tip and the oil radiator.[33]

Jimmie's second wife Marie and two assistants accompanied him on this flight. After the plane went down on its nose, Jimmie wanted to leave *El Rio Caroni* in a more dignified attitude. Using ropes, the four pulled the tail down into a normal at rest position. After three days on the plateau, they gathered their survival kit containing a month's supply of food that was always in the plane on bush flights and began a two-week journey on foot back to their base camp. They discovered no gold on the mountain.

The discovery of the falls and the plane crash have, mistakenly, been described as having both happened during the same flight, but it did not happen that way. The events were separated by four years.[34]

Jimmie returned to the United States in 1937 to fulfill another contract training Chinese pilots. He also bought a new bush plane, a Hamilton

CHAPTER 4

H-47. It was an all-metal airplane, a preference of Jimmie's since airplane fabric rots quickly in the South American jungle. This plane was registered NC854E. Jimmie and Marie flew the Hamilton to Venezuela in 1939.[35]

Jimmie would return to the states from time to time over the next eighteen years, but never for very long. After 1939, he came only to visit family or ferry aircraft back across the border.

Jimmie Angel had an accident in his Cessna 180 while landing at David, Panama, in April 1956. He died on December 8, 1956, at Gorgas Hospital in the Canal Zone from injuries caused by the April accident.[36]

For his discovery of Angel Falls and work in the country, Jimmie Angel is considered a national hero in Venezuela even though the current (2015) anti-American president has been undermining Jimmie's status.

JIMMIE'S BENEFACTOR AND PARTNER at Yuba City, Dr. Julian P. Johnson, was in the local newspapers quite often. The headlines began when he opened the first hospital in Yuba City, then there was the crash of his Eaglerock biplane at Sutter City, the subsequent lawsuit, and his various battles both physical and legally with his wife, Laura. Later, there were his bankruptcy and child support trials for his daughter, Joyce Adele, and the suicide by poison of Dr. Johnson's receptionist in September 1931. Dr. Johnson's time in Yuba City ended when he closed his thriving practice on B Street in late March 1932 and fled the state as a fugitive from justice for failure to make his child support payments.[37] Joyce Adele said Dr. Johnson left her mother with debts that took many years to pay off.

Dr. Johnson left the medical profession and the United States traveling to Beas, India. There he became a follower of guru Sawan Singh. During 1933–1939, he wrote about his experiences following the Radha Soami path and about Singh.

Much of Johnson's time in India was spent writing. Altogether, he wrote four books on the Radha Soami path. The first, *With a Great Master in India*, was about his first eighteen months in India under Sawan Singh. His next two books were semi-autobiographical. The titles were: *Call of the East* and *The Unquenchable Flame*. Last, he wrote the book he is best known for: *The Path of the Masters*.

Dr. Johnson never saw this fourth work in print. He died in 1939 before it came out. There is speculation about Johnson's death. A few who knew him while he lived and worked in Yuba City for eight years said he got in a fight with another man and was killed in India. Another source on his life in India and his books stated, "... to clarify what actually happened. Apparently, Johnson got into a fairly heated debate with a younger friend ... over health treatments. During the debate Johnson either tripped or was pushed and hit his head on a rock. He subsequently died from his injuries on the way to the hospital. ... According to witnesses who were in India at the time ... Johnson's death was a tragic accident and nothing more."[38]

LT. HAROLD F. BROWN, formerly of Marysville, flew into Cheim Field in early October 1928 to meet with Roy Bostic and Ed Johnson of the Marysville airport committee. Brown was piloting an eight-passenger, Douglas C-1 transport. Accompanying him were lieutenants J. R. Hargrove, R. H. Boudreaux, and Pvt. Blaylock, a mechanic.

The officers flew to the meeting after a request from the airport committee for advice was made to the Presidio's Lt. Col. G. C. Brant, commanding officer of the 91st Observation Squadron at Crissy Field, San Francisco.[39] They came to help the airport committee lay out the field's improvement plan to meet Department of Commerce airport requirements.

The improvements could begin as soon as a lease was obtained from the estate of Heiman Cheim, who had recently died. Prior to his death, he had turned his property over to the city of Marysville to be used as an airport. However, a formal lease had to be signed before any city or government money could be spent improving the property.

Walter Lockhoof from North Sacramento flew over Marysville one October day tossing leaflets from his Eaglerock advertising airplane rides later in the week at Cheim Field. The leaflets promised that the same day he gave rides, "Reckless" Rosie Cahill would parachute from his plane onto D Street in Marysville.

Lockhoof and Cahill, as promised, flew up to Marysville from his airport at North Sacramento on the east side of the American River. Over Marysville he performed several loops to get the attention of the townspeople, and then Reckless Rosie made her jump. It went fine until her chute got snagged on a tall tree making her planned quick escape impossible. After getting her down, the police arrested her and, eventually, Lockhoof who was fined for the dangerous stunt and for littering the streets with leaflets during his first trip over town earlier in the week. How many rides he gave after this dangerous stunt is unknown.[40]

Two weeks later, Lockhoof, while carrying two passengers over the Sacramento City Airport at Del Paso Park and doing stunts, stalled at the top of a vertical climb. He fell into a spin from which he was unable to recover and crashed. Lockhoof broke his back and the back of one of his passengers. The other suffered only minor injuries. Everyone survived, but the Eaglerock was destroyed near the airport boundary. Lockhoof was unlicensed and his plane hadn't been inspected for airworthiness by the DOC.[41]

Sierra Aircraft Corporation, once represented by Jim Read before he left town, was still active at Cheim Field. In November, the company ran a newspaper ad advising readers its planes and pilots at Cheim Field were government licensed, and their pilots were ready to give flight instruction.[42]

A large celebration was held at Marysville on Armistice Day (Veteran's Day now) in 1928. After a parade and a football game between Marysville and Yuba City, boat races were held on Ellis Lake. An air show was held at Cheim Field with many airplane rides given.

During the three-day air show there was little flying activity on Saturday the tenth, but on Sunday, a Ryan Brougham from Mutual Aircraft Corporation arrived. As usual, the plane was advertised as the sister ship to Lindbergh's *Spirit of St. Louis*. The Brougham was the same basic design as the *Spirit* but was built to haul four passengers and the pilot. Unlike the *Spirit* it had a front windshield. Jess Hart flew the Ryan Brougham that day taking passengers around the Twin Cities area.

Fog over Bay Area airports forced air show performers to arrive too late to perform on Sunday. By afternoon, the fog had lifted over the bay and the aircraft that were to hop passengers arrived and began their duties immediately.[43]

One of those passengers who braved the skies during the celebration was a local newspaper columnist known as the "Rambler." He or she went up in Hart's Ryan and wrote a column in the next day's paper describing the beautiful sights the reporter saw in the Yuba-Sutter area from two thousand feet. The Rambler also reported the runway at Cheim had been lengthened to three thousand feet, and a crosswind runway was planned.[44]

A. F. Mickel, chief pilot for Capital Flying Service of Sacramento, did stunt flying for the Armistice Day Air Show in his Hisso Travel Air. Reckless Rosie Evans (Cahill) made several parachute jumps during the three-day event. Lt. Harold F. Brown and Lieutenant Hargrove returned from Crissy Field for the celebration with the big Douglas C-1 biplane, which was popular with the spectators.[45]

Two weeks after the air show, Miss Alyce Juanita Hicks of Marysville married James Warner, the American radio operator for Charles

Kingsford-Smith during his historic trans-Pacific flight earlier in the year.[46]

J. C. "JACK" ROBERTS, instructor of aeronautics at Yuba City High School, set about organizing a Yuba City chapter of the National Aeronautics Association (NAA). A few years before, Roberts worked for Jimmy Read in Modesto and organized that city's chapter of the NAA.

The NAA is an organization whose main duty at that time was the promotion of aeronautics and airports throughout the United States. The Aero Club of America evolved into the NAA in 1922. From that date to the present, the NAA has represented the Federation Aeronautique Internationale in the United States. In promoting aviation, another part of the NAA's duties were and still are to be inspector, judge, and keeper of all aviation records set in the United States.[47]

Roberts spoke to the Yuba City Kiwanis Club in December about organizing a chapter of the NAA in the Yuba-Sutter area. He said it would require at least twenty-five members to start a chapter. He explained what the organization was about and said he was a charter member in the Los Angeles chapter, the San Francisco chapter, and the aforementioned Modesto chapter. He wanted an NAA chapter in Yuba City, and he wanted an airport for the city. He showed the audience diagrams and charts of a DOC approved airport, but there was no indication that he had a specific location to recommend to the city yet.[48]

Erling S. Norby, Yuba County district attorney, was one of the other great supporters of aviation in the community. The war veteran wanted to maintain his flying proficiency as a member of the Army Air Corps Reserves. In early December 1928, he and his wife returned from San Francisco where Norby spent two days at Crissy Field undergoing flight-tests to keep his rating as a pilot in the reserves. During those two days, he qualified as a group one pilot, the highest rating. After the war, even though he supported aviation's progress in the Yuba-Sutter community, he never instructed civilian flying students.

The army informed Norby he was to report for two weeks of active duty prior to February. He notified the board of supervisors that he would probably serve active duty around the first of the year. Norby told them he could make arrangements to fly back to Cheim Field during his two weeks of duty to handle any pressing business at the District Attorney's Office.[49]

Cheim Field had a flurry of aerial activity in December after the state's flying community learned of its existence. Two Army Douglas C-1

CHAPTER 4   113

transports landed there early in the month. One of the transports flown by a Lieutenant Hansen was going to Medford, Oregon, when heavy fog forced him to land at Cheim Field. The other C-1, flown by Lieutenant Hargrove and Lt. Harold F. Brown, landed at Cheim to drop off Lieutenant Brown to spend three weeks with friends while on sick leave.

The same week, four men arrived at Cheim in two Whirlwind powered Waco aircraft. They were weekend barnstormers from Oakland Airport. One was Frank Moore, aged twenty-two, with his transport rating and three hundred hours of flying time. He was working with W. J. "Joe" Barrows, who had taught him to fly, for Pacific Coast Air Service. Joe Barrows would become a noted bush pilot in Alaska during the 1930s.

The pilot of the other Waco was Edward J. Geer, an Oakland aviator. He and Moore brought Walter Hall, the pioneer Bay Area parachutist, and H. L. Blunt, a mechanic, with them to Marysville. They did some stunt flying and a parachute jump, then gave rides throughout the weekend.[50]

A history-making aircraft arrived at Cheim Field the first week of December. It was the Travel Air 5000 monoplane in which Ernie Smith made the first civilian flight from the mainland to Hawaii. The *City of Oakland* was flown into Cheim on a Friday for local residents to examine. It remained over the weekend and was used to give rides to those who wished to purchase them. Virgil Cline, the pilot and new owner of the plane, was employed by Bay Cities Air Service at Mills Field, San Francisco. V. H. Kelly and Sam Purcell accompanied Cline to Cheim Field.

This flight may have been a bit of barnstormer scam. The original *City of Oakland* stalled into trees and crashed on Molokai, Hawaii, at the end of Ernie Smith and Emory Bronte's record flight and was totally destroyed. It was reported afterward only the engine and a few instruments were recovered. Possibly the plane flown into Cheim was a sister-ship painted to look like Smith's plane.

Sam Purcell, aboard Cline's plane when it landed at Marysville, was the same Purcell whose career began during the Exhibition Years in the Bay Area. This is one of the last references of him involved in aviation this author has found.[51]

Judge McDaniel authorized the official lease of Cheim Field to the city of Marysville. Roy Bostic and Ed Johnson were told to start construction on a planned drainage system to help make the airport usable all winter. They had already added more gravel and coal cinders to the runway surface for that very reason.[52]

P. N. Swenson, president of Yuba City Commercial Club, appointed a committee to study the establishment and location of a new airport for Yuba City. Members of the committee were: Mayor Richard Walton, Dr. Julian Johnson, Jack Roberts, Lt. M. H. Underhill, E. E. Reeves, and Jack Griffen.[53]

Swenson told a reporter in late December, a site for an airport at Yuba City had been chosen and Richfield Oil Company promised to build a beacon and a hotel on the site. He said a large acreage near town was obtainable for lease, but no location was given.[54]

The site location for the proposed airport was revealed a week later. A newspaper story was published about Lt. Harold Brown from Crissy Field landing on the proposed site for the new airport. Brown had landed with Lt. R. Lyons on Dr. Jackson's property on the southeastern city limits of Yuba City in an army plane, then departed for Cheim Field.[55]

The proposed site of the Yuba City airport was the same makeshift airfield Charles Kingsford-Smith and many other barnstormers and transient aviators had been using since 1920. It was the Jackson Bottoms land.

Jack Roberts, night school instructor of aeronautics at Yuba City Union High School, announced to the community he would be speaking about the new air commerce regulations during his next several lectures. He stated the regulations could be confusing, and anyone interested was welcome to attend.[56]

JAMES HARSHNER AND G. D. McCallum flew to Yuba City and landed at Jackson Bottoms in a Curtiss Jenny late January 1929. The object of their trip was to interest local residents in forming a flying club. McCallum was president of the Oakland Flying Club, to which Harshner also belonged. Harshner reported he had several new members already signed up for a flying club at Yuba City. The two explained to prospective members that a flying club was a cheaper way to learn to fly because the expenses were pro-rated. They boasted that of the original eight members of the Oakland club, five obtained commercial pilot's licenses.[57]

Across the river, the Marysville City Council had obtained jurisdiction over Cheim Field with Judge McDaniel's authorization of the city's lease of the property. At the January 7 city council meeting, one of the first orders of business was a motion by Councilman D. E. Bryant that the city clerk write a letter to Dr. Johnson notifying him to move his hangar to the east side of Cheim Field or remove it completely, and do it within thirty days.[58]

After Dr. Julian Johnson gave up his lease on the Sutter County Onstott

CHAPTER 4

property where Angel Airport was established, he was at a loss for a spot to park his Eaglerock. He either built a new hangar on the site of the future Cheim Airport in Marysville or acquired an existing structure already there. There had been a slaughterhouse built on the property years before. The structure must have blocked the runway or parking area for the new airport, making its removal necessary.

More evidence that Dr. Johnson may have influenced the choice for the site of the Yuba-Sutter community's second and most successful airport, Cheim Field, is revealed in a photograph taken of Dudley Cunningham in August 1927. In the photo, Dr. Johnson's Eaglerock, without wings, is parked next to a tall wooden building. Dudley is standing next to an older fellow who is working on the Eaglerock. Dudley inscribed the photograph, "My first day working at the airport." Dudley worked at Cheim Field nearly every week of his life for the next twenty-five years except during World War II, when civilian flying within 185 miles of the California coastline was prohibited. There was no other airport in the Yuba-Sutter area in August 1927. The photo must have been taken at the Cheim site.

Dr. Johnson may have unwittingly chosen the most logical site for an airport at Marysville. Operations began at the new Marysville city airport on the Cheim site in May 1928. Dudley Cunningham would later advance to being the Cheim Field superintendant around 1930 and remained so for most of the airport's twenty-five years of operation.[59]

Marysville Exchange Club members at a February 1929 meeting enjoyed a program about aviation presented by Roy Bostic, who replaced Jim Read as the Cheim Field superintendent. The main speaker was Erling Norby. Also speaking were George Boyd Jr., who was just learning to fly, and Rennie J. Mahon, the only local ex-war pilot who actually served in France. Sidney T. Leggo and Lan B. Maupin from the Sutter County community of Tudor spoke of their experiences during aviation's pioneering years of 1910–1912. Norby talked about aviation history from ancient times and included the legend of Icarus and Daedalus.[60]

DR. JOHNSON'S PROBLEMS were growing. In addition to the city of Marysville forcing him to remove his hangar, Dr. Johnson decided to divorce his wife, Laura. . They had been separated since October 1, 1928; he filed suit for extreme mental cruelty February 9, 1929. His actions, as usual, made the headlines in the local newspapers. Even though he was the Yuba County district attorney, Erling Norby represented Johnson in Sutter

Lan B. Maupin in the Curtiss Pusher copy, the Diamond, he and Bernard Lanteri built in the fall of 1910. He is shown here after the Marysville High School aeronautics students reassembled the plane, as best they could, for the Sacramento Valley Land Show at Marysville in 1930. The Diamond, in which Weldon Cooke flew to fame in 1912, has been restored by the Hiller Aviation Museum where it was on display for several years. It has since been moved to a museum on the East Coast.

County Superior Court. Dr. Johnson decided it would not be wise to represent himself in this case.[61]

JAMES HARSHNER WAS ABLE to organize the Marysville-Yuba City Flying Club by February and was soon giving flight instruction to the new club's members at Cheim Field. Yuba City High School student George Boyd Jr., a member, made his solo flight that same month. Boyd showed unusual talent for flying and soloed after only six hours of dual flying instruction from Harshner. It usually took eight to ten hours of dual before a student soloed. After ten more hours of solo flying, Boyd would be permitted to apply for his Private Pilot License. The flying requirement for a Private Pilot License would soon be increased by the DOC to a minimum thirty-two hours and eventually forty hours.

Work was still being done on the Marysville airport to improve conditions. The runway was widened in February by PG&E, which donated the labor and cinders for the job.[62]

An organizational meeting of the NAA was held at Hotel Marysville in

CHAPTER 4 117

early February. Speakers for the evening were George McCallum from Oakland Airport, who spoke on airports and DOC flying regulations. Hilton F. Lusk, aeronautics instructor from the College of the Pacific at Stockton, spoke on air law, accidents and their causes.[63]

Cheim Field became an important addition to the Marysville community. Yuba City residents grappled with the establishment of an airport on their side of the Feather River. The topic of aviation was very popular at local service club luncheons and dinners. At a February meeting of the Rotary Club in Marysville's Memorial Auditorium, Sid Leggo and Lan Maupin, once again, told their story of early flying in 1910 through 1912. Dr. Johnson and Marysville High School aeronautics instructor Herb Keeler also spoke.

Leggo spoke of helping to build an early airplane and installing a lightened automobile engine in it for power. He talked about an early air meet at San Francisco in which he flew, surviving several crashes, and how difficult it was to build an airplane then without infringing on the patent of the Wright brothers.

Maupin talked about the airplane he built in Pittsburg, California, in 1910. He claimed to have made exhibition flights in a number of Northern California towns. He said he traveled to Los Angeles and competed against some of the nation's top aviators and won the prize for staying in the air for the longest duration.[64]

It should be said that of these two early fliers who spoke often at various service club luncheons and dinners about their early flying days, Maupin's memory of who did what in 1910 through 1912 was faultier than Leggo's.

Maupin and Lanteri built the Curtiss pusher copy named the *Diamond*, but all exhibition flights of the *Diamond* were flown by the pilot Maupin and Lanteri hired, Weldon Cooke. It was Cooke who won the duration prize at the Los Angeles Air Meet of 1912 in the Dominguez Hills. The seven thousand dollars he won was split three ways between Maupin, Lanteri, and Cooke, who split his share with his mechanic.

Lt. Harold Brown was transferred from Crissy Field to March Field near Riverside in Southern California. This occurred shortly after his three weeks of sick leave in Sutter County.

On April 23, 1929, Lieutenant Brown was seriously injured when his plane suffered engine failure. Brown had to crash land on a heavily traveled street in Highland Park, six miles northeast of Los Angeles. He was flying an army observation aircraft at the time. Rather than bailout with the possibility the plane might crash into houses or cars, he decided to ride it down and control its landing. Unfortunately, there was no safe place to land; he hit telephone wires and struck one automobile. The plane was destroyed; Brown suffered a broken shoulder and other injuries. His mechanic riding in the backseat, Harry F. Doyle, was unscathed, and the driver of the car was unhurt.[65]

On May 2, Jack Roberts announced he had gathered enough members to form a Yuba City chapter of the NAA. Charter members were: Jack E. Roberts, J. W. Gould, T. F. Peters, L. D. Sapp, F. S. Poole, Dr. Julian P. Johnson, Fred F. Dahling, R. A. Schnabel, Wayne A. Dahling, Rex Burch, Hilton F. Lusk, P. N. Swenson, Nick J. Weber Jr., A. A. McMullen, L. L. Anglade, O. Ferguson, J. B. Sheridan, Clarence M. Fletcher, E. E. Reeves, Earl R. Huffmaster, G. H. Thurn, Joseph B. Taylor, Miss Estal Burch, Jack Thompson, Thomas G. Bracewell, and Edward von Geldern.[66]

During the first week of May, Maddux Airlines sent a tri-motor Ford transport to Cheim Field flown by John Guggliametti and Bud Hoover. Their mission was to give short rides above the Twin Cities on the day they arrived. The next day they gave longer rides over Lake Tahoe. The fee for the thirty-five-minute ride over Tahoe was five dollars. It was a way for the airline to get a feel for the air-mindedness of the community, as Maddux wanted to extend service to more valley towns. Other exploratory flights were made at towns in the Great Central Valley with airports large enough to accommodate the big Ford airliners.[67]

Standard Oil Company announced it was sending one of its tri-motor Fokkers equipped with loudspeakers over the Twin Cities to play music and make announcements. If possible the plane would land at Cheim. The company's other Fokker was *Standard Ethyl*. The plane with loudspeakers, named the *Voice of the Sky*, was the only talking plane in the world.[68]

In June the new Yuba City NAA chapter received its charter. To celebrate, there was a banquet held at Yuba City High School. Members, spouses, and numerous guests were invited. Jack Roberts, president of the chapter, was the evening's master of ceremonies. Once again, Lan Maupin and Sidney Leggo were principal speakers. Maupin repeated the story of the 1912 Los Angeles Air Meet where his plane took the duration prize. Leggo claimed himself to be a qualified pilot because he had "cracked-up a ship." The ship, which he built, crashed two times in 1911 during an air meet in Oakland when he failed to make the half-mile qualification flight that would have allowed him to fly in the meet's contests.

Dr. Johnson talked about his crash in the peach orchard next to Angel Airport. He told the audience he would, "... rather go through a plane wreck than an automobile wreck." Tom E. Scott, who claimed to be the first airplane owner in Marysville, and his pilot James Harshner, wished the new chapter good luck and immediately sought membership. Scott, a Marysville auto parts dealer, owned a Travel Air 2000 purchased from D. C. Warren at Oakland Airport.

Miss Estal Burch and Miss Bessie McKenna were introduced as the first women to take up flying in the Yuba-Sutter community. Vocalist, Mrs. J. R. Pappa and her pianist, Mrs. Omar Sampson (this author's great aunt) performed during the banquet.

President Roberts presented the charter to its members and said it would be hung in Yuba City's Sutter Hotel.[69]

Second Lt. Harold F. Brown was relieved of his assignment with the 53rd School Squadron of the US Army Air Corps and from flying. He was assigned to the 70th Service Squadron, which appeared to be punishment for the April crash at Highland Park.[70]

The Yuba City airport committee made their decision—the best site for a new airport was the old landing strip in Jackson Bottoms. The site was located between the west levee of the Feather River and a lower bow levee running along the eastern shoulder of Garden Highway. The land amounted to 120 acres; twenty acres were in the city and the rest in Sutter County. Dr. Jackson, the landowner, made it clear he would sell the property for three hundred seventy-five dollars per acre. The committee felt the best way to purchase the property was for the city to buy the twenty acres within city limits, and the county purchase the rest.

The committee presented their decision to the county board of supervisors on June 17. City councilman Hugh Pryce Jones, a member of the airport committee, told the board the city had discussed the possibility of a bond issue to finance the city's share of the sale. Lieutenant Underhill of local National Guard Company H, quoted the comments of Lt. Harold F. Brown, who said the site would make a good landing field. Brown had tested the air currents and found them favorable for an airport. He said a number of trees would have to be removed, but the sandy soil dried out easily after a rain leaving an excellent landing surface at all times.

The committee left the board with a request to come up with some way to acquire the property before the end of the year. The board said it would consider the request.[71]

In Marysville, Mayor Bryant received offers for an exclusive lease of Cheim Field from two separate flying businesses. After checking the city's lease agreement with the Cheim estate, it was decided not to exclusively lease the airport, but allow it open for everyone to use.[72]

Rumors circulated in the community that the wings on Tom Scott's Travel Air at Cheim Field were weak and unsafe. Scott replied the rumors were false; he said the plane was brand new. Scott, and his pilot Harshner, had the only commercial operation on the airport at that time.

Harry Abbott flew the Neilson Golden Bear airplane to the Yuba-Sutter area in June. The Golden Bear was a new design from Neilson Steel Aircraft Corporation of Berkeley. The plane, which had a fuselage covered with fabric over steel tubing, resembled closely the Ryan Brougham.

Abbott and the plane's designer, Richard F. Korman, made the trip up from Berkeley to visit Korman's in-laws at Sutter, landing in a barley field. After the visit, they flew on to Cheim to see the Lytle family. In an interview with a Marysville reporter, the "Little Colonel," Abbott discussed his planned long distance flight to Tokio.[73]

Tom Scott made arrangements with the Oakland Travel Air dealer to bring an eight-passenger Travel Air cabin plane to Cheim Field for the wedding of a Chinese couple who wanted to be married in the air. D. C. Warren, the dealer, flew the Travel Air to Marysville and carried Charlotte Yee and Thomas Woo aloft for the ceremony along with their priest and witnesses. Aerial weddings were quite popular in the 1920s and '30s.[74]

The Yuba City chapter of the NAA invited the DOC Aeronautics Branch to send inspectors to Yuba City to examine the Jackson Bottoms airport site in late July. They hoped such an inspection would speed up local approval of the project.[75]

THE FIRST AERIAL APPLICATION ON CROPS in the Sacramento Valley took place July 31, 1929. Ex-war pilot and Dole Race survivor, Livingston Irving, carried out the flight under the auspices of his company, Agricultural Aviation Activities Inc.

For the historic event, Irving dusted a thirty-acre field of beans on S. A. McKeehan's ranch in Sutter County's district seventy, near the Tarke Warehouse, east of Meridian. Irving, flying a specially equipped black Eaglerock, covered the thirty-acre field in eighteen minutes. He made eight passes over the field, which was about a half-mile long. Each pass unleased a sulfur compound swath fifty-five-feet wide for exterminating aphids and

CHAPTER 4

red spiders. Many local farmers witnessed this first-ever demonstration. Reportedly, Irving's company had contracted to dust ten thousand acres of beans in the area.[76]

In August, four navy aircraft were flying up the Sacramento Valley to Seattle when one of the pilots, Lt. F. M. Tratnell, had engine problems and force landed in a farmer's field, four miles west of Marysville. The plane was wrecked after it hit a soft spot and turned over, but Tratnell was not hurt. The other three planes made successful landings in the same field. They stayed until sunset, then the three planes and four pilots took off for Seattle.[77]

Several members of the Yuba City Chapter of the NAA painted YUBA CITY in twelve-foot letters on the roof of Nason Lumber Company at the corner of Plumas Street and Colusa Road (Highway 20). NAA chapters carried out locator sign painting in communities across the United States to aid lost aviators.[78]

By mid-August, Livingston Irving had dusted one thousand acres of beans and prune orchards. W. B. Meinet assisted Irving flying dust on crops in Sutter and Colusa counties. Crop dusting was best done in early morning when there was a light dew on plants and trees. Calm air was a requirement with onset wind forcing flying to stop. The plane had a special bin built into the front cockpit, and the dust was dropped out evenly and spread by the airstream. The pilot controlled the dust with a lever in his cockpit. His bin, later known as the hopper, held seven hundred pounds of sulphur dust.

The following farmers had their crops dusted in this historic first effort: J. L. Browning, J. Clark, S. McKeehan, Vanderford, Ferguson, Wachter, Sanborn, Ettl, Pattison, Androtti, and R. S. Faxon.[79]

A. C. Hodgkins, also known as L. C. Hoskins, who for many years lived on his ranch west of Live Oak, was associated with Sunset Flying Corporation of Oakland. He wanted to open an airport at Live Oak. To stimulate local interest in flying, he announced that on a Sunday in August, two of his planes and pilots from the Sunset company would land on the Ramsdell property north of Live Oak, and take up those who wanted to go for rides. Hodgkins had checked out the field a week earlier and found it to be suitable for landing aircraft.

The following January, he sold an OX-5 Travel Air and various equipment of his Sunset Flying Service to the Stewart brothers of Napa. Wilbur Stewart already had his pilot's license and claimed they would use the plane for private flying and carrying passengers. Nothing more was done to open an airport at Live Oak in north Sutter County.[80]

A flying club was finally organized in the Yuba-Sutter community in September 1929 after previous attempts failed. The Yuba-Sutter Flying Club chose its first officers and took possession of its first airplane during a September meeting. Club flying operations began immediately at Cheim Field under the temporary tutlage of Sacramento instructor, A. F. Mickel, until the club's instructor, James Harshner, returned from working in Oakland.

During the September meeting, the club took possession of Tom Scott's Travel Air and voted in the following officers: Herb Keeler, president; Tom E. Scott, vice president; Bessie McKenna, secretary/treasurer; and James Harshner, field manager. The rest of the club's members were: N. Dewey Ashford, E. R. Brander, William A. Brander, W. J. Illman, William S. Kent, Larry Martin, and Ed J. Weser. The club planned its first flights. It was decided that on the upcoming Sunday, Bessie McKenna, the club's only woman member, would have the honor of making the first cross-country flight to Oroville's Riley Field with instructor Mickel.

Once the plane arrived, Oroville members Illman and Martin would take flying lessons with Mickel. Passenger hops would be given at Riley Field when the club members were not using the plane for instruction. Several Marysville members said they would drive to Oroville to get experience flying out of an unfamiliar field. Riley Field, Oroville's first airport, was located four miles south of Oroville. It was a few hundred yards west of today's Lincoln Boulevard on Kusel Road.

The flying club planned an improvement program for Cheim Field with permission of the city council and Roy Bostic, airport superintendent. They announced Associated Oil Company was ready to paint the newly completed hangar, and a telephone would soon be installed. Projects requiring immediate attention were acquiring a water supply and marking the airport so it could be easily located from the air. They didn't want a recurrence of an incident like the recent navy pilot's forced landing in a farmer's field because he couldn't find Cheim Field after his engine began packing up. Lan Maupin intimated he might join the club.[81]

Three members of the club had soloed by October 5. Twenty hours of club flying time had been put on the Travel Air by then. Tom Scott had flown to Sacramento with instructor Mickel and took his examination for a Private Pilot License. DOC flight inspector Andrews was coming to Cheim Field soon, and William Brander would take his tests then for his license.

Test results for both pilots were sent to Washington, D. C. They passed and their licenses were issued from there.

The club reported their Travel Air would be flown to the Harkey property between Live Oak and Gridley where a suitable landing field was located. There the club's student pilots would practice flying from a strange field. Passenger flights would be made available at that time for the local residents.[82]

DR. JOHNSON'S MESSY divorce was playing out in the headlines of the *Marysville Appeal-Democrat* during the months of September and October 1929.[83]

Russell Hill, the pilot Dr. Johnson hired to fly his Eaglerock after Jim Read left the area for Los Angeles, returned to San Jose and began additional training with Meade & Orr Flying Service. Hill was working towards his transport license. He was granted that license in October at San Jose.[84]

Robert McCullough, the aircraft mechanic who came to the area with Jimmie Angel in 1926 and stayed loyal to Dr. Johnson after the Angel Brother's Air Circus left town, died November 2, 1929, in Marysville. McCullough, who was from Salinas, succumbed to a lingering illness.[85]

BERKELEY FLYING SERVICE Ltd. sent F. G. "Jerry" Andrews to Marysville shortly before Armistice Day to make preparations for the arrival of six aircraft from the Bay Area taking part in the Armistice Day air show at Cheim Field. A similar air show was planned at Onstott's Field near Gridley the following day.

Joining Andrews to fly in the air show was Gene LeGault, Banty Bannister, and Dick Smith, all veteran Air Service pilots from the Bay Area. Joining them was Harry W. Abbott, a pilot who had seen action in China. Abbott had flown to the Yuba-Sutter area in the past and Andrews, who had much experience as a stunt flier, flew at Cheim for the airport's dedication two years earlier.

The Marysville and Gridley shows went off according to plan with air races, aerobatic demonstrations, and parachute drops. Passenger flights were given in a Ryan Brougham and a six-place Travel Air cabin plane.

An unfortunate occurrence happened after the air show on Sunday. Andrews and Legault bought some bootleg liquor in lower Marysville late that night. That section of the city, next to Chinatown, had over a dozen brothels and several gambling halls much as it did during the Gold Rush. There were numerous speakeasies from which the pair began wandering up D Street very drunk. They decided to kick out a plate glass show window of Bradley's department store. The two men were arrested early Monday morning for malicious mischief. Their reason for kicking out the window was given to Police Judge Langdon at their trial on Tuesday—they just wanted to hear the glass fall on the sidewalk. Hugh Smythe, Bradley's store manager, did not press charges since the aviators had already paid for the damages. The judge told them he was sorry he was not formally charging them with the punishment they deserved. He called them a couple of "smart aviators" who thought they could come to a small town and act like vandals.

The two admitted they had been drinking, and they tried to kick out another window, but it would not break. The judge told them they should lose their jobs for the way they acted. Jerry Andrews told the court he had lost his position for breaking the window. It is not known whether either pilot took part in the air show at Gridley the next day.[86]

A. R. Arnot opened a new Ford auto dealership in Marysville during November 1929. To celebrate, he hired one of the largest commercial planes available to fly to Cheim Field and promote his new business. Arnot hired a tri-motor Ford airliner named the *West Wind* to be brought to Cheim from Mamer Air Service in Spokane, Washington. Vernon Bookwalter and copilot Neil Keim flew the plane into Cheim Field where it was met by several new Ford automobiles whose passengers were taken up for rides in the airliner as guests of Arnot.[87]

Yuba County District Attorney Erling Norby was very vocal in his efforts to promote aviation and building airports. He joined Ernie Smith of Hawaiian flight fame speaking to the American Legion post at Auburn about the history of aviation. Smith centered his talk around Auburn citizens needing to improve and build on the government emergency landing field near their town.[88]

Harry H. Blee, a DOC Aeronautics Branch official, sent a message to the Yuba County Chamber of Commerce in December stating Cheim Field was government approved and, with some improvements, the field could receive the highest federal airport rating.[89]

Later in December, Richfield Oil Company sent a plane with Santa Claus aboard to drop messages on small parachutes into communities throughout Northern California encouraging children to go to any Richfield gas station and receive a small gift Santa had left for them. At Yuba City, the message landed on the grounds of C. P. C. Cannery which delivered Santa's message

CHAPTER 4

to a local newspaper for publication.⁹⁰

The Yuba-Sutter Flying Club's Travel Air had been damaged in a forced landing on a rough field in late fall. The propeller and wings were damaged in the plane's forced landing near Oroville. Dudley Cunningham repaired the airframe in auto shop at Marysville High School. He completely recovered the plane with new fabric and painted the fabric with aircraft "dope." Dope fabric paint was so named because the fumes it put off could make one "higher than a kite" if there wasn't proper ventilation.

Herb Keeler, the school's aeronautics instructor, painted all parts of the Travel Air that required lacquer paint. The Brander brothers overhauled the Travel Air's motor in their auto repair shop at Tudor. Club members did all the repair work on the Travel Air and the plane was ready to fly again by the end of December. James Harshner took the plane for a successful test flight. Harshner then flew the plane to Oakland where Monte Mouton, the DOC inspector, examined the Travel Air, passed it, and assigned the letters NC to precede the registration number, which were the new international identification code for American registered aircraft. After World War II the NC identification code was changed to N.⁹¹

George F. Irvin spoke to the Yuba City Kiwanis Club in late January 1930 about the history and future of aviation. He was said to be one of the

This Travel Air 2000 was the Yuba-Sutter Flying Club's first airplane. When the club purchased a newer Spartan biplane, the Travel Air was sold to founding club member Dewey Ashford as his first airplane. He would own ten different airplanes in his lifetime.

earliest to take up flying in California. This author could find no evidence of that claim.[92]

Three members of the Yuba-Sutter Flying Club passed the tests for their Private Pilot Licenses in February. William Andrews, the DOC flight examiner at Sacramento, gave flight tests to club members Roy Westfall of Oroville and William S. Kent and Herbert F. Keeler both from Marysville. They all passed, making a total of four club members to have earned licenses. Jim Harshner was quite pleased with the results. Three more club members, Delbert Buroker, William Brander, and Larry Martin were nearly ready to take their tests. They were all flying the club's Travel Air 2000.[93]

Lt. Harold F. Brown left the Army Air Corps and took a job as general manager of Great Western Aircraft Corporation in February 1930. The company was based at Vail Field in the Los Angeles area. It was the distributor of Kari Keen aircraft.[94]

Jimmie Angel and Dr. Tien Lai Huang circa 1928.

A Thomas Morse Scout, usually called a "Tommie," similar to one flown by Jimmie Angel at Yuba City in 1926

A three-place Bristol Tourer like one flown out of Angel Airport in the fall of 1926

CHAPTER 5

Continental Air Express – Airwar over the Twin Cities – Consolidated Air Lines (CAL) begins service – CAL inauguration air show – Dewey Ashford – Yuba-Sutter Flying Club activities – Harold F. Brown's civilian flying career

"All the hammers stopped" in early 1930, according to one Yuba-Sutter resident who lived in the community throughout the Great Depression. He was referring to the hammers of carpenters building new houses in tracts around Marysville and Yuba City. Local banks went under, construction funding disappeared, and new houses were left unfinished because the carpenters couldn't be paid.[1]

The Depression didn't have a devastating effect on aviation—at least not at first—aviation was still riding the Lindbergh surge. The new technology was still attracting investors.

Continental Air Express Inc. (CAE), a new scheduled airline, began flying a route between Los Angeles and San Diego, later adding a northern route to San Francisco. The company planned to expand its routes even further.

A definitive work on US airlines states that Continental Air Express made its first flight on September 1, 1929, but there is evidence the first flight actually occurred several months before. In June 1929, Sterling Bollar, a pilot for CAE, was flying daily on the Los Angeles to San Francisco route for CAE. Reportedly, Fresno was to be added to the route, as were other Great Central Valley cities.[2]

Continental's financial director, I. N. Brunson, and W. P. Barngrover, another CAE official, came to Marysville in May 1930. They took rooms at Hotel Marysville and began making arrangements for a two-week demonstration of the service CAE planned to offer residents of the Twin Cities.

They announced that in six weeks Continental Air Express would be landing its twelve-passenger, tri-motor airliners on a regular schedule at Cheim Field to take on passengers and express freight.[3]

In the Yuba-Sutter Twin Cities' community of 1930, the population of Marysville was 5,763 and Yuba City was 3,605.[4]

Director Brunson announced to the press that Continental Air Express was the largest independent air transportation company on the West Coast. Its planes, he said, had been flying a regular service between Los Angeles and San Francisco for some time. The company planned to extend routes to Portland and Seattle. Marysville would be a logical stop on the route to Portland. The larger CAE planes would carry up to twelve passengers, and smaller planes would haul express freight and up to four passengers. The company's plan was to send one of the express haulers to Cheim Field and demonstrate to local residents and businesses the type of service CAE was offering. E. K. Fleming, a Los Angeles capitalist, was one of the chief backers of CAE. He was an officer in the company and the brains behind the organization, according to Brunson. Other company officers were H. H. Pursal, Harry Sperl, and M. G. Phillips.[5]

CAE sent a Lockheed Vega, capable of carrying freight and four passengers, to Cheim Field to gauge the community's interest in their service by giving local residents, who had never flown before, free rides to demonstrate the safety, comfort, and ease of flying in modern cabin type aircraft.

Gene A. Tigar flew the Lockheed to Cheim Field. During his first day of demonstrations, Tigar took up numerous local residents.[6]

Marysville would be the northern terminus for Continental's express route, which began in San Francisco. Its planes would then fly to Stockton, Sacramento, various unnamed west valley towns, and finally Marysville. Eventually, Willows was included in the route as part of a large loop that ended in San Francisco.[7]

While the Vega was at Cheim Field for a two-week stay, Brunson tried to find useful missions for it to fly to impress the local residents. On April 4, the Vega was loaned to the *Marysville Appeal Democrat* for any flight they would like to make. The paper decided to send local professional photographer, Henry Sackrider, to take photos of the Sierra Nevada, and then drop bundles of the morning paper at Downieville and other mountain towns. Sackrider was able to get a few shots of the Sierra Buttes (not the Sutter Buttes), but the rest of the Sierra Nevada were covered by haze. As for the newspaper drop, they couldn't find Downieville in the haze, but they did drop bundles in other communities. Sterling Boller flew the Vega on this mission.

That same day, Boller gave Sidney Leggo and Lan Maupin, the two aviation pioneers, a ride in the Vega. They compared the flight to their early flights of 1910 and 1912 during a press interview. Leggo's wife and two of her friends from the Tudor-Oswald commuinity were also given rides that day.[8]

Mr. Barngrover received a telegram from E. K. Fleming informing him the inauguration of the company's San Francisco–Sacramento–Reno route would be April 5. It also stated the Marysville route would be held up until the crosswind runway was finished at Cheim Field and the south end of the runway was widened a thousand feet. Roy Bostic, Cheim Field's airport superintendent, said work would start within the week.[9]

While visiting Marysville, Charles H. Williams, general manager of Continental Air Express, reported the company wanted to put the town on its route. It wouldn't require sales of stock, simply an upgrade of the runway. Williams' visit was made in a four-seat Sunbeam aircraft flown by Gene Tigar, chief survey pilot for CAE. D. C. "Cowboy" Warren, chief test pilot for the Sunbeam factory, rode along as a passenger.[10]

Commercial Aircraft Corporation Ltd. of Van Nuys began production of the single-engine C-1 Sunbeam biplanes for CAE. Continental started a weekend roundtrip service between San Francisco and the Lucerne Country Club at Clear Lake.

The men and planes of CAE left Marysville about April 9 never to return.[11]

It wasn't impossible to find investment money for aviation businesses during the Depression, but it was difficult to find passengers for small regional airlines. Continental Air Express made its last flight from the Bay Area in October 1930, then surrendered to bankruptcy.[12]

There was one important fact that came about from Brunson's mission to find a useable airport for CAE's planes to land. The Yuba-Sutter community learned, for the first time, Cheim Field was not the absolutely perfect landing field they were led to believe by local pilots.

The runway, a north-south single runway, was laid out in that direction to obtain the longest run of about three thousand feet. The runway was placed beside the fence marking the southern boundary of the property that Heiman Cheim leased to the city. The levee around the northeastern section of Marysville and the Cheim runway formed a shape like the capital letter

D with the straight edge of the D being the runway and the curved body of the letter the levee. The problem with the runway was it was not quite in line with the prevailing north and south winds. If there was any wind, planes had to land in a cross wind, which is more problematic than landing directly into the wind. At Cheim Field, it could be a dangerous situation if the wind was blowing hard, especially a north wind, because it would blow a landing plane into the southern boundary fence running along the runway. It was a problem the local pilots learned to deal with, but for transient pilots unfamiliar with the airport, landings could be tricky. The problem would forever plague the airport.[13]

The national passion for aeronautics was revealed locally in a survey of students done at Marysville Union High School by Richard Hardin, a vocational counselor. The school's male students were asked to list in order their occupational preferences. Jobs most desired after they graduated were: aviation, engineering, law, stock raising, electrical, and farming.[14]

The Guggenheim Foundation awarded a certificate of accomplishment for support of aviation to the Marysville Exchange Club in April 1930. Support included painting of the locater name, MARYSVILLE, on the roof of the PG&E building earlier in the year. The Guggenheim Foundation did much to promote the growth of aviation and aeronautical education during the years of 1927 through 1930.[15]

IN APRIL THE US ARMY AIR CORPS began its 1930 war games in Northern California. These air maneuvers involved a quarter of the entire Army Air Corps, which assembled at Mather Field, twelve miles east of Sacramento. Approximately one hundred and sixty army planes made up the "Red" and "Blue" air forces, which were to battle each other for three weeks in the skies over the golden state for what the local newspapers called a "mimic war."

Over forty aircraft departed Mather on April 1 to familiarize the visiting airmen with the topography of the Sacramento and San Joaquin valleys and the Sierra Nevada. This large swarm of airplanes circling towns surprised residents of Sacramento, Marysville, Lincoln, Roseville, Rio Vista, Dixon, and Woodland. Such numbers in the sky hadn't been seen over Sacramento since the Great War. At Marysville and Yuba City, the roar of multiple aircraft engines brought crowds of residents out of their houses and into the streets for a look.[16]

Two days later, the entire force of nearly one hundred and sixty planes took to the air to fly a low-level pass and review at Mather Field for the group's commander, Brig. Gen. William E. Gilmore.[17]

The next day at Marysville, fourteen army light bombers came in from the north across Cheim Field at less than seventy-five feet. They were in a line abreast formation and followed by a single observation plane whose crew was assessing the speculative damage from the formation's attack on the airfield. The first attack the group made that day was the "destruction" of rail tracks between Oroville and Marysville. After hitting Cheim Field, they hopped over the Yuba River levee and continued on south in the direction of Mather Field.[18]

Despite the army's mock air war, civilian flying at Cheim Field continued unaffected. Delbert Buroker, a young barber from Stockton, came to Marysville to learn to fly. He heard about the success of the Yuba-Sutter Flying Club and moved to Marysville temporarily while he learned to fly. He took lessons from James Harshner in the club's Travel Air. Once he soloed, Buroker looked for a plane to buy. He settled on a Travel Air used by the Oakland Flying Club and brought his new purchase to Marysville where Dudley Cunningham reconditioned the airframe. When Dudley finished, Buroker took the plane to Marysville High School and the aeronautics classes painted the airplane. Instructor Herb Keeler did the difficult lacquer painting. Once work was completed, Buroker returned in the Travel Air to Stockton where he planned to start a flying club.[19]

Herb Keeler's aeronautics classes at the high school built an improved version of the German Zoegling primary training glider. The design was constructed mainly of spruce wood. It had a wingspan of thirty-three feet and weighed 160 pounds. The plan was to launch the glider into the air with a seventy-five-foot piece of rubber shock cord. Use of an airplane to tow a glider into the air was a radical technique not yet DOC approved in the United States. In fact, it was illegal under the new air commerce regulations. The shock cord was not a very effective method for launching a glider; most pilots of the day preferred using an auto-tow launch. The auto-tow used a long rope attached to the nose of the glider at one end and the rear of an automobile at the other. The auto would speed along towing the glider to a certain height, then the glider pilot would release his end of the rope and maneuver on his own. The Zoegling flew at fifteen miles per hour and landed at twelve. It was an excellent method of teaching students the rudiments of flying.[20]

A formation of five Keystone twin-engine LB-5 heavy bombers, escorted by a single pursuit plane, flew over Marysville on April 10 and "destroyed" Cheim Field in another mock attack. They then turned southwest for Woodland and carried out a similar attack on the Woodland airport. At least that's what the army thought happened.

Learning of the intended attack, a large number of people gathered at Cheim airport to watch. They saw the bombers approach Marysville and then turn southwest before reaching Cheim Field. It turned out the pilots had orders to attack the "airport west of Marysville." The townspeople were disappointed in Uncle Sam's accuracy. They figured the bombers "destroyed" a peach orchard west of Yuba City. Cheim airport was on the northeastern edge of Marysville.[21]

One week later, twenty pursuit planes flew over the Twin Cities towards the Sutter Buttes. They planned to attack a formation of heavy bombers that had set up an attack zone around the Sutter Buttes stretching as far north as Princeton on the Sacramento River. Climbing to great height over the buttes, the fighters engaged the bombers in a large dogfight, which brought hundreds of Sutter County residents out of their houses to watch.[22]

Erling Norby made arrangements with a friend, Lieutenant McHenry, squadron commander of the 13th Attack Squadron temporarily based at Mather Field, for Norby and three other local men to ride along as observers in separate bombing planes on one of the mock war missions. The other men were Ed Johnson, Alex Arnot, and Fred H. Heiken. They flew on a two-hour mission during which the squadron flew up and down canyons in the Sierra Nevada between Grass Valley and Downieville evading the pursuit planes looking for them. The bombers flew in close formation and kept low; skimming the tree and ridgelines to avoid the pursuit planes—a tried and true tactic used even today on bombing missions. Hopefully these local men weren't superstitious. The squadron, numbered thirteen, had a unit emblem painted on the aircraft fuselages depicting a skeleton holding a blood-covered scythe.[23]

Delbert Buroker and James Harshner had to make a forced landing on April 26 near the Bear River, south of Wheatland, in Yuba County. The landing was successful and without incident. They repaired the engine and continued on to Marysville. They were flying Buroker's Travel Air, which the Stockton Flying Club was using for training. The Stockton club's flying instructor, Harshner, was formerly instructor for the Yuba-Sutter Flying Club.[24]

The Marysville City Council made a couple of proposals in May that

Twenty-three Army Air Corps Keystone LB-5 and Curtiss Condor heavy bombers over the American River flying in the direction of Yuba County during the Air Corps' April 1930 Air Maneuvers held in Northern California.

would affect Cheim Field's future. They proposed that transient barnstorming aviators flying into Cheim just to hop passengers, be charged fifteen dollars a day for use of the airport. It would stop transient pilots from competing with local pilots for passenger hops. The other proposal was to give the unpaid airport superintendent a monthly salary of forty dollars. Rental of the airport hangars was returning forty-five dollars per month.[25]

J. M. Johnson landed at Cheim in an Aeronca C-3 powered by a thirty-five horsepower motor. The high-wing monoplane was two-place and resembled its nickname the "flying bathtub." Johnson was flying the Aeronca Company's demonstrator around the United States on a promotional tour. He had flown from Watsonville en route to Chico and saw the freshly oiled runway at Cheim and decided to land. He told everyone who would listen that the plane had a top speed of eighty-five miles per hour and a service ceiling of eighteen thousand feet. He claimed he could fly thirty miles on a gallon of gas if there was no wind. He said anyone could fly the plane if they had a rudimentary knowledge of flying. He had allowed over two hundred people to fly the plane during his tour.[26]

Tom E. Scott, the first Marysville resident to own his own airplane, was killed May 4 while landing at Cheim Field in a Curtiss Robin. Scott had lived in Marysville with his wife and child for eight years.²⁷

In May 1930, a *Marysville Appeal-Democrat* editorial complained that Cheim Field was not an all-weather airport and air transport companies wouldn't use a field that was unsafe. It recommended that either Marysville or Yuba City develop an airport that was completely safe.²⁸

CONSOLIDATED AIR LINES, a new startup airline, was planning to open a route the length of the Great Central Valley from Fresno in the south to Montague in the north. Beverly Gilmore, president of the airline, announced his plan to the California Chamber of Commerce in Sacramento on May 16. In describing the service through the Sacramento and San Joaquin valleys, he said his company had examined Marysville's airport and found it suitable as a stop on the valley route.

Gilmore outlined his plan: Consolidated would purchase two Curtiss eight-passenger Kingbird aircraft to begin service from Sacramento to Marysville, Chico, Redding, and Montague. He said Consolidated Air Lines was completely funded and had no stock to sell. It was a closed corporation with eighty thousand dollars in equipment. All he asked was a little cooperation by destination cities, especially at Sacramento, the company's headquarters. The new Freeport Boulevard municipal airport there lacked facilities to make repairs.

Consolidated Air Line (CAL) officials wanted to link up flights with other airlines to Seattle at the Montague airport and at Fresno with Maddux Air Lines to Los Angeles. At Sacramento, the company would link up with Boeing Air Transport for transcontinental flights east.

Gilmore said his company had been working on arrangements at various airports for CAL during the past two months and had made a complete survey of airports along the proposed route.

Consolidated's main airliner in the beginning was the Curtiss Kingbird. Cruising at 115 miles per hour it allowed a citizen of Siskiyou County to schedule a flight to Sacramento in the morning, transact his business, and return home before nightfall. Use of one Kingbird was planned for daily operations.²⁹

Consolidated Air Lines purchased its Curtiss Kingbird J-2, powered by two Wright Whirlwind 225 horsepower engines, on September 5, 1930. It was registered NC 379N to CAL's address at the Senator Hotel, Sacramento, and licensed until September 1, 1931. It was the only Kingbird CAL would fly.³⁰

Consolidated purchased the Kingbird from D. C. Warren at Oakland. It was the first Kingbird delivered to the Pacific Coast, and only the third one built. The plane's cabin was roomy and well ventilated. The seats were arranged in four rows of two with an aisle between the seats. The left forward seat was set up for the pilot and the right seat was meant for a passenger. The concept of a copilot on smaller passenger planes was not the industry standard yet. Shatterproof glass was installed throughout the cabin for unobstructed viewing. The interior was finished in top grain leather, cloth, and walnut trim. Chairs were made of aluminum and leather upholstered with soft headrests. A lavatory compartment was installed in the rear of the passenger cabin. The instrument panel had all instruments of the day with the exception of the tachometers, oil pressure gauges, and temperature gauges. They were mounted on the engine nacelles and easily read from the pilot's seat. Complete night flying equipment was installed, which included retractable landing lights, instrument lights, and cabin dome lights.

The twin-engine placement gave improved visibility from the cockpit and a reduction of vibration and exhaust detonation. The forward position of the engines kept the distance between the centers of thrust to a minimum. If an engine quit, the airplane would keep flying like a single-engine aircraft. In tests, the Kingbird could climb on one engine after the other engine quit. The Kingbird had a top speed of 135 miles per hour and a service ceiling of 15,500 feet. Its gross weight was 6,115 pounds, its useful load was 2,260 pounds, and it could carry a payload of 1,400 pounds.

The Kingbird was a monoplane with fuselage and wings built of aluminum alloy and chrome molybdenum steel tubing. Its spars were steel and ribs were aluminum alloy. The entire plane was fabric covered.[31]

At Marysville High School, Herb Keeler test-flew the German primary glider built by his aviation classes. The flight was made on May 22, before one hundred of Keeler's aeronautics students. He made two flights in the orange and black modified Zoegling aircraft. The glider rose to a height of fifteen feet as an automobile towed it into the air. Due to a lack of any thermal lift to sustain the glider, it returned to a landing immediately after the auto-tow.[32]

Jack Beilby, a former Wheatland resident employed by a flying service and aircraft dealer at Sacramento, flew to Cheim Field the next day in a new high-wing Curtiss Robin. He planned to take up invited guests and demonstrate the new single-engine cabin plane.[33]

The Yuba City NAA chapter was chosen to officiate air races and other

A Curtiss Kingbird at Sacramento Municipal Airport in September 1931. Consolidated Air Lines had just purchased the plane for its scheduled routes throughout the Sacramento Valley.

contests planned for the dedication of the new Colusa Airport on May 30, 31, and June 1.[34]

The Marysville City Council meeting of June 2, 1930, was crucial for proponents of the municipal airport in Marysville. Officials from Consolidated Air Lines were in town and huddled with Roy Bostic trying to learn the situation with the airport. There were questions that had to be answered. Would the Cheim estate put a price on the land finally, so the city could purchase the airport site? If the city bought the airport, would it make the necessary repairs and changes to enable Consolidated to land multi-engine transports on the field? Would they address the crosswind problem?

Lt. W. J. Davies, an active-duty army aviator, and Frank Rose, a respected Oakland flier, were on the airport that day and said more drainage work was absolutely necessary to make Cheim Field usable all year round, and they suggested a triangle layout of runways to solve the crosswind problem. PG&E and Pacific Telephone told city officials once the city owned the airport they would remove the hazard of poles and overhead lines along the levee at the south end of the runway.

At this point in negotiations with Heiman Cheim's estate, it was not known what was going to happen. The city council put out feelers for other possible airport sites. Floyd Stearn had taken an option on a site along

Capital Highway, south of Sartori's dairy farm. The land belonged to Councilman Dan E. Bryant. Lloyd Morrison, Yuba County aerial deputy sheriff, had planned to offer a site at Ostrom for a joint municipal and county airport, and was promoting the site heavily. The last alternative was a site on the Reis pastureland, east of the Southern Pacific rail tracks and opposite the Sartori place, a site favored by many of those studying the various local sites.

The Cheims surprised everyone at the city council meeting when they offered to deed the hundred acres of land in question to the city for free. The only requirements they asked were: the land be passed by experts as suitable for an airport and it was always to be known as Cheim Field.[35]

CAL president Beverly Gilmore was at the city council meeting and afterward announced Consolidated had made a deal with Western Air Express to link up at Redding, instead of Montague, to transfer passengers continuing on to Seattle. He also said his airline would begin operations to and from Cheim Field in late June. He and Sterling Boller, the airline's chief pilot, were leaving in a few days for St. Louis to pick up their Kingbird transport. They planned to fly it back to Sacramento and spend a week touring the various airports CAL would be servicing. Then they would begin passenger service.[36]

There must have been a link between the defunct Continental Air Express and Consolidated Air Lines. The two companies were carrying out their air route surveys and fact-finding missions at the same time, on the same routes, and pilots Sterling Boller and Gene Tigar were working for both airlines at the same time.

A week after the all-important city council meeting, the city had to step in and make a ruling to settle a feud that reached boiling point at Cheim Field. The city ruled Cheim was a free port, charging no fees so far, but all who used the airport were expected to treat others using it with consideration.

What brought about the feud was the Yuba-Sutter Flying Club found fault with the new startup flying school of Harshner and Buroker. They made trouble for the newcomers. Harshner and Buroker started their new flying school and air taxi business using Buroker's new Travel Air on June 8. The next day members of the flying club threatened them. The city council assured Harshner and Buroker they would be protected in their right to use the airport. Harold F. Brown was informed that he and the flying club had no more rights to the field than any other fliers. The city council reported it had not been able to set rules and regulations for the airport yet, and there was no one on the field to supervise operations. Aerial Traffic Officer Lloyd Morrison was called to intervene and settle the differences between the groups, but he was unable to do anything more than prevent physical confrontation.[37]

In June a tri-motor Ford transport landed at Cheim Field. The crew said they were on their second tour of the United States. Copilot Capt. George Flaherty owned the plane. Pilot Howard F. Walsh held Transport Pilot License No. 68, a very early issue. Operations manager was C. W. Johnson, Harry R. Lee was the mechanic, and their parachutist was Bunny Willey. The five were barnstorming across the nation in the huge transport. Usually, to get a crowd interested, they performed stunts in the tri-motor then Willey jumped. The Ford would land, and hop passengers for the rest of the day. The plane had twelve seats and could hop folks by the dozen.

Unfortunately, they had come from Stockton where the day before Willey jumped in a heavy wind. When he touched down in his chute, he was drug across rough ground for quite some distance at forty-five miles per hour. After the Ford landed at Cheim, Willey was feeling sore and couldn't do any stunts or jumps.

The Ford and crew stayed two days before moving on. It's unknown whether they gave any rides while they were at Cheim. It had to be hard for five men to make enough money barnstorming in an airliner that required forty gallons of gasoline an hour for its three 220 horsepower Whirlwinds. The Ford had a fuel capacity of 240 gallons according to the crew.[38]

R. U. St. John, who was supervising engineer for the San Francisco Bay Airdrome being built in Alameda and the construction supervisor of the new Sacramento Municipal Airport, was asked to pass judgment on Cheim Field as a suitable landing field. Regardless of his opinion, the equipment and men from local construction company Hemstreet & Bell had already begun lengthening the runway, leveling the entire field, and preparing the airport to accommodate Consolidated Air Lines' transports.

Gilmore announced CAL had acquired a twelve-passenger Ford transport for its planned route between Sacramento and San Francisco. He said the expected traffic between the two cities could be more than anticipated. He spoke of a trip to Marysville on June 26, where he saw the runway being lengthened. He was satisfied the city would have the runway long enough to safely accommodate even the Ford. He complained there was still no east-west runway; the only way to take off was still northwest and southeast. He said city officials had assured him the crosswind obstacle would be dealt with soon.[39]

Clyde "Upside-down" Pangborn arrived over Marysville with his "Flying Fleet," as part of the 1930 July Fourth celebration. The Flying Fleet was a spinoff of the famous Gates Flying Circus. The three planes, painted in the distinctive Flying Fleet green and gold colors, flew in a snarling combat formation. Before landing at Cheim, they demonstrated formation maneuvers, which ended with formation dives and loops. Then, the accompanying pilots each flew a solo aerobatic routine, after which Pangborn topped off the exhibition with an upside-down (inverted flying) routine for the crowd. Jerry Smith and Ben "Diavolo" Matthews, stuntmen with the group, also made parachute jumps during the three-day festivities. Pangborn, Hugh Herndon Jr., and Ray Baumgardner, an ex-army and ex-airmail pilot, were the Flying Fleet pilots. Marysville was the sixty-second city they had performed for on their current barnstorming tour. The fleet's headquarters were at Teterboro Airport, New Jersey.[40]

Capt. Erling S. Norby traveled to Mather Field to serve his required two weeks of active duty training in July. He would command the 316th Observation Squadron of the Army Air Corps Reserves. Also a member of that squadron was 2nd Lt. John L. Ames Jr. of Live Oak. During and after the Great War, Norby served as an instructor and an assistant commander at Rockwell Field, San Diego, March Field at Riverside, and Mather Field near Sacramento.[41]

Three planes under Norby's command collided while practicing formation flying three thousand feet above the town of Folsom. The planes were in a line astern formation, and the signal was given to move into a V formation. As the planes were moving into the V, turbulence slammed the two leading planes together, and the third plane bumped the other two. The first two planes were locked together and falling as the flight crews bailed out. The third plane suffered some damage to its fabric and structure of one wing. The pilot landed successfully at Mather Field unaware his plane was damaged.

Immediately upon learning of the midair collision, Captain Norby jumped in (without noticing the damage) the third plane and took off to the crash site of the other two biplanes. He landed in a level field nearby and rushed to aid the aircrews that bailed out. All were in good condition and unhurt. The airmen were: Capt. Charles Kruse of Coyote, Lt. F. M. Gilbert of San Francisco, and Capt. J. W. McCrills and Lt. Albert Marty both of Sacramento. The third plane, which Captain Norby commandeered, was staffed by Lt. Glenn Goddard of Palo Alto and Lt. J. T. Bowden of San Francisco.

Norby was able to fly home to Cheim Field in one of the squadron's planes during his two weeks of active duty at Mather Field.[42] Unfortunately, the two weeks of active duty ended badly for Norby. On the night of August 2, he was driving into Sacramento from Mather Field with Sgt. J. H. Deholm and struck two teenage boys with his car at Fifty-fourth and J streets. There were a combination of causes for the accident such as blinding headlights and the boys were walking in the street instead of on the sidewalk, but the most condemning was Norby had been drinking. The boys were not killed, but one was seriously injured with a skull fracture. Norby arranged for the best medical care for the boys and then went to the Sacramento police station to report what happened. He was booked on a charge of driving while intoxicated and released on a one thousand dollar bond.[43]

In August there was to be an exhibition of stunt flying and a parachute jump by Wariam S. Gravelle at Cheim Field. Gravelle is believed to have been the first East Indian parachutist to perform in Northern California. Gravelle's press release said he had been a pilot four years and employed by Thompson Aeronautical Corporation since 1928. He claimed to have been an airmail pilot and to have flown in formation with Lindbergh during an air show at Cleveland in 1929. He was supposed to make his flight at Cheim Field and parachute jump on August 8. It is unknown if this ever took place.

Buroker's flying school Travel Air was damaged a few days after Gravelle's proposed jump. Harold Brown was making a night flight at Cheim Field and crashed into the boundary fence while landing in darkness. The plane was repaired and flying again within the week, but it was damaged again, in a nose over accident, while being taxied by J. Meredith on Cheim Field.[44]

Harold Brown reported the Yuba-Sutter Flying Club was incorporating as the California Aeronautical Corporation. This, he said, would allow the club to grow and take advantage of the expanding job opportunities presented by the growing aviation industry. He also said the club was buying a new Spartan biplane.[45]

The new Spartan was already on its way when the announcement was made. The club purchased the Whirlwind powered Spartan for training and passenger carrying. It was purchased through Brown, who was the Northern California dealer for Spartan aircraft in addition to being manager of the flying club. Todd Crutchfield, a Spartan Company pilot, delivered the new plane from the factory at Tulsa, Oklahoma.

The Spartan had a cruising speed of 100 miles per hour with a top speed of 122 miles per hour. It had a service ceiling of twelve thousand feet and a range of six hundred miles. It had navigation lights and a landing light for night flying and carried the basic instruments for "blind" flying. According to Brown, the plane was ideal for training purposes. By late August, two students, Larry Martin and Bill Brander, were making solo flights in the plane, and another student was ready to solo.[46]

James Harshner, instructor and chief pilot of the competing unnamed flying school at Cheim Field, acquired a new Curtiss-Wright Robin for training. The Robin, delivered to Cheim on September 7, was purchased by Duane Lueth and William Middleton, then rented or leased back to Harshner to use as a school plane. The local men purchased the OX-5 Robin from D. C. Warren Company of Oakland, the regional distributor for Curtiss-Wright.

The Robin was the first high-wing, cabin monoplane to be manufactured for sale in America. It was the forerunner of the many thousands of high-wing, single-engine cabin planes that exist in the United States today. The Robin seated the pilot and two passengers, side by side behind him, in an enclosed cabin. With no lower wing to block the view below, and the enclosed cabin keeping out the ninety-miles-per-hour wind, it ushered in a new age of flying comfort, and was perfect for sightseeing trips.[47]

Sutter Air Terminal was the next new airport in the Yuba-Sutter community. It was built across the Feather River from Cheim Field in the Nuestro District, 4.5 air miles west-northwest of Yuba City and 7.5 miles east-southeast of South Butte, the highest peak in the Sutter Buttes. The airport's opening celebration started August 28, 1930, and lasted five days. By the time it ended on September 1, an estimated five thousand people had attended. Sutter Air Terminal is listed here due to the chronology of its opening. There will be much more about the establishment of this airport in the next chapter.[48]

The Marysville City Council was informed Cheim Field needed more hangars. It became a sensitive subject when James Harshner requested that the council allow him to rent the only hangar on the field. He said it was necessary to house the new Curtiss Robin. Councilman Walter Kynoch told the council the hangar had been ordered vacated for the Sacramento Valley Land Show. He said if Harshner was allowed to use the hangar it would be unfair to others who requested use of the hangar. It was agreed that as soon as the Land Show was over, the council would decide who would rent the hangar.

Roy Bostic told the council that Harshner should be considered first to rent the hangar. He reminded them Harshner helped the late Tom Scott build the hangar, and it was Scott who left the hangar for the city. Bostic said Harshner was an aviation pioneer at Marysville, and an outstanding instructor pilot.[49]

Consolidated Air Lines received its planes and would soon begin service to Oakland from Sacramento. When Hemstreet & Bell finished scraping and leveling Cheim Field, CAL would add service from Sacramento to Marysville.

Beverly Gilmore, CAL president, flew up to Cheim Field with a party of friends and pilots in the newly delivered Curtiss Kingbird. The plane couldn't land at Cheim because the field repairs were not finished, and the runway was in a questionable state. The Kingbird circled Cheim several times, then flew across the river and landed at the recently opened Sutter Air Terminal.

Gilmore assured a local reporter that CAL would participate in the air show planned for Cheim Field during the upcoming Five Counties Fair, which was officially named the Sacramento Valley Land Show. Gilmore said CAL transports would be on hand for inspection and to haul passengers on short hops around the area.[50]

According to Gilmore, one of CAL's big tri-motor Ford's first duties would be to haul passengers from the Bay Area to Cheim Field for the Five Counties Fair at Marysville. He said a dozen families would be moved to Sacramento, where CAL would employ the men at the airline's home field. Others would work out of Terminal No. 1 at San Francisco Bay Airdrome in Alameda. Gilmore said CAL transports would leave Cheim Field regularly at 7:30 AM for Sacramento, and the last plane would leave Alameda at 4:20 PM, arriving in Marysville at 5:35 PM.[51]

Frank Zeman, a Willows parachutist, narrowly escaped death at the College City Barbecue. Harold Brown was flying the jump plane for Zeman. At three thousand feet after Zeman climbed out on the wing to jump, the harness for his outer parachute came off. If he had jumped, he would have died or suffered broken shoulders at best. The slipstream blew him against the fuselage of the plane. Zeman, holding on with one hand, was able to climb back onto the lower wing of the plane. Brown then brought

CHAPTER 5   143

the plane down and landed with Zeman riding on the wing.[52]

Lan Maupin's 1910 Curtiss copy, the *Diamond*, had been sitting in a crate in his barn at Tudor for many years. He brought it to the aeronautical class at Marysville High School in early September to be restored for display at the Sacramento Valley Land Show. After Weldon Cooke flew many exhibitions in the *Diamond*, it served as a school training plane for California Aviation Co. at its airfield in Easton. Eventually, it was dismantled and stored in Bernard Lanteri's shipyard at Pittsburg on Suisun Bay. After Lanteri died, the plane was shipped to Maupin's Tudor farm in Sutter County and stored in his barn until late summer 1930.

The high school aeronautical classes assembled the plane with Maupin's help and put new fabric on the wings. Some parts of the plane, including the engine, were missing and the students had to improvise. A motor was located in Watsonville, but it didn't arrive in time to be installed. The plane was made ready for the parade that would open the Land Show in late September.[53]

THE SACRAMENTO VALLEY Land Show included an air show and another Cheim Airport dedication ceremony (the first airport dedication ceremony was held in August 1928.), this time to celebrate the official acceptance of the airport property by the city of Marysville. On the morning of September 23, 1930, before a thousand spectators, a formation of planes flew over Cheim Field while the Marysville High School band performed stirring marches. Harry Cheim then presented Mayor Chester A. Smith with the deed for the airport land. A Ford transport broke through a ribbon held by two young women as it began rolling for takeoff. The Ford belonged to Standard Oil of California. It carried Harry Cheim, Mayor Smith, and other local officials making yet another "first" official departure from the airport.[54]

The inauguration of the first scheduled airline service to and from Marysville by Consolidated Air Lines was also part of the celebration. But, the inauguration of Consolidated Air Lines did not take place as scheduled; it was put off for two days.

The Standard Oil Ford and several other planes had flown into Cheim earlier for the dedication. The other planes were flown by: Floyd "Speed" Nolta in his Travel Air from Willows with H. J. Doty as his passenger, Jack Elliot of Oakland's Elliot & Duck Flying Service in a Travel Air cabin plane, Eddie Smith from Berkeley in a Ryan Brougham, Associated Oil sent its big

Boeing Model 40A with Emory Bronte at the controls and Marjorie Clark as a passenger, George Dixon and his passenger H. F. George came in a Curtiss Fledgling, and Chan Keeny with H. Waage arrived in a Curtiss Robin. The local planes on the field were: the Yuba-Sutter Flying Club's Spartan, the Robin Flying Club's Curtiss Robin, and Del Buroker's Travel Air.[55]

The spectators at the airport dedication watched air racing during the afternoon hours of the twenty-third. The race was over a triangular course covering a distance of twelve miles.

The first race was for aircraft powered by Wright Whirlwind J-5 or J-6 engines. Tommy Symons from Oakland won the race flying a modified Travel Air. His time around the course was five minutes and thirty-five seconds. Ken Kleaver took second place in an Eaglerock, and Harold Brown was third in the club Spartan.

A second race, a free-for-all race, was held on the same course. This time Ken Kleaver won in five minutes and four seconds with Symons taking second, and Floyd Nolta grabbed third in his Hisso Travel Air.

Tommy Symons won the dead-stick landing event by touching down thirty-five feet past the mark. Walter Hall, usually known for his parachuting exhibitions, took second place landing forty feet from the line. The only accident of the air show occurred during this contest. John Ames of Live Oak was landing without power and passed over the line crashing into the parked Spartan biplane belonging to the Yuba-Sutter Flying Club.

During the afternoon and before the races, more pilots flew in. They were: Ray Raymond and Shirley Brush in the Boeing 40A, *Standard Oil No. 2*, Tommy Symons and Ken Kleaver from Oakland, Joe Hicks in his Travel Air from Chico, Edison E. Mouton, the DOC inspector from Oakland in a Stearman, and Herb Kraft arrived, also in a Stearman, from Oakland.

After the air racers were finished roaring around the pylons, the crowd was treated to more thrills. Harold Brown demonstrated his aerobatic skills doing loops, rolls, and other daring maneuvers; he then finished his routine with an inverted pass before the crowd.

The Yuba City chapter of the NAA officiated all races with Frank Flynn as chief timer. Flynn came from Oakland in the tri-motor Ford, *Standard Oil No.1*, flown by R. S. Allen and B. F. Doolin.[56]

Inauguration of the Consolidated Air Line service to Marysville was held at Cheim Field two days after the field's dedication ceremony. It was also a part of the Sacramento Valley Land Show, which went on for three weeks. The inauguration ceremony began with the arrival of the fourteen-passenger tri-motor Ford transport that was CAL's flagship. It brought a delegation of officials from Sacramento headed by C. H. Bidwell, that city's mayor.

Chester Smith, the Marysville mayor, addressed the crowd from a platform and then his daughter, Mrs. F. J. Duff, christened the CAL Ford transport, *Pride of Marysville*, by breaking a bottle of milk (Prohibition was in effect) on its center propeller hub. Beverly Gilmore spoke to the audience about CAL's plans for the future. He said in four days the service between Sacramento and Oakland would begin with the departure of the first plane at 7:30 Monday morning. Mayor Bidwell gave a brief speech about the value of such a service and the future of air transportation. The Ford airliner was adorned with a floral wreath made by Marysville Florists for the christening.

When the speeches were finished, the Ford departed on the inaugural flight, a short hop around the area. It returned and all VIPs were driven into town for lunch at Hotel Marysville. The Curtiss Kingbird departed Cheim that afternoon with the first scheduled airmail flight from the Yuba-Sutter community.[57]

Pylon air races were held again that afternoon, and Tommy Symons won both the Whirlwind race and the free-for-all. Ken Kleaver placed third in both races, and Jack Slaybaugh was second in both races. Slaybaugh also won the dead-stick landing event.[58]

Arriving at Cheim Field for the inaugural ceremony were: a Lycoming powered Stinson belonging to Hearst Aircraft of Mills Field piloted by G. W. H. Pope, and an Eaglerock belonging to K. Neese of Oakland flown by R. C. Bucklen. Sterling Boller with A. K. Horner as copilot flew the CAL tri-motor Ford. Sterling's brother, Dana Boller, flew the CAL Curtiss Kingbird in with passengers Mrs. Sterling Boller, Miss Fay Perry of Hollywood, and Elmer Horn, chief mechanic for CAL.[59]

Aviation events planned for the duration of the Sacramento Valley Land Show included flights around the Twin Cities area by Army Air Corps planes, which were also on display at Cheim Field during the Land Show. CAL's Ford gave groups of young boys rides around the area. The boys received flying helmets as souvenirs of the flights. The little Aeronca C-3, demonstrator, was due to fly into Cheim during the three-week duration of the Land Show.[60]

On Monday morning, September 29 at 7:20 AM, Consolidated's tri-motor Ford, *Pride of Marysville*, departed Cheim Field for Oakland via Sacramento. Ten passengers were booked on this first flight. Many of them booked just for the privilege of being first. Among the passengers were: Mr.

and Mrs. E. Burger, James Griffith, H. Dunning, Capt. Weldon Brown, and A. Arnot. Pilots for the flight were Sterling Boller and Gene Tigar.[61]

Consolidated Air Lines' service was scheduled daily. After the tri-motor transport's first passenger flight on Monday, the airline switched to the Curtiss Kingbird for daily service from Marysville. On Tuesday and Wednesday, the Kingbird departed from Cheim with no passengers. Pilot Sterling Boller was the sole occupant of the eight-seat airliner.[62]

Flying operations at Cheim Field settled down after all the hoopla of September. Delbert Buroker acquired a Curtiss Robin to replace his Travel Air damaged in the collision with the Spartan during the September dedication. Buroker traded his damaged Travel Air in when he purchased the new Robin. He would use the new cabin plane for his flying school and air taxi business. He bought the OX-5 Robin from Berkeley Aviation Services.[63]

Marysville residents had a new alarm clock. At 7:20 AM, every morning, the powerful Wright Whirlwind engines on CAL's airliner were throttled up to full power for takeoff, awakening many townspeople who didn't necessarily want to be awakened that early. Although some would wait for the roar of the engines, it was their last call to "rise and shine."

Mr. Gilmore, president of Consolidated Air Lines, reduced fares between Marysville and Oakland to stimulate ridership. A one-way fare was changed to nine dollars and eighty-five cents, but it was still twice the price of rail fare between the two cities.[64]

W. C. Burroughs, a Marysville contractor, built a new double hangar next to the existing hangar at Cheim Field. The new hangar was 88-feet long and 35-feet wide. It was constructed of corrugated iron around a wood frame with chicken wire bisecting it internally into two 44 x 35 foot hangars. There was enough space between the new hangars and the older hangar to roof over and create an additional hangar if needed. The new hangars were large enough to hold the two Curtiss Robins that were permanent residents on the field. Beverly Gilmore encouraged the city council to continue the progress at the airport and build a 75 x 100 foot hangar for his airliner. He told the council CAL would make the airport the company's home field and pay 10 percent of the cost as rent for five years. Once done, he would move his mechanics to Cheim and all of his planes. The city council said they would consider the proposition, but it was never built.[65]

DR. JULIAN JOHNSON was crossing a Marysville street in early October and hit by a car. The accident occurred late at night, and he was knocked unconscious. The next day he reported it was his fault, he did not see the car coming. He suffered only minor injuries.[66]

BEV GILMORE WAS present for a proposal submitted to the Marysville City Council to install the necessary lighting at Cheim Field to allow his airliners to land safely. The proposal, which basically planned for a floodlit runway costing $1,280, was much less than past lighting proposals. In support of the lighting proposal, Gilmore told of one of his pilot's difficulties during a recent landing at Cheim. The last scheduled airliner landed each day about 5:35 PM, which was close to sunset. The days were getting shorter, and occasionally a plane would arrive late; sometimes it would be almost dark. When this happened recently, the pilot, Jack Dalbey, would not attempt the landing. He turned the controls over to Sterling Boller, the company's chief pilot who happened to be on board, and Boller made the landing. Gilmore's story was an attempt to make the council understand how important lighting was for an airport.[67]

Peter Borello of Robbins in southwestern Sutter County, made his solo flight at Cheim Field in early October. He soloed after only six hours of dual instruction with his instructor, James Harshner. He was flying the school's Curtiss Robin.[68]

Harold Brown spoke to the Achaean Club about his experiences as a lieutenant in the Army Air Corps flying patrols along the Mexican border. W. C. Owen spoke about aviation in the Army Reserves. The men spoke at a luncheon given in the Marysville Hotel.[69]

Erling Norby hired the Consolidated Air Lines tri-motor Ford to fly a party of local residents to the popular Cal–Stanford football game at Palo Alto on October 25. Palo Alto Airport was located on the Stanford campus grounds next to the football field.[70]

Once the smaller hangars were finished at Cheim Field, the city council reported financing to build a large hangar for CAL was being sought through private means. The city and county funds were exhausted, due, no doubt, to the Depression which by then was a year old.[71]

Wiley Wright, DOC aeronautics inspector, flew into Cheim Field late October to administer tests and inspect aircraft. He was flying a DOC Stearman.

Several members of Herb Keeler's aeronautics classes at Marysville High School demonstrated their glider flying abilities for the inspector and received their student permits. The school's glider had earlier been officially inspected, approved, and issued a registration number.

License tests were given to Dewey Ashford, Bill Brander, and Larry Martin, members of the Yuba-Sutter Flying Club. They all passed.

Bill Brander and his brother, E. R. Brander, also took their examinations for aircraft engine mechanics licenses, and Dudley Cunningham took the exam for an airplane (airframe) mechanics license. They all passed. Local aircraft owners could finally get their planes repaired, overhauled, and inspected without having to wait while a licensed mechanic was brought from another city to do their repairs.[72]

A caravan of seven aircraft from Fresno flew into Cheim Field on October 25 as part of an air tour that would today be called a "meet and greet" session of business heads and city officials from Fresno meeting their Marysville counterparts. From the Fresno aviation community, a few names stood out among the visitors: Senator W. F. Chandler, the donor of Fresno's city airport; Ralph Greenamyre, head of the Greenamyre Flying School; his passenger Lewis Servie, a master mechanic with the Schneider Air Service; Jack Schmitt, head of Standard Oil Company's aviation department, who flew a Stinson to Cheim; and Ralph Hall of the Richfield Oil Company, who flew a Stearman up from Fresno. Senator Chandler was believed to have flown in with Bev Gilmore, who organized the air tour and fly-in from one end of CAL's route to the other. The guests were taken to lunch then given a tour of local orchards. A dinner was given in the evening, and the guests stayed overnight returning to Fresno the following day.[73]

Two days later, Gilmore announced that Fresno would no longer be the southern terminus of Consolidated Air Lines. The airline was buying another tri-motor Ford and would be extending service to Los Angeles. Fresno celebrated the inauguration of the new southern service with a ceremony following the arrival of the Ford carrying members of the returning caravan from Marysville, including Senator Chandler and Bev Gilmore.[74]

Little was reported of Consolidated Air Lines after the southern extension of its route. Operations continued through November and possibly into January 1931. The company never purchased the second Ford. On January 28, the company's only tri-motor Ford 4AT, registration number NC4532, was repossessed. On February 20, Consolidated's lone Curtiss Kingbird J-2 suffered the same fate. The airline had no more aircraft; the disastrous economic times had broken the company and it disappeared. But it was a phoenix and would rise again.

H. A. Buroker flew into Cheim Field in his Ryan Brougham on October

28. Two other pilots, Gus Klundt and Ben Easley, accompanied Buroker. He was the uncle of Del Buroker, owner of the Curtiss Robin parked on the field at Cheim. Del and his uncle planned to work together instructing and doing air taxi work. Del hadn't obtained his commercial license yet, but was working on it. He usually hired a pilot when there was flying work to be done. With his uncle on the field, he had the help he needed.

H. A. Buroker reportedly served nineteen months in the US Naval Air Service during the Great War. Part of that time was overseas. After the war, he took up commercial flying at Bellingham, Washington. He specialized in flying people into mountainous areas of the state. He planned to specialize in flying people to Lake Tahoe and Mt. Lassen from Marysville. He voiced his hope of obtaining hangar space at Cheim Field for his Ryan.[76]

Thirty-two aircraft landed at Cheim Field on Thursday, October 30. They were part of a goodwill flight that began in Los Angeles a few days before. There were fifty-four planes on the tour when it reached San Francisco on Wednesday. From there, smaller flights broke off to go to different towns in the north state. At Cheim it took an hour to get all of the planes landed and parked. Long tables had been set up on the field. The pilots and passengers were fed cake with local peaches during their short layover. Some planes were flagged off for departure before the last arrivals had landed.

The biggest plane in the group landing at Cheim was a Boeing 40A belonging to Associated Oil Company and flown by Emory Bronte. The smallest was a Monocoupe with a fifty-five horsepower motor, flown by Sarah M. Toney. Standard Oil had three planes flying in the tour; Richfield Oil had two planes, Shell one, and Union Oil three. One fleet of eight planes was lead by a pilot flying "blind" (or on instruments as it would be described today). Gil Shelton was flying under a hood, so he couldn't see outside the cockpit. He could only see his instruments inside the plane. He flew the airplane from town to town. His copilot, Plosser, sat in an unobscured cockpit, making all of the landings and takeoffs.[77]

On the first Sunday in November, a major effort was made by Cheim Field aviators to get local residents out to the airport to watch stunt flying and buy airplane rides. It turned out to be the most successful Sunday the fliers at Cheim had ever had. Sunday was traditionally the day for pilots to give rides, lessons, and just generally show off at airports all across America. It was the workingman's only day off, and it was the only time most folks had to visit the local airport. For many fliers trying to scrape by in the 1920s and '30s, it was the one day of the week they made the income needed to live on for the rest of the week.

On this particular Sunday at Cheim, one hundred passengers made flights, twenty flying students took lessons, and eight glider students made flights in the high school glider.

Six local airplanes were flying that day, including the ex-CAL Curtiss Kingbird, which landed after dark. The Burokers had their Ryan Brougham and Curtiss Robin flying; they did a few stunts with the Ryan and hauled passengers in both. Jim Harshner gave flying lessons in Lueth's Robin.

Another airplane from outside the area arrived at Cheim that day and began giving rides. The pilot was popular with the local Hindu and Sikh residents. The local fliers complained to the city authorities, and councilman Dan Bryant came out to Cheim to investigate. He determined the outsider was not breaking any rules and could not be stopped. However, the matter would be taken up at the next city council meeting. There was a consensus among the local commercial operators that they should be better protected from outside competition.[78]

The following Sunday, the Buroker Robin with Ben Easley at the controls took off from Cheim for Sutter Air Terminal, a few miles west in Sutter County. Easley was to fetch a parachute from Harold Brown who now kept the Yuba-Sutter Flying Club's Travel Air at the new Sutter County airfield on Township Road.

Easley knew his gas was low in the Robin's main tank, so he switched to the reserve tank. Unbeknowst to him, there was water-contaminated gasoline in that tank and his engine quit. He made a successful emergency landing in a rice stubble field. He used the rice farmer's telephone and arranged for some gas to be brought out to him. He refueled and took off, but it was too late to pick up Brown's parachute. The parachute jump at Cheim didn't take place that Sunday.

The Burokers had a parachute jump planned for Armistice Day at Oroville, and they would definitely need the necessary parachutes. Their problem was new regulations from the DOC required parachute jumpers to wear a second parachute as an emergency backup, but in the Yuba-Sutter area one parachute was hard enough to find.[79]

A few days later, the other Curtiss Robin at Cheim Field was wrecked in a night landing on the field. Jim Harshner had returned about 8:00 PM with a student, Peter Borello. He was on final approach, according to witnesses at the airport, and put the Robin into a sideslip while too close to the runway. The left wing struck the ground first and the Curtiss overturned.

A sideslip is a cross control maneuver often used by the pilots of airplanes without flaps to lose altitude quickly on landing approach without gaining airspeed. It isn't a great idea to do it close to the ground particularly at night.

Harshner was injured and Borello was not. A Lipp & Sullivan ambulance arrived to pick up Harshner, but friends had already taken him to the hospital. He sustained a cut on his head and leg injuries but nothing serious. The airplane suffered about twelve hundred dollars damage. Marysville garage mechanic Duane Lueth and Bill Middleton were owners of the Robin.[80]

Dudley Cunningham was rapidly gaining a reputation as an excellent airframe mechanic. In November, he finished rebuilding the Yuba-Sutter Flying Club's Travel Air after it had been damaged in the night flying accident. He completely rebuilt the Travel Air in about one month's time. After Dudley finished rigging the plane, Harold Brown test-flew it. It was later flown to Oakland and inspected by the DOC aeronautics inspector.

This was the eighth airplane Cunningham had rebuilt. One of those was a Curtiss Jenny he rebuilt for himself. By November 1930, Cunningham had placed a bid on a wrecked Travel Air at Oakland; he planned to rebuild it for a thousand dollars and sell it for a profit. It was a method to keep income coming in during slow work periods and is used by aircraft mechanics even to this day[81]

William Swain of Marysville received his Limited Commercial License in November, after training at Curtiss-Wright Airport in San Mateo. He continued training there to obtain a Transport Pilot License.[82]

Paul H. Jenks from the Curtiss-Wright Flying Service visited Harold Brown to discuss a new business he wanted to open at Cheim Field. It was an aircraft and engine repair shop with supply sales to serve Northern California and Nevada. The Curtiss-Wright system planned to place $7,500 worth of aeronautical supplies with Brown, and Brown agreed to the plan.

The concrete floor for Brown's business was laid and plans were going ahead for an airframe shop, an aircraft engine overhaul area, a stock and parts room, and an office. Dudley Cunningham was to handle airframe repair and overhaul, and Bill and Erwin Brander would be in charge of engine repair and overhaul. The business was named the Brown Aeronautical System. Brown was already distributor of Spartan airplanes for the north state, and now an agent for Curtiss-Wright aircraft in Northern California and Nevada.

All parties approved the plan and a third aviation business was established at Cheim Field, the first and second being the Yuba-Sutter Flying Club Flight School and Harshner's flying school. Brown's new business allowed plane owners to buy their repairs and supplies locally—negating a trip to the Bay Area.[83]

The Yuba-Sutter Flying Club made significant changes in its equipment in January 1931. Harold Brown, still instructor and chief pilot for the club, influenced its members to buy a second Spartan biplane from his distributorship. First, however, they had to sell off the club's current equipment, which included the first plane acquired by the club, the Travel Air 2000 registered NC 9087, and the club's second aircraft, a Spartan biplane registered NC 62N.

CLUB MEMBER N. DEWEY ASHFORD purchased Travel Air NC 9087 on January 3, 1931. He was a charter member of the Yuba-Sutter Flying Club and came to the club with some prior flying experience. He joined the

The Johns Multiplane at Langley Field circa 1919. Dewey Ashford may have been assigned duties relating to this aircraft. At the very least he witnessed the attempts to fly the plane. It is doubtful the aircraft's three 400 horsepower Liberty engines (one pulling and two pushing) could ever overcome the drag caused by seven wings. The plane appears to have only a single place cockpit and may have been designed as a high altitude observation aircraft.

CHAPTER 5   153

At Langley Field, this was the result of the only attempt to fly the Johns Multiplane.

Army Air Service during the Great War. When the war ended, he was an enlisted man with the 126th Observation Squadron and Photo Reconnaissance School at Langley Field, Virginia. He stayed in the army until 1920 when his enlistment was up. He left the army with the rank of an E-6 sergeant. When he left, he had 120 hours of flying time, which may not have been logged. Many enlisted ground crew of flying squadrons were taught to fly by bored flying officers, who had little to do once the war ended. They would create any form of flying duties just to stay in the air.

While at Langley Field, Dewey caught the photography bug and took many photographs of squadronmates, the airfield, and the planes he rode in as an observer and photo technician. The planes were: the JN-4D & H trainers, the DH-4 light bomber, the Handley-Page HP 400, and the Martin MB-2—the latter two being twin-engine heavy bombers. Dewey was assigned duties at Langley in support of Herbert John's Multiplane, an enormous seven-winged tri-motor aircraft. The huge plane was wrecked while attempting to take off for its first flight in 1919. Further attempts may have been made in 1920, but it never took to the air.

Dewey Ashford's Army Air Service flying experience was a great help when he returned to flying a decade later. A successful orchardist, Dewey would own at least ten different aircraft during his sixty years of flying. He was devoted to aviation and always promoting it in the Yuba-Sutter community.

The following is a list of the aircraft Dewey Ashford owned and flew during his lifetime. The list was made from his flight logbook and his photo collection.

1st Flight

Log Entry	Aircraft	Engine	Registration
Jan. 3, 1931	Travel Air 2000	OX-5 90hp	NC 9087
Oct. 9, 1933	Stearman Wright	J-5 225hp	NC 6438
Jan. 26, 1935	Stearman C-3R Wright	J-6-7	NC 790H
July 4, 1936	Fairchild 24	Warner	NC 15921
Nov. 8, 1940	Waco F	Warner 125hp	NC 612Y*
Nov. 11, 1940	Luscombe Continental	75hp	NC28749*
May 5, 1946	Ercoupe Continental	75hp	NC87387
Oct. 15, 1946	Fairchild 24	Warner 165hp	NC 81322
Sept. 4, 1958	Cessna 195	Jacobs 300hp	N 9322A
No date	Cessna 210		

*Possibly he didn't own. May have been school aircraft.

THE FAIRCHILD 24, REGISTRATION NC 15921, has been beautifully restored and is displayed in the Hiller Aviation Museum at San Carlos Airport. It is in exactly the same paint scheme as when Dewey Ashford took

Dewey Ashford's Stearman C3B, reg. NC 6438, at Cheim Field, Marysville. From the right standing in front of the Stearman is Ashford, Bill Brander, and an unknown aviator.

The page from Ashford's logbook indicating that he took possession of Fairchild 24 NC 15921 on July 4, 1936. His logbook indicates he flew the Fairchild weekly, weather permitting, until August 29, 1939. He sold it soon after that date.

possession of it July 4, 1936, at San Francisco Bay Airdrome. Today the Fairchild has some small markings of a personal nature put on the restoration by the last owner, who believed the plane was his during 1936 and '37. Ashford's logbook indicates that he flew Fairchild 24, NC 15921, 250-plus hours from July 4, 1936, until his last flight in the plane on July 29, 1939. The aircraft was flown 90 percent of the time from Ashford's short dirt airstrip, sandwiched between a peach orchard and the driveway to his ranch just off Highway 99 near Tudor. The latter is no longer on the maps and is now a very small farming community nine miles south of Yuba City. The airstrip had trees and a thirty-foot high levee along the Feather River at its east end and thirty-foot high power lines at its west end. Very few other pilots ever attempted to land there. The airstrip was eleven hundred feet long and ninety degrees to the prevailing north and south winds. There are many, many photographs of NC 15921 in Dewey's scrapbook covering the three years he owned the plane, including those from a trip he and his wife, Mary, took to the Los Angeles National Air Races in September 1936. When Dewey purchased the Farchild 24 in the Bay Area in 1936, the sale was published in *Western Flying*.[84]

From August 1939 to August 1940, Dewey worked as an instructor pilot at Cheim Field training local men as pilots in the government sponsored Civilian Pilot Training Program (CPTP). Several of those men would

Dewey Ashford with two friends beside his first Fairchild 24 on his peach ranch dirt airstrip at Tudor, circa 1936.

become respected agricultural and commercial pilots in the Yuba-Sutter community after their service in World War II. The following were some of Dewey's local students in the CPTP school at Cheim Field in 1939–40: John Bowles, Ernie Williams, Nick Webber, E. Stolp, Ken Flagg, Sherman Perkins, Dumpy Clark, Ken Onstott, Pearl Moore, Tom Bowles, Albert Locati, Al Gilman, Harry Stott, Robert Clark, Barney Long, Frank Sue, Robert Klamp, Al Ayala, J. Wheeler, Bill Musladin, Cliff Moore, and Guy "Speed" Hughes.[85]

When Dewey quit instructing in August 1940, he became a founding member of the Fourth Observation Squadron of the California State Guard. He was assigned the rank of first lieutenant and made assistant to the squadron commander, Capt. A. W. Makepeace. Dewey's logbook shows a total of only three flights made under the auspices of the state guard unit. When America entered World War II, the Fourth Observation Squadron drifted into oblivion. All civilian flying was prohibited within 185 miles of the Pacific coastline. Prior to the attack on Pearl Harbor, Dewey made his last flight on December 5, 1941, in a Curtiss Robin. Since returning to flying in 1930, Dewey had flown for pleasure an average of three times a week. He loved flying and it was a major sacrifice for him to abide by the wartime flying prohibition in California. He drove to Sparks, Nevada, in April 1942 and spent a week there flying a total of ten hours. It would be three years before he flew again. From June 1945 until well into the 1970s, Dewey flew regularly, but no longer from his short dirt strip at Tudor. After he sold his second Fairchild 24 and bought a Cessna 195 in September 1958, he rented a hangar for the Cessna at Sutter County Airport in Yuba City. His airstrip at home was too small to operate the 195 safely. His ranch on Garden Highway (Old Highway 99) was sold to nonflyers after he died in 1983. His driveway airstrip was made unusable due to single rows of forty-foot eucalyptus trees planted on each side of the drive to the ranch house.[86]

Dewey Ashford was the Yuba-Sutter community's link to all of aviation's notable eras with the exception of the Exhibition Years. Dewey flew during World War I, the Golden Age, World War II, the Jet Age, and into the Space Age. He was a founding member of the Yuba-Sutter Sheriff's Aero Squadron. He kept the faith and was always willing to help the flying community; usually not as a professional but as an ardent disciple of flight.

THE YUBA-SUTTER FLYING CLUB had four members from Oroville in Butte County by January 1931. Those members, Larry Martin, William Illman, Glenn Marders, and Roy Westfall bought all the shares in the club's Spartan and started a flying club at Oroville. This was done under the leadership of Westfall. He had obtained his Limited Commercial License, which allowed him to give instruction and carry passengers within ten miles of his home airfield. (The federal government discontinued the Limited Commercial License and the Industrial Commercial License in later years. It is now known as a Commercial Pilot License.)

Glenn Marders, acting for the Oroville members, began negotiations with the city of Oroville to have Riley Field taken over by the city and a hangar built. Joining the Oroville contingent in their new club plan was Louis Cohen.

Nothing came of the attempts to get Oroville to take over Riley Field, which was actually closer to the town of Palermo. The Oroville group decided to continue flying out of Cheim Field through the wet months and move to Riley Field after the ground dried and could be put into flying condition. Meanwhile the Yuba-Sutter Flying Club purchased its new Spartan biplane from the factory through Harold Brown.[87]

Del Buroker moved his Curtiss Robin to San Joaquin County in January 1931.[88]

Marshall C. Hoppin flew into Cheim Airport in January to inspect the airport for the DOC. He met with city officials and concerned residents voicing his satisfaction with the airport and predicting it would do well in the future. He made a few suggestions to improve the field—the most important being that the all-weather runways be aligned with the prevailing winds. It is strange that after all of the city council's claims that the runway alignment would be corrected, it never was.

The day before Hoppin arrived at Cheim Field, a Lieutenant Morrow was trapped above the fog while trying to land his pursuit plane at Mather Field. He flew all the way to Marysville before finding a hole down through the fog. He landed at Cheim safely, but he got stuck in the mud taxiing from the gravel runway to the parking area. Dudley Cunningham, who by then was airport superintendent, had a vehicle at the airport and pulled the plane out of the mud. Once the fog lifted in Sacramento, Lieutenant Morrow departed for Mather.[89]

IT WAS A foggy January throughout California. On the seventeenth, a government aircraft pursued a big monoplane through the fog in a dangerous race over the Los Angeles area. The plane was suspected of smuggling Chinese into Los Angeles from Mexico. The pilots of the government plane, Gene Hensley and Robert Forsetblade, were flying for their lives after the big plane turned and dived on them repeatedly. The smuggler escaped.

Later, officials were told the plane landed near the east corner of Vail Field shortly before daybreak. Three men, possibly more, jumped from the plane and ran to a waiting car, which disappeared. Immediately, the plane roared off and was lost in the haze.[90]

LT. HAROLD BROWN reported the new Spartan biplane was on its way from the factory to Cheim Field for the Yuba-Sutter Flying Club. It was to take the place of the older Spartan sold to the Oroville club members. Brown had just returned from his two-week active duty with the Army Reserves and was getting his new business organized. He purchased a truck for the business, which he had painted in army olive drab and white lettering with the designation of Company F, 184th Infantry. Those were the numbers and markings of the local California National Guard Unit.[91]

The Oroville flying contingent suffered a setback on February 5. Their newly acquired Spartan, being flown by Roy Westfall with Glenn Marders as passenger, turned over in a landing accident. Westfall applied the brakes too soon after landing causing the Spartan to veer to the side and go over gently on its back. The two occupants were not injured, the wings had no damage, but the metal propeller was bent and the main landing gear was damaged. The Arnot Motor Company's new wrecking car was brought out to pick up the plane and move it to the hangar.[92]

HERB KEELER HELD the first meeting of a new glider club formed of night school students at Marysville High.[93]

SIXTEEN AIRCRAFT BLANKETED the state of California visiting 407 American Legion posts in February to pick up their membership lists and deliver them to Mills Field. Harold Brown flew the club's new Spartan to take the lists to Mills for the Yuba-Sutter post.[94]

On March 4, 1931, Harold Brown married Miss Thelma Anderson of Marysville in Reno, Nevada.[95]

Consolidated Air Lines had ceased operations by March. With the Depression weighing heavily on the Yuba-Sutter community, people could not afford to travel, especially, by airplane. However, Gene Tigar, formerly a pilot with CAL, and J. L. Costello came to Marysville and announced they were advance men for a new airline service to be provided by First National Airways of America. They said the new service would cover the same routes as those covered by CAL.

First National Airways, the two men reported, had two subsidiary airlines already in operation. One was British Columbia Airways Ltd. and the other was Guatemala Air Service. Was this a reappearance by Jimmie Angel?

Tigar and Costello said the airline would use a six-passenger tri-motor aircraft on its routes. They said the company controlled the factory that built the tri-motors.[96]

This sounds much like the company that bought the Zenith Albatross tri-motor transport, which Jimmie Angel had a hand in. The Albatross was so underpowered six passengers were all that could be carried if adequate fuel was on board.

George Boyd Jr. and Rennie Mahon flew to Vancouver, B.C., from Marysville in early March. Boyd was a licensed commercial pilot; however, he was going to Vancouver as a mechanic to possibly service two planes piloted by students from the Curtiss-Wright Flying School at San Mateo. Mahon was the son of Judge K. S. Mahon and had flown during the Great War. He took the opportunity to fly with Boyd just to see Canada.[97]

HAROLD BROWN WAS having great success selling Spartan airplanes to his students. He sold one to a group of Colusa flying students and began instructing them in it. By March, two of the students, Michael O'Hair and Alfred Abreu, had passed their tests for their private licenses. Wiley B. Wright, the Western states chief of the DOC Aeronautics Branch, gave them their licenses at Cheim Field.[98]

City Councilman Walter Kynoch announced the appointment of Dudley Cunningham to be the official superintendent of Cheim Field. He would occupy the new office building completed in March. Frank Cheim donated a can of paint to cover the interior of the new building. The city council ordered an official register kept to record all aircraft movements to and from the airport.[99]

Alvin Parker and A. V. Ellis flew from Reno, Nevada, to Cheim Field to take instruction from Harold Brown. The two pilots from Reno needed advanced training to obtain their Transport Pilot Licenses. Parker already had an Industrial Commercial License and Ellis, a Private Pilot License. They flew over from Reno in a Hisso powered Travel Air, which would remain at Cheim Airport while they were taking instruction.[100]

Brown reported another new Spartan aircraft would be arriving at Cheim Field in late March. When it arrived, he planned to take the Spartan he was using at Cheim and move it to Colusa Airport for use there. He had a large group of students in Colusa and was spending half his time there. He took two of the Colusa students, L. R. Zumwalt and Noel Helphenstine, on an overnight cross-country flight to Oakland.

Brown said many of his Colusa students came to Cheim Field on Sundays to fly. Work on a diagonal runway at Cheim was to start soon. Some wag said the grass was getting high enough at Cheim it could interfere with the airplanes' propellers, and how nice it would be if a flock of sheep could be brought in to eat the grass.

Local golfers were making use of Cheim Field as a driving range. Reportedly, they were careful to watch for landing planes![101]

A new Whirlwind Spartan biplane arrived at Cheim Field for the recently named Brown Aeronautical System (for Harold Brown). It was flown from the factory at Tulsa, Oklahoma, in early April.[102]

George Boyd Jr., a graduate of the Yuba City High School class of 1929, spent a year at University of California, Berkeley. He then enrolled with the Curtiss-Wright Flying School at San Mateo Airport and was granted his Private Pilot License in March 1931.[103]

Parachutist Frank Brooks of Portland, Oregon, gave an exhibition of his

CHAPTER 5   161

skills in April at Cheim Field. Aerobatics and passenger rides were carried out on a Sunday in conjunction with his parachute jumps. Brooks claimed to have been making jumps since 1901 when he began jumping from balloons. In his exhibitions, he made single jumps, double jumps (cutaways), and triple jumps. During a triple jump, he displayed red, white, and blue parachutes. In his thirty years as a parachutist he claimed to have made 2,457 jumps.[104]

Varney Air Service inaugurated its Marysville–Sacramento–San Francisco air transport service at Cheim Field on April 15, 1931. Many dignitaries climbed out of five planes at noon that day and gave speeches. Daily service would have planes arriving in Marysville from San Francisco Bay Airdrome, Alameda, at 2:45 and 7:00 PM. Planes would leave Cheim Field for Sacramento at 7:45 AM and 5:00 PM making two trips daily. Planes used on the route would be single-engine, high-wing, Stinson Detroiters, which could carry three passengers, two pilots, and a load of freight. Important among the day's guests were Franklin Rose, vice president of Varney, and Charles E. Wilkins, Varney traffic manager for the Sacramento Valley.[105]

Hemstreet & Bell Construction Company completed the new runway at Cheim aligning it with the prevailing winds 90 percent of the time. It was 450 feet wide and 3,000 feet long. Its direction was still northwest by southeast. When there was no wind, it was expected most pilots would use the old runway because it was nearer to the hangars, better constructed, and would require less taxiing. The entire field was level and hard, and landings could be made in any direction. It was believed the runway alignment problems were finally solved. They weren't. Pilots ignored the newer runway and after a while it was forgotten to have even existed.

One of the hangars was lengthened eight feet to enable use by larger aircraft. Restrooms were built, and lights were put in the office, shop, and hangars at Cheim.[106]

Ralph Morrison made a flight from Cheim Field to the Lockheed factory in Los Angeles in just three hours. Ken Snyder of Marysville was a passenger in Morrison's Lockheed Vega for the trip. Morrison made the trip to Los Angeles to have the repairs made by Dud Cunningham on his Vega inspected by factory experts.

Morrison had flown into Cheim on April 11 from Mills Field, San Francisco, and damaged the Vega on landing. Dudley made repairs to his plane, and Morrison felt the factory should check them out. They did and Dudley received high praise for his work from the people at Lockheed. They were surprised Dudley was able to make such excellent repairs without the proper equipment or previous experience in the wood monocoque construction used in building the Vega.[107]

Bill Swain, son of W. B. Swain of Marysville, flew a new Travel Air from the factory at Wichita, Kansas, to the Curtiss-Wright Flying School at San Mateo Airport in late April. Swain had a Limited Commercial License and was working on his Transport Pilot License at San Mateo.[108]

A Stinson cabin plane used for business flights by the Marysville construction company, Hemstreet & Bell.

Left to Right: Nelson Dewey Ashford, Owen "Pearl" Moore, and John "Slim" Davis show off their new uniforms of the 4th Observation Squadron, Calif. State Guard in August 1940.

CHAPTER 6

Sutter Air Terminal is founded – Yuba-Sutter aviation in the first years of the Depression – Consolidated Air Lines' rebirth and Twin Cities aviation in the remaining Depression years – Cheim Field aviators prepare for war

The opening of Sutter Air Terminal, Yuba City's second airport, happened as Marysville's Cheim Field was preparing for its second dedication and the inauguration of Consolidated Air Lines.

Discussions were held at Yuba City service club meetings for two years about opening another airport in their town after Dr. Johnson closed Angel Airport in early 1927. When the stock market crashed in October 1929, Yuba City officials were negotiating with the family of Dr. Jackson for a city airport site at Jackson Bottoms in southeastern Yuba City. Negotiations failed and neither the city nor the county acquired the property. The land, however, was ideal for an airport and had been used as such many times in the past.

Yuba City Commercial Club members led by President P. N. Swenson were determined Yuba City would have an airport. In May 1930, attorney Lloyd Hewitt filed articles of incorporation in Sacramento for Sutter Air Terminals Inc. to provide for and equip an airport for Yuba City at a future date. Capitalization was set at one hundred thousand dollars. The corporate directors were J. H. Francisco, P. N. Swenson, Charles Moore, and James C. Nason. All were local men with the exception of Francisco, the chief financial backer. At Commercial Club meetings several airport locations were suggested, and the importance of an airport to the commercial well-being of Yuba City influenced every airport discussion.[1]

J. H. Francisco, whose residency was not revealed, returned to Yuba City in May from Sacramento where he had been arranging financing for a

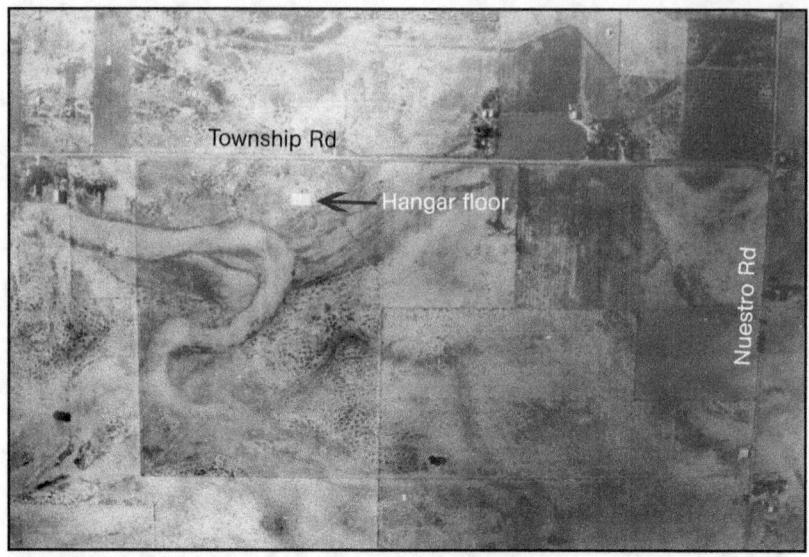

The Sutter Air Terminal site in 1937 with only the concrete hangar floor remaining. The runways developed in 1930 were no longer visible.

proposed airport at Yuba City.[2]

Sutter Air Terminals Inc. secured a lease for 135 acres of land from E. H. Galbraith in the Nuestro District five miles west of Yuba City not exactly in town and closer to the town of Sutter thus the name. Galbraith agreed to be paid 10 percent of profits earned by the airport as payment for the lease. Mr. Francisco found a contractor who would level the land for runways and take stock in the company as payment. Francisco was the only officer in the company being paid a salary. His plans for the airport included three runways, an administration building, and several offices. Tests were run by Richfield Oil Company on the soil to deduce whether it was conducive to runway oiling. The soil proved ideal for oiling.[3]

During the week of June 20, Harold Brown inspected the runways at Sutter Air Terminal. The former military pilot was impressed with the site and the general appearance of the airfield. The runways had been surveyed and staked in preparation for grading. The main runway was diagonal, running northwest to southeast. It was 4,000 feet long and 500 feet wide. Another runway running north and south was 2,950 feet in length and 250 feet wide. The third runway running east and west was 2,560 feet long and 200 feet wide. The runways all crossed at their centers in the shape of an X and served all prevailing winds encountered on the site. They were arranged in such a manner that a minimum of taxiing would be necessary for an airplane to reach its takeoff point or a hangar. Construction of the hangars and other buildings was planned for the near future.[4]

Henry Sackrider went up with Harold Brown in the Yuba-Sutter Flying Club plane in June 1930 and photographed the Feather River for the board of supervisors. The supervisors were trying to obtain federal money to correct the Feather River channel near Nicolaus Bridge to stop the damage that occurred during high river levels nearly every winter. Their flight is believed to be one of the first made from Sutter Air Terminal runways.[5]

The Sutter Air Terminal airport was officially opened June 28, 1930. During the weekend opening celebration, an air show was planned featuring stunt flying, parachute jumps, and passenger flying. At least ten airplanes were expected to fly in for the opening including three from Clover Field in the Los Angeles area. Location for the Sutter Air Terminal airport was precisely given as one mile north of Colusa Highway on the Franklin-Pennington-Live Oak Highway. Today that location would read: one mile north of Highway 20 on Township Road, just north of the new paved bicycle path, which was the old Sacramento Northern Railroad bed. There is a trucking company where the airport hangar was located, and the rest of the 135 acres is still used for farming. The site is three-and-a-half air miles east of Sutter.

Even though ten airplanes were expected to show for the airport opening, a much smaller number actually arrived. Possibly, as few as four aircraft were on the field Sunday. It turned out six planes expected to come from Sacramento didn't because of a program planned at a Sacramento airport being visited by a baby blimp.

A large number of motorists came. By afternoon several hundred spectators were on the field and events went on as planned. Brownie Roy parachuted from Robert West's plane. Harold Brown put on an aerobatic display in the club's Travel Air. Cliff Burroughs and Bill Briggs from Los Angeles flew passenger hops throughout the afternoon.[6]

Due to the poor showing of aircraft and spectators at the opening air show for Sutter Air Terminal, the July meeting of the Commercial Club was spent planning a bigger and better dedication for Sutter Air Terminal. The club, whose president P. N. Swenson was also vice president of Sutter Air Terminals Corporation, decided to sponsor a new dedication air show and make sure it was better promoted and advertised than the first. The club would correct a big problem learned from the opening show—road signs at key intersections directing spectators to the new airport were needed.

Members of the club volunteered to obtain and set the signs.[7]

The new air show would be held August 28–September 1, 1930. The dedication for the new airport on Township Line Road, five miles northwest of Yuba City, would be an unprecedented five-day celebration. In advance, one thousand automobile stickers would be sold for a dollar fifty each. The sticker would allow a carload of visitors to come and go during all five days. The money raised from these stickers would allow J. H. Francisco, now the airport manager, to hire a squadron of planes from the Bay Area to provide stunt flying and passenger hopping throughout the five days.[8]

In July two tractors belonging to Charles Hammond were hired to further level and develop the airfield in preparation for the thirty aircraft expected to fly in for the dedication.[9]

By the eighth, the tractors were doing excellent work grading the runways. A waterwell was drilled and an electric pump installed, which would allow the runways to be watered down once the grading was done. Gravel was spread on the aircraft tiedown area and on the entrance into the site from Township Road in an effort to keep the dust down. George Johnson from PG&E put up poles lighting the newly poured concrete hangar floor to be used as a dance floor, and floodlights were set up to aid night landings. Comfort stations and a small administration building were under construction. A Yuba City contractor, C. Fesler, poured the concrete floor for a large hangar 120 x 75 feet (to be built later) and costing $1,650.

Harold Brown was appointed aeronautical advisor for the event. He called most airports in Northern California inviting anyone interested to the dedication. Brown flew to bigger airports like Oakland and personally invited aviators. He estimated forty aircraft, including military planes, would fly in for the dedication.

Paul Schreck, leading the Sacramento KFBK radio station orchestra, would provide music nightly for dances held on the new concrete hangar floor.[10]

On Thursday, opening day of the dedication, there was little flying activity. The much advertised wedding of Miss Frances Schroder to H. V. Baker took place at the new airport, and a night dance was held on the new hangar floor. J. H. Francisco opened his small administration office and was trying to sell Sutter Air Terminals Inc. stock to finance a hangar on the new floor and oil the runways.

By Friday there were two airplanes on the field. Harry Shan was there with his Stearman from Oakland, as was the ubiquitous Harold Brown in the Yuba-Sutter Flying Club's Spartan biplane. Visitors danced to Schreck's orchestra again on Friday night while Harold Brown gave night rides in the Spartan.[11]

Saturday began on a more positive note after the big tri-motor Ford, *Standard of California*, landed mid-morning. Later in the day, the Ford made a short flight over Yuba City and Marysville with W. H. Haines, district manager for Standard Oil, and Elias Gardner, manager of the Twin Cities Standard Oil plant, aboard. Richard S. Allen was flying the Ford with H. R. Raymond as copilot.

Two hours after the Ford arrived, three Army Air Corps planes flew in from March Field at Riverside. Leading the flight was Lt. W. J. Davies. Floyd Nolta from Willows in his Travel Air, and Hans Kirchner from Oakland in a Waco flew in around noon. The OX-5 Travel Air, which Del Buroker had recently purchased from the Oakland Flying Club, arrived a short time later.

Events on Saturday were overshadowed by the expected arrival of Governor-elect James Rolph Jr., who was invited to the celebration by Sutter County Supervisor Ed Reeves. Rolph sent a last minute telegram stating he would be unable to attend. Flying events planned for the day, including air races and a dead-stick landing contest, were on schedule, as was a night dance to Schreck's orchestra.[12]

On Sunday, several aerial events were held. The most notable result was Leo Moore from Sacramento landing his Romair biplane precisely on the mark—winning the dead-stick landing contest. Harold Brown put on an impressive aerobatic exhibition in the club's Whirlwind Spartan, and parachute jumps were made during the day from Floyd Nolta's Travel Air.

Army Douglas O-2 observation planes from March Field were a big hit with the crowd. They drew large numbers of spectators to their static display on Saturday and Sunday. They were bigger and faster than any of the commercial planes on the field with the exception of Standard Oil's Ford.

The pilots of the Ford, Allen and Raymond, told airport officials, prior to departing for home Sunday evening, that the new airport's layout and size were impressive. It could handle the largest transports in use. Activities on Sunday concluded with a night dance to Schreck's orchestra.[13]

The final day of the dedication, Monday, September 1, was highlighted with the departures of the army's three O-2s and the few remaining commercial pilots gave occasional passenger rides during the day before finally departing.

P. N. Swenson estimated attendance for the five-day celebration at around five thousand. It was impossible to get an accurate count; no admission was charged. Stock in Sutter Air Terminals was not sold during the event even though Mr. Francisco tried.[14]

The only mishap happened when Hans Kirchner, carrying two passengers, landed short of the runway after a midnight flight in his Waco. He crashed through the property boundary fence, entangling his propeller and damaging his biplane. It was possible the floodlights mounted in the center of the airfield didn't provide adequate visibility for landing on the runway's threshold, or they may have blinded Kirchner.

Regardless, the DOC Aeronautics Branch pulled Kirchner's pilot license for one month, which was the time it took Dudley Cunningham to repair Kirchner's Waco.

While Dudley was repairing the biplane, Kirchner asked Ed Von Geldern, the Yuba City engineer, to paint a red dragon on the fuselage of the green Waco. Von Geldern had an affinity for dragons and alligators. Not long before, he released some alligators into the Feather River at Yuba City. It seems he had them tethered in the river, and the largest, a six-footer, broke his tether and escaped. Von Geldern released the rest to join the escapee. The story of Von Geldern's alligators came to light after J. R. Beyer killed a four-foot gator with an iron pipe along the Yuba City waterfront in April 1930.[15]

Two weeks after the dedication of Sutter Air Terminal, the Yuba-Sutter Flying Club elected Erwin R. Brander president, replacing Herb Keeler. C. W. Reed was elected vice president and business manager. Bill Brander became secretary. The club reported acquiring the new Spartan and selling the damaged Travel Air after rebuild to Dewey Ashford. It was revealed that the club paid for the concrete floor used for dancing during the dedication. A hangar was to be built on the floor for the club's planes and not for Sutter Air Terminal's business offices. Construction of the hangar had already begun.[16]

A newspaper report about Harold Brown's flight at the College City Barbecue implied Brown and the club's new Spartan were now based on Yuba City's new Sutter Air Terminal airport. There had been serious differences between the Yuba-Sutter Flying Club and the James Harshner-Duane Lueth flying school over use of Cheim Field in Marysville.

A week later Ed Reeves and A. R. Arnot joined Harold Brown in the Spartan for a flight to inspect Oakland and San Jose airports for ideas to apply to Yuba City's new airport.[17]

A month-and-a-half after the dedication of Sutter Air Terminal airport, corporation vice president P. N. Swenson was arrested for passing a bad check. Swenson was a Yuba City real estate and insurance broker, and president of the Commercial Club. He had been the most vocal Sutter Air Terminals Corporation officer, speaking to many service clubs throughout the area in support of the new airport.

Swenson was indicted by the grand jury on ten charges of issuing fictitious checks and grand theft. Once in court, he pleaded guilty to one charge of issuing a fictitious check, and the other nine charges were dismissed. The judge sentenced Swenson to prison at San Quentin for one to fourteen years on the check charge. He was paroled at Christmas after a year of incarceration.

Prior to going to court, Swenson resigned as president of the Commercial Club and the club disbanded. During the meeting in which it disbanded, the club reformed into a new club with new officers. The club, which had taken on the Sutter Air Terminal project as a crusade, issued a new mission statement. The new Yuba City Commercial Club would operate on the principles of practical cooperation and sound business ethics, rather than on "visionary plans and projects."[18]

When Swenson resigned as vice president of the Sutter Air Terminals Corporation, J. B. Taylor was chosen as his replacement.[19]

Tom Krull, a Sutter County resident, said the Sutter Air Terminal airport developed on Township Road (the old Franklin-Live Oak Highway) existed until the mid-1930s. Krull lived in a house, which still exists, at the intersection of Nuestro and Township roads. The house was right across from the northwest threshold of the airport's longest diagonal runway. Krull remembered only a single runway in use when he lived there. That runway ran parallel to Township Road, and the hangar with the concrete floor was on the east side of the runway putting the runway very close to Township Road. Krull's childhood bedroom was upstairs. He remembered looking out his window and watching an airplane take off right over his parent's house on a regular schedule. He couldn't remember whether it was a daily occurrence or weekly.[20]

No record of a regular air service operating from Sutter Air Terminal airport has been found. Local residents remember the hangar burning down around 1935, but no corroboration of that fire has turned up. By 1937, only the concrete hangar floor still existed. The rest of the property was barren with no other evidence it had ever been an airport.[21]

IN THE DOLDRUMS of the Great Depression, commercial aviators took whatever flying jobs they could find wherever they found them. Audrey D. Durst, a lead pilot for Pan American Airways, was at one time the owner of Wild Rose Dairy near Marysville. In April 1931, he was flying twice a week from Brownsville, Texas, to Vera Cruz, Mexico, and once a week from Brownsville to San Salvador.[22]

Jimmie Angel was depicted with two of his fifteen Chinese student pilots in a newspaper photograph. The two students are shown examining a machine gun while standing with Angel in front of an aircraft. The students, wearing Chinese military uniforms, were said to have learned aerial machine gunnery, mapping, bombing, and combat flying over the past year from Angel. They were planning to return to China to be commissioned officers and instructors in the Chinese Air Force.[23]

Sterling and Dana Boller, once pilots for defunct Consolidated Air Lines, were well-known in Marysville and Yuba City. In May 1931, they lost their brother Vernon D. Boller in a crop dusting accident. Vernon was flying for Aerial Crop Dusting Corporation of Los Angeles dusting for insects on an orange grove at Porterville. His plane carried eight hundred pounds of sulphur when Boller was just beginning a pass at two hundred feet to dust trees on D. A. Bassett's ranch. He "swooped" down, according to witnesses, "clipped a branch off a roadside tree, and nose-dived into the orange orchard." He was found sitting upright, dead from a broken neck, his hand gripping the control stick.

The Boller family previously suffered unusual tragedy. During the Great War, Vernon D. and his father, Vernon B. Boller, were military pilots in France. Both were shot down on the same day. The father was killed, but the son was unhurt. Theirs was a truly unique situation. It is doubtful there were many, if any, other fathers and sons simultaneously flying combat during the war, much less shot down on the same day. To make things worse for the three brothers, their mother was killed in France when the hospital she was working in as a Red Cross nurse was shelled by German artillery and destroyed. (There has to be a movie script somewhere in this story.) [24]

By 1932, Sterling and Dana Boller were flying air transports for a new airline—Century Pacific Lines.

The first Varney Air Service planes to Marysville from Oakland arrived at Cheim Field despite a rainstorm that hit the area just before their arrival time, and then the planes departed on schedule May 13, 1931. The heavy storm lasted a couple of hours leaving a sheet of water on the runway at

Cheim. The Varney planes' landing gear sent up rooster tails of water spray as they landed and departed. Clay Allen was flying the Varney transport that departed for Sacramento at 5:00 PM, and Joe Taff piloted the last Varney flight of the day into Cheim Field at 7:00 PM.

Varney Air Service announced its freight and passenger rates on May 13. Packages of five pounds sent from the Bay Area to Marysville cost the sender $1.25, plus $0.15 per additional pound. An order telephoned at noon could be delivered to a Marysville business by 3:00 PM. Passenger fare to Sacramento from Marsville was $8.00 round-trip or $5.50 one-way. A trip to Oakland cost $20.00 round-trip and $12.00 one-way; to San Francisco it was $22.50 for a round-trip and $13.00 one-way.

Livingston Irving dusted peaches on Jackson-Diggs' ranch in Sutter County that same day. The one hundred-acre orchard was completely dusted in little over an hour. Irving dusted with sulphur and lead arsenate for the peach twig borer and mildew. Farm adviser R. H. Klamt watched the dusting and declared all trees thoroughly covered by the airplane.[25]

Two new airplanes were flown into Cheim Field from the Spartan factory in Tulsa, Oklahoma, the evening of May 14. Harold Brown was flying the new biplane. A. Dickinson, the factory pilot, arrived in a monoplane, a prototype four-place, low-wing, fabric covered design that preceded Spartan's beautiful all metal Executive monoplane of later years. Dickinson was flying the first Spartan monoplane to visit California. Both planes were demonstrators and Cheim Field was their home base while in the north state.[26]

The first package sent via the new Varney Air Service arrived on May 16. It was for Bradley's Department Store in Marysville from a supplier in San Francisco.[27]

The new runway at Cheim Field was partially oiled, and more work on the airport would be carried out the coming summer. Work to fulfill the city's plans was completed, and the airport in excellent condition. The entire field was smooth and hard; landings and departures could be made in any direction. Low spots in front of hangars were filled in with crushed rock, and a coat of oil was applied to hold down dust as planes taxied. Standard Oil Company donated the oil.[28]

Official inauguration of Varney service occurred on May 18. Two Varney Stinson Detroiters flew into Marysville at 3:00 PM. A strong north wind delayed their arrival by fifteen minutes. Franklin Rose, president of Varney Air Service, was at the controls of one Stinson. Mrs. Rose was his passenger. The initial plan had been for Mrs. Rose, a pilot herself, to lead the two

Stinsons to Cheim Field in her Kittyhawk biplane, but high winds forced a change of plans. Joe Taff, who made his home in Marysville, flew the other Stinson with a load of express freight from the Bay Area. City Councilman Walter Kynoch and mayors of the Twin Cities made speeches welcoming the new service.[29]

Herb Keeler and his aero students at Marysville High School and Yuba Junior College built another glider. It was an American designed Cadet-2 with a wingspan of thirty-nine feet. Towed aloft by an automobile, it had the ability to stay up five minutes in calm air. Other glider designs could only stay up about ninety seconds in calm air. The Cadet-2 weighed 285 pounds without a pilot. Keeler reported the glider was strong enough to be towed behind an airplane, but that was still against DOC regulations.[30]

After minor surgery in September, George T. Boyd Jr. of Yuba City returned to the Curtiss-Wright Flying School at San Mateo.[31]

Ross Trowbridge, manager of Jackson-Diggs' ranch, said dusting the orchard saved time by eliminating the need to stop irrigating and breaking down checks for spray rigs.[32] Livingston Irving's crop duster pilot, Al Polk, crashed in the Jackson-Diggs orchard south of Yuba City. Polk had ended a dusting pass, and his engine lost power while flying at eighty-five miles an hour four feet above the orchard. He turned to make an emergency landing in a nearby bean field, but the engine restarted. He turned even further thinking he could make it back to his landing field, then the engine failed again. He pancaked the plane into a small field. The plane was badly damaged, but Polk suffered only minor injuries.

A Boeing Model 80 tri-motor biplane airliner belonging to Boeing Air Transport crashed April 20, 1932, after pilot Harry Huking tried to land on a meadow next to the Yuba River in the Sierra Nevada during a blizzard. The plane hit high-tension wires and fell into the river. Eight passengers and a copilot were on board. There were no reports of fatalities or damage.[33]

A bizarre parachute jump ended in Sutter County May 19, 1932. Madame Samandra Braescu, champion European parachutist, bailed out of an airplane east of Winters in Yolo County at an altitude of twenty-four thousand feet and landed in a wheat field near Tudor.

Braescu believed she had set a new parachute record. She told a reporter she was in the air almost an hour. A strong south wind carried her away from her jump point to Tudor. George Mortell of Tudor Mercantile Company found her uninjured after she landed. She spoke almost no English making it difficult for anyone to learn what had happened to this woman who unexpectedly floated from the sky.

The pilot of the jump plane was Harry Brashardt of San Francisco. He landed at Sacramento and was told Braescu had come down much further north. She would be driven to Cheim Field at Marysville where he could retrieve her. The two had begun their flight from Alameda Airport. The pilot said he could see Napa, Sacramento, and Clear Lake equidistantly from his plane when she jumped. He estimated the strong south wind carried Madame Braescu forty miles northeast to Tudor.[34]

Madame Braescu, a twenty-three-year-old Romanian, said she already had the women's altitude record of twenty thousand feet in Romania, and jumped from twenty-two thousand feet at Miami, Florida, in January. She had made several unsuccessful attempts to break the world's record of twenty-three thousand feet. She told a reporter, "American parachute ees not good, German good." To emphasize her words, she tossed the American chute away from her. She held a German chute above her head pointing to the name on the bag, HEINECKE, GERMANY. She said when she jumped and pulled the D ring on the American chute, it did not open. She dropped like a rock, and her pilot lost sight of her. She pulled the ring on her reserve chute, and the canopy opened properly.

She said it was very cold and she got sick on the decent swinging back and forth in the turbulent air. She had oxygen, which she discarded when she jumped. Mortell and L. O. Laughlin, a Tudor merchant, were among the first to reach her after she landed in the wheat field. She just missed getting tangled in power lines near her landing. She was very weak. Laughlin helped her get out of the parachutes and she removed her outer fleece-lined leather flying suit.

Brashardt, her pilot, was low on fuel when she jumped. It had taken two hours to climb his Cessna monoplane to twenty-four thousand feet. He flew to Mather Field and refueled. It was there he was told of her safe landing. He said he had two altimeters in his Cessna, and even though she jumped from an indicated twenty-four thousand feet, he said his type of altimeters were inaccurate at such high altitudes. He said the Department of Commerce was going to check the sealed barograph he carried in the Cessna for an accurate reading of his highest altitude. Whether she set a record that day or not is unknown. There was no world organization recording jumps by parachutists.

An Internet search identifies Madame Braescu as Smaranda Braescu who also used the alias Maria Popescu, was known as the "Queen of the

Heights." A Romanian, born in Moldavia in 1897, she was a pioneer aviatrix and said to have become the first Romanian women parachutist in 1928. She is reported to have been a 1931 European parachute champion with a jump from six thousand meters and a 1932 world parachute champion with a jump from 7,200 meters. (The latter jump was probably the one that ended near Tudor).

It is claimed that Madame Braescu was a fighter pilot in World War II, then became a freedom fighter with the anti-communist underground in Romania. She died at Cluj in February 1948 and was buried under an assumed name so the communists could not punish her protectors.[35]

The day after Madame Braescu's landing at Tudor, the fire bell sounded at Marysville's fire station alerting the city. Schools were dismissed and businesses and offices were vacated. Most of the townspeople of Marysville and Yuba City went out into the streets and peered upward. The object of their interest soon appeared. It was the USS *Akron*, a massive two-city block-long dirigible, belonging to the US Navy. It had been sent to the West Coast on a publicity junket. City officials were advised it was coming only a half-an-hour before it arrived. Seeing it approaching from the south, firefighters rang the bell to alert the city at 11:15 AM. Hundreds of people ran to their telephones and called friends and relatives to tell them about the approaching dirigible. So many calls were made the fifteen women at the telephone company's switchboard were swamped. They were unable to get out of the building and see it themselves.

The *Akron* passed over Marysville heading north at two thousand feet. It overflew the towns of Live Oak, Gridley, and then Oroville. Around noon it passed over the Twin Cities once again, this time at a lower altitude.

The *Akron* had departed the naval air station at Sunnyvale (now Moffett Field), at 8:38 AM with its crew of seventy men and a delegation of twenty-four newspaper reporters on board. It flew over Bay Area and valley towns to Sacramento where it circled for fifteen minutes. Then it headed north, unexpectedly, to Marysville and Yuba City. After passing over Marysville the second time on its return to Sunnyvale, it turned towards Woodland. Apparently, it did not fly over Chico. Phone calls came into the Twin Cities switchboard from Chico asking what had become of the dirigible.

The *Akron* was described as the largest aircraft ever built. Its length was 785 feet by 138 feet in diameter. The interior of its outer skin contained 6,500,000 cubic feet of space for helium gas. Inside its body, in addition to the giant gasbags, it carried four Curtiss F9C-2 Sparrowhawk fighters, which could depart from the airship and return to a trapeze that retracted the fighter into the body of the airship while it was in flight. On a single load of fuel for its engines, the *Akron* could travel across the continental United States three times or 10,580 miles. It had the ability to fly at a top speed of eighty-four miles per hour. It carried sixteen heavy machine guns for protection against enemy aircraft.

The helium used for lift was obtained almost exclusively from wells in Texas, which gave the United States control of a most valuable asset in airship technology. Helium, unlike hydrogen gas, is not combustible and therefore much safer to use in airships. The Zeppelin dirigibles flown by the Germans during and after the Great War used hydrogen gas for lift and burned easily when struck by an incendiary bullet.

The huge airship was built in Akron, Ohio. It was housed on the West Coast in an enormous hangar built at Sunnyvale. The hangar still exists on Sunnyvale's Moffett Field and is one of the largest in the world. It is in danger of being torn down, and there is an active group trying to save the hangar for posterity.[36]

MARYSVILLE PUT ON an old-fashioned Fourth of July celebration in 1932, "Guaranteed to kick Old Man Depression into the famous Yuba River." During festivities, an air show was to be held, but names of the pilots who took part are unknown.[37]

Franklin Jones, a native of Meridian in Sutter County, was laid to rest in the town's cemetery in early July. He died in an airplane crash while attempting to land near the resort at Buck's Lake in Plumas County. There was no designated airfield there, but he thought he could land in a meadow near the lake. At his funeral in Meridian, a formation of five planes piloted by his friends from Summit Flying School at Sacramento Municipal Airport flew over the service in tribute to him.[38]

That same month, Harold Brown had to herd sheep to the opposite corner of a pasture he wanted to land in near Gridley. Brown was flying H. J. McManus and C. W. Basset to Basset's ranch in the Manzanita District of Butte County after their car broke down near Marysville. Once over his ranch, Brown decided the Campbell field that adjoined Basset's property looked safer for landing purposes, but it had sheep grazing on it. Brown got them all herded into one corner with his airplane and then landed. When he touched down, the plane felt like it was going to be shaken apart; the ground was deceptively rough. Brown got the plane stopped without turning over and was congratulated for his expertise by his appreciative passengers.[39]

Joe Taff, brother of Mrs. Harold Moore of Sutter County, flew Will Rogers from Hollywood to Marysville in January 1933 for a newspaper convention being held there. The famous cowboy humorist and movie star came to address the convention. He reported the storm he flew through over the Tehachapi Mountains with Taff was more thrilling than a flight over the Andes.[40]

Roy Nicholson was contracted to fly rice seed onto fields in the Sutter Basin on April 1, 1933. About ten thousand acres were to be planted, mostly by his airplane. Seeding rice was done cheaper by plane than the older ground method and it was done much faster. Nicholson had the ability to sow six hundred pounds of rice in six minutes evenly over the field. Nicholson was a Sacramento aviator based at the municipal airport on Freeport Boulevard in Sacramento. Charlie "Red" Jensen was Nicholson's mechanic and swamper during the early 1930s.[41]

Lan B. Maupin reported the plane he and the late Bernard Lanteri built in Lanteri's machine shop during aviation's pioneering years would be placed in a glass house on display at the Oakland Municipal Airport.

What was unusual about Maupin's announcement was that for the first time in three years of speaking to various service clubs about his accomplishments in the early days of aviation in California, he finally admitted publicly that a young man named Cook (It was actually spelled Cooke, Weldon Cooke.) flew the plane. Maupin gave the plane credit for the early records and air meets in which it took part. No longer did he take the credit for the records and air meets in which the *Diamond* was flown. Unfortunately, he didn't directly credit Cooke either; but it was Cooke who flew the plane in all of the meets, and flew all of the record flights set by the Curtiss copy Maupin and Lanteri built. The plane was named the *Diamond* (or *Black Diamond*) for the town in which it was built. In 1909 Black Diamond changed its name to Pittsburg, California. Maupin and Lanteri built the Curtiss copy there in 1910.

Maupin admitted that Cooke was known in Oakland as a pioneer aviator, and Cooke, who was killed in a crash in 1914, should be honored along with the airplane in the airport museum. He added that he himself would be the guest of honor for his part in Oakland's aviation history.[42]

Joe Taff, the Varney airline pilot, who once lived in Marysville, was involved in a serious crash of an airmail plane he was flying with copilot Paul Preston. The plane lost power and crash landed in a swamp north of New

Orleans, Louisiana. In addition to mail and the copilot, Taff had the line superintendent, Ben Catkin, aboard as a passenger. The three men survived the crash landing with minor injuries, but they were in a desperate situation. After walking for several hours through the swamp and traveling only a mile, they found a deserted cabin and tried to light a fire to signal for help, but their matches were too wet. Spending the night in the cabin, they signaled every fifteen minutes with their only flashlight. A Coast Guard cutter finally picked them up. After spending thirty hours in the swamp, Taff had to recuperate from swamp feet and an infection from the swamp water. It was an unlucky week for Taff. A few days after crashing in the swamp, he was reinjured when an inexperienced pilot he was accompanying turned their plane over on the ground.[43]

Elmer "Joe" DeRosa, while dusting beans in September 1934, suffered broken bones, cuts, and bruises after striking a power pole guy wire with the wing tip of the cropduster he was flying for Ray Nicholson of Sacramento. The contract called for him to apply sulphur dust on a bean field at the Pieratt brothers' farm, south of Marysville. He started dusting at 4:00 AM. An hour later he clipped the guy wire. The plane kept flying, but the controls were inoperable. The plane continued a short distance, then dove into the center of the bean field. Nicholson was working on the ground as DeRosa's swamper, loading dust and flagging to keep the plane's passes straight. He saw the crash from the airstrip on the edge of the field. Louis Pieratt arrived on the scene and had the Lipp & Sullivan ambulance rush DeRosa to Rideout Hospital. Later, he was transferred to a hospital in Sacramento.[44]

Robert L. Campbell, a DOC inspector, came to Marysville in November to see how work was coming on Cheim Field. He was checking the work because it was being paid for with SERA funds from the federal government specifically for airport improvement. He conferred with Phil Divver the Marysville city engineer in charge of the work at the airport. Cheim Field had two runways in those early years, which were being improved and graded. Also, drainage was being upgraded for the entire field. Campbell told Divver more money was available because Cheim was on the map of strategically placed airfields in the state.[45]

Hawley Bowlus came to Marysville in October 1934 and spoke to the aviation class at Yuba Junior College about glider flying. Bowlus was the foremost authority on soaring in America. He once was an airframe worker at Ryan Aircraft and helped build Lindbergh's *Spirit of St. Louis*. Later, Lindbergh brought his wife to Bowlus' gliding school in Southern California where they both learned to fly gliders. Bowlus opened a factory in the San Fernando Valley to build gliders, and Herb Keeler, instructor of aeronautics at Yuba College and Marysville High School, spent a summer working at Bowlus' factory learning everything he could about gliders. It was there he bought a two-seat German glider kit to take back to Marysville for his aviation classes to build.

Bowlus' trip to Marysville wasn't just to speak to the students but to help them get started correctly in building the German glider. At Yuba College, Bowlus showed several films on gliding to the entire student body during a special assembly. One reel showed a student being taught to fly a glider. Another film was of Col. Lindbergh and his wife's first glider flights. He told the assembly about his perception of commercial possibilities for gliders and explained how an airplane could tow loaded gliders in a train just like locomotives pull freight cars. It had already been done, he said, with gliders six hundred feet apart in a V formation, but he said towing loaded gliders was only in the experimental stages.

Bowlus said that in 1933 he designed, built, and flew a glider named the *Albatross*. He made a record flight of 150 miles in the new glider. He cited the current glider records: 238 miles was the longest flight, 9,600 feet was the highest flight, and the longest time anyone had stayed aloft was 47 hours and 36 minutes.[46]

In November 1934, Keeler's aeronautics class at Yuba College began building the German sailplane. Instruction for flying the glider would begin after construction was completed.[47]

A year later, Peach Bowl Gliding Club was making auto-tows with its glider at Cheim Field. Members of the club were Boyd Benham, Larry Walton, Buzz Rose, and George Herr (this author's uncle).

Boyd Benham was preparing to fly the club's glider one November day in 1935 at Cheim. He was strapped in the glider. The car pulling him for launch inched forward to take the slack out of the towrope pulling it taut. "Stop!" yelled Benham. He got out and everybody crowded around asking what was wrong. "Just a little pin (fell) out of the rudder strut."

A reporter asked, "What would have happened if you went up without it?" The rudder would have come off, and there would have been a loss of control.

The pin was found, put in place, and the tow began. The car pulled the glider along. At thirty miles per hour the glider lifted off the ground. By the time the car reached forty miles per hour, the glider was so high in the air the towrope was beginning to pull the nose down—so Benham released the rope, turned downwind, and made a good landing. Next, Larry Walton made a flight that ended with the glider stopping one foot from a deep drain ditch paralleling Brown's Valley Road (Highway 20) by the airfield.[48]

CONSOLIDATED AIR LINES (CAL) miraculously rose from bankruptcy in May 1934. Harold Brown, William W. Lawrence, and John P. Waage acquired the company's name and purchased a used Buhl CA-5 Air Sedan from the D. C. Warren Company at Alameda.

The five-passenger Buhl biplane, known as the *Angeleno*, was flown for a world's endurance record on July 12, 1929. Set over Culver City in the south state, the record was 246 hours and 43 minutes. Loren Mendell and Pete Rinehart who flew the *Angeleno* for the record that day, used air-to-air refueling to keep the Buhl aloft.

In the Buhl, Brown and Waage flew charter flights and a scheduled run between Sacramento and Alameda. Passengers then boarded the Loening amphibians of Air Ferries Ltd. for the short cruise from Alameda across the bay to San Francisco.

In September 1934, Consolidated increased its fleet by purchasing a Fokker Super Universal, an eight-passenger, single-engine, high-wing monoplane from Glendale aircraft broker Charlie Babb. Babb had acquired the airliner from Northwest Airways just two weeks prior to selling it to Consolidated. With CAL, the Fokker carried the number two painted on the nose with the name *Silver Eagle*.

On December 4, 1935, Consolidated Air Lines, Inc., reorganized as the Consolidated Aviation Corporation. Officers of the corporation were still Harold F. Brown and John P. Waage with Norman McKay and Mitchell Tyson joining them. The Buhl and the Fokker were also transferred to the new corporation on the same date.[49]

Don C. Reath came to Marysville in February 1935. He claimed he was a member of the National Air Pilots Association promoting a St. Patrick's Day air show at Cheim Field. He proposed an aviators' ball the night before the air show, and he planned to bring pilots from around the state to participate in air races and other events during the show. He said there would be a delayed parachute jump, a bomb-dropping contest, and an OX-5 race. George Zelk, a local highway patrolman who kept his airplane at Cheim Field, said his plane was powered by an OX-5 and considered fast; he wanted to be in the race.

Reath said famous air-racing pilot Lee Miles was going to race at Cheim St. Patrick's Day. George Zelk said he would fly Reath to neighboring airports to help stimulate interest in Marysville's air show.[50]

Curley Graham, who was giving flying lessons at Cheim Field, said he would be taking part in the events. Graham also instructed at Sacramento Municipal Airport. He claimed to have soloed a hundred student pilots without an incident.

Reath deceived the entire community. The aviators' ball was held at Marysville's Memorial Auditorium on the evening of March 16. Attendance at the ball was very poor. Money from the ball's admission fees was supposed to pay for the air show acts to take place the following day. So little money was made from the ball even the dance orchestra couldn't be paid.

The next morning, Sunday, after the St. Patrick's Day parade through downtown Marysville, many locals drove to the northern outskirts to watch the air show. Hundreds of cars lined Brown's Valley Road waiting to turn into the parking area at Cheim Field. Denny McAuliffe, the only traffic officer on hand, soon became swamped and unable to control the traffic.

Reath and his assistants, H. H. Hall, J. H. LaVerne, and D. J. Marcus, were supposed to be there to help manage the air show. Dudley Cunningham, Cheim Field's superintendent, telephoned Western Hotel where Reath and his men were staying in an attempt to locate them. He was told Reath and his men had left for the airport at 2:00 PM. Cunningham realized the organizers of the meet had "flown the coop." He called all of the pilots together and told them the situation. Most agreed to go ahead with the schedule regardless of whether they were paid or not.

George Zelk, Capt. Buck Boatsman, and Jack Scofield, state highway patrol officers, hurried to the scene and straightened out traffic problems.

After the parade downtown ended, passenger flying at the airport had begun. Cunningham and pilots came to an agreement on what was to be done after the unexpected departure of Reath and associates. George Zelk, "Speed" Nolta, and Cunningham talked to C. N. Dalbey, a radioman who agreed to donate his loudspeaker system. The three men arranged for the air races and the stunt flying to take place as originally planned with the pilots and performers knowing there would be no pay for race winners or the stunt flyers. One performer even agreed to do his skywriting service without pay. Dewey Ashford assisted in making these arrangements and agreed to fly an aerobatic exhibition. Other pilots who agreed to fly aerobatic exhibitions without pay were Harry Cham and Bill Fillmore from Oakland. The only stunt that didn't take place that day was the parachute jump. It didn't seem fair to ask a jumper to risk his life for no money.

There were three thousand spectators at Cheim to watch twenty airplanes take part in the St. Patrick's Day air show. Other pilots who took part in the air show were: A. L. Reese, J. Hudson, Ingvald Fagerskog, and Ivor Whitney, all from Sacramento; Mike O'Hair of Colusa; A. L. Scott of Oroville; and Vern Heaton and Dan Best from Woodland.[51]

Harold F. Brown of Consolidated Air Lines was at Cheim Field in his company's Fokker Super Universal on Sunday morning of the air show, but he wasn't there for the festivities. A. L. Scott wasn't there for air racing.

Scott had chartered the Fokker *Silver Eagle* to drop supplies to miners working a mine he owned in the Sierra Nevada, twenty minutes flying time east of Oroville. Scott's Cascade Mine was snowbound by twelve feet of late snow in steep mountains.

Brown had flown the Fokker up to Oroville from his company base at San Francisco Bay Airdrome, Alameda, earlier that morning. At Oroville he loaded the supplies to be dropped to the miners and their families marooned at the mine. Relief pilot John P. Wagge, and third crewmember Fran Mary, accompanied Brown on the flight. Directions given the aircrew to find the mine were inadequate, and supplies were not dropped. The *Silver Eagle* returned to Oroville Airport. John Waage went to the Oroville Court House to study contour maps in the surveyor's office, helping him find the mine. On the second flight of the day, Waage may have been pilot-in-command when the Fokker left Oroville for the mine. To make sure they found the location, they took along the miner who had walked out of the snowbound mountains to notify authorities they were running out of food. A. L. Scott, the owner, also went on the second flight.

This time they found the mine with help from the miners themselves. They had built a fire to help pilots find them. Once a drop zone was determined, food packages were dropped. The miners had disappeared to avoid being stricken by the falling supplies. Packages hit the snow and sunk deeply out of sight. Grateful miners soon retrieved the parcels, which included a leg of beef and the Sunday newspapers.

After the supply drop was made, the *Silver Eagle* returned to Cheim Field and took part in the air show activities.[52] Brown would do another rescue a month later when the eighteen trapped miners needed twelve hundred pounds of food and mining equipment.

In March 1935, Mexican bandits kidnapped Louis Vremsak, a California aviator and mining engineer, in Zacatecas state, Mexico. He was rescued by federal troops March 25. Vremsak was well known in the Yuba-Sutter community. A year before he and his two companions were kidnapped, he had spent two months flying his own plane out of Cheim Field dusting crops.[53]

In April 1935, an unusual barnstorming pair flew into Cheim. Skipper Walker and his crew arrived in a tri-motor Ford named the *Nighthawk*. Another smaller plane of an unknown make accompanied the twelve-passenger airliner. The purpose of the planes' arrival at Cheim was to perform stunt flying in the small plane and passenger rides in the airliner. The two planes landed between rainstorms at Cheim Field during one of the wettest periods of the season—proving to Marysville city officials they truly had an all-weather airport.

Western Airplane Distributors of Kansas City, Missouri, sponsored Walker's two planes and crews. The barnstormers had an advance man who placed a newspaper ad on April 9 offering rides in a fifty thousand dollar tri-motor Ford transport. For one dollar each, passengers were offered a fifteen-mile ride during which they could view the "Floodwaters from the

Consolidated Air Lines' eight-passenger Fokker Super Universal on March 17, 1935, during an air show at Marysville's Cheim Field. The man in the white shirt and tie without a hat and coat is believed to be pilot Harold F. Brown or John Waage who, in the Fokker, flew supplies that day to miners trapped by late snows in the Sierra Nevada.

Air." (Marysville was and still is on occasion completely surrounded by flood water outside its protective levee system.) Shorter rides were offered in the smaller six thousand dollar open cockpit aircraft. The ad stated day or night rides could be taken from 1:00 PM until 10:00 PM after the Ford's arrival on April 10.

Walker and his barnstormers stayed three nights at Marysville. Night rides were very popular; the Ford went up with a full load many times after dark. Landings on the unlit Cheim runway were made by the *Nighthawk* with the aid of a few common "bomb" flares normally used on construction sites. The flares were used to mark limits of the runway.

The barnstormers left Cheim Field after the third day, flying on to a Chico airport where they would carry out their flights again on a new untried community.[54]

Jack Aulthouse, a respected crop duster pilot who had flown dust on many ranches in the upper Sacramento Valley, was killed in late April 1935 dusting a few miles south of Gilroy.[55]

Ken Kleaver, a commercial pilot from Siskiyou County, flew into Cheim Field on June 3. He was piloting a twelve-passenger tri-motor Fokker F 10 airliner. He reported the plane's current value was seventy-five thousand dollars, and it had recently been flying for General Air Lines (a name used by Western Air Express for a short time).[56]

Henry Sackrider and his wife, Delzzie, who ran a photography studio in Marysville for twenty-two years, sold the studio to Earl M. Gilley of Beverly Hills in June. Mrs. Sackrider moved to San Francisco to open a new studio. After Henry got the new owner introduced to the Marysville community, he left to join his wife in San Francisco. Delzzie Sackrider had gained worldwide attention for her photographs of dogs. Henry Sackrider had taken most of the aviation photographs in the Yuba-Sutter community from 1913 until leaving the area in 1935.[57]

Herb Keeler was granted a one-year sabbatical leave from his teaching duties at Yuba College in June. He went immediately to the San Fernando Valley where he worked for the Hawley Bowlus Sailplane Company. He had been employed there previously during the summer of 1934. He gained much skill as an aircraft builder. With his guidance, Marysville High School and Yuba Junior College aviation classes built the first two-place glider ever seen north of the San Francisco Bay Area. The sailplane was completed a few days before school let out for the summer, and Keeler made a successful flight in the craft from Cheim Field.

At San Fernando, Keeler helped Bowlus construct a new type of house trailer employing aircraft-type construction and streamlining. The trailer, designed by Bowlus, had become very popular and Keeler was told the Bowlus factory was swamped with orders for it.[58]

Independent Crop Dusting Company of Oakland transferred employee George Boyd Jr., a Yuba City native, to the Midwest. He was to introduce the California system of aerial seeding and crop dusting to Midwest farmers. The system had been practiced several years and proved to be highly successful. The company sent him to Chicago with a plane and equipment to dust a large acreage of peas grown close to the city. It was reported to be the first crop dusting carried out east of California. The reporter, obviously, hadn't heard of army experiments in the South in the early 1920s and later air work in cotton fields of Southern states.[59]

Consolidated Air Lines pilot Harold Brown was carrying sweet cargo prior to the holiday season of 1935. It was pounds and pounds of Margaret Burnham's candies. Jack Bielby, another CAL pilot and an ex-Wheatlander (California), was suspiciously gaining more weight flying the route.[60]

Consolidated Air Lines was planning to ease back into scheduled airline service. Harold Brown, one of the new officers of CAL, wrote to Marysville mayor F. H. Bartlett and informed him the airline was planning to extend its service to Marysville, Oroville, Chico, Red Bluff, and Redding with one flight daily. Brown asked the mayor in his letter if there would be any landing fee charged for the single trip to Marysville. The mayor replied no fee would be required for landing at Cheim Field.[61]

CAL had reemerged as an air taxi or charter airline in 1934 and was able to exist on a nonscheduled (later scheduled) route from its home field in Alameda to Sacramento. On May 15, 1936, the airline began a connecting route north to Redding stopping at Cheim Field at 11:00 AM on its way to Redding and at 3:30 PM on its way back to Sacramento, then on to San Francisco Bay Airdrome by 5:40 PM. Harold Brown was pilot for this new northern route.[62]

Walter Owen and Vince Vanderford (senior), Sutter and Butte county rice farmers, together bought their own airplane to plant their six hundred acres of rice in 1936. They planned to use the plane for their rice crop and any other rice grower who wanted to pay for it. Ed Kron of Turlock was hired to fly the plane.[63]

A successful air show was held at Cheim Field on the first Sunday of April 1936. Several thousand spectators assembled to watch an aerobatic exhibition and parachute jump. Many wanted to go for rides in a big tri-motor Fokker, which was accompanied by a smaller red Travel Air to Cheim for the air show. Ken Kleaver piloted the twelve-passenger Fokker and Ray Murrell flew the Travel Air. Cy Privett also flew aerobatic acts in the Travel Air, and their parachutist was Miss Dorothy Barden from Scott's Bluff, Nebraska. The other air show pilots were all from Sacramento. Ray Murrell gave rides in the red Travel Air. During each brief ride, he would do aerobatic maneuvers to thrill the folks in his plane and the spectators on the ground.

Miss Barden's parachute jump was delayed until 7:00 PM because of a strong north wind. She claimed to be very experienced with 286 jumps to her credit. But when she jumped, she opened her parachute too soon at an altitude of five thousand feet, and the wind blew her across the Yuba River into a bean field. She had a problem in March when she jumped at Needles in the south state. Her chute ripped open, and she deployed her reserve chute just in time to save herself. She suffered some minor injuries during that jump. Reportedly, she had been jumping for seven years and gained notice in 1932 after she was awarded the first parachute packer's license ever issued to a woman.

There were a dozen airplanes on Cheim Field that Sunday. A few were crop dusting aircraft in for repairs.[64]

There was some criticism about the poor condition of the field at Cheim. It was said to be inadequate for the April air show. It was a dilemma—repairs to the airfield needed to be done, but funds simply were not available for the city airport.

Looking back, it is understandable that the airport was not a high priority for the cash strapped community. The stock market had bottomed out in July 1932 and was ever so slowly beginning to climb upward. It would not return to its August 1929 high until the middle 1950s.

There was an unfortunate scam perpetrated at the April air show. Folks were told if they purchased tickets for an airplane ride, they would get to fly alongside the jump plane and watch Miss Barden make her jump; however, the jump was delayed all day due to the terrific winds. She didn't jump until 7:00 PM, but the ticket hawker kept telling people they would see her jump during their airplane ride. Most who bought rides were back on the ground before Miss Barden had even put on her parachutes.[65]

Mayor Bartlett made it known the hangar situation at Cheim Field was bad; there was only hangar space for a third of the planes based on the

A tri-motor Fokker F 10 transport flown to Cheim Field at Marysville in April 1936 by Ken Kleaver for an air show. From left to right stands Dewey Ashford, Dudley Cunningham, Dorothy Barden, Ken Kleaver, Ray Murrell, and Bill Brander.

airport. He said there was WPA (Actually SERA) money available and he wanted to get five thousand dollars from the government to build a new hangar. He said Chico was building a new hangar with WPA money and Oroville would soon follow.[66]

Once again, Vremsak Agricultural Air Service, based in Los Angeles, sent a crop dusting plane and pilot to Cheim Field to work the season dusting crops in the area. Pilot Del Hay brought, reportedly, the world's largest crop duster to the Marysville airport. The airplane was originally a tri-motor Kreutzer. Its two smaller outboard engines had been removed and a single 330 horsepower J-6 Whirlwind was mounted on the nose. In this configuration the Kreutzer could carry one ton of rice grain for seeding or the same weight of fertilizer or sulphur for dusting.[67]

Del Hay landed the modified Kreutzer, registered NR 71E, on Cheim Field the afternoon of May 1, 1936. He spent four hours and ten minutes on the fourth and the eighth flying around the area inspecting the fields he would be seeding. On May 9, he began flying on the rice seed. He flew twenty-three of the next thirty days. On only two days did he fly less than eight hours; most days he flew ten to fifteen hours a day. The flying consisted of short passes of less than a quarter mile with a 90-degree turn then a

270-degree turn at each end. Once out of seed, he would land on a nearby airstrip and load another ton of seed into the hopper bag by bag. He would take off and do it all over again. Del would start before dawn and fly until after sundown. Horsing the Kreutzer around for as many as fifteen hours a day was an incredible feat of physical strength. By June 10, he had completed his contracts and returned to Los Angeles in the Kreutzer. He brought it back to Marysville in July and August flying over twenty hours dusting crops.[68]

In August, Edwin Grant, another pilot for Vremsak Air Service, was dusting bean fields near Robbins in Sutter County when he lost power during a dusting pass and crashed in a field. He was able to get out of the crashed plane without serious injury, but the eight thousand dollar plane was destroyed by fire. Grant had just taken off with a full load of sulphur before the accident occurred. The burning gasoline ignited the sulphur making an extremely hot fire. There was nothing left of the plane to salvage. It is not known if this airplane was the modified Kreutzer airliner.[69]

Independent Crop Dusting Company in the Bay Area hired Tom Webdell of Yuba City as mechanic. Webdell learned the trade of aircraft repair while working under Dudley Cunningham and Bill Brander at Cheim Field. Webdell's first assignment for his new employer was accompanying George T. Boyd, Jr., on his previously mentioned trip to Chicago.[70]

On May 16, the first CAL charter flight from Marysville to Sacramento was made in the Buhl Air Sedan. In the Buhl, Marysville District Attorney Rucker and two other men went to Paso Robles for a convention. Bill Brander, who had just overhauled its engine, flew the three men to Sacramento. There they changed planes and flew to Oakland on the regular scheduled CAL Fokker Super Universal. From Oakland, the Fokker flew them to Paso Robles. Bill Middleton flew to Sacramento in his own plane and brought Brander back to Marysville. It was an inauspicious start for Consolidated Air Lines' reentry into Northern California airline flying.[71]

A beautiful red Lockheed Vega, with the name Earhart printed on the sides of the fuselage in large letters, was photographed taxiing to the tiedown area at Cheim Field. Was it Amelia Earhart?

The photo was taken some time between 1936 and 1942. There is a solitary male pilot in the plane. The Vega (c/n 171) was Amelia Earhart's during the years 1933 to 1936. She flew it on several record-setting flights. However, when the photo was taken at Cheim, she no longer owned or flew the plane. In 1936, Seth S. Terry of Reno, Nevada, purchased the Vega and had the name Earhart painted on its sides. He later sold it to Glover E. Ruckstell of Boulder City, Nevada, who owned it from 1939 through 1942.[72]

The official inaugural flight of Consolidated Air Lines' northern route connecting flight occurred May 18, 1936, when Harold Brown flew the airline's Fokker Super Universal into Cheim Field at 11:20 AM. He was twenty minutes late because more people signed up for the first flight than expected. He had to quickly get the Buhl and its pilot on line to accompany the Fokker to Cheim. Three passengers rode in the Buhl.

For the inaugural flight, Brown was carrying a heavy load of Bay Area newspapers in the Fokker to transfer to the Sacramento Northern Railroad for further dispersal. He had to leave a large load of auto parts for Marysville's Hust Brothers' auto parts store at Sacramento because there was no room for it. Two of the passengers who boarded in Sacramento were Mr. and Mrs. George Rich. He was eighty-one and she was seventy-nine; it was their first ride in an airplane. They were bound for Chico to visit friends and loved the sixteen-minute flight to Marysville from Sacramento. Another passenger on the inaugural flight was Miss Mary DeVoe, a stewardess for United Airlines, who was going on through to Redding. Frank Lauppe and S. C. Paxton, both from the Sacramento Chamber of Commerce, were on the flight, as was Theodore Leydecker. Marysville's Mrs. Ben Moss had a ticket for the return flight to San Francisco.[73]

A Lockheed Vega, flown by Amelia Earhart on her record setting flights, taxis into the ramp area at Cheim Field. Earhart was not flying it. A man, who purchased the Vega from her, painted her name in huge letters on the fuselage and flew around the country capitalizing on her fame.

Chapter 6

A Vultee V-1A ten-passenger airliner landed at Cheim Field in May. It was a sleek single-engine, all-metal, low-wing, retractable-gear transport that attracted a crowd of spectators. The airplane was more technologically advanced than any airplane to land at Cheim Field. It was a very aerodynamically clean design and very fast. The plane was an ex-American Airlines airliner that was sold to Idaho-Maryland Mining Company, which had a large mine near Grass Valley and a home office in San Francisco. Errol McBoyle, the company's vice president and general manager, flew often between the Bay Area and the mine. The stop at Cheim Field that day was for McBoyle to inspect some horses for sale on a nearby ranch.[74]

With the purchase of the Vultee and another very sophisticated aircraft of the times, a twin-engine Lockheed 10A, like Amelia Earhart's last plane, the Idaho-Maryland Mining Company needed an expert airframe and engine mechanic. They hired Harry Middleton.

Middleton had been working as a mechanic for Mexican airline Aerovias Centrales at that airlines' northern terminus, Grand Central Airport at Glendale. Harry and his wife, who worked as a waitress in the airport restaurant at Grand Central, wanted a quieter lifestyle, so Harry took the job with Idaho-Maryland and they moved to Grass Valley. Harry went to work for the mining company in 1936 at the company's airport, which today is the Grass Valley Airport. Harry would eventually start his own crop dusting business at Cloddy Field in Honcut, a small Butte County community near the northern Yuba County line.[75]

A military aircraft circled Marysville for two-and-a-half hours one night in late May 1936. It dropped eight flares suspended under small parachutes. Dudley Cunningham, the airport superintendent, assumed the plane wanted to land, so he lit flares along the runway to facilitate a landing, but the plane never came down. Another person who was convinced the plane wanted to land, rounded up several automobiles to come to the airport and shine headlights on the runway for the plane with the same result.

A liaison at the new Hamilton Army Air Base north of San Francisco, had warned the Marysville police department a bomber was coming to drop the flares as part of an army exercise being carried out in the area. The police didn't bother to notify the airport superintendent about the flight. The bomber circled the city from 8:00 until 10:30 PM and then returned to Hamilton Field.

Some children visiting Packard Library in Marysville saw the flares coming down and became quite excited. When one child exclaimed, "Ooooo the

Cheim Field, Marysville, looking north circa 1939. A car pulls into the airport off of the Tahoe-Ukiah Highway (now Hwy 20), which is blocked from view by the high levee that surrounds the city of Marysville. At the top center of the photograph is the local slaughterhouse, which still stands on Jack Slough Road, but in 2014 is a wood products plant. Prior to the creation of Cheim Field, an older slaughterhouse was only a short distance to the right of the airport hangars shown in this photo.

stars are falling," they all vacated the library quickly.[76]

Bill Obele, who began flying while living in Marysville, gave up professional flying. He was in Fort Pierre, South Dakota, in August 1936, and put his Eaglrock up for sale or trade with an extra OX-5 motor and a new propeller included. He wanted only $250, but he also wanted to sell an almost new Barling NB-8 Trainer for $875.[77]

In July 1936, Consolidated Air Lines purchased a large tri-motor Stinson Model U airliner from American Airways. The Stinson was a high-wing, eleven-passenger monoplane that had been recently refurbished and was radio-equipped.

New blood and a bigger airplane weren't enough to boost the airline's attraction for potential customers. In 1937, the Depression deepened, once again spelling doom for CAL. The failing company began selling its aircraft once more. The Buhl was sold to Floyd "Speed" Nolta's Willows Flying Service in December 1936. The tri-motor Stinson was sold off at the end of February 1937, and the Fokker Super Universal was the last to go in March 1937. This time Consolidated Air Lines was gone forever.

James E. "Jimmie" Read, the man most responsible for putting Cheim

Field on the map in 1928, was working as a field inspector for the DOC Aeronautics Branch by 1937 based at Union Air Terminal in the Los Angeles area. In April 1937, he was promoted to a new position as an airline inspector and remained at Union Air Terminal.[78]

Northern California counties were being mapped by air starting in the fall of 1937. The aerial mapping photography was done from fourteen thousand-five hundred feet for the U.S. Soil Conservation Service.[79]

In the spring of 1938, a gypsy crop duster, George Curtis Quick, came out from Texas in his plane to dust peach orchards in the Yuba-Sutter area. Guy "Speed" Hughes, a local pilot, worked for Quick as loader. Hughes said Quick came out every spring for several years to dust peaches. Quick, who flew in the National Air Races in the early thirties was great to work for, according to Hughes, but if he disliked you—look out. Hughes remembered a time when there were some folks Quick didn't care for parked beside the road changing a tire on their automobile, dressed in their Sunday best. Quick was dusting a field nearby when he spotted them. He turned his plane right for them, and with unusual precision dumped the rest of his load of sulphur on the hapless souls.[80]

Estal Burch, the first woman who learned to fly in the Yuba-Sutter community, married Ira Douglas Beals, an architect who worked for the firm of Goerge C. Sellon in Sacramento. They were married in December 1938. One wonders if she pursued her interest in flying after her instructor, Jimmy Read, left the area in 1928.[81]

Bill Brander, an expert engine mechanic and professional aviator, force landed his crop duster in the Arboga District, south of Marysville, in late July 1938. He was crop dusting an orchard, lost power, and force landed in a nearby alfalfa field. He skimmed over a pear orchard and a Sacramento Northern Railroad embankment before the crash landing.

He claimed the crash was a result of an attempt on his life. He reported linseed oil had been poured in the crankcase of his motor. He said his plane was kept in the hangar at Cheim Field, and even though the hangar door was locked, anyone could get into the hangar by pushing up the corrugated tin of the hangar's sidewall.[82]

On October 30, 1939, Bill Brander took off from Corning Airport in a brand new Piper Cub Coupe powered by a sixty-five horsepower motor. For some unknown reason, he attempted a roll just after takeoff and crashed. He was killed on impact.

Sutter County farmer Al Micheli and some partners owned the plane.

Brander had been teaching the partners to fly but was alone in the airplane when it crashed. Brander had Commercial Pilot License No. 18436.[83]

SEVERAL OF THE aviators who taught flying or learned to fly at Cheim Airport in 1938 and '39, later became respected commercial operators in the Yuba-Sutter community and surrounding counties after World War II. Some had crop dusting operations still in business in the 1980s and '90s. Among those in operation the longest were Tom and John Bowles, Frank Sue, John "Slim" Davis, Larry Martin, and Ken Onstott. Some of those from 1938 and '39 went into commercial flying elsewhere such as Robert Clark and Alfred Orjala. One Cheim flier, Adolph Del Pero, died during his service in World War II. Others took part in flying for the war effort with the military or as civilian instructors for military training schools or ferried lend-lease warplanes to Alaska for the Russians; these included Tom Bowles, Owen "Pearl" Moore, Nelson "Dewey" Ashford, Roger Brandt, Dick Brandt, and Sherman Perkins. [84]

Cheim Field was the only survivor of the first purpose-built, second-generation airports created in the Yuba-Sutter community in the 1920s and early '30s. Cheim survived until 1954 when the airport was closed, and the land was developed as housing tracts. A larger airport was constructed south of Marysville for the Army Air Force during World War II. It was a secondary base that was used for advanced fighter training during World War II. The air base was built near the Alicia railroad spur and, after the war, Marysville Army Air Force Base was turned over to civilian control and renamed Alicia Airport. The author would describe this as a third-generation airport. These airports included those developed for the military during the Second World War with longer runways for high performance aircraft. Most were deactivated and given to the county in which they were located or the nearest city after the war.

Brandt, Perkins & Brandt Company was the first civilian fixed base operator of Alicia Airport. The company was named for its partners Dick Brandt, Sherman Perkins, and Roger Brandt. The ex-army airfield's long paved runways faced properly into the prevailing winds, so there was no reason to keep Cheim Field with its unpaved slightly crosswind runway open. After Cheim Field closed, Alicia Airport was renamed Marysville Airport. It is now officially designated as Yuba County Airport on all air maps.

Across the river, Yuba City and Sutter County finally acquired a permanent airport in 1947. Now known as Sutter County Airport, it is located

CHAPTER 6 193

Jackson Bottoms became Yuba City Airport in 1947 and in later years was renamed Sutter County Airport. The black line drawn on the photo represents the position and length of the runway in 2014.

on the old Jackson Bottoms property where planes have been landing since 1919. It is near the corner of Second Street and Garden Highway in Yuba City and, as usual, local developers are drooling at the thought of closing the airport. The Feather River and a distance of one mile separate Sutter County and Yuba County airports.

In July 1938 Bill Brander inspects the burnt out carcass of his Waco 10 cropduster, which he escaped from after a crash landing near Cheim Field.

Del Paso Airport's Ingvald Fagerskog and his Travel Air 2000 with which he did early cropdusting and seeding in the Yuba-Sutter area.

Floyd "Speed" Nolta's Willows Flying Service Travel Air promoting an airshow at Willows in the 1930s.

CHAPTER 7

Butte County airships and aeronauts – Colonel Frank Johnson at Chico – Thaddeus Kerns – Orvar "Swede" Meyerhoffer – Butte County aviators at the 1911 San Francisco International Air Meet – Harry Roderick and Harry Newhart – The Mar/McAuliffe fiasco

Early aviation in Butte County yielded more aeronautical experimentation, remarkable aviators, and outstanding flying events during the Exhibition Years and into the 1920s, than any other county in the Sacramento Valley with, arguably, the exception of the Capital City itself. For these reasons, examination of early aviation in Butte County is the next logical step in this study. The study follows that of Yuba County where flying was first introduced in the valley, and precedes Sacramento County, the most populated county and one that was slower to embrace early aeroplane flight.

Was it something in the water in Butte County? Or was it the thought-provoking fantasy of airship sightings in 1896 and 1897 that created so much interest in aerial experimentation in the county? [1]

In a recent book about the 1896 sightings of mysterious flying objects in Northern California, we are told the first occurred in the evening of October 22. Residents of Nevada City spotted three meteors in a line streaking towards Oroville.

The next sighting was an airship seen on the night of November 17 over Sacramento. A light was observed floating over the city presumably carried by an airship invisible in the darkness. Voices were heard aboard the airship. One said, "Lift her up, quick! You are making directly for that steeple." It was reported that hundreds saw the airship before it left the city.

A description of the airship was given two days later as being, "oblong and egg-shaped with fan-like wheels on either side, whose rapid revolutions, beating the air," propelled it.

The airship sightings continued throughout Northern California until late January 1897, when the last sighting was made near Lodi. After this date, it is written that airships were reported in Texas and other states east of California during 1897.[2]

A few days after the Sacramento sightings, George D. Collins, a San Francisco lawyer, claimed to represent the inventor of the airship. He said, "It flies, it hails from Oroville," and it was, "... safely housed ... near San Francisco." He promised an exhibition soon and said the airship could be flown to New York at any time.[3]

These were bold claims made eight years before Capt. Thomas S. Baldwin made the first corroborated successful manned dirigible flight in America.[4]

Collins reported the inventor flew his airship from Oroville to Sacramento, which explained the November sightings, and then he flew on to the Bay Area landing at a secret location. The airship was described as being 150-feet long with, "... wings that flapped slowly as it rose." With this being said, there isn't much left of the story to believe, but it certainly sold a lot of newspapers in 1896 and 1897.[5]

Sightings of mysterious airships were pushed off the pages of American newspapers after the country went to war with Spain in February 1898. But it is possible the story of the strange airships with their connection to Oroville may have germinated more than a casual interest in flying in the minds of Butte County citizens.

Free ballooning and later the transitional technology of dirigible airship flying were very prominent in the north state during the first ten years of the twentieth century. Free ballooning would draw modest crowds of spectators at public celebrations, county fairs, etc., but dirigible flights were another matter. The dirigible aeronaut actually had control over his airship. He didn't just take off and blow away with the wind, as did free balloons. With enough motor power to overcome the wind, he could return to his departure point. It deepened interest in the exhibitions and opened the possibilities of taking up paying passengers.

As successful aeroplane flights didn't begin in California until 1910, the public's interest in balloons and dirigibles peaked in Northern California in 1909.

The free balloon *United States* was purchased for the Gordon Bennett balloon races by Dick Ferris. After the races, Ferris shipped the balloon

CHAPTER 7

to California where aeronauts Roy Knabenshue, George B. Harrison, and Capt. P. A. Van Tassell flew it at different venues. Knabenshue and Harrison flew the balloon on the first aerial flight over San Francisco after the great earthquake and fire of 1906.

In 1909, Van Tassell was flying an exhibition at Oroville. His free balloon, the *United States*, broke loose during a windstorm and, unmanned, flew over the Sierra Nevada to Reno, Nevada, and then drifted up to Alturas, California, finally coming to ground. Parts of the balloon were still at Alturas sixteen years later.[6]

Interest in mysterious night airship flights was still high in Chico as late as 1909. The Chico newspaper published a story about a mysterious airship flight over Worcester, Massachusetts, on the night of December 22, 1909. An airship stopped and hovered over the city briefly then departed. Two hours later, it returned and remained over the city for fifteen minutes shining a searchlight on the city, as if hunting for something while moving along very slowly at two thousand feet.[7]

Does the story sound familiar? It was very similar to the newspaper stories in California describing the airship sightings of 1896. Was this a typical story used by newspapers of the period to generate sales? Were these early UFO sightings—who knows?

By 1909 ballooning had taken on the status of a circus act. Three days after the newspaper report about Worcester, a free balloon ascension took place at a Chico park. The ascension in Chico on the wintery December day was evidence of such an act gone awry.

Captain Nemo (real name unknown) had reportedly already defied death for hours on this day, "… by walking around the block, attired in the airiest kind of garments, passing the hat four times before he secured the amount he desired, while the crowd of several hundred waxed impatient." After he gleaned all the coins he could from the crowd that Sunday afternoon, he ascended in his balloon.

Nemo, in pink tights, chorus girl stockings, and a football sweater, soared upward. The spectators were in awe. Upon reaching a thousand feet, he cut loose from the balloon and his parachute deployed.

The chute opened, "Like a boarding-house welcome on payday." Nemo did acrobatics during his descent, and finally just holding on to his trapeze bar with one hand blowing a kiss to the crowd with the other. As he landed, his parachute caught on the limbs of two elm trees in the city park suspending him thirty feet in the air with no way to get down.

He couldn't drop for fear of breaking a leg or worse, and he couldn't reach the limbs of either tree to climb down. By this time, the crowd was yelling advice to the suspended aeronaut none of which was useful.

It was then things got out of control. Reportedly, "Perry Benje, a lineman in a semi-pickled state ... offered aid. He was to be a hero. He secured a rope, announced his intention and, after a short delay in order to give the moving picture men a better chance to make a profit, Benje started to climb the tree to throw the stranded aeronaut a rope. The lifeline was scorned by Nemo and the lineman repaired to the ground."

Benje got angry and yelled up at Nemo all sorts of disagreeable insults. The language was shocking to the mixed company of spectators causing police to intervene.

A reporter wrote, "After a severe clubbing, Benje's mouth was hushed and he was ... off to jail."

After Benje was removed from the scene, Nemo was still stuck in the tree. Some in the crowd thought they would have to shoot Captain Nemo to get him down. Finally, an Italian sailor appeared, removed his shoes, shinnied up the tree, and handed Nemo a rope. Nemo came down and was very thankful, but still he passed the hat once more; this time it was for the sailor. The crowd eventually drifted away. The balloon had floated on by itself coming down at Fourth and Main streets after being badly torn by tree branches.[8]

The next day, after paying his ten-dollar bail, Benje was released from jail. He said, "Never again will I play the part of the hero, no Carnegie medals for ... muh!"

FIVE WEEKS AFTER Glenn Curtiss made the first successful aeroplane flight in California at the Dominguez Hills Air Meet on January 9, 1910, one of his neophytes, Frank H. Johnson, made the first successful aeroplane flight in the Sacramento Valley at Marysville. One week later, he did the same in Butte County.

On February 19, 1910, Johnson flew before a crowd of over one thousand at Chico's Speedway Park. He was flying his new factory built Standard Model Curtiss biplane, colloquially known as a Curtiss Pusher.

Johnson's flights at Chico were very short straight flights made at low altitude in a level attitude usually without turns. His flights, which took place on Saturday and Sunday, were technically successful, but as entertainment a reporter called them a joke. He wrote, "... in all fairness to the enthusiastic young man, who has spent large sums of money in endeavoring to become an aviator ... Several dashes were made across the oval of the Speedway grounds, yet upon only one occasion ..." did Johnson rise from the ground. On Saturday, he rose to fifteen feet and immediately dropped back to the ground. A wire breaking loose in the wing rigging caused the fast descent. The wire had gone into the spinning propeller and wrapped around the propeller hub cutting through the propeller blade causing the engine to lose power.

After Johnson was forced to land, the strong wind subsided and the air was perfect for flying, but the damaged plane had to be repaired. Once repairs were finished, Johnson attempted a takeoff. He just couldn't get enough thrust to break free from the ground. Flying was cancelled for the rest of the day.

Even the Speedway management was disappointed in Saturday's performance; so much so, they announced Saturday's ticket stubs would be honored with Sunday's tickets, hoping Sunday's performance would be more successful. Track management also stated if Sunday's performance was as bad as Saturday's, Johnson should quit the exhibition business until he acquired an aeroplane capable of handling a common breeze or until he learned to fly properly. Johnson later blamed excessive wind and bad gas acquired in Chico for his poor performance.

Speedway employees confirmed Frank Johnson had flown as high as two hundred feet during his test flights after assembling the Curtiss Saturday morning,. So, Johnson made successful flights on the nineteenth. Unfortunately the flights were before spectators arrived.[9]

On Sunday, a crowd of around one thousand came to the Speedway, but Johnson's flights were a repeat of Saturday's pitiful performance. He roared back and forth across the racetrack only to jump fifteen feet into the air and then settle back to the ground.

The only excitement at Chico Speedway on Sunday happened when Otto Klemmer, driving a sixty horsepower automobile at high speed carrying four passengers around the track, lost control and wiped out six lengths of fence. No one was injured.

Some sixty diehards stayed at the track after the six-car Northern Electric train pulled away from the Speedway for downtown Chico. They were hoping to see a more successful flight by Johnson, but it was not to be. Northern Electric sent no more cars for them, and they walked the two miles into town rather than wait for the regularly scheduled Western

Pacific train at 6:50 PM.[10]

Frank Johnson said early in his career, he was not flying exhibitions for the money, which was wise because it was difficult for early exhibition flyers to get any money from spectators. Many racetracks around the country being used as first generation airports had eight- to ten-foot boundary fences surrounding them to discourage spectators from watching the horse or auto races for free. Why purchase tickets for grandstand seating if you could watch an aeroplane fly from outside the track's fence for free? Flying low to stay beneath the fence tops may have been Johnson's lame effort of forcing folks in the "cheap seats" to buy tickets for his exhibitions.

Another possible reason for Johnson's low flying was his fear that the boundary fence around the track was too high to get over if his engine quit. If that happened while he was outside the track, he would have to glide down without power and land on rough ground; the track was often the only unencumbered level ground to land on.

Julius Schubert, Johnson's mechanic, explained the San Rafael millionaire pilot's poor showing at Chico. Schubert reiterated the broken wire for Saturday's aircraft failure. For Sunday's poor showing, he claimed they were unable to get decent quality gasoline in Chico. He said the gas would not flow through the needle in the plane's carburetor properly.

Schubert, who worked for Glenn Curtiss at the Curtiss factory, could make or repair every part of the Curtiss aeroplane Johnson was flying. Schubert knew the plane inside and out. By allowing one of his New York factory employees to be Johnson's mechanic in California, Glenn Curtiss must have considered Johnson's exhibitions of first flights in the Sacramento Valley important to his company.

Getting over boundary fences was a problem for Johnson. He had hit the fence at Marysville's racetrack a week earlier. A week after his unsuccessful Chico show, he performed the same low flights over the track at Woodland. There he had his plane moved outside the fence and made five flights—one nearly a half-mile in length. On his last flight at Woodland, he just barely cleared the fence while landing back inside the track.[11]

Businessmen from Redding wanted Johnson to make first flights there, but when they tried to get Johnson to sign a contract stating he would fly to an altitude of at least one hundred feet, he wouldn't sign. Apparently he only felt comfortable flying close to the ground, as he had done most of his flights in Northern California.[12]

A few days after Johnson's flights at Chico, it was reported a farmer

CHAPTER 7   201

south of Oroville saw what he thought might be a campfire burning on his property. After rushing to the scene, he discovered a large partially inflated balloon burning on the ground. The gasbag had obviously been used for an ascension miles away and recent high winds carried the balloon to his farm. The farmer extinguished the fire and kept the huge silk bag at his ranch until someone showed up to retrieve it.[13]

Thaddeus Kerns, a Chico teenager, was the first Butte County resident to build and successfully fly an aeroplane. Following him into the air later was Orvar S. T. "Swede" Meyerhoffer, and then possibly Harry Newhart. Also in the mix were local entrepreneurs, Clarence "Candy" Howard and Lawrence Gardella, who tried to purchase or build an aeroplane after witnessing Johnson's exibition in February 1910.

Reportedly, George C. Allen of Chico secured a Curtiss aeroplane agency a week before Frank Johnson flew at Chico's Speedway Park. Allen announced he would be able to sell planes to anyone who wanted to purchase a machine, just as soon as the factory could get the machines to him. It was a pipe dream and nothing ever came of his agency claim.[14]

An unnamed Oroville man negotiated with Frank Johnson on February 18 to buy an aeroplane, but they were unable to agree on terms.[15]

The two wealthy Oroville businessmen, Candy Howard and Lawrence Gardella, were still trying to obtain an aeroplane as soon as possible. Howard went to San Francisco to negotiate for a machine for Gardella and himself. A few local residents wondered how Howard and Gardella planned to use the aircraft. Some thought Gardella would use it to transport himself to his gold dredger at Kentucky Ranch, southeast of Oroville near Wyandotte.[16]

Howard and Gardella founded Western Aviation Company of Oroville in February 1910. The purpose of the company was to acquire an aeroplane and begin flights within ninety days at Oroville. They planned to hire someone to fly the plane. Exhibition flights were to begin as soon as their pilot learned to fly it. Howard and Gardella were obviously impressed by the exorbitant fees aeroplane pilots and owners were getting for exhibition flights in the Bay Area and the rest of the country. They wanted some of that "big" money.

In San Francisco, Candy Howard tried to obtain a Farman biplane from France by negotiating through overseas cables. He and Gardella had settled on a Farman biplane because they had been told many of the successful flights made to date were flown in Farmans. Some early Farman biplanes were built without the lateral control of wing warping or ailerons. When turning, this model Farman did not bank, it skidded around in a flat turn. Because of this lack of lateral control, the aeroplane was touted as not infringing on the Wright brothers' patent. The Oroville men thought the Farman could be flown in air meets, contests, and for hire without the worry of getting sued by the Wrights. But Howard and Gardella were unable to obtain a Farman.[17]

In a March press release, Western Aviation Company wrote it was swamped with applications from people wanting to learn to fly and become the company's pilot. Initially, the best applicant was Jack Cobb. Cobb had experience as a balloonist, and he was knowledgeable in the use of machinery. Those qualities plus his daring attitude made him an outstanding applicant.[18]

The two entrepreneurs had great difficulty obtaining an aeroplane for their projected exhibition business. Locals poked fun at them. The Oroville newspaper, which had been reporting on the sighting of Halley's Comet for about a week on its front page, broached the question was it Halley's Comet they were watching or the headlight on Candy Howard's flying machine?[19]

Howard and Gardella's desires to get into exhibition flying were thought to be dashed after their request to the Wright brothers was returned with the message the Wrights would not sell an aeroplane to anyone who planned to use it for exhibition purposes. The only machines they would sell were those intended strictly for private use.[20]

Jack Cobb also contacted the Wrights asking if it was difficult to learn to fly their aeroplanes. He was dealt a bit of salesmanship from Alpheus Barnes, secretary of the Wright Company, who told him, "We ... believe that anyone can learn to fly successfully within a very short time—say a week." The Wright aeroplanes with dual hand levers were never easy to fly.[21]

Western Aviation Company of Oroville considered purchasing a machine from Glenn Curtiss, but Curtiss, it was discovered, was involved in a patent infringement suit brought against him by the Wrights. The Western Aviation Company did not want to become involved in a lawsuit, so a Curtiss aeroplane was out of the picture.[22]

While Howard and Gardella were trying to buy their way into the flying game, a few Butte County teenagers were entering it by the tried and true method of glider flight.

Thaddeus Kerns, John Dreiss, and another set of Wright brothers, Hiram and John (no relation to Wilbur and Orville) set out to fly gliders built

Chapter 7   203

by their own hands.

Thad Kerns was the first to get into the air after he constructed a glider and flew it from a tall water tankhouse next his Shasta Road home near Chico. He soared out several hundred feet before coming to ground. Before building his glider, Kerns amused the Chico community by flying a small, powered model aeroplane.

Not long after Kern's successful glider flight, John Dreiss, who lived on Park Avenue in Chapmantown, completed construction of the airframe of a glider. He planned to fly it as soon as he could get the wings covered with fabric.[23]

Both the Kerns and Dreiss glider designs were biplane gliders with small tail fins mounted on a beam fuselage. The pilot rode suspended under the wings in the manner of a hang glider. The two wings were mounted one above the other in a configuration known as the (Octave) Chanute truss design, a strong, successful engineering design.

Two days after Kerns' success from the tankhouse roof and Dreiss' airframe completion, John and Hiram Wright made a successful flight in their new glider.

With six boys pulling the glider against the wind on a long rope, the glider was launched into the air, and on its first flight it reached a height of forty feet. Hiram made the first flight, but when the craft began its descent he panicked and jumped from the glider at a height of fifteen feet. He was uninjured, but the glider suffered a little damage. The boys planned to fly it again the following day.[24]

A Sacramento newspaper reporting on the flight stated Thad Kerns, who had already built an aeroplane, would make the repairs to the damaged glider. Upon news the glider would fly again the next day, the women of Chico expected a rain of boys from the sky.[25]

In August, a man in Stirling City, east of Chico in the Sierra Nevada portion of Butte County, climbed the stairs to the third floor of the Mercantile Building and there he stepped out of a window into what he believed was a waiting airship. The forty-foot fall to ground left him uninjured. It appeared John Barlycorn was involved.[26]

THADDEUS KERNS, THE SIXTEEN-YEAR-OLD Chico boy who had been trying for some time to make a successful flight in his homemade aeroplane, was at last successful on September 8, 1910. He made two flights on the Speedway racetrack at a height of ten to fifteen feet above ground. The next day he claimed to have made three or four short flights at the Speedway, smashing his rudder on the ground while landing after the last flight. He said it would be repaired and ready for more flights on the tenth.[27]

The above report from a Sacramento newspaper on the tenth, doesn't jibe with Butte County reports of the same events.

A Butte County reporter stated that Thad Kerns announced to the citizens of Chico he would make a flight from the Speedway Park racerack in his recently completed aeroplane on September 11. On that day, Kerns sped around the track many times, but he did *not* rise from the ground. Afterward, he reported he was not discouraged and would keep trying until he made his machine fly.[28]

The aircraft Kerns was attempting to fly was a copy of the very popular Standard Model Curtiss also known as the Curtiss Pusher. It was a successful design, easier to fly than the Wright aircraft and the most copied design in America during aviation's Exhibition Years (1909–1914).

This was the same Curtiss design Frank Johnson brought to Chico in February to make his less-than-spectacular "first" flights. It was a proven design used for outstanding flights in the hands of Glenn Curtiss, Bud Mars, Charles Willard, Eugene Ely, the exceptional Charlie Hamilton, and later the astounding Lincoln Beachey.

Drawings and plans for the Curtiss were published in *Popular Mechanics*, *Boy's Life*, *Scientific American*, and Victor Loughead's book, *Vehicles of the Air*, as early as 1909.

Throughout America during the Exhibition Years, do-it-yourself aviators built copies of Curtiss' design and Glenn Curtiss didn't seem to mind. Also, it was easier to build than the Wright aeroplane with its complicated twin propellers that needed long bicycle chains running from the engine to the propellers. A big reason to copy Curtiss rather than the Wrights was because the brothers cared very much if someone copied their design, and they had a nasty tendency to slap a court injunction on anyone they caught building a copy of their aeroplane, especially if it was to be flown for profit.

Thad Kerns' first successful aeroplane, the Curtiss copy, was underpowered with its twenty-five horsepower Gray Eagle motor, but it would fly.

On September 12, Thad was making more circuits on the Speedway track. An Oroville reporter wrote that some of Thad's circuits were on the ground, and some were above ground. He was flying! Or was the reporter imagining flight? A Chico reporter wrote that Kerns didn't get off the ground that day.[29]

CHAPTER 7   205

On Monday, the nineteenth, Kerns was again at Speedway attempting to fly. On one attempt his aircraft rose three feet above ground and was caught by, "... a current of air and turned turtle, the propeller being broken by the impact with the ground." Thad was thrown from the aircraft, but not injured. He said he would repair the machine and make another attempt in a few days. Actually, it took Kerns over a month-and-a-half to repair the extensive damage to his Curtiss.

E. O. Klepphahn, an electrician at the Colgate power plant, was building a biplane behind the hotel at Dobbins in October 1910. Julius Bocher was assisting in the construction. The pair claimed to have a thirty horsepower motor, which weighed only fifty pounds, to power the machine. No further reports of their efforts have been found.[30]

ORVAR MEYERHOFFER OF OROVILLE travelled to Sacramento where he witnessed Charlie Hamilton's unusual talent as an exhibition flier at the California State Fair. Orvar was said to have excellent mechanical abilities, and while at the fair he was able to "minutely" inspect Hamilton's aircraft. It was later reported that Ovar was to go up with Hamilton, but before that planned ride, Hamilton suffered a near fatal crash at the fair.

Orvar began building a small model aeroplane, which, if successful in flight, he planned to build and fly a full-sized version. If the model flew successfully, financing would be available immediately to build the full-sized machine, Orvar told a reporter.[31]

A few weeks later, Arthur Irving built and flew a model biplane at Oroville using a ten-foot rubber band to power its propeller. Irving hadn't perfected a control system, but felt it could be accomplished when building a larger example. After a successful flight of eighty-five feet, the model was displayed in the window of Thunen's Cyclery in Oroville. Nothing came of Irving's design, which was based on the Wright Flyer.[32]

The model built by Meyerhoffer was completed by November, and Orvar was showing it around Oroville and presumably giving successful flying exhibitions. The designer and his model impressed Lawrence Gardella and Candy Howard. The three men got together and formed Western Aviation Company. The capital stock was fixed at seventy-five thousand dollars. The purpose of the company was to manufacture flying machines, operate and sell such machines, and give public exhibitions in those machines.

On November 1, City Attorney Carleton Gray prepared the articles of incorporation for the Western Aviation Company, and the company announced a plan to place on the market a new aeroplane invented by Orvar Meyerhoffer. The aeroplane was a triplane of original and unique design. A patent was said to be pending and construction was to begin on the plane soon. The sale of stock would insure enough capital to guarantee construction.[33]

Two days later work began on Western Aviation Company's Meyerhoffer aeroplane in San Francisco, and Orvar made arrangements to use the Pleasanton racetrack for test flights when the machine was finished.[34]

At Thaddeus Kern's camp, repairs were completed on his Curtiss by early November. He announced he was ready to continue his attempts to make a completely successful flight. These were to be his first attempts at flying since his serious crash on September 19 at the Speedway track.[35]

On Sunday, November 13, Kerns was circling the racetrack at Chico's Speedway Park partially on the ground and at times rising several feet into the air. His longest sustained flight of the day was an eighth of a mile at a height of four to ten feet. Further flying was stopped due to the radiator on Kerns' overheating engine being too small. Kerns was reported to be seventeen years old and had begun building his machine more than a year before.[36]

Later in the month, Western Aviation Company added J. M. Chubbuck and M. Schubener to its board of members, increasing it from three to five.[37]

Meyerhoffer's aeroplane was completed on December 4 with its engine installed and ready to fly, but the attorneys charged with obtaining the patent for the machine had not been heard from. Test flights were still planned for the Pleasanton racetrack, and if satisfactory the plane would be entered in the San Francisco International Air Meet to be held in Tanforan Park at San Bruno in January 1911.[38]

A few days later vital information was reported about Meyerhoffer's aeroplane. Even though Orvar did much of the labor himself, the machine was said to have cost four thousand dollars and was built under supervision at California Aero Manufacturing and Supply Company (CAMASCO) in San Francisco. Amongst the Bay Area flying community, the machine was known as a mono-bi-triplane and was inspected by various "experts" who believed the design would be a success. Meyerhoffer told the press he had had many offers by various experts and adventurers to make the first test flight, but Orvar said only he would make the test flight.

Cleve Shaffer, the Bay Area aviation journalist and Pacific Aero Club official, published the best description of the Meyerhoffer triplane in

These Illustrations show the evolution of the three Standard Model Curtiss biplanes built and flown by Thaddeus Kerns during his flying career. They also reflect the design changes of the factory built Standard Model Curtiss aircraft during aviation's Exhibition Years (1909-1914).

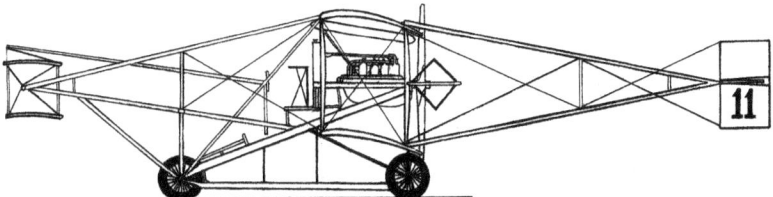

Kerns' first Curtiss copy had the "box kite" appearing elevators mounted on long booms protruding out in front of the pilot and the nose wheel. This configuration created much drag and weight to a design that was already an induced drag nightmare. This first aeroplane, which Kerns began building in the spring of 1910, was not his first flying machine. He had built a glider before this Curtiss copy. A 25 hp. Gray Eagle motor powered his first Curtiss and it got him off the ground but just barely. He had only a few miles per hour between his stall speed and his cruise speed at full throttle. On hot days or with poor gasoline, he couldn't get off the ground at all. He may have upgraded this model with a 40 hp. Elbridge engine in mid-1911. Kerns flew this machine at the San Francisco International Air Meet at Tanforan Park in January 1911. Assigned race number 11 in the amateur class, he was able to get into the air, but each time he got up he crashed on or before landing becoming ineligible for any prize money.

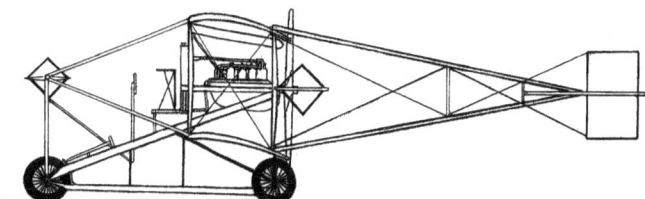

Kerns discarded the "box kite" elevators and long booms when he built his second Curtiss in February 1912 under the guidance of the Brewer brothers at their shop in Berkeley. Kerns copied the latest Curtiss design coming out of the factory with its single plane elevator mounted on short booms directly over the nose wheel.

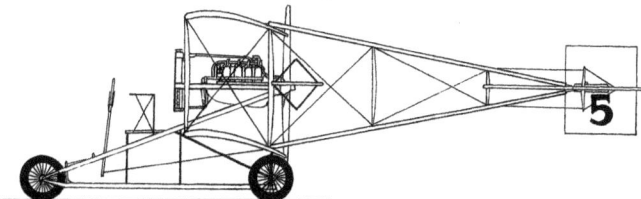

In September 1912, Kerns completed his third Curtiss copy. Again mirroring the models coming from the Curtiss factory at Hammondsport, New York, Kerns discarded the front elevator configuration and moved the elevators to the rear (tail) horizontal stabilizer, which became common practice on nearly all subsequent aircraft designs. This model of the Curtiss with the elimination of all forward booms was described as a "headless" model. Kerns flew the "headless" Curtiss in the third San Francisco International Air Meet held at Tanforan Park on Christmas Day in 1912. Assigned race number five, he made many successful flights in this aircraft.

Aeronautics a few months after the Tanforan meet. He wrote the machine had been called a biplane, a following plane, and a multiplane, but it was technically a triplane. The machine had a forward elevator mounted on long booms and then two wings mounted in tandem like Montgomery's glider, the *Santa Clara*; however, a sixty horsepower six-cylinder Elbridge two-stroke engine, weighing 250 pounds was mounted in the four-foot space between the two top wings. The aft wing had a large cutout in its center for the pusher propeller. Under the motor and five feet below the tandem wings was a third wing. The wings were thirty-two to thirty-three feet long and held in a strong triangular truss giving the plane a V appearance when viewed from either side. The rear tandem wing was set at an angle of incidence much greater than the front and lower wings. The rear wing, with the propeller cutout, extended two feet further out than the other wings. The two panels of the rear wing sloped up slightly towards the propeller cutout giving the wing an inverted dihedral (anhedral) shape. To Shaffer this seemed a detriment by lessening the lifting efficiency.

Two- by six-foot ailerons were mounted on either side between the front and lower wings and pivoting on the front spars. These were operated like those on Curtiss aircraft except that instead of the shoulder yoke, a belt was buckled around the pilot under his arms.

The camber (curvature) of the wings flattened out from the center towards the wingtips. The wings were single surfaced being covered with Naiad fabric tacked only to the underside of the ribs and to the front spar, then laced to the ribs and at the rear to a wire that ran through holes in the trailing edge of the ribs. A drumhead-like tightness resulted from this construction. No wire was used in the rigging, only stranded steel Roebling "Aviator" cable. An unusually strong oak engine mount braced by sixteen-gauge steel tubing held the Elbridge motor, which turned an eight-foot prop at fifteen hundred rpm providing 420 lbs of thrust. An El Arco radiator cooled the engine. Controls for the elevator, rudder, and ailerons worked the same as on Curtiss aeroplanes. Three twenty-inch CAMASCO wide-hub wheels supported the triplane with no shock absorbers. Brakes were installed on the front and rear wheels.[39]

Swede Meyerhoffer got impatient and decided to try flying his plane from the marshy Alameda mud flats rather than make the trek east over the mountains and use the Pleasanton racetrack. He assembled the plane on the mud flats, started the engine, and began a takeoff run. After traveling about two hundred yards, the wheels of his machine bogged down to the hubs in

Chapter 7

At Venice, California, Orvar S. T. "Swede" Meyerhoffer stands next to his Standard J-1, which had "Venice Aero Police" painted in huge letters on the fuselage. He is said to have been the first aerial policeman appointed in the state. Orvar had the longest and most successful flying career of Butte County's pre-Great War aviators.

the soft spongy soil. He tried again the following day with the same results. Finally, he packed up his plane and entrained for Pleasanton.[40]

It is hard to believe Meyerhoffer thought he would be able to fly his plane on his first attempt. One would have thought Orvar learned from the various "experts" hanging around the CAMASCO shops when he was building the triplane, that he would need to spend time "grass cutting" to learn to use the controls and develop a "feel" for the machine.

On December 15, Meyerhoffer was reported to have left the ground during an attempted flight and reached a height of forty feet; then brought the machine back down to a landing. Later in the day, he made another flight. The success of the second flight at Pleasanton prompted Candy Howard to send a telegram to Lawrence Gardella in Oroville stating, "Second flight grand success. Adjusting and making necessary changes. Will fly again Saturday. Very much pleased with trial. Meyerhoffer shows great nerve. C. E. Howard."

A telegram sent earlier by Howard conveyed the intense interest in the flights by Pleasanton residents who, supposedly, tore down sections of fencing around the track to watch Meyerhoffer test fly his plane.

The day of his first flights, Meyerhoffer named his aeroplane *California*. However, *California* was never mentioned again in reference to his plane.

During his last visit to Oroville, Meyerhoffer was optimistic he would fly. He was confident he would bring his plane back to Oroville and make numerous flights once he had learned to fly the plane with ease.[41]

A description of the Pleasanton test flights by Meyerhoffer was published in the *Pleasanton Times* and quoted in the *Oroville Daily Register* on December 19, 1910. "The 90 [sic] horsepower multiplane, designed by Orvar Meyerhoffer of Oroville and which was tried out here at the Pleasanton Training Park Thursday afternoon before a crowd of 1,500 spectators ..." was a success.

The two flights described by the *Pleasanton Times* were not flights of great altitude but did confirm Meyerhoffer's machine left the ground under its own power and would have ascended to a greater height except that Orvar, "... turned his plane's (elevators) so as to keep ..." the aircraft on the ground. Orvar was, "... fearful of his inability to keep the machine righted until he had a little more experience in the game, this (was) his first try in the air."

After this first flight, minor adjustments were made to improve the balance of the aeroplane. Then for his second flight of the day, Orvar started the motor on his machine and from his position two hundred feet east of the grandstand, he came roaring down the track. In front of the grandstand, the aircraft left the ground and rose to a height of ten to twelve feet at which time Meyerhoffer eased the plane back to the ground.

Candy Howard and Mr. Schubener of Western Aviation Inc., the company backing the aeroplane, reported they were quite pleased with the machine and the pilot's accomplishments that day.

Roy Scott, manager of California Aero Manufacturing and Supply Company, was also present for Orvar's test flights. Scott, who claimed to have made several successful flights during his career, told the press he was "more than pleased and he stated that he felt the machine would be a perfect success with very few changes." It was in Scott's CAMASCO shops that the Meyerhoffer aeroplane was built.[42]

By Christmas of 1910, Butte County had not one, but two local residents who were flying their own aeroplanes. Of course the question of control, especially in Meyerhoffer's case, begs an answer. His plane was an

CHAPTER 7   211

original design of untried aerodynamic capability. Thad Kerns was flying a tried and true Curtiss design on which he had made minor modifications.

The issue of control and ability to fly aside, two Butte County citizens had made it into the air at a time in history when successful aeroplane flight was not quite a year old in California.

A great international air meet was scheduled to take place in January 1911 at Tanforan Park, ten miles south of San Francisco. Professional exhibition aviators from the East were invited, as were professionals from England and France. The rule that most excited the two novices in Butte County was amateur aviators were invited to compete against each other for large cash prizes.

Orvar Meyerhoffer reported he and the Western Aviation Company triplane would be entering the international aviation meet. Orvar believed there would be a ten thousand dollar prize for the best flight by an amateur in a machine of his own invention. Actually, prize money for amateur flights at the Tanforan meet was awarded according to a more complicated set of contest rules and not the results of a single flight. The ten thousand dollars may have been the total amount put up for the amateur class prizes, but the cash actually awarded to the amateurs was much less.

Lawrence Gardella reported Meyerhoffer would bring the triplane back to Oroville from the Pleasanton tests to make training flights in preparation for the big meet.[43] Thad Kerns announced in early December he too would be at Tanforan Park. He planned to enter the various contests for honor and prize money. He said he had made several successful short flights, and everything he learned about flying he taught himself. He lamented never having the chance to watch professional aviators fly and was looking forward to studying their flying techniques. He saw the coming meet as a way to improve his flying skills.

Meyerhoffer did not return to Oroville to make training flights. He remained in Pleasanton modifying his triplane and making at least one more flight. This is known because he sent a telegram on December 23 to his backers in Oroville. He informed them of the flight and that he discovered the center of gravity of the triplane was too far to the rear due to the engine being moved in that direction. The telegram stated the engine would be moved forward. Despite the center of gravity problem, Orvar claimed to have flown the plane over a quarter mile at a height of seventeen feet. He explained the adjustments to the machine could only be determined by actual flight. The work of perfecting the aeroplane was progressing well, and he planned other flights soon.[44]

A reporter wrote this description of Orvar's machine: "The aeroplane built by Meyerhoffer possesses many original features, being a biplane, monoplane nor triplane, although it has three planes (wings). The main portion of the aeroplane is somewhat similar to Farman's machine, except that one-third of the top plane, above the engine and operator is missing."[45]

With the Tanforan meet only two weeks away, both of Butte County's aviators were flying, however, Thad Kerns was first into the air and was much more in control of his machine than Orvar Meyerhoffer. This was the result of Kerns' "grass cutting" experimentation so patiently carried out at the Speedway racetrack at Chico. Meyerhoffer had made only a few low-altitude hops, straight without turns, at Pleasanton.

Prior to the meet at Tanforan Park in San Bruno, Glenn Curtiss and two of his professional aviators, Charles F. Willard and J. C. "Bud" Mars, flew a three-day exhibition at Fresno on December 16, 1910.

Charles Willard was Glenn Curtiss' first student and the most experienced professional of the Curtiss exhibition fliers. He had recently gained fame for his flying exhibitions at Los Angeles and Pasadena. He was also chief attraction at the Fresno exhibition where he made two cross-county flights; one was twelve miles in length and the other twenty-five. He made both flights without a hitch. Willard became a rarity among the early exhibition flyers—one of the very few who would live a long and full life.

J. C. "Bud" Mars made more flights at Fresno than Willard or Curtiss. During one flight, he dropped bombs to demonstrate how an aeroplane might be used during wartime. His bombs landed successfully on a target from a height of one thousand feet.[46]

Mars thrilled the crowd at Fresno after his engine quit as he was climbing to set a Pacific coast altitude record. He had just climbed through four thousand feet when he lost power. He dramatically made a steep dive back to the landing field. He, "... narrowly missed plunging into a row of automobiles that lined the starting field. He tilted his (elevators) abruptly, however, and swerved around, coming to ground safely." Even though his failed record attempt was said to be accidental, many of the spectators believed the steep descent was planned.[47]

Glenn Curtiss brought Bud Mars to California as a member of the newly organized Curtiss Exhibition Team because Curtiss' most popular exhibition flyer, Charlie Hamilton, had jumped his contract. Unfortunately for Curtiss, Mars would also jump his contract just two weeks before the

Tanforan Park air meet.

Mars threw over his five thousand dollar contract with Curtiss to fly at Tanforan, and took a fifty thousand dollar contract with Capt. Thomas S. Baldwin to tour the Orient as Baldwin's headline act. By Christmas, Mars had departed on the SS *Wilhelmia* for Asia accompanied by Baldwin and two mechanics. Curtiss was upset. He had intended Mars to be his star attraction at Tanforan. He said, "Mars has cast discredit upon the Curtiss camp by failing to keep his agreement," and he concluded wistfully, "Mars, whom I taught to fly."[48]

Mars was the emerging headliner for Curtiss before he left to join Baldwin. With Hamilton already gone, Mars was to become the risk taker of the Curtiss team. Mars left Curtiss and the United States at a critical time in exhibition flying. Stars were emerging from each of the competing exhibition teams. From the Wright team, Arch Hoxsey and Ralph Johnstone were providing the thrills, much to straight-laced Wilbur and Orville's dissatisfaction. The Moisant team had John Moisant, soon to die in a crash, and the great French aviator, Roland Garros, thrilling crowds. Curtiss had been depending on Charlie Hamilton and the emerging Mars.

With Mars and Hamilton gone, Curtiss could only provide his own safe and sane flying, which was no longer enough to satisfy the crowds. He had Charles Willard and Eugene Ely, both of whom were excellent flyers, but they were not thrill seekers. Lincoln Beachey was new with Curtiss and still considered a novice. However, Beachey would soon become the greatest exhibition pilot in the world—but in January 1911 he was just starting his career flying aeroplanes, and although a professional aeronaut he was registered as an amateur aviator at Tanforan.

FLYING AT THE San Francisco International Air Meet at Tanforan Park started the afternoon of January 6, 1911. The park was next to the small community of San Bruno. Today it is the Tanforan Shopping Center, one mile west of the threshold of San Francisco International Airport's runway One Zero Left.

The most spectacular flights of the first afternoon were trial flights by England's James Radley in his Bleriot XI monoplane and France's Hubert Latham in his Antoinette monoplane. The two men flew over the city of San Francisco, Goat (Yerba Buena) Island, the Wharf, the rail lines of Oakland, and ships moored in the bay. The first flight across the bay was made on this day.

Events officially began Saturday, January 7. By the eighth, Orvar Meyerhoffer could wait no longer; he had to show everyone what he could do. He pulled his machine from the temporary tent hangar provided by the army and began making ready to fly. The first flying period assigned to amateur class aviators had just begun.

Orvar started the engine of his triplane, climbed aboard, and began his takeoff run. It was reported, "He was too impatient to get off the ground and when he tilted his altitude plane (elevator) too sharply the aircraft bucked like a bronco and came down on all fours so hard that one of the running wheels was crushed. Several wires running to the rudder were broken and one of the main supporting rods twisted." Another report described the same event: "Meyerhoffer came out in a natty varnished biplane and landed in a sad heap in the bottom of the swale. It looked rather bad for Meyerhoffer. ... The mules attached to the army ambulance were on the gallop for the scene of the wreck when the megaphone man announced: 'There's no harm done the aviator. He's perfectly safe.'"

Orvar had attempted his takeoff downwind, a big no-no in the flying game. One always takes off into the wind, unless there is little or no wind. There was substantial wind blowing that day. A reporter wrote, not once during the nearly month-long air meet did any other aviator make such a foolhardy mistake. Down in "Calamity Gulch," as the swale became known, Meyerhoffer's aeroplane was reduced to junk and his flying ability was definitely in question.

The Meyerhoffer debacle occurred just after Jack Vilas, in the towering eleven hundred-pound aerial oddity known as the Lamburth Multiplane, made the first of many attempts to fly. John Montgomery, the respected college instructor, glider pilot, and designer, tellingly declared the Lamburth the wave of the future for aeroplane design. This declaration by Montgomery, considered by some on the West Coast as the "father of aviation," reveals his actual knowledge of aeronautics may not have matched the reputation claimed later by his disciples.

For the rest of the month, Lamburth's multiplane made run after run in attempts to fly, only to find it was bound to the ground forever. Its antics caused the spectators to roar with laughter, setting a humiliating tone for others in the amateur class when they demonstrated their planes and their abilities.

Meyerhoffer's performance, following Vilas' in the Lamburth, did little to change the crowd's attitude towards the amateur aviator class at Tanforan.[49]

Chapter 7

Most of the attempts to fly by the amateur aviators were indeed laughable. The exceptions among the amateurs were Lincoln Beachey, a "ringer" from the Curtiss team; Hugh Robinson, another Curtiss pilot; Fred Wiseman from Petaluma, truly a self-taught novice with exceptional flying ability; and another self-taught novice with some flying experience, Oroville's Thaddeus Kerns. Also in this group would be Clarence Walker a San Francisco novice.

When it was time for Thad Kerns to fly, the crowd was displaying a contemptible attitude towards the amateurs. One reporter wrote, "… it was considered [a] 100 to 1 bet that Thad Kerns, the sixteen-year-old Chico birdling, would not do any more than start his engine. Kerns pushed his modified Curtiss …" out onto the field. He "propped" the engine to start it. In the meantime the crowd was getting somewhat unruly. There was much laughter and carrying on. Then Kerns climbed in and took off. The laughing and jeering stopped and became wild applause. He had flown several hundred yards when a gust of wind pushed him down into the ground." The same reporter also wrote, "Some day if he doesn't get killed, young Kerns is going to be as good as the best of them and … his daddy who has frowned on his flying … will be proud of him and maybe the citizens of Chico will make a niche for him in a local hall of fame. … What Kerns accomplished would have made Glenn Curtiss or the Wright brothers envious only a few years ago, and if a few more American boys shall turn out work of the Kerns class, the captains of the airship industry will have to look well to it."[50]

Kerns made his last flight at the meet a few days later—a successful takeoff flying over Calamity Gulch, where Meyerhoffer's flying efforts and those of several other novice pilots had ended abruptly. It appeared Thad would clear the swale successfully, but one of his wheels hit the crest of a hill and the Curtiss slammed nose-first into the ground. It appeared to be a fatal crash. The army sent the freight wagon to retrieve the corpse, but to everyone's surprise Kerns survived the crash with only minor injuries. He told a reporter, "I had a much worse wreck than this up at Chico."

On the same day, George Loose, a San Francisco amateur, also crashed. He was not seriously injured, but his aeroplane and engine, both designed and built by Cleve Shaffer, was destroyed. Fred Wiseman was the only amateur to make a successful flight that day. He exhibited professional qualities and made a sixteen-minute circling flight to different altitudes.[51]

Professional pilots from the Wright and Curtiss exhibition teams made flights of over three hours in duration. But, James Radley stole the show that day when he left the exhibition area over Tanforan Park and flew to different points across San Francisco Bay.

Amateur class aviators who won prize money during the meet were Hugh Robinson, winning the most money, a total of $1,333; then came Fred Wiseman winning $1,200; then Lincoln Beachey who won $800; and winning the least was Clarence Walker with $250. The rest of the amateurs won nothing.

Butte County's two birdmen, Meyerhoffer and Kerns went home broke with smashed aeroplanes; however, they were alive and much wiser. During the meet, they rubbed shoulders with the finest professional aviators in the world including Glenn Curtiss, an icon in the aviation world. Information and connections the two Butte County pilots gained at the Tanforan meet were invaluable. The experience would boost their careers by making them better fliers and better aeroplane builders.

Three of the four money winners in the amateur class were flying Standard Model Curtiss aeroplanes or copies of the same. The only aeroplane flying successfully from Butte County was Thaddeus Kern's Curtiss copy. However, Kern's Curtiss with its twenty-five horsepower Gray Eagle Motor was seriously underpowered and on hot days couldn't get off the ground.

During the Tanforan meet, Oroville citizens received information about it from the Western Aviation Company and Orvar Meyerhoffer. A company press release to Butte County newspapers stated heavy rains fell during the meet preventing Orvar from flying due to dampness loosening the glue in his machine's wooden joints. This report was made on Tuesday, January 10. The reality was Meyerhoffer had already crashed and severely damaged his plane two days before.

On January 20, a puzzling article was published stating Eugene Ely, one of the lead exhibition pilots on the Curtiss team who, only two days before, had landed his Curtiss on a makeshift flight deck of a US warship for the first time, said he had full confidence in Meyerhoffer's aeroplane and would be willing to fly it. Meyerhoffer claimed to have refused Ely's offer, stating he would be the first to fly the triplane.[52]

First to fly? What about the "successful" flights at Pleasanton reported in the Oroville newspapers in which he claimed to have made successful flights in his triplane?

It appears someone in Western Aviation Company was in such a hurry to associate Ely's fame and expertise with the Meyerhoffer aircraft, he forgot important previously published elements while drafting his scenario.

Western Aviation reported it would bring the Meyerhoffer machine

CHAPTER 7

home to Oroville for further testing. The reality was Lawrence Gardella left Oroville on February 2, 1911, for San Francisco to bring the remains of the triplane back to Oroville.

Meyerhoffer returned to Oroville on February 7. The aircraft arrived by rail four days later and was taken to the Kentucky Ranch gold dredger where it was to be rebuilt and "adjusted" in the dredger's machine shop. Further flights were to be made there.

Meyerhoffer supposedly had a photo, which no longer exists, of the triplane taken at Tanforan. The aeroplane was flying at a height of fifteen feet. It is inconceivable that the photo was taken at Tanforan. Meyerhoffer's plane crashed while attempting to take off. The machine needed to be completely rebuilt—it was beyond simple repairs.

It was rebuilt and was reported as having made another flight with Meyerhoffer at the controls in late February. The flight was observed by a large number of spectators who traveled from Oroville to Kentucky Ranch to witness the first flight of the rebuilt machine. Everyone agreed it was a good place to fly from with the dredger's machine shop nearby if repairs were necessary.

During this flight, after reaching "express train" velocity in a cow pasture, Meyerhoffer left the ground after a lengthy three-quarter mile run, then he

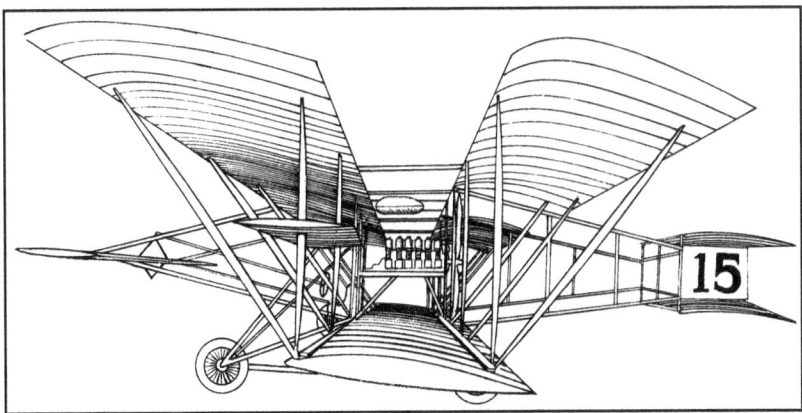

The Meyerhoffer V-Plane, which Orvar attempted to fly at the San Francisco International Air Meet at Tanforan Park (San Bruno) in January 1911. Meyerhoffer was reported to have made at least two very low-level, short, straight hops with no turns at Pleasanton in Alameda County just prior to the air meet at Tanforan Park. At Tanforan in the amateur class, he was assigned identification (race) number 15. For his first flight at Tanforan, he tried to take off downwind and crashed in "Calamity Gulch" severely damaging his plane and eliminating his further participation in the air meet.

immediately set the machine back on the ground. Witnesses of the flight or "hop," which might be more accurate, were sure the aircraft was flyable, but they thought Meyerhoffer was afraid to leave the ground for the height necessary to make an adequate test flight.[53]

Meyerhoffer reportedly made two flights in March. The first was one hundred yards at a height of fifteen feet witnessed by several unnamed citizens. Lawrence Gardella saw the second flight and claimed Orvar flew a distance of two hundred feet at a height of twenty feet. These "flights" should be considered uncontrolled hops. The plane made no turns and did not rise out of what today is known as "ground effect," a cushion of air as high as the length of the airplane's wingspan. Interestingly, the flight of one hundred yards at a height of fifteen feet made on March 12 was reported as the first "successful" flight of the Meyerhoffer airplane. After all that was claimed before, was March 12 the triplane's first successful flight?

A curious report was published in the May issue of *Aeronautics*, which stated Meyerhoffer had been making some good flights at Oroville, but on his last flight he suffered an accident. After a good flight of a half-mile, his triplane's wheels struck a tree causing the plane to noseover into the ground. The belt that activated the ailerons strapped to Orvar's chest saved his life. In the ensuing crash, Orvar was violently thrown forward but the belt kept him in the aeroplane. The triplane was not badly damaged, which was said to be a tribute to its strong construction.[54]

No date was given when Meyerhoffer crashed, but the following suggests the crash occurred before April 1911 when flying experiments with the Meyerhoffer triplane were terminated according to Western Aviation officials. Reportedly, the aeroplane, which cost several thousand dollars to build, would be placed in storage until Orvar Meyerhoffer returned from a Curtiss flying school where *he would learn to fly!* Flights of the triplane were intended to resume once Meyerhoffer returned to Oroville, but he never did.[55]

HARRY RODERICK AND HARRY NEWHART, two Oroville chauffeurs, built a model aeroplane, fifty inches long with a wingspan of forty-six inches. A compressed-air motor powered the model plane. It was successfully demonstrated for a newspaper reporter on March 15. It flew with ease after a takeoff run of twelve feet. The model was said to have an automatic balancing device better than most in use. The two designers were bringing in a draftsman to make drawings so they could apply for a patent. They planned

CHAPTER 7 219

The Roderick and Newhart triplane at the Kentucky Ranch dredger's machine shop where it was built. (The Kentucky Ranch site was in the eastern foothills about six miles south of Wyandotte off Dunstone Drive.) The Western Aviation Company's owners, Lawrence Gardella and Candy Howard, replaced Orvar Meyerhoffer and his triplane with Roderick and the Newhart brothers and their triplane. Both triplanes made short hops, but no successful sustained flight has been adequately corroborated. Roderick's triplane was constructed with parts and materials from Meyerhoffer's plane owned by Gardella and Howard's Western Aviation Company.

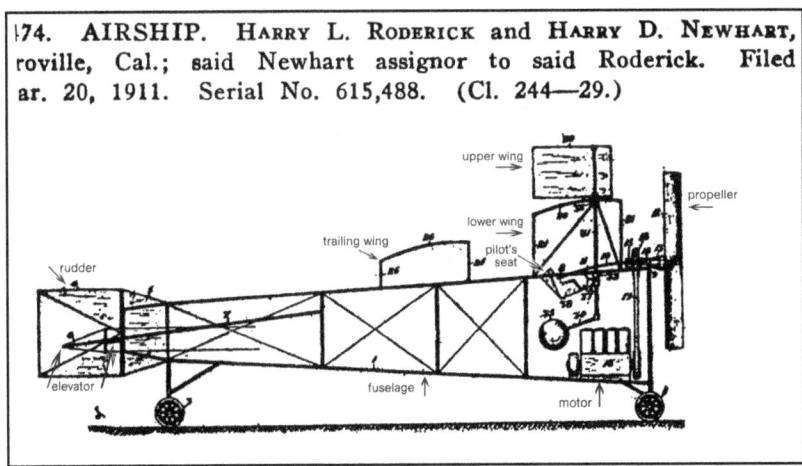

The patent drawing for the Roderick and Newhart triplane filed March 20, 1911, serial number 615,488 (Cl. 244-29) and published in the June 7, 1920 issue of *Aerial Age Weekly*.

to build a full-size example of their design.[56]

The Meyerhoffer aeroplane remained at the Kentucky Ranch dredger site in the possession of Western Aviation Company until April 1911. The company officers, now excluding Orvar Meyerhoffer, decided to back the new Oroville aeroplane designers, Newhart and Roderick, in their efforts to build a new and different aircraft design. Actually, Roderick and Newhart designed the new aeroplane, but Newhart built the machine with a colleague, Fred Hobsen.

Western Aviation provided the new builders use of Gardella's machine shop at Kentucky Ranch. Also, they were given permission to use the engine and airframe materials from the Meyerhoffer triplane. Consequently, the plane was dismantled and its parts and pieces were used in the new Roderick and Newhart machine.[57]

A patent drawing of Harry L. Roderick and Harry D. Newhart's new aeroplane design was published in *Aerial Age Weekly*. Patent No. 1,175,474 was filed on March 20, 1911, "... to Roderick and Newhart of Oroville; said Newhart assignor to said Roderick. Serial No. 615,488 (Cl.244-29)."[58]

There are two photographs of the Roderick and Newhart aircraft extant in Butte County, which are incorrectly identified. They are unquestionably this aircraft, as they match the patent drawing from *Aerial Age Weekly*. The photographs are identified as the first (1910) of Thad Kern's planes. In this author's opinion it is the aeroplane designed and built by Roderick and Newhart in the spring of 1911.[59]

At this point in time, W. P. Hammon, one of Butte County's most influential capitalists, decided to compete with Western Aviation and backed a "Mr. Murray, the dredgerman" [sic], who had designed an aeroplane and built a small model of the design. Reportedly, a number of patents related to the design had been secured, and a number of prominent local capitalists were named who would be purchasing stock in the machine. But Murray and his machine enjoyed a brief flash of publicity, then were never heard of again.[60]

In October 1911, Harry Newhart was said to have made a trial flight in his new aircraft for Western Aviation Company officials. The flight was sustained over a distance of four hundred yards at a height of ten feet. Unfortunately, Western Aviation's new winged hope never flew again. Shortly after its first flight, it was destroyed in a windstorm.[61]

Harry Newhart left the Kentucky Ranch site a few days after the windstorm and traveled to Sacramento where he planned to build another flying machine. He told a reporter before leaving he "... was personally satisfied in his own mind, even if others were not, that his machine was a success in every way." It is possible he went to Chapell & Brainard's aviation shop at Target, a rail stop (no longer in existence) a few miles northwest of

CHAPTER 7 221

Sacramento, located in the middle of today's Sacramento Bypass, a winter flood zone area.[62]

Thaddeus Kerns made his longest flight to date, a distance of three miles in October 1911; he rose to an altitude of one hundred feet during the flight.[63]

On July 3, 1911, Butte County citizens witnessed their first professional flying exhibition, and a spectacular one it was. Chico city officials hired one of Glenn Curtiss' top fliers, Eugene Ely, to fly an exhibition. Ely had emerged from the January Tanforan air meet a national hero after making the first landing of an aeroplane on a warship.

Ely's Chico flights took place at Speedway Park racetrack. Thad Kerns was also hired to fly. A crowd of five thousand assembled to watch the famous aviator and their local birdboy. Three- to five-car Sacramento Northern Electric Railroad passenger trains were running up the valley, packed to suffocation with people. A number of Chico residents walked over two miles south, past Edgar Slough, to Speedway Park to avoid riding the overcrowded trains.

Ely made two flights, each fifteen minutes long, thrilling the crowd. On his second flight, he raced an automobile around the track. It was a Studebaker EMF 30 driven by H. J. Corcoran of Chico.

Corcoran in his Studebaker beat the flying machine by driving the mile distance in one minute and eighteen seconds. Ely later reported he was nursing a sick motor, which was firing on seven of its eight cylinders. Before, after, and in between Ely's aeroplane flights, harness races were held to entertain the large crowd that filled the grandstand and much of the area surrounding the racetrack.

Ely flew exotic stunts developed by other members of the Curtiss Exhibition Team with whom he had trained, and he threw in a couple of maneuvers that were exclusively his. The crowd loved his display. Ovations were common after each flight.

When Thad Kerns' turn came to fly, he gave his engine the gun and scooted around the track. At times he rose about three feet only to settle, embarrassingly, back onto the track. Reportedly, his poor showing was due to engine problems. But it was more probable that a lack of horsepower on a hot July day was the reason he couldn't get off the ground.[64]

In October 1911, Oroville's Western Aviation Company made its last flight with Roderick & Newhart's aeroplane; Thad Kerns completed his longest flight and sadly, Eugene Ely died flying an exhibition at Macon, Georgia.[65]

Kern's October flight was made to a point three miles from his Shasta Road home and back without incident. During the flight, he reached heights of two hundred to three hundred feet. This achievement was reported in the Chico newspaper along with a story of how he first got his name in the paper.

As the story goes, Kerns was known around Chico as, "... a natural genius with machinery." Before he built his first aircraft and took up flying, Kerns had repaired an old automobile that had confounded every automobile mechanic in Chico. It became their "Jonah." Kerns fixed the auto and even drove it to Redding for a Fourth of July celebration and then drove it back to Chico.[66]

Kerns increased his longest flying distance to ten miles later in October. Even though his engine had the capacity to take him further and faster, he said he would proceed slowly and carefully in his experiments learning gradually to master the air. Kerns is believed to have upgraded the powerplant in his Curtiss by installing a forty horsepower Elbridge motor.[67]

Thaddeus distributed a press release in November to Northern California newspapers stating he was embarking on a career as professional exhibition aviator. He further reported he would be making his first professional exhibition flight at Marysville on November 17. After that, he planned to make his way to Los Angeles and take the flying test for an ACA/FAI pilot's license. Eventually, he wanted to go to Panama to compete for the (rumored) ten thousand dollar prize for a flight from the Atlantic Ocean to the Pacific across the Isthmus of Panama.[68]

EXPANDING ON AN INCIDENT briefly described in an earlier chapter, a strange headline graced the Oroville newspaper on November 18. It read: "AVIATOR TO BRAVE SIERRAS BY FEATHER RIVER ROUTE—BUD MARS SELECTS THANKSGIVING AS DATE FOR FLIGHT—expected to pass through Oroville about 4 o'clock in afternoon—PLANS ARE COMPLETE—Birdman will test Thaddeus Kerns' machine in Marysville Sunday."

It appeared the famous Curtiss exhibition flier, J. C. "Bud" Mars, who held assorted flying records, would attempt to cross the Sierra Nevada by following the Western Pacific rail tracks through the mountain range. As the report stated, he would begin his crossing flight at Sacramento on Thanksgiving and pass through Oroville on his way up the Feather River Canyon towards Nevada. A few days before that attempt, Mars was to try out Thad Kerns' Curtiss at Marysville. Mars' machine was down for repairs,

CHAPTER 7   223

said the report, but repairs were to be completed by Thanksgiving Day.[69]

On the morning Mar was to try out Kerns' plane, he made even more promises of aerial feats. In Sunday's paper, Bud Mar reported he was planning several exhibition flights that afternoon from Marysville's Knight Park in Thad Kerns' biplane. One of the flights planned was around the Sutter Buttes.[70] It is interesting the Marysville paper referred to the Bud Mar without the s at the end of his name, and the Oroville paper spelled it Mars like the famous flier.

Was Kerns in on this bit of hokum or was he as surprised as everyone else? Evidence supports the latter. On the date Mars promised a flight at Marysville, Kerns was there with his biplane, but Mars was a no-show.

A large crowd of spectators had arrived at Knight Park on Sunday afternoon of the nineteenth to see the great Bud Mars. As usual for a flying exhibition there, most of the spectators were sitting on the levees, which bordered the racetrack on two sides. How many actually paid to sit in the grandstand inside the track is unknown.

What they saw that Sunday was not the famous Curtiss exhibition pilot, but the seventeen-year-old Chico aviator, Thad Kerns, with his biplane. They waited hours for Mars to show, but he never did. Finally, after many of the spectators had given up and were starting to leave, Kerns started the engine on his plane; he was determined to give the crowd a show. The engine was running roughly at first, but Kerns got it to smooth out. He took off and turned to the northeast passing the slaughterhouse and flying out about three miles in a wide circle there, landing back on the racetrack. He had ventured as high as one hundred feet during the flight. The crowd went home somewhat satisfied.[71]

At first it was a mystery why Bud Mars didn't show for his promised exhibition. Later cracks in his story began to appear. It was revealed Mars was an alias for a man named McAuliffe. A newspaper reported Marysville as Mars' hometown. It came out later the real J. C. "Bud" Mars never used the name McAuliffe nor did he ever live in Marysville.

Thad Kern's budding professional career was taking off. His next paid exhibition was scheduled to take place just two weeks after the Marysville episode. He would fly at Woodland's racetrack on December 3.

Kerns arrived in Woodland December 1 with Ted Orr of San Francisco who was helping to arrange a program of events for the afternoon of Thad's exhibition flight. He was hoping to arrange motorcycle and auto races to fill out the program.

Thad told a Woodland reporter, who came out to the racetrack to interview him as he assembled his aeroplane, his plane would be ready for inspection by the end of the day. He said the local residents were welcome to come out to the track and examine the aeroplane, which he had built himself. He said this was the third aircraft he built, and even though he was only in his teens he had been experimenting with flight for several years in Chico. With his current aeroplane, he reported he made ten successful flights ranging from three to ten miles. During his interview, Kerns said he was trying to earn enough money to build a first class flying machine.

The reporter wrote that Kerns possessed, "... supreme confidence in his ability to fly under any ordinary circumstances, he is a very modest young man, and creates a very favorable impression."[72]

The following day an ad ran in the Woodland paper announcing a "Grand Airship Flight, December 3, 1911 at The Race Track by Thaddeus Kerns In His Biplane – 2:30 o'clock – Admission 50 cents – Children under 6 free [sic]."

Following his exhibition, the paper reported the seventeen-year-old Kerns had made a, "... highly successful flight at the racetrack." There was a large crowd, but, as usual, only about half paid to watch the show. The rest watched from outside the track. Many people were anxious to watch the boy risk his life but were unwilling to pay the fifty-cent admission fee. The excuse of many was they were "stung" or felt taken by the poor showing of Frank H. Johnson when he flew at the same track a year before.

Before his exhibition flight, Kerns inspected every part of his machine at 2:30 PM. At 3:00 he hand-propped his engine, calmly climbed into the seat, and took off. Skimming along the track, he headed north. Just before reaching the three-quarter turn of the track he pulled the nose of the plane up and climbed. He flew away from the track two miles, to the edge of Yolo Orchards, and turned back following the county road until he was opposite the grandstand. He turned directly at the grandstand and buzzed the spectators. The crowd cheered as he passed over waving to them. He banked around and made a perfect landing in a clover patch one hundred yards from the judges' stand. Kerns had a broken wire and a loose stay due to landing on the rough ground, but they were minor problems. His six-mile flight seemed to satisfy everyone watching the performance.

A reporter, though very impressed with Kerns' flying and demeanor, did comment that Kerns' machine seemed crudely constructed and none too strong.[73]

CHAPTER 7

Even though Kerns should have suspected something wasn't right about Mar/McAuliffe, his next involvement with Mar/McAuliffe again turned out badly. Kerns signed a contract to perform with McAuliffe at Buffalo Park in Sacramento December 16–17, 1911. This time Mar would not be using Thad's aeroplane. Mars struck a deal to use the biplane built (but not yet flown successfully) by Chappell and Brainard of Sacramento. It was also a Curtiss copy.

The Chappell-Brainard biplane may have had a serious flaw in its wing design and, most likely, could never be flown successfully, but that didn't matter to Mar/McAuliffe. On the afternoon of December 16, Mar/McAuliffe was exposed as a phony. It happened that the real J. C. "Bud" Mars was in San Francisco, not far from the show, visiting friends. He helped expose the impersonator. It was also revealed that McAuliffe didn't even know how to fly an aeroplane!

Thaddeus tried to save the situation at Buffalo Park, but high winds prevailed making it too dangerous to fly. After a couple of hours waiting on the winds to die, Kerns made a few runs across the park—never leaving the ground.[74] In 1912 a man named H. De La Mar was living in San Fransisco at the Grand Central Hotel. He was trying to insert himself in the aviation community without much luck. He was thought to be Mar/McAuliffe.

According to a brief mention in *Aero*, Thaddeus flew an exhibition at Stockton in December 1911.[75]

Kerns made one of the longest flights of his career on Christmas Day, 1911. He stayed up for eighteen minutes and climbed to an altitude of fifteen hundred feet above Chico.[76]

Sacramento Municipal (now Executive) Airport circa 1938.

Taken at Langley Field, Virginia, in 1918 or 1919, the 126th Observation Squadron in which Dewey Ashford served during the Great War is depicted here. The aircraft are all JN-4s with the exception of the Thomas Morse Scout fighter in the very front lower right. Jimmie Angel had one at Yuba City, which he kept in Dr. Johnson's hangar. It was destroyed when the hangar was blown down by a freak windstorm in November 1926.

CHAPTER 8

Orvar Meyeroffer and his new aviation business – California Aviation Company customers – Thad Kerns' flying career – Hamilton, Scott, and Martin fly at Chico – Kerns' last months

Orvar Meyerhoffer left Oroville with less than pleasant memories. He wrote the following to Thaddeus Kerns one year after leaving Oroville: "Do not be bashful Thaddy whenever you want ... anything ... write us and you can have it. You know Thaddy all the return favor I want is that you fly over the town of Oroville as I intended to do and tell everyone in that town to go chase themselves and that the more anyone up in that country hates me the more I like it. You know Thaddy I have my reasons, especially, Candy Howard and that bunch—they have my great love."

Meyerhoffer was paid seven thousand dollars for his share of Western Aviation Company when he either left the company or was forced out by the company's board members.

At the time he wrote the above to Kerns, Orvar was a managing partner in the California Aviation Company. The company was one of a few in the Bay Area that sold aeronautical supplies to aviators, aeronauts, and aircraft builders.[1]

Orvar had gone into business with E. H. Thompson, a former employee of California Aero Manufacturing and Supply Company, the company that built Orvar's triplane. Meyerhoffer and Thompson began operating as the California Aviation Company in late summer or early fall of 1911. Their place of business, showroom, and manufacturing plant was located at 743 Gough St., San Francisco.

By November 1911, California Aviation Company (CAC) was building a Standard Model Curtiss biplane copy for Miss Margaret Murphy of San

Francisco and a number of gliders for local soaring enthusiasts. The company was the north state distributor for the Roberts aero motors that were quite popular with aviators of the day. In the few months they had been in business, CAC had already sold one Roberts motor.[2]

If Orvar actually went to the San Diego Curtiss flying school on North Island to learn to fly properly as he said he would when he left Oroville, no record of it has been found. Ed Thompson, Orvar's business partner, may have helped him learn to fly on their new company's expansive airfield recently opened on the Easton Estate near Burlingame, south of San Francisco.

Meyerhoffer learned the skill of aeroplane construction when he helped build his triplane in the shop of California Aero Manufacturing and Supply Company during November and December 1910. Then, he was under the watchful eye of Roy Scott. Cleve Shaffer was president of the company, but Scott handled day-to-day operations at the shop.

After Orvar left Western Aviation and Oroville in March 1911, he moved to San Francisco. There he took a job using his new skills to build aeroplanes and gliders for Roy Scott. We know this because in February 1912, after he went into business with E. H. Thompson, Orvar wrote the following to C. E. Conover Company, one of his suppliers: "I, O. S. T. Meyerhoffer for some six months or so had charge of the construction department of the California Aero (Manufacturing and Supply) Company; Roy Scott, manager and know that you got stung for expressage (freight charges) at least on some cloth (aircraft fabric) but you are only a drop in the bucket for I personally have a clear labor claim of over $100 that I have so far been unable to collect, although due over a half year ago and it is in the hands of a good lawyer. Mr. Scott is sued for something like $8,000 [sic].

"As far as the California Aviation Company goes I wish to state that we do not owe anyone a single cent in the world and have a good and only place of its kind in San Francisco and at present have nine machines under construction [sic]." This letter was written in response to negative reports California Aviation Company had received from suppliers when the company was mistaken for Roy Scott's bankrupt California Aero Manufacturing and Supply Company.[3]

On the same subject, S. R. Timothy received a letter from California Aviation Company informing him, "We won our case against Roy (Scott) and he is out on $200 bail, still lawyers cost like …"[4]

A followup note from CAC to Conover stated, "California Aero

CHAPTER 8

(Manufacturing and Supply) is out of it, in the hands of the sheriff, and most of their stock we bought [sic]."[5]

By April 1912, California Aviation Company had built nine flying machines and had contracts to keep the company going for six months.[6]

THE FOLLOWING IS A LIST OF SUPPLIERS and business contacts for California Aviation Company dated 1912. The first list is Book C and then there is Book D. The latter book has some of the same names as Book C, but with more updated information, such as addresses and brief relevant facts. Information in the square brackets [ ] is additional information inserted by the author. The lists are presented here exactly as found with misspellings and other errors included.

Book C 1912 – Roy F. Brewer – 1619 Grove St., Berkeley – [The lead Brewer brother who was principally an aircraft builder in the East Bay and also did some flying. He is believed to have overseen Thad Kerns' building of Kerns' second Curtiss copy.]
Carl Brown – Sacramento inventor of Octo-Plane
Jules Brule – Oakland Motordome – [Didier] Masson Mechanician
P. J. Butler – Vallejo
H. A. Byrnes – San Francisco – Building a Bleriot copy
H. W. Blakeley – New Columbus Hotel – Sacramento St., San Francisco – [Quite active Bay Area aviator]
Boukard & Gandy – Clay St., San Francisco – Monoplane
Capt. [Thomas] Baldwin – Box 78 Madison Square, New York – [Daredevil aeronaut and aviator, a most important transitional figure from balloons to aeroplanes]
E. H. Belinsay – Marlet St., San Francisco
Ivy Baldwin –1117 Union St., Alameda [Real name William Ivy, he was a stunt balloonist who joined the US Army during the Spanish-American War and, as a sergeant, had his balloon brought down by enemy ground fire making him the first US Army airman to be shot down in combat. After the war, he was hired by Tom Baldwin to fly exhibitions as an aeronaut. Later, he went on his own and changed his name to Baldwin linking himself to the famous Captain Tom Baldwin. Eventually, he learned to fly a Curtiss Pusher and did a little exhibition work in Northern California.]
G. L. Beldochi – 716 Fulton St., San Francisco – San Francisco Aero Club

[glider club] bought Ohrts glider
V. Belingsay – Basoett St., Petaluma – Elbridge engine & triplane
Frank Beam – Oak Park [Possibly in Sacramento], California
C. A. Bosworth with Aero – Sherwood Bldg, San Francisco
California Aviation Society – W. H. Hellman Bldg, Los Angeles
Joe Carnan – Haight St., San Francisco – Dirigible
L. D. Coller – Yreka – Tandem Biplane
Weldon B. Cooke – 2244 Mongolia St., Oakland – [A record setting aviator who became famous in Bay Area.]
P. L. Criblett – 1376 Third Ave., Sunset Dist., San Francisco – [He flew out of Cavalry Flat at the Presidio or at least he tried.]
H. De La Mar – Grand Central Hotel, San Francisco
Chas. H. Dobson – Glenn County Garage, Willows
I. J. Durant – 2258 Lincoln Ave., Alameda – 8-cyl, Hall-Scott motor and plane – [possibly Cliff Durant]
S. Doi – Van Ness Ave., San Francisco
Roy E. Drake – 1002 J St., Sacramento
J. F. DeVilla – 66 Joost St., San Francisco [He flew or tried from Cavalry Flat and was said to procure aeroplanes for Pancho Villa.]
Fred Dover – Octavia St., SF – Has original [design] model wants to build
F. C. Dittman – 11th St., Sacramento
Eames Tricycle Co. – 1714 Market St., San Francisco [Another, possibly more important, aeronautical supply house]
William English – Monadnoc [Built an unsuccessful helicopter]
Will L. Frew – Concession manager California Aviation Society – W. H. Hellman Bldg, Los Angeles
Albert S. Frye
Dick Ferris – General Manager California Aviation Society – 305 H. W. Hellman Bldg, Los Angeles – [The most important aviation promoter on the West Coast. He managed all the early air meets in the Dominguez Hills near Los Angeles and many in the north state.]
Roy Francis – Hotel Belmont, San Francisco – [A pioneer Bay Area aviator.]
C. R. Gray – Precita Ave., San Francisco – 1911 Model [Curtiss ?]
Dr. P. George – Marysville – Int. Machine
Norman Green – Geary St., San Francisco
I. R. Gates – Sutter St., San Francisco – [He did some early flying in the Bay Area. He was an important early aviation promoter and later

founded the Gates Flying Circus.]

John Glang – 5th St. San Mateo – propeller maker

J. Gandy – Clay St., San Francisco – Monoplane

Gilmore Airship Company – Box 532 Grass Valley – [Lyman Gilmore talked a good line, made no manned flights, and sold worthless company stock.]

Lowell Hall – Oak St., Oakland – Motor

Jack Handy – Santa Rosa – Bought [Fred] Wiseman's Plane

John W. Hudson – Garage – Gough & Buchanan, San Francisco – [Unsuccessful aeroplane builder and aviator]

Frank H. Johnson – 320 Sansome St., San Francisco – [A famous Bay Area aviator who flew "first" flights in many towns of Northern California. Most of his "firsts" were low, short, and uninspiring.]

Thaduis S. Kearns [Thaddeus Kerns] – RFD #1, Chico – [A proficient teenage aeroplane builder and amateur aviator.]

Geo Loose – Eddy St., SF – [An early San Francisco glider pilot who built modified Demoiselle designs. He had a little success as an aeroplane builder.]

Jack McFadden – Manager [for Fred] Wiseman and salesman for A. Meister & Sons of Sacramento

Ollie Merle – Alameda Ave., Alameda – Interested in 20 HP [motor]

Morrel[l] – 1432 56th Ave., Oakland – [He is believed to be the Morrell who built and flew the huge sausage shaped balloon over Oakland in 1909. It deflated and partially came to ground on its first flight.]

L. B. Maupin – Antioch – [Maupin was half owner and a builder of the Curtiss copy that Weldon Cooke flew so successfully in 1910 – 1912.]

Miss Margaret Murphy – Hayes St., San Francisco – [CAC built a Curtiss copy for her, but no record has been found of her flying it.]

J. C. McTarnahan – 630 Van Ness, San Francisco – [An active aviation promoter, manager, and occasional aviator.]

A. Marchettie – Interested in a Bleriot

Ray L. Mattison – Santa Maria – Monoplane of own design

Ohrt Bros. Aero Mfg & Supply Co. – 1825 McAllister St., San Francisco – [An unknown aviation manufacturing and supply company whose success or lack of is unknown.]

C. S. Osbourne / Woodland Auto Co. – Woodland

E. Osterman – San Jose – Curtiss Motor

Juan Posados – California St., San Francisco – [A South American

aviation student.]
A. C. Peterson – 3rd St., Eureka
Geo Potatato – San Francisco – Reuteuber Motor
J. T. Seeley – Hotel Haywards, Los Angeles
Roy Scott – Franklin 931 (phone number only) – [Scott was manager of the California Aero Manufacturing and Supply Co.]
L. P. Signar – Sutter St., San Francisco – Demoiselle Motor for sale
H. Shick – 10th Ave., San Mateo – Bleriot type with Woerner
Geo Scarf – Nevada City
W. C. Scott – Santa Rosa
C. Schiette – Grove St., San Francisco – Elbridge Motor
Sam Sellack – 5th Ave., San Francisco
Gus Seyfried – Cook St., San Francisco – Building a Bleriot – [A well-known aviation enthusiast in Bay Area.]
R. R. Short – Pasadena
Sacramento Aerial Co. – 1002 J St., Sacramento
Cleve T. Schaffer – 331 Octavia St., San Francisco – [A Pacific Aero Club officer, occasional glider pilot, and president of the California Aero Manufacturing and Supply Co. 1910 – 1912.]
K. Sato – Oakland – Engine
T. C. Starr – Weber St., Stockton
L. Sully – Mill Valley
A. A. Sutro – 1207 Stanyan St., San Francisco – [Son of an ex-mayor of San Francisco, he was a mechanic for Bob Fowler, later built and flew a floatplane extensively as the first aviation concessionaire for the Panama-Pacific International Exposition.]
Frank T. Takahashi – Sonoma City, Sonoma Co.
R. S. Timothy – Burlingame – [aeroplane builder]
L. A. Froberg – Richmond – [An aeroplane builder and aviator at Richmond]
Baison S. Unemara – Haight St., San Francisco
Geo A. Von Ofen – Lyon St., San Francisco – Roberts Motor
Clarence H. Walker – San Mateo
Geo Wagner – Ellis St., San Francisco – Biplane
Fred Wiseman – Sacramento, – Aviator – [He was the most successful Northern California amateur aviator at the 1911 Tanforan meet. He flew the first official US Postal Service sanctioned airmail flight in February 1911 between Petaluma and Santa Rosa, his hometown. It took

Chapter 8

him two days to complete the 15 mile flight. He built and flew a Farman copy with Curtiss add-ons and may have gone into a short-lived aviation business in Sacramento with the Meister family.]

Walter Woerner – Boston Ave., Oakland – [He was a partner in a Bleriot with a Mr. Shick of San Mateo.]

Rex Young – Jackson St., San Francisco

Book D 1912 – California Aviation Company – suppliers and bus. contacts

E. H. Armstrong – Grass Valley – Business Manager Gilmore Airship Co.

Lloyd Bertand – Pierce St., SF – Send lumber for Headless [Curtiss biplane]

E. S. Brainard – Sacramento – [Pioneer aircraft builder in Sacramento]

Frank Bryant – 630 Van Ness, SF – [The premier SF Aviator and Instructor]

California Aviation Company, Inc. – Capitalization $10,000 – stockholders / H. E. Ruggles, F. J. Crisp, James Leach, F. C. Jordan refer Sacramento Mercantile Company – [Assumed to be the stockholders in Thompson and Meyerhoffers' company]

Chappell & Brainard – Sacramento – 1/14/12 – Field about mile long & ½ mile wide recommended by Kerns – [The premier aircraft builders in Sacramento from 1911 to 1917. This airfield was one they established at the Target railstop, which no longer exists but was located in what is now the flood zone of the Yolo-Sacramento Bypass.]

Walter Edwards – Madera – [A known aviator of questionable intelligence. He contracted with the Santa Cruz Water Festival promoters to crash his aircraft into the ocean following a 200-foot vertical dive. Meyerhoffer wanted to buy out his contract to keep him from killing himself. Someone stopped the stunt. Edwards was only to be paid if his plane went completely underwater!]

Eaton Bros – Los Angeles – [Very early aeroplane builders led by Warren Eaton, who was a mechanician for some famous flyers, such as, Lincoln Beachey.]

A. J. Evans – Golconda, Nevada

Roy Francis – 1120 Post St., SF – [Francis was one step behind Frank Bryant at the beginning of Bay Area aviation, but was a success, particularly, in the very early flying of multi-engine aircraft.]

A. E. Fredrickson – Page St., SF

F. Fripp = Del Ora – SF? Wright type – no engine

J. R. Froberg – 21st St., Richmond – [Aircraft builder and aviator]

E[rle] S[tanley] Gardner – Attorney at Law – Oxnard –[Orvar Meyerhoffer and Erle Stanley Gardner became friends when they both lived in Oroville before Gardner became a famous author and Meyerhoffer an aviator.]

Gilmore Airship Co. – [Lyman Gilmore wrote 31 letters to CAC, all of them were about making and purchasing one propeller for his bogus aeroplane. Other than aeronautical enthusiasm, his only aeronautical success was flying early model aeroplanes.]

William Gonzales – 435 16th Ave. Richmond [dist.] SF – [One of two brothers who built a Demoiselle copy, which is now housed at the Hiller Air Museum in San Carlos.]

Tom D[uck] Gunn – Aviator – 5th an Webster St., Oakland – [A successful Chinese aviator who flew in many of the California air meets of 1912 and 1913]

C. A. Hall – Ellis St., SF – Building a Curtiss Bipe with a Maximotor 1/30/12

W. G. T. Hamilton – Hamilton Aeroplane Co. – Riverside

Miss Violet Hansen – Guerrero St., SF – To sew cloth [She was hired to stitch aircraft fabric when needed.]

Robert Harvey – Golden Gate Ave., [SF] – Looking for Teddy [Kerns]

E. B. Heath – Vehicle Co.

Held Promoting Co. – 36th St., Oakland

Harry Holmes – Fresno CA – Licensed aviator used to fly for Remington

E. L. Howard M. D. – Steiner St., SF – Antoinette Machine

G. E. Hughes – Stockton – Has Curtiss ready for motor

Thad Kerns – RFD #1, Chico – New Address 2917 Newbury, Berkeley – Stinger WH

J. R. Lagrive [Aviator] 1246E Webster St. [Stockton]

Henry J. List – SF – School Course

W. P. Lindsey – LA – Parachute Jumper

E. C. Loring – Sec'y 4th of July committee for celebration at Calistoga

Oakland Amateur Aero Club – Bay City Model Aeroplane Contest May 18, 1912 OAAC Aerodrome at Fruitvale

Matthew Mellard – 821 – 8th St. Sacramento – [He possibly built and flew a Curtiss copy at Sacramento.]

Didier Masson – San Rafael – [Masson was a French aviator who flew throughout California and elsewhere in America during the exhibition

years. He went on to fly with the Layfaette Escadrille in WWI.]
Peerless Iron Works – Sacramento [Chapell and Brainard business name]
Fritz Schiller – Nieuport – [This may be the same Schiller who started one of the earliest flying schools in the Los Angeles area at the Dominguez Hills.]
Chappell & Brainard/Peerless Iron Works – Sacramento – Have machine – no engine – wants second hand engine – refer H. De La Mar – has Gray Eagle Motor
P. H. Shuey – Mission St., SF – [J.] De Villa's place of business
Gus Strohmeier – Sec'y Sacramento County Fair Assn
W. H. Tunison – Hotel Wellington – Geary St., SF – [This may be the same Tunison who built a Farman copy for or with Didier Masson.]
C. C. Wing – Washington – SF
R. M. Workman – Sycamore St., Chico
Wycoff – Safety Aero Machine Co. – Santa Cruz
Y. Zahinovich – Firebaugh[7]

THE LISTS AND LETTERS to and from California Aviation Company's suppliers, business contacts, and customers are fascinating. This collection is a relatively new addition to the archives of the California State Library. It provides additional insight into many well-known Northern California aviation personalities such as Meyerhoffer, Gilmore, and Kerns, but also reveals names that were unknown before. Some may have been just tire kickers and had nothing to do with the active aviation scene in the north state. Others might have been active but managed to stay out of the newspapers and aviation trade magazines of the day. The lists reveal more aviation activity in the Sacramento area than previously revealed in available sources.

Reading these lists, one is taken back in time and can look through the papers of an emerging new company at the center of the new technology in Northern California. Many of those who showed interest in flying and those who pursued the science and art of flying in the San Francisco Bay Area and beyond are included here.

Certain letters provide very useful information about California Aviation Company, Orvar Meyerhoffer, and CAC customers.

A letter from CAC to John C. Handy reveals that in the spring of 1912 CAC was begging aviators with even the slightest flying experience to fill contracts with the many north state towns clamoring for exhibitions on the Fourth of July. Interested flyers were told that to get paid they only had to make one flight of ten minutes duration. Unfortunately, for most of the inexperienced aviators available in the Bay Area, ten minutes in the air in their crude machines was as difficult to achieve as ten hours.[8]

Another letter tells of Orvar's brother, Allen Meyerhoffer, who remained in Oroville after Orvar quit Western Aviation Company and left town.[9]

A CAC letter sent to Thad Kerns care of Chapell and Brainard of Sacramento on December 18, 1911, reveals Kerns spent time observing and learning about aeroplane construction and flying from Chapell and Brainard.[10]

CAC received a postcard to Meyerhoffer from E. E. Kerns, Thad's brother, on February 28, 1912. Kern's family took great interest in his flying.[11]

Kern's March 8, 1912, letter to CAC reveals more about the three aircraft he built in his lifetime. He wrote, "... met old friend [Phil] Parmalee ..." Kerns boasted of a fifteen-mile flight he made in his new machine. Kerns may have met Phil Parmalee at an air meet Parmalee flew in Sacramento a few days before. It is of interest that Kerns commented in his letter about making the fifteen-mile flight in his *new* machine. This machine was the one he built in Berkeley under the guidance of the Brewer brothers. Thad had built one underpowered Curtiss copy in Chico and then he built his most successful Curtiss design in Berkeley, which was better constructed and had a more powerful Roberts engine.

CAC correspondence confirms Thad Kerns was sent a contract to fly an exhibition at Calistoga. The date was probably for July 4, 1912. Kerns was to be paid five hundred dollars for the contract through CAC. It required that he be bonded, which was standard procedure for aerial exhibitions. The main stipulation was Kerns must make at least one flight of at least ten minutes in duration before he was to be paid.[12]

Later correspondence tells of Kerns smashing his propeller at Calistoga. One wonders if he completed his exhibition and was paid.

There were few aviators available for exhibitions in Northern California and there was much competitive rumormongering. CAC, in a letter to their engine supplier Roberts Motor Co., refuted Ivy Baldwin's claim the Roberts motor wouldn't get Kerns off the ground at Chico as, "... a pure downright lie and nothing but pure bull."[13]

A CAC rep wrote to Roberts, "Kearn's [sic] new backer was in and wants us to handle him and receive one-third and we will probably do this as he uses a Roberts motor."

The CAC rep went on, "... working with McTarnahan and [Roy] Francis and [Frank] Bryant for 40 percent," and, he wrote, the "Vrang Brothers and [W. H.] Blakely are rustling hard to raise money to buy a Roberts [motor]."[14]

Orvar was the representative who wrote most of CAC's letters to suppliers and customers. He wrote to Maximotor Company that CAC had built a Standard Model Curtiss copy for Harvey Francis and George Van Ofen. He also mentioned CAC's newest flying field at Firebaugh, which was four miles wide and twelve miles long and had, "... perfectly level ground of hard packed alkali sand without a fence or any obstacle whatsoever and a better place to try out [an aeroplane] than any we have seen in the United States."[15]

A CAC letter to the Dougherty Bicycle Company of Fresno orders tire patching materials and other miscellaneous items to be expressed to CAC at Firebaugh.[16]

Firebaugh may have been the location where Meyerhoffer polished his flying skills. Orvar wrote that by mid-May 1912, he had made two fifteen-minute flights in a plane CAC built for Francis and Van Ofen. It was equipped with a secondhand Maximotor and flew well.[17]

Aero reported CAC had, "... recently tested a Curtiss type biplane built for Francis and Van Ofen. The flights were made at the company's new field at Firebaugh, where a branch school is being opened. Meyerhoffer flew in circles the first day, made some figure eights on the second, and a trip over the town of Firebaugh on the third." Orvar had learned to fly "properly" by June 1912.[18]

Meyerhoffer planned to leave around the first of September to fly an exhibition in Amador County. He was to fly the Curtiss that CAC built for Francis and Van Ofen. It was equipped with a Roberts engine. It is not known if Orvar carried out this plan.[19]

The Curtiss biplane that Orvar's partner Ed Thompson flew at Elko, Nevada, in July, had been shipped by rail back to California Aviation Company in San Francisco.[20]

The September trip to Firebaugh had definitely been a learning experience for Orvar. Meyerhoffer and Ed Thompson returned from Firebaugh only after they flight-tested three aeroplanes. One was a Bleriot XI copy flown by Meyerhoffer and powered by a Roberts four-cylinder, fifty horsepower motor. The second was a Curtiss biplane flown by Thompson and powered by the same motor. Beison Unemura flew a plane, designed and built by CAC, which had a biplane center section and monoplane wings. The fuselage was similar to that of the Bleriot and was partially covered with fabric. The wingspan was twenty-eight feet, the chord was five-foot six inches, and the gap between the wings at the center section was eight feet. The plane's length was eighteen feet. The control system was the same as on Curtiss aeroplanes, and the machine was equipped with a fifty horsepower Elbridge motor. Unemura had placed an order with CAC for three more machines of the same design.[21]

Ed Thompson signed a contract to fly at the town Sisson (renamed Mount Shasta in 1922) on September 29. He would fly the exhibition in a CAC Curtiss copy.[22]

There was an air meet for local Bay Area aviators scheduled for November 24, 1912, at Ingleside Coursing Park, a San Francisco racetrack south of Sloat Avenue and the Great Highway. The meet was organized by California Aviation Company. Those flying were Roy Francis with his twin-tractor Gage biplane; Harry Crawford in a biplane; Miss Catherine Thompson with a biplane; and a parachute drop from an aeroplane by Ivy Baldwin. From CAC, Edward Thompson would fly a Curtiss and Orvar Meyerhoffer a monoplane. It is not known whether this meet actually took place, and if it did it was the last time Thompson and Meyerhoffer would fly together as CAC owners.

By the end of 1912, Meyerhoffer had sold out to his partner and left California Aviation Company. He moved from the Bay Area to the warmer climes and clearer skies of Southern California.

In Butte County, there was a familiar face in the flying game; A. L. Smith the Oroville man who assisted Thad Kerns in his flying endeavors when he could. Reportedly, Smith had finished the construction of a flying machine, which he planned to keep in his barn near Palermo, south of Oroville, while carrying out test flying.[23]

Smith told a reporter that even though a number of aviators had come from Butte County, Oroville would have its first aerial exhibition on March 3, 1912, when he would fly over the city. The newspapers and trade magazines were hornswoggled. There was no flight on that date.[24]

At the end of March, Smith was still purchasing metal parts from the Eames Tricycle Company of San Francisco for a Farman biplane copy he was building. In the first week of April, a report in *Aero* claimed Smith was still hard at work on the biplane. It is doubtful that Smith ever finished the Farman. Arthur Smith became very busy as Thad Kerns' mechanic after Kerns began his professional exhibition career.[25]

Ed Workman, another Butte County aeroplane builder, was said to be building his second flying machine in Chico; it was also a Farman biplane.

CHAPTER 8   239

An R. M. Workman of Chico was in the book D 1912 list of the California Aviation Co. papers.[26]

THAD KERNS WAS SPENDING more and more time away from his Chico home pursuing a career as aviator. He didn't find the expertise he needed with Chappell and Brainard at Sacramento. He realized the key to expanding his flying career was to involve himself in the Bay Area flying scene. There, men like the Brewer brothers in Berkeley, and his old friend from Butte County, Swede Meyerhoffer of San Francisco's California Aviation Company, could help him.

In early June 1912, Thad was flying his old Curtiss at CAC's new flying field at Easton, known today as the Easton Addition in west Burlingame. Kerns had purchased a four-cylinder Roberts from CAC, which they recently installed in his old Curtiss after removing the underpowered Gray Eagle engine. He intended to fly for his Aero Club of America pilot's license within the week, and he was scheduled to fly on the Fourth of July at Calistoga for a guaranteed purse. For some unknown reason, Kerns never flew for his ACA/FAI pilot's license.[27]

While flying at Easton, Kerns sold his older Curtiss through CAC and began his professional exhibition career in a new Standard Model Curtiss copy. Victor Morris Smith Jr., a twenty-year-old engineering student at Stanford University, bought Thad's old Curtiss.

Smith moved the Curtiss to his family home near Mountain View in the Bay Area. Two days later, July 13, Smith put on his Stanford red sweater with CLASS OF 1914 emblazoned on it and took off from home to fulfill an obligation to fly over Stanford University and the city of Palo Alto.

Immediately after takeoff at 10:00 AM, Smith put on a short exhibition over Mountain View, then headed for Palo Alto. He passed over Mayfield, then over Stanford University where he followed University Avenue to Ravenswood. He was approaching a landing field at Ravenswood when he hit turbulence and lost control. His Curtiss went into a dive and crashed in a prune orchard. His mother, who had been following Victor's flight in her automobile, saw the plane go out of control at a height of seventy-five feet. Smith was seen hanging from the underside of the plane for an instant, then appeared to throw himself clear of the machine into the possible safety of a prune tree. He missed the tree and hit the ground resulting in his death.

Smith had planned to make several flights out of the makeshift landing field at Ravenswood that Saturday and then more the next day, but it was not to be.[28]

The winds on the day of Smith's final flight were reported to be treacherous. Smith told spectators at Mountain View before he took off, he would be making a record-setting flight. Smith, while at Curtiss Aviation School in San Diego, held the record for flying figure eights as well as the amateur speed record. On June 15, he was said to have qualified for his pilot license at the Curtiss school and returned to Stanford. However, Victor M. Smith is not listed among the early aviators who obtained their ACA/FAI pilot licenses.[29]

Jumping from a Curtiss Pusher prior to an inevitable crash was not an unusual occurrence. The Standard Model Curtiss was known as a pilot killer due to the heavy engine mounted right behind the pilot's seat. In a nose down crash, the engine would brake loose from the wooden airframe and hurtle into the pilot's back crushing him into the ground. Many a Curtiss pilot's escape plan was to throw himself clear at the last second to avoid being crushed. Unfortunately, Smith misjudged his height or ran out of luck.

Thaddeus may have felt guilt over the death of Smith. If so, it was misplaced. Smith's Curtiss had a fifty horsepower motor on it when Smith crashed, not the twenty-five horsepower motor Thad used most of the time he flew it. The additional horsepower should have made the plane much safer to fly. CAC refurbished the plane before selling it to Smith, which also would have made it safer.

Smith had gone to Curtiss Aviation School in April to learn to fly. As mentioned, Smith set records while at the school on North Island at San Diego. This was the finest flying school on the West Coast, so Smith did not lack training.

Even so, Thaddeus never told his parents to whom he sold his first Curtiss nor did they know of Smith's fatal crash. They would learn about the sale and Smith's death under unfortunate circumstances one year later.

THAD KERNS DID NOT FLY for Chico's Spring Festival of 1912. The largest flying exhibition ever held north of Sacramento in California took place during the festival. The exhibitions, a new attraction for the festival, were flown May 3–7.

On May 4, Kerns attended the big flying exhibition at Speedway Park, south of Chico's city limits. He was not asked to fly. As a spectator, he mingled freely with the mechanicians working for Charlie Hamilton and Glenn Martin, picking up timely suggestions and advice from the veterans.

CHAPTER 8   241

Kerns had already announced the day before he would attempt to fly his machine from his Shasta Road home to the aviation field. If the flight was successful, he hoped he would be added to the list of performers at Speedway Park. It is not known if he made the flight, but he did not fly during the Spring Festival air meet.[30]

During the late winter months of 1912, an elite group of exhibition flyers, mostly from the East, were carrying out their trade in the warmer climate of California. Much of their exhibition flying was done in Northern California. In February, Lincoln Beachey, Blanche Scott, Farnum Fish, and Tom Duck Gunn performed at the Emeryville racetrack near Oakland. Early March found Farnum Fish, Blanche Scott, Glenn Martin, Charlie Hamilton, Phil Parmalee, and Horace Kearney flying together in a large air meet at Sacramento's racetrack in Agricultural Park (the old state fairgrounds).

Charlie Hamilton stayed in Sacramento until March 14 when he flew his larger version of a Standard Model Curtiss, the *Hamiltonian*, to Marysville where he flew exhibitions on March 17 and 18.[31]

When the annual Fiesta Aborea, or Spring Festival, was held at Chico in May 1912, most of the elite exhibition pilots had left the West Coast for the gradually warming, more populated, and more profitable eastern half of the United States. Three who remained behind to fly for the Chico festival were Charlie Hamilton, who had a national reputation as a fearless and outstanding exhibition flier; Blanche Scott, who in September 1910 became the first American woman to fly solo; and Glenn Martin, who was an excellent "fancy flying" exhibition pilot from Southern California.[32]

The three fliers began their exhibitions May third at Speedway Park, and the usual attendance problem occurred. More people watched the flying from outside the fence for free than those who bought tickets for grandstand seats inside the fence.

The festival committee scolded the local population in the following day's newspaper. A committee spokesman said, "We put the price of admission ... down to as low ... as possible. ... Automobiles are not taxed; there is no fifty-cent comeback fee for the grandstand—the one fee does it all, and we are presenting birdmen who give thrills. ... We do think that our own people ought to play fair, buy a ticket, and come inside ... We know there are some who cannot in justice to their families pay the price and we are pleased that they can see something of the aviation stunts, but it takes a lot of nerve for persons who can afford automobiles and fine horses and buggies and the fronts of prosperous people to swarm about the outside of an aviation field to get a free show. Its not the right spirit."³³

The flying events on May 3 proved Glenn Martin and Charlie Hamilton had two very different styles of flying. Both styles kept the crowd spellbound; Martin flew a very cool, collected, and scientific exhibition. His every movement was very controlled and thought out, whereas Hamilton flew like a reckless and daring fanatic. A reporter wrote of Hamilton, "He goes into his work with teeth set and face drawn, feeling as much as does his audience the thrills he occasions. His actions are not studied, as are Martin's, he moves on impulse, but both obtain the same result; stir the primal instinct in man or woman that delights to see a fellow being flirt with death."

Martin opened the air show. He took off and circled the racetrack at two hundred feet and came down for a perfect landing. Then Hamilton took off and, like Martin, tested the air. It was decided the air was too rough for Miss Blanche Scott to fly, and the audience was very disappointed.

The two aviators then took off simultaneously, circled the track, and began to race neck and neck. Hamilton's plane was faster, and he gained an extensive lead after which each aviator flew his most daring stunt maneuvers.

Martin began these maneuvers with an "ocean roll" by flying downward at an angle of forty-five degrees and then pulling upward at the same angle with an accompanying side dip. Hamilton flew just over Martin's head in a direct line. Martin dropped down almost to the ground and flew past the grandstand at a speed of sixty miles per hour pulling up abruptly to just miss the fence surrounding the track.

After finishing their stunts, they landed on the track, but Hamilton had a bit of a problem. He insisted on touching down right in front of the grandstand with his plane heading for the same surrounding fence. He shouted to his mechanicians, "Grab her," which they tried to do. Despite their efforts, the plane struck the fence with a loud, "Thwack." Hamilton had jumped clear, as Curtiss pilots tended to do in such situations, and was not injured, but the plane was damaged. It took an hour of hard work to get it flyable for the last exhibition of the day.

Martin's last flight of the day began with his ascension to over one mile above the racetrack. The large number twelve on the underside of his lower wing became invisible to spectators. He then shut off his motor. It was dead quiet on the track. Women in the audience shut their eyes and one screamed. He then spiraled with his wings almost perpendicular to the ground. At the last second, he pulled the plane out of its spiral, flattened his powerless glide, and touched down directly in front of the crowd. They loved it.

Hamilton still had half an hour's hard repair work to go before he was able to get up for his last flight of the day. When he did get into the air, he flew an exhibition of dives and circles for the crowd, but his routine seemed anti-climactic after Martin's thrilling death spiral.

After Hamilton finished his flight, the crowd dispersed quickly in their rush to catch the last Sacramento Northern cars back to Chico and the surrounding communities.[34]

The next day Martin and Hamilton repeated their stunts and added a few new maneuvers of interest. The crowd was pleased to watch Blanche Scott's flying. After taking off, she showed great confidence in her flying ability. She circled the racetrack several times then demonstrated a few sharp dips after which she came down and landed, "… with the grace of a veteran."

Hamilton flew a five-mile race against an automobile driven by A. S. Jones. The Stirling City train happened by on the tracks next to Speedway Park while Hamilton was performing. On an impulse, he dropped to within a few feet pursuing the train for half a mile. He was so close to the cars some brakemen, who were riding on top, sought shelter from the pursuing aeroplane. Motorcycle races finished out the day at the racetrack.

The aviators flew again on a third day. At the conclusion, Martin and Miss Scott had their machines "knocked down" for the Southern Pacific rail trip back to Los Angeles. They planned to catch *The Owl* train at Sacramento to complete their trip south. Martin told a reporter his next flight would be crossing the channel from Balboa to Santa Catalina Island, a distance of twenty-six miles. He was anxious to get back to his aeroplane shop near Hollywood. He said he was looking forward to designing and building an aeroplane with a 240 horsepower engine for Charlie Hamilton to fly in the upcoming Gordon Bennett Cup Race at Chicago in August.[35]

Martin did not build a Gordon Bennett racer for Hamilton and there was no 240 horsepower motor light enough for use on an aeroplane in 1912.[35]

Hamilton and Martin made several new friends in Chico during the days they were there, as did their mechanicians. L. Stearns was working for Martin and Scott, and J. Doty had been with Hamilton since Charlie quit flying dirigibles and took up flying aeroplanes. The two mechanics were honored with a banquet at Brennan's Café on the evening of May 8. The men were scheduled to leave the following day with Stearns going to Balboa and Doty to Sacramento.

This exhibition by famous fliers may have spawned the Chico legend that continues to this day that one of the Wright brothers flew into Patrick Field and stayed at the Patrick's home. Another version of the legend has one of the Wrights flying an exhibition at Chico.

First, let's rule out Wilbur Wright. He died in Dayton, Ohio, of typhoid in May 1912 and the airport known as Patrick Field didn't exist until the 1920s. Orville Wright quit flying aeroplanes prior to America's entry into the Great War, so he couldn't have flown into Patrick Field. The second version of the Wright legend concerning one of them flying an exhibition at Chico is not possible. There is no evidence that the Wrights themselves ever flew an exhibition west of the Mississippi River. Chico brothers Hiram and John Wright flew their glider at Chico in April 1910. Maybe that is where the legend began.

It is possible that an aviator may have flown an aeroplane built by the Wrights at an exhibition in Chico during the Exhibition Years, but this author has found no evidence of such a flight.

What may have happened, instead, was one of the fliers who flew for the 1912 Spring Festival exhibition at Speedway Park across the state highway from the Patrick property, may have stayed with the Patricks while he was performing at the Speedway.[36]

Earlier in the week, Charlie Hamilton took the train down to Sacramento and signed a contract with the Tuesday Club to fly a three-day exhibition there beginning May 10. Barney Oldfield, the most famous auto racer in America, would race Hamilton during flying exhibitions at Sacramento's Agricultural Park racetrack. Proceeds from the races were to go to a fund for orphans.[37]

Charlie Hamilton did something most exhibition fliers would not. Whenever possible, he preferred flying to his exhibition jobs rather than ship his plane by rail like other professional aviators.

At 11:35 in the morning of May 9, Hamilton departed Chico's Speedway Park in the *Hamiltonian*. In twelve minutes, he was over Tres Vias. At 12:05 he passed by Gridley, and shortly after that he began having engine problems. He landed near Live Oak at 12:09. He worked on his engine for six hours before getting it running properly. He took off from the Live Oak area at 6:15 PM and passed by Marysville twenty minutes later, making no stop. He was determined to get to Sacramento.

It was 7:00 PM when Charlie passed East Nicolaus while fighting a vicious headwind. At 7:20, due to the headwind, he was forced to land at Riego, out of gas. Charlie then boarded the Sacramento Northern electric train, whose rails he had been following from Chico. Leaving his plane at Riego, he proceeded by train to Sacramento. He would return and fly his biplane into Sacramento the next day. His journey gives one the essence of flying cross-country in 1912.[38]

Charlie Hamilton was determined to make as much money as possible whenever he took a contract for a big meet. He traveled to as many small towns around the big meet as he could, setting up later exhibitions that were close enough to fly to in the *Hamiltonian*. By eliminating the need to use rail transport, and the necessity of "knocking down" (dismantling) the *Hamiltonian* for rail travel, he saved a lot of money.

A month-and-a-half after Charlie Hamilton flew at Chico for the Spring Festival, his wife left him and took a job working in a department store in Sacramento. Charlie went back East doing what he did best, exhibition flying, which brought him more fame, wealth, and trouble. Mrs. Hamilton stated, "It is true I have left my husband. I am earning my own living, now." She said Charlie's heavy drinking was the reason she left him. When she left him previously in Florida, he was in the, "... throes of delirium tremens." Now she was thinking of applying for a divorce. She and Charlie had been married for five years and, according to her, they were happy until Hamilton became a famous aviator.[39]

IN THE LAST week of September 1912, Thad Kerns brought his newest Curtiss copy to Sunset Aviation Field on the marshy tidal flats of Alameda.

He and his mechanic had built the Curtiss in ten days at Berkeley in the Brewer brothers' shop. The new Curtiss had an upper wingspan of 33 feet 6 inches, and 31 feet 6 inches for the lower wing. The chord (width) of the wing was 5 feet 2 inches and the gap between the upper and lower wings was 5 feet. The length of the machine was 24 feet from the tip of the front elevator to the end of the tail rudder. A Roberts four-cylinder, fifty horsepower motor powered the biplane, and its fuel tank held twenty gallons of gas. The Roberts drove a seven-foot propeller.

On his first flight, Kerns stayed up for seven minutes circling the airfield several times. Two days later, he was up doing the same. He told onlookers he'd be making flights daily for the next two to three weeks. This was confirmed in the first week of October.[40]

Kerns was still making practice flights at Sunset Field, November 2, when he took off while J. F. DaVilla was working on his Nieuport monoplane on the ground below. During his ten-minute flight, Kerns flew over Recreation Park where the Alameda-Reno football game was being played.[41]

There was an air meet for local aviators at Ingleside Coursing Park in southwestern San Francisco November 24, 1912. Kerns did not participate. However, his ex-Butte County colleague, Orvar Meyerhoffer, flew a monoplane at the meet, probably a CAC Bleriot XI copy.[42]

Thad Kerns was still making practice flights from Sunset Field at Alameda in early December 1912.[43]

He made a flight over Chico on February 12 and dropped copies of the *Chico Record* from an altitude over one thousand feet.[44]

Kerns gave a successful exhibition at Chico in late March 1913 before starting on a barnstorming trip from Chico to Sacramento. He had made arrangements to fly an exhibition at Knight Park, Marysville, on March 30.

Regarding Kerns' barnstorming tour mentioned in chapter one: Thad took off from Chico on March 24 for the planned tour getting as far as Gridley—a distance of twenty-eight miles—before bad weather forced him to land. Flying from Biggs, he arrived over Gridley and circled the town before weather conditions forced him to land in Onstott's pasture northeast of the city limits. The next day a large crowd gathered to watch, as Kerns flew an exhibition for them from Onstott's field. The Gridley paper reported Kerns was a pleasant looking fellow, who had the knack of making friends wherever he travelled.

Onstott's pasture was ideally located and used as a landing field at Gridley for many years eventually becoming the quasi-official airport for the town.

Kerns continued his tour on March 26. He took off from the pasture and set out for Live Oak, eight miles south, on his way to Marysville. After ascending to two hundred feet Kerns hit an "air pocket" (downdraft), and his Curtiss was sucked straight down hitting the ground so hard the wheels of his biplane were driven into the ground. The machine was heavily damaged, but Kerns suffered only a few scratches and bruises. Only his flying skill and coolness in operating his plane kept him from serious injury.[45]

Thaddeus spent the next two weeks rebuilding and repairing his biplane at Live Oak. On April 9, he flew the Curtiss to Marysville for a belated exhibition. With unusual skill—or recklessness—he arrived at Marysville from Live Oak after dark.

Sometime during the next few days, he finally completed his contract at

Marysville by flying an exhibition over the city from the racetrack at Knight Park. There is no evidence he continued his fragmented barnstorming tour on to Sacramento.[46]

Thad made several flights at the Rose Grower's Carnival at Princeton on May 5. He flew west from Chico to the Sacramento River town.

In June, Kerns arrived by rail in his hometown from San Francisco, where he had taken his Curtiss and expanded his career as a professional exhibition flyer. He told a reporter he would be leaving Chico in August on an exhibition tour of the larger towns in southern Canada. His plan was to fly with six other aviators, but he did not name them. He said his tour manager had eight cities signed to contracts and would have more signed soon. He expected to fly on the coming Fourth of July, probably somewhere in the Midwest, but the final arrangements hadn't been made, and the location of this exhibition hadn't yet been decided.[47]

A letter was once displayed in the Chico Air Museum written May 1, 1913, from Ivan Gates and Max Friedman, air show impresarios, to Thad asking him to sign and return an enclosed contract for his participation in an air meet at Santa Rosa (possibly on July 4, 1913). Other contracted participants mentioned in the letter were Silas Christofferson and Tom Gunn. If the next report of Kerns' activity is true, it is very unlikely he took the Santa Rosa job.

Reportedly, "… the California flyer shipped his machine to the Cicero flying field," near Chicago by rail from the West Coast, "… but he did not stay, as he left for Emporia, Kansas to fill a July 4 date. He will make Cicero his base for the season, however."[48]

Something happened to Thaddeus during his tour of the Midwest. He flew successful exhibitions at Emporia, Kansas, on July 4 and 5, and returned home to Chico July 14. He did not stay at Cicero for the season.

At his home on Shasta Road, Kerns and his mechanic Arthur Smith unpacked his Curtiss the day after he returned from Kansas. They assembled the aeroplane in a field across from the Kerns' family home. The machine was inspected for safety, then Kerns took the plane up for a test flight.

He flew west to the Sacramento River five miles away. There, he turned north flying at an altitude of a thousand feet. He swung the machine eastward towards his departure point and made some dips losing several hundred feet of altitude. A few people on the ground waved to him and he waved back. He flew over Miss Mary Sheffer's house, a girlfriend who lived nearby, and waved to her after making another dip.

As Thad leveled out from the dip, the lower wing gave way and, reportedly, the front lower "wind bar" (wing spar?) broke. The wing hit the propeller blades, creating a horrific noise from the prop chewing up the wood of the wing, which caused many witnesses on the ground to believe the machine had exploded. At this point in the Chico newspaper's description of the accident, the reporter bluntly wrote, "Recklessness was not the cause of the accident."

The stricken biplane made "... a half turn, then shot forward to the left, crossing the roadway. It struck the ground almost one hundred yards ..." from where the wing collapsed. "J. T. Henderson and Earl Morton were the first to reach the aviator. They removed the plane's (wings) from his back and the rods from his body." In addition to those wounds, Kerns suffered the Curtiss pilot's curse. He was crushed by the radiator and engine that sat just inches behind his seat.

Thad's mother was watching his flight from the family home nearby. Mercifully, a tree obstructed her view when the plane hit the ground. She was unable to fathom the truth and was in a daze when she learned of Thad's death. B. S. Kerns, her husband, was in Shasta County visiting two of his other sons when the crash occurred.

The following day an extensive press release was given to both of the principal Butte County newspapers, the *Chico Record* and the *Oroville Mercury*. It was a carefully prepared report of the accident and a surprisingly extensive and accurate biography of Thad's flying career. It stated: "Only yesterday the young aviator decided to give up his chosen profession for another branch of the same dangerous sport, carrying passengers on a hydroplane. He and Arthur Smith planned to take a vacation next month and then return to Chico and build a hydroplane." Arthur Smith was described as a mechanic and electrician who worked for Kerns, and was one of those who saw the crash.

Reportedly, everyone who saw the accident agreed the rear portion of the aeroplane came apart in pieces with sparks flying from the engine. The engine did not explode. It was found intact except for small cracks in the cylinders. The propeller chewed up the wood framework and came apart scattering wood and fabric as far as seventy-five to eighty yards away from the accident site.

The report continued: "Kerns always realized the danger of aviating, but the sport fascinated him. He often remarked that he would get killed if he stayed with it, but it was all in the game, he said. A year ago, his father offered him $10,000 if he would give up flying, but the offer was not accepted."

The newspaper claimed this was Kerns' first serious crash, which was not really true. He had crashed several times, usually while landing. Maybe the reporter felt those didn't count, but it was true he had never been seriously injured in a crash.

The paper did reveal he was almost killed in Kansas clearing some tall trees on takeoff. Kerns had been complaining his four-cylinder engine was underpowered and this author believes that when he took off at Emporia, Kansas, elevation 1,206 feet, on a hot July fourth, his takeoff distance was doubled due to the hot, humid, less-dense air, probably surprising him. Also his rate of climb would be less than what he was accustomed to and be quite disturbing when confronted with tall trees on takeoff. The fact that all of his exhibitions would be flown from the higher elevation airports of the Midwest plus the effects of the hot, humid summer air, he may have reconsidered flying exhibitions in his underpowered Curtiss and returned to Chico early from his tour of the Midwest.

The obituary reported Thad had quit high school after his first year and built his first aeroplane, a Curtiss copy, powering it with a two-cylinder thirty horsepower Elbridge motor. Kerns abandoned the first Curtiss for one of "stronger construction in 1911." A four-cylinder forty horsepower Elbridge motor powered the second Curtiss. "He made many successful flights. He was still dissatisfied with the power of the engine, however, and so he removed it and put in a four-cylinder Roberts engine of fifty horsepower."

"A pupil of Kerns, named Smith (Victor Smith), made a flight at the annual rugby game between Stanford and California at Palo Alto in November 1911, in the Chico boy's machine. He met with an accident when near the athletic field and fell to his death. The biplane was demolished but the engine was made useful again by replacing two cylinders."

This was how Kerns' family learned about Victor Smith although Thad's obituary stated, "His father learned of it through a supply house in San Francisco some time later."

In the obituary the destruction of Kerns' second Curtiss and the death of Victor Smith doesn't jibe with the Palo Alto newspaper report at the time of Smith's death. The two accounts differ as to who owned the Curtiss at the time of the crash. The Kerns obituary mentions there was a rugby game between the two colleges going on, which would suggest Smith may have been performing for the rugby fans, and if Smith had learned to fly at the Curtiss Aviation School at San Diego, why would he be a pupil of Thad Kerns?

Victor Smith was killed in July 1912 and not November 1911.

The Kerns obituary went on: "A third biplane of the same model (Curtiss) as the first two was built at Oakland (actually in nearby Berkeley) a year and a half ago. The damaged engine was installed in it. Kerns has used the same aeroplane ever since and has had remarkable success with it. He built all of his own flyers. This last one, which was smashed yesterday, is said to have been too light for practical flying."

It is difficult to understand how Kerns with his constantly expanding knowledge of aircraft construction could build an aeroplane too light for practical flying. Who in Butte County would have had the expertise to make this deduction? This author believes the supposition may have come from Kerns' companion and mechanic, Arthur Smith. As we shall see, the friend, who was about to embark on a vacation with Kerns before he died, made some critical comments to the press about his friend immediately after the crash.

Continuing with the obituary: "Kerns was a boy of exemplary habits and unlike most aviators he was not conceited over his ability to fly. He is survived by his parents Mr. and Mrs. B. S. Kerns, five brothers and three sisters. ..."[49]

A coroner's inquest was held over Kerns remains at a local funeral parlor on the evening of the sixteenth. The inquest ruled Thad's death was accidental, "... caused by falling from an aeroplane which collapsed in the air while he was flying two miles north of Chico near Shasta Road."

The coroner stated, "It would be proper to include in the verdict recommendations against permitting persons to fly in unsound airships. ..." Arthur Smith stated during the inquest, he (Smith) "did not believe that the frame of the planes (wings) was strong enough, but as no previous accident occurred, the same woodwork was kept until the time of the accident."

Following the inquest, Kerns' mechanic said he believed, "... the aeroplane would have been condemned by any inspector or commission had such an examination been compulsory, but in the absence of such a law, the aviator used his own judgement."

This comment makes one wonder if this was just Smith's opinion of the state of current aviation technology. Was Smith trying to cover his own work or was Kerns truly negligent in his construction methods? Regardless of the reason, if it was so badly constructed, why did Smith continue to help Kerns to his demise?

The report goes on: "Smith was on the stand for more than half-an-hour, describing the construction of the Curtiss biplane. He told of the weight and strength of the different parts and answered the coroner's questions in regard to the legal status of aviation.

"Smith said that promoters of all big aviation meets examine the different flying machines before they leave the ground in order to prevent accidents caused by weak or faulty construction. Further than that there is no regulation and an aviator's license has no standing in the eyes of the law."

The report continued with Smith stating, "... navigation on water is regulated and ... there are severe restrictions on automobiling, but flying in the air, which is far more dangerous, may be indulged in by anyone without restraint. Smith said that other lives could be saved by legal regulation and that the science should not receive the discredit which it receives by unnecessary casualties."

At this point in the inquisition, Albert Wahl, a juror, became sick from having to look at Kerns' mutilated body for half an hour. He had to leave the proceedings. In his place, coroner John Wallace swore in a new juror who had heard the previous testimony and had seen the body.

John Kerns, an older brother, testified Thad was "... intensely interested in aviation since he was fourteen years old and that it was his life ambition to become a great aviator. He said both his parents tried to dissuade the boy in his work in that direction but to no avail. He was always skillful as a mechanic and carpenter and before his mother knew it he had his first aeroplane almost completed, three years ago. John Kerns said his father made several inducements to Thaddeus to give up flying, at one time promising him a farm."[50]

Thad's mother and other family members requested the remains of his biplane be burned. The engine and radiator were moved from the wreck to the Kerns' farm, and every piece of the remaining aeroplane was burned.[51]

There was an undated reference in the Chico paper to the *Willows Journal*, which stated, "Many Willows people while examining his machine (during an exhibition there) ... were struck by the weakness of the thing. The bolts used in some vital parts were merely stove bolts. Some cotter pins holding important bolts were broken out. The machine looked to be a death trap.

"Asked why he didn't make it stronger with better bolts, etc. Kerns said: 'It's all right. I used to be afraid of its weakness, but I'm not any more.' He had become accustomed to danger."[52]

Thaddeus Steven Kerns' funeral on the morning of July 18 was held at the family home and was one of the largest in Chico in many years. Chico had lost its talented and dedicated premier aviator.[53]

Willows Airport in 1995 where the local pilots, lead by the Nolta brothers, put on the finest annual airshows in Northern California during the 1930s.

A Boeing Model 40 used to fly the mail and two to four passengers on the San Francisco–Chicago airmail route from 1927 well into the 1930s landing at Mather Field and later Sacramento Municipal Airport.

CHAPTER 9

Orvar Meyerhoffer after leaving the Bay Area – Lyman and Jeanette Doty learn to fly

Orvar "Swede" Meyerhoffer left San Francisco in late 1912; Northern California would never again be his permanent residence. He moved to sunny, fog-free, Southern California.

Orvar said he was in Venice, California, at year's end 1912, and the chief of police made him the world's first aerial cop. Other reports imply he was given the badge in Venice at a later date. There is a photo extant of Orvar receiving his badge in Venice from the mayor while standing next to his Martin TT biplane in 1918.[1]

Meyerhoffer's whereabouts through 1913 and most of 1914 are not clear, but in December 1914 he and Knox Martin opened a flight school and passenger service on San Diego Bay under the leadership of Tony and Roger Jannus. The Jannus brothers, in January 1914, had started America's first scheduled airline between Tampa and St. Petersburg, Florida.[2]

A handbill for the new flying service at San Diego listed the company name in bold letters as, "Jannus Brothers Flying Boats." Also listed were the pilots Tony Jannus, Roger Jannus, Knox Martin, and Jay D. Smith. Orvar S. T. Meyerhoffer was listed as company manager.

The company was not a scheduled airline like the St. Petersburg–Tampa operation, but it was a flying school and more importantly an air taxi service. A customer chose where he wanted to fly while sightseeing around San Diego Bay, and depending on his choice he was charged ten to twenty-five dollars for the flight.

Customers were assured their pilot would, "… strictly adhere to your wishes regarding altitude and general character of flight. We will keep within five feet of the water if you desire, or ascend to a thousand feet." The company claimed to have carried thirty-one hundred passengers during 1914 and "... every one delighted." Actually, they were referring to the passengers carried at their Florida operation.[3]

The San Diego air taxi service and flight school, managed by Meyerhoffer, flew passengers in a Benoist flying boat with pilot Knox's name written across the upper nose of the fuselage near the plane's two seats.[4]

During the two months the Jannus brothers' air taxi was in service, they carried over seven hundred passengers. In February 1915, J. D. Smith crashed their only flying boat into the bay ending flying operations.[5]

Orvar Meyerhoffer jumped at the opportunity and started his own air taxi service at San Diego. He obtained a Curtiss flying boat and docked it at Market Street just as the Jannus operation had previously. During his first six months of flying operations, Meyerhoffer carried more than two thousand passengers. He allowed passengers to have their pictures taken in the flying boat with him after the flight—for a price of course.

Meyerhoffer had his nickname "Swede" painted in the same place on his Curtiss as Knox Smith had on Jannus' Benoist.[6]

On December 16, 1915, Meyerhoffer's air taxi operations came to an abrupt halt. He crashed his flying boat into the San Diego Bay, and his passenger, seventy-five-year-old Lucie Comstock of San Diego, was killed.

Meyerhoffer and his passenger crashed into the bay from an altitude of one hundred feet. Mrs. Comstock died as she was taken from the wrecked flying boat to receive medical aid on the nearby battleship USS *Oregon*. Orvar suffered a bad gash over his right eye and sprained his ankle.

After Meyerhoffer spoke to the press, it reported, "The aged woman became hysterical as the big flying boat began climbing skyward and clasped him convulsively with the result that the machine became uncontrollable."

That story differed greatly from those told by the closest witnesses—the crew of the SS *Glacier* anchored near the crash site. Members of the crew declared the upper left wing of the flying boat biplane collapsed as Meyerhoffer was making a right turn, and the flying boat with Meyerhoffer standing upright and screaming as loudly as possible plunged nose first downward into the bay.

Meyerhoffer's version described what happened in more detail claiming: "We had reached an altitude of about one hundred feet when Mrs. Comstock grabbed me. Realizing the danger of taking my hands off the control wheel, I shouted for her to keep her seat. Instead she stood upright and clasped me tightly. The machine made a sudden lunge. I remember nothing more until I found myself clutching one of the struts and learned from the bluejackets who were swarming about in small boats that my aeroplane was wrecked and my passenger was somewhere in the debris."[7]

In 1916 Meyerhoffer established an unofficial altitude record at Los Angeles. Orvar, flying a Curtiss Pusher with a sixty horsepower motor, climbed to nineteen thousand feet over the city. It seems impossible that a Standard Model Curtiss could achieve this height, but it's the claim Orvar made.[8]

Al Wilson, who became a well-known movie pilot in the 1920s and '30s, said he worked for the H. V. Schiller Flying School as a mechanic's helper in trade for flying lessons. He learned to fly in Schiller's Bleriot XI monoplane with no onboard instructor (the "grass cutting" method of flying instruction was used). He later transferred to a school at Riverside flying one of the first dual control Standard Model Curtiss Pushers for training students. He said it was there, about 1914, that he completed his flying training under the instruction of Swede Meyerhoffer.[9]

The city of Venice had, as already noted, appointed Orvar Meyerhoffer as California's pioneer aerial policeman, probably before the Great War. Four years after the war, the Venice police chief would appoint George E. Stephenson, Hubert Kittle, and Frank Clarke as members of its aerial police.[10]

In December 1916, Meyerhoffer was trying various schemes to get passengers to fly with him. One unusual scheme was fishing from a seaplane.

Orvar's plan was different from other aerial fishing trips. He would fly out over the ocean and locate schools of fish, something that fishermen had never been able to do quickly. He flew his hydroplane five hundred feet above the calm waters near Catalina Island. After spotting a school of fish he would land an appropriate distance away, drift slowly over the fish, and he and his passenger would enjoy, "… all the thrills of fighting albacore with light tackle."[11]

It was believed Orvar taught Frank Clarke, the number-one first-call motion picture stunt pilot of 1920 through the '30s, to fly at Venice in 1918.[12]

By May 1918, Orvar was instructing at Riverside for Riverside Aircraft Company's flight school under its manager Mr. Bowen. Earlier in February, the government had chosen a flying field site at Riverside (March Field). Meyerhoffer may have instructed there after the base was built.[13]

Orvar reached the pinnacle of his career on November 23, 1918, when he and another pilot, Aaron R. "Bob" Ferneau, took off from a makeshift landing field at Goleta in the Lockheed brothers' F-1A on what was hoped to be a spectacular transcontinental flight to Washington D. C.

Unfortunately, a rocker arm failed in one of the Lockheed's two Hall-Scott L-6 engines, and the pilots were forced to land at Tacna, Arizona, just over six hours after leaving Goleta.[14]

The aircraft they were flying began its existence as the Lockheed F-1, designed mostly by John Northrop while working for Allen and Malcom Lockheed. The brothers' intentions were to sell the big flying boat to the US Navy for use in the war. Even though the F-1 could carry an unusually heavy load, the navy wasn't interested.

After the Lockheed brothers delivered the big biplane to the navy for testing at San Diego by flying the 211 miles from Santa Barbara to San Diego nonstop in 181 minutes, the navy wasn't impressed.

The Lockheeds didn't let the navy's rejection deter them. They decided to spend an additional ten thousand dollars and have Northrop convert the seaplane into a land plane. They planned a transcontinental flight with only two stops to promote the newly designated F-1A as a mail transport for the government.[15]

The plan was the big plane, with its ninety miles per hour cruising speed and twelve hundred-mile range, would be flown to the East Coast in thirty to thirty-five hours with two fuel stops.

The November transcontinental flight would follow the "southern route." Meyerhoffer and Ferneau would fly at low altitude and navigate by following rail lines. This early form of IFR flying, known as "I follow railroads," should not be confused with today's IFR flying meaning instrument flight rules. The flight was well planned and was to have help from the Santa Fe and Southern Pacific Railroad companies. They agreed to light fires at regular intervals along the rails. A cache of gasoline would be placed at Deming, New Mexico, and Cairo, Illinois, for the two necessary fuel stops.

The F-1A was to carry a sack of mail that contained a letter from the Santa Barbara postmaster to the postmaster general in Washington. Another account claimed the plane carried a letter from Mary Miles Mintner, a silent screen star, to President Woodrow Wilson. Miss Mintner often appeared at promotional events for the Lockheed company. In fact, she christened the F-1A at its rollout ceremony earlier in the year.

Orvar Meyerhoffer, one of the most experienced pilots in the country, was chosen to fly the F-1A as lead pilot with Bob Ferneau as copilot. The

Chapter 9

Hall-Scott Motor Company had Leo Flint, one of its mechanics, join the crew to maintain the two Hall-Scott 150 horsepower L-6 engines.

The F-1A was flown from the Lockheed factory site at Santa Barbara to a longer field near Goleta for its scheduled departure November 20.

It began raining on the seventeenth and turned the makeshift airfield at Goleta into a loblolly of mud. The Lockheed had to be removed from the morass in which it had sunk. A farmer and his tractor were hired to pull the six thousand-pound biplane to firmer ground. The tractor went down to its hubs. Another farmer, less technologically refined, brought in his eight-horse team of plow horses and worked the F-1A out of the mud.

At 5:05 AM on November 23, the Lockheed staggered off the pasture at Goleta into the dark damp morning. The crew fought heavy winds, clouds, and turbulence on the flight over Ventura, Santa Paula, and Saugus Junction before reaching Colton after three hours. There they spotted a railroad signal fire indicating their flight path over the mountains. The sky cleared and the Lockheed passed over Yuma in mid-morning. It was unseen by the residents due to a violent dust storm in progress.

Headwinds reduced the F-1A's groundspeed, forcing the crew to plan an unscheduled fuel stop at Gila Bend, Arizona. Near Gila Bend, the Lockheed lost power in its right engine. Meyerhoffer made a good landing on rough ground near Tacna, Arizona. The only damage during the landing was torn fabric on one wingtip, and the tip of the tailskid snapped.

The tailskid needed to be welded, so the crew walked to the abandoned railroad station at Tacna and flagged down the next westbound train back to Yuma.

At Yuma, Leo Flint got the skid welded and was able to catch an eastbound train back to Tacna, reattach the tailskid, and fix the right engine. In Tacna, Swede and Ferneau filled holes and broke down ridges and ruts to clear a makeshift runway. They raised the Lockheed and placed wooden planks under its wheels to get it out of the soft sand.

The following morning, the crew boarded the Lockheed and took off. They followed the Southern Pacific tracks for Gila Bend. Townspeople and local ranchers had gathered to watch the big Lockheed land. Just before 10:00 AM the plane came into sight. Once the crew found what appeared to be a safe spot to land, they did so. It was November 26, and they were behind schedule. After refueling the plane, the crew and some townspeople began clearing off a safer runway for the Lockheed's departure.

Once ready, Meyerhoffer gave Ferneau the signal to take off and the copilot opened the throttles. As the F-1A began moving, some hothead in an automobile began to race along side the aircraft. As the Lockheed was about to lift off, the auto cut in front of the plane. To avoid hitting the car, the pilots aborted the takeoff by intentionally ground looping the big biplane and missing the car. The plane came to an abrupt halt off the prepared runway with a blown tire.

Luckily, Flint had packed a couple of spare tires on board for such emergencies, which were common in the early days of flying considering the poor to non-existent landing fields available.

Now the problem for the crew was the plane was stuck at a bad angle for takeoff. Once again, the crew and townspeople cleared a suitable runway. By the time the tire was changed and the runway cleared, it was dark. Night cross-country flights were out of the question in these early days of flying. Aeroplanes of the day had no lights, few instruments, and no navigational aids. The departure of the F-1A would have to wait until morning.

A crowd gathered at dawn on the makeshift airfield. Once again, Meyerhoffer gave the go signal and the throttles were opened; the big biplane lurched along the improvised runway picking up speed. It lifted off perfectly for a good takeoff. Within seconds, the right engine quit again.

There was little choice but to crash land straight ahead, down a riverbed, and into sand dunes. The nose slammed into the ground, and the plane came to an abrupt halt with its tail in the air. The fuel tank in the fuselage broke loose and smashed into Leo Flint. Ferneau jumped down from his position pulling Flint and Meyerhoffer with him from the smashed front cockpit. Fortunately, there was no fire.

Flint was unconscious. Meyerhoffer was dazed, and Ferneau had minor bruises from his lap belt, the only belt that held. Orvar collapsed from internal injuries, and a few minutes later he and Flint were taken to a nearby makeshift medical station.

Ferneau made the necessary arrangements relating to the crashed Lockheed, after getting rail transport for Flint and Meyerhoffer to a hospital in Phoenix. Later, they were moved to Los Angeles. Flint's recovery was lengthy. He lost sight in one eye. Meyerhoffer recovered quickly and was flying again soon.[16]

Another report of the attempted transcontinental flight agrees that the F-1A covered 415 miles from Goleta to Tacna in six hours and ten minutes. But the report claims that during the last takeoff from Gila Bend, a mesquite bush fouled a propeller and the big plane went up on its nose in

CHAPTER 9

the dry creek bed. This report claims Orvar, Ferneau, and Flint escaped injury, and the wrecked Lockheed was loaded on a rail car and returned to the factory in Santa Barbara. There it was converted back to its original flying boat configuration and used to hop passengers from the beach at Santa Barbara.[17]

Swede Meyerhoffer took part in another great adventure when he joined Barr's Flying Circus. This group was organized at Venice Field, also known as Ince Field for its current owner Thomas H. Ince, the successful Hollywood movie director.

The flying circus was organized at Venice in October 1919 and staffed by professional pilots Swede Meyerhoffer, Frank Clarke, Mark Campbell, and Howard Patterson. The group had contracts to perform for fairs at Phoenix and Tucson, Arizona.

A big air show was scheduled at Phoenix Airport, also known as Fairgrounds Airport, during the Arizona State Fair. Barr's Flying Circus would provide the air show, which was said to include Ormer Locklear, the most famous American postwar aerial stuntman of the day.

Besides Locklear's stunts, an important event of the fair was the Trans-Desert Air Race. This race would be flown from Venice to Phoenix to open the Arizona State Fair. The governor of Arizona was to fly with the winner after the race.

For the race, R. E. Goldsworthy would be flying a Canuck, (a Canadian Jenny), and Burt Barr's pilot, Swede Meyerhoffer, would also fly a Canuck. The other entries were Barr's Flying Circus pilots Clarke, Campbell, and Patterson. They were flying Jennies.

The racers flew from Venice Field to El Centro. The next morning they departed El Centro for Yuma except for one nameless contestant, who had gotten disoriented on takeoff and flew south into Mexico. Conditions at the border were sensitive and Mexican troops opened fire on the interloper with their rifles. He quickly realized his mistake and turned east to find Phoenix. After he eventually landed at Fairgrounds Airport in Phoenix, he discovered eight bullet holes in his wings.

The other contestants landed at Yuma for fuel and flew on to Gila Bend utilizing IFR (I Follow Railroads), which led them to Gila Bend. There they refueled and left the IFR route, proceeding to Phoenix on a compass course, a chancy undertaking in 1919 over unknown desert terrain.

Howard Patterson won the race, but what he won is unknown, and no time was given for his efforts. He reported he was just lucky he didn't have a forced landing and managed not to get lost.

On November 5, Swede Meyerhoffer took a Phoenix reporter up for a ride. Six days later Burt Barr, manager of the group, castigated Phoenix, for having an airport that was too narrow and impossible to find, before his pilots left.[18]

There is a photograph in D. D. Hatfield's, *Los Angeles Aeronautics 1920–1929* showing Swede Meyerhoffer in a dark business suit and fedora with a group of aviators. They are standing in front of a biplane up on its nose from an obvious accident. The names of the men from left to right are: Mr. Hosick, Waldo Waterman, R. E. Goldsworthy, Frank Clarke, Jimmie Hester, Wallace Timm, Joseph Hoff, Clarence Prest, Swede Meyerhoffer, Harry Sperl, Al Wilson, George Stephenson, Otto Timm, and Mark Campbell. They are standing in front of Clarence Prest's self-designed biplane *Poison* after a bad landing at Venice Airport that the photo caption states occurred in September 1920. Swede Meyerhoffer died in July 1920, so the picture couldn't have been taken in September 1920, but was probably taken about the time of the Trans-Desert Race to Phoenix, as all the pilots from that race except Howard Patterson are in the photograph.[19]

SWEDE MEYERHOFFER FLEW from San Francisco to Willows to deliver a four-passenger Lincoln-Standard biplane to the Moffett and Hunt Airplane Company from Walter T. Varney, the regional dealer for Lincoln-Standard Aircraft. Even though it was reported Moffett bought the airplane from Varney, available information suggests the plane was rented or leased to the Willows company.

The date was May 23, 1920, when Meyerhoffer arrived in Willows. The local paper reported Swede as, "... one of the best known aviators in the United States ... Meyerhoffer claims to be the oldest (flyer) in the United States having started on his career in the air in 1902 [sic]. He has made more forced landings without accident than any aviator in the world and claims he has been in the air longer than any three aviators in this country." Swede was such a modest fellow.

The article continued with Swede's daily routine in Willows: "He spent Sunday teaching the Moffett company's pilot the points of the machine and was in the air nearly the entire day. This morning C. Burmeister, the rice man who takes great interest in aviation, made a flight with Meyerhoffer in the new machine, and flew to an altitude of 10,000 feet."[20]

Two months later, Meyerhoffer was returning from a passenger hopping tour in Oregon when he suffered a horrible accident. He fell into the spinning propeller of the Moffett and Hunt Varney Lincoln-Standard at McArthur, California. The prop severed one arm and broke a leg. Meyerhoffer died a few days later on July 20, 1920, in Fall City, Oregon, where he had been taken for medical care.

The Willows newspaper reported Swede was on his way to San Jose to fly in an air meet to which he was committed and was mortally injured hand-propping his plane at McArthur. The reporter got it right when he wrote Meyerhoffer began flying in 1912, but Meyerhoffer's claim to having more flying time than any pilot in America was pure speculation. Unfortunately, Butte County's second aviation pioneer had "gone west." [21]

I. M. Hunt, Moffett's partner in the company, drove to McArthur to retrieve the Lincoln-Standard that Swede was flying. Hunt was back in Willows by July 22.[22]

Meyerhoffer had been scheduled to fly a Lincoln-Standard for Walter Varney at the Sciots' air meet in San Jose. He had been flying in the San Jose area for at least three months prior to his death and had flown in an air meet there during that time.

Orvar Meyerhoffer in a Walter Varney owned Lincoln-Standard biplane. Orvar flew this plane on a barnstorming tour through California's far northern counties and into Oregon in July 1920. This photo was taken of him at Ft. Bidwell, CA, a few days before he was mortally injured at McArthur while hand propping the Lincoln-Standard.

Meyerhoffer was said to have been of Swedish royal birth, but renounced all his titles when he applied for citizenship in America. His 1920 death notice also claimed that he served as an aerial policeman in Venice in 1912. It stated he was the only aerial policeman in the world at that time. His altitude record over Los Angeles was said to have occurred in 1915. During the Great War, he was said to have served as a civilian instructor of aviation in the south state until the war ended, then he went back to civilian flying.[23]

Another description of Swede's demise claims he rented the Lincoln-Standard from Walter Varney, and the Varney mechanic, who accompanied Meyerhoffer, stepped up to prop the airplane only to have Swede growl at him, "Get outta there. I crank my own damn windmill!" He did just that, but he lost his balance and the prop caught his shoulder. Swede went forward into the prop, and a blade hit him in the back causing serious injuries from which he died.

Varney had warned the mechanic to keep his telegrams to Varney during the trip with Swede short, "ten words or less," because they were expensive. So, of Swede's accident, he wired Varney: "Swede cranked prop. Prop killed Swede. Send new prop." Varney was incredulous at the graveyard humor of the nine-word telegram and had it hanging in his office for many years.[24]

THE NEXT AVIATORS from Butte County to gain prominence during aviation's early years were Lyman and Jeanette Doty. They were brother and sister from Biggs, a small farm town four miles north of Gridley in southern Butte County.

Lyman and Jean, as she was known, were born in 1890 and 1891, respectively. They both graduated from Gridley High School. She attended Chico Normal School and taught at Biggs Elementary School for a while. The pair attended the University of California at Berkeley. Their parents were William and Cecelia Doty, owners of a large hardware store in Biggs, which their grandfather opened in 1876.

Lyman Doty announced in February 1916 he was going to become a professional aviator and would soon leave for San Francisco (actually Redwood City) to learn to fly at the Christofferson Aviation School. Silas Christofferson, who ran the school, was known throughout the north state for his exhibition and passenger flying prior to and during the Panama–Pacific International Exhibition of 1915. Lyman planned to learn all aspects of flying and the aviation business, which he would make his lifelong career.[25] In April, he sent photographs of himself flying one of the Christofferson

CHAPTER 9

In this photo, students, alumni, and instructors pose at the Christofferson Aviation School in Redwood City during June 1916. Standing from left to right: Unknown, Lyman Doty, Jeanette Doty, unknown, unknown, Silas Christofferson, Helen Hodge. Kneeling from the left: Unknown, unknown, Frank Bryant, Joe Boquel, Art Lim, B. Takaeshi. The two in front are unknown.

training planes to his father.

Lyman W. Doty received his ACA/FAI license No. 549 in July 1916. Silas Christofferson recommended Doty be hired by the army as a flight instructor to train new pilots for the aviation branch of the Signal Corps. Silas said Doty was one of his best students, and he would be, "... especially competent to instruct others." [26]

Doty was among the first group of three pilots to graduate from Christofferson Aviation School after it had moved to its final location in Redwood City. Guy H. Slaughter of the Pacific Aero Club was the local flying examiner representing Aero Club of America. He tested Doty, Gus Jamieson, and Ralph Hansen on June 29, 1916. They passed with ease.[27]

Jeanette Doty joined Christofferson's school in July to learn to fly like her brother. Lyman was her mentor and she adored him. That month it was reported Jean was "... the latest addition to the grass cutter class. Monday morning she will start in her course of instruction with the hopes of some day doing stunts in the exhibition line with her brother." [28]

Jeanette is third from the left in a photo taken of unamed Christofferson students and instructors at the Christofferson Aviation School in

Redwood City, published in the July 17, 1916, issue of *Aerial Age Weekly*. Helen Hodge is also in the photo. She was a Bay Area resident who learned to fly at Christofferson School the same time as Jean Doty.

A large advertisement in the *Gridley Herald* of October 7 exclaimed, "Doty Will Fly! Lyman Doty, one of our former high school boys, has become an expert air pilot, a member of the Aero Club of America, and will give an exhibition flight at 2 o'clock at the Gridley baseball grounds immediately preceding the Baseball Game—Gridley vs. Oroville [sic]." It advertised there would be, "Thrilling, Daredevil Antics." [29]

Doty's Curtiss arrived late at Gridley by rail, and the flight couldn't take place at 2:00 PM. It was 5:00 PM when Doty took off from the Gridley baseball field. He turned north and circled Gridley overtaking a murder of crows while climbing to three thousand feet. After demonstrating some safe and sane maneuvers, he descended and landed on the baseball field stopping at the same spot from which he had taken off. Reportedly, "He was given an ovation by his friends who crowded about to shake his hand. He did not try any fancy flights for which his friends were thankful." [30]

Lyman, Jeanette, and several others witnessed Silas Christofferson's fatal crash in a military biplane of his own design on November 1, 1916. The crash happened at noon on Silas' airfield in Redwood City. He had climbed, "… several hundred feet, then something went wrong, it is uncertain what. He volplaned down, and overturned a hundred feet high and fell …" to the ground. He died of internal injuries an hour later at a nearby hospital. Born in Des Moines, Iowa, and later moved to Portland, Oregon, Silas was twenty-six-years-old and a respected pioneer in the Bay Area aviation community.[31]

In November, Lyman Doty needed to obtain a license from the San Francisco Police Department that would allow him to carry passengers from the Christofferson Aviation Camp in the sand dunes near the end of Sloat Boulevard at Ocean Beach, San Francisco.

A police officer arranged to meet Lyman on Ingleside Beach (possibly the name for what is now known as Ocean Beach). Doty was to give the officer a ride to demonstrate his ability and skill in carrying passengers in his Curtiss Pusher.

The officer who showed up was Sgt. John J. Casey, a giant of a man weighing 225 pounds. The passenger's seat next to Lyman had to be widened two inches to accommodate Casey. Before taking off, Casey told Doty if he didn't bring him back alive, he wouldn't get his license!

Lyman took off with Casey, using the damp packed sandy beach nearest the water as his runway and ascended into a fog bank. He carefully turned around and brought the officer down safely landing on the same section of beach. Sergeant Casey granted his license but wondered why the ride had been so short.[32]

In December a newspaper reported, Jeanette Doty would "… be graduated on Christmas Eve from the Christofferson School of Aviation near San Francisco. Her venture after securing her license will be a flight from San Francisco to Los Angeles." That report was premature to say the least.[33]

Lyman and Jeanette learned to fly on the reliable but well-worn Standard Model Curtiss copies still in use as late as 1917 in American civilian flying schools. The Curtiss JN-4s were being built, but they weren't yet available to civilian flight schools. Foreign governments and the US military were snapping up the JNs for the war effort as fast as they came out of the Curtiss factory at Buffalo, New York.

Jeanette didn't take her license test on Christmas Eve; she hadn't acquired enough flying experience. That evening, her brother had a very close call in his Curtiss.

Lyman had volunteered to fly as part of a program held at the Palace of Fine Arts in the western section of the Marina District of San Francisco. The program, sponsored by the San Francisco Art Association, was to welcome the Christmas season. There were municipal band concerts and other activities throughout the day of December 24.

Lyman's part of the program was to take off from the Christofferson hangar at Ocean Beach and fly to the Column of Progress next to the San Francisco Yacht Harbor. There he was to drop a wreath of flowers on top of the 180-foot column. The purpose of this effort was, "… to arouse enthusiasm in favor of the preservation of the column dedicated to aviation." The wreath was a token of respect to all those aviators who had died during the development of the new technology. The Column of Progress and the Palace of Fine Arts were the only two edifices left on the old grounds of the Panama-Pacific Exposition. There was much civic interest in preserving the two structures.

Today only the rebuilt Palace of Fine Arts remains. The Column of Progress was saved until 1925, then torn down supposedly because too many drunk drivers were running into it at night.

San Francisco's first municipal airport was created next to the Marina Green in 1919, and the column, which Doty wanted to dedicate to aviation, was a virtual hazard as it sat on the western end of the airfield. All pilots departing Marina Field into the prevailing wind blowing in from the sea had to be wary of the towering column as they turned onto their course heading.

Unfortunately for Lyman, his plan for the dedication flight over the column began to unravel after he arrived at the Christofferson hangar on Ocean Beach. He discovered the wind was blowing strong from the ocean. At 2:00 PM, his scheduled departure time, the wind was blowing fifty miles per hour down the Marina! Lyman took off in a preliminary flight. After landing in the terrific wind, his biplane tangled with an obstruction. Repairs were made promptly. Lyman still planned to drop the wreath on top of the column.

J. C. Irvine, president of the Pacific Aero Club, asked Doty to consider the dangerous high winds before proceeding. Doty was insistent and took off with the wreath at 3:30 PM.

Lyman's departure in the strong wind was uneventful. He circled the column and tried to throw the huge wreath over the top of the column. Reportedly, "As he cast the wreath as a token of respect to the group of fearless aviators whose lives had been snuffed out, his engine suddenly (quit)." Doty was descending and at an altitude of only one hundred feet.

Lyman maintained his calm and control of the Curtiss, but there was no possibility of returning to Ocean Beach. He force landed wrecking his biplane when the wheels of his plane sank into soft ground instead of running on the ground's surface.

Lyman sprained his right ankle and had cuts over his left eye. The Curtiss suffered serious damage. Lyman's father had driven down from Biggs to watch his son's flight, and he rushed Lyman to Park Emergency Hospital in the family automobile. A doctor examined Doty and found no broken bones or obvious internal injuries.[34]

Mayo H. Boulware, another Biggs resident, signed up in January 1917 for flight instruction with the Christofferson Aviation School at Redwood City.

Jean Doty, J. O. Jensen, and Sam Mustain were to take their flight tests for graduation in January. In February they were to take the tests for their ACA/FAI licenses. Students at the Christofferson School were taught in classes of three, so it was not unusual for them to take their flight tests at the same time. They were to fly for Guy Slaughter, the Pacific Aero Club member, who gave the ACA/FAI flight tests in Northern California.[35]

In early February, Jensen and Mustain took their flight tests for Slaughter, but Jean Doty did not. No reasons were given for her absence at the time.[36]

In March, Jean Doty's continuing status as a student at the Christofferson School of Aviation was confirmed by a newspaper article about a cat that had adopted the school and its flying students. It seems the cat was named "Sir Thomas Aviator" by Miss Doty who planned to make the name authentic by taking the cat up for a ride in the school's Curtiss.

Even though Sir Thomas loved the aviators dearly on the ground, he held no affinity for them or their machines once in the air. When Jean left the ground with the cat in her lap, he decided he had had enough and jumped clear of the plane from an altitude of ten feet. From that time on, whenever an aeroplane engine was started, Sir Thomas scrambled into the rafters of the hangar. He resisted retrieval with an arched back and much hissing.[37]

Mayo Boulware and Michael Brown took their flying tests in March for Guy Slaughter at the Redwood City airfield. Michael Brown was lauded as being an outstanding student. Everything he did during his test was above the average student's flight test results.

Mayo Boulware made his test flights after Brown. Boulware was said to be as good a student pilot as Brown. Boulware reportedly, "… proved himself a capable flyer. Going through his paces with a skill that shows he is well fitted for the career he intends to take up, that of a professional exhibition flyer." [38]

Mayo H. Boulware received ACA/FAI license No. 696, and Michael Brown received license No. 697.

Michael Brown of San Mateo went on to become a successful attorney and an outstanding early pilot in the Bay Area. Mayo Boulware joined the Army Air Service after America entered the Great War. He passed on in Butte County in 1973.

In March Jean Doty sent a telegram to President Woodrow Wilson offering her services as a volunteer pilot. The self-proclaimed eighteen-year-old (she was actually twenty-six) aviatrix said if the military would not take her she planned to join the Army Aviation Reserve Corps. She said, "I believe I am as capable of performing scouting, observation, piloting, or other military duty as any man flyer." Jean made these comments to a reporter at the St. Francis Hotel in San Francisco.

She continued, "I have been flying since last August, when I joined the Christofferson Aviation School at Redwood City. I have made a study of the science of aeronautics, have studied closely the feats of the military aviators in Europe and I understand my machine well enough to make any repairs that a man is expected to make. I have always been mechanically inclined, and have driven and repaired my own automobile for years. If I had the tools I could build an aeroplane, including the motor, which is something most aviatrixes cannot do. I became a 'bug' on aviation through watching Art Smith fly at the exposition, and determined to master the air. If I can serve my country well, I hope they give me a chance."

Jean was a native daughter and attended the University of California. On March 23, 1917, it was reported she would take her flying test for an ACA/FAI license, "... a week from Sunday... at Redwood City." [40]

A few days later it was reported, "Christofferson aviation field will be the center of considerable interest Sunday morning (April 1) when Miss Jeanette Doty, Chico girl [sic], is scheduled to make her test flight for a pilot's license before Guy T. Slaughter of the Aero Club of America." [41]

On Monday, April 2, 1917, an article ran under the headline, JEAN DOTY LATE, LOSES AIR HONOR. Then a smaller headline said, GIRL OVERSLEEPS, FAILS TO PUT IN APPEARANCE ON TIME FOR TRIAL ARMY FLIGHT.

The report explained, "She overslept. Everything was in readiness for her at 8 o'clock yesterday morning. Frank Bryant, chief instructor at the Redwood City school, was in the field, Guy T. Slaughter, of the American Aero Club was there to watch her flight and determine if she was worthy to have the license and a big crowd of the curious were in attendance. But Miss Doty was not in evidence.

"At 10:30 AM, she arrived in a car driven by her brother. By that time the wind was gusty and howling at fifty-five miles per hour. Miss Doty was eager to go up anyway. She said she would rather pass the examination when conditions were difficult, and she wasn't afraid. But though she begged hard, Instructor Bryant would not consent to the tryout."

Bryant said to her sarcastically, "You are speaking of joining an army aviation corps, eh? Well, the first thing in the army is promptness, understand? We'll try another day for your graduation. I'll let you know when." One wonders if she hadn't bruised some male egos with her comments to the press at the St. Francis Hotel.[42]

Jeanette never took her license test. A few days later on April 6, America entered the World War. Years later she said she made a promise to her family not to pursue a career in aviation due to the danger involved and that was why she didn't pursue her license.[43]

Lyman and Jeanette with Harry Christofferson and J. R. Struble were

CHAPTER 9   269

scheduled to fly during the April 22, 1917, Column of Progress ceremonies held on the Marina's old exposition grounds. The committee organizing this ceremony was made up of Frank Bryant, Bob Fowler, Roy Francis, E. T. McGettigan, and J. C. Irvine. The purpose of the event was to raise funds for, "... the perpetuation of the column as a lasting monument to the men who have given their lives to the cause of aeronautics."[44]

America had entered the Great War before the above announcement was declared. Flight training at Redwood City airfield went into overdrive and it is doubtful the Column of Progress ceremonies ever took place. The declaration of war may also have been partially to blame for Jeanette not getting another chance to take her license test. Jeanette Doty stopped flying when war was declared.

After the war, in September 1919 Jeanette married Morris Caldwell, a captain in the US Army Engineers from New York City. She did take up flying gliders in the 1960s and won various soaring badges. She passed on in July 1972 at Merrick, Nassau, New York.[45]

A few days after he had rushed his sister to the airfield at Redwood City with the hope that she would be allowed to take her examination flight, Lyman Doty appeared in the newspaper again.

This time he had taken a famous movie actress, Miss Mary Miles Minter, for an aeroplane ride from the Ocean Beach aviation camp. This was the Christofferson hangar where several Christofferson pilots used the damp sand as a natural runway. They sold aeroplane rides to the public at this site.

Doty and Minter took off from the Christofferson site and flew south following the coastline. They decided to land on a point of beach jutting out into the sea a mile or so south of the Ocean Beach aviation camp. The sand where they landed was soft and much like quicksand. Once the Curtiss stopped rolling, it sank into the sand above the wheel hubs.

Lyman and Miss Minter stayed with the aeroplane doing everything they could to get the engine started and the plane moving again. It was hopeless. The tide was coming in and shrinking the size of the beach to a thin strip of land. Waves were splashing against the nearby rocks.

It was time to abandon the Curtiss and get to safety. Doty struggled and managed to get Miss Minter to dry land. They climbed a steep bank with its crumbly rock breaking in their hands. They made it to the Ocean Shore Railroad tracks after hiking through extensive vegetable fields. Miss Mintner arrived home long after darkness fell.

Lyman reported he would lead a party of men back to the beach after sunup to retrieve the Curtiss. The results of their efforts to salvage the Curtiss are unknown.[46]

Mary Miles Minter was a silent film star who, at one time, was Mary Pickford's biggest competition in Hollywood. She was very interested in aviation and aviators. She may have become an aviatrice herself. It was reported she qualified for a pilot's license later in 1921, but her parents objected and prevented her from ever taking the controls of a plane again.[47]

William Desmond Taylor, a movie director was said to be her lover. He was killed on William Randolph Hearst's yacht during a boating trip in the early 1920s. Minter and Thomas Ince, who founded Venice Airport, were also aboard. The murder was never solved, and there were rumors of involvement with the occult, drugs, and multiple love affairs. Afterward Miss Minter's career went into a spiral and never recovered.[48]

Lyman Doty, flying his Curtiss Pusher, "bombed" the city of San Francisco in June 1917. The aerial attack was a stunt to promote the sale of Liberty Loan Bonds to finance America's participation in the World War. Doty flew out of a fog bank over Ocean Beach and circled the Civic Center while dropping paper reproductions of regulation three-inch cannon shells, each with the inscription, YOUR COUNTRY NEEDS YOUR HELP. BUY YOUR LIBERTY BOND. DO YOUR BIT. DO IT NOW.

Doty turned towards the shopping district with his bombs, and then returned to the Civic Center where he performed a thrilling death drop. The large crowd gathered below him gasped with amazement as he pulled out of the drop and landed in the middle of Grove Street. Mayor Rolph, Adm. Charles F. Pond acting president of the Pacific Aero Club, Col. William A. Glassford, and several other members of the Liberty Loan Committee were there to meet Doty when he landed. The dignitaries congratulated him after which he bought a Liberty Bond and returned to his plane and took off for the Ocean Beach aviation camp.

Before Doty began his mission, he was met by Miss Lucy Catlin dressed as the Goddess of Liberty. It was she who supplied him with the Liberty Loan bombs.

While he was up "bombing" the local citizens, three hundred Boy Scouts equipped with more bombs and Liberty Loan posters were soliciting door-to-door asking the public to buy bonds, so the soldiers going to France would be adequately equipped to fight.

One wag wrote, "Either you must buy all the bonds you can afford to buy of this issue and the next one, or you will be taxed on everything from

CHAPTER 9   271

your shoestrings to your teeth-fillings. You will be taxed, taxed, taxed for the next twenty years, until you will be sorry that you own anything, that you eat anything or that you wear anything." [49]

There were several Liberty Loan drives during and after the Great War. Aviation exhibitions were an essential part of every drive.

In August, Lyman joined the US Army Air Service as a flying officer. Doty was honing his aerobatic skills in preparation for the Air Service by flying daily exhibitions over Redwood City. Frank Bryant, his flying instructor, would critique and advise him after each exhibition.[50]

Doty joined the Air Service in mid-1917 as an instructor in aerial gunnery at Kelly Field, Texas. Later he served as a test pilot and amassed fifteen hundred hours of flying time by the end of the war. He was discharged from the army on December 6, 1918, and joined the US Air Mail Service.[51]

On December 18, 1918, the Air Mail Service attempted to open an airmail route between New York and Chicago. There were problems. The first occurred when officials arrived at Grant Park, Chicago, on the morning of the eighteenth. For the first departure from Chicago to New York, there was no aeroplane to fly the mail.

Lyman Doty had left Elizabeth, Ohio, the day before to ferry the plane from Cleveland to Chicago. On the way, Lyman landed at Defiance, Ohio, for fuel. Just after touching down, a woman carrying a baby ran in front of him causing him to swerve to miss her. He crashed into a fence, damaging the plane, but suffered no injuries. The plane Doty was flying was intended for the inaugural morning flight from Grant Park. Another plane was summoned, and the mail finally left Chicago by late afternoon.[52]

A contemporary account of the above incident stated Doty was flying a reserve plane and after landing near Painesville, Ohio, the plane turned turtle. The crash occurred during the day, and the only damage was a broken prop.[53]

The beginning of the New York–Chicago run was a chaotic time for the Air Mail Service. The pilots were flying de Havilland DH-4 ex-army bomber biplanes and a handful of Curtiss R-4 training biplanes. Standard Aero at Elizabeth, Ohio, had modified some of the DH-4s making them safer to operate. The R-4s didn't last long; they were totally inadequate for flying the mail.

The DH-4 modifications by Standard were minor fixes. The majority of the work done on the planes was assembling the DHs from their shipping crates. Instructions had been given that each DH engine and airframe was to be closely inspected. Then the planes were to be test flown for 4.5 hours prior to being handed over to route pilots.

The testing appears to have been done by the route pilots and exposed dangerous flaws in the engines and airframes of the "modified" DHs. Complaints about the planes were numerous, but they continued to be flown.

One pilot wrote: "The whole plane in general is constructed of the cheapest material I have ever seen used in the manufacture of an airplane. Soft wood such as pine has been used where ash or some other equally as strong wood should have been used." He also said that holes had been drilled in the airframe that weakened the entire structure.

Lyman Doty was landing a Standard built DH-4 at Belmont Park on Long Island, New York, December 28, 1918, when his landing gear collapsed causing the plane to skid along the ground on its fuselage before destroying itself. Lyman suffered major injuries. Shortly after the crash, the Post Office stopped the New York to Chicago run while the accident was investigated.[54]

Doty was flying from the front cockpit of DH-4, No. 24238. He was crushed between the gasoline tank and the engine during the crash. Later modifications to the DHs in airmail service would put the pilot behind the gas tank, but Lyman would never enjoy that modification.[55]

Lyman suffered a skull fracture and was unconscious for three days. After he woke up he had a partial loss of memory for another two weeks. He wasn't released from the hospital until February 1919. It took three more months for him to recover from the crash.[56] Doty returned to his family home in Biggs during the second week of March to recuperate on furlough from the Air Mail Service and wasn't due back until May.

Upon his return, the Gridley newspaper reported that Doty only had a slight accident and had suffered a sprained wrist and fractured skull. Jeanette Doty remained in New York to visit relatives and protect her brother's interests. Doty intended to remain in the flying game and planned to return to New York in April to be reassigned to airmail routes.[57]

After his return to Biggs, it wasn't long before Lyman was in the Bay Area visiting his old haunts and seeing old friends. On April 9, his parents returned home from San Francisco after several days there. Lyman accompanied them home staying a few days in Biggs before returning to New York to resume his flying duties.[58]

In May he took his first flight physical since the accident. The doctor wouldn't pass him because he had fractured nasal bones that caused a deviated septum and put possible pressure on the right eyeball fouling his distance judgment. Lyman had a successful operation to correct the problem, and he passed his next flight physical. He was ready to fly again in July. He had fought hard to return to his job flying mail.[59]

From May 15, 1918, to May 15, 1919, Lyman Doty had completed a total of five flights for the US Air Mail Service. Three were perfect flights and two were uncompleted for a total of 369 miles. The two uncompleted flights would have been the one that ended in the crash at Defiance, Ohio, and the other would be the flight ending at Belmont Park, New York. His lack of completed flights and miles flown were due to the long recuperation required after his crash at Belmont Park.[60]

On October 14, 1919, Lyman Doty was killed at Catonsville, Maryland, near Baltimore, while flying airmail from Washington, D.C., to New York. Dispatches received in San Francisco reported he crashed at the Rolling Road Golf Course.[61]

Doty was flying an Air Mail Service Curtiss R-4, No. 32. The caretaker at the golf course saw the R-4 flying in thick fog extremely low over the grounds when it hit a tree. The plane fell to the ground and turned over, catching fire. Due to the flames, the caretaker was unable to help the pilot. The Air Mail Service sent pilot Sam Eaton to accompany Doty's remains to his hometown of Biggs.

Otto Praeger, assistant postmaster general, and known as the "Father of the Air Mail Service" wrote William Doty, Lyman's father, that Lyman, "... was dependable, courageous and of the highest integrity, and died at his post of duty. His career is worthy of emulation, and no doubt must be a source of pride to his family." Mr. Doty wrote Praeger back thanking him for his kindness and sadly concluding, "He was all I had."[62]

Del Paso Airport was the municipal airport for Sacramento from 1919 until the current Executive Airport opened in 1930.

This photo depicts an Army Air Service DeHavilland DH-4 at Langley Field in 1919. DH-4s were used by Air Service forest fire patrols over the timberlands of California, Oregon, and Washington in 1919–1921. They were also the U. S. Air Mail Service's primary mail carrier from 1919 to 1925.

CHAPTER 10

Army Air Service begins forest fire patrols – Fire patrols of 1919 – Oroville opens an airport –Army fire patrols at Oroville – Fire patrol moves to Redding – The Air Service, dissatisfied, moves from Redding to Red Bluff – Fire patrols of 1920 at Red Bluff – Fire patrols of 1921 at Corning – Fire patrols from 1925 and beyond

In October 1918, a forest fire destroyed more than ten thousand acres of timber in northern Minnesota. It was seen as a great loss of wood needed for the war effort. Chief Forester Henry S. Graves of the US Forest Service requested the Army Air Service help to minimize the occurrences and severity of forest fires. In March 1919, the secretary of war ordered the director of the Air Service, Major Gen. Menoher, to supply planes, pilots, and landing fields for the purpose of carrying out forest fire patrols over California and Oregon timberlands.[1]

The order would have the immediate effect of expanding the number of airports in northern and central California. The Army Air Service in effect created new landing facilities in Butte, Tehama, and Shasta counties of the northern and northeastern regions of the Sacramento Valley. In those regions the US Army influenced local authorities to develop airports and emergency landing fields for its planes that would ultimately be used by civilian fliers long after the army's forest patrols had ended.

Even though the patrols were planned as a wartime effort, the war ended before the patrols started. The patrols became part of the Army Air Service's postwar efforts to be useful in peacetime by introducing new aeronautical technology developed during the war but not yet available to civilians, such as aerial reconnaissance, aerial photography, and mapping. Forest fire reconnaissance was carried out after the war as long as the army had available funds for the operation. The US Forest Service, though needing the patrols, made it quite clear to the army it had no money available for fire patrols.[2]

AERIAL FIRE PATROLS began in the south state on June 1, 1919. Army patrol pilots flew Curtiss JN-4Hs, the only planes available for the patrols at this early date. In some areas army observation balloons were used to spot fires.

Patrols began in Oregon and Northern California in mid-August. The planes available for those patrols were JN-4Ds and JN-4Hs. By the end of September, the more powerful and faster de Havilland DH-4s became available for fire patrol work.[3]

Lt. Donald Cathcart spotted the first forest fire of the operation in early June from an observation balloon tethered at an elevation of fifteen hundred feet on the Lucky Baldwin Ranch at the foot of the Sierra Madre in Southern California.[4]

Mather Field, near Sacramento, was the main base of operations for fire patrols in the north state. By June 21, twenty-one flights were made over the National Forests with four fires detected and reported to the US Forest Service in Placerville. Mather Field pilots had flown a total of three thousand miles in fifty-three hours of flying time by that date.[5]

By August 9, Mather pilots flying in Oregon detected twenty-eight fires in twenty-eight flights and in Northern California, five fires in twenty-eight flights.[6] The army's fire patrols of 1919 needed satellite airfields for refueling and repairing patrol planes originating from Mather Field.

The forest patrol flight route out of Mather for the north state extended northeastward over El Dorado and Tahoe National forests in a large semicircle starting from Mather, curving to the northeast over the Sierra Nevada and then curving back northwestward to the edge of the Sacramento Valley at Oroville—a distance that comfortably fit the range of the JN-4s used during the first months of patrols.

The plan was for a patrol to make its northern flight from Mather in the morning, and after refueling and lunch at Oroville, return to Mather following the same track southward.

ON MAY 22, 1919, Sergeants Buckley and Clark departed Mather in a JN-4 for Oroville. It was a dual-purpose flight. First it was to convince the citizenry of Oroville to locate and establish a permanent landing field

CHAPTER 10 277

for the army's fire patrol aircraft. Secondly, it was to fly the route the patrol planes would take to establish the route's feasibility.

After their morning departure, Buckley set a course for Placerville. At Placerville, he turned towards Auburn and from there he made continuous course corrections flying the JN over Colfax, Grizzly Flat, Grass Valley, Nevada City, Strawberry Valley, and eventually landing at Oroville. The pair arrived at 1:00 PM in Oroville after a nonstop flight of 2.5 hours. They would return to Mather over the same route.

At Oroville, Buckley and Clark met with William Boucher, head of the chamber of commerce, and made the army's request that a suitable landing field be established. Boucher immediately set to work finding a field. He asked former Lt. Henry Wolfe, who was with the Army Air Service in France during the war, to help him locate an airport site. Wolfe was manager of Sunical Packing Company at the time.

The site selected was level ground in the El Medio District near the Oroville city limits. The site, south of Oroville, had once been the little town of Independence, a "haphazard settlement created about 1850," between the railroad tracks of the Western Pacific and Southern Pacific Railroad companies. The southern end of the runway crosses today's Kusel Road. At the north end there is a commercial salvage business. One can just make out the old runway right-of-way in Google satellite photos on the Internet.

In 1901, the property belonged to Ed H. Riley, and in 1919 the new airfield was named for the Riley family. The Oroville Realty Company managed the property and gave the chamber of commerce permission to do with it as they wished. The ground could be developed as a landing field at little expense. The army required a field fifteen hundred feet by eight hundred feet with the long side in line with the prevailing north and south winds.

Boucher notified Mather the airfield would be ready in time for the first official patrol on June 1, 1919. Fire patrol flights would be made daily until the fire season ended in October.[7]

The southern patrol route would be flown daily from Mather Field and end at Sonora or Toulumne in the mountains east of San Joaquin Valley.[8]

In the north from Mather, a fire patrol plane would arrive at Oroville between 11:00 and 11:30 AM each day and depart Oroville for the return patrol landing at Mather Field two hours later. Riley Field was soon reported in excellent condition and ready for service.[9]

OROVILLE in letters sixteen-feet square and one hundred fifty-feet

This is a 2014 aerial view of the Riley Field site on Kusel Road. Opened for the Army Air Service in 1919, it was Oroville's only airport until the current airport opened in 1935. There is evidence that it may have been used as an airfield as early as 1911–1913.

long was painted on the roof of the Exposition Building in Oroville to help aviators identify the city.[10]

SERGEANT BUCKLEY MADE THE FIRST official fire patrol flight in Northern California on June 1. He flew the same route from Mather to Oroville as mentioned above and spotted two fires, one was six miles from Colfax and the other near Forbestown. Buckley made the flight in one hour and fifty-five minutes. He left Riley Field just before 1:00 PM for his return patrol back to Mather. The Forest Service had not known of the fire near Colfax and sent fire crews out immediately to fight it.

Frank Haynie of the Forest Service, met Buckley when he landed his Jenny at Oroville. Haynie, Boucher, and nearly fifty residents from Oroville and Palermo were on hand to meet the first patrol plane. The field was only a mile and a-half north of Palermo. Haynie confirmed that the Forest Service would be installing a telephone at the new landing field allowing aviators to make their patrol reports to the Forest Service immediately upon landing. Buckley told the gathering he would be flying the northern patrol flights on alternating days with Lieutenant Gardner.[11]

A few days after the initial fire patrol flight, an anonymous letter to the local newspaper complained that for too long Palermo had been left out of the advertising when olives and oranges raised in the Palermo area were sold to the Eastern markets as "Oroville products" at best, and, worse yet, as "Southern California fruit." The complaint went on and pointed out the naming of Palermo as a "… suburb of Oroville by ambitious real estate agents, while we are supinely willing to be the tail of Oroville's kite, we cannot submit [to] supplying a landing station for the airplanes; when as a matter of fact, long before there was any prospect of a regular air service, the airplanes that made exhibition flights here chose 'Riley's Field' as the most desirable place in this vicinity in which to alight. As this location is almost a half mile [sic] from Palermo we claim the honor, and it is up to the citizens of Palermo to purchase a lot of lime and mark in letters of glaring white that can be read from the planet Mars, the words, 'Riley's Field, Palermo,' or in other words literally put Palermo in the 'lime-light' and in the years to come 'Riley's Field' may become as far famed as 'Mather's Field' [sic]." [12]

It is obvious that some citizens of Palermo resented being referred to as a suburb of Oroville; they saw themselves as more of a sister city. The letter also makes it obvious that the Riley Field land was the closest, sizable, level ground to the city of Oroville for an airport. Oroville is located in a rugged area of the Sierra Nevada foothills. The letter confirms that a number of aviators during the Exhibition Years used the field for their flights. Kerns, Fowler, and other exhibition flyers may have used the field then.

When Lt. Col. Henry L. Watson asked the Chico Chamber of Commerce to aid in establishing an airfield in early June, the matter was put on the agenda at the next meeting. Watson was in a command position at Mather Field and trying to stimulate the growth of airports in the north state.[13]

On June 9, Oroville Chamber of Commerce Secretary Boucher wrote a letter to Captain Glidden of the Army Air Service requesting the proposed transcontinental flight be routed into California by way of Oroville. He wrote that Western Pacific Railroad had a rail line pilots could follow directly from Winnemucca, Nevada, to Oroville. He also noted Oroville had just complied with the army's request for a landing field.

That same day, Sergeant Buckley was doing descending loops and rolls in his Jenny as he let down from high altitude at the end of his patrol flight. He lost several personal items from his pockets while over Oroville. He requested that if found, the money, pocketknife, and other items should be sent to the chamber of commerce for him to collect.

Also on the ninth, a flight of eight aircraft on their way from Mather to Portland flew over Oroville. The planes were scheduled to participate in the Rose Festival at Portland.[14]

Lt. E. F. Evans flew up to Oroville from Mather on a familiarization flight in early June but was unable to find Riley Field. He landed somewhere between Oroville and Wyandotte slightly damaging his plane. He contacted Sergeant Buckley at Riley Field. Buckley and Cpl. H. B. Fisher flew out to guide him to Riley. After refueling, Evans took Cpl. Fisher with him to Mather Field, and Buckley flew his daily fire patrol route to Mather.[15]

Civilian aviators Ross Gardner and Charles McHenry Pond severely damaged their plane while landing at Riley Field on June 10. Flying up from Stockton, the two were not familiar with the airport and flew too far up the runway before touching down. They ran off the runway into a ditch at the northern end of the field shattering the prop and wiping off their landing gear and a lower wing. Luckily, neither man was injured. A flatbed truck took the wrecked biplane to Feather River Garage in Oroville for repairs.

Ross Gardner, who was piloting the damaged civilian Canuck was well known in Oroville; it had been his home a few years before. He had left town and gone into the aviation business eventually taking a responsible position with the federal government. He was chief government inspector at the Curtiss Aeroplane Company during the war. His passenger, Charles Pond, was his new postwar business partner. Pond had been the chief civilian flying instructor at Mather Field during the war.

Gardner and Pond were on a promotional tour for an airline they were creating. They were purchasing a multi-engine, eight-passenger Curtiss Eagle, which they intended to fly on a regular schedule the length of the Great Central Valley and into Los Angeles. (See chapter 11.)[16]

In June, Sergeant Buckley took Boucher, the chamber secretary, up in an army JN for Boucher's first airplane ride. They flew over the Wyandotte District, then further into the Sierra Nevada. Boucher said it was impossible to describe the grandeur of the trip. He did say the air was quite choppy, and the Jenny would drop two or three feet then bounce upward the same distance. He felt that someday, "… we will be bonding ourselves to build better aerial paths than we now have, particularly in the mountains."

Boucher's ride was sanctioned by Mather command to show appreciation for the work the Oroville community had done laying out Riley Field and establishing the first aerial locator (roof sign) west of the Rocky Mountains.[17]

Sergeant Buckley snapped one of the first aerial photographs of Oroville a few days before. It was taken north of the Exposition Building. It depicted the Western Pacific rail yard, local olive processors, and the word OROVILLE on the Exposition Building roof.[18]

Raymond Gardner, a local man, was reported as having been commissioned as an ensign naval aviator at San Diego. He was being discharged from service soon and planned to return to the University of California to complete his law degree.[19]

Another Oroville man, Ken Leggett, who had been an army flier since the start of the war, was about to lead a flight of army aircraft on a grand aerial survey of the United States. Leggett had gained an excellent reputation in the Air Service and planned to make it his career.[20]

Sergeant Buckley treated the citizens of Oroville to another display of aerobatics on June 22. He lost his hat while flying at ten thousand feet returning from a fire patrol. The hat was floating down towards the ground with Buckley diving his JN after it. He, "... looped the loop, corkscrewed, nose dipped," and every other maneuver he could think of to recapture his hat, but each time he got close enough to grab it, turbulence from his prop would blow the hat away from him. Hundreds of spectators in Oroville, who watched his crazy flying, were greatly entertained even though they didn't realize he was chasing his hat.[21]

Lt. Walter Beck from Palermo, a respected veteran of the war, was discharged from the army and back in Oroville by late June for a short stay. He had been assigned to the 372nd Aero Squadron in France and arrived at Bordeaux in October 1918. He "enjoyed many hours flying over the war torn battlefields of Europe." It is unknown whether he was a pilot or an observer.[22]

On July 4, 1919, the *Oroville Daily Register* reported, "Oroville not only produces the earliest oranges in the state, has the largest olive pickling plants in the world, some of the best (olive) orchards in California, and has the first aviation landing field in the North (state), but can also boast of having the first Chamber of Commerce manager in the northern part of the state to ride in a government plane." After it became known William Boucher had taken his flight with Sergeant Buckley, the army received many requests from other California chamber of commerce heads wanting rides.[23]

A baseball game was proposed to pit the local Oroville Olives (no pun intended) against the Mather Field Flyers, but a problem arose when the army team insisted on a guarantee of expenses for sixteen players, plus 50 percent of gate receipts from the game and the dance afterward.[24]

After further negotiations, the baseball game was played July 13. Folks gathered either at the local baseball field or at Riley Field for the arrival of the Mather Field baseball team. The team was preceded by four army JNs flown up from Mather to put on an exhibition of aerobatics and give rides to a select group of Oroville city officials. A civilian pilot, Ogle Merwin, flew his Jenny up to Riley Field to give paying customers rides.

The government JNs were led by Lt. J. Parker Van Zandt, followed by the other three pilots: lieutenants W. C. Goldsborough, E. C. Batten, and Charles A. LaJotte. That morning, the four planes flew over Palermo, Wyandotte, Thermalito, Oroville, and Pentz to drum up interest in the baseball game. They then buzzed the baseball diamond thrilling the fans.

That afternoon, Lieutenant Batten, whose nickname was "the Flying Fool," brought spectators to their feet several times with his aerobatic display over the baseball field. Later, he flew over and dropped several baseballs to the army players on the ground. They used the balls to beat the Oroville Olives eleven to one.

Ogle Merwin and E. H. Pendleton gave fifteen-minute rides to many Butte County residents for ten dollars each. After Oroville, they moved on to Chico, Red Bluff, and Redding on a barnstorming tour.[25]

Two men who went up with Merwin may have been owners of the land on which Riley Field was located. Their names were Tom Riley and J. E. Riley.[26]

Lt. Edward V. Wales, a few days later, was returning from fire patrol at eleven thousand feet and decided to lose altitude in a spectacular manner. He did loops and rolls while descending seven thousand feet. He then set up a long glide to land at Riley Field.[27]

By July 21, 1919, the army's forest fire patrols had flown over ten thousand miles and reported over twenty forest fires. While flying JN-4Hs (180 horsepower Hisso powered JNs) and a few JN-4Ds (ninety horsepower OX-5 powered JNs), the army's patrol pilots had to make only two forced landings; demonstrating that JNs were dependable when cared for properly.[28]

Lieutenant Batten repeated his aerobatic display in a JN on the twenty-fourth. It was a pattern local citizens were beginning to expect from the fire patrol planes as they came down from the high altitude necessary to safely carry out their patrol flights over the Sierra Nevada.[29]

E. H. Pendleton, manager of the aviation field at Del Paso Park, Sacramento, and his pilot, Ogle Merwin, returned to Riley Field on July 25 and flew passenger hops for the next three days. They planned to barnstorm on

CHAPTER 10   283

to Redding and Red Bluff over the next several days. They would return to Oroville then hit Chico and Marysville again on their way back to Del Paso Park. Pendleton planned to send a plane from Sacramento once a week to Riley Field. If his plan was adopted, passengers and possibly mail would be carried. The plan was never adopted.[30]

Sergeant Buckley made a forced landing in the Nevada desert in early August. He was flying from Mather Field to Reno for undisclosed reasons. After crossing the Sierra, his engine began running roughly. Over the desert, he decided to put the plane down immediately. He checked the engine to find the problem and, much to his surprise, he discovered the fuel tank empty.

At first Buckley wasn't sure what he should do. He needed gasoline, so he started walking with hope that he would find a farm or ranch somewhere. After about eight miles, he came upon a farm. There he purchased some gasoline, trekked back to his plane, and took off for his next stop. When he arrived, he reported the forest fire that had been burning near Colfax for the previous twelve days was finally under control.[31]

On August 12, Sergeant Buckley announced he had purchased his own Jenny and would be hopping passengers from Riley Field at Oroville starting in September.[32]

Also on the twelfth, Lieutenant Van Zant and Major Christie discovered a dead man in the Feather River near their swimming hole by the Oroville auto camp. There was no identification on the body.[33]

Lt. Kenneth Leggett, son of Mr. and Mrs. J. H. Leggett of Oroville, departed Hazelhurst Field, New York, on August 14 in the lead plane of the Army Air Service's "All-American Pathfinders" Squadron in an attempted transcontinental flight to the West Coast. Leggett was flying as an observer in a JN-4 flown by Lt. C. K. Guenther. The squadron's mission was to gather information about the best aerial routes and landing fields en route to the coast. In addition, they were to carry out mapping duties and experiments in night photography and colored lights to visually guide aviators at night. Their airplane would precede the rest of the squadron.[34]

Lieutenant Leggett, who was actually flying one of the planes according to a report, sent his father a map of the Pathfinders' route. He said the mission would take about twelve months to complete. In addition to mapping and establishing routes and airfields, they were also doing recruiting work during the trip.[35]

If the "All-American Pathfinders" reached California—specifically the

Sacramento Valley—in December, they were to stop at Red Bluff, Marysville, Sacramento, San Francisco, and their final destination, San Diego.[36]

Oroville Chamber of Commerce Secretary Boucher joined several other chamber leaders around the north state and objected in writing to a proposed government decree to close Mather Field. A telegram was sent from the chamber leaders to each US congressmen representing the north state.[37]

Sergeant Buckley thrilled the people of Oroville on August 15 by flying his Jenny under the Feather River Bridge with a clearance of only a few feet.[38]

Lt. James S. Krull with a passenger, State Forester G. M. Homans, took off from Riley Field in mid-August on a return flight to Mather. As their JN reached one hundred feet, the engine began running roughly forcing them to land immediately. There was no damage to the plane nor injuries to the men on board. The purpose of the flight was to familiarize Homans with the conditions of the forest on the Mather patrol route. The state of California was considering taking over local fire patrol duties after Arthur W. Ford was recently named fire patrolman for Butte and Yuba counties.

When Krull reported to the press his forced landing, he mentioned the army was introducing de Havilland DH-4 aircraft into service for the fire patrols. Until then, only Curtiss JN-4s had been used for fire patrol. The DH would carry a pilot and observer and could be equipped with a radio, according to Krull. This was the same Lieutenant Krull who made the first flight into Yosemite Valley on May 27, 1919. He flew from Merced to Yosemite in an hour and five minutes, a distance of sixty miles climbing eleven thousand feet to clear the mountains surrounding the valley.[39]

Seven army JN-4s made 482 flights over California National Forests reporting sixty-eight fires during their first two months of patrols. Four of the JNs from Mather Field patrolled the northern forests; two JNs from March Field, Riverside, and one JN from Rockwell Field, San Diego, covered the central and southern forests.[40]

Lieutenant Leggett and his observer of the Pathfinder Squadron were nearly killed after their biplane brushed a power line at Altoona, Pennsylvania, and caught fire. They had just departed from Altoona and were circling the town when they hit the wire. The fuel tank caught fire instantly. The burning plane crashed from seventy-five feet, but both men were uninjured due to the low altitude. A new aircraft was flown to Altoona, and the two were on their way in a few hours.[41]

The Army Air Service planned to expand its surveillance of the

CHAPTER 10

California National Forests by sending a squadron of de Havilland DH-4s to Redding. They were to patrol the northern, northwestern, and northeastern forests of California.

Additional patrols operating from Mather Field would fly the routes previously flown by the Oroville JNs. Replacing the JNs with DHs would give pilots a much longer range and move their refueling and lunch stop to Red Bluff.

Central California was patrolled by DHs based at Fresno. Their flights would take them over Hume, behind Sequoia Park, and around the Sierra Nevada to a landing in Bakersfield. Another patrol would cover the Kings River territory. Eventually a dozen DH-4s were involved in the fire patrols over California.[42]

DURING THE SHORT TIME the fire patrols existed in the summer of 1919, they converted from Jennies to DH-4s and left Oroville for a new northern terminus at Redding. The army would soon abandon that city suddenly and move its fire patrol DHs to Red Bluff. The story of this continuous state of flux reads like a war battle plan.[43]

Lieutenant Van Zandt's engine quit at five thousand feet during a flight near Oroville on September 27. He was flying above a cloud layer twenty-five hundred feet thick when an oil line broke on his engine covering the aircraft and pilot with hot oil. He was afraid he would have to let down through the cloudbank, which in this pre-instrument flying era of aviation was dangerous.

At the last second, he found a sucker-hole down through the cloud layer and guided his powerless airplane towards it. He stayed in the vertical shaft running down through the clouds; then emerged a half-mile from a farmhouse. He made a perfect dead-stick landing near the house, repaired his oil line, added oil, started the engine, and took off for Oroville—a very lucky aviator.[44]

Lt. E. C. Kiel landed ahead of the other West Coast fliers at Roosevelt Field, New York, on October 12, 1919, at the end of the first lap of the army's Transcontinental Reliability and Endurance Race. This race, mostly entered by military pilots, was flown from both coasts to the opposite coasts and back. It was a handicap race with several different types of airplanes involved. Lieutenant Kiel from the army's forest patrol won his first lap, but the overall winner of both the eastern and western laps across the nation was Lt. Belvin Maynard.[45]

With the end of the fire season for 1919 approaching, an erroneous report was released stating Oroville's airport was to be closed. The press issued a correction immediately. Even though fire patrol season was ending, Riley Field was not closing. In fact, Riley Field would continue to serve the Oroville area until the current airport was founded in the early 1930s. Admittedly, there were times during those years when Riley Field wasn't cared for and was suitable for emergency landings only.[46]

Even though Oroville had provided the army with a suitable airfield, the army moved its northern terminus for Mather's fire patrols from Oroville to Redding. The reason was clear; the fire patrols were upgrading to the DH-4 bomber, which had a considerably longer range than the JN-4 trainer. The DH's cruise speed of one hundred miles per hour was twenty-five miles per hour faster than the Jenny.

POSTWAR FLYING AT REDDING was really a story of the creation of airports. Until August 1919, there was an aviation field there, but it was dangerously short and poorly developed. A. S. Jones of Chico came to Redding in late July 1919 looking for a landing field. He lectured the city in a newspaper interview saying, "The municipal airplane field, in a very short time will be just as necessary as the automobile camping ground, and a number of cities already have them laid out. The air tourist soon will be coming in numbers and the towns which have the fields naturally will get their attention and business."[47]

Mr. Jones was mistaken about "air tourists" but not about airplanes coming to Redding. However, the airplanes would belong to the army and barnstormers, not tourists. The army had already been to Redding in July, and barnstormers arrived less than a week after Jones made his comments.[48]

When city officials learned a barnstormer was en route to Redding to give a number of eager citizens rides in his airplane, a more suitable landing field was found. Redding, like Oroville, was a rugged rocky location with hills. It was difficult to find a large level piece of land for an airport, but one was found on property belonging to the Menzel family.

C. E. Bennett of Chico Contracting Company sent a scraper to the Menzel property on a Saturday morning in late July 1919 and leveled a landing strip forty by fourteen hundred feet. E. H. Pendleton and his pilot, Ogle Merwin—barnstormers from Sacramento—began their operations from Menzel Field immediately. They took up more than two-dozen passengers in their Curtiss JN in early August.[49]

A few days later, the army arrived once again. This time five army fire patrol planes arrived in formation. They were on their way to Eugene, Oregon, to begin a six-week forest patrol duty over that state's timberlands. The city of Redding had been warned well in advance of their arrival, but there was a problem. The Menzel's, for unknown reasons, said their field was not available for the army flight.

Once again, C. E. Bennett was called. Mayor Norton of Redding, assisted by August Griswoldt, quickly found another airfield site on West Placer Street atop Johnson Hill. Bennett came in with his scrapers, wagons, auto trucks, and twenty-five workmen to create what was reported the best landing field in the far north state. Government and commercial flyers were given use of the field for free.[50]

When the five patrol planes arrived on their way to Eugene and landed at the West Placer Street airfield, it became known Charles A. LaJotte was one of the pilots. He had flown at Redding two months before during the Good Roads Celebration. The other fire patrol pilots were lieutenants A. Goodrich, C. H. Ridnaur, C. E. Batten, and William Goldbourgh. Each carried a sergeant mechanic in their passenger cockpits.[51]

The Redding city clerk received a wire from Mather Field on August 18 that Redding would soon be the northern terminus for army fire patrol planes operating from Mather. The army planned to send four DH-4s to the city's new airfield.

The new West Placer Street airfield was soon to have a gas and oil station installed for use by the army's planes. A phone line was to be installed, and it was believed the army would send up marking materials and other equipment to facilitate the landing of fire patrol aircraft.[52]

In mid-August the Sacramento civilian aviator, E. H. Pendleton, crashed his Jenny near Hamilton City while carrying two women passengers. He was returning from a flight to Chico and his engine quit. They hit the top of a eucalyptus tree while descending from four hundred feet. After crashing into the tree, his Jenny slowly slid down it to the ground. The tree, near Hamilton City's sugar company plant, saved the pilot's and passengers' lives. Pendleton claimed water in his gas tank caused the engine to quit, and he was flying into a strong headwind.[53]

Five DH-4s from Mather Field landed at Redding the week of August 20 to refuel and make a few small repairs. The planes and their crews were headed to Salem, Oregon, where they were to replace the JN-4s being used for forest patrol flights from that city.

The DHs were under the command of Major A. D. Smith who, as he flew over Redding, spotted the new airfield on West Placer Street and realized it was too small to safely land the DHs. He changed the plan to land there and redirected the flight of five across the river to land at Menzel Field.

At Menzel Field, Major Smith had Lt. Ned Schramm go with Redding official August H. Gronwoldt to inspect West Placer Street airfield and suggest changes to make it usable. The lieutenant explained to Gronwoldt the new field must be seven hundred fifty feet wide and twenty-five hundred feet long, and a landing tee placed in the middle of the field. Once those changes were made, Lieutenant Schramm said he would be delighted with the new field. The five-plane flight made the trip from Mather in an hour and thirty-six minutes. Their next stop was Roseburg, Oregon, then on to Salem where they were to arrive just before dark.

In addition to Smith and Schramm, the other pilots in the flight were: Lt. H. W. Webb, Lt. W. A. Wright, and Lt. G. O. McHenry. Three enlisted support personnel accompanied the five pilots.[54]

Lt. S. O. Carter, flying a DH-4 to Salem from Mather, was unable to find the airfield at Redding. He needed to land and refuel if he were to continue. He gave up looking for the airfield on West Placer Street, but he did find a likely landing field on the Bassett property, south of town. He made his approach to land, but upon touching down Carter could see there was little runway left. He slammed the throttle to full power and got off before he ran out of runway. He made a circut of the field. He believed he had landed long and overflew too much runway before touching down, so he decided to try again. He touched down once more, only this time he ran out of runway and went through a heavy wire fence ending upside down in a ditch. The landing gear, propeller, and one wheel on his DH were badly damaged, but Carter was uninjured. Spare parts were shipped up from Mather the next day for repairs.[55]

Seven Curtiss JN-4s carrying nine men under the command of Major A. D. Smith landed at Redding's West Placer Street airfield the next day. Smith and his detachment of pilots and mechanics were returning to Mather Field with the Curtiss JNs replaced by the five DHs Smith's men had flown to the Salem forest patrol base earlier in the week. The JNs were to fly forest patrol duty out of the Redding base for three or four days until more DH-4s could be flown up from Mather to replace the Jennys at Redding.

The JNs had no difficulty landing at West Placer Street airfield. They were smaller and lower powered than the DHs and required less distance to land. Major Smith was quite perturbed upon hearing of Lieutenant Carter's crash. Carter was flying Smith's personal aircraft. He was to use that particular DH, as unit commander, for trips to and from Mather on his inspection trips of fire patrol bases around the north state.

The route fire patrols were to fly from Redding was being drawn up. Soon the pilots would begin patrols. Pilots flying the patrols were: Major Smith, lieutenants Schramm, H. W. Webb, W. A. Wright, G. O. McHenry; sergeants C. A. LaJotte, V. Thomas, R. P. Blandon, and C. D. Leonard.[56]

At times there were critical gasoline shortages in America following the war's end. It was particularly bad in the small towns of Northern California. At Redding on August 29 it "... continued to be serious. Except for a little at the service stations, there was not a gallon in town. And the service station supplies were very meager. The seven airplanes which are doing forest patrol work from here were supplied with 'case gas' to make it possible for them to go out. One of the (gas) companies has seven tank (rail) cars at Roseville on the way and at least one car is expected in today. It is expected that conditions will return to normal within a few days."[57]

R. F. Hammatt of the US Forestry Service, and Col. H. H. Arnold, commander of the Army Air Service Western Department, met in Redding at the end of August to work out the details of operating fire patrols out of Redding's West Placer Street airfield.

Arnold was expected to arrive on the evening of the twenty-ninth in a La Pere fighter plane from the as-yet-unnamed Presidio airfield. Because of the small size of West Placer Street (WPS) airfield, the WPS aviation officers moved the landing tee across the river to Menzel Field, giving Arnold a longer airstrip to land on.

After the meeting, Hammatt reported the fire patrols would run from Redding to Alturas, and another from Redding to Yreka. A third would run from Redding to Lakeport in Lake County with Redding being the northern hub of all operations and supplies. Lt. E. C. Kiel would be in charge of the Redding flights. What the aviation officers were not sure of was "... a safe landing place for the big government machines (DH-4s)."[58]

COLONEL ARNOLD RETURNED to Redding the first week of September, accompanied by Major Smith and seven DH-4s. Three of the DHs led by Smith moved on to Roseburg, Oregon, where they would carry out fire patrols, and the other four would stay at Redding to fly patrols. Colonel Arnold was to return to his headquarters at the Presidio. Forestry official R. F.

Hammatt headquartered in Redding for a few weeks.[59]

Lieutenant Schramm and his mechanic Sergeant McKee flew a DH-4 on the inagural fire patrol to the Montague area on September 7. The patrol route for the area ran from Redding–Montague–Lakeport and back to Redding in one day. The pair made the trip to Montague in fifty-five minutes and reported two forest fires. The landing field at Montague had only been open for short time. Lieutenant Schramm said the ground and surroundings made the field a perfect landing strip. The town of Montague had placed gas, oil, a telephone, and emergency equipment on the field for the fire patrol.[60]

Lt. E. C. Kiel flew a DH-4 from Redding to Alturas in an hour and thirty minutes. He carried R. F. Hammatt as his passenger. The town of Alturas was deserted during the plane's presence on the nearby airfield. The residents of the Modoc County seat were all at the airport looking over the army DH-4 with its four hundred horsepower Liberty engine. Most of the residents had notified each other by telephone that the big plane had landed, and they should hurry to the airport if they wanted to see it.

Kiel and Hammatt departed Alturas after a three-hour stay. They made their return flight by a different route flying over Grizzly Peak, east of McCloud in Siskiyou County, and followed the divide between the Pit and McCloud rivers.

There was quite a lot of aerial activity at the Redding airfield that day. There were eleven planes on the field—then they all departed. Four returned to Mather Field, three left for Eugene, Oregon, another with Colonel Arnold and Major Smith on board took off for Portland, Oregon, and two left on fire patrols. The last two went to Yreka then to Orleans in the extreme western part of Siskiyou County. Later they flew to Lakeport and back to Redding by way of Weaverville.[61]

The army recruiting office in Redding was notified by wire that fireworks were being sent up from the Presidio for the welcome home celebration for returning servicemen on Admission Day, September 9, 1919. The forest patrol planes based at Redding were ordered to carry out a mock aerial combat over Redding for the afternoon's entertainment. The DH-4s were to carry the fireworks over the city and "… cast them adrift in the air currents." One wonders, who thought of having a fire prevention unit casting fireworks from airplanes during the late summer heat over a California mountain town?[62]

Lt. A. Goodrich, with forest ranger Lorenzen of Sisson as observer, flew to Alturas in mid-September. Goodrich flew very low over Muck Valley between Fall River and Bieber hoping to see evidence of a large meteor that shook up local residents the previous afternoon. They failed to see any evidence of the meteor. The remarkable spectacle was the talk of nearly everyone in the north state.[63]

A DRAMATIC CHANGE OCCURRED when Lt. E. C. Kiel arrived at Redding early on September 15, after a short trip from Red Bluff. He told his pilots orders had been issued to vacate the forest patrol base at Redding immediately and move to Red Bluff. After weeks of flying fire patrols out of Redding, army operations at the West Placer St. airfield were being moved elsewhere.

Lieutenant Kiel was blunt when he spoke to reporters, "Owing to a poor landing field and the (lack of) proper help from the local citizens in making a permanent place for the airplanes, the government ordered the post patrol moved to Red Bluff Wednesday morning, September 17."

During operations at Redding, the army had five to twelve aircraft on the field. At short notice, all equipment for the airplanes was being packed for shipment via express rail on Tuesday afternoon, and the planes would fly to their new base on Wednesday.[64]

By September 18, all planes of the forest patrol had moved to their new field in Red Bluff. The pilots were happy with their surroundings; the new field was spacious, long, and level. There were no hills near the field like the Redding airport. No fire patrols were cancelled during the move.[65]

The army's daily forest fire patrols during the final two months of the 1919 fire season, September 1 through October 31, covered fifteen out of the seventeen national forests in the state of California. Army JNs and DH-4s flew over 210.5 million acres of national forests. The lumber protected by the fire patrols was valued at 210 million dollars. During the entire fire season of 1919, the fire patrols suffered one fatality and six aircraft accidents requiring major repairs.[66]

For the army's involvement in forest patrols during the 1919 fire season, twenty-seven aircraft flew from six bases in California and Oregon. They made 709 flights and discovered 570 fires.[67]

The Army Air Service airfield on the Presidio grounds at San Francisco was named Crissy Field on November 3, 1919, for Major Dana H. Crissy who was killed in October at Salt Lake City while flying in the Transcontinental Reliability and Endurance Race.

As the state of California prepared for the 1920 fire season, the Army Air Service authorized, in March 1920, training twenty-two civilian foresters in forest fire observation technique from airplanes at a special school opened on March Field at Riverside in the south state.

The US Forest Service would pay for the six-week course. The army would continue to supply planes and pilots for the fire patrols, but the forest service would pay its observers.[68]

The 91st Observation Squadron at Crissy Field was ordered to transfer its eighteen airplanes to US Forest Service fire patrols for the 1920 fire season on May 1, 1920. Two of the aircraft would be equipped with wireless telegraphy, which was to be used to contact land stations at specific locations. Aircraft for the northern fire patrols would come from the 91st Squadron at Crissy Field. In the south state, planes would come from the 9th Squadron at Rockwell Field, San Diego.

The school at March Field for new civilian forest service observers was teaching not only the finer points of aerial observation, but also wireless telegraphy.

FOR THE 1920 FIRE SEASON, there were to be four flights of four DH-4 aircraft based at four stations around the state: Red Bluff, Mather Field, Fresno, and March Field. Two planes would be sent on patrol daily from each station. The two wireless equipped planes were to be roving aircraft with no permanent base. They would go to wherever forest fires were burning. Other landing fields for the patrol aircraft fuel stops would be at Rockwell Field, San Diego; Montague in Siskiyou County; Lakeport in Lake County; Alturas in Modoc County; Sonora in Tuolumne County; Bakersfield; and Santa Barbara.

A daily wireless report was to be compiled from all patrols and sent to Colonel Arnold at his headquarters on Crissy Field.

Directing fire crews by aerial wireless radio had been tried unsuccessfully during the 1919 fire season on the Angeles National Forest fire. However, the problems were supposedly fixed, and the process would be tried again.[69]

At Oroville, the site of so much aerial activity the previous fire season, the residents learned future fire patrols would be landing at Red Bluff or returning to Mather; they would not be landing at Oroville except in an emergency.[70]

A fire patrol DH-4 made a forced landing at Dana, a small community north of Fall River Mills, on May 28, 1920. The DH needed new parts to

CHAPTER 10 293

fly out of its predicament and return to Red Bluff. A call was made to Red Bluff to send a plane with spare parts.

Army aviator M. F. Robbins with his observer, C. A. Fritiofson, flew a second DH with the parts to Dana. On landing, Robbins hit a patch of soft ground and his DH went tail over nose destroying the fuselage and wings of the aircraft. The two men suffered no serious injuries with only Fritiofson's flying goggles broken. The first plane that force landed was able to utilize the undamaged spare parts and take off returning to base. What was left of Robbin's DH was loaded on an army truck and driven back to Red Bluff via Redding.[71]

Lt. Lowell H. Smith, one of the contestants of the 1919 Transcontinental Reliability and Endurance Race, was placed in charge of the Army Air Service fire patrol flight based at Eugene, Oregon, in June 1920. Smith would soon be known in Butte County as vice president of Friesley Company, which would build the Friesley airliner near Gridley.[72]

Ten army pilots assigned to the fire patrol planes based at Red Bluff spotted and reported thirty-five forest fires by mid-June 1920. Three of those fires, located east of Red Bluff, were still burning as of June 18. There was one accident during that period; a DH-4 crashed into another while landing at Red Bluff. There was damage to the planes but no injuries to the fliers.[73]

A DH-4 carrying three men took off from Red Bluff at 2:30 in the afternoon of July 10. Within six minutes, the big biplane was a smoking pile of rubble with the crew dead! It was the worst accident that would befall the Air Service aviators of the forest fire patrols in all their years of service over the nation's forests.

Sgt. Wayman Haney piloted the ill-fated DH. The rest of his crew were army observer Cpl. Antonio Salcido and civilian observer Benjamin H. Robie. While climbing out after takeoff, Haney fell into a spin at a dangerously low altitude of four hundred feet; the plane erupted instantly in flames from nose to tail. Witnesses on the ground were stunned watching the three men frantically getting out of their seat belts as their clothes and hair began to burn. In the short time it took the plane to fall from four hundred feet totally out of control, it did a succession of loops before hitting the ground nose first shattering into small bits and pieces.

The commander of the fire patrol flight, Capt. W. J. Hoover, recovered the bodies of the crew and drove them to the Red Bluff airfield.

Lt. H. E. Halverson of the Army Air Service at Crissy Field reported

Haney was one of the best enlisted pilots and was unable to say what caused the accident.[74]

It should be noted that the DH-4 had a nasty reputation for catching fire. After the war, the army had a number of the DHs modified to alleviate the fire problem, but it is unknown if Haney was flying a modified DH-4. If it was the usual fuel leak problem that brought Haney down, it could explain the abrupt maneuver he performed to get the plane on the ground fast after the leaking gasoline was detected.

The residents of Alturas purchased land for a new airfield in July 1920. The forty-five acre site they bought would be available, not only to the forest fire patrols, but also to any commercial or private pilots who wished to land there.[75]

Lt. Lowell H. Smith, as already noted, was in command of a flight of DH-4 fire patrol planes at Medford, Oregon. Smith convinced the community to convert a section of Medford's new county fairgrounds into an aviation field. He informed the residents there were five planes under his command. Two planes would be used each day to patrol the forests of Oregon and the extreme northern part of California. He predicted the Medford base would have seven hangars and a wireless station.[76]

The US Forest Service declared that from July 16–31, fire patrol planes, based originally at Mather Field, reported seventeen of the nineteen fires spotted in all patrol areas of the Pacific coast. Eleven of those were reported by radio, which were by then carried on all aircraft used for fire patrols.[77]

The success of the fire patrol in Northern California was indicated by the following statistics: 33 percent of the 196 fires spotted by the aircraft from Mather Field were accurately reported to within one-quarter of a mile from their exact location determined later by ground survey crews. An additional 19 percent of the fires were reported to be within a half-mile from the exact location. Ten percent were spotted by aerial patrols before rangers even knew they existed, and 43 percent (eighty-four fires) were reported by radio while the planes were still airborne. District Forester Paul G. Redington reported these statistics in late September 1920.[78]

In October, after the final fire patrol flight of the season was made, results for the 1920 fire season were made public. The patrols in the north and south state flew 2,457 flights over a distance of 202,000 miles. The crews discovered and reported 442 fires. During those flights, three men died in six major accidents. No other serious injuries occurred to the aircrews.[79]

For the upcoming fire season of 1921, the Army Air Service requested

CHAPTER 10   295

five reserve squadrons be made available for patrol duty.[80]

Citizens of Oroville, Redding, and Red Bluff had developed airports for their communities very early in the development of aviation infrastructure in Northern California. The sole reason for this early development in 1919 and 1920 was entirely to meet the needs of the US Army Air Service in its lopsided partnership with the US Forest Service to protect the valuable forest resources of the Western states.

IT WAS CORNING CITIZENS' TURN to step up to the plate for the 1921 forest fire season and create a new northern terminus for fire patrols in the north state.

Forty DH-4s were shipped to Mather Field on April 1, 1921, for use by the 9th and the 91st Aero Squadrons for forest fire patrol. Another fifty DHs were being assembled and overhauled for fire patrol duty if needed for the upcoming fire season. Five service squadrons were to operate out of Mather for this duty with another two squadrons to be added at a later date.

Headquarters for fire patrol operations would again be Mather Field. Patrols would be based at Rockwell Field and March Field for the south state; Fresno and possibly Santa Barbara for the central state; and Mather Field and Red Bluff (the latter replaced by Corning), as bases for the north state patrols.[81]

In May, Colonel Arnold, Air Service commander of the 9th Corps Area, announced from Crissy Field that fifty DH-4s would begin patrols over California forests from Mather Field on May 20. Planes from the 91st Aero Squadron would begin patrols over Oregon forests and on the Olympic Peninsula of Washington that same day.

There had been some doubt there would be forest fire patrols by the Air Service in 1921 due to the absence of congressional appropriations to finance the army's protection of the national forests. Arnold's announcement erased all doubts for the Western states.

Patrols in Washington would operate from the airfield at Ft. Lewis. Those flying over Oregon timberlands would operate from bases at Eugene and Medford. According to Arnold, those patrolling California forests would fly from the same fields as stated above with the exception of Santa Barbara, which was changed to Bakersfield. There would be thirteen patrols made up of three planes each.[82]

When operations began in 1921, the landing fields to be used were Mather Field and Corning in the north; March Field and Visalia in the south. Central state bases were, as originally planned, to be Fresno and Bakersfield. Auxillary bases were designated at Covelo, Montague, and Alturas in the north. Chowchilla was added with Santa Barbara in the central and south state.[83]

After the northern most patrol base in California was changed from Red Bluff to Corning at the last minute, the good citizens of Corning under the direction of Warren N. Woodson, Corning's city father, acted quickly.

Woodson described the events in a brief history he wrote for the local paper years later: "Public spirit smoothed a runway in the 160-acre field, which adjoined the town on the north. Lumber barracks were erected and a well drilled by Corning. The flyers flew around Corning for the summer, frightening hens until egg production was severely effected and white laundries were impossible as well as destroying a number of olive trees by accidental landings."[84]

This fire patrol airfield was not to remain the town's airport for long. Later, Woodson founded a new airport named Woodson Field, of course, and it remains Corning's municipal airport to this day. It is located near the northeast corner of Corning, just one mile east of the army's fire patrol airfield built in the northwest corner of town in 1921.

In late May 1921, seven DH-4s flew into the newly developed fire patrol airfield at Corning. They were from the 9th Aero Squadron with Lt. John Morgan commanding the seven-plane patrol. In later years, Major John Morgan would become executive officer of the Army Air Corps' Randolph Field in Texas.

One of the pilots under Lieutenant Morgan's command at Corning was Lt. T. Claude Ryan who piloted DH-4 No. 13. This was the same T. Claude Ryan who later, as a civilian, would start the first scheduled landplane airline service in the United States from San Diego to Los Angeles in March 1925. His partner in that endeavor was B. F. Mahoney, one of his former flying students. They designed and built the Ryan M-1, used as a mail plane by fledgling airmail companies, and later built the M-2 for the same purpose. In 1926, they designed and built the Ryan B-1 Brougham, an advanced four-place cabin plane, a version of which became the *Spirit of St. Louis* flown by Charles Lindbergh. During World War II, Ryan built the PT-22 primary trainer.

Ryan's early years, as an aviator, are most informative. His flying career started when he became an army aviator after the end of the Great War. He graduated from flight training at March Field in 1921 and decided to

CHAPTER 10

take an option the army offered new graduates from primary training that year. Instead of going to advanced flight training at Kelly Field in Texas, one could choose to fly forest fire patrols over the timberlands of California, Oregon, and Washington. Ryan chose the forest patrol.

Ryan was sent to Mather Field for ten hours of training on the Liberty-powered DH-4. He learned not only to fly this powerful biplane but also the finer points of observation flying and fire patrol techniques. He was then assigned to Lieutenant Morgan's patrol squadron and put in charge of his own plane, a mechanic, and an enlisted observer who also acted as fire lookout and radioman.

Ryan thought he was a pretty hot pilot with no fear, so he chose plane number thirteen as his mount. He flew it the entire 1921 season without a serious problem.

After the squadron was established on their new airfield at Corning, they learned their patrol routes. Ryan's route was nearly five hundred miles, which he was to fly every other day. For his patrol, he would depart Corning and take up a heading northwest to the Oregon state line where he would turn east to Montague. There he would land to refuel and eat lunch, then fly back to Corning via Mount Shasta.

Ryan would fly his DH at ten thousand feet for most of the patrol. He would be over timber-thick mountains with few places to land. There were only two emergency fields available to him the entire patrol. His plane was equipped with a radio, and amateur radio operators would act as receiving stations for the fire patrols.

Even though Ryan never had any problems with old No. 13, some of the other patrol pilots had frequent forced landings. As the season neared its end, the forest service cleared a number of new emergency landing strips, and Ryan was given the job of finding these strips and making the first landings on them to determine if they were satisfactory. He spent the remainder of the fire season on this duty without incident and greatly improved his flying skills.

He did have a scare over a dangerous section of forest after his engine stuttered a bit, and he had to put the plane down. Luckily, he was near the emergency strip at Orleans in the Klamath National Forest. He was forced to make three passes at the strip before he pancaked the plane onto it. Ryan and his observer were both amazed the landing gear held; it was the shortest landing he ever made. When Ryan began flying patrols on this route in June, the only other emergency landing field besides Orleans was at Gravelly Valley.

Fire season ended in October with Ryan and his squadron returning to Mather Field where he remained until January 1922 when he left active service.[85]

Two of Ryan's squadron mates, who flew the same route as Ryan, were not so lucky. On September 4, pilot Sgt. Clement J. Whistle and his observer, Robert Noupe, possibly a Forest Service employee, had just taken off from Montague when their DH-4 burst into flames. They were about five hundred feet above ground when the plane exploded and crashed. Both men were killed.[86]

The 15th Aerial Photo Section based at Crissy Field made a photo survey in late November of the area between Ft. Bragg, Montague, and Mather Field. The purpose of the survey was to furnish data to determine the value of the forest patrol operations during the past summer of 1921.[87]

The final report on operations was announced in December 1921. The Air Service fire patrols reported six hundred fires in California during the fire season, and four hundred and eighty fires were reported from the planes by radio. Fifteen radio stations worked with the army reporting those fires. The aircrews operated from March Field, Visalia, Mather Field, and Corning. About thirty DH-4s were used for fire patrols during the entire season.[88]

The Air Service used personnel and planes from only the 9th and the 91st Aero Squadrons to make up the smaller forest patrol flights. In these patrol flights there were twenty-six officers, twenty-four flying cadets, and 466 enlisted men. The cost of the fire patrols to the Air Service for the 1921 fire season was $128,528 with twenty-five planes lost or seriously damaged in crashes during which four men were killed.

A government report on the army forest patrols stated there were no efforts made by any government department to utilize the Air Service for forest patrols during 1922. Funds for the Army Air Service and the US Forest Service had been cut to the bone that year.[89]

In 1923 the message from Washington, D.C., was the Forest Service would not be able to use army aircraft for fire patrols. There were no available funds. It was the same story in 1924.[90]

IN 1925 ARMY FOREST FIRE PATROLS were reinstated but on a much more limited basis. It was announced in May there would be two patrol bases in California from which nine planes would fly. Griffith Park, Los

Angeles, would be one base and Mather Field the other. There would be three additional bases from which an additional nine planes would patrol Oregon, Washington, Idaho, and Montana. The army would make all patrols available on July 1.

Regular fire patrols would not be flown over the forests. The planes would be made available for special flights during times of high fire danger and for reconnaissance missions over large fires in progress. As in the previous years, Paul G. Redington, the California district forester, would be in charge of the Pacific coast patrols.[91]

Special flights during times of high fire danger included those needed to confirm ground reports of a fire, those required for detailed observations after electrical storms, and when smoke prevented ground lookout stations from locating a fire.

The bases and pilots involved in the 1925 fire season were: Mather Field–N. W. Potter and Paul A. Andert; Griffith Park–C. N. James; Eugene, Oregon–A. R. DeGarmo and A. R. Loomis; Vancouver, Washington–S. D. Priestly and D. G. Logg; and Spokane, Washington–M. E. Meer and R. M. Freng.

Lt. Lloyd Barnett of Crissy Field was chosen as liaison officer between the Air Service and the Forest Service. Eight of the planes involved were from Rockwell Field, San Diego, and the ninth was from Salt Lake City.

Emergency landing fields were located throughout the Western states and were adequately marked.[92]

Captain Potter and Lt. Andert were pilots for the Mather Field fire patrol flight. The flight's mechanics were O. C. Hanson, C. DeVelschow, and Ben Torrey. Captain Potter was well known in Western aviation circles, and Ben Torrey would become legendary as the manager and chief pilot of Woodson Field at Corning throughout the 1930s.[93]

In 1926 the forest fire patrols were organized the same as 1925. The same fire bases were used and most of the same crews. At Mather Field, Lt. Paul A. Andert was put in charge of patrol flight, and Lt. C. A. Burrows was in charge of patrol flight at Griffith Park. Once again, Lt. Barnett was liaison officer at Crissy Field supplying aircraft used by the patrol flights.[94]

The army was not used for forest fire patrols in 1927. In 1928 the service was contracted out to civilian businesses. For Northern California, the service was contracted to Pacific Coast Air Service headquartered at Oakland Airport. The company's chief pilot, Joe Barrows, accompanied by J. W. Nelson of the US Forest Service, made the first patrol over Tahoe National

Forest. Pacific Coast Air Service's flight was made in a Whirlwind powered Romair biplane. The company had recently purchased two Romairs from Pacific Air Transport. The first flight was a six hundred-mile trip over national forests in the Sierra Nevada and took less than six hours. Joe Barrows was not only chief pilot but also operations manager for the company.[95]

Pacific Coast Air Service was also awarded the contract for fire patrol in 1929. In 1928 the company was credited with saving thousands of acres of timber. The company's planes were not only utilized for detecting fires, they also transported fire crews to landing strips closest to fires.[96]

Forest fire patrols for the 1930 fire season may have been reduced due to the onset of the Depression. However, it is known that an unnamed flying service from Palo Alto was hired in August to patrol forest fires already burning. Fifty-two lightning fires were started after a particularly bad electrical storm over the Klamath and Trinity National Forests. Five hundred men were fighting twenty forest fires in those areas. More fires were burning in the Hayfork–Mad River area, sixty miles west of Red Bluff. Twenty-one fires were burning in the Happy Camp district. Ten were burning in the Scott River Valley, and one at Summit Lake. Arsonists were plaguing the Pit and McCloud river area. There was another fire burning along a seventeen-mile front near Oroville. It burned off much of the brush on Table Mountain north of Oroville.[97]

Information conflicts as to the state of forest patrols in the 1931 fire season. The regional forester at San Francisco was waiting to receive bids for the Federal Forest Service Air Patrol. Bids were due by March 24. Only three planes were to be hired. Two would operate from Oakland or San Francisco to cover the north state and one plane would cover the south state.[98] Another report suggests the military were involved in forest patrols, at least in the south state. Lt. C. A. Burrows, a pilot for the California National Guard, was said to be flying a National Guard Douglas observation plane out of Los Angeles Municipal Airport on fire patrol duty. He was cooperating with the state division of forestry by observing progress of current forest fires.[99]

Associated Air Service Ltd. on Goddard Field, Palo Alto, was awarded the contract for forest patrols north of the Tehachapi Mountains during the 1932 fire season. The contract stated Associated Air Service had to have two aircraft with at least 220 horsepower engines on call for the northern forests at all times during fire season—the pilot's duty was determining the direction and spread of large fires when smoke or fog blocks visibility of the mountaintop lookout sites. Pilot's duties were carry messages, transport officials, and haul supplies to firefighters during active fires.[99]

The US Forest Service conducted aerial tests in September 1937 using airplanes to direct firefighters from the skies. Tests were also carried out using aircraft to drop chemical bombs and water to extinguish or retard forest fires. Fred W. Funke, a forestry official, reported the tests were satisfactory.[100]

In September 1939, James Trenham took over Duck Air Service at Oakland. He assisted the Forest Service fighting forest fires and was in command of the fire patrol base at Red Bluff Airport. The Duck Company had eight airplanes in its fleet. The company's tri-motor aircraft was said to be the only large transport in the region available for charter work. The original owner of the company, William R. Duck, was killed in a plane crash in May 1939.[101]

Emmet E. Fall was flying for a company, probably Duck, with a fire patrol contract for the Forest Service during the 1938 and 1939 fire seasons. The company was paid twenty dollars per hour for each single-engine plane and eighty-four dollars per hour for the company tri-motor aircraft. The pilots received two to five dollars per hour for their work in the air. By 1938 and '39, fire patrol duties and procedures had changed considerably from what they were in 1920 and '21.

Major duties of the patrol pilots in the late thirties were resupplying the firefighters and watching for spot fires after an initial blaze began. Aerial resupply of food and materials for firefighters, usually within a few hours, became an enormous advantage over resupply by mules, which took as long as a week. This fast resupply of fresh meat, eggs, and vegetables kept the fire crews' energy levels high. Fire fighters in better physical condition were able to save more timber.

The pilots' work was dangerous; they had to drop bundles of supplies slowed by crude drag parachutes onto ridgeback and canyon bottom drop sites. The latter were the worst; they were usually obliterated from view by thick smoke.

Fall described his job, "In the old days flying forest patrol meant cruising over the area and spotting fires, but now we do all kinds of jobs. Last year (1938) when the Pacific Coast was hit by the worst forest fires in thirty-five years was the first time firefighters at the front were fed entirely by food dropped from planes. Each plane took care of 2,500 men. We had five ships flying from dawn to dark. We dropped more than twenty-five tons of food and supplies. To show how much faster we were, it took the mules four days to a week to return our chutes."

Later he wrote the new flying chores were varied. One minute the planes were wallowing in the rough air above the smoke spotting new fires and next, the pilot would be dropping food to firefighters, or hay and water for their mules. Later, he might be flying an injured firefighter to the nearest town or flying the fire crews' mail to the nearest post office.

Fall wrote about flying out of the Montague and Orleans airfields on missions into the Trinity Alps. He wrote of radios being used by the Forest Service to communicate with airplanes, and he wrote of the biggest item hauled in his plane a 350-pound tool grinder used to sharpen the fire crews' axes.

He described food bundles and how they were prepared for the drop. Each bundle weighed seventy pounds, light enough for the ranger assisting the pilot to handle and push out the door. The bundles were wrapped in heavy burlap with a square of muslin attached by ropes at each corner forming a crude parachute. An unusual rope grouping opened the chute so the bundle fell easily to the ground. Drop planes flew low when the bundles were pushed out.

Fall wrote with a little humor about the deadly game of fire crew support. At one particular drop site, a family of bears sometimes beat the fire crews to the bundle and ran off with the fresh meat. Crews at another drop site near Orleans requested their bundles be dropped from a higher altitude so the harder impact would tenderize the meat.[102]

Corning Airport in 1990, which became an important fuel stop for early airliners flying down the Pacific northwest route.

CHAPTER 11

Postwar civilian flying at Oroville – E. H. Pendleton – Ogle W. Merwin – Friesley Aircraft Corporation – Bond Spencer, designer, builder, pilot – Friesley development

Oroville had developed Riley Field rapidly for the Army Air Service to use as a fire patrol base. It was ready for use by army JN-4s by June 1, 1919. North state civilian pilots, who were mostly all ex-military fliers flying ex-military JN-4s and Standards, soon learned of the field's existence. As mentioned, there is evidence the property was used as a landing field, possibly as early as 1911 during the Exhibition Years. By the middle of 1919, early barnstormers found Oroville with its Riley Field a new market to tap.

One of the first civilian planes to land at the new postwar Riley Field was the aforementioned Canuck flown by Ross L. Gardner and Charles McHenry Pond. Their disastrous landing on June 10 had left an unfavorable impression of civilian pilots on local residents. Pond and Gardner came from their home field in Stockton searching for possible landing sites for their airline venture. After spending two weeks in Oroville repairing their Canuck, they returned to Stockton June 25.

Gardner and Pond left a redeemingly favorable impression on the community when they departed—they carried the first letter to be dispatched from Oroville by air. It was mailed from the *Oroville Register* to the *Stockton Record*. The letter had airmail postage affixed and was properly cancelled.[1]

Gardner and Pond landed at Pond Field in Stockton two hours and ten minutes after leaving Oroville with more than one letter. Additional letters were from the Oroville Chamber of Commerce to the chamber in Stockton, from the Oroville sheriff to the Stockton sheriff, letters for the Knights of Pythias and to Stockton banks, and a parcel post box of cherries to Ruth Single from a friend in Oroville. Gardner had been sworn in as Oroville's deputy mail carrier. All letters bore the correct airmail postage and cancellations.[2]

THE NEXT NOTABLE PRESENCE of civilian aircraft at Riley Field following the crash of Gardner and Pond was the arrival of E. H. Pendleton and Ogle Merwin on July 13 in their Curtiss Jenny. Pendleton was manager of the new airport at Del Paso Park, eight miles northeast of Sacramento. Ogle Merwin was his chief pilot. Both men were accomplished pilots. In their civilian JN they followed several army fire patrol Jennies from Mather Field to Oroville. The army planes were headed to Riley Field to put on an air show. Knowing army pilots were not allowed to take up civilians, other than approved VIPs, Pendleton and Merwin went to give rides to locals willing to pay for their first airplane rides. Merwin flew the JN while Pendleton took the money, organized the passengers, and helped them in and out of the Jenny.[3]

E. H. Pendleton, who claimed to be director of aviation in Sacramento, told Oroville city officials that Sacramento had the only municipal landing field in the state at Del Paso Park. He said even San Francisco didn't have a municipal airfield. If Riley Field was made the municipal airport for Oroville, he said the government would eventually transfer its rights to Riley Field to the city now that the war was over. The airport would be turned over if the city built hangars and other facilities. If these conditions were met, the city would earn considerable profits from the airfield.

It was at this point in his monologue that Pendleton offered to send a plane to Oroville once a week to carry mail between Oroville and Sacramento. If a local flying operator was found, Pendleton promised to withdraw and let the local operator take charge of the field. Oroville officials did not accept Pendleton's offer.[4]

Unfortunately, Pendleton was wrong on a couple of his facts. The airport located at Del Paso Park wasn't officially designated as the municipal airport for Sacramento until the mid-1920s even though it was supported financially by the city from 1919. San Francisco had a de facto municipal airport, Marina Field, from 1919 until 1924.[5]

Postwar civilian commercial aviation began at Oroville's Riley Field when Ogle Merwin gave ten dollar rides to a number of Oroville residents during that air show in July 1919. Business was so good, Merwin stayed at Oroville an extra day to give rides to those who came too late to ride on the weekend.⁶

To Merwin, the age of his passengers was of little consequence during his stay in Oroville. He took up Lena Cress, the daughter of L. M. Cress, who was only five years old.

Merwin moved on to fresh pickings. He flew into Thomasson Field, near the south Chico city limits, on state Highway 99 (Midway road today).⁷

E. H. Pendleton did his best to convince city officials in Chico, Oroville, and Gridley of the necessity to create suitable airfields for aircraft, which he claimed he could provide for mail and passenger service. He promised Gridley residents he would send a plane to their city to give practical demonstrations, in other words an air show and passenger hopping, if they were favorably inclined towards his suggestion. He was told the Gridley Chamber of Commerce would take up the matter soon.⁸

Pendleton kept pushing the various communities to construct landing fields because he wanted to establish weekly airplane flights throughout the north state carrying passengers and mail.⁹

Pendleton reported he was establishing a passenger service from Oroville to Red Bluff for a fare of ten dollars.¹⁰

Pendleton's name was on the front page of Oroville and Chico newspapers on a weekly basis, sometimes twice and three times a week throughout the months of July, August, and September 1919. He tried desperately to push north valley towns into accepting passenger and mail service by his Sacramento based JN-4s. He implied the US government would pay the cities twenty dollars a month for use of a hangar on any municipal airfield built, which was untrue. He tried to convince large local farmers they needed his planes to carry out their daily land and crop inspections. He was everywhere trying to sell flying to north valley residents, but their numbers dwindled when it came time to vote for money to develop airports.¹¹

Sergeant Buckly purchased his own airplane in August so he could hop paying passengers between missions for Air Service forest patrol.¹²

On August 13, E. H. Pendleton, as previously mentioned, crashed his JN, while carrying two women passengers near Hamilton City.¹³ Pendleton's next big push for aerial passenger service came the second week of September. He announced he was starting a passenger service between Oroville and Chico. One of his planes, flown by J. M. Fetters, would make the first flight of the hourly service, which would begin on the upcoming weekend. The flight was estimated to take thirty minutes. If the short haul flights were a success, Pendleton planned to extend them to the Bay Area within a few months.[14]

For the ten dollar fare the Oroville–Chico flight would depart from Riley Field and land at Morehead Field, west of Chico (possibly where today's Ranchaero Airport is located).[15]

If demand was high enough for the Oroville–Chico service, Pendleton promised to bring more planes and pilots up from Sacramento, and he would reduce the fare to four dollars.

To purchase a ticket for the new passenger service, one had to buy it from the Chico Chamber of Commerce at the Elks Club on Second Street in Chico.[16]

The Chico–Oroville air service lasted one day, September 13, and what a day it was. It began when J. M. Fetters flew his first passenger from Chico to Oroville in the morning. Frank B. Durkee, secretary of the Chico Chamber of Commerce, was chosen to be the first passenger because of his efforts helping to get the passenger service started. After Fetters landed at Riley Field and the official ceremony opening the new air service was concluded, Pendleton approached Fetters with new instructions.

Pendleton had received a message from his boss, Frank McManus, who owned the planes and aviation business that Pendleton managed. The message was for Fetters and his mechanic, Berger Johnson, to immediately bring the JN home to Sacramento, change planes, and fly to Reno to fulfill a new contract flying for the Nevada State Fair. The two men departed Oroville for Sacramento at once. They landed at Del Paso Field, Sacramento in mid-afternoon.

For Fetters and Johnson, that was the end of the story. Presumably, they took off for Reno in a different JN, hopefully, one with a 180 horsepower Hisso engine to get them over the Sierra Nevada. The ninety horsepower OX-5 model JN made a trip to Reno a real white-knuckle affair.

For residents of the Oroville–Chico area, it was quite a different story. A few minutes after Fetters took off from Riley Field, a huge ball of flame dropping from the afternoon sky was seen not only from Oroville and Chico, but also from points as far southeast as Colfax. Oroville witnesses of the ball of fire were convinced it was Fetter and Johnson's JN going down in flames.

Search parties headed by Pendleton and others rushed out into the foothills in the direction of Bidwell Bar looking for the crashed Jenny. They searched all afternoon but found nothing. Some thought Fetters might have returned to Chico, so a search party was sent to Morehead Field finding no one.

Captain Voss at Mather Field telephoned Frank Durkee in Oroville and expressed his fear that one of his forest patrol JNs from Oroville was the ball of fire reported. He was relieved when told it wasn't an army patrol plane lost. Durkee became worried about the plane that was searching for Fetter's plane.

Pendleton returned from the search around 6:00 PM and told everyone he thought Fetters and Johnson must have been burned alive. He then called the Sacramento office of his employer; he was told Fetters and Johnson had arrived on time, and the plane in question was sitting on the field at Del Paso Airport. Somehow, earlier communications had failed to reveal this information. At 7:00 PM the search was called off; the plane and crew were reported safe.

Although several people around the countryside had called and reported a plane going down in flames, it was actually a rare daylight sighting of a large meteor that left a trail of flame and smoke, which was visible for five minutes.

Due to McManus signing the lucrative contract with the Nevada State Fair, the air service between Oroville and Chico, thought to have been only temporarily suspended, was never resumed.[17]

EVENTUALLY, OGLE MERWIN'S LUCK ran out as he was flying duck patrol over the flooded rice fields on the Parrott Grant lands, west of Chico, in mid-October 1919. While cruising five feet above the rice chasing ducks away, his engine sputtered and lost power causing his plane to drop into the water. The JN was broken up badly; burying its nose in the rice and muck. Merwin suffered lacerations on his eyes and nose. The Jenny was later pulled from the mucky ooze by a Caterpillar tracklayer tractor. Merwin said, as soon as the plane was repaired, he would be back in the air chasing ducks.[18]

A week later, due to the severe damage to his JN, Merwin decided to leave the Butte County rice fields. He had run his total flying time up to 750 hours. He refuted a statement that ducks gradually become accustomed to the airplanes and showed little fear when the planes were near. Merwin asserted, "On the contrary, the use of an aeroplane for patrol purposes proved very effective in the rice fields. The birds take flight immediately upon the machine's approach."[19]

He left for Sacramento October 22 after completing his contract for duck patrol with the landowner, Parrott Investment Company. After his accident, Merwin's mechanics, Mark Wood and C. Gerdon, repaired the Jenny in ten days. When he left for Sacramento, Merwin had two small scars on his face from the October crash, his only flying accident to date. His engine was "hitting on all twelve" when he taxied the length of Morehead Field and took off for Sacramento.

Later, when asked about the safety of airplane racing and stunt flying, Merwin said, "I do not favor aviation races or spectacular flying for it discourages and retards the promotion of commercial aviation on a sane basis." About his duck patrols, he said, "The work on the Parrott Grant (Rancho Llano Seco) has demonstrated the airplane may be used commercially to advantage. We successfully kept that large rice area free from ducks for nearly a month."

What he said next was most telling about the deterrent method of the airplane in chasing ducks. He was again referring to ducks becoming accustomed to the planes when he said, "It would be just as sensible to say that a child will become accustomed to being shot through the head with a loaded gun. The plane runs into flocks of ducks, killing the birds by the score. Ducks fly fast, but not fast enough to escape an airplane."

When Merwin departed Morehead Field for Sacramento into a stiff south wind, he had two suitcases and a thirty-pound fish strapped outside the cockpit of the Hisso powered JN. He caught the fish in the Sacramento River earlier that day.[20]

The North American Air Line Association (NALA) considered constructing a large airfield near Oroville. It was to be a part of a network of airports linking the Pacific coast to the Atlantic coast. This was made known to the Oroville Chamber of Commerce when it received a request that a representative be sent to an NALA meeting in Kansas City on November 15.

If Oroville would build an airport of the proper size, NALA would list it on the main airplane route across America from east to west. NALA claimed such an airport would add much business to the community in the years to come.[21]

Was this request part of Alfred Lawson's premature efforts to create his transcontinental airline service in the United States? He had recently taken part in the first flight of his big Pullman cabin, twin-engine, biplane transport named the Lawson *Air Line*. A very similiar plane would be built in Butte County by Bond Spencer for Harold Friesley.

Use of a landing field for an airline at Oroville came up once more in

June 1920. R. L. Gardner of Stockton suggested the city construct an emergency landing field at Oroville for the airline he and his partner, Charles McHenry Pond, had planned.[22]

THE FRONT PAGE of the *Redwood City Standard*, September 25, 1919, had a long print column with the headline, REDWOOD SELECTED AS BIG AVIATION TERMINAL. Next to this long column was a much shorter one with smaller headline print stating, 17-MONTH-OLD BABY TAKES RIDE IN AEROPLANE HERE.

The long column explained A. W. Lawson's negotiations with Gordon Ferrie, president of Redwood Aviation Company, to make the airport at Redwood City the western terminus for Lawson's planned New York to San Francisco airline service. These negotiations were Lawson's attempt to pit the Redwood City airfield, which at the time was the finest in the Bay Area, against Marina Field, much closer to the center of San Francisco, for the honor of being the terminus for his transcontinental air service.

The shorter column told of Harold Friesley and his two daughters, Ruth and Eleanor, going for their first airplane ride at Redwood City with pilot Frank Bryant.[23] Evidence suggests Harold M. Friesley, or Herold as his name is sometimes spelled, in early 1919 became interested in the business possibilities of aeronautics, the new technology that proved effective in the Great War.

After Friesley hired Frank Bryant to take him and his two girls for their airplane ride, he became a true believer in aerial transportation. He was determined to build a large airplane that could move numerous passengers at once to their destination; not just the one or two passengers carried by most existing airplanes of the day. He wasn't quite sure how to accomplish this. He decided it would be best to get into the flying game and learn how to bring his idea of air travel to fruition.

During the following year-and-a-half after his ride with Bryant, Friesley, a wealthy pottery manufacturer from Berkeley, built an airport, Friesley Field, two miles directly south of the city of South San Francisco. (It was very close to the threshold of today's runway, One Zero Left, at San Francisco International Airport.) He started a flying school and air taxi service with three Jennies flying from his South San Francisco airfield and from Marina Field on the old Panama-Pacific International Exposition grounds in San Francisco. While attending to his new flying service, he began construction of a multi-passenger transport plane with an uncanny resemblance to Alfred

Lawson's *Air Line* transport.²⁴

Friesley Field near South San Francisco remained a usable airfield as late as September 1924, when Lt. Leigh Wade made an emergency landing there in the Douglas World Cruiser *Boston II*. Wade was headed for Crissy Field with the other two World Cruisers when he had battery problems and had to land. The three Douglas World Cruisers were nearing the final leg of their mission to be the first airplanes to circumnavigate the earth.

Wade's September 25 emergency landing of *Boston II* was witnessed by "Hollywood Pilot" Paul Mantz who happened to be driving by Friesley Field on the Bayshore Highway and saw Lieutenant Wade coming down to land on the abandoned airfield. He pulled over to watch the troubled plane and was soon helping the crew of *Boston II*. Mantz drove Wade to a nearby garage to acquire the battery needed to get the Douglas back in the air.

Coincidently, Lt. Lowell Smith, commander of this flight around the world, was once vice president of the corporation that built Friesley Field where Wade landed. Wade made it to Crissy Field that day and rejoined the others. The Douglas World Cruisers and crews would make it to Seattle, completing their famous record-setting flight September 28, 1924.²⁵

Lieutenant Smith gave the impression he was a silent partner in the Friesley Corporation. What he brought to the table is unknown and purely speculative. He was assigned to the Presidio in San Francisco after the World War, and he was there during the Air Service's construction and implementation of the Presidio airfield that would be named Crissy Field. He first made the newspapers in San Francisco for flying photographs of the Dempsey–Willard prizefight from Ogden, Utah, to the Presidio airfield for the *San Francisco Examiner*. The US Air Mail Service had flown the photos from Chicago to Ogden, but in July 1919 that's as far west as the airmail service came. The army allowed Lt. Smith to fly to Utah and bring the photos to San Francisco. This flight was said to be the stimulus for bringing the airmail from Ogden to San Francisco a little over one year later.²⁶

Lowell Smith from Battle Mountain, Nevada, came to broader public attention a few months later when he took part in the Army Air Service's Transcontinental Reliability and Endurance Race when he won the first leg. He managed to fly both the east and west legs of the race across America in a DH-4. Some pilots in the race were not so lucky. Major Dana Crissy was killed during the race, as was Lt. E. V. Wales of Mather Field's forest patrol. For his efforts in the grueling contest, Smith lost twenty-five pounds of body weight.²⁷

Smith's biggest career triumph began when as a lieutenant, he took over command of the Army Air Service's "Around the World Flight" in April 1924. Major Fredrick Martin, the first commander of the flight, crashed in Alaska. Smith assumed command of the remaining three Douglas World Cruisers. The flight was a major success for the United States and the Air Service. Smith's reward from the army was promotion to the rank of captain. He was jumped over a thousand senior candidates on the promotion list. The other world flight officers were jumped over five hundred senior candidates to higher ranks as their rewards.[28]

When Friesley's airliner made its first "official" flight on April 17, ten thousand people journeyed to the second Friesley Field, developed two miles south of Gridley in Butte County. There they witnessed the airliner's flight and a planned air show. Eddie Rickenbacker with Reed Chambers, Eddie's good friend and wingman from the World War, flew up from Durant Field, Oakland, in a Durant company white and blue Standard J-1.

There is a group photo extant of Rickenbacker and Chambers standing in front of the Friesley Falcon airliner. Chambers is listed as representing Durant Aircraft Corporation. Among those also in the photo are Lt. Lowell Smith, the Friesley vice president, there from his active duty post at Mather Field, and Lt. H. Halverson from Crissy Field, who flew in from their respective army airfields. Bond Spencer, the designer, builder, and test pilot of the Falcon, is in the photo with his employer, Harold Friesley, and others.[29]

Some of the local folks in the Gridley area are convinced Eddie Rickenbacker was involved in the Friesley project. It has been said Rickenbacker owned property in the Gridley area. Unfortunately, land records from that period were destroyed in a fire. Supposedly, Rickenbacker convinced a number of local ranchers to buy stock in the Friesley company. Some say Rickenbacker convinced Friesley to hire Bond Spencer to design and build his airliner, but that claim doesn't fit the timeline for Rickenbacker's presence in the San Francisco Bay Area.

Whether Rickenbacker influenced anyone in the Gridley area to buy stock in Friesley is questionable. Wherever he went, Eddie Rickenbacker, as a representative for General Motors (GM) at the time, was making speeches to promote GM's new line of Sheridan automobiles, but his talks usually turned into speeches promoting aviation and its future. He surely delivered such a speech in the Gridley area for the local GM dealership.

Friesley Aircraft Corporation was first incorporated in mid-1919 and reincorporated in early 1920. The original target date for the first flight of the Friesley BS-1 "Aircar," as it was originally named for its designer Bond Spencer, was September 1, 1920.[30]

Rickenbacker did not move to the Bay Area until September 1920. It is doubtful he had much influence over Friesley prior to then. However, once he arrived, it is certain he took great interest in the Friesley project. Rickenbacker and his 94th Aero Squadron buddy from the war, Reed Chambers, were quietly looking for such an airline project in which to involve themselves. Cliff Durant, Rickenbacker's boss at GM and founder of Oakland's Durant Field, also wanted to be in the airline business.

During the period 1920–1921, Cliff Durant hired a Los Angeles aeronautical engineer and designer, Waldo Waterman, to design and draw up plans for a twin-engine passenger aircraft to be built by Durant Aircraft Corporation of Oakland. Waterman did so and was paid for his efforts by Durant. What Durant did with those plans is unknown.[31]

As for Friesley's choice of Bond Spencer to design his airliner, that suggestion may have come from Lowell Smith. When the company was created, Lt. Smith was on active duty with the Army Air Service at Crissy Field and would have known Spencer earlier during the latter's army service.

The choice of Spencer might supply an answer as to why the Friesley and Lawson airliners were so similar in design. Spencer graduated from Brown University and learned to fly in 1914. He designed and built his own airplane before the war. During the war, he became an army pilot and was one of the top test pilots at McCook Field, where most of his three thousand hours of flying time were amassed. During the war, McCook was the test center for the Army Air Service. It was the equivalent of today's Edwards Air Force Base. Spencer left the military in early 1919 as one of the pilots with the most flying hours in the Air Service.

It was common practice during the Great War to assign manufacturing rights to several companies not just the company that originally designed the airplane to be produced. Spencer knew that and may have assumed the practice would be carried over into civilian manufacturing after the war. The Lawson Air Line passenger transport had already flown successfully when Harold Friesley decided to build a passenger plane capable of carrying a dozen people and hired Bond Spencer to carry out that decision. Once hired to build such a plane, Spencer may have figured what better way than to copy the most successful and only purpose built, fourteen-passenger aircraft flying in America.

Friesley may have even been given tacit permission to copy the Lawson plane from Lawson himself by not legally interfering with Friesley's construction. Friesley often stated his plane was planned to fly the San Francisco to Portland route, thus being no competition for Lawson's New York to San Francisco route. Gardner and Pond with their smaller eight-passenger Curtiss Eagle had planned for the route from San Francisco to Los Angeles to be the domain of their California Air Transport Company. Was it just coincidental that both Friesley Company and California Air Transport planned to use San Francisco, the terminus for Lawson's transcontinental airline, as a terminus for their airline routes?

HAROLD M. FRIESLEBEN, born in 1892, was the son of Daniel Friesleben who, when he died in 1897, was said to be Oroville's wealthiest citizen. Harold went on to graduate from the University of California at Berkeley. In 1917 he changed his name to Friesley because of anti-German sentiment in America brought about by the Great War.[32]

The Friesleben family, whose wealth came from hotels, real estate, farming, and a dry goods store, moved to San Francisco from Oroville the year Harold was born. He was schooled in San Francisco, but spent many of his summers and vacations on the family ranch at the confluence of Honcut Creek and the Feather River in Butte County.

After graduating from the University of California at Berkeley and with a sizable inheritance from his father, Harold went into various entrepreneurial endeavors. When he began his investing career in aviation, it was reported he was in the pottery manufacturing business.

Entering the flying business, as mentioned previously, Friesley purchased a trio of Jennies and built a large hangar near the city of South San Francisco. There he began construction of his large multi-engine passenger plane.[33]

BONIFIELD MELVILLE SPENCER was the designer and hands-on builder of the Friesley transport. After leaving the Army Air Service, Bond Spencer, as he was known, was first reported flying in the Bay Area in May 1919. He joined Pacific Aviation Company to do aerial photography for various advertising jobs and to haul passengers throughout California. Spencer was chief pilot for the company whose main purpose was photographing cities, towns, real estate developments, rivers, lakes, irrigation projects, farms, ranches, and estates.[34]

Raymond Duhem of Duhem Motion Picture Company in San Francisco and Adolph Sutro founded the Pacific Aviation Co. This was the same

Ray Duhem who filmed from Robert Fowler's Gage-Fowler biplane as they flew the length of the Panama Canal in April 1913.[35]

Pacific Aviation Company hired Spencer in the spring of 1919. Sharing flying duties with Spencer was pioneer San Francisco aviator Sam Purcell, who was also listed as a chief pilot with military experience. The company purchased two Glenn Martin TT three-seat biplanes for photo work and hopping passengers. Company headquarters was at the old McMaster horse barns on Thirteenth Street at Richmond in the East Bay. The two pilots began making air taxi flights across the bay from Oakland to San Francisco for ten dollars per person.

In May 1919, the company began one of the first newspaper delivery services by air from San Francisco's Marina Field across the bay to Richmond.

Pacific Aviation made much of its revenue by hopping passengers. A handbill for the flights stated, "You may now take an Aeroplane Ride over Richmond. Fly over Santa Fe shops, the Standard Oil Refinery is 2000 feet below, while Oakland, Berkeley, San Francisco and the islands of the bay and Marin County views are plainly visible SAFE, SANE flying for passengers. $10 a flight. Field is at 1st and Ohio Streets" [sic].[36]

By August 1919, Spencer and Purcell had carried five hundred passengers in their Martin TT biplanes.[37]

There is a photograph extant of Bond Spencer sitting in his Martin TT handing a bottle of serum to a Stockton physician. The story behind this photo began when the physician's patient needed a serum for rheumatism of the heart and none was available in Stockton. The physician called the manager of the local Owl Drug Company; they in turn called the San Francisco office and had the drug raced from the San Francisco pharmacy to Marina Field. There it was handed to Spencer for a quick fifty-minute flight to Stockton's Pond Field. White sheets were placed as field markers to help Bond find the landing field, as he had never been there before. He found the field, and the patient got the serum that saved his life. Of course, the newspaper claimed it was the first such lifesaving flight ever made.[38]

Pacific Aviation Company was first listed in the 1920 San Francisco phone book with an address of just Marina Field. It would continue to be listed for the next few years, but by then Bond Spencer had moved on to bigger things.

Bond remembered meeting Friesley for the first time in late 1919. "He was then interested in building and organizing a passenger and air mail line to northern points. It was not long before I became chief engineer and general manager of the Friesley Aircraft Company. I set to work immediately on preliminary plans and after sketching features and characteristics to win the approval of Mr. Friesley, we began to make definite plans for actual construction."

Spencer's design for the Friesley airliner utilized the latest innovations in aviation technology for a 1919 design. The plane would have twin motors, and the passenger cabin would be completely enclosed with headroom for passengers. It was a biplane with dual controls for more than one pilot. It had an adjustable stabilizer (trim) to ease the pressure on the controls. Passengers and pilots would look out through clear vision windows, and there were no exposed control wires. Double rudders gave excellent rudder control at low speeds with help from the aircraft's twin engines. Balanced controls would assure the ability to operate on one motor if necessary. Double landing gear under each engine supported the plane's twelve-passenger capacity. It could carry fifteen if necessary.

Ten years later, when Spencer wrote the above about the Friesley, the design features were commonplace on most aircraft, but when the Friesley was built, they were definitely innovations.

Spencer had the following to say about the construction of the Friesley. "The enormous amount of intricate metal and woodwork would tax the patience of any man. I was a champion welder by the time the fittings were brazed and welded. The modern airplane (in 1929) is built of small steel tubing compared with (in 1920) our heavy motor bracing, landing gear struts, and other parts. We had to cut parts out of large strips of 3.5 percent nickel alloy steel. I think we used half-a-million hack saw-blades and our hands bore mute evidence of the rough treatment to which they had been subjected. The drilling of the 2.5 x 7 inch solid ash bearers for the two Liberties was a mean job and we had no machine tools to help us."[39]

Conditions under which the Friesley was built were not always the best. Spencer, in a 1921–'22 advertisement for Valentine's Valspar, a high-grade wood varnish used in the construction of wooden airplanes, revealed that, "… when the question of varnish came up there was no hesitation as to what to use. Valspar is used by preference on all our ships and always has given complete satisfaction. Due to the fact that the ship was varnished under the worst possible conditions—heavy rains and in a building exposed to the weather—the behavior of Valspar was simply wonderful.[40]

"One of our last concerns was regarding the fueling system, which consisted of two tanks, one in each upper (wing) panel next to the center. These were connected to two large tanks covering the entire bottom of the cabin. In the top section of the instrument panel were overflow glass gauges to indicate to the pilot that the gravity tanks in the center section were feeding the engines as they were being kept full from the main tanks by wind driven pumps located outside in the slip-stream of the propellers. The excess from the gravity tanks went to main tanks instead of the engine."

Once flying tests were begun, Spencer found that during take off, "... it was only necessary to put the stabilizer [trim] as far forward as possible and retard [the trim] about one-half turn of the wheel when the ship was loaded normally. The tail was in the air in a level position after a run of one hundred feet. As [soon] as you pulled it off, [you] ran the stabilizer [wheel] back approximately a half turn. In decent weather you could set the tail at a fair lift and retain a determined climb with no manual attention necessary [hands off]."[41]

An early mention of the Friesley plane came in the May 1920 issue of *Pacific Aeronautics* which reported the Friesley was designated BS-1 Aircar—for Bond Spencer number one. The BS-1 was reported to be practically finished and ready to start passenger service that month. A photograph was published with the press report showing the right side of the cabin with passengers sitting in wicker chairs as if ready for flight. Obviously the plane was not ready for flight, as there were no wings, nor any glass in the windows.

The report listed the headquarters address of Friesley Aircraft Corporation as 703–704 Phelan Building, San Francisco. It mentioned the plane was being built in San Francisco for a passenger service between San Francisco and Portland and the company had a 150-acre flying field on the highway directly south of South San Francisco. It reported the BS-1 was being built there. A flying school was active there with student pilots studying aeronautical theory, as well as gaining actual flying experience. Passengers were taken for short "hops" from the field in Curtiss JNs. Harold Friesley was listed as company president and L. Ponton de Arce as sales manager.[42]

The report featured an excellent photograph of the Friesley hangar at the South San Francisco location. The company had not yet moved to Butte County, and there wasn't a hangar of that size at Marina Field in San Francisco until the US Air Mail Service hangar was built later. Marina Field is mentioned in the report because Friesley Company pilots used it for air taxi and passenger hopping operations during 1920 and 1921.

There were various pilots flying for Friesley Company in May 1920. For the automobile show held at Chico in late spring of 1920, Rex Johnson from Marysville was granted the airplane passenger-carrying concession at the temporary airfield developed next to the auto show's tents. He hired three pilots and planes from Friesley Aircraft Company of San Francisco. The pilots, all ex-military aviators, were: Lt. Bunny Woodworth, Lt. Lynn Melendy, and Capt. J. McGraves.[43]

After the company's second incorporation and its move to Butte County, Bunny Woodworth would replace Ponton de Arce as Friesley's sales manager.

On May 26, 1920, there was a report that a twelve-passenger airplane was parked at Friesleben's ranch, fifteen miles north of Marysville on the east side of the Feather River. The report should have said parts of a twelve-passenger airplane were parked on the ranch.[44]

The reasoning for Harold Friesley moving the entire aircraft manufacturing division of Friesley Company from South San Francisco to the family ranch at Central House in Butte County is uncertain. He stated in an interview with the editor of the *Gridley Herald* there were three reasons for the move. The first was the countryside terrain presented few natural or man-made obstructions for airplanes. The second was similar to the first in that the flat areas made quick landings possible for emergency adjustments to the airframe and power plants. The last reason was that year-round good weather made test flying of the airliner possible at anytime.

Friesley ended the interview with remarks about his company negotiating contracts for the construction of a dozen airliners. He again gave the completion date for his plane as September 1, 1920. These last comments were meant to entice new stockholders, but it reveals there wasn't anyone in the company who had a realistic view as to how long it would take a new untried company to build a multi-passenger air transport unlike anything ever built in the western United States.

About this same time, Australian pilot Charles Kingsford Smith made a request to a big Northern California fliers' club for financial backing to build a large plane for his proposed long-distance flight. Club officials told him later, they had decided to support an American consortium involving World War ace Eddie Rickenbacker. Could this consortium have possibly been the Friesley Company?[45]

If acquiring new investors was Friesley's reason for departing San Francisco, and it probably was, as financial markets were taking a nosedive in the postwar depression of 1920–'21 making new investors scarce, then Friesley left town just in time. However, his company would soon suffer a tremendous blow that would add more inducement to move his business out of the Bay Area.

On June 30, Dan Lane, an aviator who had been hired by the Friesley Company just three days before, flew a company JN into overhead electrical wires while trying to land on the east end of the runway at San Francisco's Marina Field. Lane and his two passengers were all killed in the fiery crash that followed. The plane came down on the old Panama-Pacific International Exposition's wooden ferry piers outside the airport's eastern boundary. One of the passengers was the pilot's ten-year-old cousin, Paul Lane, and the other was a man named Herman L. Tucker.

Grafton T. Reed, a mechanic and local manager for Friesley Company, told reporters Lane was an ex-army pilot who had flown in France during the war. He also had flying experience in the East before moving to San Francisco. James Wormuth, another ex-army pilot working for Friesley, told the deputy coroner he helped start Lane's aircraft for him. He said the plane was in perfect order before taking off. He said Lane took off from the middle of the airfield to the west, which, although not the safest idea, was standard procedure at Marina Field. Lane flew a circular pattern around the airport at low altitude, as if unable to climb. Planning to land, he first had to pull up and over the ten thousand-volt electric lines at the east end of the field. He couldn't make it and flew into the wires, which tore a heavy power pole off at its base as his plane fell in flames.

Another witness said the same pilot in the same plane had similar problems the day before. Then, Lane had taken up Lucy Branham, head of the American Woman's Emergency Committee. Something went wrong just after takeoff, and the pilot had to go around and land, just barely clearing the same wires. They had a jarring landing after which they took off again and were able to climb up to altitude while heading for the Civic Auditorium. Once over the auditorium, Miss Branham dumped propaganda leaflets from the plane onto the delegates of the Democratic National Convention taking place below. The leaflets exhorted the government to lift the Russian embargo currently in effect. The next day at the time of the crash, Herman Tucker was planning to throw out more of the same leaflets.

A spokesperson for Friesley Aircraft Corporation admitted the aircraft that crashed did belong to the company, but arrangements for the flights were not made with the Friesley people. He said the Curtiss JN had been loaned to Lane, and Friesley Corporation was in no way connected with Lane's arrangements.

At San Francisco during the first months after the wartime flying ban was lifted, Friesley operated passenger-carrying planes, but several months before the accident occurred the company suspended such flights devoting their energies to sales and manufacture of their large multi-engine airplane. The spokesman for the company claimed it loaned several of their JN-4s to local aviators for passenger flights.[46]

Newspaper reports of the accident at the Marina mistakenly described the pilot as flying a Friesley aircraft, not a Curtiss JN. It would be natural for an uninformed potential stockholder to assume the aircraft was a Friesley design built by the company making it that much harder for the company to find new investors in the Bay Area. Thus it may have been the best decision for Friesley to move his manufacturing operation to the family ranch in Butte County.

A week after the crash, the coronor's jury held its inquiry and made the following recommendations. The jury urged that legislation be passed eliminating overhead wires near airfields to prevent such accidents in the future. It recommended laws requiring the registration of all airplane passengers and consent of a minor's legal guardian before they be allowed to ride in airplanes.[47]

Even though the Marysville newspaper ran a brief mention at the end of May about Friesley Company moving to Butte County, it wasn't announced in the San Francisco press until the first week of August, more than a month after the horrible Marina Field crash.[48]

The Friesleben family ranch was located twelve miles north of Marysville, fifteen miles south of Oroville, and the nearest town, Gridley, was five miles to the west across the Feather River. Most of the reports on the progress of Friesley airliner construction came from the *Gridley Herald*.

Friesley released a statement in late August to the *Herald*, which read as a headline: FRIESLEY OPENS COMPANY STOCK TO THE GENERAL PUBLIC. The article under the headline stated how much the stock would cost and what a deal investors would be getting if they purchased stock soon.[49]

In September, Friesley held a contest that would award a twenty-five dollar prize to the person who submitted the best name for the Friesley airliner.[50]

A Friesley spokesman reported in October the company moved its main office from the Phelan Building in San Francisco to the First National Bank

Building in Gridley. Company officials were listed as: Harold M. Friesley, president; Lt. Lowell Smith, vice president; Bond M. Spencer, chief engineer and designer; Bunny Woodworth, sales manager; and Grafton "Wally" T. Reed, mechanic and company aerial photographer.[51]

Before Friesley moved his aircraft's construction from the Frisleben family ranch across the Feather River to Gridley, Daniel Patrick Corcoran, a local banker and rancher, met Harold Friesley and Bond Spencer while visiting the ranch to see the plane being built there. During conversation, Friesley told Corcoran his company was in serious need of a large section of unobstructed level ground for a landing field, a large hangar, and a machine shop for the purpose of manufacturing and test-flying multi-engine airplanes. They wanted the land to be near the Gridley rail stop in Butte County.

Corcoran agreed to lease a 185-acre parcel of land on his family's C. P. Corcoran property, two miles south of Gridley on the west side of the rail tracks and the state highway, to Friesley Aircraft Company. Cutting and clearing some of the oak trees on the land began immediately preparing the ground as a landing field for large aircraft. Plans were drawn up for construction of a hundred by three hundred-foot hangar.

Local contractor George Tolley and several of his employees were to leave on October 16, 1920, to tear down Friesley Company's hangar at the South San Francisco airfield and ship the lumber and equipment by train to the new Gridley airfield.[52]

Two large signs were erected on the state highway (Highway 99 now) announcing the location of Friesley Aircraft Company to the motoring public. The new factory and airfield site was another reason for the move from the family ranch. The new plant's very public location next to a major artery was more beneficial for stock sales. As one report stated, "High pressure salesmen were imported from Southern California to extract the necessary 'moola' from the farmers, businessmen, transients et al [sic] who showed interest in the project. These salesmen went about their work with a flare. They wore bleached Director's jodhpurs, shiney, above the calf boots or puttees, open-throated shirts and drove sporty cars. They also lived in the Gridley Hotel and were being subsidized by sales commissions. Money for the Corporation was limited [sic]."

"Eventually, they returned to Hollywood or Bel Air or wherever, and when newspaper ads brought feeble responses, construction of the Falcon hit a new low." [53]

The winners of the airplane-naming contest were Joseph H. Manford of Marysville and Miss Irma Dodge of Gridley. Each submitted the name Friesley Falcon, which was chosen by the judges as the new name for the airliner. They split the twenty-five dollar prize.

Some of the other names submitted were: Diplax Elisa (latin for Dragonfly); Friesley Cloud Bug, Friesley Cuckoo, Friesley Skylark, Friesley Rocket, and the San Porto (for the plane's route—San Francisco to Portland).

The Falcon's power plants arrived at Gridley in late November. At the train station sat two twelve-cylinder, water-cooled, four hundred horsepower Liberty engines. The Packard Motor Company built the motors for use by the US Navy during the war. The war ended and the engines were never taken out of their crates nor did they leave the country. Friesley purchased them as war surplus from the Navy. Before they were shipped to Gridley, they were uncrated and tested by navy aircraft mechanics on November 2, 1920.

When the motors arrived at the train depot in Gridley, it was discovered there was no equipment on hand to move the heavy crated motors from the railroad flatcars to the depot warehouse. After much head scratching, the move was completed. The two engines would eventually be hauled to the new Friesley Field south of Gridley.[54]

Bunny Woodworth, Friesley sales manager, reported the first plane built would be followed by construction of eleven more. He claimed five of that number had already been sold, a typical salesman's ploy to spark sales but simply untrue. Reportedly, sales price for each plane was forty-five thousand dollars.[55]

Construction methods at the Friesley plant were primitive; there was no heavy mechanical equipment available for milling and drilling nor were there bending presses. Bond Spencer had to do all the work necessary with hand drills and bending frames. It was said, "The plane is perhaps better for the conscientious hand labor put into it; for each piece of wood and metal has been tested and inspected and reinspected time and time again."[56]

Hauk and Smith, owners of Chico Westwood Auto Stages, reportedly placed an order for two Friesley Falcons on January 1, 1921. As soon as the planes could be delivered, they wanted to start an air service between Chico and the lumber town of Westwood. The trip into the Sierra Nevada would be cut from a seven-hour ride in an auto stage to one hour by air.[57]

Even if the planes were delivered, which they weren't, weather conditions in winter would have made such flights very difficult if not impossible. The sale was never completed.

The first Friesley test of the Liberty motors was in February and went well; Friesley and Spencer were pleased. The landing field west of the hangar/manufacturing plant was being prepared for the upcoming trial flights of the Falcon.[58]

The first flight of the Falcon was drawing near and rumors were flying. Many local citizens visited Friesley Field on Sunday, March 6, hoping to see some flying activity. A rough estimate placed the number of visitors that day at two thousand. It was said that at one period during the day, one hundred automobiles were parked along Highway 99. At sundown there were still five hundred people watching work going on at the hangar. Auto traffic got very congested, and two traffic officers had to take control of the situation on the highway.[59]

This was the Friesley Company's first hangar at Friesley Field two miles south of San Francisco from mid-1919 until October 1920 when the hangar was dismantled and moved to the new Friesley Field, two miles south of Gridley in Butte County.

Marina Field, San Francisco's first municipal airport (1919-1924), it was here the Friesley Falcon ended up before being shipped to China in 1922.

CHAPTER 12

The Friesley Falcon flies – Friesley hires Roy Francis – Bond Spencer after the Falcon – The Friesley Falcon finale – Oroville flying activities after the forest patrol moves on

It was said the Friesley Falcon first flew on April 8, 1921. The flight occurred during a fast taxi test, a flight-testing procedure in which an airplane is run on the ground at just under flying speed. This allows the pilot to check out the various systems on the plane and develop a feel for the controls. Bond Spencer was carrying out such a test with Grafton Reed riding along as mechanic. The plane felt responsive and Spencer couldn't resist the urge to get it into the air; he pushed the throttles to full power and "let her go."

The Falcon lifted off easily at around forty miles per hour. Spencer took the plane up to five hundred feet and flew straight and level for three miles. The Falcon was responding well to control inputs. The unofficial first flight was going fine until one of the Liberty engines began to miss. Spencer immediately landed the plane in a level field on Richard Johnson's ranch in Sutter County.

Spencer and Reed checked out the troublesome engine and discovered the oil pump was developing too much pressure and forcing more oil into the engine than required. The excess oil was fouling the spark plugs. After cleaning the plugs, the Falcon was flown back to Friesley Field and adjustments were made to the oil system.

Spencer was happy with the flight and said later, "The Falcon is perfectly balanced and it takes off in less distance than the smaller Curtiss (JN-4) planes and can be landed at a relatively slow speed."

The above description of the Falcon's first unofficial flight was a compilation of a 1921 Friesley press release and contemporary newspaper reports.[1]

In actuality, the unofficial flight of the Friesley Falcon most likely took place on April sixth and not the eighth for the following reasons. The description of the first flight published in the *Marysville Appeal* on April 7 states the flight took place at "Friesley Field yesterday afternoon." The first flight story in the *Gridley Herald* on Saturday, April 9, stated: "Friesley Aircraft Corporation Wednesday decided to make a test flight," in the Falcon. Wednesday was April 6.[2]

The company press release of the first flight published by at least three Northern California newspapers wasn't credible. It reported Spencer leveled off in the Falcon at two hundred feet after taking off. Why would the pilot of an aircraft on its first flight climb to only two hundred feet, a dangerously low altitude should anything go wrong with the aircraft? All pilots know altitude is insurance on any flight. If problems arise during a flight, the more altitude the pilot has, the longer he or she can problem solve and find a safe place to land.

The press release used the word "perfect" flight several times. It would be unusual for any first flight to be perfect, and in fact, the *Gridley Herald* reported the Falcon's first flight did not go perfectly. Bond had to set the Falcon down on Johnson's ranch with fouled spark plugs.[3]

The press release stated the first flight ended back at Friesley Field; it never mentioned the emergency landing made on Johnson's property.[4]

Russ Christian, son of the family with whom Bond Spencer lived while he was staying in Gridley, confirmed the emergency landing Spencer made to repair the Falcon's engine during that first flight. About the incident, he later reported, "One night my dad was awakened about 3:00 AM by Spencer, who had a hold of Dad's knee and trying to awaken him. The year was probably 1920 [sic]. No one in Gridley locked their doors in 1920. We didn't even have keys to the doors in our eleven-room house.

"When Dad was fully awake, Bond told Dad that the Falcon had been completed but they didn't want the public to know before an anticipated announcement in the papers with a grand celebration and demonstration. He said that he purposely waited until dusk to give the plane its 'hopping' tests, reasoning that visibility would be poorer at that time and fewer people would be about to witness it. He told Dad, 'these tests involve giving the plane enough power to lift it briefly off the ground then shutting off the power to allow the plane to settle.

"It was performing beautifully and then 'catastrophe' of a sort. It didn't drop back as planned and was heading for the barbed-wire enclosure of the field, so I gave it the gun and jumped the fence. The plane was behaving so beautifully, I decided to extend the test flight. Somewhere north of Sacramento, the plugs fouled up and I landed in a wheat field. I walked away until I hit a highway where, after a long hike, I was able to thumb a ride to Gridley. I would like you to drive me to the hangar where I can get some longer plugs and then, drive me to the plane where I can exchange the plugs and try and get the plane back in the hangar before anyone sees it.

"I believe those huge Liberty motors were twelve-cylinder jobs and to exchange all those plugs with only my non-mechanical dad to assist him, had to consume a lot of sweat and time. But they made it and Dad experienced an unplanned adventure allotted to no other human being. The Good Old Days, indeed."[5]

The cat was out of the bag. The Marysville paper reported on April 9 that Spencer made another half-hour flight in the Falcon on the eighth. He took along a passenger, E. C. Taylor, an officer of the Rideout Bank of Gridley. The article did not lack humor in its description of the flight. It contained the following: "Now Captain Spencer is somewhat familiar with airplanes, having been 2,500 hours in the air, and having traveled some 250,000 miles by air during that time, but Taylor is far more familiar with banking methods than with tailspins. It is reported that as soon as Captain Spencer shot the Falcon off the grounds, that Taylor 'wanted the captain to stop the ship,' and offered to trade the entire bank for one single foot of solid ground."

Spencer landed the Friesley in another farm field then took off demonstrating to the banker the Falcon could land almost anywhere. He then flew the airliner back to Friesley Field. Spencer would make similar flights to work out minor problems before the official first flight scheduled for April 17, 1921.[6]

The April 17 official first flight was scheduled during a grand air show and celebration at Friesley Field. Pilots from all around the state planned to fly to Gridley for the official first flight of Friesley's new passenger plane. Bunny Woodworth, sales manager and public relations expert, sent invitations to prominent airman throughout the north state and to all of the state's aircraft manufacturers asking them to send representatives to the launching of the Falcon.

Henry Laugenour, manager of Producers' Film Company of Oroville, was coming with his cameramen to film the Falcon's flight and the stunt flying planned for the celebration. A full reel of movie film would be taken and shown in weekly newsreels playing at the local theaters. The film would also be used as part of a travelogue movie that Laugenour was making showing points of interest in Butte, Yuba, and Sutter counties to promote the Sacramento Northern Railroad.[7]

The event was expected to attract several thousand people. The South Butte Post of the American Legion in Gridley was chosen to handle security as well as food and beverage concessions. The Gridley Woman's Club served the food and drink with the Legion providing eighteen mounted security officers for crowd control and parking. Reportedly, there would be commercial civilian pilots giving airplane rides, and military pilots providing stunt-flying exhibitions.[8]

To encourage local residents to buy Friesley stock, there was an extensive five-page article about aviation, its progress, and its business potential in the biweekly *Gridley Herald*.[9]

On the day of the official first flight and air show, an estimated ten thousand people attended in two thousand automobiles. Another estimate claimed seventeen thousand people with four thousand cars attended.

The following pilots and their planes visited Friesley Field that day:

- From Sacramento's Mather Field: Sergeant Ekerson with an observer flew up in a DH-4; Sergeant Arndt came in a DH-4; Lieutenant Jones was in an SE-5; and Lt. Lowell Smith, vice president of Friesley Corporation, arrived in one of the army's captured German Fokker D. VII fighters.
- From the Presidio's Crissy Field, came lieutenants Halverson and Maxwell in a DH-4.
- From Oakland's Durant Field, Eddie Rickenbacker flew in with Reed Chambers in a Durant H. S. Standard.
- From Redwood City's Redwood Field, H. G. Andy Andrews flew in with G. D. Oster, salesmanager for the Varney Lincoln Standard dealership. Lester Shone came up from the same airport in a Varney Lincoln Standard.

Some of the above aviators kept the crowd interested by demonstrating their aerobatic prowess prior to the flight of the Falcon. Andy Andrews made several flights during the day carrying paying passengers around the

Gridley area.

In late afternoon, Miss Alyse Monteverdi of Sacramento and Miss Bettie Jellinek of San Francisco carried out the official christening of the Falcon. Then, Bond Spencer, Harold Friesley, and Grafton Reed climbed into the Falcon and the twin Liberties were started.

Bond lifted the Falcon off the airfield at 3:45 PM. Initially heading to the south, Bond began a wide 180 degree left turn while climbing to seven hundred feet. He flew over Gridley and then made a wide turn back towards the field descending to land in front of thousands of thrilled spectators.

Spencer later told a reporter the speed of Falcon was remarkable. He cruised at eighty-five miles per hour and was forced to throttle back constantly to avoid going too fast for the photo ship flown by Sergeant Ekerson carrying a cameraman who was taking pictures of the Falcon on its "first" flight.

The official "first" flight of the Falcon is often said to have taken place on April 20, but that's not true; it happened on the seventeenth. The *Gridley Herald*, which gave the best description of the day's activities, was published only twice a week and did not report the story until April 20, thus the confusion of dates.[10]

Russ Christian described the day as follows:

> After much ballyhoo in the area papers and a couple feature stories in the big city papers, the stockholders and the public in general were given the date of the Falcon's inaugural, which was awaited with anticipation, curiosity and all the accompanying emotions.
>
> In addition to the Falcon's premiere, there was the added attraction of Spencer's World War One buddies. The group included our country's aces, not the least of whom was the great Eddie Rickenbacker, as well as other training associates.
>
> On that great day in the morning, they began arriving early by plane. What would you expect? Many were flying foreign planes that they had brought back from overseas. … They were all lined up along the edge of the field, elbow to elbow, so to speak. There was dust everywhere, what with all these alien props beating the air as their owners gunned the planes' motors to clear their throats, so to speak.
>
> The highest visibility was attained by the crown jewel, The Friesley Falcon. Spencer had previously wheeled it into a preeminent position where the admiring stockholders could feast their eyes on

their vanished investments.

After the usual introductions of all the important people who had a part in this great production and the way-too-long acknowledgements by the introduced, many of whom, actually did little or nothing toward this culmination. Then those really entitled to credit, were introduced and allowed to say a few words. 'The fewer the better' was the feeling of many of the assembled thousands who were standing in the hot sun with bladder pressure at an all time high. There were no commercial portable potties in 1920.

Many of the dignitaries and their friends had dressed, fitting their stature. Almost like going to a wedding. Blue serge suits with vests, yet and when the big moment arrived and those big Liberties were cranked-up, their large props loosened and pried out any stray dust that had been missed by the smaller planes. Blue suits became gray and it was impossible to distinguish the North from the South. Coughing, sneezing with cause, and crying without sadness.

The Falcon was designed to carry twelve passengers. When Spencer was set to take off, I don't think he was fully loaded but I don't remember who his passengers were. I believe his head mechanic was one. I'm sure Spencer was thinking of that early morning landing in that wheat field north of Sacramento and didn't want a repeat performance.

The plane behaved beautifully. Thousands applauded and hundreds yelled. The plane made a very brief flight, returned, landed without incident. More applause, followed by the exodus, sans Moses, sans alcohol, although I'll bet Bond or his friends had a bottle stashed somewhere, for medicinal purposes only, mind you. 'Prohibition' Remember?

Bond Spencer was a good many years ahead of his time. The world felt no pressing need for multi-passenger airplanes. There were no airlines and no commercial companies in need of Falcons. The Falcon had become a white elephant.[11]

FRIESLEY COMPANY CALLED a public meeting in Gridley four days after the big celebration and inaugural flight. A spokesman opened the meeting with a statement that Friesley and his associates had invested sixty thousand dollars in the airplane, then Harold Friesley spoke to the local businessmen who had gathered for the meeting. He told them, in so many words, the design and construction of the Falcon was a wise move, and they should get behind the company because other communities were interested in having the company in their towns. For the company to grow, he said it needed a fully stocked machine shop, which would require more investors. The new shop would cost fifty thousand dollars. With the inclusion of those who signed up for stock at the meeting, there were a total of fifty local men who invested in the Friesley Falcon.[12]

Roy Francis, recently hired by Friesley, arrived at Friesley Field the first week of May 1921. Francis was a pioneer aviator in the Bay Area, but more importantly to Friesley, he was one of, if not, the most experienced multi-engine pilots in America. He had just finished his wartime hitch with the Army Air Service that included an unsuccessful attempt to fly an army twin-engine Martin MB-1, heavy bomber, across the United States.[13]

Capt. Roy Francis with Major W. H. Frank, Lt. Coe, Lt. T. F. Gilmore, and Lt. E. E. Harmon flew a Martin bomber from Washington, D.C., to Macon, Georgia, in seven hours and fifty minutes for a new nonstop record in May 1919. Distance was 650 miles. Average speed was 82.98 miles per hour.[14]

Initially, the army had planned for Francis to fly across the Atlantic Ocean in a Martin bomber, but the selected Martin needed more flight tests before embarking on such a long flight over water. The US Navy's NC-4 flying boat completed the first transatlantic flight on May 31—stealing the thunder from any Atlantic flights planned by the army. The Army Air Service's plans were changed and Francis was assigned to fly a Martin MB-1 on a one-stop (at North Platte, Nebraska) transcontinental hop on June 10, 1919.

Unfortunately, it took the Martin factory until June 14 just to get the bomber ready for flight-testing at McCook Field, Dayton, Ohio. On June 15, British pilots Alcock and Brown flew the Atlantic nonstop from Newfoundland to Ireland in a Vimy bomber.

Additional work had to be done on Francis' bomber while it was at McCook, causing more delays. On June 25, Francis flew the Martin to New York where his proposed transcontinental flight came to naught when the plane was wrecked in its hangar at Hazelhurst Field by severe winds.[15]

Captain Francis got another chance to make a transcontinental flight in a Martin bomber on October 15, 1919, competing in the army's Transcontinental Reliability and Endurance Race. Unfortunately, Francis crashed the plane at Yutan, Nebraska, while landing in the fog and hitting telegraph wires. Damage to the plane was severe enough to put him out of the race, but there were no serious injuries. He and his crew removed one of the Martin's Liberty engines and shipped it to another army racer, Lt. Belvin Maynard, whose engine failed and forced him down only ten miles from Francis' crash site. Maynard switched engines and went on to become the overall winner of the race in an army DH-4.[16]

Roy Francis left the military shortly after the conclusion of the Transcontinental Reliability and Endurance Race and returned to the Bay Area. Friesley hired Francis to take over Spencer's duties as pilot of the Falcon.

Difficult flights to a large air meet at Woodland and another near Francis' old stomping grounds at Marina Field, San Francisco, were planned for the Falcon. The company may have wanted a hometown hero to present the plane at Marina Field. Part of Friesley's plan was taking up full loads of passengers in the Falcon at these events. Having the notable and more experienced multi-engine pilot fly the Falcon gave a perception of additional safety.[17]

Francis carried out familiarization flights in the Falcon soon after his arrival at Gridley. He reported the plane had a better rate of climb and was more stable in flight than any multi-engine plane he had ever flown. He said he shut down one engine and flew the plane on the remaining engine. The Falcon, he said, "behaved splendidly," on one engine. Francis took the plane up to ten thousand feet during high altitude tests, and the engines behaved normally. Even though Liberty engines were low compression motors and not built for high altitude work, Francis said "… their performance was particularly gratifying." The Falcon attained 125 miles per hour over a measured course during speed tests along the state highway.[18]

On May 7, 1921, Roy Francis flew a planeload of passengers to Woodland's Yolo Fliers' Club airfield for what was the largest (at the time) postwar civilian air meet in the entire state of California.[19]

Three days before flying to Woodland, it was decided an auction would be held to sell seats on the Falcon for a later first cross-country flight to San Francisco from Gridley. The flight was scheduled for May 15 to attend a Pacific Aero Club air meet at Marina Field. It is unknown whether the reasoning behind the auction was to make more money for the company or an attempt at an equitable solution to satisfy the many local investors' desire to be among the first to travel cross-country in the new plane.[20]

Regardless of the reasoning, the first bid to win a pair of seats came from

Mr. and Mrs. Gerald Chalmers. Mr. Chalmers just happened to be the most vocal Gridley supporter of Friesley's company. Mr. Chalmers was also given a seat in the Falcon for the trip from Gridley to the Yolo Fliers' Club meet taking place a week before the San Francisco trip.

The trip to Woodland had dual purposes. First was promoting the Falcon amongst possible wealthy investors of the Yolo Fliers' Club. The second purpose was checking the plane's handling with a three-quarter-passenger load of eight in preparation for the upcoming longer flight to Marina Field.

Passengers for the Woodland trip were: Mr. Gerald Chalmers; L. C. Taylor, the banker; Mr. and Mrs. Grafton T. Reed, the company's chief mechanic and his wife; Miss Bertha Graf; Earl Porter; Cliff Strother, an assistant mechanic; and Harold Friesley.

Bond Spencer and his wife, in the company's JN-4, accompanied the Falcon on its thirty-minute flight. Although the Spencers departed fifteen minutes before the Falcon, Bond barely beat the faster Falcon to Woodland. Twenty-five different types of aircraft had gathered there. Spencer flew the company Curtiss Jenny in a twenty-five-mile pylon race and took third place.[21]

The trip to San Francisco began May 15, 1921. It was the first extended cross-country flight by the Falcon and first flight to the Bay Area. The Falcon's landing at Marina Field was the first appearance of a multi-engine, twelve-passenger airliner to the San Francisco Bay Area. Roy Francis, pilot for the company's landmark flight, carried a full load of Friesley Company men and investors as passengers.

The Falcon left Friesley Field at Gridley just after 1:00 PM and overflew Woodland's Yolo Fliers' Club Field on its way to Suisun City where Francis landed and topped off the fuel tanks in case the infamous San Francisco fog had settled and required the Falcon to divert to another airfield.

Fog was not a problem. The Falcon circled over the city at five thousand feet. At 5:15 PM Francis landed the big biplane at Marina Field. A large crowd of spectators, photographers, and newspapermen were on hand to greet the disembarking passengers.[22]

The Falcon and crew remained in San Francisco nearly two weeks taking up VIP guests that had been or could be helpful to the company. On Thursday, May 26, Bond Spencer took over as pilot-in-command and flew the Falcon from Marina Field down to Redwood City Airport.

At Redwood City, VIP rides were once again given before fog closed in and halted activities. Fog kept the Friesley grounded a day longer than planned. The Falcon and its passengers left Redwood Field a little after 5:00 PM Friday for Stockton, landing there at 6:00 PM. While crossing the hills and mountains of the Coast Range between the two cities, Spencer ran into the roughest turbulence he had ever experienced. He encountered a fifty-five mile per hour headwind at six thousand feet. Wind speeds were as high as forty-eight miles per hour at Stockton Aviation Center (AKA Farris Field) when the Falcon landed.[23]

The next day, the Falcon was fueled and prepared for departure to Gridley. At 7:00 AM, it left Stockton Aviation Center with Spencer at the controls. Friesley crewmembers Grafton T. Reed and Clifford Strother were aboard, as was L. A. Pingpank of Gridley, and two new passengers, Mr. and Mrs. F. W. Farris. Mr. Fauna Farris was manager of the Stockton Aviation Center and sowed a crop from an airplane for the first time in the Great Central Valley during January 1923—it was winter wheat at Tracy.

Spencer flew the airliner through severe rainstorms climbing as high as eight thousand feet to escape the worst of the turbulence. He landed at Mather Field along the way to check the plane over and get some new data on government regulation of wireless use. Spencer got everyone back on board, fired up the two Liberties, and flew home.[24]

The successful junket to San Francisco covered a distance of 1,162 miles, and took twelve hours and thirty-five minutes flying time. The Friesley Falcon pilots gave rides to seventy-five people from the Marina and Redwood City airfields.[25]

IN JUNE, ONE of the most impressive items built in the woodshop program at Marysville High School was a model airplane. Student Dudley Cunningham made a wooden model replica of the Friesley Falcon. Cunningham was preparing to build a full-size airplane using a forty horsepower motor for power. It is unkown whether he ever built the larger plane, but seven years later Dudley tore down an old Jenny and totally rebuilt it. He then learned to fly in that Jenny.[26]

Dudley became a superb airplane mechanic specializing in wood and fabric repairs. He stayed in Marysville and developed a notable reputation for rebuilding the wooden wings used on the popular Travel Air and Stearman crop dusting aircraft used by local ag-flying businesses in the 1930s, '40s and '50s. Cunningham was chosen to be superintendent of Cheim Field in Marysville for most of the time it was in operation. He was truly a link to the Golden Age of aviation in the Yuba-Sutter community.

CHAPTER 12   333

Dudley's Friesley model ended up at the Mary Aaron Museum in Marysville where it was seen in storage in the 1960s. A similar model of the Friesley Falcon now hangs in the lobby of the Hiller Air Museum at San Carlos.

In July 1921, Yuba County Supervisor W. J. Forbes, Marysville City Councilmen L. B. Crook, Matt Arnoldy, and Frank Booth with Francis Arnoldy, Matt's six-year-old son, all went for an evening flight in the Falcon with Friesley Corporation president Harold Friesley. Frank Merril of the Friesley Company and C. R. Bishop also rode along. Roy Francis piloted the airliner. Francis once told a reporter he was the first to fly an airplane into the Sacramento Valley in 1909 in a plane he built himself. The date was incorrect, but he often made this claim when talking to news reporters. The facts are: he hadn't yet learned to fly aeroplanes in 1909, and he didn't fly his Gage biplane in the Sacramento Valley until he and Frank Bryant barnstormed through it in January 1912.[27]

The Falcon was flown often during June, July, and August taking up various VIPs (possible investors) over the local counties of Butte, Yuba, and Sutter. The Falcon made two flights on August 7, 1921, that will long be remembered by residents of the three counties. Bond Spencer and copilot Roy Francis, flew the Marysville Merchants baseball team from Friesley Field, Gridley, to Yolo Fliers Club Field, Woodland, to play the Woodland American Legion baseball team.

The flight to Woodland took the Falcon only thirty minutes at a cruising altitude of three thousand feet. At Woodland, a large white tee in the center of a circle made the landing field visible to Spencer and Francis from several miles out. (Yolo Fliers Club Field still exists; it is Woodland's city airport located four miles west of town.)

The Marysville team was taken to the ball field nearby for the game, which they lost to Woodland 15–5. In their defense, two of Marysville's key players did not make the flight. It was reported they were sick.[28]

A famous photograph is included here of the Marysville Merchants baseball team standing in front of the Friesley Falcon prior to departure from Gridley. Fourteen men and a young batboy are lined up in front of the plane with six bags and suitcases of equipment. Roy Francis is third from the left, Bond Spencer is fourth, and Grafton Reed is fifth in the photo. The implication is that all these people got on the plane and flew to Woodland. Henry Sackrider, a professional photographer in Marysville, took the photograph, and it has been published countless times in newspapers, books, and magazines.

The Marysville Merchants Baseball Team prior to their departure in the Falcon from Friesley Field, Gridley, for a game at Woodland on August 7, 1921. It was thought to have been the first time a baseball team was flown to a game, unfortunately, that was not true.

The other photograph of the Marysville baseball team standing in front of the Falcon was taken at Yolo Fliers Club Field, indicated by gently rolling hills and oak trees immediately behind the plane. There are only ten men lined up in front of the Falcon. There are from the left the two pilots, Francis and Spencer, the mechanic Reed, then seven team members wearing the identical clothes they wore when they left Gridley. The bags, batboy, and four team members are missing. It would be safe to say, only ten men flew to Woodland for the game in the Falcon. The equipment, batboy, and other players may have travelled by car.[29]

The claim made locally, and again recently in a book on local baseball history, and in most publications that have published Sackrider's photo, is that this was the first time a baseball team travelled by airplane. As much as one local fellow hates to be the bearer of bad news, this author found the claim not true.[30]

The August 25, 1919, *Aerial Age Weekly* states, "During a recent railway strike ... The Post Field Aerial Baseball Club [at Fort Sill, Oklahoma] was carried in Curtiss planes [probably JN-4s] to and from Marlow, Oklahoma, in order to play a game scheduled there." This was two years before the baseball team flew to Woodland in the Friesley airliner.[31]

Roy Francis, piloting the Falcon, took up eight passengers on August

9 including S. G. Patrick, a Marysville reporter who wrote a glowing article about how comfortable the Falcon was in flight. Patrick wrote, "No better method of viewing the country could be had and there is no doubt that before long this method of transportation will be as popular here as it is abroad where transportation ships [airplanes] are running on regular schedule.

[The Falcon] "... is not only suitable for passenger traffic, but with a slightly altered body would be, according to the specifications of government, [a] bombing plane." Harold Friesley, himself, couldn't have written a better sales pitch for the Falcon.[32]

More advertising in the guise of a legitimate newspaper article was published locally a few days later. It stated, "Daily flights are being made by the big Falcon airplane of the Friesley Aircraft Corporation, which are becoming popular with the people of Yuba, Sutter and Butte counties. Employees of the Friesley Aircraft Corporation are always ready to make flights in the big Falcon and each evening the big plane is filled with pleasure seekers enjoying a soar among the clouds getting a birds-eye view of the beautiful

Later on August 7, the Marysville baseball team arrived at Woodland's Yolo Fliers Club Field. There are five fewer team members in this photo than their Gridley departure photo. Were these the only team members that actually departed Gridley or were these all that could safely be carried back to Gridley due to the August afternoon heat?

Sacramento Valley. Thursday night H. H. Wolfskill, James and Barbara Barr, Howard, Ruth, and Gordon Harter, William Gern and daughter Elsie made the trip in the big plane."[33]

Friesley Company almost lost a mechanic in August when Clifford Strothers of Chico was pulled from the San Francisco Bay after a hydroplane he was flying collapsed a wing and dove into the water from two hundred feet. George Butler, who had helped him rebuild the Curtiss hydroplane at Redwood City, was in the plane with Strother. They went down offshore near Redwood City. Workers from the local Alaska Codfish Company rescued the two. Both men were tangled in the wreckage and difficult to extract. They were exhausted and had to be put under a doctor's care.[34] Strother worked with Bond Spencer and Grafton Reed building the Falcon in Gridley.

By August, Spencer and Roy Francis made sixty-nine flights in the Friesley Falcon. All were made without accident or damage to the big airliner. During those flights, they carried over four hundred passengers. In a demonstration, the Falcon flew on just one engine, and the company claimed it was the only plane of its kind able to do that.[35]

Bond Spencer, who contributed more than anyone in the creation of the Falcon, announced on August 16 he was leaving the Friesley organization effective in four days. Roy Francis would be solely responsible for flying the Falcon after Spencer was gone.[36]

Spencer was through with the Friesley, but he had made many friends in the Gridley area. Some thought he was an engineering genius. He decided to stay in the area a while and pursue his other great interest—radio. Radio, like aviation, was another emerging technology, which Spencer felt could be an important career choice. Radio enabled him to utilize his engineering degree from Brown University, as did aviation, but radio was a much safer environment.

Meanwhile, the Falcon made very few flights in late August and September. On September 28, 1921, the Friesley Falcon was flown out of its Gridley airfield and the Sacramento Valley forever. That day Roy Francis, with Grafton Reed as passenger, flew to Marina Field in San Francisco. Harold Friesley was already in San Francisco and told a reporter the Falcon would be shown to local capitalists interested in aviation.[37]

While at Marina Field, the Falcon made some unusual flights during October. On two occasions, it was used to drop one thousand free meal tickets to jobless and homeless men in the South of Market Street area of San Francisco. On the first drop, Col. H. H. Arnold accompanied pilot Francis. The tickets were for a free meal at Teck's Eat Shop on Third Street. The idea was to alleviate some of the suffering caused by the economic depression of 1920–21. The meal ticket drops may have been the Falcon's last flights in the United States.[38]

Early airline development in America was stalled due to: the lack of aviation regulation by the government; the inability of flying businesses to obtain insurance coverage; the absence of airports and airline infrastructure; and the sharp jolt to the national economy from the 1920–21 depression. Lack of airline infrastructure included not only multi-passenger transports but also ground crews and service equipment. France and Britain in 1919 were the only countries to develop scheduled air service of multi-passenger aircraft so soon after the Great War.[39]

LESS THAN A month after Bond Spencer realized the worsening financial condition of Friesley Company, he and G. J. Chalmers opened The Precision Shop. Chalmers, a successful farmer in the nearby Manzanita District, had invested heavily in the Falcon. He believed in Spencer's abilities, and together they planned a top-of-the-line machine shop where Spencer would do work for local farmers, while building wireless radio equipment for sale.

In September, Spencer travelled to San Francisco and ordered equipment for the new shop. He came back from the city with a contract for $1,500 of wireless apparatus to be built by his new business.[40]

At some point in Spencer's stay in the Christians' home during his pursuit of a career in early radio, Russ remembered a conversation between his dad and Spencer. Spencer said, "All my pals and flying acquaintances have been killed stunting planes. I shall never stunt another plane!"[41]

Historian James Lenhoff of Butte County was very specific about Spencer's radio career. He wrote, "The first radio broadcasting station between Sacramento and Seattle was KFU located in Gridley. KFU commenced operation on a wavelength of 510 meters, with 100 watts of power on 2 March 1922." The station's owner was The Precision Shop owner Bond M. Spencer. KFU operated about three months. Spencer, at The Precision Shop, also built radios for sale at prices ranging from $26.50 to $300. The shop was located at Sycamore and Virginia streets in Gridley.

Excerpted and edited from the *Gridley Herald* of March 4, 1922, Lenhoff wrote: "On Wednesday, March 1, 1922, Capt. B. M. Spencer of The

Precision Shop in Gridley received a government license as one of fourteen broadcasting radio stations of the Pacific Coast. The first scheduled concert from the local station was transmitted on March 2, 1922. Practically all parts of Northern California can receive the signal. Spencer's first application to build a wireless station was denied, the reason given was that stations in Sacramento and the Bay Area were adequately serving Gridley."[42]

When Bond Spencer left the Gridley area is unknown, possibly in 1923. Did he return to the Bay Area? His name doesn't reappear in the newspapers or aviation trade magazines until September 1928 when he was mentioned as being a member of the 476th Pursuit Squadron, Army Reserve, based at Clover Field in Southern California. It was reported that every member of the 476th held a commercial transport license and most were engaged in current commercial operations.[43]

It is believed that Bond moved to Glendale and was hired by a music company to manage the company's radio department.[44]

In October 1928, Bond Spencer and Allan Barrie were added to the instructing staff of the American Aircraft School of Flying at Los Angeles. When hired, Spencer was said to be a former DOC aviation inspector. He couldn't have worked as an aviation inspector for the DOC more than two years—the DOC only began hiring aviation inspectors in January 1927.

Reportedly, Spencer delivered the first in a series of lectures to fifty students of the American Aircraft School of Flying. He was scheduled to give lectures once a week on various aviation ground school subjects.[45]

Spencer got into movie flying about late 1927. Dick Grace, the veteran movie stunt flyer, approached him with an offer to join a group of fliers he was assembling to do film work. It was during the time Howard Hughes was filming *Hell's Angels* and had most of Hollywood's stunt pilots working for him. There were few left for the rest of the filmmakers, so Dick Grace put together what he first called, his "Buzzards." Later, he would very dramatically call them the "Squadron of Death."

Grace whose business specialty was crashing airplanes for the Hollywood cameras already had two experienced movie pilots with him, Ross Cooke and C. K. Phillips. He needed more pilots to handle the film work coming in and hired five new pilots: Charles Stoffer, Frank Baker, Del Hay, E. D. Baxter, and Bond Spencer.

Dick Grace worked on *Wings*, the first picture to require an entire squadron of planes. Hughes' picture required more planes and pilots than Hollywood could muster. Later, First National Studio decided to make the film *Lilac Time*, which would require a squadron of planes and pilots. Dick Grace was hired by the director to supply the planes and pilots for *Lilac Time* and that's when he first assembled his Buzzards. Grace had only recently recovered physically and financially from his unsuccessful attempt to fly from the Hawaiian Islands to California prior to the Dole Race.

Ross Cooke was made flight commander of Grace's movie squadron, and Garland Peed was hired to orchestrate Grace's aircraft crashes. Hal Rouse was in charge of the aircraft while on the ground, and a Sergeant Costenborder was hired as mechanic to keep the planes flying.

Before Grace hired the five new pilots, he made sure of their flying abilities by requiring they fly tail chase with him. If the new pilot stayed on his tail for the entire flight, he was hired.[46]

It is believed Grace renamed his Buzzards the Squadron of Death because of the attrition rate of his pilots. More than half of the members were killed in a relatively short time. He doesn't say how Bond Spencer crashed, but he does state in his book, *I Am Still Alive*, that at one point after Ross Cook was killed doing a film for Fox Studios, only three of the original Buzzards were still around, Charlie Stoffer, Del Hay, and himself.[47]

Some reports state Bond crashed and was seriously disabled while flying in the movie *Lilac Time*. This does not jibe with Dick Grace's comments in his book. He wrote the first of the Buzzards to be killed was E. D. Baxter, who died when a student froze on the controls of the plane they were flying and crashed. The crash happened, "Shortly after we finished *Lilac Time*." Grace doesn't mention in his book any disastrous crash by Spencer during the filming of *Lilac Time*.[48]

An article in *Skyways* No. 18 gives an even different account of Bond's accident. It states Spencer crashed on November 10, 1928, following a day of filming a Tom Mix movie near Saugus. With filming over for the day, Spencer took off in an OX-5 Waco biplane. He had climbed to about a hundred feet when his engine quit. He hit some trees during the forced landing and suffered serious skull injuries.

Mrs. Bertha Buchart, his mother, had him admitted to Patton Hospital at Patton in San Bernadino County. It was the location of a state mental hospital for many years. He died August 19, 1933, at Patton Hospital. He was forty years old.[49]

Spencer wrote an article about the Friesley Falcon titled, "A Transport of Yesterday." It was published in *Western Flying* in August 1929.[50]

The *Gridley Herald* reported on April 26, 1929, that B. M. Spencer, a

Friesley associate, crashed while making the movie *Lilac Time*.

THE BEGINNING OF THE END for the Friesley Falcon, and the company that built it, became evident in January 1922, when the *Herald* published a fateful message to the Gridley citizenry. The headline was simple, To SELL ASSETS TO PAY DEBTS. Not what a stockholder in any company wants to read over his morning coffee.

The accompanying article notified the public there was to be a Friesley Aircraft Company stockholders' meeting at 2:00 PM on January 31 in the Kuhl Building, San Francisco. It was a sad message for Gridley area stockholders. The first item mentioned was Harold M. Friesley's twenty-two thousand dollar bill presented to the company. He claimed it was for money loaned to him by friends and placed in the company's treasury. In addition there were outstanding debts totaling nine thousand five hundred dollars.

The article stated the assets of the company would be sold and they were: the large Falcon airplane, a smaller airplane (JN-4), one large wooden hangar, plus miscellaneous machinery and hand tools. Money from the sale would be used to pay debts.

The Friesley Company had sold fifty-two thousand dollars worth of stock to over 150 stockholders. Most of them lived in Butte, Yuba, and Sutter counties. The rest were from San Francisco and southern Oregon.

G. J. Chalmers, one of the largest stockholders, called a stockholders meeting in Gridley on January 28. At least thirty stockholders attended and denounced Friesley's attempt to draw on the sales of assets to pay off unsecured loans. Chalmers was elected as the stockholders' representative to go to the Bay Area and protect their interests.[51]

It was reported the Falcon was in San Francisco, and if anyone was interested in purchasing the plane it was ready to fly.[52]

The following creditors came to the meeting in San Francisco with their claims: Grafton T. Reed, $1,000 for labor; Roy Francis, $1,100 for services; Butte County Lumber Yard, a large claim for materials; Standard Oil Co., $500 for gas and oil; Attorney Stainhar, $1,500 for legal services in the formation of the corporation; and there were further miscellaneous small claims.

At the meeting, Chalmers offered to buy the small plane but was refused. Reed and Francis' lawyer demanded an audit of the company's books. Reed and Francis were protected by the labor laws of California and therefore preferred creditors.

Chalmers assumed that after the sales of the company's assets were made and the creditors were paid off, the stockholders would get what was left.[53] On February 22, the creditors filed a petition asking the US District Court to declare the company bankrupt.[54]

The Falcon, which cost forty thousand dollars to build, was sold to representatives of the Chinese government for three thousand dollars in May 1922.[55] By August the Friesley Falcon and six Curtiss JN-4Ds were being prepared for shipment to Fuchow, China. Great China Airways, a once legitimate company that had been revived as a shell company, bought the planes for Chinese leader Sun Yat-sen.

One of Sun Yat-sen's officers, Gen. Yang, asked Harry W. Abbott, and ordered the ten Chinese pilots that he trained at Courtland, California, in March 1922, to travel to the arms factory at Fuchow. The men had trained not only as pilots but also as aircraft mechanics and were to assemble the six Jennys and the Friesley Falcon. They were to test fly them and have the JN-4s ready to bomb Canton. The Falcon was to be used to haul drums of gasoline to the numerous coastal fuel stops for the JN-4s while they made their way to bomb Canton.

How much of this operation actually took place is only speculative, as the warlord targeted for bombing at Canton had left the city by the end of January. The Jennys were moved elsewhere in 1923, and the Friesley Falcon was never heard of again. Pilots Dan Davison, Guy Colwell, and mechanic Arthur Wilde from San Francisco's Marina Field, traveled to China with the Falcon. They didn't fair so well. Colwell and Davison died there from typhoid; only Wilde made it back to San Francisco.[56]

Harold Friesley and his Falcon failed to ever haul a single passenger from San Francisco to Portland. Such passenger service would have to wait another seven years.

Alfred Lawson was never able to captain his Lawson *Air Line* on a transcontinental passenger flight.

Charles McHenry Pond and R. L. Gardner were able to fly a few passengers between San Francisco and Los Angeles in their Curtiss Eagle before it crashed—bankrupting their dream.

In 1928, they were all on the sidelines as the Boeing Model 80As of Boeing Air Transport, Bach Air Yachts of West Coast Air Transport, and Ford 4-ATs of Maddux Air Lines—all tri-motor airliners—began the multi-passenger service they prematurely attempted in 1921.

As if to wipe out the existance of the Friesley Falcon, on March 25, 1923, a fire was discovered burning in the second story of the Corcoran residence on Corcoran and Miller property, three miles south of Gridley. Part of this property had been leased to Friesley Corporation for its airfield and the factory hangar where the Falcon was built. Dan Corcoran was the last factory manager for Friesley Company.

Dan, his family, and a ranch employee were just sitting down for lunch when Mrs. Corcoran went upstairs and found a fire burning. Dan ran up to put it out using two fire extinguishers only to discover it burning elsewhere. A strong north wind intensified the fire, which eventually burned the family's home, a tank house, the bunkhouse, a chicken house, hog shed, and a large cow barn, one right after the other. It was believed a defective stove flue caused the fire. Destroyed in the fire were all the Friesley factory drawings and blueprints of the Falcon by Bond Spencer. The company's papers and records plus most of the company's photographs also went up in flames.[57]

Others involved in the development of the Friesley Falcon include Roy Francis who, by 1930, was superintendent of Mills Field, which eventually became today's San Francisco International Airport.[58]

Grafton T. Reed, the longest serving Friesley employee, learned to fly at the Summit Flying School in Sacramento with instructor Ivor Whitney and was granted his Private Pilot License in the fall of 1931. He eventually obtained his commercial license and was working as a flight instructor in the 1930s and early '40s. He was killed in an airplane crash near his hometown of Auburn.[59]

In July 1931, a labor war took place on the T. B. Hutchins' ranch in the Central House district near the Friesleben property. Irate workers girdled 150 prune trees killing them all. Two months before, four hundred peach trees were girdled on Corcoran's ranch, where Friesley Field had been ten years before.[60]

There were few newspaper reports of aviation activities in and around small cities and towns of the Sacramento Valley from 1922 through 1926. Reasons for this are varied and subject to conjecture.

Aerial activity in the north state during those years consisted mainly of barnstormer flights and army forest fire patrols, which the army was phasing out. There was no airline activity. The only flying schools that were active were in the more densely populated areas like the Bay Area and Sacramento.

It is difficult to know how much barnstorming activity really went on in the Sacramento Valley. There were no regulations governing the pilots, planes, or their activities during the postwar years. Until 1927, there were

CHAPTER 12 343

no government watchdogs to monitor activities of the various gypsy fliers roaming the countryside.

After the war ended, barnstormers were able to get ten dollars per person for a ten-minute airplane ride. For that kind of money, a pilot would place newspaper ads telling local folks when he would be visiting their town along with where to find him and the price of a ride. For this reason, it is possible newspapers stopped sending out reporters to cover the barnstormers flights as editors realized aviators would pay for newspaper space when they came to town.

By 1922 pilots were only getting five dollars a ride and by 1926 they were giving rides for as little as two and a-half dollars. Later on, the price of rides dropped to a penny a pound. Pilots could no longer afford newspaper advertising, and the papers were no longer willing to publish the information for free. Thus there is little known about the activities or even the identities of many of the barnstormers during 1922–1926, lean years for barnstormers.

In 1927 the Aeronautics Branch of the Department of Commerce was activated, and new federal flying regulations enforced by DOC inspectors began to put the squeeze on this popular form of unregulated and dangerous flying activity. Barnstorming was practically eliminated by the mid-1930s.

AT OROVILLE IN THE FALL OF 1926, Dr. Julian P. Johnson, president of California Airways at Yuba City, announced he would be starting an air service between Redding and San Jose in the near future. He asserted that Oroville would be one of the daily stops made by his three-seat Bristol Tourer biplane. He emphasized how comfortable the passenger cabin was in the Tourer.[61]

Johnson, while promoting his California Airways Company, spoke to the Fellows Club of Oroville. He stipulated in his talk that Oroville was well situated for an airport. Dominic DiFiore, one of Johnson's pilots, also spoke, as did Albert Lane an aviator from Willows.[62]

In the summer of 1928, Oroville lost one of its distinguished citizens when Harry E. Higgens, a steel manufacturer and local rancher, was killed in an air crash at Palo Alto. Milo Campbell was flying the ill-fated Pacific Coast Air Service Fairchild in which Higgens was killed.[63]

Standard Oil's aviation chief reported in September that a new airport was needed in Oroville. He claimed that the old airport, Riley Field, was a poor facility, according to pilots who used the field. They all agreed it was too small.⁶⁴

Don Castle of the California Association of Professional Aviators, came to Oroville to promote an air show planned for Chico September 29–30, 1928. Castle, chief pilot for Sierra Aircraft Corporation of Chico, said he would fly Don Cornell to Oroville and land on Facher's field, west of Oroville. Tex Frolich, a local pilot, planned to represent Oroville in the Chico air show by flying his Whirlwind powered Travel Air.⁶⁵

R. U. St. John, district engineer for Standard Oil Company, arrived in Oroville on the afternoon of September 13 to help the chamber of commerce select a new site for Oroville's municipal airport. He was flying his Swallow biplane.⁶⁶

John E. Tremayne of Oroville flew his Waco to Oakland and took the test for his Transport Pilot License.⁶⁷

In February 1929, Capt. A. F. Eagle of the Army Air Corps, made the none-too-careful observation that the flat top of Table Mountain, immediately north of Oroville, was an excellent natural site for a municipal airport. The DOC planned to send airport inspector A. H. Waite to potential Oroville and Grass Valley airport sites in October.⁶⁸

In November, Oroville Chamber of Commerce members painted the word OROVILLE across the roof of the Exposition Building to help fliers identify the city. Boy Scouts did the painting. Elks Lodge and the chamber provided the paint.⁶⁹

After inspecting the Table Mountain airport site, Waite ruled it unsuitable. The only safe landing area on the mountain was too small for an airfield.

Ted R. Smith, born in Oroville in 1906, graduated from the Boeing School of Aeronautics in 1929. By 1935 he was working for Douglas Aircraft Company of Los Angeles. In 1939 he was group leader at Douglas in charge of A-20 bomber fuselages. He was project engineer on the A-26 from 1941–1945. After WWII, he started Aero Design & Engineering Corporation and designed all of the Aero Commander twin-engine executive aircraft. His last design produced was the Smith Aerostar, a very fast and sleek executive aircraft.⁷⁰

The West America Air School's Sacramento staff spent the 1930 Fourth of July at Oroville arriving in two planes and staying several days.⁷¹

Riley Field was well established as the airport for the Oroville community. Today its still undeveloped ground is visible at Kusel Road just west of Lincoln Boulevard. J. H. Kerrigan, agent for the six men who financed the airport, told the press that credit for the improved condition of the airport belonged to contractor C. W. Wood from Stockton who, in September 1930, donated labor and equipment to regrade the landing field. It had fallen into serious disrepair in the years since the army utilized it as a forest patrol base.[72]

By January 1931, Riley Field's dirt runway was once again in bad condition from the winter rains, so the Yuba-Sutter Flying Club, led by its Oroville members, approached the city of Oroville and requested the city take over Riley Field. No action was taken. The members realized they would have to continue using Cheim Field in Marysville throughout the winter.[73]

Ray Westfall, an Oroville pilot, ground looped the Yuba-Sutter Flying Club's Spartan biplane at Cheim Field in February, damaging the landing gear. His passenger was Glenn Marders.[74]

In late May 1932, a rare kidnapping by airplane occurred in Oroville. Herbert Koch visited the Glen Sheets' residence on Montgomery Street to see his three-year-old daughter, Gwendolyn. She was staying with the Sheets family—his estranged wife's parents.

Even though Koch had once taken his daughter away without the mother's permission, the grandparents allowed Koch to see Gwendolyn and let him inside. He told them he brought a necklace and asked permission to put it on her. While slipping it around the girl's neck, he snatched Gwendolyn and ran out the back door. In the alley behind the house, a car was waiting with its engine running. He jumped in with the little girl. The driver, Earl Waller, sped off towards Riley Field.

The Sheets called the police and local traffic officer Carl Rabe arrived. Rabe, on a motorcycle, followed the getaway car's tire tracks to Riley Field. Just as Rabe entered the airport grounds, Koch and his daughter took off in a biplane flown by A. N. "Shorty" Hall headed for Oregon.

It is not known if Koch made it to Oregon and kept his daughter. The previous time he took her was in a car and he was brought back to Oroville—not on a kidnapping charge—but on an unpaid traffic ticket warrant. The judge couldn't act on the kidnapping charge because there had been no divorce, separation, or restraining orders filed in the marriage.[75]

A. N. Hall was believed to be the first commercial pilot to come to Oroville with the idea of starting a permanent flying business there. For his business, he was flying the biplane belonging to Oroville resident and Yuba-Sutter Flying Club member, W. J. Illman.[76]

In early September, Hall flew Illman's biplane, a Whirlwind powered

Spartan, to Portola Airport to give sightseeing rides during the Labor Day celebration. He took aboard three passengers, Virginia Gibbs James, sixteen, her sister, Helen Gibbs James, seventeen, and Maurice Murray, twenty-five. The Spartan with a 165 horsepower motor was only certified to carry a pilot and two passengers, not three.

Four minutes after take-off, Hall reached an altitude of 750 feet. Without warning, the aircraft lurched nose-down in a spin. A witness said Hall pulled out of the spin going to full power. The plane went back into a spin. When Hall realized a crash was inevitable, he switched off the magnetos to prevent fire. At one point, Virginia James rose up from her seat, and an instant later the plane crashed into the ground killing all of the passengers. Hall lived a short while then slipped into a coma and died at the local hospital.

DOC inspector E. E. Mouton flew up from Oakland the next morning. Although he had yet to examine the crash, he delivered a bitter diatribe against pilots who overloaded their airplanes in spite of ATC load carrying limits for planes.

Shorty Hall, forty-four, was from Kentucky and had twelve hundred hours flying time. He was a good pilot known for his safe flying technique. He came to Los Angeles area in 1927 and obtained his Transport Pilot License. He moved to Oroville in 1931 with two grown daughters, a three-year-old granddaughter, and wife. He was trying to make a go of the town's first flying business—giving instruction to several local pilots including James A. McNeil, an Oroville airplane owner.

Hall didn't have a plane of his own. He rented or leased Bill Illman's Spartan for his business. The Spartan once belonged to the Yuba-Sutter Flying Club. Illman testified at the coroner's hearing his plane had all its required equipment including seat belts for the passengers.[77]

A. L. Scott, an Oroville automobile dealer, bought a new four-place Waco cabin biplane in November 1933. He intended to use it for pleasure flying. Unfortunately, since he had no adequate airfield locally, he had to park at Cheim Field in Marysville, a forty-five-minute drive from Oroville.

Scott reported, in the first week of December, his plane had been flown to San Francisco and later to Rio Vista. He had plans to take it to Merced and then to an air show at San Mateo. Larry Martin, an Oroville pilot, flew Scott's plane for him. Martin, a longtime Yuba-Sutter Flying Club member, had seven years of pilot experience. Scott was learning to fly and planned to get his license soon.

Scott's blue Waco was equipped with landing lights for night flying. It had navigation lights and a radio capable of both short wave and entertainment band reception. The cabin biplane cruised at 125 miles per hour with a top speed of 150 miles per hour. It carried electric fired flares for emergency night landings when away from airports.[78] With his new purchase and his newfound passion for flying, A. L. Scott would become one of the city's leaders in the quest for a proper municipal airport at Oroville.

During the first week of December 1933, Harold F. Brown* met twice with members of the Oroville Chamber of Commerce to discuss his plans to start an airline operation serving Oroville. He reported he would name his new airline Capitol Speed Lines. The plan did not come to fruition. Many believed it was because Oroville lacked a suitable landing field.[79]

Harold Brown was one of the founders of Consolidated Air Lines, which flew a regular schedule from Marysville to Sacramento and on to the Bay Area in 1930. Prior to 1930 Harold Brown was well known in the area for his service as flying instructor and mentor for the Yuba-Sutter Flying Club.

That first week of December, Eugene L. Vidal, director of aeronautics for the Department of Commerce, announced plans for a network of airports around the United States. Every city and town in America was asked to submit an application for funds to create an airport on municipally owned ground or to upgrade an existing but inadequate landing field. The funds were allotted by the federal government and provided by the DOC Aeronautics Branch through the Civil Works Administration (CWA). The purpose of the allotted funds was two-fold: stimulate flying and, most importantly, create construction jobs.[80]

Butte County's three largest cities, Oroville, Chico, and Gridley all wanted a share of the funds. However, Oroville didn't own the land on which Riley Field was located, which made it ineligible to receive the government's money.

Secretary of the Oroville Chamber of Commerce, R. C. Ramsey, announced the following week he was reopening negotiations with the Crocker Estate in San Francisco for a certain property on which to build a new municipal airport for Oroville. The chamber had begun negotiations for the property three years before.[81]

The Hangar Club, an aviation club formed by fifty-four high school boys, announced to anyone who would listen, "Oroville needs that airport." The boys contributed nickels towards advertising in the local newspaper exclaiming their opinion. The club's officers were Richard Hughes, Clifford

Hills, and Albert Martin. Members met twice a month to hear talks on aviation related subjects.[82]

A. L. Scott and R. C. Ramsey lead a delegation to San Francisco to dicker with Crocker Estate representatives over acquisition of the desired property. The site, south of the highway lateral and three miles west of Oroville, is the location of the present day Oroville Airport. Another site being considered at that time by the chamber of commerce committee was south of Power House Hill west of Oroville.[83]

Capital Speed Lines of San Francisco was planning to provide air service to Oroville by the middle of the following month, said William H. Royle, company manager, while in Oroville December 18. Royle was visiting to inspect possible landing fields for passenger service. He said company planes would already be landing at Oroville if there was a suitable airfield. He told city officials his company was ready to send its experts to Oroville to lay out the runways and facilities for free if the Crocker site was chosen.

Royle reported his company was already flying planes between Sacramento and San Francisco and hoped to be flying two planes per day to Marysville, Oroville, Chico, Red Bluff, and Redding on its valley schedule. He said his company would be flying two Wacos on the valley schedule, and when passenger traffic increased and airfields were improved, a switch would be made to bigger Lockheeds. Capital Speed Lines was, presumably, the same non-existent Capitol Speed Lines that was represented earlier in the month by Harold F. Brown. The results were, unfortunately, the same.[84]

The Oroville City Council approved the purchase of 165 acres of land located in the triangle formed by the state highway and the Haselbusch county road, two miles west of Oroville city limits. The council authorized payment of $1,750 to Crocker Estate for the airport site.

It was discovered the city did not have funds to pay for the land. An arrangement was made for A. L. Scott and the *Oroville Mercury Register* newspaper to loan the city money. The land would be deeded to the city immediately. Oroville would repay its two benefactors in monthly installments. The city met all requirements to apply for CWA federal grant money for airport construction.[85]

R. C. Ramsey, secretary of the Oroville Chamber of Commerce, sent an application for CWA funds to Capt. B. M. Doolin, DOC airport inspector, on December 26. Ramsey cited advantages of the airfield's location. It was near the state highway, it lacked obstacles in all directions for considerable distances, and it was opposite Reno on the lowest passage over the Sierra

CHAPTER 12   349

Nevada into the Great Central Valley on a direct route between the airport at Susanville to San Francisco.[86]

Oroville was awarded the funds. It was the eighty-fifth city to indicate an interest in the federal airport funds, the fifteenth city to submit an application for the funds, and the first city to have its airport project approved. When the new Oroville Municipal Airport held its official opening in June 1935, the federal government had spent $20,818. Oroville had put in $5,294 including the cost of the land. Most of the federal money went for labor costs as required by CWA (later SERA).

During May 1935, a number of naval aircraft and army multi-engine bombers made their way to the newly opened Oroville Airport for the dedication air show scheduled for June 1, 1935. For the dedication, five Army Air Corps Martin B-10s of the 11th Bombardment Squadron from the army's recently opened Hamilton Field in Marin County, took off from the new Oroville runways. Circling the airport several times, the big twin-engined bombers eased into one large formation. They then headed for the coast to take part in planned army war maneuvers.

Once the bombers were out of sight, A. L. Scott, chairman of the airport committee, introduced J. C. Nisbet, chairman of the day, to the celebrating crowd. Nisbet reviewed many of the efforts of getting the airport developed. Then he introduced his young daughter, Gertrude Nisbet, who was to break a bottle of champagne on the bumper of the announcement truck to christen the Oroville Municipal Airport. She needed a little help from her father to break the bottle, and Gertrude's second attempt was successful. Next, Nisbet introduced Mayor Al Hoke who accepted the airport for the city of Oroville.

William Royle took over announcing following the speeches of officials. He talked about the efforts to get the airport developed as a federal project. He announced the various events the rest of the day. He personally knew the pilots and planes arriving from the Bay Area, and gave a running commentary about whomever was in front of the spectators at any given moment. Royle was considered the best air show announcer in the north state.

At 3:00 PM "Iron Hat" Mylon Johnston arrived and soon began his stunt flying routine. He flew his aerobatic displays in a small Aeronca C-2, which was a high-wing monoplane that resembled a flying bathtub. The spectators who lined the two runways, which were layed out in the form of a large X each thirty-one hundred feet long, were thrilled by the day's events. The air show was repeated the following day.[87]

Three years later, the main hangar at Oroville Airport caught fire shortly after 4:00 AM, July 26, 1938. It was completely destroyed, including eight airplanes inside. When state forest service firefighters arrived, the building was totally engulfed in flames. Larry Martin reported there was no electricity to the building, thus no wiring to catch fire. He also said there were no oily rags or papers in the building. A state forest ranger found no batteries in the remains that could have started a fire.

Most of the planes that burned were based at the airport, but two were transients. Lyle Perrine of Corning had stopped overnight in his new Porterfield Zephyr monoplane to visit relatives. He had it housed overnight in the hangar. The Porterfield was so new it had been flown a total of only 6.5 hours when it burned. Bill Miller of Chico owned the other transient aircraft destroyed in the fire.[88]

The Oroville Airport would have another official opening in 1941 after undergoing a complete facelift with lengthened runways, taxiways, numerous new hangars, and other structures, as America prepared for another war.

---

*Harold Frederick Brown was born January 17, 1905. Raised in Oakland, he enlisted in the Army Air Corps circa 1927 and was sent to Kelly Field in Texas for flight training. He was in a training group of 100 men of which only seven graduated. Brown was the top of the class. In April 1929 he crashed while flying an Air Corps observation plane in Southern California. His observer, Lt. Harry Doyle, suffered a broken shoulder. The plane crashed because of a broken gas line. Brown resigned from the Air Corps in August 1929. In 1930 he was an airport manager living in Montebello. In early 1930 a passenger Brown was flying tried to commit suicide by jumping out of the plane. Brown threw the plane into a steep bank, which forced his passenger against the fuselage. Brown grabbed his leg and threw the man into the front seat. He tried to jump again, and Brown stunned him with a blow to the head with a fire extinguisher then made a safe landing. In 1935 after his and John Wagge's Consolidated Air Lines went bankrupt, Brown went back into the military. He joined the Marine Corps Reserve. By 1951 he was a full colonel in the Marines, retiring from the Corps in 1961. He passed on in July 1966.

Oroville's current (1994 photo) city airport opened in 1935.

CHAPTER 13

Postwar aviation at Chico – Merwin and Pendleton – Flying at the Chico Auto Show – More barnstormers – Jimmie Angel at Chico – Royle Air Lines – Sierra Aircraft Corp. at Chico – Garrison Patrick

Lieutenant R. E. Gay, son of George H. Gay of Chico, made the first US Air Mail Service flight between Memphis and Knoxville, Tennessee, after the conclusion of the Great War in the remaining days of December 1918.

Gay was flying a JN-4 that had a speed of seventy-five miles per hour. He commented, "When we get Liberty engines, a greater speed will be attained." He was looking forward to the day the Air Mail Service would give him a Liberty-powered DH-4 to fly mail at one hundred miles per hour.[1]

Lt. Col. Henry L. Watson an Air Service officer at Mather Field, in June 1919, sent the Chico Chamber of Commerce a request the city establish a proper airplane landing field. The secretary of the chamber soon after announced, "The matter of securing a permanent landing place for airplanes," at Chico would be discussed at the next chamber of commerce meeting.[2]

The local newspaper speculated, "As Chico was the largest city between Sacramento and Portland," the request from Watson must be related to possible airmail routes being planned, but a more likely reason was the Air Service's need for more landing fields for the newly activated forest fire patrols being carried out by aircraft from Mather Field.[3]

Chico businessman Ben E. Crouch was in Sacramento that June and missed his train for San Francisco. He had to attend an important corporation directors meeting. Frantic to get there in time, he learned of an airplane at a local airfield leaving for the Bay Area in a few hours. Crouch immediately sought out the pilot and requested a ride to San Francisco. Within minutes he was winging his way to the Bay Area in the plane's spare cockpit, and arrived in time for his meeting. He said the plane reached the city in less than one hour.[4]

Crouch later admitted he was a flying convert and became interested in the Earl Cooper Company, a new business selling ex-military airplanes to private individuals. The company had offices in Sacramento and San Francisco. Company salesmen were selling off a large inventory of army surplus JN-4D Jennies and Standard J-1s that had been sold back to the Curtiss Company and were being offered to the public.[5]

In fact, Curtiss Aeroplane and Motor Company had purchased an entire lot of planes from the US government for the following prices. Eleven hundred Standard J-1s were purchased for two hundred dollars each, which was about 4 percent of the price the government paid for them. Sixteen hundred Curtiss JN-4s were purchased for four hundred dollars each, 8 percent of what they cost the government. Four thousand, six hundred Curtiss OX-5 motors were bought for four hundred dollars each, which was 19 percent of the government's cost.[6]

In July a newspaper report reiterated that anyone buying an airplane would be required to obtain a license once they became qualified pilots. This requirement was brought to the fore because during a recent parade down Fifth Avenue in New York City, a reckless civilian pilot flew his hydroplane up and down the avenue at less than five hundred feet above the heads of the spectators. The culprit had no license.

During the World War, a regulation had been passed allowing civilian pilots to fly during the wartime ban of civilian flying if they had a license issued by the Joint Army and Navy Board of Aeronautic Cognizance. The application for such a license could be obtained from the board's office in Washington, D.C.[7] The Aero Club of America's ACA/FAI license was not recognized by the federal or state governments.

The problem with this early attempt at government licensing of aviators was with the end of the war and a flood of ex-warplanes hitting the civilian market, very little was said about the need for a license. It was discovered the Army Navy Board licenses, which were issued without cost, were not backed by any government enforcement. There would be no effective license requirement by the federal government for aviators until the passage of the 1926 Air Commerce Act with the enforcement of its licensing regulations beginning in July 1927.

On July 14, 1919, E. H. Pendleton, manager of the Sacramento city landing field in Del Paso Park, as mentioned, came to Chico as the advance man for ex-Lt. Ogle Merwin, who arrived the following day at Thomasson Field south of town on the state highway. Merwin, who the day before was hopping passengers at Oroville, planned to hop passengers at Chico in his Jenny. Pendleton, who during the war headed the mechanical department at March Field, reported Merwin was trained as a pilot during the war at March Field and Wright Field.[8]

Merwin gave fifteen people their first airplane rides on July 15. One of those was Melvin Deter, who paid one dollar a minute for his first plane ride. The following day Merwin dropped copies of the *Chico Record* from his plane at S. T. Mason's store in the nearby community of Durham. Later, he took up Miss Mabel Mitchell of Golden Poppy Café, who tossed out promotional leaflets over Chico.[9]

For several days, Merwin gave fifteen to twenty rides a day at Thomasson Field including a free ride to Herbert Mitchell, a young Chico boy who had sold his bicycle for ten dollars to go for a ride in Merwin's Jenny. Mrs. J. M. Deter went for her first ride in an airplane, and J. W. Broyles, a farmer, was flown over his threshing crew working a field near Nord.

Merwin returned to Oroville after several days at Chico taking along Prescott Carmack, a Chico man who had been an army sergeant pilot recently discharged from Mather Field. Mechanic Berger Johnson from Sacramento joined Merwin on his last day in the county during which Merwin gave the landing field owner, Verne Thomasson, a free airplane ride. In all, Merwin gave over ninety rides in his biplane at Chico. After hopping passengers at Oroville once again, he returned to Sacramento with a passenger, Mark H. Wood, who was interested in learning to fly and possibly buying an airplane.[10]

Mark Wood took the train back to Chico. Before leaving the Sacramento airfield in Del Paso Park, Wood had toured the airplane repair shop of McManus' and Merwin's flying service. During the World War, Frank McManus worked for Liberty Iron Works in North Sacramento building Curtiss JN-4D training planes for the army. He was later hired by the army to take charge of the repair shops at Mather Field. After the war ended, he and Merwin purchased JN parts from Liberty Iron Works and began building and repairing JN-4 aircraft in their shop at Del Paso Airport.[11]

Ben Crouch became associated with Earl Cooper Company, the distributor of Curtiss airplanes in Northern California. In late July 1919, he urged the city of Chico to establish a landing field as soon as possible. He suggested a location adjoining Bidwell Park that was not in agricultural use. He claimed the list of airplane owners in the state was increasing quickly and had passed the one hundred mark. Earl Cooper Company was offering completely reconditioned Curtiss JN-4s for immediate delivery at three thousand dollars and up.[12]

Sacramento Aviation Company pilot Ogle Merwin and its manager, E. H. Pendleton, introduced commercial aviation to Butte County citizens after the war. Merwin pursued an aggressive campaign of hopping passengers at Oroville and then Chico, the two largest towns in the county.

He was not the first to fly in Butte County following the war. Obviously that honor fell upon the previously mentioned army forest fire patrols flying from Oroville's Riley Field. However, the army pilots were not allowed to take civilians for rides in army planes, unless the civilians were army approved VIPs. If the rides were approved, they were free. The army brought the first airplanes to Butte County after the war, but the citizens could only watch them fly. It was Merwin who allowed them to enjoy the thrill of actually flying.

Merwin returned to Chico from Sacramento on July 29, 1919. He had placed an ad in the Chico newspaper, which stated, FLYING—RETURN ENGAGEMENT OF ONE DAY FOR PASSENGER CARRYING PLANE—TUESDAY, JULY 29—ALL DAY AT THOMASSON FIELD.[13] E. H. Pendleton drove to Chico in advance of Merwin's arrival and immediately called Mark H. Wood and H. K. Sears to ask if anything had been done about a permanent landing field for the city.

Wood and Sears were on the airport committee of the Chico Chamber of Commerce. Pendleton reminded them (erroneously) that, "The government is establishing a number of reserve fields and Chico, as one of the most important towns in the north (state), should not be without such a field. By establishing a chain of (landing) stations, the Sacramento Valley could have a weekly passenger air service and an aerial mail service."

The army was helping cities establish airfields in the valley, but they were few and used as bases or emergency landing fields for the forest patrol. The army had no interest in airmail or passenger flights. Since the cities had to choose a location and develop the airfields, the airfields could be shared for any purpose the cities desired.

When Merwin flew into Chico for his second round of passenger hops, he brought Martin J. Pendleton, the four-year-old son of E. H. Pendleton,

CHAPTER 13   355

and Merwin McDonald, his nephew.[14]

Wood and Sears were to meet with the Chico Board of City Trustees the evening of August 5 to request the board consider establishment of a municipal airfield for Chico. They suggested dire consequences if the airfield was not established.

They told the board the federal government would pay twenty dollars per month for a hangar on a new city airport. They must have gotten the idea from a similar payment to Oroville for a forest patrol hangar at Riley Field. Of course, the forest patrol would not have paid for a second hangar at Chico; patrols weren't flying there.

Wood and Sears next claimed airmail service would bypass Chico if it did not have a suitable airfield. This was a possibility if the airmail ever came to the north valley, but regularly scheduled direct airmail flights to north valley towns never happened regardless of their airports nor were they ever contemplated. An airmail letter mailed from a valley town was carried by ground transportation to designated airmail fields at Sacramento or the Bay Area for transcontinental transportation after September 1920

The two men updated the board about city airport progress around the north state—emphasizing Oroville and Sacramento already had municipal airfields. They pointed out Colusa, Red Bluff, and Redding residents had taken the necessary action to establish city airports. What they may not have said was those airfields were created because the army requested and needed them for fire patrols.[15]

Sam Purcell flew into Morehead Field at Chico in August 1919. He was trying to pick up some fast cash hopping passengers while waiting until his contract to scare ducks off local rice fields began. He managed an interview with the Chico newspaper, which included a photograph of his Martin TT biplane in flight.

Purcell accurately recounted his flying career. He was a prewar aviator who began flying in 1912. He would be at Morehead Field for the purpose of carrying passengers, and claimed he was the first flier to scare ducks off a rice field. After an airplane scared them off, he said they would remain out of the field for two or three days. "They don't get used to a plane like they did the scarecrow." Purcell predicted a high demand for aerial duck patrols during the 1919 rice season saying they could save rice worth thousands of dollars.

A local farmer said if planes were effective keeping ducks off rice fields, farmers would no longer have to use rockets and searchlights to scare away waterfowl. But this was the first year of the airplane experiment and until it was thoroughly tested some farmers would contnue using their old methods of keeping birds away.

Purcell, who reported having 4,560 flying hours, said his Martin TT biplane had seats for three passengers and reiterated he would be at Morehead Field five more days giving rides. His Martin was a dark color overall with number 395 painted five feet across in white on each top wingtip. The number was his wartime pilot's license number; he was one of the few who obtained a license from the Joint Army and Navy Board of Aeronautic Cognizence during the war.

In the article about Purcell, the beauty of Chico from the air was described. Frank B. Durkee, secretary of the Chico Chamber of Commerce, had gone up with Purcell. What impressed Durkee most were, "... the wonderful shade trees along Chico's streets and the parks. We must preserve these trees and plant more of them. Next come the rows and rows of green orchards, and to the west one could see the green of the rice fields on the Crouch and Phelan ranches and on the Parrott Grant (Rancho Llano Seco). It certainly is great."[16]

O. Rice, an aviator flying for E. H. Pendleton, landed at Thomasson Field to take James Mills Jr. over his ranch near Hamilton City in Glenn County. Mills had never seen his ranch from the air and was looking for possibile airfield locations on the ranch. He wanted to learn to fly and use an airplane to help manage his large holdings, so he wouldn't have to drive so much each day.[17]

Sam Purcell was flying passengers from a specially prepared field on Mills' ranch August 10 when his engine quit forcing him to land in a sugar beet field causing damage to his Martin. After the rough landing, his passengers, Miss Helen Torrey and Tracey Mills, wanted to know why they didn't get their money's worth. He nonchalantly remarked, "Water in the gasoline got into the carburetor, causing the engine to miss." Miss Torrey, a senior citizen, said, "Is that all? Well, next time you have an airplane accident to stage, let me bring a photographer along so I may send a picture to my friends."[18] Purcell had to ship his plane by rail to San Francisco for repairs. He said he would return to Chico in about ten days with a new plane.

Ogle Merwin was back on the scene and announced he was opening a passenger service for tourists who arrived by train at Chico on their way to the resort at Richardson Springs north of town. The tourists got off at the Sacramento Northern train station in Chico, and Merwin would fly them

CHAPTER 13   357

to the resort from Morehead Field. Merwin's first passenger to Richardson Springs was James Patterson of Sacramento. Merwin sent his master mechanic, G. W. Eldred, to help Lee Richardson choose a suitable landing site for his plane at the resort.[19]

The matter of a permanent landing field for Chico was brought to the fore on August 13. Another newspaper article reported city board of trustees must align Chico with the efforts of towns like Redding, Red Bluff, Oroville, Colusa, Marysville, Willows, and Woodland. They all provided landing fields for pilots.

The report stated ten airplanes landed at Redding the previous week on their way to Portland. They didn't stop at Chico because there wasn't an adequate airfield for them. It was reported a transcontinental flight would take place within the next thirty days, and the fliers would be stopping at Redding. If Chico had a permanent airport, planes might stop in the City of Roses (AKA City of Trees). Upcoming airmail flights would pass by Chico due to the lack of a permanent field claimed the report.

Ogle Merwin went to Chico to evaluate the airport situation. While there, he talked with C. E. Bennett, manager of Chico Contracting Company. Bennett's company had just leveled and graded a landing field for the city of Redding. He offered to do the same for Chico if the city trustees or anyone else would provide land for an airport.

Mark Wood said there was an ideal site available, which could be leased long-term for a moderate sum. It was just off the highway near Chico in the old Carly tract. It would provide for a three thousand-foot runway with plenty of room for hangars and equipment. Wood said planes as big as the Handley Page and Caproni bombers would be able to land on the site.[20]

Wood, always the aviation enthusiast, next found himself at Richardson Springs helping Chester Eldred clear an area for Ogle Merwin to land his Standard biplane near the resort. Merwin, Eldred's employer, planned to depart Moorehead Field at 10:00 AM the following day and arrive at Richardson Springs six minutes later. Eldred reported a first-class landing field had been prepared two miles below the springs.

Owner Lee Richardson, who had previously made the six-minute flight from Chico to his resort, reported Merwin could fly passengers from Sacramento to the springs in an hour and ten minutes, instead of the four-hour trip it usually took riding from Sacramento by rail and then from the station by automobile. The Sacramento–Richardson Springs fare for the trip was one dollar per minute. In total, one trip would cost seventy dollars. If three passengers traveled together, the fare ran less than twenty-five dollars each.

Merwin made a perfect landing at the Springs and carried several passengers on flights to Morehead Field.[21]

Merwin flew passenger hops from the new field at Richardson Springs on August 16, 1919. Passengers had a choice of flying over Chico, Feather Falls, or the Feather River Canyon. Merwin flew about twenty-five passengers including Lee Richardson, Harry Fraser, and visitors from the resort. He concluded his service at the end of the day and returned to Sacramento.

Merwin scheduled the first freight hauling air delivery in the area on the following Monday. He would fly Jack Patterson from Chico to Sacramento with a consignment of hats for his hattery in the Capital City.[22]

On September 13, a meteorite fell over the Butte County area. The flaming object was thought to be the Jenny flown by J. M. Fetters with his passenger Berger Johnson. (The incident was covered in chapter eleven.)[23]

Three pilots and their planes were hired to fly at the Durham Community Barbecue in late September at Durham, a small town six miles south of Chico. The pilots did stunt flying for the crowd and gave airplane rides.[24]

E. J. Moffett of Colusa had reportedly signed contracts with various Colusa County rice farmers to chase ducks out of their rice fields with his two Curtiss JN-4 aircraft. Butte County rice growers took notice and began making similar arrangements.

H. O. Jacobson, director of the Pacific Rice Growers' Association, was quoted at the end of September saying if it required fifteen, or even two hundred airplanes to drive ducks out of Sacramento Valley rice fields it would be done. When asked about the efficiency of airplanes eradicating ducks from fields, Jacobson described the Lake Charles region of Louisiana, which included an army flying field. Daily use of training planes drove all of the birds away from the surrounding rice fields.[25]

Ogle Merwin had contracted with the Parrott Grant rice growers of Butte County to chase ducks with his Standard J-1. He was making a low-level run over a rice field on October 13 and lost control of his biplane for a split second. Merwin crashed in the standing water. He was cut about his nose and body, but his injuries were not life threatening. His airplane, however, was severely damaged.[26]

As mentioned earlier, Merwin had second thoughts about flying duck patrols and left the Butte County rice fields for good on October 23, 1919.[27] Merwin once said, "The plane runs into flocks of ducks, killing birds by the score. Ducks fly fast, but not fast enough to escape an airplane." The

CHAPTER 13   359

constant bird strikes on his airplane were so dangerous they had to have a demoralizing effect on the pilot.[28]

An aviator named Eldridge was doing loops and spins over the city of Chico April 17, 1920, causing most citizens to stop what they were doing and strain their necks looking high into the sky at Eldridge's antics. Dr. A. R. Waters saw the exhibition, and as chairman of the ordinance committee for the city board of trustees, he decided such displays were too dangerous to be done directly over the city. After a number of complaints from local citizens, he decided he would present the problem at the next board meeting.

Waters reported he would prefer the state pass a law prohibiting stunt flying over cities to save small towns from the trouble of passing local ordinances to the same effect. However, since the state had done nothing to prevent such actions by errant aviators, he believed small towns must act. Waters' last report recommended the board should at least pass an ordinance prohibiting pilots from flying dangerously low over the city.[29]

EARL COOPER, THE FAMOUS RACE CAR DRIVER and Curtiss airplane dealer, with his partner Ben Crouch, a Chico capitalist, flew from San Francisco to Chico in Cooper's company airplane in early May to close a deal for a large exhibition space at the Chico Auto Show to be held that month from the nineteenth to the twenty-third.[30] Cooper reserved a frontage area of sixty feet in the exhibition tent for his Curtiss JN-4s. He displayed his refurbished airplanes in the company of various new automobiles.[31]

The Chico Auto Show was a big boost to the community. Every effort was given to make it a success. A landing site for airplanes was developed next to the show grounds. The runway for Cooper's airplanes was laid out diagonally across the rear of the high school site thanks to the courtesy of the Chico Board of Education, which gave the show's committee permission to remove five mature plum trees that presented obstructions on an otherwise perfect runway. The runway was rolled and watered to prevent dust clouds from the aircraft.[32]

Earl Cooper sent his newest Curtiss model, a large biplane called the Oriole, up to Chico the day before the show. The flight from San Francisco to Chico took two hours. When Dan Davison, an ex-airmail pilot, landed the Oriole at the show site, its wings were removed and reassembled after the plane was rolled into the exhibition tent.

The Friesley Aircraft Corporation sent its business manager, Bunny Woodworth, to Chico by rail on the El Dorado Flyer from San Francisco.

Lynn Melendy would fly a company plane into the show grounds the following day from the Bay Area. They would be selling company stock to finance construction of the Friesley airliner. The only plane they had to display was a company JN-4.

Rex Johnson, a Marysville pilot who obtained his license from the Christofferson Aviation School in Redwood City before the war, had been awarded the airplane passenger-carrying concession for the auto show. E. F. Fordyce and I. J. Wrightman finished development of the landing field on May 18 the same day the Oriole came to town. The runway, behind the show tents, was seven hundred- to eight hundred-feet long.[33]

Chico realtor O. E. Tracy made a deal with the passenger concession for Lynn Melendy, who was hopping passengers at the show, to fly prospective customers over certain properties Tracy had for sale if they wished to see them from the air.[34]

Arrivals at the Chico Auto Show, who wanted an airplane ride, were asked to follow arrows posted along Chico's Esplanade in their cars to the flying field at the Reed property on Richardson Springs Road near the state highway. It was decided at the last minute not to use the makeshift runway developed behind the tents on the auto show grounds. The runway was a little short for passenger carrying. Tickets for airplane rides were sold at the show and at Reed's field.

Lee C. Dibble, who had been an instructor in night flying at March Field during the war, would fly the Curtiss Oriole at the auto show. He took passengers up for rides from Reed's field, and gave exhibition flights each day at 2:00 PM. His flights included a number of spectacular aerobatic stunts to thrill the crowd. Dibble remained at Chico for the duration of the show.[35]

The Curtiss Oriole was the first new postwar Curtiss design produced for the civilian market. The biplane was powered by a 160 horsepower Curtiss C-6 engine giving it a cruising speed of seventy-seven miles per hour and a maximum speed of ninety-seven miles per hour—far less than the 150 miles per hour speed quoted in a local newspaper. The plane carried two passengers on staggered seats in the front cockpit. The pilot sat in the rear cockpit. It had a cruising range of 388 miles. A service ceiling of 12,850 feet would, as the newspaper reported, get it over the Coast Range and the Sierra Nevada but just barely. The plane had a wingspan of forty feet or thirty-six, feet depending on which model was purchased. Its length was twenty-six feet.

The Oriole was reported to be as comfortable as a modern automobile and featured a slow landing speed. The plane had a very unusual add-on, an electric starter, which made it ideal for landing in areas where there were airports with no personnel to hand prop the engine.[36] The self-starter was a unique addition for 1920. Electric starters were not included on civilian light aircraft until the mid-1930s.

The Oriole was not successful on the aircraft market because its initial sales price was $9,850. A Curtiss factory refurbished JN-4D sold for one-third the price of a new Oriole. The national policy of dumping surplus wartime aircraft on the civilian market killed the success of new postwar models until the late 1920s when surplus ex-war planes became worn out beyond repair.[37]

Earl Cooper made a plea to the city during an auto show interview in which he emphasized the necessity of a permanent airport at Chico. He said there were over two hundred commercial aviation businesses flying planes in the state of California and more would be coming. These aircraft needed a permanent designated place to land at every town. He said doctors, lawyers, and businessmen were turning to flying as an expedient method of travel. Cooper made the bold statement that a, "… huge eight-passenger plane is operating down the San Joaquin Valley between Stockton and Los Angeles in a passenger carrying business, which promises to surpass all expectations." He was referring to the efforts of Charles McHenry Pond and R. Gardner with their Curtiss Eagle, which Cooper sold them. Their effort was admirable but ultimately unsuccessful.[38]

One year later there was some success establishing a landing field at Chico. H. E. Ward, head of the local airport committee, announced that a temporary city-supported landing field would be developed on ground adjoining Edgar Slough, south of the city limits. The Thomasson brothers, owners of the land, donated the property to the city for all aviators to use if they wished.

The airfield would be marked with a large C, sixty feet in diameter, indicating Chico, and within the C would be a wind tee, which was standard equipment on all government designated airports. The whitewashed C could be seen easily from the air.

The Thomasson airfield was supposed to be temporary until a permanent landing field could be developed on ground adjoining the golf links—land set aside by the park commission for that purpose.

The permanent field next to the golf course would not be ready by the week of May 18, 1921, but work was said to begin at once to put it in condition for landing airplanes. The same emblem and wind tee would be used on the permanent field as was used on Thomasson Field.[39] This permanent field would never be developed.

CHARLES R. PARMELEE, A NOTED WAR FLYER, came to Chico June 7, 1921, to fly an aerobatic exhibition under the auspices of the Gates-Morris Aviation Company of San Francisco. Parmelee was flying a three-seat Martin TT, according to Ivan R. Gates, who reported the Martin TT was a San Francisco police department machine recently used to track down criminals from the air.

Jinx Jenkins was Parmelee's parachutist for the exhibition. He was said to be the new "Locklear" with his wing-walking stunts and parachute drops. Ormer Locklear, the most famous stunt pilot and wing walker of the day, had recently died during a stunt. As Locklear's replacement, Jenkins performed for only a year until the dangerous profession took his life.

The land on both sides of Edgar Slough near the old state highway, now known as Midway, were the sites of most aeronautical activity occurring at Chico from 1911 until 1935: (1) was the site of Chico's auto and horse racing track known as Speedway Park—it was Chico's first flying field; (2) this was the site of Thomasson Field (possibly a little closer to the 1919 Chico city limits), some believed at the time this would become Chico's municipal airport; (3) this area was also used as a landing field in 1919–1920; (4) Patrick Field was located here—the runway's northern threshold was very close to Hegan Lane; (5) there is evidence that the ground between Hegan Lane and Edgar Slough was also used as a landing field.

Parmelee and Jenkins had been operating out of Thomasson Field on the old state highway (now Midway). This airfield may have been located where the fuel tank farm is today, but there is strong evidence it may have been closer to Chico's city limits of the day on the north side of Edgar Slough. A permanent airport was later developed further south of the tank farm along the old state highway on property belonging to the Patrick family and managed by Garrison Patrick. The Patrick airport was in operation through the 1960s.[40]

Parmelee and Jenkins were originally scheduled to fly for only one day at Chico, but interest was so great they stayed four more days hopping passengers and flying daily exhibitions at Thomasson Field.[41]

Dwight Clark, a boy from Chico, had taken up the dangerous profession of wing walking. Reportedly, he started this work in Sacramento and later moved to San Francisco where there was more opportunity.[42]

Ivan R. Gates of the Gates-Morris Company brought Jinx Jenkins back to Chico in late August 1921 for another round of aerial exhibitions in Butte County. This time his pilot was Emmett Tanner who flew loops and spins over the city before landing on a makeshift landing strip on the north side of Edgar Slough and south of city limits probably Thomasson Field. The month before, Tanner flew his Curtiss Jenny four times under the Sacramento River Bridge at Red Bluff.[43] As an army aviator, Tanner had flown with Major Carl Spatz in the 1919 Transcontinental Reliability and Endurance Race.

Tanner told a reporter he and Jenkins arrived for the exhibitions late because they were replacing the worn out engine in his plane with a new one at San Francisco. Thorton "Jinx" Jenkins, with Emmett Tanner in the cockpit, would soon carry out the most dangerous stunt ever done during the barnstorming days of the 1920s. On August 27, 1921, Jenkins purposely jumped from Tanner's airplane without a parachute at Chico.

While he was performing his wing-walking exhibition in late evening, Jenkins dropped from Tanner's Curtiss at very low level intending to land in a haystack at Sears Field. For three days the two men had been performing at Sears Field, east of the state highway (Midway) on the north side of Edgar Slough and south of the city limits. On this last day of the exhibitions, they decided to step up the thrills.

Jenkins jumped without his chute at 7:15 PM. He hit and rolled along the ground through several somersaults before landing in the haystack. It was said the approaching darkness made an accurate drop impossible. As

Tanner guided the Jenny towards the haystack at sixty miles per hour, Jenkins dropped from the trapeze he was holding on to and struck the ground "with a thump" and then catapulted into the haystack.

The crowd felt sure he had been killed. They gathered around him as he was lifted to his feet. He refused further help and limped off in search of his mechanic.

The same stunt was to be done the next morning for a movie crew. Whether it was or not is unknown. Jenkins and Tanner remained one more day at Chico giving rides before moving on to fulfill their next commitment.

Jenkins was killed during a later exhibition at San Jose. Before his death another stuntman, Wesley May, sent Jenkins' bosses, Ivan R. Gates and Clyde Pangborn, a cold-blooded but pragmatic telegram reading, "When Present Wing-Walker Is Killed. I Want The Job."

May got the job and was a daring parachutist, but he too was killed within the year. The job was so dangerous there was a constant turnover of wing-walking parachutists. Gates was spending too much money having his handbills reprinted with each new parachutist's name, so he decided to use a stage name, the Great Diavolo, for all of the parachutists. The posters and handbills never had to be changed. It was a grim business.[44]

The farmer who raised alfalfa on the field Tanner was flying from at Chico sued him for seventy-five dollars. Farmer George Pegden said exhaust sparks from Tanner's plane caused his haystacks to burn. The case was going to court until Pegden learned he had served in the same squadron with Tanner during the war. The two men settled the case amicably out of court.[45]

Dwight Clark, the eighteen-year-old Chico boy who had taken up wing walking, died at the Dalles, Oregon. He had performed as stuntman for pilot Charles Parmelee at Pendleton, Oregon, where he contracted lockjaw and died. His funeral was held in Chico on August 30. Emmett Tanner dropped flowers over the grave from his Jenny during the service.[46]

Jack Shalk, a wing walker who claimed to have performed for the movie cameras in Hollywood, came to Chico in late May 1923 to perform an exhibition of aerial stunts. Sierra Aircraft Company of Sacramento sent Shalk and two of its pilots, Ive McKinney and Bob Clohecy, to Chico to perform. They flew their Jennies out of Vern Thomasson's airfield.

While making his way to Chico, Bob Clohecy had flown into a rainstorm north of Marysville then turned around and landed there. He made it to Chico the following day.

During their exhibition over Chico, Shalk descended a rope ladder below one of the Jennies and hung by his teeth as the plane flew over the crowd. He also hung by his knees below the Jenny and did several other stunts. The men were on a barnstorming tour of the north state for two weeks. They reported they would be returning to Chico and do even more dangerous stunts.[47]

Ive McKinney was soon hired by Clyde Pangborn and Ivan Gates to join their flying circus and barnstorm across the United States with the group. McKinney stayed with Gates Flying Circus until its demise, and was killed later while flying his Swallow in an air race at Teterboro, New Jersey.[48]

Jack Shalk returned to the Chico area on June 30, 1923. He and his pilot, Ingvald Fagerskog from Sacramento's municipal airfield in Del Paso Park, flew over the various cities and towns of Butte, Tehama, Glenn, Yuba, Colusa, and Sutter counties dispersing handbills from the air advertising a big three-day celebration at Chico for the Fourth of July.[49]

Flight activity was busy in May through August 1923 at Sierra Airport, a few miles south of Chico. Albert Hastings, president of Sierra Aircraft Corporation, acquired the airport for his company operations. It was the landing field on the Patrick property. The airport served Sierra Aircraft Company until at least October 12, 1928, when a powerful windstorm did a lot of damage to the airfield and its occupants.

W. J. "Joe" Barrows became a legendary bush pilot in Alaska, but before he found his calling as a bush pilot, Barrows had been knocking around the western United States in a Jenny hopping passengers and doing any other jobs he could to keep flying. In August 1924, he wrote to his future wife Mary that he would be leaving home in the Bay Area to fly up the Sacramento Valley searching for flying jobs.

Barrows started his search at 5:00 AM and reached Stockton around noon. After refueling, he proceeded to Sacramento where he rested and let the summer afternoon heat dissipate. He took off for the north valley in early evening. His engine burned a valve; stranding Barrows in Chico for six weeks while he tore down his engine, waited for parts, and worked in a local garage for food and gas money. He wrote to Mary, "Even if my plane were repaired there is no business here carrying passengers. People aren't sold on aviation. There is a pilot here now with a plane and he is almost starving."[50]

William J. Obele, a flier from Sacramento, signed a contract with the commander of the Chico American Legion Post No. 17 in October 1924 to fly an aerobatic and wing-walking exhibition at Chico for the upcoming

Armistice Day festivities. If the weather was decent that day, Obele promised a plane-to-plane transfer by an expert wingwalker.[51]

JIMMIE ANGEL CRASHED ON AN AIRFIELD one mile south of Chico on November 24, 1924. He had just put his airplane into a spin to demonstrate the maneuver to his passenger Robert Broderick. As a safety precaution, before they had taken off, Angel removed the passenger's control stick. However, Broderick apparently panicked when the plane started spinning and jammed his feet against the rudder bar, and Angel could not recover from the spin.

Their flight had started several minutes earlier in a relatively peaceful manner. After a normal departure from the airfield, Angel climbed to fifteen hundred feet and executed an Immelman maneuver reversing his direction. Numerous people in the business district witnessed them flying over Chico. Next, Angel put the plane into the spin from which he planned to recover just above the threshold of the runway making an immediate and, usually, impressive but very dangerous landing.

As the spin progressed, Angel saw Broderick brace himself in the front cockpit. When Angel started his recovery movements using the stick and rudder bar, he realized Broderick had both of his feet braced against the rudder bar giving the plane full left rudder and rendering the bar useless.

Broderick didn't seem to hear or understand Angel's cries to release the rudder bar. Somehow Angel was able to stop the spin at an altitude of about fifty feet! He gave the plane full power and pulled back on the stick to slow the descent. The plane hit wing first in a glancing blow then crashed in a heap.

Before the wreck, rancher T. B. McDaniels and others could hear Angel screaming at Broderick to take his feet off the rudder bar. The airplane ended up in pile of broken wing struts with a twisted metal engine cowl. Broderick suffered cuts and bruises to his head, but no serious internal injuries or broken bones. He spent the night at Enloe Hospital.

The crash happened a little before noon. After a brief checkup at Enloe, Jimmie Angel was on his way to Sacramento to arrange for another airplane. There was an effort to salvage the engine from the wrecked biplane, but a fire had started and the plane was partially consumed. Harry Zink, a local photographer, took several shots of the crashed airplane including the fire that partially destroyed it. They were immediately enlarged and put in the window of the R. F. Roberts Company.[52]

One month later, Jimmie Angel reported he and several mysterious unnamed businessmen from Sacramento, San Francisco, and Chico were planning to start passenger service between Chico, Sacramento, and San Francisco. Angel said the service would start in fifteen days, and Chico might be the company headquarters; if not, Sacramento would be the main office. He said negotiations were under way to establish a local airfield for the company's operations where hangars could be built to house two airplanes that would fly from Chico, twice a day, to southern ports. Lincoln Standards with 220 horsepower Hisso motors were chosen for the service. These planes could haul five people and two hundred pounds of baggage at one hundred miles per hour, enabling the flight from Chico to San Francisco in 1.5 hours. The planes, Angel said, were currently being reconditioned at the Angel brothers' shop in Sacramento.[53]

Jimmie Angel was arrested in Sacramento, a few days later, on an outstanding warrant from Mt. Ada, Arkansas, but, even though he got out of the charge and jail, nothing more was reported in Chico about his plan to start a local passenger service. A year and a-half later he would sell a more reduced scheme to Dr. Julian Johnson and other citizens of Yuba City and Marysville.[54]

Western Flying published in June 1926, the following information about Chico Municipal Airport: Location—".5 mile S (south) of Town. It is 1500' x 900' Trees on S side."[55] This location, if correct, sounds more like Thomasson Field than Patrick Field.

Twin brothers Thomas and John Penfield of Paradise built and flew an airplane of their own design. It is known only as the 1926 Penfield Aircraft.[56]

One of the airports used at Chico during the years 1926–1927 deteriorated to such a degree it was declared useless. In early 1928, forty young Chico area men sought to start a flying club. According to club leader Allen Miller, members wished to associate themselves with the American School of Aviation. Miller said the club intended to hire a licensed pilot to come to Chico weekly and give flight instruction. However, the club's most important duty, he said, was establish a permanent airport at Chico.[57]

Once again the Chico City Council began looking at possible sites for a municipal landing field. On February 7, the council discussed in detail the site proposed near the golf links at Bidwell Park. They didn't make any decision except to continue site discussions at their next meeting.[58]

In June 1928 Albert Hastings filed papers in Oakland for Sierra Aircraft

Company to incorporate. Hastings, company president, reported his headquarters would be at Oakland Airport, and Sierra Aircraft would replace Golden State Aircraft Company as the Northern California distributor for Alexander Eaglerock airplanes.[59]

There was talk in Chico about possibly issuing bonds to raise eighteen to twenty thousand dollars to purchase and develop the airport already established. Air traffic between Marysville and Chico was frequent enough due to the activities of Sierra Aircraft Corporation, which had an office at Marysville and a branch at Chico on the Patrick Ranch.[60]

A Chico airport was surveyed and mapped by Butte County engineer H. H. Hume. Reportedly, the field would soon be ready for traffic.[61]

On July 4, the *Chico Record* reported, "Since the establishment of the Chico airport [Thomasson], many planes have visited this city according to Allen E. Miller, a member of the Chico Aero Club which has been keeping in touch with all arrivals from the air."

In the preceding weeks, John Tremayne had flown his Waco 10 into Chico from Oroville; Don Cornell of Sierra Aircraft Corporation, flew an Eaglerock up from Marysville; a Jenny flew in from Sacramento; Foster and Atherly arrived in a Swallow from Oakland; and an Eaglerock from Vallejo with several other planes had flown in for a short stay. Captain Eagle, an army pilot, took up a member of the Chico Aero Club. Several Chico residents went for short hops over the town, and J. T. Delany made a flight to Willows and back on business.

A wind sock was erected on a twenty-foot pole at the airfield to assist incoming and outgoing pilots with the wind direction.

"The news that Chico has an airport is spreading rapidly over the state and Aero Club members believe that it will be but a short time until great passenger and mail planes will be stopping here daily."[62]

A public plea was made in early July 1928. All interested persons with trucks were needed for one night at the Chico airport south of town near Edgar Slough. They were asked to help the chamber of commerce and the Chico Aero Club clear the airport's landing ground of rocks, which could interfere with airplanes. One runway was said to be in fine shape, but the new runway to be laid out was covered with rocks.[63]

WILLIAM H. ROYLE MET with the Chico Chamber of Commerce and assured them he would open a flying school—a satellite school of Royle Air Lines in Oakland. Royle, a successful aviation businessman, was commanding officer of the 316th Observation Squadron of the US Army Air Corps Reserve at Crissy Field. He saw service with the British and French armies during the war where he was gassed and wounded. He was president of the Pilots and Operators Association of the Oakland airport, and had been a member of the committee that authorized construction of Oakland Municipal Airport.[64]

Royle and Bernard Foster signed a contract with the city of Chico allowing Royle Air Lines to start a flying school at the Chico airport.[65]

In August, Jerry Andrews, a licensed transport pilot for Royle Air Lines, arrived at the Chico airfield in a new Swallow to be used for training at the new school.[66]

Royle Air Lines was not an airline service like we know today. It would more accurately be described as a flying service that flew charter flights and carried out flight instruction. It did not fly regularly scheduled passenger flights nor would it in the future.

It is confusing, but there were actually two airports developed over the years south of the Chico city limits. One of the airports, Thomasson Field, was one mile southeast of the then city limits and used by Royle Air Lines.

The "Oakland Gang" in 1928. These East Bay aviators flew in nearly every airport dedication air show in Northern California in the twenties and early thirties. They are from left to right: Jerry Andrews, Denny Wright, Bill Royle, Louise McPhetridge (Thaden), Swede Leomintine, Bill Fillmore, Swede Anderson, Barney Foster (Major Foster), Banty Bannister, and Ray Bowman.

This would be the quasi-municipal airport favored and supported by the city chamber of commerce and the Chico Aero Club.

The other airport was located about four miles south of the city limits and was occupied by Sierra Aircraft Corporation. This was located on the Patrick family property west of the state highway (Midway).

The following were flying students who trained at those Chico airports in the fall of 1928: Allen Miller, James Carnahan, Dr. R. E. Haslett, Byron and Harold Durff, George Sisk, Jerome Schwartz, Harold Graves, James Kidwell, Wesley Hersperger, Gillette Stanford, Silas Weahunt, and Bud Carpenter.[67]

In early September, Richfield Oil Company brought its big tri-motor Fokker F. VII to Chico's Municipal Airport on a promotional flight. The airport's runway had to be lengthened six hundred feet to accommodate the big airliner. That gave Thomasson Field, Chico's closest airport, a runway length of twenty-two hundred feet.

Much was made of the amenities built into the tri-motor airliner's fuselage, and its fantastic cost of ninety-five thousand dollars. Thomas J. Fowler, an army veteran, piloted the Fokker for Richfield. Many local officials and their families from Chico and Oroville were given rides in the big plane. Among the various VIPs, who went up in the Fokker, was Butte County veteran war flier, Victor Strain, and his wife. After the war, Strain kept a Jenny on his ranch in southern Butte County near the Yuba County line.[68]

A Sacramento newspaper story reiterated that Chico, indeed, had two airports citing slightly different facts concerning them. It stated the airport used by Sierra Aircraft Corporation was located only two miles south of town, while the other airport was literally on the 1928 southern edge of Chico. Local promoters claimed that in the near future this latter airport would be municipally owned.

The location of the latter airport (the Thomasson site) was cited as immediately north of Edgar Slough on the state highway and was being promoted by public-spirited citizens. They had an option on the thirty acres of land with the offer of forty additional acres. They planned to form a holding committee to control and develop the airport until the city could take it over as a municipally-owned enterprise.

The runway at this airport was twenty-two hundred feet long laid out in the direction of prevailing winds, which are north and south. Future plans for the airport included building an additional runway giving the layout of runways a fan shape, allowing airplanes to land from several directions. The twenty-two hundred-foot length would allow planes as large as tri-motor airliners to land.

The holding committee planned to pursue establishment of an airmail service allowing Chico to connect with the transcontinental airmail service at Sacramento.[69]

The Chico Aero Club was reorganized in September 1928 and renamed Butte County Flying Club. Dr. R. E. Haslett was elected president; J. E. Schwartz was elected secretary-treasure. Schwartz, James Kidwell, and James Carnahan were appointed to draw up a constitution and bylaws for the club. The other charter members were: Harold and Byron Durff, Rolla Lucas, Hayden Rhoy, George Clark, Mrs. R. E. Haslett, George Sisk, Ray Steinberger, William E. Wright, Harold Graves, Howard Jenkins, and Allen Miller.[70]

Jerry Andrews, chief pilot for Royle Air Lines, moved a new plane to Chico from Oakland at the end of September. He reported the plane had a speed of 140 miles per hour and the trip from Oakland took an hour and seven minutes. He assured everyone his company would be at Chico permanently, and he would be in charge of operations. He reported, "Many students have waited for assurance of a permanent location before signing up for lessons. I can assure them that we are here to stay."

There was a plan afoot to have, what many were led to believe, an opening celebration and air show for the newly named Chico Municipal Airport, north of Edgar Slough at the southern border of town, on September 29 and 30. The promoter for this air show was Don Castle (AKA Don Lake). He was spokesman for the California Association for the Promotion of Aeronautics or CAPA, but he was actually promoting the air show on behalf of Sierra Aircraft Corporation.

Castle was in Oroville September 11, 1928, promoting the Chico air event. He also was making arrangements with Sheriff C. W. Toland to have Don Cornell, chief pilot for Sierra Aircraft Corporation at Chico, appointed Butte County's aerial deputy sheriff. Castle announced that afternoon he would fly Cornell to Oroville and land on Eacher's field, west of the city at 2:00 PM, and a delegation would meet Cornell for a brief deputizing ceremony.

Castle said Tex Frolich, who would be flying a Whirlwind powered Travel Air biplane in the air show, would be representing Oroville. He also said he would choose an Oroville girl as air queen for the event at Chico.[71]

It is difficult to understand what Castle was trying to achieve in Oroville that day. None of what he said or did in Oroville happened, other than there was an air event at Chico on September 29 and 30.

The aforementioned air show at Chico's municipal airport was a disaster. Not only was it not a community event to dedicate a new municipal airport for the city, it appears to have been just a money making event for various commercial pilots who came to the event with no other reason than to give passenger rides. There was no air show.

George N. Mitchell, a professional parachutist and pilot from Mills Field, San Francisco, told a reporter he was with a group of pilots who came up from Mills Field. "We were led to believe that it was a community event, and while we were not actually told so, we presumed that we were to come to Chico to dedicate a municipal airport since it is in only that class of activities that Mills flyers participate. We had five men on the field. Thor Polson, Ernie Voss, Sandy Derenzo, Oscar Rutjin, and C. B. Briggs. The first three mentioned flew while the rest of us stood by and looked on."

Mitchell continued, "It was simply a cutthroat proposition, competition between commercial flyers to see which could get the most passenger business. There were no events or stunts that cannot be seen any day at any active aviation field.

"Frankly, we are ashamed of our participation in the affair. And we would like to have an opportunity to come to Chico some time in connection with the municipal airport to redeem ourselves and our organization in the minds of those who financed and witnessed a private money-making enterprise believing it to be a community activity."

All of the Mills Field private pilots mentioned above were present when Mitchell made his statements. They were unanimous in their approval of all he said.[72] Mitchell and C. B. Briggs had flown to Chico in the passenger cockpit of Thor Polson's Hisso powered Travel Air.[73]

Among independent pilots who took part in the frenzy of hopping passengers that day was North Sacramento's flying barber, Walter Lockhoof.[74]

Don Castle, promoter of the dubious Chico event, had recently promoted an air show at Cheim Field in Marysville. The success of that show enabled Castle to hoodwink everyone involved with the Chico event. However, the promoter didn't leave town without some repercussions.

Castle was arrested for being "drunk and disorderly" on October 1. When presented with his hotel bill in the lobby of Hotel Oaks in Chico, he spoke in a foul manner to the proprietor, Mrs. DeGuines. She promptly swore out a warrant for his arrest for using offensive language in her presence. Chico

CHAPTER 13

police were unable to locate him for the arrest. Tom Marlor, Castle's attorney, paid his client's bail at the police station. Castle appeared in court, admitted he had been drinking, but claimed his gin had been drugged. He voluntarily pleaded guilty was fined twenty-five dollars and released.

On the same day, Chico printers Miline and Johnson filed suit against Castle to recover $79.10 in unpaid printing promoting the air show. Charges were also filed against him for parking a car belonging to Jerome E. Schwartz in a private driveway and on the street after 2:00 AM. These charges were dismissed.

Don Castle made quite a splash in Chico while promoting his flying "event," but surely his event left a black mark on aviation with city officials for some time.[75] Castle was promoting the infamous Chico air show under the auspices of Sierra Aircraft Corporation, operating from its own exclusive airport a few miles south of the newly opened municipal airport. Six thousand people from Chico and the surrounding towns showed up for the air show, which they believed was to be an official dedication of the city's new airport.[76]

Two weeks after the infamous air show, severe winds swept through the Chico area. The steel and wooden hangar at Sierra Aircraft's airfield on the Patrick property was lifted by the wind and set down nineteen feet south of its original site. An Eaglerock had been parked in the hangar but was removed only minutes before the severe wind carried the hangar.

The hangar remained intact during its forced move until a few minutes later when another gust took the building twenty feet into the air and smashed it back to earth leaving just bits and pieces of lumber and iron.

Not a single light bulb in the building was broken, nor was a can of black powder explosive stored there disturbed. If anything had stricken the can, there could have been a mighty explosion.[77]

Jerry Andrews was still in charge of the Royle Air Lines flying school and charter business in November at Chico Municipal Airport. He carried out this work in the Hisso powered Swallow.[78]

A West Coast Air Transport Company tri-motor Bach airliner departed Corning Airport on November 2, 1928, at 7:15 PM after a refueling stop. The plane was on its regular run from Portland to San Francisco. Pilot L. C. Goldsmith after passing Fairfield realized the weather report given him over the phone at Corning was either incorrect or the weather had changed rapidly. Goldsmith was trapped over a layer of fog. He decided to turn around and head back to Corning but was blown off course.

About 9:00 PM some residents of Chico heard a plane pass overhead in a northerly direction. The airliner crashed a short time later on a pine covered ridge four miles northeast of De Sabla, a mountain community. Everyone on board miraculously survived, but five of the eight were injured. The two pilots, who suffered only a few scratches, walked through the forest in the dark to find help. They were successful. The four most seriously injured passengers were taken to a work camp known as Camp One and given first aid treatment. As the sun rose, it was possible to get everyone to Enloe Hospital in Chico where they received medical care.

One passenger, Ben Silver, had lost his shoes during the crash, borrowed a pair from a patient in Enloe, and left without telling anyone who he was or where he was going. He stirred up a hornet's nest by leaving without consulting the staff.

He explained later he left the hospital after refusing to enter the Emergency Room, because a relative had died after entering an emergency room, and he didn't want the same fate. He had a painful but not life threatening scalp wound and made his way home to San Francisco.

The traumatic event ended well, but for a couple of days the Northern California newspapers ran full-page headlines about the missing airliner, the story of the crash, and the missing hospital patient.[79]

A photograph was published in the *Chico Record* of the Penfield twins who lived in Paradise between Chico and De Sabla. It depicted them shaking hands in front of their aircraft at Oakland Municipal Airport in mid-December. The brothers were working as movie pilots for Howard Hughes' production of *Hell's Angels*. The Penfields had just landed after carrying out a dogfight sequence for the film. John's plane had German markings, and he fought against his brother, Tom, whose plane had British markings. The newspaper photo showed them congratulating each other for coming through the choreographed battle sequence unscathed.[80]

ALBERT HASTINGS OF SIERRA AIRCRAFT CORPORATION flew into the Sierra airport at Chico with Santa Claus as his passenger in December. Santa would be driven by car to the city park to meet Mayor Waters and City Manager Morrison. After greeting all the children at the park, he was taken to The Fair Store and picked out hundreds of toys to hand out to local children on stage at the National Theater in Chico on December 24. A complete motion picture was filmed by L. C. Cook of Santa's arrival at Sierra Aircraft's airport and greeting children in the plaza. The motion picture

CHAPTER 13 375

would be shown on screen at the National Theater throughout the 1928 Christmas season.[81]

Local aviation enthusiasts organized a flying club in May 1929 headquartered in Chico. It was, undoubtedly, the same men who started the first two clubs. The aero club's territory was expanded with each new organization. First it was the Chico Aero Club, then the Butte County Aero Club, and with this last reorganization they called themselves the Northern California Aero Club.

Joe Hicks, who possessed a Transport Pilot License, was one of the club directors. He promised ground school and light plane classes for members who wished to fly and qualify for their commercial licenses.[82]

He is the same Joe K. Hicks who was to become manager of Reno Municipal Airport in the early 1960s. He was a member of a small group of men who founded the Reno National Air Races in 1964.[83]

Demise of Sierra Aircraft at Chico was front-page news May 24, 1929. It stated, "Airplane passenger service and instructional flying will be discontinued at the Sierra Aircraft Corporation field, south of Camino, it was learned yesterday." Camino was the Sacramento Northern rail stop, south of the Speedway stop, and directly across the old state highway from the Patrick family home, which still exists as a historical site. The rail line paralleled the old state highway (Midway) into Chico.

At the closing of Sierra Aircraft Corporation at Chico, the local paper reported, "The ship that formerly was stationed at the port has been removed and the hangar has been torn down. Albert E. Hastings, who headed the organization, left some time ago for San Diego to take an additional flying course, and since that time Joe Hicks has been in charge of the field." [84]

In 1929 Galt High School, south of Sacramento, developed an aviation program, which was recognized nationally as the finest in the country. It was also one of the earliest. Many high schools in the state, especially those in close proximity, desired to emulate Galt's direction in teaching this important emerging vocational subject.

Frank Parker, a member of the Chico Board of Education, and Clyde Dahlman, a teacher at Chico High School, met with J. C. Beswick, the state commissioner of vocational education, in Sacramento on May 27, 1929. Earlier in the day, the two men visited the aeronautics class at Galt High School and Galt Junior College. At their meeting, Beswick gave Mr. Dahlman authorization to spend two weeks of August in San Diego acquiring the necessary equipment to conduct an aeronautics class at Chico High

Franklin Rose, one of the most famous postwar Bay Area aviators, headed a committee, which recommended in 1929 that the city purchase the site where today's Chico Municipal Airport is located. The Great Depression intervened and six years passed before it was finally acquired.

School in the fall.

The board members approved the class on May 28. They wanted students to learn the fundamentals of flying, but only ground school was to be taught, which included how to build and maintain airplanes. Unlike Galt, Chico board members were totally opposed to actual flying being taught to the young students.[85]

Three Liberty aircraft engines arrived at Chico High School for use in the fall of 1929. They were to be utilized by aeronautics students as part of the auto mechanics department.

The motors came from Rockwell Field, San Diego. They were obtained through a government program that specifically targeted high schools and colleges around the country to receive some of the thousands of war surplus Liberty engines for educational training. They were practically free; schools paid only the packing and shipping fees to obtain the engines.[86]

On the first Sunday in June 1929, during the dedication celebration for the opening of Willows Airport in Glenn County, an air race was flown between Willows and Chico.[87]

Northern California Airways Inc. brought a Travel Air to Chico for commercial air taxi and instructional work in September 1929. Bob Strief, manager of the Redding airport, would fly the plane at Chico. The company planned to establish a flying school if a suitable field could be found. It seems clear that a permanent airport for the city had not been agreed upon by that date.[88]

A 160-acre airport site was chosen in November for Chico; four-and-a-half miles north of the city. A committee of experts, including Frank Rose, general manager of Varney Air Service of Oakland, chose the site. Cost to develop the airport was estimated to be about fifty thousand dollars.[89] Little evidence of this plan going forward at the time is found, but the location is right for the Chico Municipal Airport in use today.

Ken Kleaver of Dunsmuir, flying an Eaglerock and Leo Moore from Sacramento in his Romair biplane, departed Del Paso Field for Chico in late November. There they flew in an air show promoted by the noted parachutist Sig Smith.[90]

An airplane was reported flying over Richardson Springs and later Paradise on Sunday morning, December 15. What made this remarkable was cloud layers blanketed the Sacramento Valley, and visibility was extremely limited due to a winter storm. Later, citizens of Chico learned the identity of the visitor.

The aircraft was a Pacific Air Transport Boeing Model 40 mail plane flown by J. Crandall and carrying 450 pounds of mail in the big single-engine biplane's cargo compartment. He was flying the Los Angeles to Seattle run. He had taken off from Oakland for Medford and was forced to the east by the storm. He got lost in the clouds and tried to climb above them. At twelve thousand feet his plane had accumulated so much ice it stalled and went into a spin. Crandall managed to get out of the spin and found himself between two strati of clouds. He glimpsed a town through a hole in the cloud layer below him and began to circle. He saw an emergency airfield and landed. He confirmed his location upon landing as Magalia. He took on thirty gallons of fuel and departed for Redding where he remained until the storm passed.

When asked why he didn't land at Chico, he said he could have but was unable to find a suitable landing field. Crandall also said he had three passengers ready to go at Oakland, but he refused to take them because of the dangerous storm in progress. He departed from Magalia at 1:30 PM for Redding where the mail was put on a northbound train.[91]

NORTHERN CALIFONIA AIRWAYS leased the old Sierra Aircraft Corporation airfield on the Patrick property, south of the city, in late 1929 or early 1930. The company had an office, a hangar, and seven student fliers being trained in the company's Travel Air 2000. Its corporate officers were E. J. Elfendahl, president; ex-Lt. Joe K. Hicks, vice president; Watson L. Johns, secretary; and Robert E. Haslett, treasurer.[92]

W. Garrison "Pat" Patrick III was not listed as an officer but held an interest in the business. He owned half of the company's Travel Air biplane and the airport property, which his forefathers had acquired in the 1800s from John Bidwell, the founder of Chico. Garrison Patrick died in November 1981. It was then reported that Patrick at age twenty-five opened the first airfield in the area in 1929. It was obviously not the first airfield in the area, and it is doubtful that 1929 was Patrick's first involvement in flying and the aviation business.[93] He may have been involved earlier.

Northern California Airways suffered a serious setback when its president, James Elfendahl, crashed the company's Travel Air just after sundown February 13, 1930. Pilot Elfendahl, twenty-one, and passenger Percy Little, twenty-three, died the next evening in Enloe Hospital. The other passenger, Clifford Squier, twenty-two, was in and out of a coma. His ultimate fate is unknown.

Elfendahl had inherited twenty-two thousand dollars when he turned twenty-one. He immediately went into a partnership with Garrison Patrick purchasing the Travel Air. He acquired part of the airport and began taking flying lessons. He had over fifty hours flying time when he died.

When the accident occurred, Elfendahl was flying 250 feet above the airport. Suddenly his plane went into a spin from which he was unable to recover. It was believed he was preparing to land. He had lived in the Chico area for four years while attending Chico State Teachers College.[94]

Following Elfendahl's death, Patrick soured on flying. However, he got back into the game some months later and bought another Travel Air 2000 from D. C. Warren Co. at Oakland Airport. In the 1930s, Patrick Field became part of the Curtiss-Wright chain with a school of aeronautics and a dealership that sold and serviced Curtiss-Wright aircraft. Garrison Patrick was listed as manager on company business cards.[95]

The second Travel Air purchased by Garrison Patrick may have been the plane Joe Hicks flew from Lordsburg, New Mexico, to Los Angeles—stopping at Davis-Monthan Airport in Arizona for fuel on May 28, 1930. Hicks was flying Travel Air NC 663H, presumably from the Travel Air factory at Wichita, Kansas, to his home field listed in the Davis-Monthan Airport daily register as Chico, California.[96]

In early December 1933, the Chico Chamber of Commerce decided to appoint a delegation to attend a Sacramento meeting of the state chamber of commerce where Department of Commerce officials would talk about CWA/SERA funds available through the DOC for development of municipal airports.

The Chico delegation was seeking a five thousand dollar grant, as was the delegation from Oroville.

Before the delegation left for Sacramento, the Chico Chamber of Commerce had to choose a site for the delegation to list on the application for the federal grant. Sites considered were the present Patrick airport property; the old city sewer farm; the DeGarmo ranch; the Eaton property on Richardson Springs Road; and a site on Shasta Highway, which was offered as a direct donation to the city by R. C. Hurst.[97]

The chamber decided not to apply for the federal grant money because the city was unable to buy a site; the Depression had deeply stressed its finances.

By April 1935, Chico's financial status had improved. It was able to purchase a 160-acre parcel for the city's permanent municipal airport in use today. It is believed this airport site, purchased from Lessie J. Garner for twenty-four hundred dollars, was the same site recommended to the city in November 1929 by Frank Rose, general manager of Varney Air Service, and his committee of experts.

The first runway was graded the same month the site was purchased, and airplanes began using the new airfield immediately. In June 1937, the next improvement was authorized by the city manager who allocated $1,480 to construct the first building on the site, a new hangar. In September 1937, the first airport manager was hired. The city's municipal airport was by then on equal footing with Patrick Field, which had been in use since the 1920s.

The War Department announced in August 1941 the municipal airport would become the new Chico Army Airfield. During World War II, it was used as a flight school. Army flying students who successfully completed primary training were sent to Chico for basic flight training.

From Chico they would go on to advanced training in other parts of the nation. The student fliers at Chico Army Airfield took their instruction in Vultee BT-13 aircraft. The BT-13 was nicknamed the "Vultee Vibrator," a plane loved by a few and disliked by most who flew it. The army's flying school at Chico opened in April 1942.[98]

Chico's current municipal airport (1994 photo) was opened in 1935. In 1941 the U.S. Army announced the airport would soon become Chico Army Airfield, which explains the huge landing pad west of the main runway.

A Ford Tri-motor transport believed to belong to Golden State Airways parked on Patrick Field near Chico, circa 1930.

CHAPTER 14

Early fliers and barnstormers at Gridley – Friesley's influence – The California Association for the Promotion of Aeronautics – Harvey Bolton

Gridley was the third largest city in Butte County in 1910. During the early years of aviation, it was little more than a village. Its residents were more familiar with the nearby Sutter County towns of Live Oak and Yuba City than Butte County's largest towns, Chico and Oroville, located farther away. In the early 1920s, Gridley was included in the city directory for Yuba and Sutter counties because of its close proximity to them.

The first airplane to land at Gridley was flown by Thaddeus Kerns in 1912. He was forced to land his Curtiss Pusher after his engine quit during his previously mentioned cross-country flight to Marysville from Chico.

Gridley's next aerial event occurred in October 1916. Lyman Doty, a former resident of the nearby Biggs community, brought his Curtiss Pusher by rail from Redwood City. Doty assembled his machine, then flew an exhibition at Gridley's baseball field for the citizens and his many friends.[1] (Lyman Doty's aviation career is described in chapter nine.)

After Doty's 1916 exhibition, there were few if any notable flying events at Gridley until after the Great War. Sergeant Major Clark and Sergeant Buckley flew a JN-4 from Mather Field to Gridley in early June 1919. They were searching for a field where several aircraft could land on June 18, Picnic Day, when planes from Mather were to fly an aerial exhibition at Gridley. They made a good landing at Parkside. They decided the site, with a little preparation, would be adequate for the army aircraft.[2]

The same month, Sergeant Buckley just happened to be flying over Honcut, east of Gridley, and saw a field on fire near town. He dove his plane low over Honcut. After many townspeople came outside their homes to observe the noisy interloper, he threw out a message that fluttered down to H. A. Brown. Brown told everyone around him the pilot saw a fire burning nearby in a field. The townspeople jumped in their cars, rushed to the fire, and soon had it under control.³

During the Twenty-third Annual Picnic Day, a four-plane formation of planes from Mather Field arrived and landed on the Parkside grounds at Gridley. Later that day, the aviators flew exhibitions over town. Capt. F. S. Voss, piloting a Jenny, was in command of the flight. Sergeant Major Clark rode along with Voss as his mechanic. Flying a second Jenny was Lt. G. Gardner. Sgt. Frank McKee flew the third JN. Lt. C. F. Dexter and Sergeant Saxe were in the last plane. They thrilled the picnic crowd with formation flying and formation maneuvers. The next morning Sergeant Buckley, a member of the army fire patrol based in Oroville, flew over early and performed stunts for the picnickers. He did not land afterward. Instead, he turned toward the Sierra Nevada and resumed his patrol duty. A civilian airplane from Stockton was on the scene giving rides to a few of the thousands of people who attended Picnic Day festivities.⁴

E. H. Pendleton came to Gridley from Sacramento in July 1919 to speak at a gathering of local residents about the necessity of preparing and maintaining a landing field at Gridley.⁵

Ogle Merwin, a Sacramento flier affiliated with Pendleton, occasionally carried out passenger flights at Gridley between duck patrols in Butte County before he gave up the dangerous duck patrols in October 1919.⁶

In April 1920, an unnamed aviator parked his airplane on Onstott Field, north of Gridley, and proclaimed he would be making several flights around Gridley, all while flying under the power lines along Biggs Road.

It is quite possible this flyer was Charles Kingsford-Smith, who at that time was keeping one of E. J. Moffett's JN-4s at Jackson Bottoms in Yuba City. He was using the plane to barnstorm small towns in the area while waiting to fulfill contracts to fly duck patrols in Glenn and Colusa counties.⁷

DURING 1920–1921, THERE WAS MUCH FLYING ACTIVITY in the Gridley area by Friesley Aircraft Corporation's aircraft. The Friesley company, whose story has already been told in a previous chapter, had landing fields at Friesleben's ranch on the east side of the Feather River and at the company's plant and airfield two miles south of Gridley, west of the river.

In February 1921, Bond Spencer, chief pilot for Friesley Aircraft Corporation, made a flight in one of the company's Jennies that forever endeared the company to the Gridley community.

The American Legion post in Gridley had arranged a shipment from San Francisco of victory medals, awarded to local World War veterans, to the legion post at Sacramento. The post was to hand deliver the medals to Gridley. But, unknown to the Gridley post until the last minute, the Sacramento post had been ordered closed down, and the medals were not shipped.

C. W. Johnson, commander of the Gridley post, called the army officer in charge of the medal distribution in San Francisco and asked if he could deliver them in time for the award ceremony at Gridley. The officer said yes, if airplane transportation could be arranged from Crissy Field.

Johnson telephoned Lt. Lowell H. Smith asking if something could be done. Smith was both commander of the 91st Squadron stationed at Mather Field and vice president of Friesley Aircraft Corporation. Smith contacted Col. H. H. Arnold at Crissy Field asking for help.

Arnold acted immediately and Lindeman, the officer with the medals, was flown from Crissy Field at 3:00 PM in a de Havilland DH-4 to Mather Field. The pilot of the DH-4, Lt. F. J. Fowler, after landing at Mather, transferred Lindeman to a waiting army Curtiss JN-4 piloted by Lt. Edward D. Arndt. The JN-4 left Mather for Gridley. Arndt was unfamiliar with the area and figured he would land at Live Oak, six miles south of Gridley.

Bond Spencer realized the army pilot would probably have difficulty finding a place to land, so he took off in the Friesley JN-4 and intercepted the army JN near Live Oak. He guided the army plane to Friesley Field where both planes landed at 5:10 PM. The army pilot, Arndt, later praised the service rendered by the Friesley employees, and although the field was a little wet and soft, he explained that once it had dried and was graded it would be a good landing field.

Lindeman was able to hand out the medals that night at the American Legion awards ceremony in Gridley. He said he gave out more medals in Gridley than he had given at a recent Stanford University ceremony.[8]

The Friesley company kept aviation alive in southern Butte County throughout much of 1920 and all of 1921. The tide turned when the company declared bankruptcy in early 1922. Many of the Gridley community's citizens who invested in Friesley stock were left with bad feelings towards the aviation community. Little interest in aviation was shown in the Gridley area until the "surge" in aeronautics following Lindbergh's flight to Paris in May 1927.

Harvey Bolton, a local farmer's son who was quite popular in Gridley, traveled to Los Angeles to learn to fly at the Aero Corporation of California flying school. Bolton passed the tests for his Private Pilot License at the Aero Corporation's airport on South Western Avenue, Los Angeles, in August 1927.[9]

Biggs High School, a few miles north of Gridley in Butte County, was reported to be one of the first high schools in the northern valley counties to offer a class in practical aeronautics. W. E. Wright began teaching the class in September 1927. Wright had served in the British Royal Flying Corps in Egypt, North Africa, Italy, and France during the Great War.[10]

Famed movie stunt pilot Dick Grace was invited by the South Butte Post of the American Legion to Gridley to perform an aerobatic exhibition on November 5. His latest film, *Wide Open*, in which he was the star, was to be shown that night at Gridley Memorial Auditorium. It was assumed he would speak about his attempt to fly from the Hawaiian Islands to California prior to the Dole Race in August. Grace failed to show at Gridley citing problems with his airplane and injuries suffered in a recent plane crash he performed for a movie shoot. Crashing airplanes was his specialty in Hollywood.[11]

Fred Dixon, a San Rafael cattleman, attended a Gridley Rotary Club luncheon meeting in March 1928. He told the gathering that within the next five years every California community would have an airport or be left out of future progress and development. He said if the community would provide a place to land, he would fly up from San Rafael for the next luncheon.

At the same meeting, Del Delehanty of Sacramento spoke for a few minutes about the Capital City's plans for a municipal airport. Fred Onstott was chairman of the Rotary Club meeting.[12]

A few weeks later, the Rotary Club luncheon featured a talk about aviation by R. Grover Powers, the Colusa postmaster. Powers learned to fly during the World War and continued flying until 1923. He spoke mainly on the advantages of future aircraft designs that could rise and land vertically.[13]

C. W. Miller, a Gridley realtor, leased twenty-two acres for the city to construct an airport. It was a tract of land located between the Libby, McNeil and Libby Cannery and Vermont Street. The property was large enough to handle all commercial and locally owned airplanes. This land offer was not pursued by city of Gridley officials.[14]

Talking to the Gridley Community Club on September 18, 1928, about the city's need for an airport were Don Castle, of the California

CHAPTER 14

Association for the Promotion of Aeronautics (CAPA); Don Cornell and Jerry Schwartz, employees of Sierra Aircraft Corporation at Chico; and P. Carney, field man for CAPA.

The men tried to convince the Community Club that the city should have an air show and an airport dedication on October 6 and 7, which was the weekend following the air show and dedication at Chico. Since the city had no official airport to dedicate, they suggested the popular landing strip on Fred Onstott's ranch, a half-mile north of Gridley, be dedicated on that weekend. Space required for an airport—a runway twenty-five hundred feet long by five hundred feet wide—was not a problem on the large Onstott field. The only problems were it didn't belong to the city and they weren't paying Onstott anything to use the field.[15]

Don Castle and Jerry Schwartz harangued Gridley service clubs with speeches about the progress of aviation, the necessity of every small town to develop an airport, and what a great stimulus for local interest in aviation an air show would be.[16]

The three men were trying to set up a series of air shows, one at Cheim Field, Marysville, which they held in early September 1928, another at Chico on September 29 and 30, and a third at Gridley in early October.

The air show at Marysville was a true airport dedication and opening. With large community support, the air show portion was a great success. Everyone involved made money. The upcoming air show and dedication to be held at Chico the end of September would be a disaster, as mentioned previously. It was not an official opening and there was no air show, just passenger hopping. But the Chico event had not been held yet, so the people of Gridley had only the success at Marysville as reference. Gridley town leaders acquiesced—the October air show was a go.

Leo Moore, a Sacramento commercial pilot, was to fly the aerobatic performance at Gridley's Onstott Field October 5, 6 and 7.

Moore and his mechanic Leo Lane arrived on Friday the fifth in Moore's *Miss Sacramento*, a blue Travel Air biplane. Moore and Lane wouldn't make the same mistake made at Chico the week before. Stunt flying was definitely provided for the spectators at the air show. Friday afternoon Moore's mechanic tried his hand at wing walking. Moore also did a brisk business hopping passengers that day. Saturday he gave more rides. On Sunday, Moore did a few aerobatic stunts for the crowd and then continued hopping passengers.

Throughout the weekend, Leo Moore emphasized how safely he flew.

He told a reporter he was a government-licensed pilot with three to four thousand flying hours to his credit. He also said in eleven years of flying he never had an accident; not even a blown tire. This latter statement would come back to haunt him.

On one of his Sunday passenger hops, he struck a rice check (berm) with the wheels of his Travel Air, wiping one wheel off the fuselage and slamming the nose into the ground shattering his prop. Mrs. J. C. Brokaw and her daughter were his passengers. No one was hurt. Moore got a new prop from Marysville and amazingly had *Miss Sacramento* ready to fly in a few hours.

Leo Moore was owner and chief instructor of his flight school, Moore School of Aviation, at Del Paso Airport near Sacramento. He told a reporter the three hundred pilot members of CAPA had chosen him to fly the aerobatic exhibitions at Gridley. He also said he wanted to open a branch flying school at Gridley.[17]

The local newspaper published a photograph taken at Onstott Field of P. Carney, Charles Chase, Herman Ohrt, Milt Brown, two unamed pilots, and Don Castle standing in front of a Sierra Aircraft Corp. Alexander Eaglerock. The unidentified pilots were probably Don Cornell and Jerry Schwartz.[18]

Once again Don Castle, promoter of the air show, was served with a summons and an attachment of personal property including his car. Constable Tom Elliott and Gridley Chief of Police C. H. Miller carried out the service on Saturday during the air show. The summons was carried out on Don Lake, an alias for Don Castle, Byron Lake, his partner in the air show promotions, and Miss Claire Jacks, Castle's secretary. The summons was part of the original attachment taken out after the Chico air show by Milne and Johnson printers of Chico.[19]

An aerial locator sign was painted on the roof of a garage in Gridley. It named the town and an arrow pointed towards Onstott Field.[20]

George Frates, chairman of the Gridley Armistice Day celebration, signed a contract with Berkeley Aviation Service for an air show at Gridley on November 11, 1929. He was assured five planes from Berkeley Airport would take part in the air show. Pilots would be Col. Harry Abbott, Gene LeGault, Jerry Andrews, Bante Bannister, and Dick Smith and Walter Hall would make parachute jumps. Although five planes were to fly in formation over the morning parade, if they did the local newspaper failed to report it or any news of the air show.[21]

Cloddy Field was the airport for the small community of Honcut in south Butte County. Harry Middleton opened a crop dusting business there in the 1940s, but it was said to have been in use since the '30s. It was a rough strip, as this author will attest to having landed there in the early 1970s. It is no longer in use.

Harry Middleton's Eaglerock cropuster on Cloddy Field at Honcut in the 1940s.

HARVEY BOLTON, THE young man from Live Oak who was a Gridley favorite, finished his pilot training at Aero Corporation of California in the south state. A photograph in *Aero Digest* listed him as a pilot or an instructor for Aero Corporation of California in August 1928. The magazine photo of him included Paul E. Richter Jr., Lee Willey, Charles Witmer, Lee Flannigan, and Jack Frye. Frye later became head of the TWA airline, and Richter was his right-hand man in management of the airline.[22]

Harry Middleton by the rudder of his Eaglerock duster. He moved to Butte County in the late 1930s and went to work for the Idaho-Maryland Mining Co. at Grass Valley as their aircraft mechanic. On the company's airfield, which is now Grass Valley Airport, Harry kept the company's Vultee V-1A and Lockheed 10 in top flying condition.

By November 1929, Bolton was flying a tri-motor Kreutzer for Hawaiian Airways.[23] In April 1930, one of the Hawaiian Airways' two Kreutzer trimotor air coaches made a forced landing. Further airline operations had to be suspended. The company's two pilots, who alternated inter-island flights, were chief pilot Harvey Bolton and W. D. Cannon Jr. of San Diego.[24] A month later, Hawaiian Airways was flying again

W. N. Morgan of Merced-Wawona Air Lines at Merced came to Gridley in March 1930 to interest local rice growers into hiring his company to sow their rice seed. The company offered to sow rice by plane at one dollar per acre. The grower had to provide a landing field two thousand feet long by two hundred feet wide. Morgan boasted one of his planes had sown forty-eight tons of rice in twenty-seven hours. Sowing by airplane allowed rice to grow on land that could not have otherwise been seeded. Morgan signed a contract with O. H. Vanderford, a grower west of Gridley, to seed a field for him.[25]

Ford Presley, a student at the University of California and son of Gridley residents Mr. and Mrs. B. F. Presley, passed his government exam for a pilot's license with the remarkable score of 100 percent in September. He

Before he moved to California, Harry Middleton worked in Mexico, as a mechanic, for Aerovias Centrales, a Mexican airline and a subsidiary of Pan American Airlines. While there he befriended James Giffin, a pilot for one of the many mining companies in Mexico. In this remarkable photo, Giffen sits with his foot on a stack of gold bars, each purposely made to be too heavy for one man to carry or steal. The Mexican Indian next to Giffin was his loyal helper and was said to follow Giffin's Boeing Model 40, on foot, during each gold delivery. It would take him a week trekking over rugged mountains to meet up with Giffin. Apparently, he didn't like to fly.

Frank Gallison's Merced-Wawona Airlines Waco 10 during the first rice seeding operation in Butte County (late April 1930) on the O. H. Vanderford Ranch.

was one of nine with a score of 100 percent out of six hundred people who passed the test.[26]

Gridley city officials were still being urged to establish a municipal airport by members of the Rotary Club after the members listened to another speech by Colusa postmaster Grover Powers, in December.[27]

J. E. Frazier, a state assemblyman from Gridley, flew from Sacramento with fellow congressman Dan W. Emmett in April 1931 to the latter's home in Santa Paula. There they met a Richfield Oil Company tri-motor transport carrying Governor Rolph to Los Angeles. After the meeting, they returned to Sacramento that same evening.[28]

Lt. Harold F. Brown carrying two passengers, Clarence Bassett and H.

J. McManus, flew from Marysville to Bassett's ranch near Gridley in July 1932. He landed in a nearby field on the Campbell property after buzzing the field twice to get the sheep to move away from his landing area.[29]

In December 1933 when Oroville was applying for the CWA/SERA money to construct an airport, and Chico was considering doing the same, the Gridley Community Club members declared airports were becoming a necessity for the progress of every community. They wanted to pass a resolution to go after the federal money being offered to build or repair local airports. If Gridley officials did apply for federal grant money, they didn't get it. Gridley didn't own a municipal airport site, which was a requirement of grant regulations.[30]

HARVEY BOLTON DIED on the morning of May 6, 1935, in the crash of a Douglas DC-2 airliner he was flying for TWA. He was the son of Mr. and Mrs. F. C. Bolton of Live Oak where he was raised. Live Oak is located in Sutter County, two miles south of the Butte County line. The Boltons were better known among Butte County residents than those in Sutter County.

Bolton's crash would shake the foundations of the emerging airline industry and the Department of Commerce Aeronautics Branch that would regulate it.

Bolton was flying a twin-engine Douglas DC-2 on the TWA route from Los Angeles to Kansas City, Missouri, on the night of May 5 through the morning of May 6. He was scheduled to land in Kansas City at 2:55 AM to refuel, but dense fog at the Kansas City airport made landing impossible. He radioed he had two hours of fuel left and then proceeded to an alternate airport at Kirksville, where he thought he could land. Reportedly, he tried to find a hole in the fog to get down through but was unable. He then let down on instruments hoping to spot the runway; his fuel was about gone.

A newspaper report contradicted itself stating that after failing to get down at Kansas City, two hours passed with occasional radio calls from Bolton to ground stations. His fuel supply dwindled. He was thirty miles from his alternate landing site, and there was no break in the fog. The Douglas crashed a short time later killing five people, seriously injuring six, and two others suffered lesser injuries. All were passengers and aircrew.

Of the passengers, most were Hollywood executives and technicians on their way to a film shoot. One passenger was nationally known—US Senator Bronson Cutting, a Republican from New Mexico. He became the first prominent US politician to die in an airplane crash.[31]

Bolton was mortally injured. His copilot, Kenneth Greeson, was killed instantly. TWA pilot Frederick Whitten, a good friend of Harvey Bolton, accompanied Bolton's body to Live Oak and spoke at his friend's funeral on May 11.

Due to the death of such a prominent public figure as Senator Cutting, there was public outcry for a government investigation into the crash, and a strong desire to fix the blame. When Frederick Whitten got up to speak at his friend's funeral, there had already been an editorial in the Marysville newspaper. Luckily, it did not cast any ill will towards the pilots who died in the crash. That would come later.

Whitten expressed his appreciation for the editorial and then told the mourners unpublished facts about Bolton and the crash. He said Bolton was, "One of the most efficient and dependable pilots flying for Transcontinental and Western Airlines." Whitten said that without a doubt after Bolton was unable to land at Kansas City, he was sure he had enough fuel to make it to an airport where he could safely land.

At this point, Whitten believed the wind had changed and blew with such strength Bolton's ground speed was reduced to the extent he was forced to crash land short of the runway near Kirksville.

Apparently, Bolton had not turned on his landing lights when he made his final descent, leading some reporters to assume he unknowingly flew the airliner into the ground. Whitten explained, "We never turn on our landing lights in a fog. To do so produces a blinding glare that hinders instead of aids in landing."

About Bolton, Whitten said, "When rescuers arrived he was still conscious and took charge of the work, directing that passengers be first attended to, and refusing aid for himself." Bolton said, "Never mind me, look after my passengers." He repeated this as long as he was conscious. "Bolton was not lost." Whitten said loudly for all to hear. "He was right on the radio-beam and was bound for Kirksville, but his gas gave out before he could reach the landing field."[32]

These were the earliest months of the airlines' use of instrument landing approaches, as they are called today. The jargon of airline pilots in 1935 called such an approach to landing, as being or landing "on the beam," the radio beam.

As flying accidents happen, they are normally in the headlines for a few days and then quickly disappear. But due to the death of Senator Cutting and four others, the crash was still in the newspapers three years and five investigations later. The investigations, "... into airline safety ... would ultimately revolutionize the industry and indirectly bring about the passage of the Civil Aeronautics Act of 1938." [33]

At the time of the accident, Bolton had over two thousand hours flying time of which 714 were in the DC-2. He had scored 100 percent on his written IFR tests in late 1934. TWA took special pride in the IFR (Instrument Flight Rules) abilities of its pilots. Bolton was considered one of the best of the best.

Why was Bolton assigned to fly special VIP charter flights? Surely it was because of his proficiency, but also he had a relationship with TWA president Jack Frye and Paul Richter, going back to when all three were pilots for Aero Corporation of California in 1928, which must have influenced the decision to give Bolton plum assignments.

This flight, which would take Bolton and Greeson back to their home field, was boarded at 4:00 PM on May 5 at Grand Central Air Terminal, Glendale. Bolton took off a short time later.

In those early days, not all airlines had cabin attendants. It was copilot Greeson's responsibility to see to the passengers' comfort, including serving supper.

Bolton landed at Albuquerque, New Mexico, just after 9:00 PM, and Senator Cutting boarded the aircraft.

The flight to Kansas City was routine. Bolton's TWA flight six was just minutes behind flight eight, a DC-2 piloted by J. D. Graves. The weather was clear until Bolton passed Wichita, then he went on instruments because of fog. From this point, the only facts known are Bolton was unable to land at Kansas City and switched to Kirksville as his alternate destination. It was also known he had trouble locating the low-power NDB (nondirectional radio beacon) at Kirksville. The range of the NDB was only twenty-five miles, and on this particular night it may have been reduced to two miles.

The last weather report issued before the crash said Kirksville had a cloud ceiling of twelve hundred feet and visibility of five miles. Bolton should have been able to land at Kirksville.

Historian George E. Hopkins wrote in his book *Flying the Line*, it was then that, "... something went wrong. At less than two hundred feet above ground level ... flight six was still in and out," of fog unable to establish visual ground contact. Occasional breaks in the fog revealed no sign of Kirksville's beacon.

It was later determined there were only two possibilities for what happened next. The first was Bolton saw what he thought was a suitable spot for a forced landing and decided to land before he ran out of fuel, which meant he would still have some control in the landing. Evidence supporting this possibility—he had turned on the seat belt light before impact. The second possibility—he unknowingly flew the airliner into the ground. The evidence supporting this possibility was no power reduction was made before the plane hit the ground. One passenger thought the landing lights came on once, but were turned off just before impact. The DC-2 hit the ground, flipped over, and broke apart.

Bolton, as he struggled painfully among the dead and injured, repeated over and over, "My God, these poor people." He told those around him he had run out of gas. An investigation determined the plane had thirty gallons left in its tanks. There was much confusion and, mortally injured, there was little time left for him to explain his plan for the forced landing. Bolton refused medical care until everyone else on the plane was moved to the hospital. He died on the way to the hospital from internal injuries.

Three weeks after the crash, the DOC Aeronautics Branch investigation ruled the cause was "pilot error." It was then that all hell broke loose.

The Air Line Pilots Association (ALPA), lead by David Behncke, was attempting to unionize airline pilots during the 1930s. Its success was hit and miss. At the time of Bolton's crash, most of TWA's pilots had joined a company union set up by Jack Frye. The TWA Pilots Association was started in December 1933, when David Behncke was threatening a national strike. Seventeen TWA pilots remained loyal to ALPA's goals, but the majority agreed to join a company union. It is believed Harvey Bolton was one of the seventeen.

Behnke went to bat for the deceased Bolton as soon as the DOC's finding was released. The number of "pilot error" findings for airline pilots in accidents during the 1930s was an open wound among the airline pilot community. The pilots wanted the DOC bureaucracy examined as closely as pilots were examined during accident investigations. To Behncke, it wasn't right that DOC was allowed to investigate itself.

During the eight years prior to Bolton's crash, there were over one hundred fatal accidents in the airline industry and DOC blamed the majority on "pilot error." The DOC never assumed any degree of responsibility for even one of the fatal accidents.

Bolton's crash was investigated by Congressional committees nearly a half dozen times over the next few years, but the DOC Bureau of Air

Commerce wasn't exonerated from blame this time.

David Behncke never revealed for certain that Bolton was a member of ALPA, as the list of members in the early days of the union was kept secret to protect the pilots. But it was believed Behncke would have gone to bat for Bolton regardless of his membership.

Behncke did not believe Bolton was completely at fault for the accident. Poor weather forecasting and bad radio maintenance at Kirksville gave the DOC a share in responsibility for the accident. Behncke had the DOC on the defensive. Just hours after the crash, Behncke told reporters, "A tired pilot is an unsafe pilot. The pilots believe that fatigue is an important factor in accidents."

A DOC Bureau of Air Commerce regulation limited airline pilots to flying no more than eight hours in any twenty-four-hour period. Bolton had exceeded those eight hours when he crashed. Behncke reported TWA regularly flew its pilots longer than eight hours—disregarding the DOC regulation.

Airlines got away with flying their pilots long hours because DOC's Director Eugene Vidal of the Bureau of Air Commerce issued special waivers to the airlines relaxing the regulation.

Behncke kept up a constant attack in the press.

Several congressmen, who hadn't realized that Vidal had the power to waive the eight-hour rule, began to apply pressure on Vidal. At the end of May 1935, Vidal canceled all waivers to the eight-hour rule.

Behncke's call for an independent investigation of the crash rattled congress, and DOC officials realized they couldn't make Bolton their only scapegoat. The DOC added TWA to share the blame with Bolton and his copilot Greeson. DOC listed several rule violations to support its new findings.

Secretary of Commerce Daniel Roper, Vidal's boss, told the press, "In my opinion the crash was due chiefly to bad weather." Then he hit TWA with heavy fines, opening the airline to negligence lawsuits.[34]

TWA officials suspected low-level DOC employees of lying to their bosses when the DOC disputed Bolton having received instructions to divert to Kirksville.

The DOC agreed some of the infractions against the pilots were unrelated to the accident, which made the case against TWA stronger. Of these infractions, Bolton was a few days past his due date for his quarterly physical. The DOC waiver allowing Bolton to fly more than eight hours during a twenty-four-hour period required the copilot to have a Scheduled Air Transport rating. Greeson didn't have a Scheduled Air Transport rating.

TWA's Frye and Richter knew Behncke was right. They were going to need an independent investigation, and the senate authorized it. In the meantime, a predecessor of the Federal Communications Commission declared, "The root cause of the crash was due to the company's radio system," and hit TWA with forty-five violations to Communications Commission rules.

The Copeland congressional committee spent seven months listening to everyone who had anything relevant to say about the accident. Its final report was nearly a complete vindication of Bolton, Greeson, and TWA. The DOC was cited for inefficiency as the principal cause of the accident. TWA's infractions were merely contributing factors. About Bolton and Greeson, the committee said, "No one could possibly allege carelessness, lack of loyalty to duty, selfishness, or a character that would shirk. They were 'let down,' the victims of fallible ground aids to navigation in which they trusted implicitly."

The Copeland committee led Congress to drastically change the government's regulation of aviation in America by passing the Civil Aeronautics Act of 1938. This law took control of commercial and private aviation out of the hands of the Department of Commerce and into the hands of a new agency, the Civil Aeronautics Administration, which would be renamed, years later, the Federal Aviation Agency.

The new law also created the Air Safety Board, an independent group of three investigators, one of whom was Tom Hardin, the first vice president of the Air Line Pilot's Association, and a pilot for American Airlines. The Air Safety Board was the forerunner of today's National Transportation Safety Board (NTSB), which investigates all airline accidents.

The most damning evidence against the DOC in what history has labeled the Cutting Crash, was DOC's order to airport managers at secondary airports, like Kirksville, to reduce their beacon light wattage to save the DOC two thousand dollars a year on its electrical bills. Sadly, one wonders if Bolton and Greeson knew this as they struggled to see the rotating beacon in the fog at Kirksville before they crashed.[35]

For further examination of the Cutting-Bolton crash, the book *Bonfires to Beacons* by Nick A. Komons is recommended. It is a careful dissection of the accident with a full explanation of the political power struggles, which influenced the people involved in the various committee investigations that followed. It also gives a more thorough perspective of the DOC officials who were involved before, during, and after the crash.

The deaths of Harvey Bolton and, sixteen years earlier, Lyman Doty reveal tragic coincidences between the two. Bolton was involved in the creation of what would become the first successful airline pilots union, ALPA. He was born in Live Oak, and died trying to land his plane in fog.

Lyman Doty, who may well have been part of the first strike by professional (airmail) pilots in the summer of 1919, was born and raised in Biggs just ten miles from Live Oak. Doty was flying for the US Air Mail Service when the pilots struck for safer planes, safer weather flying procedures, better pay, and the creation of a pilots' union.[36]

The airmail pilots' strike was only partially successful, and Doty saw little of the results. While flying the mail in October 1919, he also died trying to land in fog. Both Doty and Bolton rest among the giant evergreen trees in the Gridley-Biggs cemetery.

A Curtiss R-4, similar to the plane Lyman Doty was killed in while flying the airmail near Baltimore, Maryland, in October 1919.

The de Havilland DH-4 above was typically used to fly the airmail from 1919-1927, but, sadly, Lyman Doty drew an obsolete R-4 for his last flight.

The U.S. Army gave Marysville Army Airfield to the city and county after WWII ended. It was first named Alicia Airfield then Marysville Airport and finally its current name — Yuba County Airport.

In the early 1950s the main hangar and control tower at Marysville Airport burned down in a spectacular fire.

Endnote Source
ABBREVIATIONS

Abbreviation -- Magazine or Journal

AAHS Journal -- American Aviation Historical Society Journal
AAM -- American Aviation Magazine
AAW -- Aerial Age and Aerial Age Weekly
AD -- Aero Digest Magazine
Aero -- Aero Magazine (As of July 1912 Aero became Aero & Hydro)
Aero & Hydro -- Aero and Hydro Magazine
Aeronautics -- Aeronautics magazine
Air and Space -- Air and Space Magazine
AF -- Air Facts Magazine
Aviation -- Aviation Magazine
Diggin's -- Butte County Historical Society Quarterly
PA -- Popular Aviation Magazine
PAC A -- Pacific Aeronautics Magazine
PF -- Pacific Flyer Magazine
Skyways -- Skyways Journal
The Ace -- The Ace Magazine
WF -- Western Flying Magazine

Abbreviation -- Newspapers

BWN -- Biggs Weekly News
CDS -- Colusa Daily Sun
CO -- Corning Observer
CR -- Chico Record
DC -- Daily Californian
GAH -- Galt Herald
GH -- Gridley Herald
LA Ex -- Los Angeles Examiner
LMRR -- Los Molinos River Rambler
MA -- Marysville Appeal
MAD -- Marysville Appeal Democrat
MD -- Marysville Democrat
MED -- Marysville Evening Democrat
NYS -- New York Sun
ODR -- Oroville Daily Register
OE -- Oakland Enquirer
OM -- Oroville Mercury
OMR -- Oroville Mercury Register
OT -- Oakland Tribune
PAlto -- Palo Altoan

PR -- Porterville Recorder
RBDN -- Red Bluff Daily News
RCD -- Redwood City Democrat
RCFP -- Redding Courier Free Press
RDC -- Redding Daily Courier
RDI -- Richmond Daily Independent
SB -- Sacramento Bee
SCF -- Sutter County Farmer
SCIF -- Sutter County Independent Farmer
SDI -- Stockton Daily Independent
SF Call -- San Francisco Call Bulletin
SF Ch -- San Francisco Chronicle

SF Ex -- San Francisco Examiner
SIF -- Sutter Independent Farmer
SJMH -- San Jose Mercury Herald
SU -- Sacramento Union
TDJ -- Turlock Daily Journal
VMD -- Visalia Morning Delta
WDD -- Woodland Daily Democrat
WDJ -- Willows Daily Journal
WDR -- Woodland Daily Register
WFR -- Western Flyer
WH -- Washington Herald

Yuba County Airport is in the center of this 1994 photo with Marysville in the top right corner and Yuba City is in the top left corner with Sutter County Airport (Jackson Bottoms) closest to the Feather River.

ENDNOTES

Chapter 1

1. *CDS*, June 12, 1929; *MD*, May 28, 1897.
2. *Aeronautics*, May 1910, p. 169; *MA*, Feb. 13, 1910.
3. *SB*, Feb. 9, 1910.
4. *ODR*, Feb. 10, 1910; *ODR*, Feb. 14, 1910.
5. *MA*, Feb. 13, 1910.
6. *CR*, Feb. 18, 1910.
7. *SU*, Feb. 13, 1910.
8. *SB*, Feb. 14, 1910.
9. *MAD*, Nov. 18-21, 1911.
10. *MED*, Mar. 15–18, 1912.
11. *SB*, Mar. 4, 1912.
12. *MED*, Mar. 15, 1912.
13. *MED*, Mar. 11 & 18, 1912; *SB*, Mar. 4, 1912.
14. *MED*, Mar. 25 & 27, 1913.
15. *MD*, Mar. 28, 1918; Maurer, p. xxi.
16. *MD*, July 17, 1918.
17. *MD*, July 24 & 25, 1918.
18. *MD*, Aug. 6, 1918.
19. *MD*, July 28, 1918.
20. *MD*, Aug. 8, 1918.
21. *MD*, Aug. 13, 1918.
22. *MD*, Aug. 19, 1918.
23. *GH*, Aug. 21, 1918.
24. *MD*. Aug. 21, 1918.
25. *MD*, Sept. 5, 1918.
26. *MD*, Sept. 9 & 16, 1918.
27. *MD*, Sept. 5, 1918.
28. *MD*, Nov. 16, 1918.
29. *MD*, Nov. 19, 1918.
30. *MD*, Dec. 10, 1918; Maurer, p. 20.
31. *MD*, Dec. 10, 1918.
32. *MD*, Jan. 22, 1919.
33. *AAW*, May 13, 1918, p. 455; Sloan, p. 408; *MD*, April 17, 1919; *MD*, Jan. 3, 1919; *MD*, Jan. 23, 1919.
34. Delay, n. p.
35. *MD*, Mar. 14, 1919.
36. Todd Bihlman Interview, Mar. 19, 1999.
37. Maurer, pp. 19-20.
38. *MD*, Apr. 30, 1919.
39. *MD*, May 8, 1919.
40. *MD*, July 22, 1919.
41. *MD*, Aug. 1, 1919.
42. *MD*, Aug. 2, 1919.
43. *MD*, Aug. 2, 1919; *MD*, Apr. 3, 1920.
44. *MD*, Apr. 5, 1920; *MA*, Nov. 9, 1920.
45. *MAD*, June 25, 1930; Von Geldern, Rick, Interview, Mar. 7, 2000.
46. Mackersey, p. 49.
47. *MAD*, Apr. 7, 1920; Von Geldern, Rick, Interview, Mar. 7, 2000.
48. *MAD*, Apr. 17, 1920.
49. *MAD*, Apr. 18, 1920.
50. *MAD*, Apr. 19, 1920.
51. *MAD*, Apr. 23, 1920.
52. Mackersey, p. 32.
53. *MAD*, Apr. 27, 1920.
54. *AAW*, May 10, 1920, p. 280; Bruce, pp. 2-5.
55. *AAW*, June 21, 1920, P. 586.
56. *SB*, June 23, 1920.
57. *SB*, June 27, 1920; Kingsford-Smith, p. 20.
58. Mackersey, p. 50; Ronnie, p. 273; *WDJ*, July 15, 1920.
59. Mackersey, p. 50.
60. *MD*, Dec. 20, 1927; MD, Jan. 17, 1928.
61. *MD*, June 15, 1920.
62. *MD*, Apr. 7, 1921; *MD*, Apr. 19, 1921.
63. *MD*, June 16, 1921.
64. *MD*, July 2, 1921; *MD*, Sept. 27, 1921.
65. *MD*, Aug. 15, 1921.
66. *MD*, Aug. 6-8, 1921.
67. Griffin, *Skyways*, No. 18, p. 46.
68. *SU*, Mar. 8, 1923; *AAW*, Aug. 25, 1919, p. 1099.
69. *MD*, Mar. 20, 1923.
70. *MD*, Mar. 22, 1923.
71. *MD*, Mar. 23, 1923.
72. *MD*, Mar. 21-22, 1923.
73. *MD*, Apr. 25, 1923; Cleveland, pp. xii & 133; Komons, p. 111.
74. *MD*, May 23, 1923.

75. *MD*, May 19, 1923.
76. *MD*, May 22, 1923.
77. *MD*, May 23, 1923.
78. *MD*, May 25, 1923.
79. *MD*, June 3, 1923.
80. *MD*, July 30, 1923.
81. *MD*, Aug. 1, 1923.
82. *MD*, Aug. 2, 1923.
83. *MD*, Aug. 10 & 17, 1923.
84. *MD*, Sept. 6, 1924.
85. *MD*, Feb. 17-19, 1925; Glines and Cohen, p. 64; Waterman, p. 134.
86. *MD*, Feb. 19, 1925.
87. *MD*, Feb. 21, 1925.
88. *MD*, Feb. 5, 1925; *SU*, Dec. 30, 1924.
89. *MD*, Feb. 4, 1925.
90. *MD*, Mar. 19, 1925; *WF*, Jan. 1926, n. p.
91. *MD*, Feb. 6, 1926.
92. *MD*, Mar. 28, 1925.
93. *MD*, Jan. 5, 1926.
94. *MD*, Mar. 10, 1926.
95. *MD*, June 9, 1925.
96. *SCF*, Jan. 8, 1926.
97. *MD*, July 1, 1926.

Chapter 2

1. Hatfield, *Los Angeles Aeronautics*, p. 99.
2. *MD*, Apr. 19, 1926.
3. *MD*, Apr. 17, 1926.
4. *MD*, Apr. 21, 1926.
5. *MD*, Apr. 22, 1926.
6. *MD*, July 2, 1926.
7. *MA*, July 3, 1926; Norby Collection at Community Memorial Museum of Sutter County.
8. *MA*, July 7, 1926.
9. Ibid.
10. *MA*, July 22, 1926.
11. MA, Sept. 10, 1926; Angel, *Terrae Incognitae*, Apr. 2012, pp. 17-20.
12. Ibid.
13. Slonniger, p. 48.
14. Letter to author, dated Feb. 20, 2014, from Karen Angel, daughter of Jimmie Angel's youngest brother Clyde Angel.
15. Slonniger, p.48.
16. Angel, *Terrae Incognitae*, Apr. 2012, p. 18.
17. *CR*, Nov. 27, 1924; *CR*, Dec. 28, 1924.
18. *CR*, Jan. 6, 1925.
19. *SU*, Jan. 7, 1925.
20. *SU*, Dec. 29, 1924.
21. *SU*, Jan. 1, 1925.
22. *SU*, Jan. 18, 1925.
23. *SB*, May 11, 1925.
24. Minor, p. 68; Larkins and Reuther, *San Franciso...*, p. 18.
25. *RDI*, June 2, 1923.
26. *AAW*, July 26, 1920, p. 694
27. *RDI*, Mar. 26, 1925; Bastin, p. 56.
28. *RDI*, May 8, 1925.
29. *RDI*, June 10, 1925.
30. Ibid.
31. *RDI*, June 13, 1925.
32. *RDI*, June 27-29, 1925; *OT*, June 27, 1925.
33. *SJMH*, June 4, 1926.
34. *SJMH*, June 5-6 & 12, 1926.
35. *SJMH*, June 15, 1926.
36. *SJMH*, June 19, 1926.
37. *SJMH*, June 19, 1926; Smith, *Fly The Biggest ...*, pp. xii, 24-26.
38. *MD*, Aug. 24, 1925.
39. *MD*, June 17, 1926.
40. *MA*, Aug. 5, 1926.
41. *MA*, Aug. 7, 1926.
42. *MA*, Aug. 5, 1926.
43. *MA*, Aug. 8, 1926.
44. *MA*, Aug. 14, 1926.
45. *MA*, Aug. 17, 1926.
46. *MA*, Aug. 18 & 26, 1926.
47. Ibid.
48. *MA*, Aug. 22, 1926.
49. *MA*, Aug. 20, 1926.
50. *MA*, Sept. 2, 1926.
51. *MA*, Sept. 4, 1926.
52. *MA*, Sept. 18, 25, & 26, 1926.
53. *MA*, Sept. 30, 1926.
54. *MA*, Sept. 10, 1926.
55. *MA*, Oct. 10, 1926.
56. Ibid.
57. *MA*, Oct. 8, 1926.
58. *MA*, Oct. 14, 1926.
59. *MA*, Oct. 16, 1926.
60. *MA*, Oct. 20, 1926.
61. *MA*, Oct. 9, 1926.
62. *MA*, Oct. 9, 1926; *SCF*, Oct. 15, 1926.
63. *MA*, Oct. 17, 1926; Robert Staight, Interview, May 16, 1999; Compton newspaper, undated circa 1926-1927, via Karen Angel.
64. *MA*, Oct. 19, 1926; *ODR*, Oct. 20, 1926; *SCF*, Oct. 22, 1926.
65. *SCF*, Nov. 12, 1926.
66. *MA*, Nov. 27, 1926.
67. *Marysville City Directory*, 1927; Robert Straight Interview, May 16, 1999. *MA*, Dec. 2, 1926; *SCF*, Dec. 3, 1926; Robert Straight

Interview, May 16, 1999.
68. *MA*, Dec. 2, 1926.
69. Ibid.
70. *MA*, Dec. 18, 1926.
71. *SCF*, Dec. 24, 1926.
72. *MA*, Feb. 11 & 26, 1927.
73. *MA*, Mar. 25, 1927.
74. *MA*, Apr. 2, 1927.
75. *MA*, Apr. 24, 1927.
76. *MA*, Feb. 9, 1927; *MA*, May 4, 1927.
77. *MA*, May 4, 1927.
78. *MA*, June 26, 1927; Grambow, p. 27; Workman, p. 23 & 26.
79. *MA*, Aug. 10, 1927.
80. *MA*, Aug. 19, 1927.
81. *MA*, Aug. 21, 1927.
82. *MA*, Oct. 22, 1927.

Chapter 3

1. *MA*, Oct. 25, 1927.
2. Herr, H. T. Ted, Interview, Jan. 7, 1999.
3. *MA*, Aug. 25, 1927.
4. *MA*, Nov. 7, 1927.
5. *MA*, Dec. 2, 1927.
6. *MA*, Dec. 10, 1927.
7. *MA*, Dec. 19, 1927.
8. *MAD*, Dec. 20, 1927.
9. *MAD*, Dec. 28, 1927.
10. *MAD*, Jan. 11, 1928.
11. *MAD*, Jan. 12, 1928.
12. *MAD*, Jan. 14, 1928.
13. *MAD*, Jan. 17, 1928.
14. *MAD*, Jan. 19, 1928.
15. *MAD*, Jan. 23, 1928.
16. *MAD*, Jan. 26, 1928.
17. Ibid.
18. Ibid.
19. *MAD*, Feb. 3, 1928
20. *MAD*, Feb. 27, 1928.
21. *MAD*, Mar. 2, 1928.
22. *MAD*, Mar. 5, 1928; *MAD*, Apr. 28, 1928; *MAD*, May 1, 1928.
23. *MAD*, Mar. 19, 1928.
24. *MAD*, Apr. 17, 1928.
25. *MAD*, May 7, 1928.
26. *WF*, June 1928, p. 68.
27. *MAD*, May 25, 1928.
28. *MAD*, June 4, 1928.
29. *MAD*, June 5, 1928.
30. *MAD*, June 8, 1928.
31. Hatfield, *Los Angeles Aeronautics*, p. 51; *MAD*, June 6, 1928.
32. *MAD*, June 14, 1928.
33. *MAD*, June 29, 1928.
34. *MAD*, June 29, 1928.
35. *MAD*, July 3, 1928.
36. *MAD*, June 29, 1928.
37. *MAD*, July 2, 1928.
38. *MAD*, July 10, 1928.
39. *MAD*, July 11, 1928.
40. *MAD*, July 12, 1928.
41. *MAD*, July 19, 1928.
42. *MAD*, July 30, 1928.
43. *MAD*, Aug. 10, 1928.
44. *WF*, Aug. 1928, p. 86.
45. *SB*, Aug. 9, 1928; *SU*, Aug. 10, 1928.
46. *MAD*, Aug. 22, 1928.
47. *MAD*, Aug. 23, 1928.
48. Ibid.
49. *MAD*, Aug. 24, 1928.
50. Ibid.
51. *MAD*, Aug. 25, 1928.
52. *MAD*, Aug. 27, 1928; *SU*, Aug. 27, 1928.
53. *SB*, Aug. 27, 1928.
54. *MAD*, Aug. 20, 1928.
55. *MAD*, Aug. 27, 1928.
56. *MAD*, Sept. 3, 1928.
57. *MAD*, Sept. 20-21, 1928.
58. *MAD*, Sept. 21, 1928.
59. *MAD*, Sept. 28, 1928.

Chapter 4

1. Sterling, p. 155; *WF*, Mar. 1939, p. 7. Read's name in photo caption is Reed. This may be a mistake or Read may have legally changed it to fit the more accepted pronunciation of Reed.; Ricklefs, p. 31.
2. *WF*, Feb. 1927, p. 16.
3. *VMD*, July 22, 1927.
4. Robert Straight Interview, May 16, 1999.
5. Angel, Karen, Letter to author, Feb. 20, 2014.
6. *WF*, Mar. 1928, p. 57; Department Of Commerce Aero Bulletin no. 20, p. 9; Richfield Oil Co., *1929 Aviation Guide*, p. 4.
7. *WF*, Mar. 1928, p. 54; Richfield, *Aviation Guide*, p. 12; Shell, *Airports 1936*, p. 44.
8. *WF*, Mar. 1928, p. 38; Robert Straight Interview, May 16, 1999.
9. *WF*, Apr. 1928, p. 56.
10. Hatfield, *Los Angeles …*, p. 131; *SF Ch*, Apr. 17, 1928; *Aviation*, Apr. 2 & 20, 1928; *WF*, May 1928, p. 70.
11. *MAD*, Apr. 16-18, 1928.
12. www.articles.latimes.com/2006/jul/02/local/me-then2; Tomlinson, p. 43; *WH*, Dec. 5, 1931; *SF Ch*, Apr. 18, 1928.

13. *SF Ch*, Apr. 24, 1928.
14. *SF Ch*, Apr. 26, 1928.
15. *SU*, May 7, 1928.
16. *MAD*, May 16, 1928.
17. Hatfield, *Los Angeles Aeronautics*, p. 142; *WF*, Sept. 1928, p. 244.
18. *AD*, Jan. 1928, p. 94.
19. *MAD*, Sept. 4, 1928; *RDC*, Sept. 4, 1928; *CR*, Sept. 5, 1928; *PF*, Oct. 1928, p. 18.
20. Harry Middleton Interview, Nov. 7, 2000; Department of Commerce Extract via Richard S. Allen.
21. *AD*, Jan. 1929, p. 98; Hatfield, *Los Angeles Aeronautics*, p. 147.
22. *AD*, Feb. 1929, p. 140; *AD*, Mar. 1929, p. 106.
23. *WF*, Jan. 1928, p. 25; Bell, p. 315; Smith, *From Jennies ...*, p. 72.
24. Casey, *Flying As It Was*, p. 114.
25. *NYS*, Dec. 15, 1930; *MAD*, Dec. 13, 1930; Casey, *Flying As It Was*, pp. 114-115; Smith, *From Jennies To Jets*, p. 87.
26. Casey, *Flying As It Was*, p. 115; *NYS*, Dec. 15, 1930.
27. *WFR*, Jan. 1989, p. 44; Casey, *Flying As It Was*, p. 115.
28. Angel, Karen. Letter to author, Feb. 20, 2014.
29. Ibid.
30. Shell, *Airports 1936*, p. 15.
31. *MAD*, May 7, 1931, FAA Inactive Files via Richard S. Allen and Gary Kuhn.
32. Angel, *Terrae Incognitae*, Apr. 2012, p. 20.
33. Angel, *Terrae Incognitae*, Apr. 2012, pp. 18 & 24; Angel, Karen. Letter to author, Feb. 20, 2014.
34. Ibid.
35. Angel, Karen. Letter to author, Feb. 20, 2014.
36. Angel, *Terrae Incognitae*, Apr. 2012, pp. 40-41.
37. *SIF*, Sept. 18, 1931; *SIF*, Apr. 1, 1932.
38. Joyce Adele Johnson Telephone Interview, Sept. 29, 2000; Internet website, http://www.angelfire.com/electronic/awakening101/jpjohnson.html
39. *MAD*, Oct. 13, 1928.
40. *MAD*, Oct. 17 & 20, 1928.
41. *MAD*, Nov. 12, 1928.
42. *MAD*, Nov. 6, 1928.
43. *MAD*, Nov. 12, 1928.
44. Ibid.
45. *WF*, Dec. 1928, p. 115.
46. *MAD*, Nov. 24, 1928.
47. *WF*, Dec. 7, 1928, p. 120.
48. *MAD*, Dec. 7, 1928.
49. *MAD*, Dec. 4, 1928.
50. *MAD*, Dec. 7, 1928.
51. *MAD*, Dec. 8, 1928.
52. *MAD*, Dec. 8 & 14, 1928.
53. *MAD*, Dec. 8, 1928.
54. *MAD*, Dec. 20, 1928.
55. *MAD*, Dec. 27, 1928.
56. *MAD*, Jan. 12, 1929.
57. *MAD*, Jan. 23, 1929.
58. Marysville City Council Meeting Minutes for Jan. 7, 1929.
59. Note on back of photo taken of Dudley Cunningham in 1927 in Community Memorial Museum of Sutter County.
60. *MAD*, Feb. 1, 1929.
61. *MAD*, Feb. 15, 1929.
62. *MAD*, Feb. 15, 1929.
63. MAD, Undated.
64. *MAD*, Feb. 28, 1929.
65. *LA Ex*, Apr. 24, 1929; *TDJ*, Apr. 24, 1929.
66. *MAD*, May 2, 1929.
67. *MAD*, May 6, 1929.
68. *MAD*, May 7, 1929.
69. *MAD*, June 10, 1929; *PF*, June 1929.
70. *WF*, June 1929, p. 108.
71. *MAD*, June 17, 1929.
72. *MAD*, June 25, 1929; *MAD*, June 12, 1929.
73. *MAD*, June 25, 1929.
74. *MAD*, June 26, 1929.
75. *MAD*, July 27, 1929.
76. *MAD*, July 30-31, 1929.
77. *CR*, Aug. 4, 1929.
78. *SCF*, Aug. 9, 1929.
79. *MAD*, Aug. 16, 1929.
80. *SCF*, Aug. 23, 1929; *MAD*, Aug. 29, 1929; *WF*, Feb. 1930, p.146.
81. *MAD*, Sept. 17, 1929.
82. *MAD*, Oct. 5, 1929.
83. *MAD*, Oct. 28, 1929.
84. *PF*, Nov. 1929, p. 20.
85. *SCF*, Nov. 8, 1929.
86. *MAD*, Nov. 8-9 & 12, 1929.
87. *MAD*, Nov. 9, 1929.
88. *SB*, Nov. 12, 1929.
89. *MAD*, Dec. 2, 1929.
90. *SCF*, Dec. 20, 1929.
91. *MAD*, Dec. 21, 1929; *SCF*, Jan. 3, 1930.
92. *SCF*, Jan. 31, 1930.
93. *MAD*, Feb. 19, 1930.
94. *WF*, Mar. 1930, p. 90.

Chapter 5

1. H. T. Ted Herr Interview, Jan. 7, 1999.
2. Davies, *Airlines of the United States* ..., p. 595; *PF*, July 1929, p. 21.
3. *MAD*, Mar. 24 & 31, 1930.
4. Marysville City Directory, 1934.
5. *MAD*, Mar. 24 & 31, 1930.
6. *MAD*, Mar. 24, 1930.
7. *MAD*, Mar. 27, 1930.
8. *MAD*, Apr. 4, 1930.
9. *MAD*, Apr. 5, 1930.
10. *MAD*, Apr. 9, 1930.
11. *WF*, June 1930, p. 118; Bell, p. 80.
12. Davies, *Airlines of the United States* ..., p. 59.
13. *MAD*, Mar. 28, 1930.
14. Ibid.
15. *MAD*, Apr. 5, 1930.
16. *MAD*, Mar. 31, 1930; *MAD*, Apr. 1, 1930.
17. *MAD*, Apr. 3, 1930.
18. *MAD*, Apr. 4, 1930.
19. *MAD*, Apr. 7, 1930.
20. *MAD*, Apr. 9, 1930.
21. *MAD*, Apr. 10-11, 1930.
22. *MAD*, Apr. 17, 1930.
23. Ibid.
24. *MAD*, Apr. 26, 1930.
25. *MAD*, May 3, 1930.
26. *MAD*, May 4, 1930.
27. *MAD*, May 6, 1930; *SCF*, Mar. 28, 1930.
28. *MAD*, May 15, 1930.
29. *MAD*, May 17, 1930; *SCF*, May 23, 1930.
30. *Skyways*, Jan. 2001, p. 53.
31. *PF*, Nov. 1930, p. 9.
32. *MAD*, May 23, 1930.
33. Ibid.
34. Ibid.
35. *MAD*, June 2 & 3, 1930.
36. *MAD*, June 3, 1930.
37. *MAD*, June 10, 1930.
38. *MAD*, June 16, 1930.
39. *MAD*, June 25, 1930.
40. *MAD*, July 3, 1930; Cleveland, p. 124.
41. *SCF*, July 18, 1930; *MAD*, July 19, 1930.
42. *MAD*, July 25, 1930.
43. *MAD*, Aug. 4, 1930; *CR*, Aug. 5, 1930.
44. *MAD*, Aug. 19, 1930.
45. *MAD*, Aug. 20, 1930; *PF*, Sept. 1930, p. 22.
46. *MAD*, Aug. 26, 1930.
47. *MAD*, Sept. 1930; *PF*, Oct. 1930, p. 21; *PF*, Dec. 1930, p. 24.
48. *MAD*, Sept. 2, 1930.
49. *MAD*, Sept. 23, 1930.
50. *MAD*, Sept. 12, 1930.
51. *MAD*, Sept. 13, 1930.
52. *MAD*, Sept. 15, 1930.
53. *MAD*, Sept. 19, 1930.
54. *MAD*, Sept. 23, 1930.
55. Ibid.
56. *MAD*, Sept. 24, 1930.
57. *MAD*, Sept. 25, 1930.
58. *MAD*, Sept. 26, 1930.
59. *MAD*, Sept. 26, 1930; *SCF*, Oct. 3, 1930.
60. *MAD*, Sept. 26, 1930.
61. *MAD*, Sept. 29, 1930; *PF*, Oct. 1930, p. 21.
62. *MAD*, Oct. 1, 1930.
63. *MAD*, Oct. 2, 1930; *PF*, Nov. 1930, p. 28.
64. *MAD*, Oct. 9, 1930.
65. *MAD*, Oct. 10, 1930.
66. Ibid.
67. Ibid.
68. *SCF*, Oct. 10, 1930.
69. *MAD*, Oct. 10, 1930.
70. *MAD*, Oct. 16, 1930.
71. *MAD*, Oct. 17, 1930.
72. *MAD*, Oct. 23, 1930.
73. *MAD*, Oct. 25, 1930.
74. *MAD*, Oct. 27, 1930.
75. *Skyways*, Jan. 2001, p. 53.
76. *MAD*, Oct. 29, 1930.
77. *MAD*, Oct. 39 & 31, 1930.
78. *MAD*, Nov. 3, 1930.
79. *MAD*, Nov. 10, 1930.
80. *MAD*, Nov. 11, 1930.
81. *MAD*, Nov. 19, 1930; *PF*, Dec. 1930, p. 20.
82. *PF*, Dec. 1930, p. 20.
83. *MAD*, Dec. 8, 1930.
84. Delay, n.p. (N. Dewey. Ashford entries); N. Dewey Ashford scrapbook, and logbook copies in author's possession; Yuba-Sutter Flying Club Aircraft Logbook copy in author's possession; *WF*, Aug. 1936, p.40.
85. N. Dewey Ashford Flight Logbook no. 2 copy in author's possession.
86. N. Dewey Ashford Flight Logbook no. 2 and scrapbook copies in author's possession.
87. *MAD*, Jan. 2, 1931; *PF*, Jan. 1931, p. 22.
88. *MAD*, Jan. 9, 1931.
89. *MAD*, Jan. 14, 1931.
90. *MAD*, Jan. 17, 1931.
91. *MAD*, Feb. 5, 1931.
92. *MAD*, Feb. 6, 1931.
93. Ibid.
94. *MAD*, Feb. 19-21, 1931.
95. *PF*, Mar. 18, 1931, p. 17.
96. *MAD*, Mar. 5, 1931.
97. *SCF*, Mar. 11, 1931.

98. *MAD*, Mar. 18, 1931.
99. *MAD*, Mar. 25, 1931.
100. *MAD*, Mar. 27, 1931.
101. *MAD*, Mar. 31, 1931.
102. *PF*, Apr. 8, 1931.
103. *MAD*, Apr. 1, 1931.
104. *MAD*, Apr. 11, 1931.
105. *MAD*, Apr. 15, 1931; *PF*, Apr. 22, 1931, p. 11.
106. *MAD*, Apr. 16, 1931; *PF*, Apr. 22, 1931, p. 11.
107. *MAD*, Apr. 21, 1931.
108. *MAD*, Apr. 24, 1931.

Chapter 6

1. *SCF*, May 9, 1930.
2. *MAD*, May 30, 1930.
3. *MAD*, June 4, 1930; *SCF*, June 7, 1930.
4. *SCF*, June 27, 1930.
5. *SCF*, June 20, 1930.
6. *MAD*, June 24 & 30, 1930.
7. *SCF*, July 4, 1930.
8. *SCF*, July 25, 1930.
9. *MAD*, Aug. 1 & 23, 1930.
10. *MAD*, Aug. 8, 12, & 23, 1930.
11. *MAD*, Aug. 28-29, 1930; *SCF*, Aug. 29, 1930.
12. *MAD*, Aug. 30, 1930; *PF*, Sept. 1930, p. 33.
13. *MAD*, Sept. 1, 1930.
14. *MAD*, Sept. 2, 1930; *PF*, Oct. 1930, p. 21.
15. *SCF*, Sept. 2, 1930; *SCF*, Apr. 25, 1930; *MAD*, Oct. 1, 1930.
16. *SCF*, Sept. 12, 1930; *PF*, Nov. 1930, p. 23.
17. *WDJ*, Sept. 15, 1930; *SCF*, Sept. 19, 1930.
18. *SCF*, Nov. 21, 1930; *SCF*, Dec.19, 1930.
19. *SCF*, Nov. 21, 1930.
20. Tom Krull Interview, Oct. 10, 2000.
21. H. T. Herr Interview, Jan. 7, 1999.
22. *MAD*, Apr. 27, 1931.
23. *MAD*, May 7, 1931.
24. *MAD*, May 12, 1931.
25. *MAD*, May 15, 1931.
26. *MAD*, May 16, 1931.
27. *MAD*, May 18, 1931.
28. *MAD*, May 19, 1931.
29. Ibid.
30. *MAD*, May 23, 1931.
31. *SCF*, Sept. 11, 1931.
32. *SCF*, July 3, 1931.
33. *AD*, Aug. 1932, p. 29.
34. *MAD*, May 19, 1932.
35. *MAD*, May 20, 1932; www.flickr.com/photos/costi-londra/333199625
36. *MAD*, May 20, 1932; Flynn, n. p.
37. *SCF*, July 1, 1932.
38. *RBDN*, July 9, 1932.
39. *MAD*, July 23, 1932.
40. *SCF*, Jan. 26, 1933.
41. *SCF*, Feb. 23, 1933.
42. *SCF*, Oct. 12, 1933; Gillis, p. 584.
43. *SIF*, July 6, 1934.
44. *SIF*, Sept. 14, 1934.
45. *SIF*, Nov. 13, 1934.
46. *SIF*, Oct. 12, 1934.
47. *SIF*, Nov. 27, 1934.
48. *SIF*, Nov. 15, 1935.
49. *Skyways*, Jan. 2001, pp. 51-53.
50. *MAD*, Mar. 4, 1935.
51. *MAD*, Mar. 18, 1935.
52. *SIF*, Mar. 19, 1935; *MAD*, Mar. 18, 1935.
53. *SIF*, Mar. 26, 1935.
54. *MAD*, Apr. 9, 11, & 13, 1935.
55. *SIF*, Apr. 30, 1935.
56. *MAD*, June 3, 1935; Davies, *Airlines of the United States ...*, p.196.
57. *SIF*, June 4, 1935.
58. *MAD*, June 18, 1935.
59. *SIF*, June 28, 1935.
60. *WF*, July 1936, p. 34.
61. *MAD*, Apr. 13, 1936.
62. *SIF*, May 5, 1936.
63. *SIF*, Mar. 20 1936.
64. *MAD*, Apr. 3 & 6, 1936.
65. *MAD*, Apr. 9, 1936.
66. Ibid.
67. *SIF*, May 8, 1936; A. T. Del Hay Jr., Flight Logbook.
68. Hay Jr., Flight Logbook.
69. *SIF*, Aug. 28, 1936.
70. *SIF*, June 9, 1936.
71. *MAD*, May 16, 1936.
72. Allen, p. 214.
73. *MAD*, May 18, 1936.
74. *MAD*, May 16, 1936.
75. Middleton, Harry, Interview, Mar. 3, 1999.
76. *MAD*, May 20, 1936.
77. *AD*, Aug. 1936, p. 93.
78. *WF*, May 1937, p. 58.
79. *SIF*, Oct. 1, 1937.
80. Hughes, Guy "Speed," Interview, Jan. 24, 1999.
81. *SIF*, Dec. 30, 1938.
82. *RBDN*, July 20, 1938; *SIF*, July 22, 1938.
83. *AF*, Dec. 1939, p. 27.
84. Thomas Bowles Scrapbook Copy

Chapter 7

1. Busby, p. 249.
2. Busby, pp. 249-251.
3. Busby, pp. 252.
4. Crouch, *The Eagle Aloft*, p. 528
5. Busby, pp. 254-255.
6. *The Ace*, Aug. 1925, p. 13.
7. *CR*, Dec. 23, 1909.
8. *CR*, Dec. 28, 1909.
9. *CR*, Feb. 20, 1910; *ODR*, Feb. 21, 1910.
10. *SB*, Feb. 21, 1910.
11. *CR*, Feb. 24, 1910; *SB*, Mar. 14, 1910.
12. *ODR*, Feb. 23, 1910.
13. *ODR*, Feb. 26, 1910.
14. *ODR*. Feb. 15, 1910.
15. *ODR*, Feb. 19, 1910.
16. *ODR*, Feb. 21, 1910.
17. *ODR*, Mar. 4, 1910.
18. Ibid.
19. *ODR*, Mar. 11, 1910.
20. *ODR*, Mar. 21, 1910.
21. *Air and Space*, Feb. 3, 2003, p. 78.
22. *ODR*, Mar. 21, 1910.
23. *ODR*, Apr. 14, 1910.
24. *ODR*, Apr. 16, 1911.
25. *SU*, Apr. 16, 1910.
26. *SB*, Aug. 15, 1910.
27. *SU*, Sept. 10, 1910.
28. *CR*, Sept. 13, 1910.
29. *ODR*, Sept. 13, 1910.
30. *ODR*, Sept. 20, 1910; *ODR*, Oct. 6, 1910.
31. *ODR*, Sept. 21, 1910; *OE*, Dec. 12, 1910.
32. *ODR*, Oct. 25, 1910.
33. *ODR*, Nov. 1, 1910.
34. *ODR*, Nov. 3, 1910.
35. *ODR*, Nov. 9, 1910.
36. *ODR*, Nov. 15, 1910
37. *ODR*, Nov. 23, 1910.
38. *ODR*, Dec. 3, 1910.
39. *ODR*, Dec. 6, 1910; Smith, *Aircraft Piston Engines*, pp. 16-17; *Aeronautics*, May 1911, pp. 175-176.
40. *ODR*, Dec. 12, 1910.
41. *ODR*, Dec. 16, 1910.
42. *ODR*, Dec. 19, 1910.
43. *ODR*, Dec. 20, 1910.
44. *ODR*, Dec. 9, 1910; *ODR*, Dec. 24, 1910.
45. *OE*, Dec. 12, 1910.
46. *OE*, Dec. 17, 1910.
47. *OE*, Dec. 17&19, 1910.
48. *OE*, Dec. 24, 1910.
49. *SF Ch*, Jan. 9, 1911.
50. *SF Ex*, Jan.17, 1911.
51. *ODR*, Jan. 24, 1911; *CR*, Jan. 24, 1911.
52. *ODR*, Jan. 20, 1911.
53. *ODR*, Feb. 27, 1911.
54. *ODR*, Mar. 14, 1911; *ODR*, Mar. 18, 1911; *Aeronautics*, May 1911, p. 183.
55. *ODR*, Mar. 20, 1911.
56. *ODR*, Mar. 16, 1911.
57. *ODR*, Apr. 13, 1911.
58. *AAW*, June 7, 1920. P. 436.
59. Herr, Allen, *Diggin's*, Vol. 47, No. 3 & 4, pp. 52-53.
60. *ODR*, Apr. 6, 1911.
61. *ODR*, Nov. 17, 1911.
62. *ODR*, Nov. 20, 1911.
63. *CR*, Oct. 18, 1911.
64. *SB*, July 4, 1911; *CR*, July 5, 1911.
65. *ODR*, Oct. 20 & 25, 1911.
66. *ODR*, Oct. 18, 1911.
67. *ODR*, Oct. 25, 1911; *Aero*, Nov. 4, 1911, p. 96.
68. *ODR*, Nov. 10, 1911.
69. *ODR*, Nov. 18, 1911.
70. *MAD*, Nov. 18, 1911.
71. *MAD*, Nov. 21, 1911.
72. *WDD*, Dec. 1, 1911.
73. *WDD*, Dec. 4, 1911.
74. *SU*, Dec. 17, 1911.
75. *Aero*, Dec. 30, 1911, p. 261.
76. *Aero*, Jan. 13, 1912, p. 301

Chapter 8

1. California Aviation Company (CAC) letter to Thaddeus Kerns, April 2, 1912.
2. *Aero*, Dec. 16, 1911, p. 216.
3. CAC Papers, Feb. 26, 1912.
4. CAC Papers, Jan. 1, 1912.
5. CAC Papers, Jan. 4, 1912.
6. CAC Papers, Apr. 1, 1912.
7. CAC Papers, Book C & D.
8. CAC Papers, May 14, 1912.
9. CAC Papers, Mar. 4, 1912.
10. CAC Papers, Dec. 18, 1911.
11. CAC Papers, Feb. 28, 1912.
12. CAC Papers, July 4, 1912.
13. CAC Papers, July 17, 1912.
14. CAC Papers, Aug. 2, 1912.
15. CAC Papers, Apr. 23, 1912.
16. CAC Papers, May 17, 1912.
17. CAC Papers, May 14, 1912.
18. *Aero*, June 15, 1912, p. 263.
19. *Aero and Hydro*, Aug. 31, 1912, p. 484.
20. *Aero and Hydro*, Aug. 31, 1912. P. 485.
21. *Aero and Hydro*, Sept. 7, 1912, p.505.

22. Ibid.
23. *Aero*, Feb. 10, 1912, p. 388.
24. *Aero*, Mar. 2, 1912, p. 441.
25. *Aero*, Mar. 30, 1912, p. 516; *Aero*, Apr. 6, 1912, p. 23.
26. *Aero*, Feb. 17, 1912, p. 401.
27. *Aero*, June 15, 1912, p. 263.
28. *SF Call*, July 14, 1912; *PAlto*, July 19, 1912.
29. *Aero and Hydro*, July 27, 1912, p. 385.
30. *CR*, May 4, 1912.
31. *MD*, Mar. 11, 1912; *MD*, Mar. 15, 1912; *MD*, Mar. 18, 1912.
32. *CR*, May 4, 1912; Lebow, p. 133.
33. *CR*, May 4, 1912.
34. Ibid.
35. *CR*, May 7, 1912.
36. *CR*, May 9, 1912.
37. *CR*, May 8, 1912.
38. *CR*, May 10, 1912.
39. *CR*, June 29, 1913.
40. *Aero and Hydro*, Sept. 28, 1912, p. 565; *Aero and Hydro*, Oct. 5, 1912, p. 12.
41. *SF Call*, Nov. 3, 1912.
42. *Aero and Hydro*, Nov. 30, 1912, p. 163.
43. *Aero and Hydro*, Dec. 7, 1912, p. 190.
44. *Aero and Hydro*, Mar. 1, 1913, p. 402.
45. *MA*, Mar. 25-27, 1913; *Aero and Hydro*, Apr. 12, 1913, p. 22.
46. *MA*, Apr. 10, 1913; *MA*, Apr. 13, 1913.
47. *CR*, June 17, 1913.
48. *Aero and Hydro*, July 5, 1913, p. 272.
49. *CR*, July 16, 1913.
50. *CR*, July 17, 1913.
51. *OM*, July 17, 1913.
52. *CR*, July 18, 1913.
53. *CR*, July 19, 1913.

Chapter 9

1. *AAW*, Aug. 9, 1920, p. 738; Alexander, p. 48.
2. Reilly, p. 133.
3. Reilly, p.170.
4. Reilly, p. 168.
5. Ibid.
6. Pescador and Renga, p. 26.
7. *SF Ex*, Dec. 17, 1915.
8. *AAW*, Aug. 9, 1920, p. 739.
9. Wynne, p. 6.
10. Wynne, p. 30.
11. *AAW*, Jan. 1, 1917, p. 408.
12. Wynne, p. 11.
13. *AAW*, May 13, 1918, p. 439; *AAW*, Feb. 18, 1918, p. 1038.
14. Boyne, p. 15.
15. Boyne, pp. 14-15.
16. Reinhold, pp. 139-142.
17. Allen, p. 7.
18. Wynne, p. 7; Reinhold, pp. 58-59.
19. Hatfield, *Los Angeles Aeronautics*, p. 79.
20. *WDJ*, May 24, 1920.
21. *WDJ*, July 21, 1920; *SJMN*, July 21, 1921.
22. *WDJ*, July 22, 1920.
23. *SJMN*, July 22, 1920.
24. Cleveland, p. 58.
25. *GH*, Feb. 26, 1916.
26. *GH*, Apr. 22, 1916; *GH*, July 1, 1916.
27. *RCD*, July 13, 1916.
28. *RCD*, July 21, 1916.
29. *AAW*, July 17, 1916, p. 531; *GH*, Oct. 7, 1916.
30. *GH*, Oct. 11, 1916.
31. *GH*, Nov. 1, 1916.
32. *SF Ex*, Nov. 28, 1916.
33. *GH*, Dec. 20, 1916.
34. *SF Ex*, Dec. 25, 1916; *GH*, Dec. 27, 1916.
35. *RCD*, Jan. 25, 1917.
36. *RCD*, Feb. 12, 1917.
37. *RCD*, Mar. 17, 1917.
38. *RCD*, Apr. 5, 1917.
39. *RCD*, Apr. 5, 1917; Robie, p.267.
40. *SF Ch*, Mar. 23, 1917.
41. *SF Ex*, Mar. 31, 1917.
42. *SF Ex*, Apr. 2, 1917.
43. Oakes, p. 23.
44. *RCD*, Apr. 12, 1917.
45. www.soaringmuseum.org/halloffame/chronlist.htm
46. *SF Ex*, Apr. 6, 1917.
47. *AAW*, Apr. 24, 1922, p. 150.
48. Boyne, p. 11; Louvish, p. 194.
49. *SF Ex*, June 6, 1917.
50. *SF Ex*, Aug. 22, 1917.
51. *GH*, Oct. 15, 1919; Leary, *Aerial Pioneers*, p. 108.
52. Leary, *Aerial Pioneers*, p. 70.
53. *AAW*, Dec. 30, 1918, p. 810.
54. Leary, *Aerial Pioneers*, p. 72.
55. Leary, *Aerial Pioneers*, p. 108; Smith, *From Jennies ...*, pp. 166-167.
56. Leary, *Aerial Pioneers*, pp. 108-109.
57. *GH*, Mar. 12, 1919.
58. *GH*, Apr. 9, 1919; *GH*, Apr. 12, 1919.
59. Leary, *Aerial Pioneers*, p. 109.
60. *AAW*, May 26, 1919, p. 545.
61. *SF Ex*, Oct. 15, 1919.
62. Leary, *Aerial Pioneers*, pp. 109 & 253.

Chapter 10

1. Maurer, pp. 131-132.
2. *AAW*, Feb. 10, 1919, p. 1072.
3. *AAW*, May 19, 1919, pp. 500 & 502; Maurer, p. 132.
4. *AAW*, June 16, 1919, p. 673.
5. *AAW*, July 7, 1919, p. 806.
6. *AAW*, Aug. 25, 1919, p. 1099.
7. *ODR*, May 23, 1919, *GH*, May 24, 1919; *ODR*, July 19, 1930; Information compiled by Forrest D. Dunn, ANCRR, 1977.
8. *AAW*, June 2, 1919, p. 575.
9. *ODR*, May 30, 1919.
10. *ODR*, May 31, 1919.
11. *ODR*, June 2, 1919.
12. *ODR*, June 6, 1919.
13. *CR*, June 6, 1919; *ODR*, June 7, 1919.
14. *ODR*, June 9, 1919.
15. *ODR*, June 10, 1919.
16. *ODR*, June 11, 1919.
17. *ODR*, June 12, 1919.
18. Ibid.
19. *ODR*, June 16, 1919.
20. *ODR*, June 18, 1919.
21. *ODR*, June 24, 1919.
22. *ODR*, June 25, 1919.
23. *ODR*, July 4, 1919.
24. *ODR*, July 7, 1919.
25. *ODR*, July 14, 1919; *ODR* July 16, 1919.
26. *ODR*, July 15, 1919.
27. *ODR*, July 19, 1919.
28. *ODR*, July 22, 1919.
29. *ODR*, July 24, 1919.
30. *ODR*, July 28, 1919.
31. *ODR*, Aug. 8, 1919.
32. *ODR*, Aug. 12, 1919.
33. *CR*, Aug. 13, 1919.
34. *ODR*, Aug. 14, 1919.
35. *ODR*, Aug. 18, 1919.
36. *CR*, Aug. 22, 1919.
37. *ODR*, Aug. 15, 1919.
38. *ODR*, Aug. 16, 1919.
39. *ODR*, Aug. 18, 1919, *AAW*, June 9, 1919, p. 628.
40. *ODR*, Aug. 22, 1919.
41. *ODR*, Aug. 27, 1919.
42. *CR*, Sept. 10, 1919.
43. *CR*, Sept. 17, 1919.
44. *GH*, Sept. 30, 1919.
45. *ODR*, Oct. 13, 1919.
46. *ODR*, Sept. 17, 1919.
47. *RCFP*, July 28, 1919.
48. *RCFP*, July 23, 1919; *RCFP*, Aug. 1, 1919.
49. *RCFP*, Aug. 2, 1919.
50. *RCFP*, Aug. 6, 1919.
51. Ibid.
52. *RCFP*, Aug. 19, 1919.
53. *RCFP*, Aug. 16, 1919.
54. *RCFP*, Aug. 23, 1919.
55. *RCFP*, Aug. 27, 1919.
56. *RCFP*, Aug. 28, 1919.
57. *RCFP*, Aug. 29, 1919.
58. Ibid.
59. *RCFP*, Sept. 6, 1919.
60. *SU*, Sept. 8, 1919.
61. *SU*, Sept. 9, 1919.
62. *RCFP*, Sept. 6, 1919.
63. *SU*, Sept. 16, 1919.
64. *RCFP*, Sept. 15, 1919.
65. *SU*, Sept. 18, 1919.
66. *OT*, Dec. 7, 1919
67. Grey, C. G., Editor, *Jane's All The ... 1920*, n. p.; *AAW*, Mar. 15, 1920.
68. Grey, C. G., Editor, *Jane's All The ... 1920*, n. p.; *AAW*, Mar. 15, 1920; Haller, p. 28.
69. *SU*, Apr. 4, 1920; *AAW*, Apr. 19, 1920, p. 193.
70. *ODR*, May 15, 1920.
71. *RCFP*, June 2, 1920.
72. *RCFP*, June 15, 1920.
73. *SB*, June 18, 1920.
74. *SF Ex*, July 11, 1920; *RCFP*, July 12, 1920.
75. *AAW*, Aug. 2, 1920, p. 707.
76. *AAW*, Aug. 30, 1920, p. 833.
77. Ibid.
78. *WDJ*, Sept. 25, 1920.
79. *The Ace*, Oct. 1920, p. 22.
80. *AAW*, Dec. 6, 1920, p. 355.
81. *AAW*, Apr. 4, 1921, p. 78.
82. *SF Call*, May 14, 1921.
83. *SDI*, June 1, 1921.
84. *CO*, July 23, 1936.
85. *PA*, May 1939, p. 11.
86. *SF Ex*, May 9, 1921.
87. *AAW*, Nov. 28, 1921, p. 269.
88. *AAW*, Dec. 12, 1921, p. 327.
89. *AAW*, Mar. 13, 1922, p. 15.
90. *SB*, Apr. 19, 1923.
91. *CO*, May 23, 1925; *CO*, June 24, 1925.
92. *MD*, June 24, 1925.
93. *The Ace*, Aug. 1925, p. 12.
94. *SJMH*, June 13, 1926.
95. *WF*, Aug. 1928, p. 68; *AD*, Aug. 1928, p. 286.
96. *SB*, May 29, 1929.
97. *OT*, Aug. 18, 1930.
98. *PF*, Mar. 18, 1931, p. 12.

99. *SB*, Sept. 16, 1931; *RBDN*, July 22, 1932.
100. *SCIF*, Sept. 17, 1937.
101. *AAM*, Sept. 15, 1939, p. 18.
102. *PA*, Oct. 1939, p. 28.

Chapter 11

1. *ODR*, June 23-24, 1919.
2. *ODR*, June 26, 1919.
3. *ODR*, July 14, 1919.
4. *ODR*, July 15, 1919.
5. Ibid.
6. *ODR*, July, 19, 1919.
7. *ODR*, July 15, 1919; *ODR*, July 28, 1919; *CR*, July 16, 1919.
8. *ODR*, July 23, 1919.
9. *ODR*, July 28, 1919.
10. *ODR*, July 30, 1919.
11. *ODR*, Aug. 9, 1919.
12. *ODR*, Aug. 12, 1919.
13. *ODR*, Aug. 14, 1919.
14. *ODR*, June 11, 1919.
15. *CR*, June 12, 1919.
16. *ODR*, Sept. 13, 1919.
17. *CR*, Sept. 14, 1919; *ODR*, Sept. 15, 1919.
18. *ODR*, Oct. 15, 1919.
19. *ODR*, Oct. 23, 1919.
20. *CR*, Oct. 23, 1919.
21. *ODR*, Oct. 24, 1919.
22. *ODR*, June 8, 1920.
23. *RCD*, June 25, 1919.
24. *RCD*, June 25, 1919; *PAC A*, May 1920, p. 109; *GH*, Apr. 6, 1921.
25. Dickey, p. 49; Dwiggins, p. 12; Glines and Cohen, p. 133.
26. *ODR*, July 12, 1919; *SF Ex*, Sept. 12, 1920.
27. *OT*, Oct. 22, 1919.
28. Maurer, p. 186; *SU*, Dec. 30, 1924.
29. *AAW*, May 16, 1921, p. 226.
30. Griffin, *Skyways*, No. 17, p. 33, *PAC A*, May 1920, p.109.
31. Waterman, p. 151.
32. Daniel N. Frieslaben Family Group Sheet (Genealogical Study) via James Lenhoff.
33. Ibid.
34. *AAW*, May 26, 1919, p. 532.
35. Letter from the Community Memorial Museum of Sutter County, Jan. 8, 2002; Burden, p. 108.
36. Letter from the Community Memorial Museum of Sutter County, Jan. 8, 2002; *AAW*, Aug. 4, 1919, p. 967.
37. *AAW*, Aug. 4, 1919, p. 967.
38. *SER*, June 28, 1919.
39. *WF*, Aug. 1929, p. 148
40. Hatfield, *Aeroplane Scrap Book*, p. 46.
41. Spencer, *WF*, Aug. 1929, p. 150.
42. *PAC A*, May 1920, p. 109.
43. *MD*, May 17, 1920.
44. *MD*, May 26, 1920.
45. Gwynn-Jones, p. 93.
46. *SF Call*, July 1, 1920; *SF Ch*, July 1, 1920; *SF Ex*, July 1, 1920.
47. *SF Ex*, July 4, 1920.
48. *SF Ch*, Aug. 5, 1920.
49. *GH*, Aug. 25, 1920.
50. *GH*, Sept. 11, 1920.
51. *GH*, Oct. 2, 1920.
52. Griffin, *Skyways*, No. 17, p. 34.
53. Christian, *GH*, undated.
54. *GH*, Nov. 19, 1920; *GH*, Nov. 30, 1920.
55. *GH*, Dec. 2, 1920; *MA*, Dec. 3, 1920.
56. *GH*, Dec. 15, 1920.
57. *ODR*, Jan. 3, 1921.
58. *GH*, Feb. 25-26, 1921.
59. *GH*, Mar. 6, 1921.

Chapter 12

1. Griffin, *Skyways*, No. 17, p. 37.
2. *MA*, Apr. 7, 1921; *GH*, Apr. 9, 1921.
3. *GH*, Apr. 9, 1921.
4. *MD*, Apr. 8, 1921.
5. Christian, *GH*, undated.
6. *MA*, Apr. 9, 1921.
7. *MA*, Apr. 12-13, 1921.
8. *GH*, Apr. 13, 1921.
9. *GH*, Apr. 16, 1921.
10. *GH*, Apr. 20, 1921.
11. Christian, *GH*, undated.
12. *GH*, Apr. 23, 1921.
13. *MD*, May 7, 1921.
14. *AAW*, July 27, 1919.
15. Maurer, p. 25.
16. Maurer, p. 35; Friedman, *Aviation History*, Nov. 2010, p. 54.
17. *MD*, May 7, 1921.
18. *GH*, May 11, 1921.
19. *GH*, May 11, 1921.
20. *MD*, May 4, 1921.
21. *GH*, May 11, 1921.
22. *GH*, May 18, 1921.
23. *GH*, June 1, 1921.
24. *SR*, May 29, 1921; *GH*, June 1, 1921.
25. *GH*, June 1, 1921.
26. *MD*, June 16, 1921.
27. *MD*, July 19, 1921; *Aero*, Jan. 13, 1912, p. 299.

Endnotes

28. *MD*, Aug. 6, 1921; *MD*, Aug. 8, 1921.
29. Yolo County Archives, Woodland CA, photograph of Friesley Falcon and Marysville Baseball Team.
30. Jang, p. 13.
31. *AAW*, Aug. 25, 1919, p. 1099.
32. *MD*, Aug. 10, 1921.
33. *MD*, Aug. 13, 1921.
34. *CR*, Aug. 16, 1921.
35. *MD*, Aug. 15, 1921.
36. *MD*, Aug. 16, 1921; *GH*, Aug. 17, 1921.
37. *GH*, Oct. 1, 1921.
38. Griffin, *Skyways*, No. 18, pp. 47-48.
39. Leary, "Prologue," by W. David Lewis, *From Airships To Airbus*, p. xii.
40. Griffin, *Skyways*, No. 18, p. 47.
41. Christian, *GH*, undated.
42. James Lenhoff Letter to author, Aug. 30, 2004.
43. *WF*, Sept. 1928, p. 300.
44. Letter from Community Memorial Museum of Sutter County, Jan. 8, 2002.
45. *WF*, Oct. 1928, p. 76.
46. Grace, p. 140-141.
47. Grace, p. 224.
48. Grace, p. 155.
49. Griffin, *Skyways*, No.18, p. 47.
50. *WF*, Aug. 1929, p. 148.
51. Griffin, *Skyways*, No. 18, p. 49; *MD*, Jan. 31, 1922.
52. *GH*, Feb. 1, 1922.
53. *GH*, Feb. 4, 1922.
54. *GH*, Feb. 22, 1922.
55. *GH*, May 24, 1922.
56. Andersson, pp. 22-23; Paul Chesebrough Album; Mattison, *PF*, May 1929, p. 9.
57. Davies, *Airlines of the United ...*, pp. 70, 588; *GH*, Mar. 28, 1923.
58. *AD*, June 1930, p. 136.
59. *SB*, Oct. 14, 1931; Tom Bowles scrapbook copy.
60. *WDJ*, Aug. 1, 1931.
61. *ODR*, Oct. 9, 1926.
62. *ODR*, Oct. 13, 1926.
63. *SB*, Aug. 13, 1928.
64. *MAD*, Sept. 8, 1928.
65. *ODR*, Sept. 11, 1928.
66. *ODR*, Sept. 13, 1928.
67. *WF*, Sept. 1928, p. 188 & 250.
68. *PF*, Feb. 1929, p. 22; *SB*, Oct. 2, 1929.
69. *SB*, Oct. 16, 1929.
70. *PF*, Nov. 1929, p. 22, Grambon, p. 414.
71. *SB*, July 11, 1930.
72. *PF*, Sept. 1930, p. 22.
73. *MAD*, Jan. 2, 1931.
74. *MAD*, Feb. 6, 1931.
75. *SB*, May 27, 1932.
76. *ODR*, Sept. 7, 1932.
77. *ODR*, Sept. 6-7, 1932; *SB*, Sept. 6-7, 1932.
78. *OMR*, Dec. 8, 1933.
79. *OMR*, Dec. 4, 1933; *OMR*, Dec. 6, 1933.
80. *OMR*, Dec. 9, 1933.
81. *OMR*, Dec. 11, 1933.
82. Ibid.
83. *OMR*, Dec. 12, 1933.
84. *OMR*, Dec. 19, 1933.
85. *OMR*, Dec. 21, 1933.
86. *OMR*, Dec. 26, 1933.
87. *OMR*, June 1, 1935.
88. *RBDN*, July 26, 1938.

Chapter 13

1. *GH*, Jan 4, 1919.
2. *CR*, June 6, 1919.
3. *ODR*, June 7, 1919.
4. *CR*, June 25, 1919; *ODR*, June 25, 1919.
5. *CR*, July 4, 1919.
6. *ODR*, July 2, 1919.
7. *ODR*, July 11, 1919.
8. *CR*, July 15, 1919.
9. Komons, pp. 86 & 96; *CR*, July 16-17, 1919.
10. *CR*, July 18-20, 1919; *CR*, July 22, 1919.
11. *CR*, July 23, 1919.
12. *ODR*, July 25, 1919.
13. *CR*, July 29, 1919.
14. *ODR*, July 30, 1919.
15. *CR*, Aug. 3, 1919.
16. *CR*, Aug. 5, 1919.
17. *CR*, Aug. 9-10, 1919; *ODR*, Aug. 9, 1919.
18. *CR*, Aug. 12, 1919.
19. *CR*, Aug. 13, 1919.
20. Ibid.
21. *CR*, Aug. 14, 1919.
22. *CR*, Aug. 16, 1919.
23. *CR*, Sept. 14, 1919.
24. *SU*, Sept. 23, 1919.
25. *CR*, Sept. 25, 1919; *ODR*, Sept. 29, 1919.
26. *CR*, Oct. 14, 1919; *ODR*, Oct. 15, 1919.
27. *ODR*, Oct. 23, 1919.
28. *CR*, Oct. 23, 1919.
29. *CR*, Apr. 18, 1920.
30. *MAD*, May 6, 1920.
31. *CR*, May 6, 1920.
32. *CR*, May 18, 1920.
33. *CR*, May 19, 1920; *CR*, May 23, 1920.
34. *CR*, May 19, 1920.

35. CR, May 20, 1920.
36. CR, May 23, 1920; Roseberry, *Glenn Curtiss*, pp. 174-176.
37. Roseberry, *Glenn Curtiss* ..., p. 174.
38. CR, May 23, 1920.
39. CR, May 18, 1921.
40. CR, June 7, 1921; CR, June 9, 1921.
41. CR, June 10, 1921; CR, July 24, 1921.
42. CR, July 24, 1921.
43. CR, Aug. 26, 1921.
44. Cleveland, pp. 47 & 54.
45. CR, Aug. 31, 1921.
46. CR, Aug. 30-31, 1921.
47. CR, May 19-21, 1921.
48. Cleveland, p. 141.
49. CR, June 23, 1923.
50. Worthylake, p. 6.
51. CR, Oct. 9, 1924.
52. CR, Nov. 27, 1924.
53. CR, Dec. 28, 1924.
54. CR, Jan. 6, 1925.
55. WF, June 1926, n. p.
56. Bell, p. 225.
57. SB, Feb. 3, 1928.
58. SB, Feb. 8, 1928.
59. MA, June 27, 1928.
60. AD, July 1928, p.108.
61. PF, July 1928, p. 16.
62. CR, July 4, 1928.
63. CR, July 8, 1928.
64. CR, July 18, 1928.
65. CR, Aug. 1, 1928; RCFP, Aug. 1, 1928.
66. CR, Aug. 12, 1928.
67. WF, Sept. 1928, p. 303.
68. CR, Sept. 2, 1928.
69. SB, Sept. 12, 1928.
70. CR, Sept. 23, 1928.
71. ODR, Sept. 11, 1928.
72. ODR, Oct. 1, 1928.
73. WF, Nov. 1928, p. 78.
74. SB, Oct. 3, 1928.
75. MA, Oct. 1, 1928; CR, Oct. 2, 1928.
76. AD, Nov. 1928, p. 950.
77. MA, Oct. 12, 1928.
78. WF, Nov. 1928, p. 70.
79. CR, Nov. 2-3, 1928; GH, Nov. 6, 1928.
80. CR, Dec. 15, 1928.
81. Ibid.
82. PF, May 1929, p. 21
83. 1965 Official Reno National Air Race Program, p. 6.
84. CR, May 24, 1929.
85. CR, May 29, 1929.
86. CR, May 30, 1929.
87. CR, May 31, 1929.
88. PF, Sept. 1929, p. 20.
89. PF, Nov. 1929, p. 20.
90. SB, Nov. 20, 1929; WF, Jan. 1930, p. 118.
91. SB, Dec. 17, 1929.
92. WF, June 1930, p. 96.
93. CR, Nov. 20, 1981.
94. MAD, Feb. 14, 1930; GH, Feb. 18, 1930.
95. PF, Apr. 22, 1931, p. 17; Sperlin, *Diggins*, V.52 No.2 & 3, p. 39.
96. www.dmairfield.com
97. ODR, Dec. 7, 1933; SB, Dec. 7, 1933.
98. Nathan, *Diggins*, Vol. 30, No. 1, pp. 4-5.

Chapter 14

1. GH, Oct. 7, 1916.
2. GH, June 7, 1919.
3. GH, July 14, 1919.
4. GH, July 18, 1919.
5. ODR, July 23, 1919.
6. GH, Oct. 25, 1919.
7. MD, Apr. 23, 1920.
8. GH, Feb. 26, 1921.
9. WF, Aug. 1927, p. 30.
10. SF Ch, Sept. 6, 1927.
11. MD, Oct. 28, 1927, MD, Nov. 4-5, 1927.
12. GH, Mar. 24, 1928.
13. GH, Apr. 14, 1928.
14. MAD, Apr. 21, 1928.
15. GH, Sept. 18, 1928.
16. GH, Sept. 14, 1928; GH, Sept. 18, 1928; GH, Sept. 21, 1928.
17. GH, Oct. 5, 1928; GH, Oct. 9, 1928.
18. GH, Oct. 9, 1928.
19. GH, Oct. 16, 1928; CR, Oct. 9, 1928.
20. SB, Mar. 13, 1929.
21. GH, Nov. 8, 1929; MAD, Nov. 9, 1929.
22. AD, Sept. 1928, p. 530.
23. MAD, Nov. 5, 1929.
24. WF, May 1930, p. 116.
25. GH, Mar. 7, 1930.
26. SB, Sept. 23, 1930.
27. PF, Dec. 1930.
28. MAD, Apr. 14, 1931.
29. MAD, July 23, 1932.
30. OMR, Dec. 13, 1933; OMR, Dec. 15, 1933.
31. MAD, May 6, 1935; MAD, May 8, 1935.
32. MAD, May 13, 1935.
33. Hopkins, p. 79.
34. Hopkins, pp. 24-30 & 84-89
35. Hopkins, pp. 89-90.
36. Hopkins, p. 24.

BIBLIOGRAPHY

Alexander, Carolyn Elayse. *Venice*. San Francisco, CA: Arcadia Pub. 2004.
Allen, Richard Sanders. *Revolution in the Sky*. Brattleboro, VT: The Stephen Greene Press, 1961.
Andersson, Lennart. *A History of Chinese Aviation*. Taipei, Taiwan: AHS of ROC, 2008.
Bastin, Donald. *Richmond*. San Francisco, CA: Arcadia Publishing, 2003.
Bell, Dana. *Directory of Airplanes: Their Designers and Manufacturers*. London: Greenhill Books, 2002.
Boyne, Walter J. *Beyond The Horizons*. New York: St. Martin's Press, 1998.
Bruce, J. M. *Avro 504K*. Hertfordshire, Great Britain: Albatros Productions Ltd., 1991.
Busby, Michael. *Solving the 1897 Airship Mystery*. Gretna, LA: Pelican Pub. Co., 2004.
Burden, Maria Schell. *The Life and Times of Robert G. Fowler*. Los Angeles: Borden Publishing Company, 1999.
Casey, Gerry A. *Flying As It Was*. Blue Ridge Summit, PA: TAB Books, 1987.
Cleveland, Carl M. *Upside-Down Pangborn*. Glendale, CA: Aviation Book Co., 1978.
Crouch, Tom D. *Wings*. New York: W. W. Norton & Co., 2003.
Cummins, Julie. *Tomboy of the Air*. New York: Harper Collins Publishing, 2001.
Davies, R. E. G. *Airlines of the United States Since 1914*. Washington, D.C: Smithsonian Institute Press, 1998.
Delay, Peter J. *History of Sutter and Yuba Counties California*. Los Angeles: Informational Record Company, 1924.
DeVries, Col. John A. *Alexander Eaglerock*. Colorado Springs, CO: Wolfgang Pub. 1994.
Dickey, Philip S. III. *The Liberty Engine 1918-1942*. Washington, D. C: Smithsonian Institute Press, 1968.
Dwiggins, Don. *Hollywood Pilot*. Garden City, NY: Doubleday & Co., 1967.
Flynn, Mike. *The Great Airships*. United Kingdom: Sevenoaks Publishing, 1999.
Francillon, Rene J. *Lockheed Aircraft Since 1913*. UK: Putnam Aero Books, 1987.
Gardner, Lester D. *Who's Who in American Aeronautics 1925*. 2nd Ed., Los Angeles: F. Clymer Publishing, 1925.
Gillis, Mabel R. (1939 Editor) *The WPA Guide To California*. Reprint, New York: Pantheon Books, 1984.
Glines, Carroll V. *Around The World In 175 Days*. Washington D. C: Smithsonian Institute Press, 2001.
Glines, Carroll V, and Stan Cohen. *The First Flight Around The World*. Missoula, MA: Pictorial History Publishing, 2000.
Gordon, Marjorie. *Changes in Harmony*. Northridge, CA: Windsor Publication, 1998.
Grace, Dick. *I Am Still Alive*. New York: Rand McNally Co., 1931.
Grambon, Marion E., Editor. *Who's Who In World Aviation*. Washington, D. C: American Aviation Publishing, 1958.
Grey, C. G. (Editor). *Jane's All The World's Aircraft 1927*. London: Sampson, Low, Marston & Co., 1920.
Gudde, Erwin G. *California Place Names*. 4th Ed., Berkeley, CA: University of California Press, 1998.
Gwynn-Jones, Terry. *Wings Across the Pacific*. Atgen, PA: Schiffer Military/Aviation History, 1995.
Haller, Stephen A. *The Last Word in Airfields*. 1st Ed., San Francisco, CA: San Francisco National Park Service, 1994.
Haller, Stephen A. *The Last Word in Airfields*. 2nd ED., San Francisco, CA: Golden Gate National Parks Association, 2001.
Hallion, Richard P. *Legacy of Flight: The Guggenheim Contribution to American Aviation*. Seattle WA: University of Washington Press, 1977.
Hallion, Richard P. *Taking Flight:Inventing The Aerial Age From Antiquity Through The First World War*.

New York: Oxford University Press, 2003.
Hatfield, D. D. *Aeroplane Scrap Book*. Inglewood, CA: Northrop University Press, 1975.
Hatfield, D. D. *Los Angeles Aeronautics 1920-1929*. Inglewood, CA: Northrop Univesity Press, 1973.
Hearn, Peter. *Sky High Irvin: The story of a parachute pioneer*. London: Robert Hale Publisher, 1883.
Hopkins, George E. *Flying The Line*. Washington, D. C: ALPA International, 1982.
Howard, Edwin T. *Travel Air Digest*. St. Louis, MO: Howard Pub., 1992.
Irvine, Eastman E., Editor. *The World Almanac and Book of Facts for 1940*. New York: New York World-Telegram Publishers, 1940.
Jang, Michael. *The Local Nine*. San Francisco: Preston House Books, 2003.
Juptner, Joseph P. *U. S. Civil Aircraft Series*. Blue Ridge Summit, PA: Tab Aero Division of McGraw-Hill, 1993.
Kingsford-Smith, Charles. *My Flying Life*. Philadelphia: David McKay Co., 1937.
Komons, Nick A. *Bonfires to Beacon*. Washington, D. C: Smithsonian Institute Press, 1989.
Larkins, William T. and Ron Reuther. *San Francisco Bay Area Aviation*. San Francisco, CA: Arcadia, 2007.
Leary, William M. *Aerial Pioneers*. Washington, D. C: Smithsonian Institution Press, 1985.
Leary, William M., Editor, *From Airships To Airbus*. Vol. 1, Washington, D. C: Smithsonian Institution Press, 1995.
Lebow, Eileen F. *Before Amelia*. Washington, D. C: Brassey's Inc., 2002.
Lewis, W. David. *Eddie Rickenbacker*. Baltimore, MD: Johns Hopkins University Press, 2005.
Lincke, Jack R. *Jenny Was No Lady*. New York: W. W. Norton & Co., 1970.
Lipsner, Capt. Benjamin B. *The Airmail*. New York: Wilcox and Follett Co., 1951.
Louvish, Simon, *Cecil B. DeMille: A Life In Art*. New York: Thomas Dunne Books, 2007.
Lyman, Robert H., Editor. *The World Almanac and Book of Facts for 1929*. Reprint, New York: The New York World Publishers, 1929.
MacDougall, Curtis D., Editor. *Chicago American National Almanac and Year Book for 1938*. Chicago: National Survey and Sales Corp., 1937.
Mackersy, Ian. *Smithy*. London: Warner Books, 1999.
Marysville City Directory 1927 & 1934.
Maurer, Maurer. *Aviation in the U. S. Army 1919-1939*. Washington, D. C: Government Printing Office, 1987
McNally, Ward. *Smithy*. Cranbury, NJ: A. S. Barnes & Co., 1967.
Minor, Woodruff. *Pacific Gateway*. Oakland, CA: Port of Oakland, 2000.
Norlie, Eric R. *The Chico User's Guide*. Chico, CA: Cognitive Think Inc., 2006.
Oakes, Claudia M. *United States Women in Aviation Through World War I*. Washington, D. C: Smithsonian Institution Press, 1985.
Payne, Lee. *Lighter Than Air*. Revised Edition, New York: Orion Books, 1999.
Peek, Chet. *The Forgotten Barnstormer*. Norman, OK: Three Peaks Pub., 2110.
Pescador, Katrina and Alan Renga. *Aviation In San Diego*. San Francisco, CA: Arcadia, 2007.
Reilly, Thomas. *Jannus an American Flier*. Gainsville, FL: University Press of Florida, 1997.
Reinhold, Ruth M. *Sky Pioneering*. Arizona: University of Arizona Press, 1982.
Richfield Oil Co. *Aviation Guide*. Publisher Not Indicated, August 1929.
Rickenbacker, Edward V. *Rickenbacker*. Englewood Cliffs, NJ: Prentice-Hall Inc., 1967.
Ricklefs, Jim. *Quiet Birdmen – San Francisco Hangar*, Privately Published, Date Unkwn.
Robie, Bill. *For The Greatest Achievement*. Washington, D. C: Smithsonian Institute Press, 1993.
Ronnie, Art. *Locklear: The Man Who Walked On Wings*. New York: A. S. Barnes & Co., 1973.
Roseberry, C. R. *Glenn Curtiss: Pioneer of Flight*. Garden City, NY: Doubleday & Co., 1972.
Shell Oil Co. *Airports 1936 Edition*. Hackensack, NJ: Airport Directory Co. 1936.
Sloan, Jr., James J. *Wings of Honor*. Atglen, PA: Schiffer Military History, 1994.
Slonniger, Jerrold E. *One Pilot's Log: The Career of E. L. "Slonnie" Slonniger*. Charlottesville, VA: Howell Press, 1997.
Smith, Herschel H. *Aircraft Piston Engines*. New York: McGraw-Hill Book Co., 1981.
Smith, Steve L. *Fly the Biggest Piece Back*. Missoula, MA: Mountain Press, 1979.
Smith, Vi. *From Jennies To Jets*. Fullerton, CA: Sultana Press, 1974.

Spearman, Arthur Dunning. *John Joseph Montgomery 1858-1911:Father of Basic Flying*. Santa Clara, CA: University of Santa Clara, 1967.
Sterling, Bryan B. and Frances N. Sterling. *Forgotten Eagle*. New York: Carroll & Graf Publishing, 2001.
Tomlinson, D. W. *The Sky's The Limit*. Philadelphia: Macrae-Smith Co. Publishers, 1930.
Waterman, Waldo Dean and Jack Carpenter. *Waldo: Pioneer Aviator*. Carlisle, MA: Arsdalen, Bosch & Co. Publishers, 1988.
Workman, Lottie Lathrop. *Memories of Hammonton*. Wheatland, CA: Consolidated Lithograph, Date Unknown.
Worthylake, Mary M. *Up In The Air*. Bend, OR: Maverick Publications, 1988.
WPA Writers Project. *The WPA Guide to California*. Reprint, New York: Pantheon Books, 1984.
Wynne, H. Hugh. *The Motion Picture Stunt Pilots and Hollywood's Classic Aviation Movies*. Missoula, MA: Pictorial Histories Publishing Co., 1987.

Articles from Journals and Quarterlies

Allen, Richard S. Two Little Airlines (Consolidated), *Skyways*, Jan. 2001, No. 57: 51-53.
Angel, Karen, Why the World's Tallest Waterfall is Named Angel Falls. *Terra Incognitae*, Vol. 44 No. 1, April 2012: 16-42.
Christian, Russ, Oxymoron, *Gridley Hearld*, undated, n.p.
Friedman, A.M. & A. K., The Great Transcontinental Air Race, *Aviation History*, Nov. 2010: 50-55.
Griffin, Larry and Helena. Log of the Friesley Falcon, Part I, *Skyways*, Jan. 1991, No. 17: 33-39.
Griffin, Larry and Helena. Log of the Friesley Falcon, Part II, *Skyways*, Apr. 1991, No. 18: 42-50.
Herr, Allen, The Dawn Of Aviation In Butte County. *Diggin's*, Butte County Historical Society Quarterly, Vol. 47, Nos. 3 & 4: 52-53.
Nathan, ElRoy N., Development of the Chico Army Air Base. *Diggin's*, Butte County Historical Society, Vol. 30 No. 1: 3-14.
Spencer, B. M., Transport of Yesterday, *Western Flying*, Aug. 1929:150.
Sperlin, Lucy, The Wright-Patrick House and Its Inhabitants. *Diggin's*, Butte County Historical Society Quarterly, Vol. 52, Nos. 2&3: 19-39.

Interviews

Todd Bihlman, Oct. 10, 2000
H. T. Ted Herr, Jan. 7, 1999.
Guy Speed Hughes, Aug. 14, 2002.
Joyce Adele Johnson, Telephone Interview, Sept. 29, 2000.
Thomas Krull, Oct. 23, 2000.
Harry Middleton, Nov. 7, 2000.
Clyde Moore, Jan. 2000.
Robert Straight, May 16, 1999.
Sutter County Planning Dept. Employee, Dec. 3, 2000.
Vince Vanderford (II), Feb. 1998.
Rick Von Geldern, Mar. 7, 2000.

Private Papers

Tom Bowles Scrapbook (Copy in author's possession).
California Aviation Company (CAC) Papers. Boxes 2494, 2498 & 2499; California Room, California State Library, Sacramento, CA.

Websites

www.angelfire.com/electronic/awakening/101/jpjohnson.
www. articles.latimes.com/2006/jul/02/local/me-then 2.
www.dmairfield.com
www.flickr.com/photos/cost-londra/333199625
www.soaringmuseum.org/halloffame/chronlist.html

PHOTOGRAPH CREDITS

The search for the photographs in this book began in 1999, and through the years the following individuals and organizations have been kind enough to permit me to use photographs from their family albums or archives. Their names are followed by the page numbers of their photographs.

Wendelin Edward Beochanz collection – Page 126 (middle)
Todd Bihlmann holder of the George Bihlmann collection – Page 17
Community Memorial Museum of Sutter County – Page 116
Tom Feusi holder of the Dewey and Mary Ashford collection – Pages 125, 152, 153, 154, 155, 156, 186, 226, 276, 334
Donald B. Gray, Exec. Dir. of Crissy Field Aviation Museum Assn. – Pages 322 (bottom), 397 (top)
Guy "Speed" Hughes – Page 193
Glen A. Lane, holder of the Albert H. Lane collection – Page vi
James Lenhoff – Pages 6, 7, 219, 397 (bottom)
Joyce Adele Johnson – Page 42
Mary Aaron Memorial Museum – Pages 89, 96, 182, 188, 190, 194 (top)
McClellan Aviation Museum – Page i, 133
Carol McKibben holder of the Dudley Cunningham collection – Pages 72, 73
Meriam Library, California State University Chico – Page xii, 261, 380 (bottom)
Ben Middleton holder of the Harry Middleton Collection – Pages 387 (lower photo), 388, 389
David Nopel holder of the John Nopel Collection – Page 4, 252, 429
Pacific Aeronautics magazine (1920) – Page 322 (top)
Pacific Flyer magazine – Page 273
Karen Ripley holder of the Avis Sutfin Bielefeld collection – Page 88
Sacramento Archives and Museum Collection Center – Pages 38, 136, 194 (middle), 225, 335
San Diego Air and Space Museum Library and Archives – Pages 3, 52, 107, 209, 369
Pat Titus, holder of the Bee Brandt collection – Page 398
Rick Von Geldern – Von Geldern Engineering – Pages 13, 21
Bill Wedderien holder of the W. E. Wedderien collection – Page 390
Gordon Werne – Pages xiv, 126 (top), 162 (top), 194 (bottom)

All other photographs are from Allen Herr's collection. Pages 37, 207, 217, and 430 are illustrations by the author who also created the front and back cover art.

INDEX

Entries are for the persons mentioned in this book

Abbott, Harry, 120, 122, 133, 142
Abreu, Alfred, 160
Alcock, Capt. John, 25, 329
Allen, Clay, 171
Allen, George C., 201
Allen, Richard Sanders, xiv
Allen, Richard S. "Dick," 89, 167
Allinio, A. Peter, 48–53, 60
Ames Jr., Lt. John L., 139, 144
Anderson, Irene, 92
Anderson, Rob, 27
Anderson (Brown), Thelma, 159
Andert, Paul A., 299
Andrews, F. G. "Jerry," 123, 124, 369, 371, 373, 373, 386
Andrews, Henry Gay "Andy," 48, 70, 326
Andrews, William, 122, 125
Androtti, 121
Angel, Clyde, 44
Angel, Eddie, 46, 51, 52, 58, 64, 98, 99, 103
Angel, Goldie, 43
Angel, James Crawford, 39–68, 97–109, 159, 170, 351, 366, 367
Angel, Karen, 43
Angel, Margret Belle Marshall, 43
Angel, Marie, 44, 108
Angel, Parker, 58
Anglade, L. L., 118
Annear, John, 53
Anthony, Lou, 29
Armstrong, E. H., 233
Arndt, Lt. Edward D., 383
Arndt, Sergeant, 326

Arnold, Col. H. H. "Hap," 289, 290, 295, 337, 383
Arnoldy, Francis, 333
Arnoldy, Mat, 76
Arnoldy, Mayor, 15, 20, 28
Arnot, A. A., 124, 132, 146, 168
Ashford, N. Dewey, 18, 122, 125, 148, 152–157, 168, 180, 186, 192
Atherly, 368
Attwood, Harry, 8
Aulthouse, Jack, 183
Ayala or Orjala, Al, 156, 192
Babb, Charles, 179
Bach, Morton, 99
Baker, Frank, 338
Baker, H. V., 166
Baldwin, Captain Thomas S., 2, 196, 213, 229
Baldwin, Ivy (William Ivy), 2, 236
Baldwin, Lucky, 276
Bannister, Banty, 123, 369, 386
Barbour, Bob, 89
Barden, Dorothy, 185, 186
Barger, E. L., 50
Barhan, Jack, 51
Barnes, Alpheus, 202
Barnett, Lt. Lloyd, 299
Barngrover, W. P., 127, 129
Barr, Barbara, 336
Barr, Burt, 259, 260
Barrie, Allan, 70, 71, 338
Barrows, Mary, 365
Barrows, W. J. "Joe," 113, 365
Bartlett, Mayor F. H., 184
Basset, C. W., 175
Bassett, Clarence, 390
Bassett, D. A., 170
Bassford, J. C., 59
Batten, Lt. E. C., 282
Baumgardner, Ray, 139

Baxter, E. D., 338, 339
Beachey, Lincoln, 204, 215, 216, 241
Beals, Ira Douglas, 191
Beam, Frank, 230
Beck, Lt. Walter, 281
Behncke, David, 394–396
Beilby, Jack, 135, 184
Beldochi, G. L., 229
Belingsay, V., 230
Belinsay, E. H., 229
Benham, Boyd, 178, 179
Benje, Perry, 198
Bennett, C. E., 286, 287, 357
Benson, Lester, 96
Benton, William, 100
Beri, William, 100
Bertand, Lloyd, 233
Best, Dan, 181
Beswick, J. C., 375
Beyer, J. R., 168
Bidwell, C. H., 145
Bidwell, Mayor, 145
Bihlmann, George H., 17, 18
Bishop, C. R., 333
Blake, T. M., 30
Blakely, H. W., 229
Blandon, Sgt. R. P., 289
Blaylock, Private, 110
Blee, Harry H., 124
Blunt, H. L., 113
Boatsman, Capt. Buck, 180
Bocher, Julius, 205
Boggs, Marshall, 48
Boller, Dana, 145, 170
Boller, Mrs. Sterling, 145
Boller, Mrs. Vernon B., 170
Boller, Sterling, 127, 129, 137, 145–147, 170
Boller, Vernon B., 170
Boller, Vernon D. ---170
Bolton, Harvey, 381, 383, 384, 388, 391-397

— 417 —

Bolton, Mr. and Mrs. F. C., 391
Bookwalter, Vernon, 124
Booth, Councilman, 28
Booth, Frank, 333
Booth, H. W., 51, 52
Boquel, Joe, 263
Borello, Peter, 147, 150, 151
Bostic, Roy, 82, 94, 95, 110, 113, 115, 122, 129, 136, 142
Bosworth, C. A., 230
Boucher, William, 200, 277, 278
Boudreaux, Lt. R. H., 110
Boukard, 229
Boulware, Mayo H., 266, 267
Bowden, Lt. J. T., 140
Bowen, Mr., 255
Bowles, John, 156, 192
Bowles, Tom, 156, 192
Bowlus, Hawley, 177, 178, 183, 184
Bowman, Ray, 369
Boyd Jr., George, 19, 159, 160, 172
Bracewell, Thomas G., 118
Bradley's, 124
Braescu, Madame Samandra (alias Maria Popescu), 172–174
Brainard, Ernest S., 220, 225, 233, 235, 236, 238
Brand, L. C., 34
Brander, E. R., 122, 125, 148, 157, 168
Brander, William A., 122, 125, 126, 141, 148, 151, 154, 155, 168, 186, 187, 191, 192
Brandt, Dick, 192
Brandt, Lt. Col. Gerald C., 110
Brandt, Roger, 192
Branham, Lucy, 318
Brashardt, Harry, 173
Brewer, Roy F., 207, 229, 236, 239, 245
Briggs, Bill, 165
Briggs, C. B., 372
Broderick, Robert, 366
Brokaw, Mrs. J. C., 386
Bronson, Mrs. Eva, 69, 70
Bronte, Emory, 113, 149
Brooks, Frank, 160, 161

Brooks, Tyrell, 29
Brown, Carl, 229
Brown, Charles, 29
Brown, H. A., 382
Brown, Harold F., 93, 110–114, 117, 119, 126, 137, 140–144, 147, 150–152, 157–160, 164– 168, 171, 172, 179–182, 188, 347, 390
Brown, Michael, 267
Brown, Milt, 386
Brown, Sir Arthur W., 25, 329
Brown, Weldon Capt., 145
Browning, J. L., 121
Broyles, J. W., 353
Brule, Jules, 229
Brunson, I. N., 127, 128
Brush, Shirley, 144
Bryant, Councilman Dan E., 137, 150
Bryant, Frank, x, 11, 236, 263, 268, 269, 271, 309
Bryant, Mayor, 120
Buchart, Mrs. Bertha, 339
Buck, George, 51
Bucklen, R. C., 145
Buckley, Sergeant, 19, 276–284, 381
Bunnell, Dr. Sterling, 49
Burch, Estal, 89, 191
Burch, Rex, 118
Burger, Mr. and Mrs. E., 145
Burmeister, C. ---260
Burnham, Margaret ---184
Burns, Joseph M., 34
Buroker, Delbert, 126, 131, 132, 137, 140, 144, 146, 150, 167
Buroker, H. A., 148–150
Burroughs, Cliff, 165
Burroughs, Eleanor, 92
Burroughs, W. C., 145
Burrows, Lt. C. A., 299
Butler, George, 336
Butler, P. J., 229
Byrnes, H. A., 229
Cahill (Evans), "Reckless" Rosie, 110
Caldwell, Morris, 269
Campbell, 175, 391
Campbell, Mark, 259, 260
Campbel, Milo, 343

Campbell, Robert L., 177
Cannon Jr., W. D., 388
Carmack. Prescott, 353
Carnahan, James, 370, 371
Carnan, Joe, 230
Carney, P., 385 386
Carpenter, Bud, 370
Carter, Lt. S. O., 288, 289
Casey, John J., 264
Castle, Don, 87, 89, 95, 344, 371–373, 384–386
Cathcart, Lt. Donald, 276
Catkin, Ben, 177
Catlin, Lucy, 270
Chace, C. H., 11–16
Chalmers, Mr. and Mrs. Gerald, 331, 337, 340
Cham, Harry, 180
Chambers, Reed, 311, 312
Chandler, Senator W. F., 148
Chanute, Octave, 203
Chapell, Ernest, 220, 225, 233, 235, 236, 238
Chase, Charles, 385
Cheim Harry, 143
Cheim, Frank, 160
Cheim, Heiman, 76, 77, 87, 94, 95, 129, 136
Christian, Russ, 324, 327, 337
Christie, Major, 283
Christofferson, Harry, 268
Christofferson, Silas, ix, x, 247, 262,–264
Chubbuck, J. M., 206
Clark, Dumpy, 156
Clark, Dwight, 363, 364
Clark, Ernestine, 50
Clark, George, 371
Clark, J., 121
Clark, Marjorie, 144
Clark, Robert, 156
Clark, Sergeant, 276, 277
Clark, Sergeant Maj. 381, 382
Clarke, Frank, 104
Cline, Virgil, 113
Clohecy, Robert J., 31–33, 364
Coats, Arthur, 65
Cobb, Jack, 202
Coe, Lieutenant, 329
Coffee, H. L. "Bud," 21
Cogswell, E. P., 68
Cohen, Louis, 157
Coller, L. D., 230

Index

419

Collins, George D., 196
Colwell, Guy, 341
Comstock, Lucie, 254
Conover, C. E., 227
Cook, Councilman, 28
Cook, L. C., 374
Cooke, Ross, 338, 339
Cooke, Weldon, 117, 118, 143, 176, 230
Cooper, Earl, 352, 353, 359, 361
Copland, 396
Corcoran, C. P., 320
Corcoran, Daniel Patrick, 320, 342
Corcoran, H. J., 221
Cornell, Don, 83, 84, 344, 371, 386
Cornwell, W. H., 95
Costello, J. L., 159
Counter, Carol, 92
Crandall, J., 377, 378
Crawford, Harvey (or Harry), 103
Cress, L. M., 305
Cress, Lena, 305
Criblett, P. L., 230
Crisp, F. J., 233
Crissy, Maj. Dana H., 291, 310
Crocker, 348
Crook, L. B., 333
Crosby, Carl, 54
Crouch, Ben E., 351–353, 359
Crutchfield, Todd, 141
Cunningham, Allen, 18
Cunningham, Dudley, 28, 72, 73, 81, 83, 115, 125, 131, 148, 151, 158–162, 168, 180, 186, 187, 189, 332, 333
Cunningham, Lottie, 28
Curtiss, Glenn, vii, ix, 198, 200, 202, 204, 212, 213, 216, 221
Cushman, Lieutenant, 93
Cutting, Senator Bronson, 391, 392, 396
Dahling, Fred F., 118
Dahling, Wayne, 118
Dahlman, Clyde, 375
Dalbey, C. N., 180
Dalbey, Jack, 147
Danley, Jewel, 89

Daugherty, Earl, 100
Davies, Lt. W. J., 136
DaVilla, J. F., 230, 246
Davis, John "Slim," 192
Davison, Dan, 341, 359
De Arce, Ponton, 316, 317
De La Mar, H., 225, 230
DeGarmo, 379
DeGarmo, A. R., 299
DeGuines, Mrs., 372
Deholm, Sgt. J. H., 140
Del Pero, Adolph, 192
Delany, J. T., 368
Delehanty, Del, 384
Derenzo, Sandy, 372
DeRosa, Elmer "Joe," 177
Deter, Melvin, 353
Deter, Mrs. J. M., 353
DeVelschow, C., 299
DeVoe, Mary, 188
Dexter, Lt. C. F., 382
DiFiore, Dominic, 54, 55, 58, 59, 62–64, 343
Dibble, Lee C., 360
Dickinson, A., 171
Dittman, F. C., 230
Divver, Phil, 177
Dixon, Fred, 384
Dixon, George, 144
Dobson, Chas. H., 230
Dodge, Irma, 321
Doi, S., 230
Doolin, B. M., 144
Dorme, Ray, 66, 67
Doty, Cecelia, 262
Doty, H. J., 143
Doty, J., 243
Doty, Jeanette (Jean), 253, 262–268, 272
Doty, Lyman W., 253, 262–273, 381, 397
Doty, William M., 262, 273
Dougherty, 237
Dover, Fred, 230
Dowell, Red, 22, 23
Dowling, Lieutenant, 51
Doyle, Anita, 92
Doyle, Harry F., 118
Drake, Roy E., 230
Dreiss, John, 202, 203
Drennan, E. W., 79
Dreyfus, Felix, 87
Duck, William R., 301

Duff, Mrs. F. J., 145
Duhem, Raymond, 313
Duke, Richard, 49
Dunning, H., 145
Durant, Cliff, 311
Durant, I. J., 230
Durff, Byron, 370, 371
Durff, Harold, 370, 371
Durkee, Frank B., 306, 307, 356
Durst, Audrey D., 170
Duservoir, Julius, 63
Dutro, Leslie, 98
Eagle, Capt. A. F., 341, 368
Eames, 230, 238
Earhart, Amelia, 187, 188
Easley, Ben, 149, 150
Eaton, 379
Eaton brothers, 233
Eccles, Robert, 98
Edwards, J. Spaulding, 71
Edwards, Maj. A. J., 39
Edwards, Walter, 233
Eich, Allen, 29
Eich, Harvey, 29
Eich, Warren, 29
Eich, Wilton, 29
Eichwaldt, Alvin, 72
Ekerson, Sergeant, 326, 327
Eldred, Chester, 357
Eldred, G. W., 357
Eldridge, Lieutenant, 359
Elfendahl, E. J., 378
Eliel, Leon T., 85
Elliot, Jack, 143
Elliott, Tom, 386
Elliott, Milton "Skeets," 26
Ellis, A. V., 160
Ely, Eugene, 204, 216, 221
Emmett, Assemblyman Dan W., 390
Emmons, Maj. Dellos C., 14
English, William, 230
Erwin, William P., 71–73
Ettl, 121
Evans, Lt. E. F., 280
Facher, 344
Fagerskog, Ingvald, 70, 181, 365
Fall, Emmet E., 301
Fallon, L. J., 81
Farrel, Capt. Louis, 101
Farris, Mr. and Mrs. Fauna

W., 332
Farrow, E. W., 49
Faxon, R. S., 121
Faxon, Sergeant, 51
Ferguson, 121
Ferguson, O., 118
Ferneau, Aaron R. "Bob," 256–259
Ferrera, J. S., 60
Ferrie, Gordon, 309
Ferris, Dick, 8, 196, 230
Fesler, C., 166
Fetters, J. M., 305–307, 358
Fike, Carrol, 88
Fillmore, Bill, 180, 369
Fish, Farnum, 241
Fisher, Crpl. H. B., 280
Flagg, Ken, 156
Flaherty, George, 138
Flanders, J. L., 32, 33
Flannigan, Lee, 388
Fleet, Maj. Ruben H. 11–16
Fleming, E. K. 128, 129
Fletcher, Clarence M., 118
Flint, Leo, 257–259
Flynn, Frank, 144
Forbes, W. J., 333
Ford, Arthur, W., 284
Fordyce, E. F., 360
Forsetblade, Robert, 158
Foss, E. E., 9
Foster, Bernard, 91, 94, 369
Foster, J. Rupert, 5
Fowler, Lt. F. J., 383
Fowler, Robert G., 24, 269, 279
Fowler, Thomas, 370
Francis, Harvey, 237
Francis, Roy, ix, 28, 29, 230, 233, 236, 238, 269, 329–334, 336, 340
Francisco, J. H., 163, 166, 168
Frank, W. H., 329
Fraser, Harry, 358
Frates, George, 386
Frazier, Assemblyman J. E., 390
Fredrickson, A. E., 233
Freng, R. M., 299
Frew, Will L., 230
Friedman, Max, 247
Friesleben, Daniel, 313
Friesleben (Friesley), Harold M., 313
Friesley, Eleanor, 309

Friesley, Harold M. (or Herold), 309, 316–320, 327, 328, 335, 336, 340
Friesley, Ruth, 309
Fripp, F., 233
Fritiofson, C. A., 293
Froberg, L. A., 232, 234
Frolich, H. E. "Tex," 91, 344, 377
Frye, Albert S., 230
Frye, Jack, 388, 393, 396
Fugitt, Lon C., 18
Funke, Fred W., 301
Gage, Jay, ix
Galbraith, E. H., 164
Gallison, Frank, 390
Gandy, J., 229, 231
Gardella, Lawrence, 201, 205, 209, 211, 217
Gardner, Earle Stanley, 234
Gardner, Elias, 167
Gardner, Lieutenant, 19, 278
Gardner, Lt. G., 382
Gardner, Raymond, 281
Gardner, Ross, 280, 303, 304, 309, 341, 361
Garner, Lessie J., 382
Garros, Roland, 213
Gates-Morris, 362, 363
Gates, Ivan R., 31, 230, 247, 363–365
Gay, George H., 351
Gay, Lt. R. E., 351
Geer. Edward J., 113
George, Dr. P., 230
George, H. F., 144
Gerdon, C., 308
Gern, Elsie, 336
Gern, William, 336
Giblin, Tom, 23
Giffin, James, 389
Gilbert, Lt. F. M., 139
Gilbert R. W., 52
Gilhausen, Al, 76
Gill, Catherine, 19, 24
Gillet, Governor, J. N., 4
Gillette, Stanford, 370
Gilley, Earl M., 183
Gilman, Al, 156
Gilmore, (Lyman), 231, 234, 235
Gilmore, Beverly, 134, 137, 142, 145–148

Gilmore, Brig. Gen. William E., 131
Gilmore, Lt. T. F., 329
Glang, John, 231
Glass, Mr. and Mrs. Don, 106
Glassford, Col. William A., 270
Glidden, Captain, 279
Goddard, Lt. Glenn, 140
Godfrey, Thomas J., 1
Goebel, Art, 59
Goebel, Les, 59
Goldsborough, Lt. William C., 282
Goldsmith, L. C., 373
Goldsworthy, Lt. R. E., 259, 260
Gonzales, William, 234
Goodrich, Lt. A., 287, 290, 291
Gornall. Langer, 104
Goss, Fire Chief, 88
Gotwals, Cliff, 29
Gould, J. W., 118
Grace, Dick, 338, 339, 384
Graf, Bertha, 331
Graham, Curley, 180
Grant, Edwin, 187
Gravelle, Wariam S., 140
Graves, Harold, 370, 371
Graves, Henry S., 275
Graves, J. D., 393
Gray, C. R., 230
Gray, Carleton, 205
Gray, Dr. E. E., 80
Green, Norman, 230
Greenamyre, Ralph, 148
Greeson, Kenneth, 392, 393, 396
Griffen, Jack, 114
Griffith, James, 145
Griswoldt, August, 287, 288
Guenther, Lt. C. K., 283
Gugliametti, John, 51
Gunn, Tom Duck, 234, 241, 247
Haines, W. H., 167
Hall, A. N. "Shorty," 345, 346
Hall, C. A., 234
Hall, H. H., 180
Hall, Harold, 53, 58, 98, 99
Hall, Lowell, 231
Hall, Ralph, 148
Hall, Walter, 113, 144, 386
Haller, Stephen A., xi

Index   421

Halverson, Lt. H. E., 293, 311, 326
Hamilton, Charles K., 6–9, 204
Hamilton, Mrs. Charles, 245
Hamilton, Frank, 2
Hamilton, W. G. T., 234
Hammatt, R. F., 289, 290
Hammon, W. P., 220
Hammond, Charles, 166
Handy, Jack (John C.), 231, 235
Haney, Sgt. Wayman, 293, 294
Hansen, Lieutenant, 113
Hansen, Ralph, 263
Hansen, Violet, 234
Hanson, O. C., 299
Hardin, Richard, 130
Hardin, Tom, 396
Hargrove, Lt. J. R., 110
Harkey, 123
Harmon, Lt. E. E., 329
Harrison, George B., 197
Harshner, James, 114, 126, 131, 132, 137, 141, 142, 147, 150, 152, 168
Hart, Jess, 111
Harter, Gordon, 336
Harter, Howard, 336
Harter, Ruth, 19, 336
Harvey, Robert, 234
Haslett, Dr. R. E., 370, 371
Haslett, Mrs. R. E., 371
Hastings, Albert E., 83–87, 365–368, 374, 375
Hatfield, D. D., 260
Hauk and Smith, 321
Hay, Del, 187
Haynie, Frank, 278
Hearst, William Randolph, 270
Heath, E. B., 234
Heaton, Vern, 181
Heddinger, George A., 91
Heiken, Fred H., 132
Held, 234
Helphenstine, Noel, 160
Hemingway, Frank W., 99
Hemstreet & Bell, 138, 142, 161
Henderson, J. T., 248
Hensley, Gene, 158
Herman L. Tucker, 318
Herndon Jr., Hugh, 139

Herr, Allen, xii, 427
Herr, George, 178
Herr, H. T. "Ted", xiv
Herr, Kathleen H., xiv
Hersperger, Wesley, 370
Hester, Jimmie, 260
Hicks, Alyce Juanita, 111
Hicks, Joe K. ---144
Higgens, Harry E., 343
Hill, Russell A., 76–80, 95, 123
Hodge, Helen, 263, 264
Hodgkins, A. C. or Hoskins, L. C., 121
Hoff, Joseph, 260
Hoffman, K. K., 43
Hogland, Lt. A. F., 11, 12
Hoke, Mayor Al, 349
Holmes, Harry, 234
Homans, G. M., 284
Hoover, Capt. W. J., 293
Hopkins, Capt., 93
Hopkins, George E., 393
Hopkins, Sam, 105
Hoppin, Marshall C., 157, 158
Horn, Elmer, 145
Horner, A. K., 145
Hosick, Mr., 260
Howard, Clarence "Candy," 201, 205, 209, 210
Howard, Dr. E. L., 234
Howell, Harriett, 54
Hoxsey, Arch, 213
Hoyt, Fred, 35
Huang, Maj. (or Dr.) Tien Lai, 103
Hudson, J., 181
Hudson, John W., 231
Huffmaster, Earl R., 118
Hughes, G. E., 234
Hughes, Guy "Speed," 156, 191
Hughes, Howard, 338, 374
Huking, Harry, 172
Hume, H. H., 368
Hunt, Irwin W., 261
Hurst, R. C., 379
Hust brothers, 188
Hust, Charles, 29
Hutchins, T. B., 342
Illman, William, J., 122, 157, 345, 346
Ince, Thomas H., 259
Ingle, Gladys, 39
Irvin, George F., 135

Irvine, J. C., 266, 269
Irving, Arthur, 205
Irving, Livingston, 120, 171, 172
Irwin, Jack, 58
Jacks, Claire, 386
Jackson, Dr., 22, 114, 119, 163
Jackson, Larry, xiv
Jackson, Sheriff George, 45
Jacobs, J. J., 82
Jacobsen, Lieutenant, 16
Jacobson, H. O., 358
James, C. N., 299
James, Helen Gibbs, 346
James, Virginia Gibbs, 346
Jamieson, Gus, 263
Jannus, Roger, 253, 254
Jannus, Tony, 253, 254
Jellinek, Bettie, 327
Jenkins, Howard, 371
Jenkins, Thorton "Jinx," 362
Jenks, Paul H., 151
Jensen, Charles "Red," 176
Jensen, J. O., 266
Jensen, Martin, 86, 87
Johns, Herbert, 152, 153
Johns, Watson L., 378
Johnson, Berger, 306, 307, 358
Johnson, C. W., 138
Johnson, Dr. Julian P., 41, 42, 55, 56, 58–86, 95–97, 109, 110, 114–119, 123, 146, 163, 343, 367
Johnson, Ed, 19
Johnson, Frank H., 2–6, 198–200, 204, 224, 231
Johnson, George, 166
Johnson, J. M., 133
Johnson, Joyce Adele, 109
Johnson, Mrs. Laura, 95
Johnson, Pat, xiii
Johnson, Rex, 317, 360
Johnson, Richard, 323
Johnson, Siri, 92
Johnston, Mylon "Iron Hat," 349
Johnstone, Ralph, 213
Jones, A. S., 243
Jones, Franklin, 175
Jones, Hugh Pryce, 58, 119
Jones, Lieutenant, 326
Jordan, F. C., 233
Kearney, Horace, 241

Keeler, Herbert, 85, 122, 125, 126, 131, 135, 147, 159, 168, 172, 178, 183, 184
Keeny Chan, 144
Keim, Neil, 124
Kelly, Bryden, 29
Kelly, Lt. Oakley G., 34
Kelly, V. H., 113
Kent, William S., 122, 126
Kerns, B. S., 248
Kerns, E. E., 236
Kerns, J., 251
Kerns, Mrs. B. S., 248
Kerns, Thaddeus S., 6–9, 201–207, 211, 212, 215, 216, 221–227, 229, 231–241, 245–252, 279, 381
Kerrigan, J. H., 344
Kidwell, James, 370, 371
Kiel, Lt. E. C., 285, 289–291
Kingsford-Smith, Sir Charles, 21–27, 79, 317, 382
Kirchner, Hans, 168
Kirk, Gus, 75
Kittle, Hubert, 255
Klamp, Robert, 156
Klamt, R. H., 171
Kleaver, Ken, 144, 145, 183, 185, 186, 377
Klemmer, Otto, 199
Klepphahn, E. O., 204
Klundt, Gus, 149
Knabenshue, Roy, 2, 197
Knight, D. E., 14
Koch, Herbert, 345
Komons, Nick A. 396
Kraft, Herb, 144
Kron, Ed, 184
Krull, Lt. James S., 19
Krull, Tom, 169
Kruse, Capt. Charles, 139
Kynoch, Mayor Walter, 95
LaJotte, Charles, 104, 282, 287, 289
La Pierre, Wentella, 51
LaFortune, Darrell, 90
Lagrive, J. R., 234
Lake, Bryan, 95, 386
Lake, Don, 371
Lamburth, 214
Lamkin, W. L., 62
Lane, Albert, 343
Lane, Dan, 318, 319

Lane, Leo, 385
Lane, Paul, 318
Langdon, Police Judge, 124
Lanteri, Bernard, 116, 117, 143, 176
Latham, Hubert, 213
Laugenour, Henry, 325
Laughlin, L. O., 173
Laughlin, Norman J., 34
Laughlin, Willis, 29
Lauppe, Frank, 188
LaVerne, J. H., 180
Lawrence, William W., 179
Lawson, Alfred W., 308–310
Leach, Jack, 103
Leach, James, 233
Lee, Harry R., 138
LeGault, Gene, 123
Leggett, Lt. Kenneth, 281, 283, 284
Leggett, Mr. and Mrs. J. H., 283
Leggo, Sidney T., 115, 118, 129
Lenhoff, James, xiv, 337
Leomintine, Swede, 369
Leonard, Sgt. C. D., 289
Leroy, Robert, 98
Lewis, Walter, 20
Leydecker, Theodore, 188
Lim, Art, 263
Lindbergh, Charles A., 77, 111, 127, 140, 177, 296, 383
Lindeman, 383
Lindsey, W. P., 234
List, Henry J., 234
Little, Percy, 378
Locati, Albert, 156
Lockheed (Loughead), Allen, 156
Lockheed (Loughead), Malcom, 156
Lockhoof, Walter, 110, 111, 372
Locklear, Ormer, 25
Logg, D. G., 299
Long, Barney, 156
Long, James, 63
Long, Lt. L., 13, 15
Loomis, A. R., 299
Loose, George, 215, 231
Lorenzen, Ranger, 290
Loring, E. C., 234
Loughead (Later Lockheed),

Victor, 204
Lueth, Duane, 141, 150, 168
Lundgren, T. S., 104
Lusk, Hilton F., 117, 118
Lyons, Lt. R., 114
MacCracken, 107
MacCracken, William P., 32
Macready, Lt. John A., 34
Mahon, Judge K. S., 159
Mahon, Rennie J., 18, 115, 159
Mahoney, B. F., 296
Makepeace, Capt. A. W., 18, 156
Manford, Joseph H., 321
Mantz, Paul, 310
Manwell, Clyde, 29
Marchettie, A., 231
Marcus, D. J., 180
Marders, Glenn, 156, 158, 345
Marias, 94
Marler, Tom, 373
Marlor, T. S., 91
Mars, J. C. "Bud," 212, 213, 222, 223, 225
Mars/McAuliff, Bud, 6–8, 223, 225
Marshall, Mrs. Ester, 59
Marshall, Mrs. J., 67
Martin, Eddie, 104
Martin, Glenn, viii, 240–243
Martin, Gornall and Abergast, 104
Martin, Knox, 253, 254
Martin, Larry, 122, 126, 141, 148, 151, 154, 155, 168, 186, 187, 191, 192
Martin, Maj. Fredrick, 34
Martin (Angel), Virginia, 45
Marty, Lt. Albert, 139
Mary, Fran, 181
Mason, S. T., 353
Masson, Didier, 229, 234
Mather, Lt. Carl, 10
Matthews, Ben "Diavolo," 139
Mattison, Ray L., 231
Maupin, Lan B., 115–118, 129, 143, 176, 231
Maxwell, Lieutenant, 326
May, Wesley, 364
Mayberry, James, 83, 84
Maynard, Lt. Belvin, 285, 330
Mazo, Gen. Francisco R., 102
McAuliffe, Denny, 180

INDEX

McBoyle, Errol, 189
McCallum, G. D., 114
McCoy, Sheriff C. J., 87
McCrills, Capt. J. W., 139
McCullough, Robert, 58, 66, 71, 83, 123
McDaniel, Eugene, 95
McDaniels, T. B., 366
McDonald, Merwin, 355
McFadden, Jack, 231
McGettigan, E. T., 269
McGraves, Lt. J. ---229
McHenry, Lieutenant, 132
McHenry, Lt. G. O., 288, 289
McKay, Norman, 179
McKee, Sgt. Frank, 19
McKeehan, S. A., 120, 121
McKenna, Bessie, 119, 122
McKinney, Ive "Joe, 30–33, 364, 365
McManus, Frank, 306, 307, 353
McManus, H. J., 175
McNeil, James A., 346
McPhetridge (Thaden), Louise, 91, 369
McTarnahan, J. C., 231, 236
Meade & Orr, 123
Meade, Hudson, 82
Meek, W. M., 14
Meer, M. E., 299
Meinet, W. B., 121
Melendy, Lt. Lynn, 317, 360
Mellard, Matthew, 234
Mendell, Loren, 179
Mendoza, John, 54
Menoher, Maj. General, 275
Menzel family, 286, 287
Meredith, J., 140
Merle, Ollie, 231
Merril, Frank, 333
Merwin, Ogle, 282, 286, 303–307, 351–358, 382
Mess, Lieutenant, 20
Meyerhoffer, Allen, 236
Meyerhoffer, Orvar S. T. "Swede," 201, 205– 212, 214, 216–220, 227, 228, 235–239, 253–262
Meyling, Chris, 51
Micheli, Al, 191
Mickel, A. F., 111
Middleton, Harry, 43, 52, 189,

387–389
Middleton, Mrs. Harry, 189
Middleton, William, 141, 187
Miles, Lee , 180
Miline and Johnson, 373
Miller, Allen E., 367, 368, 371
Miller, C. H., 386
Miller, C. W., 384
Miller, Bill, 350
Miller, Lt. H. C., 34
Mills Jr., James, 356
Mills, Tracy, 356
Ming, Charley, 40, 41, 98
Mintner, Mary Miles, 256, 269, 270
Mires, Roy, 21
Mitchell, George N., 41, 372
Mitchell, Herbert, 353
Mitchell, Mabel, 353
Mix, Tom, 339
Moffett, Edmund J., 22–26, 260, 261, 358, 382
Moisant, John, 213
Monteverdi, Alyse, 327
Montgomery, John J., 2, 208, 214
Moore, Cliff, 156
Moore, Frank, 113
Moore, Leo, 91–95, 377
Moore, Mrs. Harold, 176
Moore, Owen "Pearl," 156
Morehead, 306, 357, 358
Morgan, Lt. John, 296, 297
Morgan, W. N., 388
Morrel, 231
Morrison, Aerial Traffic Officer Lloyd, 137
Morrison, City Manager, 374
Morrison, Ralph, 161
Morrow, Lieutenant, 158
Mortell, George, 172
Morton, Earl, 248
Moss, Mrs. Ben, 188
Mouton, E. E. "Monte," 25
Mullen, A. A., 30
Murphy, Margret, 227, 231
Murray, Maurice, 346
Murray, Mr., 220
Murrell, Ray, 185, 186
Musladin, Bill, 156
Mustain, Sam, 266
Nason, James C., 163
Neese, K., 145

Neimeyer, Henry, 20
Nelson, J. W., 299
Nemo, Captain, 197, 198
Ness, Jack, 91, 95
Newhart, Harry D., 201, 218–221
Nicholson, Ray, 176, 177
Nisbet, Gertrude, 349
Nisbet, J. C., 349
Nolta, Floyd "Speed," 143, 144, 167, 180, 190
Norby, Erling S., 18, 34, 35, 40, 63, 69, 76, 94, 112, 115, 132, 139–147,
Norins, M., 75
Northrop, John, 256
Norton, Mayor, 287
Noupe, Robert, 298
Noyes, Assemblyman Fred B., 75
O'Brien, J. S., 76
O'Hair, Michael, 160
Obele, W. J. "Bill," 32, 33, 70, 190, 365
Ohrt, 230
Ohrt brothers, 231
Ohrt, Herman, 385
Oldfield, Barney, 244
Onstott, 246
Onstott, Fred, 384, 385
Onstott, Glenn, 56, 58, 73
Onstott, Ken, 156, 192
Orjala, Alfred, 192
Orr, Ted, 223
Osbourne, C. S., 231
Oster, G. D., 326
Osterman, E., 231
Otis, G. Fred, 63, 65
Owen, Walter C., 147, 184
Owen, Wes, 75, 86
Pangborn, Clyde "Upside-Down," 31, 364, 365
Pappa, Mrs. J. R., 119
Parker, Alvin, 160
Parker, Frank, 375
Parmalee, Phil, 236
Parmelee, Charles R., 362, 364
Parrott, 356
Patrick Family, 244, 370, 375
Patrick III, W. Garrison "Pat," 351, 363, 378, 379
Patrick, S. G., 335
Patterson, Howard, 259, 260

Patterson, Jack or James, 357, 358
Patterson, R. B., 54
Pattison, 121
Paulhan, Louis, 1
Paxton, S. C., 188
Pebbles, Frank, 99
Peed, Garland, 339
Pegden, George, 364
Pendleton, E. H., 20, 282, 286, 287, 303–307, 351, 353, 354, 356, 382
Pendleton, Martin J., 354
Penfield John, 367, 374
Penfield, Thomas, 367, 374
Penney, Ted, 76
Perkins, Sherman, 156, 192
Perrine, Lyle, 350
Perry, Fay, 145
Peters, T. F., 118
Peterson, A. C., 232
Phelan, 356
Phillips, C. K. 338
Phillips, M. G., 128
Phillips, William H. (or Walter M.), 62, 68, 69
Pickford, Mary, 270
Pieratt brothers, 177
Pieratt, Louis, 177
Pingpank, L. A., 332
Plosser, 149
Polk, Al, 172
Polson, Thor, 372
Pond, Admiral Charles F., 270
Pond, Charles McHenry, 15, 280, 303, 304, 309, 341, 361
Pond, George, 26, 79
Poole, F. S., 118
Pope, G. W. H., 145
Porter, Earl, 331
Posados, Juan, 231
Post, Lt. Leo F., 15, 16
Post, Wily, 97
Potatato, Geo, 232
Potter, N. W., 299
Powell, Major, 51
Powers, R. Grover, 384, 390
Praeger, Otto, 273
Presley, Ford, 388
Presley, Mr. and Mrs. B. F., 389
Prest, Clarence, 260
Preston, Paul, 176

Price, 4
Price, S. E., 88
Priestly, S. D., 299
Privett, Cy, 185
Purcell, Sam, 113, 355, 356
Pursal, H. H., 128
Quick, George Curtis, 191
Rabe, Carl, 345
Radley, James, 213, 215
Ramsdell, 121
Ramsey, R. C., 347, 348
Raymond, H. R., 167
Raymond, Ray, 144
Read, James E., 34, 40, 41, 65, 69, 71–77, 79– 83, 85–87, 89, 92–94, 96, 97, 111, 112, 190
Reath, Don C., 179, 180
Redington, Paul G., 294
Reed, 360
Reed, C. W., 168
Reed, Grafton T. "Wally," 29, 318, 327, 331– 336, 340, 342
Reese, A. L., 181
Reese, L. J., 20
Reeves, E. E., 114, 168
Reis, 137
Remington, 234
Ressinger, Bernice, 15
Ressinger, Dorothy, 15
Ressinger, Manila, 15
Rhoy, Hayden, 371
Rice, O., 356
Rich, Mr. and Mrs. George, 188
Richardson, Lee, 357, 358
Richerson, O. C., 51
Richter, Paul E., 388, 393, 396
Rickenbacker, Capt. Eddie, 10, 311, 312, 317, 325
Riddle, Laura, 78
Riddle, Mildred, 86
Ridnaur, Lt. C. H., 287
Riley, Ed H., 277
Riley, J. E., 282
Riley, Tom, 282
Rind, 80
Rinehart, Pete, 179
Robbins, M. F., 293
Roberts, Jack C., 96, 112, 114, 118
Roberts, R. F., 366
Robie, Benjamin H., 293

Robinson, Hugh, 215, 216
Roderick, Harry L., 218–221
Rogers, Will, 97, 176
Rolph Jr., Gov. James, 167, 390
Roper, Daniel, 395
Rose, Buzz, 178
Rose, Franklin "Frank," 136, 376, 377, 379
Rose, Mrs. Franklin, 171
Rouse, Hal, 339
Royle, Capt. William H., 348, 349, 368, 369
Ruckstell, Glover E., 187
Ruggles, H. F, 233
Russell, Basil, 63
Rutherford, William, 81
Rutjin, Oscar, 372
Ryan, T. Claude, 296, 298
Sackrider, Delzzie, 183
Sackrider, Henry, 79, 128, 165, 183, 333
Salcido, Crpl. Antonio, 293
Salz, Ruby, 79
Sampson, Mrs. Omar, 119
Sanborn, 121
Sanders, Mr. H. A., 91
Sanders, Mrs. Sandy, 91
Sanders, Sandy, 91
Sapp, L. D., 118
Sartori, 137
Sato, K., 232
Saxe, Sergeant, 382
Scarf, Geo., 232
Schaffer, Cleve T., 206, 208, 215, 232
Schanhals, W. R., 94
Scheu, 35
Schiette, C. 232
Schiller, Fritz, 235
Schiller, H. V., ix, 255
Schillig, 2
Schmipf, Mrs. Marie, 86
Schmitt, Jack, 148
Schnabel, Carl, 63
Schnabel, R. A., 110
Schramm, Lt. Ned, 288–290
Schreck, Paul, 166, 167
Schroder, Frances, 166
Schubener, M., 206, 210
Schubert, Julius, 200
Schultz Frank, 51
Schwartz, Jerome E., 370, 371, 373, 385

Index

Schwartz, Lieutenant, 19
Scofield, Jack, 180
Scott, A. L., 181, 346–349
Scott, Blanche, 240, 241, 243
Scott, Roy, 210, 228, 232
Scott, Tom E., 119, 120, 122, 133, 142
Scott, W. C., 232
Sears, H. K., 354
Seeley, J. T., 232
Selkirk, Professor, 21
Sellack, Sam, 232
Sellon, George C., 191
Seracini, Debbie, xiii
Servie, Lewis, 148
Seyfried, Gus, 232
Shalk, Jack, 31, 33
Shan or Sham, Harry, 166
Sheets, Glen, 345
Sheets, Gwendolyn, 345
Sheffer, Mary, 247
Sheitz, Frank, 51
Shelton, Gil, 149
Sheridan, J. B., 118
Shick, H., 232
Shone, Lester, 326
Short, R. R., 232
Short, Stanley, 99
Shuey, P. H., 235
Signar, L. P., 232
Silver, Ben, 374
Silverstein, Louis, 53
Singh, Sawan, 109
Single, Ruth, 305
Sisk, George, 370, 371
Skinner, R. W., 62
Slaughter, Guy T., 263, 266–268
Slaybaugh, Jack, 145
Slonniger, Eyir "Slonnie," 44
Smith Jr., Victor Morris, 239, 249
Smith, Arthur L., 247, 248, 238, 250, 251
Smith, Capt. Lowell H., 33, 34, 293, 294, 310, 311, 320, 326, 383
Smith, Dick, 123, 386
Smith, E. M., 88
Smith, Eddie, 143
Smith, Ernie, 113, 124
Smith, Jay D., 253
Smith, Jerry, 139
Smith, Leo J., 40
Smith, Maj. A. D., 288–290
Smith, Mayor Chester A., 143, 145
Smith, Sig, 377
Smith, Ted. R., 344
Smith, W. J., 81
Smythe, Hugh, 124
Snyder, Ken, 161
Soami, Radha, 109
Sowles, Mildred, 60
Spatz, Maj. Carl (Later Spaatz), 19, 27, 363
Spencer, Bonifield Melville "Bond," 28, 29, 311, 313, 314, 316, 320–327, 331–339, 342, 382, 383
Sperl, Harry, 128
Spracklin, Dick, 81
Squier, Clifford, 378
Squires, J. W., 82
St. John, Royal U., 138
Stack, Jim, 77
Stainhart, 340
Starbuck, Art, 51
Stark, Julie, xiii
Starr, T. C., 232
Stearn, Floyd, 136
Stearns, L., 243
Steele, Dudley, 81
Steinberger, Ray, 371
Stephenson, George E., 255, 260
Stephenson, Presho, 99
Stewart brothers, 121
Stewart, Wilbur, 121
Stoffer, Charles, 338, 339
Stolp, E., 156
Stott, Harry, 156
Straight, Robert, 53, 66, 98
Strain, G., 11
Strain, Victor G., 11, 370
Strief, Bob, 377
Strohmeier, Gus, 235
Strother, Cliff, 331, 332, 336
Struble, J. R., 268
Sturtevant, E. R., 54
Sue, Frank, 156, 192
Sullivan, Farm Advisor, 24
Sully, L., 232
Sun Yat-sen, 341
Sutro, A. A., 232
Swain, Lt. John D., 17
Swain, William, 151, 162
Swenson, P. N., 114, 163, 165, 167, 169
Swift, Clarence E., 11–16
Symons, Tommy, 144, 145
Taff, Joe, 171, 172, 176, 177
Takaeshi, B. 263
Takahashi, Frank T., 232
Tanner, Emmett, 363
Taylor, E. C., 325, 331
Taylor, J. B., 169
Taylor, Joseph B., 118
Taylor, William Desmond, 270
Templeman, Donald, 82
Terry, Seth S., 187
Thayer, Schillig, 20
Thomasson, 305
Thomasson, Albert, 80
Thomasson, Otto, 80
Thomasson, Verne, 353, 361
Thompson, Catherine, 238
Thompson, Ed H., 227, 228, 237, 238
Thompson, Jack, 118
Thornbrough, Laura, 17
Thunen, 205
Thurn, G. H., 118
Tigar, Gene A. 128, 129, 137, 146, 159
Timm, Otto, 104, 260
Timm, Wally, 104, 260
Timothy, S. R., 227
Toland, Sheriff C. W., 371
Tolley, George, 320
Tolman, J. E., 96
Tomlinson, D. W., 100
Tompkins, F. V., 89
Toney, Sarah M., 149
Torrey, Ben, 299
Torrey, Helen, 356
Tracy, O. E., 360
Tratnell, Lt. F. M., 121
Trayner, Gerald, 29
Tremayne (or Tremaine), John E., 344, 368
Trenham, James, 301
Trowbridge, Ross, 172
Tunison, M. C., 104
Tunison, W. H., 235
Tusch, Mother, 51
Tyson, Mitchell, 179
Underhill, Lt. M. H., 114
Unemara, Baison S., 232, 237,

238
Van Ofen, Geo A., 232, 237
Van Tassell, Capt. Park A., 2, 236
Van Zandt, Lt. J. Parker, 282, 283, 285
Vanderford, 121
Vanderford, O. H., 388
Vanderford (Senior), Vince, 184
Varney, Walter T., 35, 46, 47, 49, 260–262
Vidal, Eugene L., 346, 395
Vilas, Jack, 214
Virden, Ralph, 67
Von Geldern, Ed, 22, 24, 168
Von Geldern, Rick, 22
Voss, Capt. F. S., 307, 382
Voss, Ernie, 372
Vrang brothers, 236
Vremsak, Louis, 181, 182, 187
Waage, H., 144
Waage, John P., 179, 181, 182
Wachter, 121
Wade, Lt. Leigh, 310
Wagner, Geo., 232
Wahl, Albert, 251
Waite, A. H., 344
Wales, Lt. Edward V., 282, 310
Walker, Clarence H., 215, 216, 232
Walker, Skipper, 182
Walsh, Howard F., 138
Walton, F. S., 64
Walton, Larry, 178, 179
Walton, Mayor Richard, 114
Warner, James, 111
Warren, D. C., 119, 129, 135, 379
Waterman, Waldo, 34, 260
Waters, Dr. A. R., 359
Waters, Mayor, 374
Watson, Lt. Col. Henry L., 19, 279, 351
Weahunt, Silas, 370
Webb, Lt. H. W., 288, 289
Webdell, Tom, 187
Weber, Nick J., 118, 156
Werlhof, Victor H., 30, 32
Werne, Gordon, xiii
Weser, Ed J., 122
West, Robert, 165
Westfall, Roy, 125, 157, 158,

345
Wheeler, J., 156
Wheeler, Julius, 75, 86, 87
Whistle, Sgt. Clement J., 298
White, L. C., 33
White, Roy, 47
Whitney, Ivor, 181
Whitten, Frederick, 392
Wilcoxen, Lewis, 29
Wilde, Arthur "Pop," 341
Wilkins, Charles E., 161
Willard, Charles F., 204, 212
Willey, Bunny, 138
Willey, Lee, 388
Williams, Charles H., 129
Williams, Ernie, 156
Williams, Red, 51
Wilson, A. J., 47
Wilson, Al, 160
Wilson, Claude, 59
Wilson, President Woodrow, 10
Wing, C. C., 235
Wingfield, Sgt. William, 19
Winn, Frank, 67
Winn, Herbert, 65
Wiseman, Fred, 215, 216, 232
Witmer, Charles, 388
Woerner, Walter, 233
Wolfe, Henry, 277
Wolfskill, H. H., 336
Woo, Thomas, 120
Wood, C. W., 345
Wood, Mark, 308
Woodson, Warren N., 63
Woodworth, Lt. Bunny, 317, 320, 321, 359
Workman, Ed, 238, 239
Workman, R. M., 235
Wormuth, James, 318
Wright brothers, 202, 244
Wright, Denny, 369
Wright, Hiram, 202, 203, 244
Wright, John, 202, 203, 244
Wright, Lt. W. A., 288, 289
Wright, Orville, vii, viii
Wright, W. E., 384
Wright, Wiley, 147, 160
Wright, William E., 371
Wright, Wilbur, vii, viii, 244
Wrightman, I. J., 360
Wyatt, Lt. Ben H., 51
Wycoff, 235

Wynns, Maj. Walter, 18
Yang, General, 341
Yates, Francis, 80
Yee, Charlotte, 120
Yerex, Lowell, 31
Young, Rex, 233
Zahinovich, Y., 235
Zelk, George ---128
Zeman, Frank ---101
Zink, Harry ---269
Zumwalt, L. R., 160

ABOUT THE AUTHOR

Allen Herr

Allen Herr performed as a professional musician while working in a family business for four decades. He minored in American history at college and has written articles on early aviation for *Air Enthusiast Quarterly*, *American Aviation Historical Society Journal*, and various Northern California historical society quarterlies.

As a private pilot, Allen has flown over eighteen hundred hours of which nearly a tenth was aerobatic time. As a member of the International Aerobatic Club, he achieved his Sportsman with Stars Certificate in competition. He has been a member of the Experimental Aircraft Association and the American Aviation Historical Society for almost forty-five years. Allen is also a member of the National Air-racing Group. An avid air-racing fan, he has attended air race week at Reno National Air Races every year since they began in 1964.

Allen lives near Yuba City, California, with his wife, Kathe (also a pilot), and their children, Bella and Skeezix.

Planes in need of repair were often transported to and from the Sacramento Air Depot (McClellan Field) by Sacramento River barges from the Bay Area to a loading dock on the Garden Highway (levee road). This took place from the late 1930s thru the early 1960s. They were then towed through Gardenland, Del Paso Heights and Rio Linda to McClellan. Photo shows Air Corps planes from the late '30s, such as, B-10s, P-36s, a Grumman Widgeon and Douglas observation plane

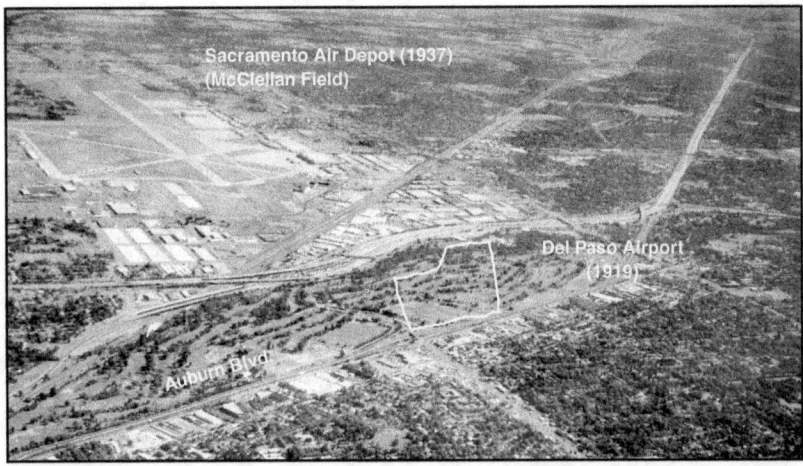

McClellan Field (Sacramento Air Depot) takes up the whole upper left quadrant of this 1994 photo; the center of the Del Paso Park golf course, running diagonally thought the center of the photo, is the location of Sacramento's (first) municipal airport, Del Paso Airport, from 1919 until April 1930.

A Bach Tri-motor on Crissy Field at the Presidio in San Francisco circa 1929. Bach's were flown by West Coast Air Transport on a route from Seattle – Portland – Corning – Sacramento – San Francisco and return from 1928 through 1931.

A painting of the author's Bellanca Decathlon from which many of the airport photos in this book were taken. The airport in the background is Sutter County Airport in 1978.

www.ingramcontent.com/pod-product-compliance
Lightning Source LLC
Chambersburg PA
CBHW051827230426
43671CB00008B/869